INTRODUCTION TO
Group Work

FOURTH EDITION

David Capuzzi
Johns Hopkins University
Portland State University

Douglas R. Gross
Arizona State University

Mark D. Stauffer
Oregon State University

LOVE PUBLISHING COMPANY®
Denver • London • Sydney

Published by Love Publishing Company
P.O. Box 22353
Denver, Colorado 80222
www.lovepublishing.com

Fourth Edition

Library of Congress Control Number: 2005926007

ISBN 0-89108-318-9

Contents

PART ONE: Foundations for Group Work   1

1 Group Work: An Introduction   3
David Capuzzi and Douglas R. Gross

2 Group Work: Stages and Issues   37
Douglas R. Gross and David Capuzzi

3 Group Work: Elements of Effective Leadership   57
David Capuzzi and Douglas R. Gross

4 **Group Work: Theories and Applications   89**
Douglas R. Gross and David Capuzzi

PART TWO: Professional Issues   121

5 **The Efficacy of Group Work   123**
Cass Dykeman and Valerie E. Appleton

6 **Approaches to Evaluating Groups   161**
Conrad Sieber

11 Psychotherapy Groups   295
Jonathan W. Carrier and Melinda Haley

PART FOUR:
Group Work in Specific Settings   321

12 Groups in Schools   323
Tamara E. Davis

Preface

The therapeutic elements of a positive group experience have been documented through empirically based research, client self-reports, descriptions by group leaders, and the emergence of paradigms derived from a variety of theoretical perspectives. These curative factors have been described by terms including acceptance, altruism, universalization, belonging, security, instillation of hope, increased awareness of emotional dynamics, and interpersonal learning, among many other descriptors. The role of professional counselors in educational, corporate, mental health, private practice, and rehabilitation settings calls for knowledge, experience, and competence in facilitating groups.

Group work is demanding and requires the professional counselor to add knowledge and skills to the foundation in individual counseling provided by coursework and supervised practice. Individuals who are trying to decide if group work is the specialization they want will find the information in this text helpful as a point of departure in the decision-making process.

The book is unique in format and content. The contributed-authors format enables state-of-the-art information by experts in their respective group work specializations. The content goes beyond that usually addressed in introductory group work texts. Chapters on group work with elderly people and their caregivers, clients who have addictions, those who have experienced a form of loss, and those who are dealing with gay, lesbian, and bisexual concerns are cases in point. This textbook includes chapters on the specialty groups (task/work, psychoeducational, and psychotherapy) identified by the Association for Specialists in Group Work (ASGW), in addition to numerous chapters on topics related to group counseling.

New to this fourth edition are reconceptualized chapters on the topics of ethical/legal considerations in group work, as well as diversity issues in group work. Also new to this edition is a part entitled *Group Work in Specific Settings,* which includes chapters on groups in schools, mental health settings, and groups in rehabilitation settings. We hope readers will find these changes of high interest and helpful in developing an appropriate knowledge and skills base.

Students enrolled in a beginning course in group work will find the book useful for the future as well as the present. The book provides a comprehensive overview of major issues connected with group work, as well as insight and practical guidelines for group work in general. We have provided the addresses of Web sites with most chapters rather than including this information as appendices at the end of the text, because Web sites usually reflect the most current best-practice guidelines, training standards, diversity competencies for group workers, and other topics.

Recognizing that one book cannot cover all the factors involved in preparing a person to be a specialist in group work, we attempt to give readers a broad perspective on group work as they begin to learn about groups. The chapters combine information on research, theory, and practice pertinent to the role of the group-work specialist. The many case studies will help the reader identify with, and make applications to, current and future clients. The text is divided into five parts: Foundations for Group Work, Professional Issues, Specialty Groups, Group Work in Specific Settings, and Group Work With Specific Populations.

Part One, Foundations for Group Work (chapters 1 through 4), covers the historical, definitive, theoretical, research, and practical perspectives that provide the foundation for all types of group work. Separate chapters are devoted to an introduction, a discussion of stages and issues in group work, elements of effective leadership, and theories and applications.

Part Two, Professional Issues, contains chapters on the efficacy of group work, approaches to evaluating groups, ethical/legal considerations in group work, and diversity issues in group work.

Part Three, Specialty Groups, addresses the three kinds of groups, other than counseling groups, identified by ASGW: task/work groups, guidance/psychoeducational groups, and psychotherapy groups.

Part Four, Group Work in Specific Settings, contains chapters on group work in schools, group work in mental health settings, and groups in rehabilitation settings. This part is especially helpful to those aspiring to practice as a group work specialist in one of those settings.

Part Five, Group Work With Specific Populations, provides valuable information to readers who are interested in designing groups for any of the four identified specific populations: groups for people who have suffered losses, groups for people with addictions, groups for elderly people and their caregivers, and groups for gay, lesbian, and bisexual clients. The chapters in this section are concrete and relevant to practice.

ACKNOWLEDGMENTS

We would like to thank the 22 authors who contributed their time, expertise, and experience in developing this textbook, written for the beginning group work specialist. And we thank our families, who provided the support to make our writing and editing efforts possible. Our thanks also go to Stan Love and the staff of Love Publishing Company for their encouragement, understanding, and editing. Without the collaboration and interest of all those whose efforts are reflected in these pages, this fourth edition would not have become a reality.

MEET THE EDITORS

David Capuzzi, Ph.D., N.C.C., L.P.C., is a past president of the American Counseling Association (ACA) and currently is a counselor educator at Johns Hopkins University. He is professor emeritus and former coordinator of counselor education in the Graduate School of Education at Portland State University in Portland, Oregon.

From 1980 to 1984, David was editor of *The School Counselor.* He has authored a number of textbook chapters and monographs on the topic of preventing adolescent suicide. His four most recently conceptualized texts are *Approaches to Group Work: A Handbook for Practitioners* (2003); *Sexuality Counseling* (2002), coauthored and edited with Larry Burlew; *Suicide Across the Life Span* (2004); and *Career Counseling: Foundations, Perspectives, and Applications* (2006), coedited with Mark D. Stauffer.

A frequent speaker and keynoter at professional conferences and institutes, David has consulted with a variety of school districts and community agencies that are interested in initiating prevention and intervention strategies for adolescents at risk for suicide. He has facilitated the development of suicide prevention, crisis management, and postvention programs in communities throughout the United States; provides training on the topics of youth at risk and grief and loss; and serves as an invited adjunct faculty member at other universities as time permits. He is the first recipient of ACA's Kitty Cole Human Rights Award.

Douglas R. Gross, Ph.D., N.C.C., is a professor emeritus at Arizona State University, Tempe, where he served as a faculty member in counselor education for 29 years. Now retired, he is living in Three Rivers, Michigan. His professional work history includes public school teaching, counseling, and administration. He has been president of the Arizona Counselors Association, president of the Western Association for Counselor Education and Supervision, chairperson of the Western Regional Branch Assembly of the ACA, president of the Association for Humanistic Education and Development, and treasurer and parliamentarian of the ACA.

Doug has contributed chapters to seven texts in counseling, youth at risk, mental health, and group work. His research has appeared in the *Journal of Counseling Psychology, Journal of Counseling and Development, Association for Counselor Education and Supervision Journal, Journal of Educational Research,* and *AMHCA Journal.* Doug provides national training for certification in the areas of bereavement, grief, and loss.

Mark D. Stauffer, M.S., is a doctoral student in the counselor education and supervision program at Oregon State University, where he is a member of the doctoral teaching staff. He specialized in couples, marriage, and family counseling during his graduate work in the counselor education program at Portland State University, where he worked as a research assistant.

Mark enjoys scholarly writing and authored a chapter in *Suicide Across the Life Span* (2004) and coauthored chapters in *Introduction to the Counseling Profession* (2005). This textbook and *Career Counseling: Foundations, Perspectives and Applications* are his first two coedited works.

At the annual convention in 2005, he was selected as a participant for the Emerging Leaders Training Program sponsored by the ACA. He has presented at regional and national professional conferences.

Mark has worked in the Portland (Oregon) metro area at crises centers and other nonprofit organizations providing counseling to individuals, couples, and families. He has studied and trained in the Zen tradition, is vitally interested in spirituality issues in counseling and the use of meditation and mindfulness in the counseling process.

MEET THE AUTHORS

Lisa Langfuss Aasheim, M.S., N.C.C., currently serves as the coordinator of family therapy at De Paul Treatment Centers in Portland, Oregon, and is a member of the doctoral teaching faculty at Oregon State University in Corvallis, Oregon. Her areas of interest and research include clinical supervision, grief and loss, premarital and marital therapy, multifamily group, multicultural supervision practices, and systemic approaches to treatment and supervision. She is passionate about addressing the ongoing developmental and supervisory needs of counselors and counselor educators so clients can best be served by enthusiastic and well-regarded professionals.

Valerie E. Appleton, Ed.D., M.F.C.C., A.T.R., N.C.C., is associate dean of the College of Education and Human Development and professor of counselor education at Eastern Washington University. She has taught school and mental health counseling for 22 years. Dr. Appleton currently is the principal investigator for a U.S. Department of Education grant titled the "Bilingual Counselor Education and School Support Project." It examines the multicultural competencies of in-training counselors and school climate changes effected by diversity education and counseling. Her grant funding and numerous research publications are in the areas of counselor education and supervision, the psychosocial aspect of trauma resolution, and art therapy. The research Dr. Appleton conducted on an intensive-care burn unit provides a unique perspective of trauma assessment and intervention.

Malachy Bishop, Ph.D., is an assistant professor in the rehabilitation counseling program in the Department of Special Education and Rehabilitation Counseling, University of Kentucky, Lexington. He received the M.S.Ed. in rehabilitation counseling from Portland State University and the Ph.D. in rehabilitation psychology from the University of Wisconsin–Madison. His research interests include the application of quality-of-life research in counseling and psychology, and the process of adaptation to disability, particularly among individuals with epilepsy and other chronic neurological conditions.

Cynthia A. Briggs, M.Ed., N.C.C., L.P.C., is a native of southwest Virginia. After completing the B.S. in psychology at Guilford College in Greensboro, North Carolina, she worked for 2 years with developmentally disabled, autistic, and head-injured adults and children. She received the M.A.Ed. in community counseling at Wake Forest University in Winston-Salem, North Carolina, and worked for 2 years as a mental health and addictions counselor. Returning to her alma mater in 2000, Cynthia took a position in enrollment and campus life administration before entering the doctoral program in counselor education and supervision at Oregon State University in 2003. Her research interests include spirituality, women's issues, wellness, and professional identity development, and she has presented regionally and nationally on these topics. Her teaching experiences include introduction to counseling, addictions, social and cultural foundations, practicum, and internship. Her current clinical experience includes career, college, and school counseling.

Jonathan W. Carrier, M.S., is a doctoral student in counseling psychology at the University of Louisville in Kentucky. As author and coauthor of several book chapters, his topics include behavioral group counseling, group psychotherapy, and the assessment of suicide and depression. Currently he is involved in research concerning adolescent employment and family functioning, family religiosity and adolescent peer group choice, and math anxiety in adult students. Upon completing the doctoral degree, Jonathan hopes to attain a position as a university professor in counseling or psychology.

Tamara E. Davis, Ph.D., is an associate professor of psychology at Marymount University, Arlington, Virginia. With nearly 20 years of experience in education, she teaches primarily graduate school counseling courses in Marymount's CACREP-accredited program. Prior to her position in higher education, Dr. Davis was an elementary and high school counselor for 9 years in Manassas, Virginia. Dr. Davis has served in many professional organizations, including serving as president of the Virginia Association for Counselor Education and Supervision, as well as the Virginia School Counselor Association. She will serve as president of the Virginia School Counselor Association in 2005–2006. Dr. Davis has presented locally, regionally, and nationally on a number of topics in school counseling, including developing resilience and handling perfectionism. Her publications include a book, entitled *Exploring School Counseling: Professional Practices & Perspectives*, in 2005. Dr. Davis has taught a school counseling specialty-specific graduate course in group counseling for 7 years and continues to work closely with school counselors in several school districts in Northern Virginia.

Cass Dykeman, Ph.D., is an associate professor of counseling at Oregon State University. Dr. Dykeman received the master's degree in counseling from the University of Washington and the doctoral degree in counselor education from the University of Virginia. He holds national certification in addictions counseling and school counseling. Dr. Dykeman is a past president of the Western Association for Counselor Education and Supervision. He has authored numerous books, book chapters, and research articles and currently teaches doctoral research methods courses at Oregon State University.

Abbé Finn, Ph.D., is a faculty member in the Counseling Department, College of Education, Florida Gulf Coast University. A graduate of the University of New Orleans Counselor Education Program, she has worked extensively in the mental health field, counseling individuals as well as groups. She has published several book chapters and has been a guest speaker at numerous national conferences. Dr. Finn has led many different types of groups and has specialized in working with groups in crisis response and with clients in addiction recovery.

Lea Flowers, M.Ed., N.C.C., is a doctoral candidate at the University of New Orleans. Her group work interests and experience include work with adult trauma victims, the adult paranoid schizophrenia population, group supervision, and psychoeducational and interpersonal skills training. She has worked in community mental health agencies and schools. Her research interests include ethics and leadership, group work, gender issues, boundaries, interpersonal communication, and counselor supervision.

Melinda Haley, M.S., N.C.C., has written several book chapters in the areas of group work, youth at risk, technology in counseling, and theory. Currently pursuing the doctoral degree in counseling psychology at New Mexico State University, her professional goals are to continue writing, obtain a tenure-track faculty position upon graduation, and work with disadvantaged populations. Her current research interests are multiculturalism in counseling, bias and racism in general, and bias and racism within the criminal justice system and its effect on minority individuals. She also is interested in researching personality disorders and how personality develops over the lifespan.

Debra A. Harley, Ph.D., C.R.C., P.C., is a professor in the department of special education and rehabilitation counseling and the women's studies program at the University of Kentucky. She has published a book entitled *Contemporary Mental Health Issues Among African Americans* (2004). In addition, Dr. Harley has published in the areas of substance abuse, cultural diversity, AIDS, and career counseling. Dr. Harley is the past editor of the *Journal of Applied Rehabilitation Counseling* and the *Journal of Rehabilitation Administration* and a former Switzer Scholar.

Barbara Richter Herlihy, Ph.D., is a professor of counselor education at the University of New Orleans. She has worked as a counselor and supervisor in schools, community agencies, and private practice, with a primary teaching and research focus on counselor ethics. Her publications include five books and numerous book chapters and articles, and she has presented workshops and seminars on ethics across the United States and internationally. She combines her work in ethics with her other research interests in feminist counseling, multicultural counseling, and counselor supervision.

Reese M. House, Ed.D., currently works as director of the National Center for Transforming School Counseling at the Education Trust in Washington, DC. He came to the Education Trust from Oregon State University, where he focused on preparing school counselors to be proactive change agents and advocates for all students. He approaches education from a critical-social perspective and with a belief in integration of theory and practice. Reese has worked extensively to upgrade standards and accreditation guidelines for counselors at the state and national levels. He works with school districts and school counselor educators to develop improved standards of practices for school counselors.

Kurt L. Kraus, Ed.D., is an associate professor in the Department of Counseling at Shippensburg University of Pennsylvania. His professional interests include ethics, clinical supervision, counseling challenging adolescents, and group work. The 2005 ASGW Fellows recipient, he currently serves on the board of directors for the National Board for Certified Counselors.

Virginia Martin, Ed.D., L.P.C., is an associate professor and coordinator of counselor education at Alabama State University, Montgomery. Dr. Martin earned the Ed.D. in counselor education from Auburn University. Her teaching specialties are developmental and abnormal psychology, group counseling, and helping relationships. Her publications are concerned with group counseling for shy people and older people, as well as treatment of specific anxiety disorders.

Susan H. Niemann, Ph.D., L.P.C., is a licensed professional counselor in private practice in New Orleans, Louisiana, with more than 10 years of experience as a mental health counselor and more than 20 years of experience as an educator. She provides individual and group counseling for adults, adolescents, and children, as well as marriage counseling, counselor intern supervision, domestic mediation, and comprehensive custody evaluation.

Dale Elizabeth Pehrsson, Ed.D., is a counselor educator at Oregon State University, where she has coordinated the community agency counseling program since 1999. She is a licensed professional counselor for advanced clinical practice, a licensed supervisor, a nationally certified counselor with approved clinical supervision certification, as well as a registered play therapy supervisor, registered nurse, and graphic artist. Dr. Pehrsson uses art, play, and therapeutic story techniques in her work with families. Her research passion is in expressive and creative uses of therapeutic interventions.

Bianca Puglia, M.Ed., is a doctoral student and graduate assistant at the University of New Orleans. Her clinical experience includes group work with individuals dealing with severe mental illness, and she has worked with substance abuse and dual-diagnosis groups. Currently she is involved with the Voices For Children project, which combines group work and creative arts for children who are dealing with family transition and custodial issues. Bianca also has extensive experience working with cultural assimilation for American and international students alike. She has presented at conferences on topics ranging from group work with patients with schizophrenia to cultural sensitivity for individuals with disabilities.

Deborah J. Rubel, Ph.D., is an assistant professor of counselor education in the new School of Education at Oregon State University. She received the master's degree in mental health counseling and the doctoral degree in counselor education from Idaho State University. Her areas of specialization are group work, multicultural/social justice counseling, and qualitative research methodology.

Conrad Sieber, Ph.D., a licensed psychologist, trained at Colorado State University and completed his internship at Ohio State University's Counseling and Consultation Service. Professionally, he has worked in higher education, K–12 schools, and private practice. His interests include counseling and education programs for diverse populations, program development, and evaluation. Currently he coordinates student assessment and program evaluation for a school district in Forest Grove, Oregon.

M. Carolyn Thomas, Ph.D., L.P.C., L.M.F.T., is a professor and coordinator of counselor education at Auburn University, Montgomery, Alabama. Dr. Thomas earned the Ph.D. in counselor education at the University of Iowa. Her specialties include group work, career development, and supervision, and her publications are concerned with group work for older people and victims of family abuse. An active leader in the ACA, the National Career Development Association (NCDA), and the ASGW, she is an ASGW and NCDA Fellow and was recognized with the Point of Light Award for her community and group work at the Montgomery Area Family Violence Program.

Ann Vernon, Ph.D., L.M.H.C., N.C.C., is professor and coordinator of counselor education at the University of Northern Iowa, Cedar Falls. In addition, she maintains a part-time private practice, specializing in work with children and adolescents. Dr. Vernon conducts workshops throughout the United States and abroad on a variety of issues pertaining to children and adolescents. She has authored the books *Thinking, Feeling, Behaving; What Works When With Children and Adolescents;* and *Counseling Children and Adolescents*, in addition to articles and chapters in books. Dr. Vernon has held numerous leadership positions in professional associations, including vice president of the Albert Ellis Board of Trustees.

PART ONE:

Foundations for Group Work

Group work encompasses many knowledge and skill modalities in which the group leader must be proficient. Part One of this text provides an overview of the historical context of group work, as well as basic knowledge and skill areas pertinent to facilitating groups.

Chapter 1, "Group Work: An Introduction," begins with foundational information and terminology. This is followed by an overview of the history of group work, examples of goals for groups, a discussion of various types of groups, models for group work, therapeutic factors in groups, personal characteristics of group leaders, and myths connected with group work.

Chapter 2, "Group Work: Stages and Issues," analyzes the stages and transitions inherent in the group experience, as well as the issues these stages and transitions present for the leader and the members of a group. After beginning with a case study — revisited at the end of the chapter — the chapter turns to the early and current conceptualizations of stage theory and members' behavior. A composite conceptualization of the developmental stages of groups incorporates definitive, personal involvement, group involvement, and enhancement and closure stages. In conjunction with each of the four stages, member and leader behaviors are identified.

Chapter 3, "Group Work: Elements of Effective Leadership," explores the styles of leadership: authoritarian, democratic, laissez-faire, leader-centered, group-centered, interpersonal, intrapersonal, and charismatic. The chapter also covers skills related to pre-group screening and organizing for groups and outlines the roles of the various members. The authors set forth the skills the group leader must master to facilitate the definitive, personal involvement, group involvement, and enhancement and closure stages discussed in chapter 2. Chapter 3 concludes with consideration of techniques for dealing with difficult members.

Chapter 4, "Group Work: Theories and Applications," takes six selected theoretical/therapeutic approaches—Adlerian, Gestalt, person-centered, rational-emotive behavior theory, transactional analysis, and psychodrama—and applies them to groups. Rather than reiterating theory available in texts on individual counseling and psychotherapy, these theoretical concepts are translated into group leader behaviors and techniques. The chapter concludes with an integrative theme considering relationship, leader role, member role, process, and outcome variables in light of the six theoretical approaches.

Group Work:
An Introduction

David Capuzzi and Douglas R. Gross

We spend a considerable amount of time in groups, whether at home, at work, at school, at social gatherings, at church, or at civic, professional, or political meetings. Of the many ways by which groups can be defined (Gladding, 2003; Johnson and Johnson, 2000), all involve interpersonal interactions. Counselors have become increasingly aware that many of the problems that bring clients to counseling are interpersonally based (Corey & Corey, 1997; Johnson & Johnson, 2000) and that, for many clients, group counseling or therapy may be the treatment of choice because of the interpersonal learning opportunities that groups provide. Group counseling fits well into the current emphasis on managed care (Kline, 2003; Sleek, 1995) because many groups can be facilitated in ways that provide brief and cost-effective assistance for participants.

Like other institutions and training activities, group counseling reflects both the culture and the history of the moment as influenced by national, regional, and local concerns (Gladding, 1999; Klein, 1985). If the 1950s symbolized the "individual in society," the 1960s "the individual against society," the 1970s "the individual's conflict with self," and the 1980s "the individual's integration into the family," the 1990s and beyond may symbolize "the individual's integration with the machine" (Shapiro & Bernadett-Shapiro, 1985).

As Capuzzi and Gross (1997) predicted nearly a decade ago, much of the work in educational, career, and day-to-day living situations in the 21st century will be done by computers; and connections among colleagues, friends, and family members will be maintained by telephone lines, word processors, and modems. The replacement of consistent social contact with friends and coworkers by the video display terminal and telecommunication networks will create a much greater need for interpersonal communication on a person-to-person basis

(Trotzer, 1999). Groups will provide an antidote to isolation, and more and more counselors, therapists, and other human development specialists will be called upon to serve as group facilitators. The counseling and human development professional faces crescendoing opportunities (Corey, 2004) and escalating responsibilities in group work.

THE HISTORY OF GROUP WORK

Group work has a long and eventful history, with milestones and changes along the way. We will trace it from its beginnings to contemporary group work.

The Beginning

Although there is evidence of the therapeutic use of groups in both England and the United States prior to the 1900s (Gladding, 1999, 2003), more formal group counseling can be traced back to the first decade of the 20th century (Gazda, 1985). In 1905, Joseph Hersey Pratt, a physician, applied the "class" method in providing assistance to patients with tuberculosis in Boston, Massachusetts. A few years later, in 1909, Cody Marsh began to offer psychiatric inpatients what could be called inspirational group lectures (Scheidlinger, 1994). He soon became known for his motto: "By the crowd they have been broken; by the crowd they shall be healed."

During the 1920s, Edward Lazell, a psychiatrist, used a similar lecture method when working with severely disturbed inpatients suffering from schizophrenic and manic-depressive psychoses. In later years, Lazell applied this didactic approach to outpatients relying upon concepts from Jungian psychology (Scheidlinger, 1994).

As noted by Rudolf Dreikurs (1932), Alfred Adler used collective therapy with families and children in his child guidance clinics in Vienna in the 1920s. Dreikurs brought these methods with him to America. His work with groups complemented that of early American group "pioneers" such as Jesse B. Davis, who used public school classrooms in Michigan as forums for vocational guidance and the followers of Frank Parsons, who worked with vocationally undecided individuals in small groups via the Vocational Bureau of Boston (Gladding, 1991, 1999, 2003). By the middle of the 1920s, Trigant Burrow, one of the founders of the American Psychoanalytic Association, had begun conducting groups for his patients, members of his patients' families, and mental health professionals (Scheidlinger, 1994). The experience, which was termed *group analysis*, replaced Sigmund Freud's emphasis on the individual intrapsychic themes with a new focus on interactive themes.

From 1908 to 1925, Jacob L. Moreno, known as the founder of psychodrama, used group action techniques in Vienna. Following his arrival in the United States, Moreno continued developing his psychodramatic techniques, and his ideas influenced later American Gestalt, existential, and encounter group movements (Gladding, 1991, 1999, 2003; Scheidlinger, 1994).

The 1930s

In the 1930s, a number of psychoanalytic clinicians began to apply Freudian principles to group work in hospitals (Scheidlinger, 1994). One of these individuals, Louis Wender, facilitated small groups in a private hospital and differentiated his approach from those of Pratt, Lazell, and Marsh by emphasizing family transference manifestation. Paul Schilder, a colleague of Wender and a research professor of psychiatry at New York University School of Medicine, also helped legitimize the growing interest in group modalities.

Among the first to apply group work to children was Loretta Bender, who pioneered children's cathartic expression in groups by using puppets. She was followed by Betty Gabriel, the first American to bring adolescents to the group experience (Scheidlinger, 1994). S. R. Slavson, a contemporary of both Bender and Gabriel and founder of the American Group Psychotherapy Association, also pioneered the use of groups for children (Slavson & Schiffer, 1975). His groups, which he called *activity therapy groups*, consisted of about eight children of the same sex and similar ages. He used handicrafts, games, and food to foster interactions, and the groups were conducted in the context of a nondirective climate. Counselors and therapists of the day welcomed Slavson's approach because they had difficulty engaging children in one-to-one "talking" sessions. Variations of activity group therapy directed at more seriously disturbed youth were soon introduced.

This early emphasis on group work with children provided the basis for the use of psychoeducational groups with children in elementary schools. In recent years, elementary school counselors have seen children in groups centering on issues of divorce, substance abuse, enhancement of self-esteem, conflict resolution, and other concerns.

The 1930s also bore witness to the inception of Alcoholics Anonymous (AA), which provides self-help support group experiences to help alcoholics maintain sobriety (Gladding, 1991, 1999, 2003). Most communities in the United States currently have AA groups.

The 1940s

During World War II, large numbers of American military personnel who were "psychiatric casualties" of the war experience were seen by military psychiatrists (Scheidlinger, 1994). As a result of sheer necessity, more and more of these psychiatrists adopted group methods. Indeed, many of the subsequent leaders of the American group work movement gained their experience in military hospitals. Among these American army psychiatrists were Samuel Hadden, Harris Pick, Irving Berger, and Donald Shaskan.

America's chief of military psychiatry during the war, William C. Menninger, believed that the practice of group work during that time constituted a major contribution of military psychiatry to civilian psychiatry. During the World War II era, Great Britain also contributed to the emerging interest in the use of groups. Joshua Bierer, S. H. Foulkes, Wilfred R. Bion, and Thomas Main all provided leadership (Scheidlinger, 1994).

Another influential promoter of group work during the 1940s was Kurt Lewin, who emphasized field theory and the interaction between individuals and their environments (Gladding, 1991, 1999; Johnson & Johnson, 2000). Much of his work was based on the ideas of Gestalt psychology, which emphasizes the relationship of the part to the whole. Lewin was influential in establishing a workshop on intergroup relations in New Britain, Connecticut, in 1946 (Gladding, 1991, 1999, 2003). Later, with the help of Ron Lippitt, Lee Bradford, and Ken Benne, he founded the National Training Laboratories in Bethel, Maine (now called NTL: The Institute for Applied Behavioral Science; Schmuck & Schmuck, 1997). The laboratories directed research on improving personal learning and organizational process in groups.

An important derivation of the work of these individuals was the training group, or T-group (Bradford, Gibb, & Benne, 1964). Participants in T-groups learn to understand themselves and others better and to develop collaboration skills. The T-groups that were popularized in later decades emphasized individual and personal growth goals, understanding of interpersonal relations, and the application of group dynamics to social change.

Two important group organizations were established in the 1940s:

1. American Society of Group Psychotherapy and Psychodrama (ASGPP), established by J. L. Moreno
2. American Group Psychotherapy Association (AGPA), founded by Samuel R. Slavson.

These same men established two important journals—*Group Psychotherapy* and the *International Journal of Group Psychotherapy,* respectively. Both journals were characterized by the philosophies of their founders (Gladding, 1991, 1999, 2003).

The 1950s

One of the first references to group work with the elderly population appeared in 1950 with the work of J. J. Geller (1950). Early efforts in this area consisted of groups in residences for older adults. Reports of this work were often anecdotal in nature and most often appeared in social work and nursing journals (Scheidlinger, 1994). The reports described groups for well-functioning elderly people, for widows and widowers, for retirees, and for people with physical and emotional disabilities. The reports pointed out the positive response of older adults to group experiences aimed at anxiety and pain reduction and social skills training. As time has passed, more and more journals have published research and practice articles for professionals who are interested in group work with elderly people (the topic of Chapter 17).

The 1950s also were characterized by the application of group procedures to family counseling (Gladding, 1997). Rudolph Dreikurs, John Bell, Nathan Ackerman, Gregory Bateson, and Virginia Satir are just a few of the notables who addressed group work with families. Most practitioners who are licensed as marriage and family therapists are familiar with the growing body of literature addressing aspects of group work with families.

The 1960s and 1970s

The 1960s were a time of great social upheaval and questioning. There were riots on university campuses and in cities as civil rights groups struggled to raise the consciousness of the nation after years of unfair discrimination and prejudice. Charismatic leaders such as John F. Kennedy and Martin Luther King, Jr., became the idolized champions and international symbols of a people's determination to change a society and to promote social responsibility. The nation united in grief-stricken disbelief as its heroes were martyred, and determination to counter the human rights violations of the decades escalated.

As the 1960s ended, the encounter group movement, emphasizing personal consciousness and closer connection with others, reached its zenith. It gradually waned in the 1970s (Kline, 2003), and events such as the first presidential resignation in the history of the United States in the aftermath of the Watergate scandal, the Charles Manson murders, the group killings at the Munich Olympics, and the rise of fanatic cults caused people throughout the country to question the extent to which permissiveness and "human potential" should be allowed to develop (Janis, 1972; Rowe & Winborn, 1973).

An important influence on group work in the 1960s was the federal legislation that created a national network of community mental health centers. Administrators, in their attempts to fill newly created positions intended to provide counseling and mental health services to the less affluent members of communities, often resorted to less-than-advisable solutions (Scheidlinger, 1994). They frequently assigned counselors and therapists whose education and supervised practice was limited to one-to-one counseling and psychotherapy to facilitate groups. When poorly run groups proved to be ineffective, and sometimes even harmful, a frantic search began for counselors and therapists trained in group work.

In addition to the group work conducted by the community mental health centers, the youth revolt kindled by the Vietnam war gave rise to many nontraditional group models that flourished outside the auspices of the mental health profession. Among the most publicized of these groups were the encounter and transcendental meditation groups. Because they functioned without adequate pre-group screening, these commercial undertakings often attracted disturbed and emotionally vulnerable participants. Many participants were harmed by membership in these groups, and a protest by qualified mental health professionals resulted in eliminating the most serious abuses by individuals who organized these community programs.

Granted, journalists of the era sensationalized the use and misuse of group approaches. Nevertheless, a number of developments in the use of groups did occur (Gladding, 1991). Most notably, Fritz Perls's applications of Gestalt theory in groups at the Esalen Institute in California, Eric Berne's application of transactional analysis to groups, William C. Schutz's contributions that stressed aspects of nonverbal communication in groups, Jack Gibb's study of competitive versus cooperative behavior in groups, Irvin Yalom's work on curative factors in groups, and Carl Rogers's encounter group philosophy all provided important insights and methods for group counselors and therapists.

As the decade of the 1970s went on, counselor education, counseling psychology, psychology, and social work departments on university campuses instituted more and more coursework and supervised experiences in aspects of group work. The Association for Specialists in Group Work (ASGW) was chartered in 1973 (Forester-Miller, 1998), and by 1974 it had become a division of the American Counseling Association (ACA) (at that time known as the American Personnel and Guidance Association). ASGW publishes *The Journal for Specialists in Group Work,* which provides group work specialists with information on research, practice, and supervision as related to group work. Similar developments also took place during the 1970s in the context of other large professional groups such as the American Psychological Association (APA) and the National Association of Social Workers (NASW).

The 1980s

Interest in group work and in working with specialized populations grew during the 1980s. Groups sprang up for alcoholics, adult children of alcoholics, incest victims, adults molested as children, overweight people, underassertive individuals, and victims of violent crimes. There were groups for elderly people, individuals dealing with death and other losses, people with eating disorders, smokers, and victims of the holocaust (Shapiro & Bernadett-Shapiro, 1985). This increasing specialization brought with it a need for higher standards for the preparation of group leaders, as evidenced by the development of ethical standards for group work specialists (ASGW, 1989) and inclusion in the standards of the Council for the Accreditation of Counseling and Related Educational Programs (CACREP) of specific group work specialist preparation guidelines for graduate-level university educators (CACREP, 1994).

The 1990s and Beyond

The escalating interest in group work and in working with special populations that became so evident in the 1980s continued into the last decade of the century. The 1983 ASGW standards for the training of group counselors were revised, and a new set of standards was adopted in 1991 (ASGW, 1991).

Whereas the 1991 standards built on the 1983 standards, emphasizing the knowledge, skills, and supervised experience necessary for the preparation of group workers, the newer standards broadened the conception of group work, clarified the difference between core competencies and specialization requirements, defined the four prominent varieties of group work, and eliminated the distinctions made previously among different kinds of supervised field experience (Conyne, Wilson, Kline, Morran, & Ward, 1993). In addition, in its 1994 revision of accreditation standards, CACREP reemphasized the importance of group work by identifying principles of group dynamics, group leadership styles, theories of group counseling, group counseling methods, approaches used for other types of group work, and ethical considerations as essential curricular elements for all counselor education programs (CACREP, 1994, 2001).

The use of groups has expanded to virtually all settings connected with counseling and therapy, as well as to schools, hospitals, and corporate environments. Group programs for individuals with chronic diseases (e.g., cancer, heart disease, AIDS), for people suffering from eating disorders, and for people involved in the recovery process connected with substance abuse, sexual abuse, and other traumas are just beginning to capture the attention of the general public. In conjunction with the escalating number of older adults in this and other countries, group approaches for working with older individuals are bound to expand (Scheidlinger, 1994). Given the current emphasis on managed care and cost-containment, the interest in group work will continue to grow and the qualified group work specialist will be in high demand.

GOALS FOR GROUPS

In the early or "definitive" stage of a group, each member has to develop a clear understanding of the goals of the group experience (Chen & Rybak, 2004; Trotzer, 1999). Members who have not developed some ownership of the reasons they are participating in the group may not make constructive use of the group experience (Corey & Corey, 1997). Group goals can be addressed in a number of ways: (a) general goals for groups, (b) goals for specialized groups, (c) goals based on theoretical perspectives, and (d) goals developed by individual members.

General Goals for Groups

Although many group work leaders believe that the goals for each counseling group should be established by the members and leaders of those groups, group work leaders have reached some consensus on general group goals (George & Dustin, 1988). In 1957, J. Frank proposed a general statement defining group goals as helping members to

- release their feelings constructively,
- strengthen self-esteem,
- face and resolve their problems,
- improve their skills in recognizing and resolving interpersonal and intrapersonal conflicts, and
- fortify their ability to consolidate and maintain therapeutic gains.

In 1963, H. C. Kelman proposed a similar set of general goals, which added the dimensions of helping members to

- overcome feelings of isolation,
- develop hope for increased adjustment,

- learn to accept responsibility,
- develop new relationship skills, and
- enhance commitment to change.

Corey, Corey, Callahan, and Russell (1982) suggested that group facilitators have two kinds of goals:

1. *General goals* have to do with establishing a psychological environment within the context of a group that is conducive to supporting members as they work toward their personal goals.
2. *Process goals* relate to teaching members appropriate methods of sharing their own concerns and providing feedback to others in the group.

This differentiation provides a helpful guideline.

Carroll and Wiggins (1997, p. 25) identified the general goals of helping the group member to

- become a better listener,
- develop sensitivity and acceptance of others,
- increase self-awareness and develop a sense of identity,
- feel a sense of belongingness and overcome feelings of isolation,
- learn to trust others as well as self,
- recognize and state areas of belief and values without fear of repression, and
- transfer what is learned in the group to the outside by accepting responsibility for solving one's own problems.

In addition, Carroll and Wiggins (1997, p. 290) proposed the following process goals as helpful to group members:

- Help members stay in the here and now.
- Prevent storytelling related to the there and then.
- Help members to confront others with care and respect.
- Learn to give nonevaluative feedback.
- Learn to risk by speaking from the first person.

Both of the above lists are only partial and could be modified in accordance with the group leader's style and philosophy, and on the type of group. For example, a group of adults who were molested as children would modify the process goals so the members could disclose there-and-then information relative to their own experiences as victims of sexual abuse, because they may not have been able to verbalize their thoughts and feelings in the past.

In any case, these goals provide general guidelines only, and the different experience and different process of each group call for flexibility in goals (Posthuma, 1999). As noted by Corey and Corey (1997) and Corey (2000, 2004), numerous generic goals can be applied to the group experience, but goals always should be selected based on the needs of those who constitute a given group.

Goals for Specialized Groups

Specialized groups often have specific goals based on the issues of individual members of the groups. The goals for a weight-loss group, for example, might be for members to identify specific reasons for why food has become such an important part of their everyday life; to discuss nutrition, exercise, and motivation; to provide understanding and support for one another's efforts; and to learn to avoid using food to manage stress. The goals for a group of incest survivors might be for members to tell about their incidents of sexual abuse; to learn that other members have similar feelings of hurt, shame, and anger; to develop trust; and to identify ways in which their earlier experiences affect their friendships and relationships with significant others. Goals for a men's group might include discussion of gender role expectations, relationships with fathers, transitions, overworking, or how to enhance self-esteem. Regardless of the specific purpose for which a number of individuals meet as a group, goals must be discussed thoroughly and understood by every group member.

Goals Based on Theoretical Perspectives

As Gibson and Mitchell (1995) noted, the theoretical orientation of the group leader can have a primary influence on group goals. The psychoanalytic, Adlerian, psychodramatic, existential, person-centered, Gestalt, transactional analysis, behavior therapy, rational-emotive behavior therapy, and reality therapy conceptual frames of reference all provide perspectives for the establishment of group goals. The following examples illustrate this point:

The Adlerian group leader may focus on

- establishing a working relationship in which the leader and the members are equal;
- aiding the members in exploring the personal goals, beliefs, feelings, and motives that are determining factors in the development of their lifestyle;
- helping members to enhance their involvement with others and to extend their social interest as it applies to self and others;
- assisting members in considering alternative lifestyles and helping them in strengthening their commitment to change.

The Gestalt group leader may focus on

- allowing members to find their own way in life and accept the responsibility that goes with it;
- aiding members in accepting all aspects of themselves and encouraging their sharing hidden and self-disguised aspects of self;
- assisting members in recognizing the blocks/barriers that impede their growth;
- helping members recognize the splintered parts of self and work toward integrating those parts.

The person-centered group leader may focus on

- establishing a facilitative climate within the group, characterized by congruence, unconditional positive regard, and empathic understanding;
- providing an environment in which all group members perceive the constructs of safety and mutual trust;
- supporting members in finding their own way in life and accepting the responsibility that goes with it;
- refraining from giving advice and direction and allowing members to positively activate their organismic valuing process.

Chapter 4 of this book provides a more comprehensive overview of theoretical perspectives as related to group counseling.

Goals Developed by Individual Members

Group participants often need assistance to personalize their reasons for wanting to be part of a group (Corey & Corey, 1997; Johnson & Johnson, 2003). Often, their goals have to be refined and clarified. The goal of "wanting to get in touch with feelings," for example, might relate to feelings of loss, anger, or guilt. A member who says she is "having trouble with assertiveness" might be talking about the workplace, the home, or the responsibilities of parenting. Another member, who says he is "having trouble with depression," could be experiencing difficult circumstances or having a chemically based, genetically linked, endogenous problem. The group leader has to help individual members continuously analyze their reasons for participating in a group to ensure that they state and realize their personalized goals.

TYPES OF GROUPS

Most textbooks for introduction to counseling courses begin the discussion of group work by attempting to make distinctions between group therapy, group counseling, and group guidance.

1. *Group therapy* typically is described as being longer term, more remedially and therapeutically focused, and more likely to be facilitated by someone with doctoral-level preparation and a more "clinical" orientation.
2. *Group counseling* usually is differentiated from group therapy by its focus on conscious problems, by its being aimed at major personality changes, by an orientation toward short-term issues, and by being less concerned with treating more severe psychological and behavioral disorders.
3. *Group guidance* describes a classroom group in a K–12 setting in which the leader presents information or conducts mental health education. In contrast to group therapy and group counseling, which generally involve no more than 8 to 10 participants, a group guidance experience could involve

20 to 40 participants, lessening the opportunities for individual participation and facilitator observation and intervention.

For the purposes of this chapter, ASGW's definitions of the four group work specialties—task/work groups, guidance/psychoeducational groups, counseling groups, and psychotherapy groups—are presented as a point of departure for classifying groups (Conyne et al., 1993). Good sources for additional reading on group types include Corey (2004), Corey and Corey (1997), Chen and Rybak (2004), Dinkmeyer and Muro (1979), Gazda (1984), Gladding (2003), Kottler and Brown (2000), and Ohlsen (1977).

Task/Work Groups

Group workers who specialize in promoting the development and functioning of task and work groups seek to support the members of these groups in improving their group function and performance. Task and work group specialists apply principles of group dynamics, organizational development, and team building to enhance group members' skills in accomplishing group tasks and maintaining the group. The scope of practice for these group work specialists includes normally functioning individuals who are members of naturally occurring task groups or work groups operating within a specific organizational context.

Graduate coursework for specialists in task and work groups should include at least one specialization course in organizational management and development. Ideally, they also should take coursework in the broad area of organizational psychology, management, and development to foster an awareness of organizational life and how task and work groups function within an organization. In addition, a task/work group specialist would benefit from developing skill in organizational assessment, training, program development, consultation, and program evaluation.

Clinical instruction for training specialists to work with task and work groups should include a minimum of 30 clock hours (45 clock hours recommended) of supervised practice in leading or co-leading a task/work group appropriate to the age and clientele of the group leader's specialty area(s) (e.g., school counseling, community counseling, mental health counseling).

Guidance/Psychoeducational Groups

Psychoeducational, or guidance groups, were originally developed for use in public schools and other educational settings (Gladding, 1999, 2003). The psychoeducational group specialist educates group participants in a specific area (Corey, 2000, 2004; Kottler, 2001) (e.g., how to cope with external threats, developmental transitions, or personal and interpersonal crises), in which participants may be informationally deficient. The scope of practice of psychoeducational group leaders includes essentially normally functioning individuals who are "at risk" for, but currently unaffected by, an environmental threat (e.g., AIDS), who are approaching a developmental transition point (e.g., new parents), or who are in the midst of coping with a life crisis (e.g., the suicide of a loved one). The primary goal in psychoeducational group work is to prevent dysfunctional behaviors from developing in the future.

Coursework for specialization in psychoeducational groups should include at least one specialization course that provides information about community psychology, health and wellness promotion, and program development and evaluation. Ideally, psychoeducational group specialists also would take courses in curriculum design, group training methods, and instructional techniques. Further, they should acquire knowledge about the topic areas in which they intend to work (e.g., AIDS prevention, substance abuse prevention, grief and loss, coping with transition and change, parent effectiveness training).

Clinical instruction for preparing to facilitate psychoeducational groups should include a minimum of 30 clock hours (45 clock hours recommended) of supervised practice in leading or co-leading a psychoeducational group appropriate to the age and clientele of the group leader's specialty area(s) (e.g., school counseling, community counseling, mental health counseling).

Counseling Groups

The group worker who specializes in group counseling assists group participants to resolve the usual, yet often difficult, problems of living by stimulating interpersonal support and group problem solving. Group counselors support participants in developing their existing interpersonal problem-solving competencies so they may become more able to handle future problems similar to those they are currently experiencing. The scope of practice for these group work specialists includes essentially normally functioning individuals with nonsevere career, educational, personal, interpersonal, social, or developmental concerns (Corey, 2000, 2004; Gladding, 1999, 2003; Kottler, 2001; Trotzer, 1999).

Graduate coursework for specialists in group counseling should include multiple courses in human development, health promotion, and group counseling. Group counseling specialists should have in-depth knowledge in the broad areas of normal human development, problem identification, and treatment of normal personal and interpersonal problems of living.

Clinical instruction for preparing to facilitate counseling groups should include a minimum of 45 clock hours (60 clock hours recommended) of supervised practice in leading or co-leading a counseling group appropriate to the age and clientele of the group leader's specialty area(s) (e.g., community counseling, mental health counseling, school counseling).

Psychotherapy Groups

The specialist in group psychotherapy helps individual group members remediate in-depth psychological problems or reconstruct major personality dimensions. Group psychotherapists differ from specialists in task/work groups, psychoeducational groups, and counseling groups in that their scope of practice involves individuals with acute or chronic mental or emotional disorders characterized by marked distress, impairment in functioning, or both (Corey, 2000, 2004; Gladding, 1999, 2003; Kottler, 2001; Trotzer, 1999).

Graduate coursework for training in group psychotherapy should include multiple courses in the development, assessment, and treatment of serious and chronic personal and interpersonal dysfunction. The group psychotherapist must develop in-depth knowledge in the broad areas of normal and abnormal human development, diagnosis, treatment of psychopathology, and group psychotherapy.

Clinical instruction for training specialists to work with psychotherapy groups should include a minimum 45 clock hours (60 clock hours recommended) of supervised practice in leading or co-leading a psychotherapy group appropriate to the age and clientele of the group leader's specialty area(s) (e.g., mental health counseling, community counseling).

Other Models for Group Work

Various other distinctions are made between types of groups (Corey & Corey, 1997; Gibson & Mitchell, 1995). For example, *T-groups* help members develop self-awareness and sensitivity to others through the verbalization of feelings. *Encounter groups*, initiated by Carl Rogers, became known as "personal growth groups" because of their emphasis upon the individual development of each of their members (Gladding, 1991). Both T-groups and encounter groups are sometimes called *sensitivity groups*.

In J. L. Moreno's *psychodrama* groups, participants stage a production in which they sometimes play themselves and sometimes play the alter egos of others. By acting out their issues and concerns and "processing" the experience afterward, members progress to higher levels of self-awareness and begin to exert more control over their emotions and behaviors.

Marathon groups, introduced in the 1960s by George Bach and Fred Stoller, are intense experiences lasting 24 hours, 48 hours, or even longer, and requiring that group members stay together for the duration of the experience. Because fatigue and intensity are built into the marathon, participants' defenses break down, truthfulness and openness increase, and personal growth can take place in a different way than in groups conducted once a week for an hour and a half. (Provisions usually are made for participants to receive individual or small-group follow-up counseling after they participate in a marathon group.)

Self-help groups are widely utilized as adjunct support for individual or group counseling or therapy conducted by professionally prepared, licensed counselors and therapists (Corey, 2000, 2004; Kottler, 2001). As Gladding (1997) noted, self-help groups take at least two forms: (a) those that are organized by an established professional helping organization (e.g., Alcoholics Anonymous), and (b) those that emerge spontaneously. Members of these groups share something in common, and the groups can be psychoeducational, therapeutic, or task-focused. Self-help groups can be powerful catalysts in helping people take charge of their lives. Some of these groups lack the advantage of having professional leaders but often compensate by having the contribution of committed and experienced lay leaders.

Closed and Open Groups

Closed and open groups are subcategories of most groups. A closed group is characterized by a membership that remains together until the group terminates. In an open group, new members are added during the life cycle of the group (Corey, 2004; Gruner, 1984).

Both the closed group and open group models have advantages and disadvantages. Open groups permit members to resolve problems and issues in their own time frame and then leave the group. New members may enter the groups as openings occur. Although new members coming in at various times may be viewed as adding stimulation to the group, the group as a whole may go through a process of regression, with accompanying fluctuations in cohesion and trust, when a new member is added.

By contrast, closed groups offer stability of membership and facilitate cohesion and trust. Because all members of a group do not progress at the same rate, however, some group members lose the advantage of being able to work hard and terminate in a manner consistent with their own ability to learn, resolve intrapersonal or interpersonal issues, and obtain closure based on an appropriate resolution (Gruner, 1984).

COMPOSITION OF GROUPS

The composition of a group has an influence on how the group functions (Corey, 2004; Perrone & Sedlacek, 2000; Waltman & Zimpfer, 1988; Yalom, 1985). Two general approaches to combining members of a group are the heterogeneous approach and the homogeneous approach.

Heterogeneous or Mixed-Gender Group

Beasley and Childers (1985) discussed five fundamental assumptions for creating groups composed of both men and women:

1. The heterogeneous group is a microcosm of society.
2. Self-defeating behavior can be identified and confronted more easily in a group approximating the composition of society.
3. The group focus is on the present rather than on the past.
4. Reality testing can and does occur.
5. The heterosexual group situation generates anxiety that produces change.

Social Microcosm

Creating a group environment that is representative of the world in which an individual interacts daily is said to maximize opportunities for learning and realizing potential (Corey, 2004; Hansen, Warner, & Smith, 1980). Not all group research, however, supports the assumption that creating such a microcosm through heterogeneous grouping promotes personal growth for women and men alike.

In some studies, women in a mixed-gender group, compared to those in all-female groups, have been seen to talk less, talk primarily to the men, share less personal information, and be less involved in topics (Carlock & Martin, 1977). Although some studies have indicated that men in heterogeneous groups are more personal and self-disclosing and initiate and receive more interaction than they do in all-male groups (Aries, 1976; Carlock & Martin, 1977; Reed, 1981), it will be interesting to see if these findings continue to be reported with the same frequency as researchers begin to study the group phenomenon created by Robert Bly and other proponents of the men's movement.

Confrontation of Self-Defeating Behavior

Based on the premise that a person's true self will emerge in a group reflecting society in general, this assumption presupposes that group members' dysfunctional behavior will become more clearly evident in a heterogeneous group than in a homogeneous group. Once the behavior surfaces, other group members, as well as the group leader, can confront the behavior and provide constructive feedback (Beasley & Childers, 1985). Some evidence supports this assumption. A person's self-perception evolves from the feedback he or she receives through the years from interacting with both men and women, so a mixed-gender group would seem to be the best avenue for clarifying self-perception. But the evidence is not unanimously supportive. For example, women could risk negative feedback by revealing characteristics such as assertiveness, competitiveness, and independence in the group (Broverman, Broverman, Clarkson, Rosenkrantz, & Vogel, 1970).

Further, the concern has been voiced that heterogeneous groups may tend to reinforce stereotypical behavior for men and for women (Reed, 1981). Group leaders should be alert to that possibility when facilitating a mixed-gender group.

Focus on the Present

Yalom (1985) maintained that a focus on the present augments a group's potency and effectiveness. This focus aids the development of each group member's social microcosm and promotes feedback, self-disclosure, and the acquisition of social skills. Because focusing on the present may be easier in heterogeneous groups than homogeneous groups (Aries, 1973), this factor should be considered when making decisions about group composition.

Reality Testing

In groups, participants can discuss new alternatives and test the reality of those alternatives by having other group members provide feedback. Reactions from both genders, in the context of a safe and well-facilitated group, may help a group member gain confidence and accept responsibility for behavior in a way that will transfer to heterosexual relationships outside the group (Beasley & Childers, 1985). If women's behaviors are circumscribed in a mixed-gender group, however, the group composition may limit women's communication and exploration of new options.

Generation of Gender-Based Anxiety

Much research shows that heterogeneous groups produce more anxiety in the members than do homogeneous groups (Aries, 1973; Carlock & Martin, 1977; Hansen et al., 1980; Melnick & Woods, 1976). Yalom (1985) contended that this anxiety is positive because change usually follows a period of anxiety and a state of ambiguity. This anxiety ideally propels members to participate in problem solving, to consider new behaviors, and so on. Active participation and interest in self-enhancement are generally valued in the context of the group experience.

Homogeneous or Same-Gender Group Composition

A homogeneous group consists entirely of members of a given population or members who share a specific need, concern, or situation (Beasley & Childers, 1985; Corey, 2004). The cohesiveness theory underlies this approach to group composition and supports the idea that similarity of members can lead to a great deal of cohesion, openness, and exploration of issues (Perrone & Sedlacek, 2000).

All-Female Groups

Some feminist groups have excluded men from membership because of the perception that men tend to dominate the conversation and the decision-making process (Bardwick, 1971). When women are in the presence of men in a group, they tend to withdraw, become passive, defer to more dominant men, and assume other patterns of communication that are different from those seen in all-female groups (Aries, 1973; Carlock & Martin, 1977).

According to some group leaders (e.g., Halas, 1973), groups composed solely of women are more conducive to change for women than are mixed-gender groups. In summarizing the research on women's consciousness groups, Kravetz (1980) reported that these groups consistently

- increased self-awareness, self-respect, and self-esteem;
- prompted greater awareness of the effects of traditional sex roles and sexism;
- increased awareness of a commonality with other women;
- improved relationships and a sense of solidarity with other women;
- showed positive changes in interpersonal relationships and roles; and
- engendered participation in work and community activities to change the options and opportunities for women

All-Male Groups

Men's groups provide opportunities for members to share the stress and anger, to discuss concerns and insecurities, and to develop the needed confidence to change their behaviors (Washington, 1982). Research such as that done by Twentyman and McFall (1975) and MacDonald, Lindquist, Kramer, McGrath, and Rhyne (1975) indicated that all-male groups helped members improve and rehearse their behaviors and confront personal issues, which resulted in improving their relationships with women. Some research (Aries, 1973; Reed, 1981) has suggested that men's self-disclosures in all-male groups frequently take the form of storytelling and metaphors with frequent references to competition, self-aggrandizement, and aggression.

THERAPEUTIC FACTORS IN GROUPS

Therapeutic factors in groups have been extensively researched and discussed for a number of years (Chen & Rybak, 2004; Shechtman & Perl-Dekel, 2000). A therapeutic factor in a group is "an element occurring in group therapy that contributes to improvement in a patient's condition and is a function of the actions of a group therapist, the patient, or fellow group members" (Bloch, 1986, p. 679). This definition is important because it helps distinguish between therapeutic factors and necessary conditions for change in a group as well as group interventions or techniques. An example of a condition for change is the presence of a group leader and group members to listen and provide feedback. An example of a Gestalt intervention or technique that a group leader might employ is "making the rounds." Conditions and interventions or techniques increase the impact of therapeutic factors in groups.

As George and Dustin (1988) noted, Corsini and Rosenberg (1955) published the first major work that presented a unifying paradigm of factors that group leaders considered therapeutic from a variety of theoretical perspectives. After clustering statements reflecting therapeutic factors, they formed the following nine-category classification system:

1. *Acceptance*: a sense of belonging
2. *Altruism*: a sense of being helpful to others
3. *Universalization*: the realization that one is not unique in one's problems
4. *Intellectualization*: the process of acquiring knowledge about oneself
5. *Reality testing*: recognizing the reality of issues such as defenses and family conflicts
6. *Transference*: a strong attachment to either the therapist or co-members
7. *Interaction*: relating within the group that brings benefits
8. *Spectator therapy*: gaining from observing and imitating fellow members
9. *Ventilation*: the release of feelings and expression of previously repressed ideas

In an attempt to further refine the classification of therapeutic elements in groups, Hill (1957) interviewed 19 group leaders. He proposed the six elements of catharsis, feelings of belongingness, spectator therapy, insights, peer agency (universality), and socialization. This was followed by the classification of Berzon, Pious, and Farson (1963), who used group members rather than group leaders as a source of information about therapeutic factors. Their classification included the following 10 factors:

1. Becoming more aware of emotional dynamics
2. Recognizing similarity with others
3. Feeling positive regard, acceptance, sympathy for others

4. Seeing self as seen by others
5. Expressing self congruently, articulately, or assertively in the group
6. Witnessing honesty, courage, openness, or expressions of emotionality in others
7. Feeling warmth and closeness in the group
8. Feeling responded to by others
9. Feeling warmth and closeness generally in the group
10. Ventilating emotions

Ohlsen (1977) proposed a very different set of therapeutic factors connected with group experiences. His list differs from earlier proposals in that it emphasizes group members' attitudes about the group experience. Ohlsen's paradigm includes 14 elements, which he labeled "therapeutic forces":

1. Attractiveness of the group
2. Acceptance by the group
3. Clear expectations
4. Sense of belonging
5. Security within the group
6. Client readiness
7. Client commitment
8. Client participation
9. Client acceptance of responsibility
10. Congruence
11. Feedback
12. Openness
13. Therapeutic tension
14. Therapeutic norms

In what is now considered a landmark classification of "curative factors," Yalom (1970, 1975, 1985, 1995) proposed a list of therapeutic elements based on research that he and his colleagues conducted:

1. *Instillation of hope*: receiving reassurance that the group experience will be constructive and helpful
2. *Universality*: developing an awareness that what seems to be a unique problem may be similar to the experience of another member of the group
3. *Imparting of information*: learning about mental health and mental illness via group discussion
4. *Altruism*: sharing with others and being willing to reach out
5. *The corrective recapitulation of the primary family group*: reliving family-of-origin conflicts and resolving them through the group
6. *Development of socializing techniques*: learning social skills
7. *Imitative behavior*: imitating positive behaviors modeled by other group members

8. *Interpersonal learning*: developing new insights and correcting past interpretations
9. *Group cohesiveness*: developing bonds of trust, support, and caring
10. *Catharsis*: sharing feelings and experiences
11. *Existential factors*: accepting responsibility for one's life, including deci-
    sions, meaning making, and spiritual dimensions

These listings represent only a few of the many possibilities for viewing the therapeutic elements of a positive group experience. Jacobs, Harvill, and Masson (1988) pointed out a number of factors that can work for or against a group. As possible contributors to a positive or a negative group experience for members, they cited and identified size, length of session, setting, member composition, level of goodwill, level of commitment, level of trust, members' attitudes toward one another, members' attitudes toward the leader, leader's attitude toward members, interaction pattern of members and leader, and stage of the group. In his discussion of factors influencing group dynamics, Gladding (1991) emphasized the importance of identifying with the group's structure, norms, power roles, group interaction, length of group, attitude, here-and-now variables, and racial and gender issues. Gerald Corey and Marianne Schneider Corey (1997, 2002) discussed therapeutic factors that operate in groups, including self-disclosure, confrontation, feedback, cohesion and universality, hope, willingness to risk and trust, caring and acceptance, power, catharsis, the cognitive component, commitment to change, freedom to experiment, and humor. Bemak and Epp (1996) proposed love as another curative factor in groups, identifying nonsexual love as a characteristic of groups that is not accessible to the same extent in other counseling modalities. Donigian and Malnati (1997) identified contagion, conflict, anxiety, and consensual validation as additional curative factors in groups. In light of the importance of therapeutic factors in group work, beginning group workers are urged to spend time reading the sources discussed here, as well as resources on the topic.

PERSONAL CHARACTERISTICS OF EFFECTIVE GROUP LEADERS

Many professionals in the field have described the personal traits and characteristics of effective group leaders (e.g., Corey, 2000; Corey & Corey, 1997; Dinkmeyer & Muro, 1979; Kottler, 1983). As expressed by Gerald Corey (1985):

> It is my belief that group leaders can acquire extensive
> theoretical and practical knowledge of group dynamics and be
> skilled in diagnostic and technical procedures yet be ineffective
> in stimulating growth and change in the members of their
> groups. Leaders bring to every group their personal qualities,
> values, and life experiences. In order to promote growth in the
> members' lives, leaders need to live growth-oriented lives

themselves. In order to foster honest self-investigation in others, leaders need to have the courage to engage in self-appraisal themselves. In order to inspire others to break away from deadening ways of being, leaders need to be willing to seek new experiences themselves. In short, the most effective group direction is found in the kind of life the group members see the leader demonstrating and not in the words they hear the leader saying. (p. 39)

Like Corey, we believe the group leader must possess certain characteristics to be effective. As Kottler (2001) noted, who you are is as important to your success as a group facilitator or leader as what you know and do in the process of working with group members. Others who have presented their views on this topic include Arbuckle (1975), Carkhuff and Berenson (1977), Jourard (1971), Truax and Carkhuff (1967), and Yalom (1975). In the following paragraphs we summarize Corey and Corey's (1997, 2002) orientation on personal characteristics of effective group leaders as a starting point for the beginning group work specialist. This point of view is congruent with ours and is similar to discussions presented by Corey (2000, 2004), Gladding (2003), and others.

Presence

The group leader must have the capacity to be emotionally present as group members share their experiences. Leaders who are in touch with their own life experiences and associated emotions are better able to communicate empathy and understanding because they can relate to similar circumstances or emotions. Group leaders must not lose perspective by being overly focused on their own reactions but, rather, allow themselves to be connected with the experience of group members in such a way that they can communicate compassion and concern and still facilitate constructive personal growth.

Personal Power

Personal power is derived from a sense of self-confidence and realization of the group leader's influence on a group. Personal power channeled in a way that enhances the ability of each group member to identify and build upon his or her strengths, overcome problems, and cope more effectively with stressors is both essential and curative. Leaders who have the most power are accepting of their own strengths and weaknesses and do not expend energy attempting to prevent others from seeing them as they are.

Courage

Group leaders have to be courageous. They take risks when they express their reactions to aspects of group process, confront members, share life experiences, act on a combination of intuition and observation, and direct group movement and discussion. These risks are the same risks that group members are expected to take. In this regard, the leader's role-modeling can help make a group more productive and better able to communicate and bond.

Self-Awareness

Serving in any kind of a counseling role would be difficult without highly developed self-awareness. In facilitating a group, personal needs, defenses, apprehensions, relationship conflicts, and unresolved issues of any kind come into play. These can enhance or detract from one's ability to lead the group, depending upon the group leader's level of awareness and the extent to which these factors make the leader's role more difficult. Many counselor education departments require that graduate students obtain personal counseling outside the department, to resolve "unfinished business" so personal issues do not impede their ability to serve constructively in a counseling role.

Belief in Group Process

Group leaders must be positive about the healing capacity of groups and must believe in the benefits of the group experience. If they are unsure, tentative, or unenthusiastic about the healing capacity of the group experience, group members will develop the same tenor. Although the outcome of a group experience does not depend totally on its leader, the leader does convey messages, both verbally and nonverbally, that impact the overall benefit of the experience.

Inventiveness

Group leaders who are spontaneous in their approach to a group often catalyze better communication, insight, and personal growth than those who rely on structured interventions and techniques. Creative leaders usually accept those who are different from themselves and are flexible about approaching members and groups in ways that seem congruent with the specific group. In addition, a certain amount of creativity and spontaneity is necessary to deal with the unexpected. In a group situation, the leader is presented continuously with comments, problems, and reactions that cannot be anticipated before a given session.

Stamina and Energy

Unlike an individual counseling session, during which the counselor listens to and interacts with one client, the group experience requires the leader to "track," remember, and diagnose several clients simultaneously. This set of circumstances requires more alertness, observation, responsiveness, proactivity, and energy. Therefore, a group leader should not overschedule groups. Many leaders prefer the co-facilitation model, in which the co-facilitator or co-leader assumes part of the responsibility for group process and observation.

Goodwill and Caring

Group leaders must place the welfare of group members first. They make sure that members are achieving the goals that have been established for the group experience. Caring about those in a group is also vital to successful outcomes. If a group leader has difficulty in this regard, he or she must evaluate what is blocking this capacity and what steps he or she can take to ensure that member needs will be met.

Openness

Group leaders must be open with and about themselves, open to experiences and lifestyles that are different from their own, and open to how the group is affecting them. Openness does not mean that the leader should reveal every aspect of his or her personal life. Rather, it can mean being open enough to give members an understanding of who he or she is as a person. The leader's willingness to be open promotes a corresponding spirit of openness and willingness to communicate among group members.

Awareness of One's Own Culture and That of Group Members

In today's multicultural society, group leaders have to be aware of diversity issues. They must understand that just as their culture influences their worldview and decision making, the same is true of the culture of each member of a given group. Cultural diversity encompasses more than ethnic influences; it also encompasses age, gender, sexual orientation, disability, and numerous other factors. Effective group leaders are sensitive to aspects of diversity and respect the differences that individual members bring to the group.

Nondefensiveness in Coping With Attacks

Members of a group often test their leaders by being critical or confrontational with the leader. These attacks can occur if the leader has made a mistake or has been insensitive. They also can occur if a member is jealous, wishes to control, or is projecting feelings about someone else to the leader. Regardless of the reason, the leader must remain nondefensive and explore the reasons for the member's behavior. To do this, the leader must have a strong sense of ego integrity and confidence. Becoming angry or refusing to explore reasons for the attack models behavior that can interfere with openness, trust, and positive outcomes.

Sense of Humor

Humor can be crucial to a group's success. Laughter can help release tension and help members retain perspective on their problems. As long as humor does not become a roadblock to doing the therapeutic work that has to be accomplished, it can be a tremendous asset to a group.

Personal Dedication and Commitment

To be effective, the group leader must be dedicated to the value of group process and be committed to continuing to develop his or her leadership skills. If the group leader believes that group membership can empower and benefit participants, his or her enthusiasm and energy will come through to participants and contribute to some of the therapeutic elements of group work discussed earlier in this chapter.

Willingness to Model

Group members learn how to respond to others in the group and how to communicate their own thoughts and feelings by watching the facilitator. The facilitators who are best at creating a safe and therapeutic "holding environment" for members to do their work also are likely to be exceptional role models for participants in their groups. Willingness to be authentic, spontaneous, and immediate in facilitating a group means being comfortable in knowing that members will imitate their communication style more and more as the group progresses.

Willingness to Seek New Experiences

The best group facilitators make a personal commitment to lifelong learning about themselves and others. A facilitator would have difficulty relating to the issues that participants bring to the group if he or she did not strive continuously to learn more and more about his or her own way of being and relating in the world and also about the contemporary struggles of clients who live in an ever-changing culture and set of life circumstances. Group workers have to remain engaged with the world around them by seeking new experiences, new people, and differing cultures, and by striving to attain ever-increasing levels of self-understanding and insight. This may require additional education, travel, introspection, personal counseling, supervision, and taking advantage of a myriad of other precipitants to expand their worldview of themselves and others.

MYTHS CONNECTED WITH GROUP WORK

Counselors who are group leaders are usually enthusiastic about the benefits to clients who participate in a small group. A group experience that is facilitated competently can engender personal growth (Capuzzi & Gross, 1997, 2001, 2005) that affects clients well into the future. Like other forms of therapeutic assistance (e.g., individual or family therapy), however, group work can be for better or for worse (Carkhuff, 1969). Many group leaders adhere to a belief system that can be challenged by empirical facts. The following myths connected with group work are given quite a bit of attention here, with the hope that group leaders will not base their practices on any belief system that is not supported by research (Anderson, 1985; Capuzzi & Gross, 1997, 2001, 2005; Kottler & Brown, 2000).

Myth #1: Everyone Benefits From Group Experience

Groups do provide benefits. Research on the psychosocial outcomes of groups demonstrates that groups are a powerful modality for learning, the results of which can be used outside of the group experience itself (Bednar & Lawlis, 1971; Gazda & Peters, 1975; Parloff & Dies, 1978). At times, however, membership in a group can be detrimental. Some research shows that 1 in every 10 group members can be hurt by the experience (Lieberman, Yalom, & Miles, 1973).

The research findings that seem to relate most to individuals who are harmed by group experience suggest two important principles (DeJulio, Bentley, & Cockayne, 1979; Lieberman et al., 1973; Stava & Bednar, 1979):

1. Group members who have the greatest potential to be hurt by the experience have unrealistic expectations
2. These expectations seem to be reinforced by leaders who coerce the group members to meet them.

To prevent harm, members' expectations for the group have to be realistic and the leader must maintain a reasonable perspective.

Myth #2: Groups Can Be Composed in a Way That Assures Success

Actually, we do not know enough about how to compose groups via the pre-group screening interview. In general, objective criteria (age, gender, socioeconomic status, presenting problem, and so forth) can be applied to keep groups homogeneous in some respects, but behavioral characteristics should be selected on a heterogeneous basis (Bertcher & Maple, 1979). The most consistent finding is that groups should be composed so that each member is compatible with at least one other member (Stava & Bednar, 1979). This composition seems to prevent the evolution of neglected isolates or scapegoats in a group. It gains additional importance when considering that the essence of group process in terms of benefit to members and effective outcomes is *perceived mutual aid* (helping others, a feeling of belonging, interpersonal learning, instillation of hope, and so on) (Butler & Fuhriman, 1980; Long & Cope, 1980; Yalom, 1975), which cannot be achieved when members feel isolated.

Myth #3: The Group Revolves Around the Leader's Charisma

Although leaders do influence groups tremendously, two general findings in the research on groups should be noted (Ashkenas & Tandon, 1979):

1. The group, independent of the leader, has an impact on outcomes.
2. The most effective group leaders are those who help the group develop so members are primary sources of help to one another

According to Anderson (1985), research on leadership styles has identified four leader functions that facilitate the group's functioning:

(1) *Providing*: This is the provider role of relationship and climate-setting through such skills as support, affection, praise, protection, warmth, acceptance, genuineness, and concern.

(2) *Processing*: This is the processor role of illuminating the meaning of the process through such skills as explaining, clarifying, interpreting, and providing a cognitive framework for change, or translating feelings and experiences into ideas.

(3) *Catalyzing*: This is the catalyst role of stimulating interaction and emotional expression through such skills as reaching for feelings, challenging, confronting, and suggesting; using program activities such as structured experiences; and modeling.

(4) *Directing*: This is the director role through such skills as setting limits, roles, norms, and goals; managing time; pacing; stopping; interceding; and suggesting procedures. (p. 272)

Providing and processing seem to have a linear relationship to outcomes: The higher the providing (or caring) and the higher the processing (or clarifying), the higher the positive outcomes. Catalyzing and directing have a curvilinear relationship to outcomes. Too much or too little catalyzing or directing results in lower positive outcomes (Lieberman et al., 1973).

Myth #4: Leaders Can Direct Groups Through Structured Exercises or Experiences

Structured exercises create early cohesion (Levin & Kurtz, 1974; Lieberman et al., 1973), helping to bring about the early expression of positive and negative feelings. At the same time, they restrict members from dealing with group themes such as affection, closeness, distance, trust, mistrust, genuineness, and lack of genuineness. All of these areas form the basis for group process and should not be hampered by too much structure. The best principle around which to plan and use structured exercises to get groups started and to keep them going can best be stated as: "Overplan and underuse."

Myth #5: Therapeutic Change in Groups Comes About Through Here-and-Now Experiences

Much of the research on groups indicates that corrective emotional experiences in the here-and-now of the group increase the intensity of the members' experience (Levine, 1971; Lieberman et al., 1973; Snortum & Myers, 1971; Zimpfer, 1967). The intensity of emotional experiences, however, does not seem to be related to outcomes. Higher-level outcomes are achieved by group members who develop insight or cognitive understanding of emotional experiences in the group and can transfer that understanding into their lives outside the group. The Gestaltists' influence on groups in the 1960s and 1970s (Perls, 1969) suggested that group members should "lose their mind and come to their senses" and stay with the here and now. Research, however, suggests that members "use their mind *and* their senses" and focus on the there and then as well as the here and now.

Myth #6: The Greatest Member Learning in Groups Is Derived From Self-Disclosure and Feedback

Most of the learning of members in a group is assumed to come from self-disclosure in exchange for feedback (Jacobs, 1974). To a large extent, this statement is a myth. Self-disclosure and feedback per se make little difference in outcome (Anchor, 1979; Bean & Houston, 1978). Rather, the *use* of self-disclosure and feedback is what seems to make the difference (Martin & Jacobs, 1980). Self-disclosure and feedback seem to be useful only when deeply personal sharing is understood and appreciated and the feedback is accurate (Berzon et al., 1963; Frank & Ascher, 1951; Goldstein, Bednar, & Yanell, 1979). The actual benefit of self-disclosure and feedback relates to how these processes generate empathy among group members. Empathy, or the experience of being understood by other members, is what catalyzes personal growth and understanding in the context of a group.

Myth #7: A Leader Does Not Have to Understand Group Process and Group Dynamics

All groups are characterized by a natural evolution and unfolding of processes and dynamics. Anderson (1979) labeled these processes and dynamics as trust, autonomy, closeness, interdependence, and termination (TACIT). Tuckman (1965) suggested the more dramatic terminology of forming, storming, norming, performing, and adjourning.

In chapter 2 we suggest four stages in the evolution of a group: the definitive stage, the personal involvement stage, the group involvement stage, and the enhancement and closure stage. Two reviews covering more than 200 studies of group dynamics and group process (Cohen & Smith, 1976; La Coursiere, 1980) revealed remarkably similar patterns (despite differences in the terms chosen as descriptors) in the evolution of group processes. To do a competent job of enhancing benefits from group participation, group leaders must understand group processes and dynamics

Myth #8: Changes in Group Participants Are Not Maintained

Groups can be powerful. Members can maintain changes for as long as 6 months to a year after a group has disbanded, even when the group met for only 3 or 4 months (Lieberman et al., 1973). The positive effects of having participated in a group can be subtle but pervasive. For example, graduate students at Portland State University who took part in a 10-week off-campus personal growth group focusing on art therapy reported that skills they learned in the group, such as the need for creativity in their lives, relaxation techniques, insight into personal family dynamics, and ways of working with daily stress, continued to be relevant and useful a year later.

Myth #9: A Group Is a Place to Get Emotionally High

Although feeling good after a group session can be a positive outcome, it is not the main reason for being in a group (Corey, 1985). Some group members have periods of depression after their group has disbanded because they don't find, on a daily basis, the kind of support they received from members of the group. Group members should be prepared for this possibility and assisted in their ability to obtain support, when appropriate, from those around them.

Myth #10: A Group's Purpose Is to Make Members Close to Every Other Member

Although genuine feelings of intimacy and cohesiveness develop in effective groups, intimacy is a byproduct, not the central purpose of the group. Intimacy develops as individual members risk self-disclosure and problem solving and other group members reach out in constructive ways (Corey & Corey, 1997).

Myth #11: Group Participation Results in Brainwashing

Professional groups do not indoctrinate members with a particular philosophy of life or a set of rules about how each member "should be." If this does occur in a group, it is truly a breach of professional ethics and an abuse of the group. Group participation should encourage members to look within themselves for answers and to become as self-directed as possible (Corey & Corey, 1997).

Myth #12: To Benefit From a Group, a Member Has to Be Dysfunctional

Group counseling is as appropriate with individuals who are functioning relatively well and who want to enhance their capabilities as it is for those who are having difficulty with certain aspects of their lives. Groups are not just for dysfunctional people (Corey & Corey, 1997).

LEARNING ACTIVITIES

In a small group, complete one of the following six tasks:

1. Examine several issues of the journals published by the Association for Specialists in Group Work, the American Society of Group Psychotherapy and

Psychodrama, and the American Group Psychotherapy Association. Discuss with the rest of the class your observations about the kinds of articles (research, theory, or practice) that characterize each publication

2. Identify as many conferences or workshops as you can that are scheduled for the next few months on the topic of group work. Prepare a description of costs, locations, dates, focus of content sessions, and so forth, and share the information with the rest of the class. Investigate the possibility of working with some of your peers to submit a program proposal for one of the conferences you have identified. Ask your professor to mentor you as you develop the proposal and serve as the content session sponsor and convener.

3. Study the ASGW definitions of specialty types of group work as described in this chapter. Identify courses, internships, and supervisors that might be available on your campus or in the local community to provide you with the knowledge and skills base to facilitate each type of group. Share your findings with the rest of the class.

4. Invite several group practitioners from the local community to make a panel presentation to your class on the topic of therapeutic factors in groups. Ask them to discuss how they structure the groups they facilitate to assure that the experience is therapeutic for group members. If the panelists conduct groups for specific populations of clients, ask them to also describe the education and supervision needed to competently facilitate such groups.

5. The discussion of personal characteristics of effective group leaders in this chapter can seem overwhelming to the beginning group work specialist. Prepare a group presentation for the class summarizing these characteristics and the kind of supervision that a group leader might need to learn to function effectively with groups. After giving the presentation, ask members of the class to share what they would be comfortable sharing about their own strengths and weaknesses with respect to the recommended characteristics and the kind of supervision that probably would be needed.

6. With the other students in your group, discuss and analyze positive experiences you have had as a member of a group. What did the facilitator of the group do that made the experience therapeutic? Could you learn to create a similar atmosphere for members of a group you were conducting? What do you see as the biggest challenge for you, personally, in this regard? What might be needed to meet this challenge? Share the results of your group discussion with the rest of the class.

SUMMARY

Group counseling has its roots in the early 1900s, when it was applied in medical settings and with children, adults, and families. The first "laboratory" group, or T-group, emerged in 1947, and groups later branched out to university and other settings. Interest in group work has increased dramatically over time, illustrated by the recent flood of self-help groups led by either professionals or lay people.

Among the goals for groups are to facilitate the release of feelings, to strengthen members' self-esteem, to help members face and resolve their problems, to help them learn how to recognize and solve interpersonal and intrapersonal conflicts, and to facilitate their maintaining of their therapeutic gains. Group goals can be addressed in a number of ways: (a) general goals for groups, (b) goals for specialized groups, (c) goals based on theoretical perspectives, and (d) goals developed by individual members.

Distinctions can be made between group therapy (more likely to be longer term and have a therapeutic emphasis), group counseling (having a focus on conscious problems and an orientation toward short-term issues), and group guidance (in which the leader presents information or conducts mental health education to a larger group). Specialized types of group experiences include sensitivity groups, psychodrama groups, marathon groups, and task groups, among others. Based on ASGW's definitions, groups can be classified into four primary categories: task/work groups, guidance/psychoeducational groups, counseling groups, and psychotherapy groups. All of these types of groups can be either heterogeneous (mixed gender) or homogeneous (same gender) and can be closed (members stay together until the group is terminated) or open (new members are added as others leave).

Therapeutic factors in a group include acceptance, altruism, universalization, intellectualization, reality testing, transference, interaction, spectator therapy, and ventilation. Translated into leader qualities, these factors entail presence, personal power, courage, self-awareness, belief in group process, inventiveness, stamina and energy, goodwill and caring, openness, becoming aware of one's own culture and that of group members, nondefensiveness in coping with attacks, sense of humor, and personal dedication and commitment.

Numerous myths commonly associated with group work, by group leaders and others, can detract from group effectiveness. Among these misconceptions are that everyone benefits from group experience, groups always have advantageous outcomes, the group revolves around the leader's charisma, group members should be limited to discussion of here-and-now experiences, and dysfunctional people are the only ones who can benefit from groups. Groups can be either powerful and growth-enhancing or stifling and hindering. The more a leader is aware of the goals, purposes, and dynamics of groups, the better equipped he or she will be to provide an optimal experience for group members.

USEFUL WEB SITES

☐ American Counseling Association *Code of Ethics*
www.counseling.org
☐ Association for Specialists in Group Work (ASGW)
www.asgw.org
☐ ASGW *Professional Training Standards*
www.asgw.org/training_standards.htm

☐ ASGW *Best Practice Guidelines*
www.asgw.org/best.htm

☐ ASGW *Principles for Diversity-Competent Group Workers*
www.asgw.org/diversity.htm

☐ American Group Psychotherapy Association &
National Registry of Certified Group Psychotherapists
www.groupsinc.org/group/ethicalguide.html

REFERENCES

Anchor, K. N. (1979). High- and low-risk self-disclosure in group psychotherapy. *Small Group Behavior, 10*, 279–283.

Anderson, J. D. (1979). Social work with groups in the generic base of social work practice. *Social Work With Groups, 2*, 281–293.

Anderson, J. D. (1985). Working with groups: Little known facts that challenge well-known myths. *Small Group Behavior, 16*, 267–283.

Arbuckle, D. (1975). *Counseling and psychotherapy: An existential-humanistic view*. Boston: Allyn & Bacon.

Aries, E. J. (1973). Interaction patterns and themes of male, female and mixed groups. *Dissertation Abstracts International, 35*, 3084. (University Microfilms No. 74-27, 772)

Aries, E. J. (1976). Interactional patterns and themes of male, female and mixed groups. *Small Group Behavior, 7*, 7–18.

Ashkenas, R., & Tandon, R. (1979). Eclectic approach to small group facilitation. *Small Group Behavior, 10*, 224–241.

Association for Specialists in Group Work (ASGW). (1989). *Ethical guidelines for group counselors*. Alexandria, VA: Author.

Association for Specialists in Group Work (ASGW). (1991). *Professional standards for the training of group workers* (rev. ed.). Alexandria, VA: Author.

Bardwick, J. M. (1971). *Psychology of women*. New York: Harper & Row.

Bean, B. W., & Houston, B. K. (1978). Self-concept and self-disclosure in encounter groups. *Small Group Behavior, 9*, 549–554.

Beasley, L., & Childers, J. H., Jr. (1985). Group counseling for heterosexual, interpersonal skills: Mixed or same-sex group composition. *Journal for Specialists in Group Work, 10*(4), 192–197.

Bednar, R., & Lawlis, G. (1971). Empirical research in group psychotherapy. In S. L. Garfield & A. E. Bergin (Eds.), *Handbook of psychotherapy and behavior change* (2nd ed., pp. 420–439). New York: Wiley.

Bemak, F., & Epp, L. R. (1996). The 12th curative factor: Love as an agent of healing in group psychotherapy. *Journal for Specialists in Group Work, 21* (2), 118–127.

Bertcher, H. J., & Maple, F. F. (1979). *Creating groups*. Beverly Hills, CA: Sage Publications.

Berzon, B., Pious, C., & Farson, R. (1963). The therapeutic event in group psychotherapy: A study of subjective reports by group members. *Journal of Individual Psychology, 19*, 204–212.

Bloch, S. (1986). Therapeutic factors in group psychotherapy. In A. J. Frances & R. E. Hales (Eds.), *Annual review* (Vol. 5, pp. 678–698). Washington, DC: American Psychiatric Press.

Bradford, L. P., Gibb, J. R., & Benne, K. D. (Eds.). (1964). *T-group theory and laboratory method: Innovation in re-education*. New York: Wiley.

Broverman, I. K., Broverman, D. M., Clarkson, F. E., Rosenkrantz, P., & Vogel, S. R. (1970). Sex role stereotypes and clinical judgments of mental health. *Journal of Consulting Psychology, 34*, 1–7.

Butler, T., & Fuhriman, A. (1980). Patient perspective on the curative process: A comparison of day treatment and outpatient psychotherapy groups. *Small Group Behavior, 11,* 371–388.

Capuzzi, D., & Gross, D. R. (1997). *Introduction to the counseling profession* (2nd ed.). Boston: Allyn & Bacon.

Capuzzi, D., & Gross, D. R. (2001). *Introduction to the counseling profession* (3rd ed.). Boston: Allyn & Bacon.

Capuzzi, D., & Gross, D. R. (2005). *Introduction to the counseling profession* (4th ed.). Boston: Allyn & Bacon.

Carkhuff, R. R. (1969). *Helping and human relations: A primer for lay and professional helpers: Vol. 2. Practice and research.* New York: Holt, Rinehart & Winston.

Carkhuff, R. R., & Berenson, B. G. (1977). *Beyond counseling and therapy* (2nd ed.). New York: Holt, Rinehart & Winston.

Carlock, C. J., & Martin, P. Y. (1977). Sex composition and the intensive group experience. *Journal of the National Association of Social Workers, 22,* 27–32.

Carroll, M. R., & Wiggins, J. (1997). *Elements of group counseling: Back to the basics* (2nd ed.). Denver: Love Publishing.

Chen, M., & Rybak, C. J. (2004). *Group leadership skills: Interpersonal process in group counseling and therapy.* Belmont, CA: Brooks/Cole.

Cohen, A. M., & Smith, D. R. (1976). *The critical incident in growth groups: Theory and techniques.* La Jolla, CA: University Associates.

Conyne, R. K., Wilson, F. R., Kline, W. B., Morran, D. K., & Ward, D. E. (1993). Training group workers: Implications of the new ASGW training standards for training and practice. *Journal for Specialists in Group Work, 18,* 11–23.

Corey, G. (1985). *Theory and practice of group counseling* (2nd ed.). Pacific Grove, CA: Brooks/Cole.

Corey, G. (2000). *Theory and practice of group counseling* (5th ed.). Belmont, CA: Brooks/Cole.

Corey, G. (2004). *Theory and practice of group counseling* (6th ed.). Belmont, CA: Brooks/Cole.

Corey, G., & Corey, M. S. (1997). *Groups: Process and practice* (5th ed.). Pacific Grove, CA: Brooks/Cole.

Corey, G., & Corey, M. S. (2002). *Groups: Process and practice* (6th ed.). Pacific Grove, CA: Brooks/Cole.

Corey, G., Corey, M. S., Callahan, P. J., & Russell, J. M. (1982). *Group techniques.* Pacific Grove, CA: Brooks/Cole.

Corsini, R., & Rosenberg, B. (1955). Mechanisms of group psychotherapy: Processes and dynamics. *Journal of Abnormal & Social Psychology, 51,* 406–411.

Council for the Accreditation of Counseling and Related Educational Programs (CACREP). (1994). *Accreditation procedures manual and application.* Alexandria, VA: Author.

Council for the Accreditation of Counseling and Related Educational Programs (CACREP). (2001). *CACREP Accreditation procedures manual and application.* Alexandria, VA: Author.

DeJulio, S. J., Bentley, J., & Cockayne, T. (1979). Pregroup norm setting: Effects on encounter group interaction. *Small Group Behavior, 10,* 368–388.

Dinkmeyer, D. C., & Muro, J. J. (1979). *Group counseling: Theory and practice* (2nd ed.). Itasca, IL: Peacock.

Donigian, J., & Malnati, R. (1997). *Systemic group therapy: A triadic model.* Pacific Grove, CA: Brooks/Cole.

Dreikurs, R. (1932). Early experiments with group psychotherapy. *American Journal of Psychotherapy, 13,* 882–891.

Forester-Miller, H. (1998). History of the Association for Specialists in Group Work: Timeline of significant events. *Journal for Specialists in Group Work*, *23*(4), 335–337.

Frank, J. (1957). Some determinants, manifestations, and efforts of cohesiveness in therapy groups. *International Journal of Group Psychotherapy, 7,* 53–63.

Frank, J., & Ascher, E. (1951). The corrective emotional experience in group therapy. *American Journal of Psychiatry, 108,* 126–131.

Gazda, G. (1984). *Group counseling* (3rd ed.). Dubuque, IA: Wm. C. Brown.

Gazda, G. M. (1985). Group counseling and therapy: A perspective on the future. *Journal for Specialists in Group Work, 10*(2), 74–76.

Gazda, G. M., & Peters, R. W. (1975). An analysis of research in group psychotherapy, group counseling and human relations training. In G. M. Gazda (Ed.), *Basic approaches to group psychotherapy and group counseling* (pp. 38–54). Springfield, IL: Charles C Thomas.

Geller, J. J. (1950). Proposed plan for institutionalized group psychotherapy. *Psychiatric Quarterly Supplement, 24,* 270–277.

George, R. L., & Dustin, D. (1988). *Group counseling: Theory and practice.* Englewood Cliffs, NJ: Prentice-Hall.

Gibson, R. L., & Mitchell, M. M. (1995). *Introduction to counseling and guidance* (4th ed.). Columbus, OH: Merrill.

Gladding, S. T. (1991). *Group work: A counseling specialty.* Columbus, OH: Merrill.

Gladding, S. T. (1997). *Community and agency counseling.* Columbus, OH: Merrill.

Gladding, S. T. (1999). *Group work: A counseling specialty* (3rd ed.). Columbus, OH: Merrill.

Gladding, S. T. (2003). *Group work: A counseling specialty* (4th ed.). Upper Saddle River, NJ: Merrill/Prentice Hall.

Goldstein, M. J., Bednar, R. L., & Yanell, B. (1979). Personal risk associated with self-disclosure, interpersonal feedback, and group confrontation in group psychotherapy. *Small Group Behavior, 9,* 579–587.

Gruner, L. (1984). Membership composition of open and closed groups. *Small Group Behavior, 15,* 222–232.

Halas, C. (1973). All-women's groups: A view from inside. *Personnel & Guidance Journal, 52,* 91–95.

Hansen, J. C., Warner, R. W., & Smith, E. J. (1980). *Group counseling: Theory and process* (2nd ed.). Chicago: Rand McNally.

Hill, W. F. (1957). Analysis of interviews of group therapists' papers. *Provo Papers, 1,* 1.

Jacobs, A. (1974). The use of feedback in groups. In A. Jacobs & W. W. Spradline (Eds.), *The group as an agent of change* (pp. 31–49). New York: Behavioral Publications.

Jacobs, E. E., Harvill, R. L., & Masson, R. L. (1988). *Group counseling: Strategies and skills.* Pacific Grove, CA: Brooks/Cole.

Janis, I. L. (1972). *Victims of group think: A psychological study of foreign-policy decisions and fiascos.* Boston: Houghton Mifflin.

Johnson, D. W., & Johnson, F. P. (2000). *Joining together: Group theory and group skills* (7th ed.). Boston: Allyn & Bacon.

Johnson, D. W., & Johnson, F. P. (2003). *Joining together: Group theory and group skills* (8th ed.). Boston: Allyn & Bacon.

Jourard, S. (1971). *The transparent self* (rev. ed.). New York: Van Nostrand Reinhold.

Kelman, H. C. (1963). The role of the group in the induction of therapeutic change. *Journal of Group Psychotherapy, 13,* 399–432.

Klein, E. B. (1985). Group work: 1985 and 2001 [Special issue]. *Journal for Specialists in Group Work, 10*(2), 108–111.

Kline, W. B. (2003) *Interactive group counseling and psychotherapy.* Upper Saddle River, NJ: Merrill/Prentice Hall.

Kottler, J. A. (1983). *Pragmatic group leadership.* Pacific Grove, CA: Brooks/Cole.

Kottler, J. A. (2001). *Learning group leadership: An experimental approach.* Boston: Allyn & Bacon.

Kottler, J. A., & Brown, R. W. (2000). *Introduction to therapeutic counseling: Voices from the field* (4th ed.). Belmont, CA: Brooks/Cole.

Kravetz, D. (1980). Consciousness-raising and self-help. In A. M. Brodsky & R. Hare-Mustin (Eds.), *Women and psychotherapy* (pp. 267–281). New York: Guilford.

La Coursiere, R. (1980). *The life-cycle of groups: Group development stage theory*. New York: Human Sciences.

Levin, E. M., & Kurtz, R. P. (1974). Participant perceptions following structured and nonstructured human relations training. *Journal of Counseling Psychology, 21,* 514–532.

Levine, N. (1971). Emotional factors in group development. *Human Relations, 24,* 65–89.

Lieberman, M. A., Yalom, I. D., & Miles, M. B. (1973). *Encounter groups: First facts*. New York: Basic Books.

Long, L. D., & Cope, C. S. (1980). Curative factors in a male felony offender group. *Small Group Behavior, 11,* 389–398.

MacDonald, M. L., Lindquist, C. V., Kramer, J. A., McGrath, R. A., & Rhyne, L. D. (1975). Social skills training: Behavior rehearsal in groups and dating skills. *Journal of Counseling Psychology, 22,* 224–230.

Martin, L., & Jacobs, M. (1980). Structured feedback delivered in small groups. *Small Group Behavior, 1,* 88–107.

Melnick, J., & Woods, M. (1976). Analysis of group composition research and theory for psychotherapeutic and group oriented groups. *Journal of Applied Behavioral Science, 12,* 493–512.

Ohlsen, M. M. (1977). *Group counseling* (2nd ed.). New York: Holt, Rinehart & Winston.

Parloff, M. B., & Dies, R. R. (1978). Group therapy outcome instrument: Guidelines for conducting research. *Small Group Behavior, 9,* 243–286.

Perls, F. (1969). *Gestalt therapy verbatim*. New York: Bantam.

Perrone, K. M., & Sedlacek, W. E. (2000). A comparison of group cohesiveness and client satisfaction in homogeneous and heterogeneous groups. *Journal for Specialists in Group Work, 25*(3), 243–251.

Posthuma, B. W. (1999). *Small groups in counseling and therapy: Process and leadership* (3rd ed.). Boston: Allyn & Bacon.

Reed, B. G. (1981). Gender issues in training group leaders. *Journal for Specialists in Group Work, 6,* 161–170.

Rowe, W., & Winborn, B. B. (1973). What people fear about group work: An analysis of 36 selected critical articles. *Educational Technology, 13*(1), 53–57.

Scheidlinger, S. (1994). An overview of nine decades of group psychotherapy. *Hospital and Community Psychiatry, 45*(3), 217–225.

Schmuck, R. A., & Schmuck, P. A. (1997). *Group process in the classroom* (7th ed.). Madison, WI: Brown & Benchmark.

Shapiro, J. L., & Bernadett-Shapiro, S. (1985). Group work to 2001: Hal or haven (from isolation)? [Special issue]. *Journal for Specialists in Group Work, 10*(2), 83–87.

Shechtman, Z., & Perl-Dekel, O. (2000). A comparison of therapeutic factors in two group treatment modalities: Verbal and art therapy. *Journal for Specialists in Group Work, 25* (3), 288–304.

Slavson, S. R., & Schiffer, M. (1975). *Group psychotherapy for children: A textbook*. New York: International Universities Press.

Sleek, S. (1995, July). Group therapy: Tapping the power of teamwork. *APA Monitor, 26,* 1, 38–39.

Snortum, J. R., & Myers, H. F. (1971). Intensity of T-group relations as function of interaction. *International Journal of Group Psychotherapy, 21,* 190–201.

Stava, L. J., & Bednar, R. L. (1979). Process and outcome in encounter groups: The effect of group composition. *Small Group Behavior, 10,* 200–213.

Trotzer, J. P. (1999). *The counselor and the group: Integrating theory, training, and practice* (3rd ed.). Ann Arbor, MI: Taylor & Francis.

Truax, C. B., & Carkhuff, R. R. (1967). *Toward effective counseling and psychotherapy: Training and practice*. Chicago: Aldine.

Tuckman, B. W. (1965). Developmental sequences in small groups. *Psychological Bulletin, 63,* 384–389.

Twentyman, C. J., & McFall, R. M. (1975). Behavioral training of social skills in shy males. *Journal of Counseling & Clinical Psychology, 43,* 384–395.

Waltman, D. E., & Zimpfer, D. G. (1988). Composition, structure and duration of treatment: Interacting variables in counseling groups. *Small Group Behavior, 19*(2), 171–184.

Washington, D. S. (1982). Challenging men in groups. *Journal for Specialists in Group Work, 7,* 132–136.

Yalom, I. D. (1970). *The theory and practice of group psychotherapy.* New York: Basic Books.

Yalom, I. D. (1975). *The theory and practice of group psychotherapy* (2nd ed.). New York: Basic Books.

Yalom, I. D. (1985). *The theory and practice of group psychotherapy* (3rd ed.). New York: Basic Books.

Yalom, I. D. (1995). *The theory and practice of group psychotherapy* (4th ed.). New York: Basic Books.

Zimpfer, D. G. (1967). Expression of feelings in group counseling. *Personnel & Guidance Journal, 45,* 703–708.

Group Work: Stages and Issues

Douglas R. Gross and David Capuzzi

As George left the group counseling classroom that evening, he thought of all of the issues the class had been discussing during the past few weeks. He would finish his program within the next year, and he knew the expectations of any position he might take would require both group and individual counseling. He felt comfortable with his individual skills, and his practicum experience had substantiated his ability in this domain, but he remained concerned about his ability to work with groups. This was his second class in groups, and there seemed to be so many things to remember, so many factors to consider, so many issues to be addressed.

As he drove home that evening, George felt overwhelmed. From talking with others in his class, he knew that many students shared his concerns. He wondered if he would ever feel comfortable with group counseling and what would happen in his internship when he would be asked to lead or co-lead groups. "Will I be able to function effectively as a group leader or a group trainer?" is a question that continued to plague him.

The concerns expressed by this hypothetical student arise for both students and trainers in the group counseling or therapy area. When Gill and Barry (1982) studied the anxiety surrounding group counseling for experienced and novice group leaders, they found that individuals selected to provide training or lead groups are immediately struck by the complexity and the challenge that groups present. Addressing group complexity, Ward (1985) stated:

> Group work is challenging and complex because groups are complex because each group member has complex thoughts, feelings,

and behaviors. The complexity is magnified many times because most group members who have psychological exploration, growth, and change as their goals interact with one another and with the group leaders in intricate patterns. In addition, if members have an opportunity to interact over a period of time, the group develops a set of overt and covert guidelines or group norms that help regulate individual behavior and interactions between and among members. (p. 59)

The challenge and complexity of group work have been further substantiated in the literature by Capuzzi and Gross (2002, 2005), Corey (2004), Corey and Corey (2002), Gladding (2003), Jacobs, Masson, and Harvill (2002), Johnson and Johnson (2003), Kline (2003), and Trotzer (1999). These authors, while addressing different facets of group work, arrived at similar conclusions related to issues of challenge and complexity. They highlighted areas such as group membership, leadership styles, group methods, issues surrounding confidentiality, resistance, silence, conflict, termination and follow-up, and stages and transitions inherent in the group experience. Add to these the complexity of each individual involved, and it is easy to see why group work generates anxiety for the leader and members and sets forth a challenge for both.

Adding to this challenge are the complexities of each individual involved and, often, the design of groups around special themes and populations, as identified in Parts Three and Four of this text. Theme- and population-specific groups often carry with them special directives related to membership, leadership, methods, process, dynamics, multicultural issues, ethics, and stages and transitions. Current group texts and journals are replete with research on themes and special populations covering topics such as HIV/AIDS groups (Smiley, 2004), groups dealing with drug and alcohol use (Gonet, 1998), grief groups in medium-security prisons (Olsen & McEwen, 2004), groups addressing eating disorders (VanLone, Kalodner, & Coughlin, 2002), groups for angry and aggressive children (Sheultman, 2001), and groups for adult survivors of childhood abuse and neglect (Choate & Hensen, 2003), and anger and anxiety in combat veterans (Deroma, Root, & Battle, 2003). With the abundance of specialized groups and their diverse directives, many group workers have questioned whether group work can even be approached from a generic perspective or whether all groups should be viewed in terms of their specialized members and purpose. The answer to this question is not readily available. It depends on the group leader's philosophical and theoretical viewpoint.

In this chapter we explore just one aspect of the complex process of group counseling or therapy—the stages and transitions through which groups move from initiation through termination. The information presented, we believe, has application across both generic and specialized approaches to group work. We begin by discussing early as well as current conceptualizations of stage development and then present the reader with our own view of this developmental process, based on our extensive literature review and experience in working with groups. Member and leader behaviors are discussed for each stage. We conclude with recommendations for how group leaders can use this knowledge of stage development to enhance member growth and leader effectiveness.

STAGES AND TRANSITIONS

The distinct stages that groups move through as they pass from opening to closure are difficult to describe in definitive terms. The nature of the group, its membership, leadership style, and open or closed nature of the group all influence the developmental process. In terms of stages of development, a closed group, which maintains the same membership through its lifetime, is more easily described than is an open group, in which members come and go. The addition of new members as old members leave complicates the developmental process. Because of the variables affecting group development, any developmental scheme must be based more upon experience than on hard-and-fast rules governing a group's development.

Further, group stages are not discrete and neatly separated. In discussing this point, George and Dustin (1988) stated:

> The stages described do not occur in discrete and neatly separated points in the life of a real group. There is considerable overlap between the stages, as groups move from one stage to the other in a somewhat jerky, hesitant manner. As a result, there may be some movement toward the next stage and then regression to the previous stage. (p. 102)

In spite of these caveats, authors have been in apparent agreement about a generalized pattern of stages and transitions in groups (Corey, 2004; Gazda, 1989; Gladding, 2003; Trotzer, 1999; Tuckman, 1965; Tuckman & Jensen, 1977; Yalom, 1995). The stages and transitions identified within this pattern are outlined in Table 2.1. Before we discuss these stages, however, we present the following background information.

Early Conceptualizations

Much has been written about the stages through which groups progress from inception to closure. In the 1940s and 1950s, Bales (1950), Miles (1953), and Thelen and Dickerman (1949) conceptualized stages of groups based on the problem-solving behaviors exhibited in task groups. In these early developmental schemas, the emphasis was on tasks the group was expected to accomplish, such as getting organized, sharing ideas and opinions, and reaching solutions through suggestions. From this task orientation they examined specific member roles in groups. Researchers then began to translate group maintenance behaviors (member behaviors utilized to either promote or impede the group's progress) into interactional behaviors, which added a dimension to the early emphasis on task behaviors. Subsequent approaches to stage development in small groups combined task and member behaviors into descriptions of group process over time.

An example of how task and member behaviors have been combined is found in the work of Bennis and Shepard (1956). Integrating the work of Bales (1953) with their own concepts, these authors developed a conceptualization of group movement based upon their observations while teaching group dynamics to graduate students. As a result of those observations, they proposed that groups generally move through six developmental phases:

1. Dependence–flight
2. Counterdependence–fight
3. Resolution–catharsis
4. Enchantment–flight
5. Disenchantment–fight
6. Consensual validation

This conceptualization indicates that groups begin in a somewhat dependent state and that they grow as group members strive to move toward interdependent functioning.

Expanding on the work of Bennis and Shepard, Reid (1965) discussed the developmental stages of groups in terms of an "authority cycle." He viewed the growth and development of the group in direct relationship to the leader's authority. Groups move from dependence upon an established leader through counterindependence and counterdependence until they establish interdependence with the original authority leader. A crisis within the group may cause it to fall back to dependence on the established leader and begin the circular developmental pattern again. Like Bennis and Shepard, Reid stressed that growth occurs in groups as the members move from degrees of dependence to degrees of interdependence.

Other writers (Bion, 1961; Gazda, 1971; Gibb, 1964; Kaplan & Roman, 1963; Mills, 1964; Ohlsen, 1970; Schutz, 1958) aided in the early development of stage theories applied to the group process. Each described the various stages through which groups progress. Their descriptions cover the content of each of the stages and also the behaviors that individual group members display at each stage.

Current Conceptualizations

The authors listed in Table 2.1 expanded upon the early theories, viewing the movement of groups from origination to termination from a stage/transition perspective. Although the authors differ in the terminology they used to describe each stage and the number of stages they delineated, a pattern emerges that emphasizes the importance of

- pre-group planning (*formation*);
- member inclusion (*orientation, security*);
- member interaction (*storming, transition, conflict, acceptance*);
- member/group cohesion (*norming, action, conflict, responsibility, cohesiveness*);

Table 2.1   *Stages/Transitions of Group Development*

STAGES/ TRANSITIONS	1	2	3	4	5	6
AUTHOR						
Tuckman (1965), Tuckman & Jensen (1977)	Forming	Storming	Norming	Performing	Adjourning	
Gazda (1989)	Exploratory	Transition	Action	Termination		
Yalom (1995)	Orientation	—Conflict—		—Cohesiveness—		
Trotzer (1999)	Security	Acceptance	Responsibility	Work	Closing	
Gladding (2003)	Forming/ Orientation	Transition Storming/Norming		Performing/ Working	Mourning/ Termination	
Corey (2004)	Formation	Orientation/ Exploration	Transition	Working	Consolidation/ Termination	Follow-up/ Evaluation

- member and group goal achievement (*performing, cohesion, working*); and
- member and group parting (*adjourning, mourning, termination, closing, consolidation, follow-up/evaluation*).

Within this pattern, there is a degree of consistency in the member behaviors characteristic of each of the stages.

Stage 1

Labeled by terms such as *forming, exploratory, orientation,* and *security,* Stage 1 incorporates both the preparatory work that has to take place prior to group formation and inclusion of members in the group process. Corey (2004) stressed the importance of the formation phase by calling it pre-group issues and making this stage separate from orientation. In this phase he included functions such as group planning, member recruitment and screening, and leader selection. The other authors in Table 2.1 discuss these same issues but combine them with orientation.

   In the pattern that emerges from the research, Stage 1 is characterized by the following member behaviors:

- Orienting self to the environment
- Testing the environment

- Identifying boundaries
- Coming together
- Seeking acceptance
- Seeking approval
- Developing commitment
- Searching for structure and meaning
- Building relationships
- Defining goals
- Building a group culture
- Exploring expectations
- Learning group functioning
- Seeking one's place in the group
- Reviewing and defining power
- Reducing tension
- Dealing with anxiety
- Exploring safety issues

Whether these behaviors are viewed from an individual's perspective or from the group's perspective, Stage 1 in group development seems to be a period of *definition* for the individual members and the group alike. Individuals are defining where and, perhaps, *if* they fit in the group, what role they will take in the group, degrees of acceptance and approval within the group, and expectations for themselves and for others as related to the group process.

If the group can be viewed as an entity unto itself, separate from its individual parts, other elements of definition appear. This entity called "group" is seeking to define its structure and meaning, functions, goals, and boundaries. Through such definition, the group attempts to build a networking system that connects its individual parts—its members. The extent of success in this endeavor often rests in the strength of the constructed network and the skills of the group leader in helping members build this network.

In addition to being a period of definition, Stage 1 is characterized by *anxiety*. The amount of anxiety seems to be related to perceptions of risk, threat, power, impact, member behaviors, leader behaviors, and expectations, either perceived or real. Anxiety seems to be present, to some extent, in the beginning stages of all groups.

Another characteristic is *dependence*. Aspects of dependence seem to be much more pronounced during this initial stage than in subsequent stages. Factors that may be responsible for this response include the unknown elements of the new group members' need to test, seek, and explore to find their place in the group, and the challenge involved in attempting to reach a definition of self in relationship to the group.

Stage 2

Labeled by such terms as *storming, transition, conflict, acceptance, orientation*, and *exploration,* Stage 2 is characterized by active personal involvement as group members begin to test their position and power in the group as well as the behavioral parameters of the group and its members. The following member behaviors are descriptive of Stage 2:

- Conflict resolution
- Conflict management
- Polarization
- Resistance
- Dominance
- Control
- Power
- Anxiety
- Defensiveness
- Struggle
- Confrontation
- Tension
- Fear
- Questioning
- Dependency

Beyond action and reaction, these terms convey interaction on the part of the individual members as they attempt to establish themselves within the group structure. The words *struggle, conflict,* and *confrontation* attest to the need of individual group members to move from the safety of passive involvement to the more risk-oriented position of active involvement. Indeed, most of the behavioral descriptors for Stage 2 signify a movement from observation to participation, and this participation is viewed in general as action oriented.

Stage 3

Terms applied to Stage 3 include *norming, action, conflict, responsibility,* and *transition*. Yalom (1995) noted that conflict is part of both Stages 2 and 3 but that the conflict associated with Stage 3 is a more productive interaction, out of which group cohesion develops. This stage often is viewed as a transitional period during which greater degrees of commitment and productive interaction take place within the group. The following behaviors are descriptive of Stage 3:

- Cohesiveness
- Standardization
- Role clarification and adoption
- Intimacy
- Problem exploration
- Action exploration
- Belonging
- Inclusion
- Solidarity
- Conflict resolution

- Helping skills
- Enhanced risk taking
- Decreased aggression
- Increased compromise
- Increased trust
- Increased self-disclosure

Activities in Stage 3 involve blending and merging. In this move from independence to more interdependence, individuality is not lost but, instead, becomes enmeshed in the group. That is, Stage 3 encompasses behaviors and activities that are more group specific than member specific. Whereas in Stage 2 individual members strive for greater self-involvement through testing, checking, and confrontation, in Stage 3 members put group purposes, processes, and membership ahead of maximizing their own development.

Stages 4, 5, and 6

Stages 4, 5, and 6 are combined here because of their overlapping nature. Words used to describe these stages include *performing, adjourning, termination, cohesiveness, work, mourning, closing, consolidation,* and *follow-up/evaluation.* Stages 4 and 5 can be considered "work intensive," as group members direct much of their effort to developing new behaviors and perspectives, resolving personal issues, and enhancing self and the group.

If this process is successful, termination and/or closure of the group would be the expected outcome. With the exception of Corey (2004), the authors in Table 2.1 implied or discussed process evaluation and planning for follow-up as part of Stage 4 or Stage 5. Corey identified these important group tasks as a separate stage, which he labeled Stage 6. He referred to this process as "postgroup" issues, giving it the same weight as he did Stage 1 "pregroup" issues. Discussing the importance of follow-up/evaluation, Corey (2004) stated:

> Just as the formation of a group and the leader's preparatory activities greatly affect the group's progress through its various stages, the work of the leader once the group has come to an end is also highly important. (p. 123)

Stage 4 has the following descriptive behaviors:

- Developing roles
- Channeling energy
- Resolving issues
- Increasing self-disclosure
- Increasing honesty
- Increasing spontaneity
- Increasing responsibility
- Increasing integration

- Increasing interpretation
- Increasing behavioral reaffirmations
- Increasing intensification of feelings
- Increasing sadness, anxiety, and dependence
- Preparing for separation
- Ending
- Evaluating
- Follow-up

With group members drawing upon the growth and development that have taken place during the previous stages, the final segment is best viewed in terms of self- and group-enhancement, closure, and evaluation and follow-up. Enhancement is seen in greater involvement and development as these apply to the group and to the individual. Group development is furthered by deeper exploration of problems, an action orientation, solidarity, integration, and problem resolution. Personal development is seen when work on honesty, spontaneity, intimacy, feelings of belonging, inclusion, and integration come to fruition.

As the group approaches culmination, the cyclical nature of group development (Capuzzi & Gross, 2005) becomes obvious. As individuals begin to see closure as a reality, loss anxiety and dependence evolve, evidenced by questions such as: Will I be able to take what I have learned and apply it outside the group? Will I be able to function without the group?

The anxiety and dependence inherent in these questions are characteristic of Stage 1 behaviors, and the leader must have the skill to turn this anxiety and dependence into positive attributes as members leave the group. In discussing the closure process, Berg and Landreth (1990) made the following observations:

> A certain ambiguity of feelings can be anticipated that approximates the grieving process. Leave taking will produce denial and withdrawal in some and elation in others. Overriding these natural feelings of loss and anticipation should be a general optimism and a sense of completion. The group leader needs to take special care in dealing fully with feelings of anxiety associated with leaving the group. (p. 109)

COMPOSITE CONCEPTUALIZATIONS

Based upon the preceding information, and calling upon our own collective experiences, we developed our own view of the developmental stages of groups. As described in the following sections, we divide the developmental process into four stages: definitive stage, personal involvement stage, group involvement stage, and enhancement and closure stage.

Definitive Stage

The definitive stage contains two definitive aspects. The first, which we label "formative/developmental," deals with all of the foundational steps that must be taken prior to the first meeting of the group. These steps include but are not limited to

1. developing a rationale for the group;
2. making decisions regarding the theoretical format to be used in conducting the group;
3. determining group logistics such as time, place, number of meetings, and open versus closed format;
4. delineating operating guidelines (ground rules);
5. recruiting members;
6. screening members;
7. selecting a group leader(s).

After successfully completing these foundational steps, the second component of the definitive stage, which we call "member inclusion," begins. Provided with the rationale, logistics, operating guidelines, and an opportunity to react to the group's structural format, members begin to define for themselves the purpose of the group, their commitment to it, their potential involvement, and how much they are willing to share of themselves. Characteristic of this component of the definitive stage are questions such as the following:

- Will this type of group help me?
- Can I fit into this type of group?
- Can I trust the leader?
- Can I trust the other members?
- Where will I find support?
- Will I be hurt by others knowing about me?
- How much of myself am I willing to share?

Dealing with these questions and the lack of immediate answers, members in the definitive stage show increased anxiety, excitement, and nervousness. The dialogue during this stage tends to be self-protective and of a small-talk, social nature as the members test the waters of group involvement. To help group members deal effectively with the definitive stage, the group leader must possess skill in dealing with such issues as trust, support, safety, self-disclosure, and confidentiality.

As noted earlier, individuals define, demonstrate, and experiment with their own role definitions; test the temperament, personality, and behaviors of other group members; and arrive at conclusions about how personally involved they are willing to become during this stage of group development. An individual's movement through this stage can be enhanced or impeded by the group's makeup (age, gender, number, values, attitudes, socioeconomic status, and so on), the leader's style (active, passive, autocratic, democratic), the group's setting (formal, informal, comfortable, relaxed), the personal dynamics the individual brings to the group (shy, aggressive, verbal, nonverbal), and the individual's perceptions of trust and acceptance from other group members and from the group leader.

The definitive stage is crucial in group development as it can determine for the individual, and, therefore, for the group, future involvement, commitment, and individual and group success or failure in the long run. Assuming that appropriate foundational steps have been taken in establishing the group, the following are member and leader behaviors descriptive of the definitive stage.

Member Behaviors

■ Members evaluate the leader in terms of skill, ability, and capacity to trust.
■ Members evaluate other members in terms of commitment, safety, and confidentiality.
■ Members evaluate themselves in terms of taking risks, sharing themselves with others, and being willing to participate fully.
■ Members search for meaning and structure within the group.
■ Members search for approval from members and from the leader.
■ Members define themselves in relationship to other members and to the leader.
■ Members define the group experience in terms of their other life experiences.

Leader Behaviors

■ The leader attempts to foster inclusion of all group members.
■ The leader explains the rules and regulations that will operate within the group.
■ The leader attempts to draw, from the members, rules and regulations that will aid their participating in the group.
■ The leader explains the structure, timelines, and leader behaviors that members can expect within the group.
■ The leader attempts to model the behaviors expected of group members.
■ The leader attempts to deal effectively with the various emotions within the group.
■ The leader discusses issues of confidentiality, behavior, and goals and expectations for the group.
■ The leader attempts to draw from the members their goals and expectations for the group.
■ The leader attempts to provide an environment that facilitates growth.

Personal Involvement Stage

Once individuals have drawn conclusions about their commitment and role in the group, they move into the personal involvement stage of group development. This is a period of member-to-member interactions, including sharing personal information and engaging in confrontation and power struggles. The stage also is characterized by the individual's growing identity as a group member. Statements such as "I am," "I need," and "I care" are characteristic of this stage of group involvement. Through their speech and behaviors, group members demonstrate the extent to which they are willing to share personally and confirm the commitment they made during the definitive stage.

The personal involvement stage is one of action, reaction, and interaction. This stage is manifested by both fight and flight as members strive to carve their place within the group. The process often involves heated member-to-member interactions followed by retreat to regroup and battle again. The battles that ensue enhance members' places within the group and also aid in firmly establishing the group as an entity in its own right.

The personal involvement stage offers the individual the opportunity to try out various behaviors, affirm or deny perceptions of self and other, receive feedback in the form of words or behaviors, and begin the difficult process of self-evaluation. Individual involvement in this stage is crucial to the eventual outcome of the group. The following member and leader behaviors are descriptive of the personal involvement stage.

Member Behaviors

- Members openly challenge other members and the leader as they strive to find their place in the group.
- Members test their personal power within the group in attempts at manipulation and control.
- Members struggle as they try to find safety and comfort in sharing themselves with others.
- Members resist integrating the feedback they receive, as the suggested changes are perceived as being too painful to implement.
- Members join with other selected members in attempting to build safety and security.
- Members increase their commitment to themselves and also to the group, its goals, and its purposes.
- Members become more willing to share themselves with others and take a more active role in the group process.
- Members expand their ability to share feelings, ideas, and needs as these relate to the group process.

Leader Behaviors

- The leader demonstrates awareness of the emotional make-up of the group and encourages affective expression.
- The leader participates in the struggle, confrontation, and conflict that are part of this stage.
- The leader communicates to the members the appropriateness of their member-to-member reactions and interactions.
- The leader allows members to move through this stage at their own pace, knowing the dangers of rushing them.
- The leader provides an environment that is conducive to greater comfort and safety.
- The leader encourages members to explore new ways of behaving within the group.
- The leader acknowledges his or her own struggles as the group moves to deeper levels of interaction.

- The leader emphasizes the importance of all members of the group aiding in the transition from definition to involvement.

Group Involvement Stage

With the information they gained about themselves in the personal involvement stage, group members move into the group involvement stage, characterized by self-evaluation and self-assessment of behavior, attitudes, values, and methods used in relating to others, and also by members' channeling their energies to better meet group goals and purposes. During this stage the member and the group become somewhat more synonymous.

Cooperation and cohesiveness gradually replace conflict and confrontation as members, who are now more confident in their role in the group, direct more of their attention to what is best for the group and all of its members. This stage reveals increasing clarification of roles, intimacy, exploration of problems, group solidarity, compromise, conflict resolution, and risk taking.

The group, with its purposes and goals, is merging with the individual purposes and goals of its members. Individual agendas are replaced by group agendas, and members identify more with the group. Members become bonded as they join forces to enhance the group and, in turn, enhance their individual selves in relation to the group. References to "insider" and "outsider" differentiate the group and others in the members' lives outside the group. Members become protective of other group members and also of the group itself.

The group and its membership take on special significance unique to those who are part of the process. The melding of member and group purposes and goals is necessary to the group's ongoing success. The following member and leader behaviors are descriptive of the group involvement stage.

Member Behaviors

- Members develop confidence in themselves and their ability to relate effectively in the group environment.
- Members develop better helping skills and apply these to working with other group members and to themselves.
- Members devote increasing energy to helping the group meet its purposes and goals.
- Members direct more attention to cooperation and cohesiveness and less to conflict and confrontation.
- Members display a perspective more characterized by belonging and inclusion than by nonbelonging and exclusion.
- Members operate more in a problem exploration/solution mode than in a problem developmental mode.
- Members provide support for other members and the group as a whole.
- Members demonstrate more solidarity, as in their view of group members and the group.

Leader Behaviors

- The leader encourages and facilitates the development of individual strengths within the group.
- The leader encourages members in their development of group identity and solidarity.
- The leader provides more opportunity for members to serve in the leadership role within the group.
- The leader gives positive direction as the members move from individual to group-directed purposes and goals.
- The leader demonstrates, in words and through his or her behaviors, the benefits to be derived from individuals working cooperatively.
- The leader demonstrates, in words and through his or her behaviors, the benefits to be derived, for individual members and for the group, from reinforcement of positive change.
- The leader becomes more involved as a participant, sharing in the changing dynamics of the group.
- The leader functions more in a helping capacity than in a leader capacity to enhance the development of individual members and the group.

Enhancement and Closure Stage

The final stage in a group's life is often described as the most exhilarating but also the saddest aspect of group work. The exhilaration stems from a combination of members' evaluation of the group process and individual and group progress, individual and group reinforcement of changes in individual members, and a commitment to continue self-analysis and growth. Members share what they believe have been significant growth experiences during the group tenure, and they receive feedback—generally positive—from other group members and the leader.

Members are encouraged to review the process of the group and to measure changes within themselves as a result of the group experience. At this stage of group development, members' statements tend to be along the line of: "I was . . . , now I am . . ."; "I felt . . . , now I feel . . ."; "I didn't . . . , now I do . . ."; "I couldn't . . . , now I can . . ." The following member and leader behaviors are descriptive of the enhancement and closure stage.

Member Behaviors

- Members evaluate the amount of progress they have made during the life of the group.
- Members evaluate the extent to which the group accomplished its purposes and goals.
- Members share their perceptions of the strengths and weaknesses of other members and the leader.
- Members share their concerns about what will happen after the group ends.
- Members attempt to evaluate the group experience in terms of their other life experiences.

- Members try to build contacts with group members and the leader that will continue after closure.
- Members start to deal with the loss that group closure will bring.
- Members consider alternative actions to take the place of what the group provided.

Leader Behavior

- The leader assists group members in evaluating their growth and development during the group's tenure.
- The leader aids group members in resolving any issues that remain.
- The leader facilitates closure early in this last stage by initiating certain activities, such as structured ways of saying good-bye.
- The leader makes sure that each member in the group receives appropriate feedback.
- The leader offers his or her view of the dynamics of the group and its members.
- The leader reviews individual members' strengths and weaknesses from his or her perspective.
- The leader encourages the emotional venting that is necessary in the closure process.
- The leader encourages each member to discuss what he or she plans to do after the group ends.
- The leader explains and encourages members to take advantage of proposed follow-up procedures that will be scheduled at specified time intervals in the future.

The movement of a group from initiation to termination varies. Groups and their individual members differ in this movement for a myriad of reasons. No single conceptualization has all the answers or addresses all the issues inherent in this developmental process of groups. The various conceptualizations, however, do provide guidelines and directions for working with groups. According to Hershenson, Power, and Waldo (1996):

> The group as a whole can be seen as passing through different periods in its life, similar to the way individuals pass through periods in their lives. When a group first forms it is in childhood, then moves into adolescence, followed by young adulthood, then adulthood, and then maturity as it is about to disband. (p. 211)

LEARNING ACTIVITIES

1. With several other students, construct what you consider to be the most effective conceptualization of the stages through which groups move. Be creative. Go

beyond what is presented in this text. As a team, present the stages and your rationale to the class.

2. Interview someone who leads groups in your community. Questions to ask might include the following:

Does knowledge of the various stages and phases of group development play a part in how you operate as a group leader? If so, how?

Do you think that such knowledge is necessary for effective leadership?

Knowing how others have described the process of group development, what words would you use to describe each stage?

Present your findings to the class in written or oral form.

3. With several other students, select one of the following: therapy groups, self-help groups, support groups, task groups, human relations/training groups, or classroom groups. As a group, determine if the stage conceptualizations presented in this chapter apply to the type of group you and your classmates selected. Report to the class your conclusions and the rationale for them.

4. Identify the stage(s) exemplified in the group counseling or therapy videos shown to your class. Provide rationales for your stage identifications. Compare and contrast your stage identifications with those of other students. Think about the role that individual perception plays in stage identification. How might this perceptual difference affect the overall leadership of a group?

SUMMARY

The concerns expressed at the beginning of this chapter by the hypothetical student, George, are legitimate. The process of group work is both complex and challenging, and the information that has been written about this process results at times in more questions than definitive answers. Novice and experienced group leaders alike strive to increase their level of comfort in leading groups. The following recommendations for group leaders summarize the information covered in this chapter.

1. Knowledge of group stages and transitions provides useful information about typical member behaviors and the developmental process of groups as they move from initiation to termination.

2. Knowledge of group stages and transitions offers the following directives:
   a. During the early stages of group development, the leader must address the anxiety and dependence of group members. One way to do this is to establish operating procedures and structures that will alleviate some of this anxiety and dependence.
   b. During the middle stages of group development, the leader should facilitate empowerment of group members as they work on personal and group issues. These are the working, or productive, stages of the group and the stages that foster both individual and group development.

    c. During the final stages, the leader must be aware of the dichotomy of exhilaration and sadness the group members feel. Allowing members to discuss and deal with both ends of this emotional continuum will facilitate positive closure.

3. Knowledge of group stages and transitions allows the leader to plan and structure the group to better meet the needs of its members.

4. Knowledge of group stages and transitions enables the leader to instruct and orient the members regarding their experiences when moving from initiation to termination of the group.

5. Knowledge of group stages and transitions helps the leader to better judge the types of individuals who would benefit most from the group experience and, accordingly, enhance the group outcome.

6. Knowledge of group stages and transitions enables the leader to better understand the cyclical nature of groups and be better prepared to deal with forward and backward movement within the group and with the behaviors and emotional reactions that can be expected throughout the group's life.

7. Knowledge of group stages and transitions allows the leader to integrate his or her experiences in a group with information from past and current research. He or she then can restructure or reconceptualize the group process to the best advantage for all.

8. Knowledge of group stages and transitions allows the leader to measure or evaluate the developmental process within his or her group by comparing it with what others in the field have reported.

9. Knowledge of group stages and transitions allows the leader to become comfortable with the overall process of group work by understanding certain dynamics that are generally predictable.

10. Knowledge of group stages and transitions offers the leader the freedom to work within the known parameters of the group process and also to create and develop his or her own conceptualizations within the process.

USEFUL WEB SITES

- □ American Counseling Association
  www.counseling.org
- □ American Psychological Association
  www.apa.org

REFERENCES

Bales, R. F. (1950). *Interaction process analysis: A method for the study of small groups.* Cambridge, MA: Addison-Wesley.

Bales, R. F. (1953). The equilibrium problem in small groups. In T. Parson, R. F. Bales, & E. A. Shils (Eds.), *Working papers in the theory of action* (pp. 111–161). Glencoe, IL: Free Press.

Bennis, W. G., & Shepard, H. A. (1956). A theory of group development. *Human Relations, 9,* 415–437.

Berg, R., & Landreth, G. (1990). *Group counseling: Concepts and procedures* (2nd ed.). Muncie, IN: Accelerated Development.

Bion, R. W. (1961). *Experiences in groups.* New York: Basic Books.

Capuzzi, D., & Gross, D. (2002). *Introduction to group counseling* (3rd ed.). Denver: Love Publishing.

Capuzzi, D., & Gross, D. (2005). *Introduction to the counseling profession* (4th ed.). Boston: Allyn & Bacon.

Choate, L. H. J., & Hensen, A. (2003). Group work with adult survivors of childhood abuse and neglect. A psychoeducational approach. *Journal for Specialists in Group Work, 28*(2), 106–121.

Corey, G. (2004). *Theory and practice of group counseling* (6th ed.). Pacific Grove, CA: Brooks/Cole.

Corey, M., & Corey, G. (2002). Groups: Process and practice (6th ed.). Pacific Grove, CA: Brooks/ Cole.

Deroma, M., Root, L., & Battle, J. (2003). Pretraining in group process skills: Impact on anger and anxiety in combat veterans. *Journal for Specialists in Group Work, 28*(4), 339–354.

Gazda, G. (1971). *Group counseling: A developmental approach.* Boston: Allyn & Bacon.

Gazda, G. (1989). *Group counseling: A developmental approach* (4th ed.). Boston: Allyn & Bacon.

George, R. L., & Dustin, D. (1988). *Group counseling: Theory and practice.* Englewood Cliffs, NJ: Prentice-Hall.

Gibb, J. E. (1964). Climate for trust formation. In L. P. Bradford, J. R. Gibb, & K. D. Benne (Eds.), *T-group theory and laboratory method: Innovation in re-education* (pp. 279–300). New York: Wiley.

Gill, S. J., & Barry, R. A. (1982). Group-focused counseling: Classifying the essential skills. *Personnel and Guidance Journal, 60,* 302–305.

Gladding, S. T. (2003). *Group work: A counseling specialty* (4th ed.). New York: Macmillan.

Gonet, A. M. (1998). Groups for drug and alcohol abuse. In K. C. Stoiber & T. R. Kratochwill (Eds.), *Handbook of group intervention for children and families* (pp. 172–192). Needham Heights, MA: Allyn & Bacon.

Hershenson, D., Power, P. L., & Waldo, M. (1996). *Community counseling: Contemporary theory and practice.* Boston: Allyn & Bacon.

Jacobs, E., Masson, R. L., & Harvill, R. L. (2002). *Group counseling: Strategies and skills* (4th ed.). Pacific Grove, CA: Brooks/Cole.

Johnson, D., & Johnson, F. (2003). *Joining together* (8th ed.). Boston: Allyn & Bacon.

Kaplan, S. R., & Roman, M. (1963). Phases of development in an adult therapy group. *International Journal of Group Psychotherapy, 13,* 10–26.

Kline, W. (2003). *Interactive group counseling and therapy.* Upper Saddle River, NJ: Merrill Prentice Hall.

Miles, M. B. (1953). Human relations training: How a group grows. *Teachers College Record, 55,* 90–96.

Mills, T. M. (1964). *Group transformation.* Englewood Cliffs, NJ: Prentice-Hall.

Ohlsen, M. M. (1970). *Group counseling.* New York: Holt, Rinehart & Winston.

Olsen, M., & McEwen, M. (2004). Grief counseling groups in a medium-security prison. *Journal for Specialists in Group Work, 29*(2), 225–236.

Reid, C. (1965). The authority cycle in small group development. *Adult Leadership, 13*(10), 308–331.

Schutz, W. D. (1958). *FIRO: Three dimensional theory of interpersonal behavior.* New York: Rinehart.

Sheultman, Z. (2001). Prevention groups for angry and aggressive children. *Journal for Specialists in Group Work, 26*(3), 228–236.

Smiley, K. (2004). A structured group for gay men newly diagnosed with HIV/AIDS. *Journal for Specialists in Group Work, 29*(2), 207–224

Thelen, H., & Dickerman, W. (1949). Stereotypes and the growth of groups. *Educational Leadership, 6,* 309–316.

Trotzer, J. P. (1999). *The counselor and the group: Integrating theory, training and practice* (3rd ed.). Philadelphia: Taylor & Francis.

Tuckman, B. W. (1965). Developmental sequence in small groups. *Psychological Bulletin, 63,* 384–399.

Tuckman, B. W., & Jensen, M. S. (1977). Stages of small group development revisited. *Groups & Organizational Studies, 2,* 419–427.

VanLone, J., Kalodner, C., & Coughlin, J. (2002). Using short stories to address eating disturbances in groups. *Journal for Specialists in Group Work, 27*(1), 59–77.

Ward, D. E. (1985). Levels of group activity: A model for improving the effectiveness of group work. *Journal of Counseling and Development, 64*(1), 59–64.

Yalom, I. D. (1995). *The theory and practice of group psychotherapy* (4th ed.). New York: Basic Books.

Group Work: Elements of Effective Leadership

David Capuzzi and Douglas R. Gross

Many factors contribute to the outcomes of group counseling (Conyne, Harvill, Morganett, Morran, & Hulse-Killacky, 1990; DeLucia-Waack & Donigian, 2004; Greenberg, 2003; Zimpfer & Waltman, 1982). Studies have focused on the relationship between group counseling outcomes and the counselor's personality (Cooper, 1977; Kellerman, 1979), the counselor's experience (Heikkinen, 1975; Wittmer & Webster, 1969), group membership (Heslin, 1964; Shaw, 1981), the leader's directiveness (Brown, 1969; Chatwin, 1972), the counselor's self-disclosure (Dies, 1973, 1977), and counselor–group interaction (MacLennan, 1975). In an interesting analysis of the bases of influence in groups, Richard and Patricia Schmuck (1997) and David and Frank Johnson (2000, 2003) concluded that group outcomes are influenced by the following aspects of the power of the group leader:

1. *Expert power*—the extent of expertise and knowledge that group members attribute to the leader. Members see the leader as having expertise that will assist them in achieving their goals.
2. *Referent power*—the extent to which group members identify with and feel close to the group leader. Generally, the more members like the leader, the more they will identify with him or her.
3. *Legitimate power*—the power attributed to the leader by group members because the leader is in the position of facilitating the group. Usually, members believe they have a duty to follow a leader whom they perceive as having legitimate power, and often this kind of leadership influence can reduce conflict or confusion in a group.

4. *Reward power*—the extent to which group members view the leader as having the ability to reward them by providing reinforcement and attention during group sessions. The more the leader is viewed as being able to dispense the reward and the less the members believe they can receive the reward from someone else, the greater will be the leader's power.

5. *Coercive power*—the extent to which the group leader is seen as having the ability to move the group in a certain direction or even "punish" group members. Coercive power often causes group members to avoid and/or to dislike the leader.

6. *Informational power*—the amount of information the leader has about the members of the group or resources that will be useful to members as they work toward a goal. The leader's power is based upon his or her ability to demonstrate knowledge and is similar to "expert" power (see #1).

7. *Connection power*—the number of close relationships the leader has developed with other professionals outside the group that may prove helpful to members of the group.

Because the leader of a group can influence the outcome of a group counseling experience in a number of ways, elements of effective leadership are important to consider for anyone who is interested in leading or co-leading a group.

LEADERSHIP STYLES

Leadership style relates to the manner in which something is said or done (Johnson & Johnson, 2000, 2003). Leadership style can be contrasted with the substance related to the leader's words and behaviors. The leader's style carries as many messages as the leader's words and actions and either adds or detracts from the credibility and legitimacy of what the leader is saying or doing.

Lewin's Three "Classics"

Discussing elements of effective leadership is not possible without understanding the contributions of Kurt Lewin and his colleagues. In the late 1930s, Lewin studied the influences of different leadership styles or patterns on groups and group members. He observed small groups of 10- and 11-year-old children who met for a period of weeks under the leadership of adults who behaved in one of three ways: democratically, autocratically, or in a laissez-faire manner (Johnson & Johnson, 2000, 2003). The impact of these leadership styles on the group members was dramatic and definite. A great deal of scapegoating, for example, occurred in groups led by autocratic leaders. Further, when some of the autocratic groups terminated, the children destroyed the items they had been making. Lewin's studies made it clear that the leader's style can greatly influence the outcomes for group members. His identification of authoritarian, democratic, and laissez-faire leadership styles provided the group leader with a point of departure for understanding this element of group leadership (Lewin, 1944).

Authoritarian Style

Authoritarian group leaders assume a position as the "expert" and direct the movement of a group. They interpret, give advice, explain individual and group behavior, and generally control most facets of group process. Professionals with strong psychoanalytic, medical, or teaching backgrounds may prefer this style of leadership Generally, the leader does little self-disclosing.

Authoritarian leaders wield a great deal of power and usually are quite safe from being personally vulnerable (Gladding, 1999, 2003). In directing and controlling the group, they typically create a structure that protects them from self-disclosing or being confronted by group members. This type of leader is sometimes referred to as a *Theory X leader* (Gladding, 1999, 2003).

Democratic Style

Democratic group leaders are more group- and person-centered in the way they interact with group members. They place more emphasis upon the responsibility of each participant to create a meaningful individual and group experience. Implicit is their trust in the ability of members and the phenomenon of the group experience. Professionals who subscribe to a Rogerian frame of reference or who align themselves with humanistic or phenomenological viewpoints are more likely than others to adopt a democratic leadership style. They are more accessible and self-disclosing than authoritarian leaders. This type of leader is sometimes called a *Theory Y leader* (Gladding, 1999, 2003).

Laissez-Faire Style

In contrast to authoritarian and democratic leaders, group leaders who adhere to the *laissez-faire* style do not provide structure or direction to a group. Group members are expected to take responsibility for making the group experience beneficial. Some group leaders (usually inexperienced) select this style in an attempt to be "nondirective" (a misnomer in and of itself), as a way to avoid decision making and enhance their likability, or because they believe a completely unstructured group works best (Gladding, 1999, 2003). Some evidence shows that many laissez-faire groups accomplish little during the life of the group. A *laissez-faire* leader is sometimes called a *Theory Z leader*.

Conclusions

Several studies, as identified by Zimpfer and Waltman (1982), have investigated the relationship between the extent to which the group leader takes an active, directive role and success with certain group members. The studies showed that low-anxiety members, for example, may do well in a group with little structure, whereas low-trust members may prefer a distinctly leader-centered group.

In discussing the authoritarian, democratic, and laissez-faire styles of leadership, Posthuma (1999) emphasizes that the leader's style has an impact on the behavior of the members of the group. Members in groups with authoritarian leaders tend to be compliant, unenthusiastic, and somewhat resentful of the leader. They may take little initiative, resist responsibility, and fail to be collaborative. Members of groups led by democratic leaders usually are enthusiastic about the group, motivated, collaborative, connected to each other, and interested in taking responsibility and initiative. Members of groups who have a leader with a laissez-faire style usually are confused and frustrated because of a lack of direction on the leader's part, not very productive, much less collaborative, and less able to take responsibility because of the perceived lack of purpose for the group.

Leader-Directed and Group-Directed Styles

Another way to conceptualize leadership styles is based on the extent to which the group is leader-centered or group-centered (Jacobs, Masson, & Harvill, 1998, 2002). In a leader-centered group, the leader is the center of focus, and he or she determines what will most benefit group members. In this kind of group, the leader may emphasize a predetermined theme, a sequence of structured exercises, or a format for each group session, and likely will direct interaction quite assertively at times. Group members are expected to cooperate with the leader and to deal with personal issues as they fit into the leader's agenda. By contrast, a more group-centered style encourages members to establish the agenda for the group and to more freely discuss personal concerns, issues, and plans. Each of these styles can facilitate the growth of group members, depending upon the group's purpose, the expectations and personalities of group members, and the leader's ability to apply techniques and interventions in a comfortable, congruent, and sensitive manner.

Interpersonal and Intrapersonal Styles

In 1978, Shapiro described two leadership styles: interpersonal and intrapersonal. Leaders with an *interpersonal* style (Corey, 2000; Gladding, 1999, 2003) emphasize the importance of understanding and processing interactions among group members and relationships that develop within a group as sessions progress. Interest centers on the nature, quality, and dynamics of the interactions among members and *what* is occurring in the here and now of the group.

Leaders with an *intrapersonal* orientation are likely to explore *why* group members make certain responses by focusing upon individual members and the conflicts, concerns, and dynamics within them. This style is directed more toward the past, and it facilitates insight and resolution of internal conflicts. At times, leaders with an intrapersonal orientation engage in individual counseling or therapy in the context of the group experience.

Charismatic Leadership Style

Group members have a tendency to admire and respect the group leader, particularly in the early stages of a group (Rutan & Rice, 1981). Group leaders may derive some of their power from a combination of traits that are particularly appealing to group members, such as being personable, having an appealing appearance, and having good verbal ability. Group leaders with charisma may inspire group members, who at times become almost devoted to them (Johnson & Johnson, 2000, 2003; Schmuck & Schmuck, 1997).

Group leaders whom members perceive as charismatic may have an advantage during the early stages of a group in terms of their ability to facilitate the work occurring at that time. If group members view the leader as an ego ideal, however, they may become dependent upon his or her leadership and initiatives. Some charismatic leaders begin to enjoy the admiration of group members to such an extent that they fail to encourage autonomy of the participants (Rutan & Rice, 1981). Group leaders, it must be stressed, should work to develop the skills they need to promote the personal growth of group members and to guide the group from the beginning to middle and later stages of the group's life.

Textbooks used by counselor education, counseling psychology, psychology, and social work programs present numerous discussions of different leadership styles that prepare professionals to do group work. One of the most integrative of these discussions appears in the Johnson and Johnson (2000, 2003) texts referenced earlier in this chapter. We recommend that you use it in conjunction with this chapter to begin evaluating and developing your own leadership style.

THE IMPORTANCE OF LEADERSHIP STYLE

Leadership styles do make a difference in how groups function, as shown by Lewin's pioneering study mentioned earlier in the chapter. After reviewing numerous studies, Stogdill (1974) reached these conclusions:

1. Person-centered styles of leadership are not always related to group productivity.
2. Socially distant, directive, and structured leadership styles that tend to promote role differentiation and clear member expectations are related consistently to group productivity.
3. Person-centered styles of leadership that provide for member involvement in decision making and show concern for the welfare of members are related consistently to group cohesiveness.
4. Among task-focused leadership styles, only the structuring of member expectations is related consistently to group cohesiveness.
5. All person-centered leadership styles seem to be related to high levels of member satisfaction.
6. Only the structuring of member expectations is related positively to member satisfaction with task-focused leadership styles.

The single aspect of leadership style that contributes positively to group productivity, cohesiveness, and satisfaction is to initiate structure by being clear about one's role as a leader and what one expects from members (Johnson & Johnson, 2000, 2003). The most effective group leaders are those who show concern for the well-being and disclosures of members and also structure member role responsibilities.

The importance of taking time to establish goals during the definitive stage of a group, as discussed in Chapter 2, cannot be overstated.

DEVELOPING YOUR OWN LEADERSHIP STYLE

You should place considerable emphasis on analyzing and developing your own style of leadership in groups. Corey (2000, 2004) suggests that this will be influenced by whether you lead long-term or short-term groups, as well as the theory base you use as the conceptual frame of reference for your work with groups (chapter 4 covers theoretical systems and their applications to groups). In addition, before you are in the position of providing leadership, you should acquire an understanding of your own inherent qualities, characteristics, and inclinations. But you will have to go far beyond assessing your personal qualities before leading a group. In addition to gaining self-awareness and an understanding of how personality traits and personal qualities can enhance or detract from what the leader contributes to a group experience, you must master a set of core knowledge and skill competencies in the process of developing a personalized leadership style.

In 2000, the Association for Specialists in Group Work (ASGW), a division of the American Counseling Association (ACA), published a revised version of its training standards entitled *Professional Standards for Training of Group Work Generalists and of Group Work Specialists.* (Parts of these standards were overviewed in chapter 1 in conjunction with the discussion of group types.) These standards specify knowledge and skill competencies, as well as education and supervision requirements. Some examples of the specified *knowledge competencies* are

- an understanding of the basic principles of group dynamics,
- an awareness of the specific ethical issues unique to group work,
- an understanding of the specific process components in typical stages of a group's development, and
- comprehension of the therapeutic factors inherent in a group experience.

Examples of specified *skill competencies* are

- the ability to explain and clarify the purpose of a given group,
- the ability to encourage the participation of group members,
- the ability to open and close sessions effectively, and
- the ability to help group members integrate and apply what they have learned in the group.

Depending upon whether the group leader wishes to be prepared at a beginning (generalist) or an advanced (specialist) level, *education* requirements range from a minimum of two group work courses to a wide range of related coursework in areas such as organizational development, sociology, community psychology, and consultation. *Supervision* requirements involve group observation, co-leading, and leading expectations, ranging from 30 to 55 clock hours (minimum) depending on the type of group work under study.

The point is that professionals who are interested in becoming competent group leaders must develop a leadership style that integrates their personal qualities with a myriad of knowledge and skill competencies engendered through master's or doctoral coursework, as well as by meeting requirements for group observation and supervised practice. In many ways, developing a leadership style is an integrative, sequential, and creative endeavor resulting in the group leader's ability to transmit knowledge and skill competencies in a unique, individualized way, linked and integrated with a variety of personal characteristics, to encourage emotional, cognitive, and behavioral changes on behalf of each member of a group.

PRE-GROUP LEADERSHIP SKILLS

Before actually conducting groups, leaders have to know how to screen potential members. This is followed by organizing the group program.

Conducting Pre-Group Screening

Group leaders have to develop expertise in screening potential group members (Chen & Rybak, 2004; Kottler, 2001; Remley & Herlihy, 2005). As noted in the *Ethical Guidelines for Group Counselors* (ASGW, 1989), leaders must screen prospective members of a group to select individuals whose needs and goals are congruent with the group goals, who will not be detrimental to the group, and whose well-being will not be jeopardized by the group experience. As Corey and Corey (1997) noted:

> We are concerned that candidates benefit from a group but even more concerned that they might be psychologically hurt by it or might drain the group's energies excessively. Certain members, while remaining unaffected by the group, sap its energy for productive work. This is particularly true of hostile people, people who monopolize, extremely aggressive people, and people who act out. The potential gains of including certain of these members must be weighed against the probable losses to the group as a whole. We also believe that group counseling is contraindicated for individuals who are suicidal, extremely fragmented, or acutely psychotic, sociopathic, facing extreme crises, highly paranoid, or extremely self-centered. (pp. 112–113)

Screening may be accomplished through individual interviews, group interviews of potential group members, an interview as part of a team staffing, or reviewing a questionnaire completed by the prospective member. Pre-group screening must provide prospective members with information about expectations for participation in the group, goals, payment methods and fee schedules, termination and referral procedures, client rights, and so on. The group leader also must inquire about prospective members' current and past experiences with counseling and provide clients with a written disclosure statement of his or her qualifications and the nature of the services to be provided. (See the ACA *Code of Ethics* as published in 2005, which addresses screening procedures.)

George Gazda (1989) made some interesting screening recommendations that also serve to establish ground rules for prospective group members. He suggested providing group candidates with the following guidelines as part of the screening:

1. Before you attend the first group session, you should establish personal goals. You will be able to refine and clarify these goals as the group progresses.
2. Whenever you contribute during a group session, you should be as honest and straightforward about yourself as possible. Success and lack of success with respect to aspects of your behavior may be important for you to discuss.
3. Listen carefully when other members of the group are contributing, and try to communicate nonjudgmental understanding and caring.
4. Do not discuss any information about other group members outside the group.
5. Attend all sessions, and arrive on time.
6. Respect your counselor's right to suggest that you terminate participation in the group if the counselor believes it is best for you and best for the group.
7. Respect the rule that no one group member can control the group and that group decisions are made by consensus.
8. Let the group counselor know if someone in your group poses a barrier, because of a prior relationship, to your open participation as a member of the group.
9. If you request an individual meeting with your group counselor, recognize that you may be asked to share the content of the discussion with the total group.
10. Be sure to be aware of the amount and schedule of fee payment for membership in the group prior to committing to group participation.

Selection of group members through pre-group screening also grants potential members the opportunity to assess their readiness for, and interest in, being a group member (Gladding, 1999, 2003). Group leaders who have not conducted a group previously should conduct pre-group screening under the supervision of an experienced group work specialist.

Organizing for Groups

A number of elements have to be considered in organizing a group or group program. These considerations include, among others, publicizing the group, attending to the physical setting, setting the length and frequency of group meetings, and determining the size of the group.

Publicizing the Group

Letting potential group members know about an opportunity to participate in a group can be accomplished in a number of ways (Gladding, 1999, 2003). If the group leader lets colleagues know about the plan to initiate the group or group program, the colleagues could help publicize the group and possibly refer clients for the pre-group screening and orientation. Although this has the advantage of personalizing the announcement and referral, it does leave the group leader and the success of the group or group program dependent on the time and opportunities that colleagues have to contribute to publicizing it. At times, the group leader already has clients—perhaps clients who have been engaged in individual counseling—who stand to benefit from membership in a group. Suggesting the possibility of group participation (provided that participation would be appropriate and pertinent to the client's reasons for engaging in counseling) is one way by which groups sometimes are formed. This approach has the advantage of being personalized, but it may have the disadvantage of reaching few potential members.

Sometimes counselors place advertisements about upcoming groups in community newspapers, or post flyers, or distribute brochures about the groups they conduct. This method has the advantage of reaching more individuals who might be interested, but it may not be comprehensive enough to answer the questions of those who might like to participate. In addition, it is important to consider the ethical aspects of advertising as addressed in the ACA *Code of Ethics* (2005).

Selecting the Physical Setting

Group sessions may be conducted in a variety of settings, as long as the room allows privacy and relative freedom from distraction for participants (Yalom, 1985). Some leaders seat participants around a circular table. Others prefer to place chairs in a circle so members' nonverbal or body language responses are observed more readily. No matter what type of seating arrangement is selected, the room has to be comfortable for the group. A group of eight members and a group leader in a room large enough to seat 30 or 40 people can be just as inappropriate and inconducive to the development of cohesiveness as a room that is too small to readily accommodate chairs for nine people. If group sessions are to be observed or videotaped, group members must give permission ahead of time and must have the opportunity to ask questions about and discuss the purposes of observation and taping procedures.

Deciding Length and Frequency of Meetings

The agency or the setting may dictate the duration and frequency of group sessions (George & Dustin, 1988), but the group leader also has to consider the purpose of the group when determining scheduling. Some groups require longer time periods and more frequent scheduling than do others. Typical groups require 1½-hour sessions to provide for a warm-up period and for the participation of each person in the group.

Sessions scheduled for more than 2 hours, unless they are designed specifically as part of a marathon group, tend to become nonproductive and fatiguing for all concerned. Groups conducted in educational settings, such as high schools and middle schools, may be limited of necessity to a 40- or 50-minute time period based upon the school's standard class schedule. Ideally, groups should meet once or twice a week to promote continuity in the group experience.

Determining Size of the Group

Yalom (1985) suggested that the ideal size of a counseling/therapy group is 7 or 8 members, with 5 to 10 members constituting an acceptable range. He noted that a minimum number is required for a group to function and interact as a group; a group of fewer than five members often results in a sequence of individual therapy or counseling sessions within the group context. As the size of the group diminishes, many of the advantages of a group, particularly the opportunity to receive validation and feedback from a microcosm of society, are lost.

Other Aspects of Organization

Following are several additional possibilities for group leaders to consider in conjunction with groups they lead or co-lead (Yalom, 1985).

1. Weekly, written summaries describing some aspects of the group experience during a given week could be mailed to group members, providing reinforcement and continuity.
2. In addition to the disclosure statement mentioned earlier, written material describing the ground rules, purposes, expectations, and so on, of the group could be distributed. Beyond providing important information, material of this nature reinforces group participants. Providing this written material after the first session may be particularly helpful because anxious members may not have been able to totally integrate information about what a group experience would be like.
3. Group members might be afforded an opportunity to see a movie or a videotape presenting information about group participation, similar to the information described in item 2.
4. Group members could be provided the option of watching videos of their own group after each session. This would give members a chance to evaluate their participation and to obtain additional feedback from other group members. As noted earlier, group members must have provided written permission before filming.
5. Group members could be offered pre-group training sessions during which they would be taught skills for self-disclosure, expressing feelings, staying in the here and now, and so forth. Obviously, this suggestion depends upon the time and resources available to the group leader and group participants and may work better in the context of inpatient rather than outpatient situations.

RECOGNIZING MEMBERSHIP ROLES

When a group is formed and begins to meet, all of the members have just one role, that of group member (Vander Kolk, 1985). As time passes, however, roles are differentiated as members interact and become more comfortable about being themselves in the group. Most groups are characterized by a combination of roles (Gladding, 1999, 2003; Posthuma, 1999; Trotzer, 1999). This combination results in a dynamic interaction among members that energizes or deenergizes the group in some way. For example, a group composed of a number of task-oriented members might identify objectives for the group experience and monitor interactions to ensure movement and progress during each session. Another group might consist of several task-oriented members and also several process-oriented members who value spontaneous interaction and disclosure. This group might find itself in conflict from time to time if task-oriented members feel time is being spent nonproductively and process-oriented members think they are not always able to complete interactions or express deep feelings without others pressuring them to refocus on the original objectives established for the session.

The group leader must recognize the types of roles that group members are taking and institute appropriate interventions to maintain balanced interaction and movement through the definitive, personal involvement, group involvement, and enhancement and closure stages of a group (described in chapter 2). One way of conceptualizing membership roles in groups is to view roles as facilitative, vitalizing and maintenance, or anti-group or blocking in nature.

Facilitative Roles

Facilitative roles serve to keep the group on task and to clarify aspects of communication. Members who behave in facilitative ways contribute to the group constructively and increase the likelihood of participation and cooperation. Table 3.1 presents examples of facilitative roles in groups.

Vitalizing and Maintenance Roles

Vitalizing and maintenance roles help develop social–emotional bonds among members of a group and usually contribute to cohesiveness and feelings of connectedness. Group members who fill vitalizing and maintenance roles usually are sensitive to the affective components of a group and respond in ways that either escalate or reduce tensions related to affective aspects of intra- and interpersonal communication. Table 3.2 summarizes selected vitalizing and maintenance roles.

Anti-Group (Blocking) Roles

Individual needs of group members (Vander Kolk, 1985) often inhibit a group's progress. Group leaders must recognize these anti-group roles and learn to diffuse

Table 3.1   Facilitative Roles in Groups

Role	Description
Initiator	Energizes the group; presents new ideas, new ways of looking at things; stimulates the group to move toward some sort of action. Responses to the initiator may be positive, if the group is ready to move ahead, or negative, if it prefers inaction.
Information Seeker Opinion Seeker	Both request data of a factual or judgmental nature from the group. Information seeker simply requires cognitive information for clarification; opinion seeker focuses on values and the group's affective aspect. Each can be facilitative when data would be helpful to the group. An information seeker, however, can dwell on data to the exclusion of affective concerns; and the opinion seeker can put people on the defensive by pressing for value judgments and self-disclosure before a member is ready.
Information Giver Opinion Giver	An information giver may spontaneously provide cognitive data or respond to the information seeker. An opinion giver may also offer values or judgments on his/her own or in response to the opinion seeker.
Elaborator	Explains and gives examples of the topic, thus developing a meaning for what the group discusses; a rationale for group ideas evolves and the elaborator suggests how the ideas might work out.
Coordinator	Acts as a reality base for the group; ties ideas to practicality, prevents meandering into unrealistic discussions; pulls together group ideas; tries to have the group organize its activities.
Orienter	Tells the group where it is in regard to goals and direction; summarizes what group has done and whether it is "on course."
Evaluator	Describes group's accomplishments and how well it is functioning; may evaluate usefulness or logic of a procedure, suggestion, or group discussion.
Procedural Technician	Carries out technical tasks (arranging chairs, brewing coffee).
Recorder	Writes down or remembers the group's decisions, plans, and suggestions.

Source: From *Introduction to Group Counseling and Psychotherapy* (p. 139) by C. J. Vander Kolk, 1985, Columbus, OH: Charles E. Merrill. Copyright © 1985 by Charles E. Merrill. Reprinted by permission of Merrill, an imprint of Macmillan Publishing Company, and the author.

problematic behaviors in individuals so the entire group does not become unproductive. Table 3.3 outlines some of the possible anti-group roles that members of a group might bring to a group experience.

Table 3.2   Vitalizing and Maintenance Roles

Role	Description
Encourager	Accepts others' ideas by praising, agreeing with, or stimulating ideas from participants; wants good feelings and a sense of security for the group. Excessive use of this role may direct attention from this person to the others.
Harmonizer	Attempts to mediate conflict and tension to keep group in harmony rather than polarized. May deal with subgroups in conflict. May brush real conflicts aside without a thorough working through.
Compromiser	Contracts with the harmonizer in cognitive orientation toward resolving group issues; may seek alternatives acceptable to the participants. When compromiser is part of the conflict, is often willing to give up status, see other points of view, or compromise in a way that resolves the problem.
Expediter	Oversees establishing group norms and guiding adherence to those norms. May try to get everyone to participate or suggest length of individual contributions. Role is similar to a leader's assistant or referee. Group members can become annoyed with someone who takes this role too seriously.
Standard Setter	Wants group process and goals to meet a criterion for acceptance by others. Sets high standards for norms and objectives. May evaluate quality of interactions. Often unsure of himself/herself; wants high standards as a means of reassurance.
Group Observer and Commentator	Notes group process, relates observations or conclusions. Contributions may be descriptive, interpretive, or evaluative. In the extreme, this member may be distancing himself/herself from the group, becoming a less involved participant.
Follower	Goes along with whatever group wants; quiet; offers little of self, preferring to be friendly observer. Usually too insecure and fearful to initiate ideas or discussion; not really a vitalizer.

Source: From *Introduction to Group Counseling and Psychotherapy* (p. 140) by C. J. Vander Kolk, 1985, Columbus, OH: Charles E. Merrill. Copyright © 1985 by Charles E. Merrill. Reprinted by permission of Merrill, an imprint of Macmillan Publishing Company, and the author.

FACILITATING THE GROUP STAGES

Understanding the developmental stages of groups helps the group leader anticipate apprehensions, needs, and fears of members of a group that has just been convened. Understanding how to facilitate the following four stages should prove helpful to the beginning group worker.

Table 3.3   Anti-Group Roles

Role	Description
Aggressor	Disagrees with ideas and discussion. May disapprove of behavior, feelings, and values. May impose beliefs or ways of doing things on others. May be jealous, insecure, need attention. Some groups fight back; others react passively.
Blocker	Stubborn about what should and should not be discussed; resists wishes of total group. Negativism can impede group progress.
Recognition Seeker	Boasts; engages in other behavior to attract group attention.
Self-Confessor	Reveals feelings and insights unrelated to group's immediate dealings. Personal expressions distract group from concentrating on its task.
Playboy	Nonchalant or cynical toward group; engages in horseplay or other behaviors that communicate lack of involvement, thus disrupting group cohesiveness.
Dominator	Tries to manipulate others to recognize his/her authority; less aggressive than manipulative. Behaviors include interrupting, flattery, asserting status, giving directions. Interferes with sense of equality among participants.
Help Seeker Rescuer	Elicits sympathy from group by excessively dwelling on personal problems, confusions, and inadequacies. Giving attention may reinforce dependent behavior. Rescuers may meet own needs by accommodating help seekers, but both roles are unproductive.
Self-Righteous	Has need to always be right and to think others are always wrong. Authority on moral issues. Does not care to be liked; wants to be respected for moral integrity. Imposes moral standards on others. Will at first be quiet, then assert position persistently without conceding or admitting error. Projects image of moral superiority that soon alienates participants. Yalom (1970) suggested these people are disturbed by feelings of shame and anger but usually believe they have no problems.
Do-Gooder	May be a modified form of self-righteous moralist who wants to do what is "right." Is helpful, kind, understanding toward others. Does not usually impose "good" behavior on others, but wants acceptance from others.
Informer	Possible variation on the do-gooder. Occurs when group members interact and know each other outside group sessions; informer shares information about someone's behavior outside the group. Purpose of "squealing" is to enhance one's status with and acceptance by others, or as act of revenge.

(continued)

Table 3.3   Anti-Group Roles *(continued)*

Role	Description
Seducer	Uses manipulations, usually in the form of active or subtle attempts to control others by getting others to reach out to him/her or pretending to be fragile. Seductive behavior also avoids genuine closeness.
Hostile or Angry Member	Manipulates others by intimidation or avoids needs such as affection. Joking, sarcasm, and ridicule are signs of hostility. Result is greater self-protection on part of other participants to avoid attacks.
Monopolist	Talks incessantly about experiences, ideas, and information that is usually only tangentially related to group goals. Self-centered talk may be set off by similarity of another member's problems with an experience of the monopolist. May tell stories, relate what he/she has read, or relate personal upheavals in great detail. At first, group is relieved to have someone carry the ball; after several sessions, there is often fighting, absenteeism, and dropouts. Leader and group must deal with underlying anxiety of the monopolist.
Withdrawn, Nonparticipating, Silent Member	Opposite end of continuum from monopolist. Nonfacilitative group members may resent these members' seeming noninvolvement or resent attention they get when other members try to draw them out.

Source : From *Introduction to Group Counseling and Psychotherapy* (p. 142–143) by C. J. Vander Kolk, 1985, Columbus, OH: Charles E. Merrill. Copyright © 1985 by Charles E. Merrill. Reprinted by permission of Merrill, an imprint of Macmillan Publishing Company, and the author.

Facilitating the Definitive Stage

As discussed in chapter 2, in the definitive stage of the group's developmental process, group members define for themselves and for each other the purpose of the group, the quality of their commitment to it, and their involvement level. Members have questions about trust, support, safety, self-disclosure, confidentiality, and many other aspects of group participation. During the initial sessions, the group leader has to be sensitive to members' questions and uncertainties and be able to model behavior that encourages constructive communication and gradual movement toward achieving individual and group goals. Several group specialists (Corey, 2000, 2004; Gladding, 1999, 2003; Nolan, 1978) have discussed the importance of mastering special skills unique to group work. Among the leader's skills vital to the definitive stage of a group are the following:

1. *Active listening*: paying attention to and paraphrasing the verbal and non-verbal aspects of communication in a way that lets members know they have been listened to and have not been evaluated
2. *Supporting*: providing reinforcement and encouragement to members to create trust, acceptance, and an atmosphere in which self-disclosure can occur when appropriate
3. *Empathizing*: communicating understanding to members by being able to assume their frames of reference
4. *Goal setting*: assisting in planning by helping members define concrete and meaningful goals
5. *Facilitating*: opening up communication between and among group members so each member contributes in some way to the group and begins to feel some involvement with others and with the group
6. *Protecting*: preventing members from taking unnecessary psychological risks in the group
7. *Modeling*: teaching members the elements of constructive communication by demonstrating desired behavior in conjunction with each interaction with group members

Certain practical tasks also must be accomplished. Establishing ground rules, for example, is something the group leader usually does during the first and, if necessary, subsequent sessions, even if some aspects have been addressed in pre-group screening. Examples of ground rules that may be established are: attendance at all meetings, no advice giving, no physical violence, no smoking during meetings, no sexual relationships with other members of the group, and no coming late (Gladding, 1999, 2003; Trotzer, 1999; Vander Kolk, 1985). The leader should explain all of the ground rules and the rationale behind each. As the group continues to meet, members may add ground rules as long as none of these rules endangers the well-being of group members.

Confidentiality (Remley & Herlihy, 2005) is another aspect of group participation that should be discussed during the definitive stage. The group leader must stress the importance of confidentiality and possible violations (as examples—talking about the disclosures of group members outside the group; telling individuals outside the group the identity of those participating in the group). This topic will receive more attention in chapter 7.

During the definitive stage of a group, members' uncertainties about what the group experience may be like are often related to their individual fears and apprehensions. Group leaders can anticipate some of the following misgivings and should help members address any that might interfere with participation (Corey & Corey, 1997):

- Concern about being accepted by other members of the group
- Uncertainty about whether other group members will accept honesty or whether their contributions must be carefully framed so others won't be upset

- Questions about how communication in the group will be different from communication outside the group
- Apprehension about being judged by other group members
- Wondering about similarities to other group members
- Concern about pressure to participate
- Uncertainty about whether to take risks
- Apprehension about appearing to be inept
- Confusion about how much to self-disclose
- Fear about being hurt by other members of the group
- Fear of being attacked by the group
- Wondering about becoming dependent on the group experience
- Apprehension about facing new insights about oneself
- Uncertainty about changing and whether significant others will accept these changes
- Concern about being asked to do something that would be uncomfortable to do

In addition to establishing ground rules, discussing confidentiality, and addressing individual members' apprehensions, the leader may wish to provide structural elements, such as leader and member introductions, exercises to be completed in dyads or triads followed by sharing in the total group, guided fantasies followed by discussion of the experience, sentence-completion exercises, and written questionnaires with subsequent discussion. Structural elements such as these can promote involvement and productivity. The amount of structure necessary to catalyze group interaction will always depend on pre-group screening, the purpose of the group, the age and functionality of group members, and the leader's style. As a rule, we recommend that the leader provide and use structure when needed but not depend on group exercises to the extent that members are unable to express their concerns, desires, and issues. The chapters addressing special populations provide numerous examples of how to structure group sessions.

Finally, the leader should think about how he or she will close the group sessions in a way that provides time for reflection, summarization, and integration. Corey and Corey (1987) have recommended setting aside at least 10 minutes at the end of each session for this purpose so group members do not feel frustrated by a lack of closure or what might be perceived as an abrupt ending. This might be an ideal time to suggest introspection, behavioral rehearsal, or other homework, if applicable.

Facilitating the Personal Involvement Stage

The personal involvement stage of a group is best depicted as one of member-to-member interactions, the sharing of personal information, confrontation with other members of the group, power struggles, and the individual's growing identity as a member of the group. This stage of action, reaction, and interaction requires the group leader to demonstrate awareness of the emotional make-up of the group and the intra- and interpersonal struggles that are part of this stage of a group. In addition to the skills discussed, the following are required of the leader during this challenging stage of group life:

1. *Clarifying*: helping members sort out conflicting feelings and thoughts to arrive at a better understanding of what is being expressed
2. *Questioning*: asking questions to gain additional information or to promote members' self-exploration and description of feelings and thoughts
3. *Interpreting*: providing tentative explanations for feelings, thoughts, and behaviors that challenge members to explore their motivations and reactions in more depth
4. *Reflecting feelings*: letting members know they are being understood in a way that goes beyond the content of their communication
5. *Confronting*: challenging members to become aware of discrepancies between words and actions or current and previous self-disclosures
6. *Initiating*: being proactive to bring about new directions in individual sharing or interpersonal communication
7. *Giving feedback*: offering an external view of how a member appears to another by describing concrete and honest reactions in a constructive way
8. *Self-disclosing*: describing here-and-now reactions to events in the group
9. *Blocking*: preventing counterproductive behavior by one or more group members

During the personal involvement stage of any group, some practical considerations must be dealt with. As self-disclosure becomes more open and interactions among members become more straightforward and more focused on the here and now, some group members may become threatened and remain silent to avoid taking risks. When this happens, the group leader should use his or her skills to acknowledge the way those members may be feeling and encourage them to participate without demanding more participation than they are able to contribute at the time. The longer members remain silent, the more difficulty they may have entering into dialogue and interacting spontaneously. Also, silent members often engender suspicion and criticism by other group members who begin to wonder why the silent members are not involved in the group.

Silence is not the only way that members who become threatened by the dynamics of the personal involvement stage react. Benjamin (1981), Corey (2000, 2004), Corey and Corey (1997), Sack (1985), and Yalom (1985) offered these additional possibilities the group leader should recognize:

1. *Intellectualization*: Members who are feeling threatened by the openness of communication may focus completely on their thoughts to avoid making connections with either their own or others' emotions. A cognitive pattern of communication should signal the leader that these members may not be comfortable with their feelings.
2. *Questioning*: Questions by members can direct the discussion to why something was said or has happened rather than on how members are feeling and

what they are experiencing now. They often ask questions to avoid dealing with their true feelings.

3. *Advice giving*: Offering advice rarely helps another group member resolve personal issues or solve problems independently, but it does provide a means for the advice-giver to avoid struggling with internal issues, empathizing, and adopting the internal frame of reference of other group members.

4. *Band-aiding*: Band-aiding is the misuse of support to alleviate painful feelings. Group members who band-aid prevent themselves and others from fully expressing their emotions.

5. *Dependency*: Dependent group members invite advice-giving and band-aiding by presenting themselves as helpless and "stuck." This, too, prevents complete and accurate self-disclosure by those who feel threatened by aspects of group interaction.

6. *Behaviors related to struggles for control*: During this stage of group development, struggles for control are common. Some of the behaviors that might surface are competition and rivalry, jockeying for position, jealousies, affronts to leadership, and arguing about the division of responsibility and decision making. The leader must be able to recognize these issues and help members talk about them.

7. *Conflict and anger*: Conflict and anger are other common responses to feeling threatened. When conflict and anger are recognized, expressed, and discussed, cohesion in a group usually increases. Participants learn that it is safe to openly disagree and express intense feelings. Further, group members learn that bonds and relationships are strong enough to withstand honest levels of communication.

8. *Confrontation*: Confrontation in a group is not helpful when the emphasis is on criticizing others, providing negative feedback and then withdrawing, or assaulting others' integrity or inherent personality traits. If, however, confrontation is presented in a caring and helpful way, it can catalyze change. For responsible confrontation, group leaders should provide members with guidelines such as the following:

   ■ Know why you are confronting.
   ■ Avoid dramatic statements about how another member appears to be.
   ■ Include descriptions both of observable behaviors and of the impact they have on you.
   ■ Imagine being the recipient of what you are saying to another member.
   ■ Provide the recipient of a confrontive statement with time to integrate and reflect. Do not expect an immediate change in behavior.
   ■ Think about whether you would be willing to consider what you are expecting another group member to consider.

9. *Challenges to the group leader*: Although a leader may feel uncomfortable when a member challenges his or her leadership, the leader must recognize that confrontation often is members' first significant step toward realizing

their independence and trust in the group. The way the leader responds to a challenge by a group member can have a powerful effect on member willingness to trust and to take risks. Leaders can be excellent role models if they respond to challenges nondefensively and ask members to talk about the thoughts and feelings behind them.

One or more members may verbally attack the group leader. Attacks usually are the result of the leader modeling some inappropriate behavior or a member's feeling threatened by the energy or interactions in the group. During the session, the leader has to work through the criticism, by encouraging those who have negative feelings toward him or her to describe those feelings. A give-and-take discussion may lead to acceptable resolution of the difficulty. If a leader does not provide opportunities for members to describe and resolve their feelings, the feelings may escalate to a point at which group sessions become counterproductive.

Facilitating the Group Involvement Stage

As explained in chapter 2, the group involvement stage is characterized by much self-evaluation and self-assessment of behavior, attitudes, values, and methods in relating to others, and also by members' channeling their energies toward meeting the group's goals and purposes. During this stage the terms *members* and *group* become somewhat more synonymous. The group, with its purposes and goals, is merging with members' individual purposes and goals. Individual agendas are replaced by group agendas, and the members identify more with the group.

Facilitating this stage of the group's life requires the leader to use all of the skills needed during the definitive stage and, from time to time, some of the skills important to positive resolution of the personal involvement stage. Additional skills that may be needed include the following:

1. *Linking*: stressing the importance of interpersonal communication within the group by connecting what one member is feeling or doing to what another member is feeling or doing
2. *Providing group identity*: encouraging members in their development of a group identity
3. *Suggesting direction*: providing suggestions as the members progress from individual- to group-directed purposes and goals
4. *Sharing leadership*: encouraging members to assume leadership responsibility within the group when appropriate
5. *Participating in the group*: involving oneself as a member of the group and sharing leadership as opportunities arise
6. *Reinforcing cooperation*: demonstrating, on verbal and nonverbal levels, the benefits of cooperative participation

During this stage, practical considerations for constructive leadership relate to the higher level of self-disclosure and intimacy that members have developed. In one situation that often arises, a member gains sudden insights as another member self-discloses and solves problems. Because members now are readily able to put aside personal agendas and listen and empathize as others in the group share during this stage, they may become aware of incidents in their own lives (e.g., interactions designed to prevent intimacy from occurring) that are emotionally laden.

At times, these memories may be extremely difficult to express and then integrate into a new perspective or set of behaviors. During these circumstances the leader must provide the safety and support needed to guide resulting disclosure and group response and interaction. Insights about previously denied experience can be powerful and difficult for an individual to handle.

During the group involvement stage, the group may be immersed in risk taking, and self-disclosure may progress more rapidly than is necessary or appropriate for the participant or the group as a whole. The leader may have to slow the rate and intensity of self-disclosure, to safeguard members from unnecessary psychological risks. Because of the cohesive atmosphere that has developed during this stage, other members may reinforce a participant's self-disclosure or offer suggestions that the leader might have to ward off to avoid escalating the risk.

Group efforts to help a member with a problem sometimes become detrimental during this stage. Unlike the advice giving and band-aiding in the personal involvement stage, these efforts are not meant to direct the group away from discussing emotional or painful issues. Instead, they derive from the strong feelings of closeness that have developed, and they follow intense discussion and thorough exploration. The problem arises when a participant receives so many suggestions for resolving a problem that he or she begins to feel confused and at a loss to deal with the many options presented. The group leader has to intervene so an option or two can be considered carefully and then either adopted or discarded. Or the leader, more appropriately, might encourage participants to discuss a specific problem or area in future sessions after they have identified their own solutions.

During the group involvement stage, group members begin discussing their desire to establish on the "outside" the same kind of cooperation, cohesiveness, and communication patterns they enjoy during their group sessions. The leader should encourage discussion, helping members to understand that they should not expect the same level of cooperation and the same level of self-disclosure in all groups. Still, they should not assume that nothing can improve in established outside circles. Members also may express how much they look forward to group sessions and how much they dislike the idea of their group terminating at some future time. This latter sentiment, which may begin to be expressed as the group moves toward the enhancement and closure stage, must be addressed.

Facilitating the Enhancement and Closure Stage

This final stage in group development is often described simultaneously as the most exhilarating and the saddest aspect of group work. The exhilaration stems from evaluation and reevaluation as members are encouraged to review the group process and to measure changes from the time they entered the group to this point just before closure and termination. The sadness centers on leaving an environment that has provided safety, security, and support and individuals who have offered encouragement, friendship, and positive feedback related to one's growth potential.

Facilitation of this stage requires the leader to draw upon the following skills in addition to any of those used during previous stages:

1. *Evaluating*: assessing both individual and group process during the group's tenure
2. *Resolving issues*: assisting individual members and the group to achieve closure on remaining issues
3. *Reviewing progress*: helping group members obtain an overview of the progress and change that have taken place since the group was initiated
4. *Identifying strengths and weaknesses*: encouraging members to pinpoint the strengths they have developed in the group, as well as the weaknesses they have acknowledged and begun to overcome, so they can apply this learning outside the group after it terminates
5. *Terminating*: preparing group members to finalize the group's history, assimilate the experience, and separate from the group as sessions come to an end
6. *Referring*: recommending possibilities for individual or group counseling after the group ends

Practical considerations for the group leader are numerous. Corey (2000, 2004), Corey and Corey (1997), George and Dustin (1988), Gladding (1999, 2003), Jacobs et al. (1998, 2002), Ohlsen, Horne, and Lawe (1988), Vander Kolk (1985), and others have discussed aspects of effective leadership associated with closure and termination. The following are some suggestions the leader can draw upon for facilitating closure and termination, although these are by no means an exhaustive listing of possibilities.

1. *Reminders*: Make sure that members are aware of the approaching termination date, to enable them to achieve the essential review and closure. This suggestion applies to groups that have a predetermined closure date established by the members themselves or by a set of external circumstances.
2. *Capping*: During the last few sessions of a group, do not encourage members to initiate discussions of intensely emotional material or to facilitate powerful emotional interchange in the group as a whole. Capping means easing members and the group out of affective expression and into intellectual consideration of progress, change, and strengths, because time is running out for processing new emotional material.
3. *Logs*: If members have been keeping written logs chronicling the group experience, suggest that they share particularly meaningful segments as the group reaches its conclusion. This can be an excellent vehicle for evaluation, review, and feedback.
4. *Unfinished business*: Ask group members to share and work on resolving any unfinished business (whether individual- or group-focused). Allow enough time for members to adequately achieve resolution.

5. *Homework*: Suggest that each group member identify, discuss, and commit to some homework to be completed after the group ends. This may help group members integrate learning and develop perspectives for the future.

6. *Making the rounds*: Offer members the opportunity to look at each person in the group and provide some final feedback (or to hand each person some written feedback). This can provide the basis for one or more sessions aimed at easing the emotions that sometimes are associated with the end of a positive group experience. To allow feedback to be discussed and processed adequately, the leader should allow more than one group session for this activity.

7. *Saying good-bye*: Allow each member to express his or her unique personality and perspective in saying good-bye when a group is ending. Suggest that members frame this good-bye as it relates to the group as a whole, to each participant, or both.

8. *Future planning*: Discuss how group members can approach the future in a proactive way. This helps participants integrate new learning and plan to meet future needs. Members need plenty of time to think about how they will function in the absence of support from the group.

9. *Referrals*: Make arrangements for members who need further counseling, whether group or individual. Discuss the possibilities during a specifically scheduled group session. Members may decide to share with the group their decision for follow-up counseling.

10. *Questionnaires*: If desired, use questionnaires to assess the strengths and weaknesses of a specific group. If these questionnaires are filled out before the group ends, share excerpts with the group, with advance permission of the members.

11. *Follow-up interviews*: Ease the apprehension often associated with the end of a group by offering the opportunity for individual follow-up sessions. Members can utilize the follow-up meeting to discuss post-group progress, difficulties, or issues, and to obtain the support they need to continue in productive ways.

12. *Group reunions*: Organize a group reunion. The reunion might be in the form of a group session, a potluck dinner or picnic, or group attendance at a lecture, for example. The purpose of the follow-up is to give members a chance to reconnect, share, and provide support and encouragement.

DEALING WITH DIFFICULT MEMBERS

At times counselors face some difficult group members—members who attempt to control or take over the group in some way. Typical patterns, presented by Carroll, Bates, and Johnson (1997), Chen and Rybak (2004), Dyer and Vriend (1973), Jacobs et al. (1998, 2002), Kottler (1994), Milgram and Rubin (1992), and Trotzer (1999), are given here, with suggestions for how the group leader might respond (Capuzzi &

Gross, 2001, 2005). The 15 examples that follow concretize the use of skills discussed for facilitating the four stages of a group.

1. *A group member speaks for everyone.*

A group member typically says something like, "We think we should . . . ," "This is how we all feel," or "We were wondering why . . ." Often this happens when a member does not feel comfortable making statements such as, "I think we should . . ." or "I'm wondering why . . ." or when a group member is attempting to garner support for a point of view. The difficulty with allowing the "we" syndrome to operate in a group is that it inhibits members from expressing their individual feelings and thoughts. The group leader might give *feedback* ("You mentioned 'we' a number of times. Are you speaking for yourself or for everyone?") or engage in *linking* ("What do each of you think about the statement that was just made?").

2. *A member speaks for another member in the group.*

Examples of one group member speaking for another are "I think I know what he means" and "She's not really saying how she feels; I can explain it for her." One member speaking for another often connotes a judgment about the ability of the other member to communicate or a judgment that the other member is about to disclose uncomfortable information. Regardless of the motivation behind the statement, the group member who permits another group member to do the talking for him or her has to assess the reason for doing this and whether the same communication patterns happen outside the group. The "talker" has to evaluate his or her inclination to make decisions for or to rescue others.

Appropriate leader skills here include *questioning* ("Did Jim state your feelings more clearly than you can?" or "How does it feel to have someone rescue you?") and making *interpretive statements* ("Did you think June needed your help?" or "Do you find it difficult to hold back when you think you know what someone else is going to say?").

3. *A group member behaves in an "entitled" manner.*

The entitled group member is someone who attempts, in a variety of ways, to keep the focus of the group on himself or herself. This member may monopolize the conversation, tell stories that are related only tangentially to the topic under discussion, arrive late or miss sessions and then expect everyone to accommodate him or her by using most of the time to bring him or her up to date, or be needy and demanding of attention a great deal of the time. As long as such a member can control the proceedings of the group, he or she can demonstrate a sense of power. Such a client must be taught the capacity for empathy and attentiveness to the needs of others, and groups can be ideal for teaching those skills.

Possible leader interventions include *modeling* ("I realize that what you are saying is important to you; perhaps we can provide you with more time after others have had an opportunity to participate in today's session.") and giving *feedback* ("Have you noticed how much time you have taken today, and how restless some other group members appear to be?"). Another option is to cue a group member to do the work ("John, you seem to be getting progressively restless as Bonnie has been speaking; tell her how you feel.").

4. *A group member remains silent.*

As noted earlier, silent group members can create difficulties for groups. A group member's silence can have many different reasons. Sometimes a member is silent because he or she cannot find the words to describe a subjective experience. Other times silence occurs because the member is observing and taking things in. If a group member lacks self-confidence and generally avoids taking the initiative in conversations, he or she may be behaving in his or her normal pattern and does not intend to be resistant or difficult. At times, however, a group may have a member who is not committed to participation and uses the silence as a means of manipulation.

In any case, when a group member *remains* silent, the possibility increases that this member eventually will be confronted, or even attacked, by other group members. Group members may begin to imagine that the silent member does not approve, has definite opinions that ought to be shared, or simply does not care about others in the group. Group leaders may have to *empathize* ("I get the feeling that it's difficult for you to speak up in a group.") or *facilitate* ("Jim, is there anything you can add to the discussion at this time?"). Although the leader may use *questioning* ("I'm wondering what you're thinking and feeling right now?") and *blocking* ("I don't think it's a good idea for you to remain so silent; others may wonder why you don't participate.") to elicit participation, these methods may engender even more resistance. Working with the silent group member can be difficult.

5. *A group member identifies a scapegoat.*

Scapegoating is a common and difficult problem for the group leader. Often, the person who is scapegoated is the target of the displaced anger of another member of the group. Something in his or her behavior has elicited the attack. Although leaders sometimes encourage group members to give feedback to the scapegoat so this member can better understand the reason others are upset with his or her behavior, they must be cautious so the scapegoat is not attacked unnecessarily.

Leaders who are not experienced group work specialists often allow the attention to remain on the scapegoat because of the interaction and participation occurring in the group. Even if the feedback is accurate, the leader is responsible for seeing that the rights of the scapegoated member are not being violated.

At times, a silent member may be inclined to support the scapegoat but needs the help of the leader to vocalize a minority point of view. To reach a constructive resolution, the leader also might ask the group members to imagine how they would feel if they were in the place of the scapegoat.

6. *A group member challenges the leader's authority.*

Because this topic is so important to the group leader, it merits additional attention in this chapter. Group members who challenge the leader's competence sometimes do so in a nonaggressive way, suggesting how the leader might be more effective. At the other end of the continuum of member behavior is the angry, hostile member who overtly attacks the leader's competency and expertise. Members usually view the leader as a source of authority, so the leader should set norms and establish leadership during the first few sessions, to stave off such challenges, at least until the group has met two or three times.

When coping with a challenger, the most important things for a group leader are to stay calm and to avoid responding defensively. A response such as, "I'm glad you're able to express those feelings. Can you tell me more about what led up to this?" implies that the leader is willing to listen to the challenger, is not going to withdraw from the confrontation, and is not going to abdicate the leadership role. Once some interchange takes place, the conflict may be seen as a misunderstanding and resolved in a way that makes the group even more cohesive and able to function constructively. In any event, the behavior the leader *models* for the group when facing a challenge is crucial to the group's future productivity and comfort levels.

7. *A group member focuses on persons, conditions, or events outside the group.*

Many times group counseling sessions turn into gripe sessions. Group members tend to enjoy complaining about a colleague, a friend, or a partner if they are allowed to reinforce one another. The difficulty with this type of interaction is that it might erroneously substantiate that others are at fault and that group members do not have to take responsibility for those aspects of their behavior contributing to their complaints.

The group leader might use skills in *initiating* ("You keep talking about your wife as the cause of your unhappiness. Isn't it more important to ask yourself what contributions you can make to improve your relationship?") or *clarifying* ("Does complaining about others really mean you think you would be happier if they could change?").

8. *A member seeks the approval of the leader or a group member before or after speaking.*

Some group members nonverbally seek acceptance by nodding, glancing, or smiling at the leader or another group member. These members may be intimidated by authority figures or by personal strength or have low self-esteem, causing them to seek sources of support and acceptance outside themselves. When a group member glances at the leader for approval when speaking, one tactic is for the leader to look at another member, forcing the speaker to change the direction of his or her delivery. Another is to give *feedback* ("You always look at me as you speak, almost as if you're asking permission.").

9. *A member says, "I don't want to hurt her feelings, so I won't say what I'd like to say."*

   Especially in the early stages of a group, this sentiment is common. Sometimes a member believes another member is too fragile for feedback. At other times the member is revealing apprehension about being liked by other group members. The group leader should explore reasons for the reticence to offer feedback. In doing so, the leader may reinforce cooperation, asking the member to check with the person to whom feedback may be directed to validate his or her fears.

10. *A group member suggests that his or her problems are someone else's fault.*

    This example may seem to overlap with the seventh one, but it presents a different problem than a group gripe session. When a group member periodically attributes difficulties and unhappiness to another person, the leader might use *blocking* ("Who is really the only person who can be in charge of you?" or "How can other people determine your mood so much of the time?"). We are not suggesting a stance that would be perceived as lacking empathy and acceptance but, rather, the leader should facilitate members' taking responsibility for themselves.

11. *A member might suggest that "I've always been that way."*

    This suggestion indicates irrational thinking and lack of motivation to change. Believing that the past determines all of one's future can limit one's future growth. The group leader must help members such as this to identify irrational thoughts that cause them to be ineffective in specific areas and learn that they are not doomed to repeat the mistakes of the past. *Interpreting* ("You're suggesting that your past has such a hold over you that you never will be any different.") and *questioning* ("Do you think everyone has certain parts of their life over which they have no control?") are possible responses to stimulate the examination of faulty thinking and assumptions.

12. *A member of the group suggests, "I'll wait, and it will change."*

    Frequently, group members are willing to discuss their self-defeating behavior during a group session but are not willing to make an effort to change outside the group. At times they take the position that if they postpone action, things will correct themselves. A competent group leader will use *initiating* to help members develop strategies for doing something about their problems outside the group and will assign *homework* as a means of tracking or checking with members to evaluate their progress.

13. *A member shows discrepant behavior.*

    When discrepancies appear in a member's behavior, the group leader must intervene. Discrepancies may arise between what a member is currently saying and what he or she said earlier, in a lack of congruence between what a member is saying and what he or she is doing in the group, in a difference between how a member sees himself or herself and how others in the group see him or her, or in a difference between how a member reports feeling and how his or her nonverbal cues communicate what is going on inside. The statements a leader uses to identify discrepancies may be *confrontational* in nature because the leader usually has to describe the discrepancies so the group member can begin to identify, evaluate, and change aspects of the behavior.

14. *A member bores the group by rambling.*

Sometimes members use talking as a way of seeking approval, and it may become "overtalk." In response, the leader might ask other members to give *feedback* to the "intellectualizer" to let him or her know how the rambling affects them. If this behavior is not addressed, other members may become angry and hostile toward the offender and toward the leader.

15. *A group member cries.*

Sometimes group leaders, especially those who are just beginning to lead groups, see the member who cries as "difficult." Maybe the difficulty is related more to the discomfort of the group leader, and his or her uncertainty about how to respond, than it is to this behavior on the part of the group member. When a member of the group cries, it could be because the member is attempting to convey feelings that are painful and anxiety-laden. Or a member might cry because what another member is sharing is similar to his or her own unresolved feelings or issues.

The leader has to decide whether to focus on the crying member. The leader should ask the member if he or she would like to process the emotions and thoughts behind the tears or let some time pass before doing so. An important consideration on the leader's part has to do with the amount of time left in the group session. If time is short, the leader may have to acknowledge the member's pain, and if the member wants to share, structure the sharing so the member deals with only one aspect of his or her feelings with the understanding that there will be time during the next session to continue.

The following are the most important guidelines for the leader:

1. Acknowledge the tears.
2. Ask for permission to work with the member and give him or her some time to regain composure, if that is what the member seems to need.
3. Avoid exploring too many areas and making the member feel vulnerable if there is not time to attain closure near the end of the session.

LEARNING ACTIVITIES

1. If you are participating in a small group in conjunction with the course you are taking on group counseling, keep a log and make entries in the log after each

small-group session. How would you describe the leadership style of the facilitator of your group? How would you describe the role you are playing as a member of the group? Is the style of the group leader one that would be natural for you? If not, how do you think your style will differ? Are you comfortable with your role in the group? If not, what would you like to change?

2. Reread the descriptions of the stages—definitive, personal involvement, group involvement, and enhancement and closure—in chapter 2. In what stage of the developmental process is your group? What observations about yourself and other group members have led you to identify this stage as characteristic of your small group at this time? What skills has the leader of your group employed to assist members at this stage?

3. Do some additional reading on the topic of pre-group screening, and evaluate the material for its applicability to the kind of group you plan to lead, under supervision, in conjunction with your practicum or internship experience. Draft a written description of the way you will do the screening, and ask other graduate students in the counselor education program for feedback and suggestions.

4. This text makes a number of suggestions for how to organize the group you are planning to conduct. Develop an outline of your plan for the type of group you will be conducting. Look at some of the chapters on specific populations in this text for some initial ideas of how you might structure each of your sessions, and include a session-by-session outline in your plan. Share your outline and ask for feedback.

5. Reread the discussion on Dealing with Difficult Members and pick the three member behaviors you think would be the most troublesome for you to handle. Think about what would make these member behaviors difficult for you. How can you improve your ability to respond to the member behaviors that you have identified? What assistance might you need from your personal counselor, or your supervisor, or both?

6. Many of the textbooks referenced in this chapter discuss membership roles in groups. Read at least three other sources that address this topic, to better prepare yourself as a group worker.

SUMMARY

The group leader's style, personality, experience, and skills have many ramifications for group experiences and outcomes. The three classic leadership styles that Lewin identified—authoritarian, democratic, and laissez-faire—may relate somewhat to the group's purpose and its composition. In another conceptualization, groups can be seen as leader-centered or group-centered. A third way of looking at leader style is to characterize it as interpersonal or intrapersonal. Group members tend to admire leaders who have charisma, though this carries the danger of the leader's relying too much on this characteristic and failing to facilitate the autonomy of group members. Leaders are encouraged to develop their own unique style through self-awareness, an understanding of their own personal traits and qualities, and the acquisition of specific skills common to all group needs.

In planning for a group experience, leaders should conduct pre-group screening, which may be done through interviews or completion of questionnaires, to select members whose needs and goals are compatible with those of the intended group and who will not be detrimental to other group members or themselves. During pre-group screening, potential members should receive full information about all aspects of the group and what to expect.

When organizing for a group, the leader has to consider the physical setting, the length and frequency of meetings, and the size of the group (within a recommended range of 5 to 10 members). Other organizational aspects may include weekly summaries, written material, movies or videotapes, and pre-group training sessions.

Among the various roles that members assume within a group are facilitative, vitalizing and maintenance, anti-group, and sub-roles of each. The leader must be able to recognize these roles and intervene appropriately. The leader also has to apply a repertoire of skills in leading each of the stages in a group's development. In a group's life, the leader likely will encounter difficult members and behaviors, which he or she must counteract to ensure that the group progresses as intended from beginning to termination. Readers should refer to the Web sites suggested in the first three chapters of the book for additional information.

REFERENCES

American Counseling Association (ACA). (1995). *Code of ethics and standards of practice.* Alexandria, VA: Author

Association for Specialists in Group Work (ASGW). (1989). *Ethical guidelines for group counselors.* Alexandria, VA: Author.

Association for Specialists in Group Work (ASGW). (2000). *Professional standards for training of group work generalists and of group work specialists.* Alexandria, VA: Author.

Benjamin, A. (1981). *The helping interview* (3rd ed.). Boston: Houghton Mifflin.

Brown, R. (1969). Effects of structured and unstructured group counseling with high- and low-anxious college underachievers. *Journal of Counseling Psychology, 16,* 209–214.

Capuzzi, D., & Gross, D. R. (2001). *Introduction to the counseling profession* (3rd ed.). Boston: Allyn & Bacon.

Capuzzi, D., & Gross, D. R. (2005). *Introduction to the counseling profession* (4th ed.). Boston: Allyn & Bacon.

Carroll, M., Bates, M., & Johnson, C. (1997). *Group leadership: Strategies for group counseling leaders* (3rd ed.). Denver: Love Publishing.

Chatwin, M. (1972). Interpersonal trust and leadership style in group counseling. *Dissertation Abstracts International, 32,* 6120A.

Chen, M., & Rybak, C. J. (2004) *Group leadership skills: Interpersonal process in group counseling and therapy.* Belmont, CA: Brooks/Cole.

Conyne, R. K., Harvill, R. L., Morganett, R. S., Morran, D. K., & Hulse-Killacky, D. (1990). Effective group leadership: Continuing the search for greater clarity and understanding. *Journal for Specialists in Group Work, 15*(1), 30–36.

Cooper, G. L. (1977). Adverse and growthful effects of experimental learning groups: The role of the trainer, participant, and group characteristics. *Human Relations, 30,* 1103–1109.

Corey, G. (2000). *Theory and practice of group counseling* (5th ed.). Pacific Grove, CA: Brooks/Cole.

Corey, G. (2004). *Theory and practice of group counseling* (6th ed.). Pacific Grove, CA: Brooks/Cole.

Corey, M. S., & Corey, G. (1987). *Groups: Process and practice* (3rd ed.). Pacific Grove, CA: Brooks/Cole.

Corey, M. S., & Corey, G. (1997). *Groups: Process and practice* (5th ed.). Pacific Grove, CA: Brooks/Cole.

DeLucia-Waack, J. L., & Donigian, J. (2004). *The practice of multicultural group work: Visions and perspectives from the field.* Belmont, CA: Brooks/Cole.

Dies, R. R. (1973). Group therapist self-disclosure: An evaluation by clients. *Journal of Counseling Psychology, 20,* 344–348.

Dies, R. R. (1977). Group therapist transparency: A critique of theory and research. *International Journal of Group Psychotherapy, 27,* 177–200.

Dyer, W. W., & Vriend, J. (1973). Effective group counseling process interventions. *Educational Technology, 13*(1), 61–67.

Gazda, G. M. (1989). *Group counseling: A developmental approach* (4th ed.). Boston: Allyn & Bacon.

George, R. L., & Dustin, D. (1988). *Group counseling: Theory and practice.* Englewood Cliffs, NJ: Prentice-Hall.

Gladding, S. T. (1999). *Group work: A counseling specialty* (3rd ed.). Columbus: Prentice Hall.

Gladding, S. T. (2003). *Group work: A counseling specialty* (4th ed.). Upper Saddle River, NJ: Merrill/Prentice Hall.

Greenberg, K. R. (2003). *Group counseling in K–12 schools: A handbook for school counselors.* Boston: Allyn & Bacon.

Heikkinen, C. A. (1975). Another look at teaching experience and closed-mindedness. *Journal of Counseling Psychology, 22,* 79–83.

Heslin, R. (1964). Predicting group task effectiveness from members' characteristics. *Psychological Bulletin, 62,* 248–256.

Jacobs, E. E., Masson, R. L., & Harvill, R. L (1998). *Group counseling: Strategies and skills* (3rd ed.). Pacific Grove, CA: Brooks/Cole.

Jacobs, E. E., Masson, R. L., & Harvill, R. L (2002). *Group counseling: Strategies and skills* (4th ed.). Pacific Grove, CA: Brooks/Cole.

Johnson, D. W., & Johnson, F. P. (2000). *Joining together: Group theory and group skills* (7th ed.). Boston: Allyn & Bacon.

Johnson, D. W., & Johnson, F. P. (2003). *Joining together: Group theory and group skills* (8th ed.). Boston: Allyn & Bacon.

Kellerman, H. (1979). *Group psychotherapy and personality: Intersecting structures.* New York: Grune & Stratton.

Kottler, J. A. (1994). Working with difficult group members. *Journal for Specialists in Group Work, 19,* 3–10.

Kottler, J. A. (2001). *Learning group leadership: An experiential approach.* Boston: Allyn & Bacon.

Lewin, K. (1944). The dynamics of group action. *Educational Leadership, 1,* 195–200.

MacLennan, B. W. (1975). The personalities of group leaders: Implications for selection and training. *International Journal of Group Psychotherapy, 25,* 177–184.

Milgram, D., & Rubin, J. S. (1992). Resisting resistance: Involuntary substance abuse group therapy. *Social Work With Groups, 15,* 95–110.

Nolan, E. J. (1978). Leadership interventions for promoting personal mastery. *Journal for Specialists in Group Work, 3,* 132–138.

Ohlsen, M. M., Horne, A. M., & Lawe, C. F. (1988). *Group counseling* (3rd ed.). New York: Holt, Rinehart & Winston.

Posthuma, B. W. (1999). *Small groups in counseling and therapy* (3rd ed.). Boston: Allyn & Bacon.

Remley, T. P., Jr., & Herlihy, B. (2005). *Ethical, legal, and professional issues in counseling* (2nd ed.). Upper Saddle River, NJ: Merrill/Prentice Hall.

Rutan, J. S., & Rice, C. A. (1981). The charismatic leader: Asset or liability? *Psychotherapy: Theory, Research and Practice, 18,* 487–492.

Sack, R. T. (1985). On giving advice. *AMHCA Journal, 7,* 127–132.

Schmuck, R. A., & Schmuck, P. A. (1997). *Group process in the classroom* (7th ed.). Dubuque, IA: Brown & Benchmark.

Shaw, M. E. (1981). *Group dynamics: The psychology of small group behavior.* New York: McGraw-Hill.

Stogdill, R. M. (1974). *Handbook of leadership.* New York: Free Press.

Trotzer, J. P. (1999). *The counselor and the group: Integrating theory, training, and practice* (3rd ed.). Philadelphia: Taylor & Francis.

Vander Kolk, C. J. (1985). *Introduction to group counseling and psychotherapy.* Columbus, OH: Merrill.

Wittmer, J., & Webster, G. B. (1969). The relationship between teaching experience and counselor trainee dogmatism. *Journal of Counseling Psychology, 16,* 499–504.

Yalom, I. D. (1985). *The theory and practice of group psychotherapy* (3rd ed.). New York: Basic Books.

Zimpfer, D., & Waltman, D. (1982). Correlates of effectiveness in group counseling. *Small Group Behavior, 13*(3), 275–290.

Group Work: Theories and Applications

Douglas R. Gross and David Capuzzi

The group-procedures class was just beginning, and Dr. Burns asked if anyone had questions about the material that the students read prior to class. Greg, a first-year student, raised his hand and said he was confused about the information dealing with theory applied to groups. When Dr. Burns asked Greg to be more specific in his question, Greg said that when he had taken the counseling theory class last semester, he had understood that the various counseling theories had been developed to work with the individual, that the research done in developing these theories was all completed on individual cases. His confusion resulted from the author of the assigned material seeming to simply transfer these theoretical concepts from the individual to the group.

Greg's question was, "How do I transfer these individual concepts into a group of eight or ten members?" Dr. Burns's response of "carefully" brought laughter from the class. He continued, however, by stating that Greg had a good question—one that continues to concern even the most experienced group leaders. The class spent most of the period discussing the issue. As with many such questions, the class arrived at no definitive answers, and every student left that evening with several questions regarding the relationship of counseling theory to group interaction and how to use individual-based approaches with groups.

This scenario probably has taken place, in one form or another, in every group class. The confusion in how to transfer individual counseling theory to groups plagues students, as well as professionals who operate in the broad arena of group counseling or therapy. Addressing this issue in 1978, Shapiro stated:

> There is an apparent paradox in the notion of group psychotherapy. The locus of therapy is the

group, and yet the group is not in need of treatment. Unless the
group in question is a natural group (family, management, etc.),
group therapists are using a group format to treat individuals.
The goal of the leader is not to alter the group per se but to
provide treatment and growth for the members of the group.
This problem is reflected in the development of therapeutic
approaches to groups. Most of the extant group therapies are
in fact individual therapies which subsequently were applied
in group settings for reasons of economy. (pp. 44–45)

This statement encapsulates one of the major dilemmas emanating from discussions of theoretical/therapeutic systems applied to groups. The dilemma revolves around the transferability of concepts, techniques, and approaches originally developed for and directed toward the individual into a group modality. Authors such as Capuzzi and Gross (2002, 2003), Corey (2000, 2004), Gladding (1999, 2003), and Yalom (1995) have all addressed the difficulties and cautions the counselor or therapist has to face when making the transition from individual to group counseling or therapy.

These difficulties and cautions should not be interpreted to mean that transferability is impossible. To the contrary, current practice indicates that all theoretical/therapeutic systems have been applied, with varying degrees of success, across both individual and group counseling or therapy. Based upon statements by Lakin (1985), Shaffer and Galinsky (1989), and Wright (1989), many of the factors that dictate the selection of one or more theoretical/therapeutic systems in the individual realm also apply in the group domain. The selection of a theoretical system is often based upon the counselor's or therapist's philosophical position and what he or she believes regarding the nature of the individual as related to development and change. This selection also may stem from an experiential position based upon the counselor's or therapist's education and working background in selected theoretical systems.

Regardless of the reasons for selecting any theoretical system, those who choose to work with groups should do so with a basis in theory. To do otherwise places the individual and group in what Corey (2004) describes as "somewhat like flying a plane without a map and instruments" (p. 51).

In this chapter we explore selected theoretical/therapeutic systems and their application to groups. This discussion is followed by an integration of the concepts and systems based on similarities in the variables of relationship, leader role, member role, process, and outcome.

THEORETICAL SYSTEMS

Although all of the major theoretical/therapeutic systems have been adapted for the group modality, we have limited our discussion to six systems that are widely accepted in the group setting and have applicability and adaptability for developing short-term group models. According to Corey (2004), "Given the managed care emphasis on being both efficient and effective, today's group leaders need to learn as much as possible about short-term groups" (p. 52). The six systems are Adlerian, Gestalt, person-centered, rational–emotive behavior theory, transactional analysis, and psychodrama. The basic concepts of each theory are presented, followed by leader dynamics and techniques drawn from these concepts that are applicable to a discussion of group counseling or therapy.

For readers who are interested in group modalities stemming from theoretical/ therapeutic systems not included in this text, we offer the following resources:

Psychoanalytic	Bemak & Epp (2001); Messer & Warren (2001); Rutan (1999)
Behavioral	Gazda, Ginter, & Horne (2001); Kalodner (2003); Spiegler & Guevemont (2003)
Existential	Bryant-Frank (2003); May & Yalom (2000); Walsh & McElwain (2002)
Reality therapy	Glasser (2000); Wubolding (2001)

Adlerian Theory

Basic Concepts

Adlerian psychology is both an individual and a social psychology. The individual aspects define humans as unified organisms whose behaviors are purposeful and goal directed and not necessarily determined by genetic endowment, environmental press, or early sexual impressions. Individuals give meaning to their lives. They have the creative power and the self-determination to influence their personal and social development and also certain events. Through their unique powers, individuals strive to achieve an identity and to belong.

According to Milliren, Evans, and Newbauer (2003), Adlerian psychology is "a cognitive, goal-oriented, social psychology interested in a person's beliefs and perceptions, as well as the effects that person's behavior has on others" (p. 91). They further conclude that it is one of the few theories interested in democratic processes in the home, school, and workplace.

The social aspects of Adlerian psychology emphasize the importance of the individual's interaction with the rest of society and rely on the premise that individuals are motivated primarily by social interest. Social interest is translated into a "need to belong."

According to Manaster and Corsini (1982), social interest is possibly the most distinctive and valuable concept in Adlerian psychology. It involves individuals' attitudes in dealing with the social world and includes concern and striving for a better world for all humans. The social connectedness and individuals' needs to be useful to others are what give people measures of happiness and success. Based upon this social interest, individuals strive to master three main tasks as they move through life: their relationships with society, work, and love.

Adler (1938) believed that feelings of inferiority are common in children because of the dependent, small, and socially inferior position they hold in the family and in society. According to Adlerians, this position provides the motivational forces of

- striving from a perceived negative (inferiority) to a hoped-for positive position (superiority) in life,
- striving in the direction of a unique goal or ideal self,
- striving to belong in one's social world,
- striving to understand one's spiritual nature, and
- striving to better comprehend the "I" and "me" aspects of self.

None of these motivating forces stands alone. They are interrelated, and movement in one area impacts movement in another.

These motivating forces are influenced by a number of factors, any one of which may encumber individuals in their development and movement toward goals. These factors include

1. fictional goals (unconscious assumptions regarding what must be done to develop worth as an individual, such as striving for superiority);
2. birth order (the individual's chronological and psychological position within the family);
3. the family constellation/atmosphere (variables related to personality, relationships, developmental issues, structural factors, attitudes and values within the family).

This planned and orchestrated movement toward goals is termed one's "style of life" and, based upon the factors identified above, may lead individuals to a lifestyle characterized by positive growth and development or to one characterized by maladjustment. The key rests with individuals and their perceptions and interpretations, which translate into assumptions and goals that direct the formation of their "style of life." According to Gladding (2003), "Lifestyles are developed early in a person's development (around age 5), but they are open to change" (p. 393).

Summarizing the major concepts underlying Adlerian psychology, Gilliland, James, Roberts, and Bowman (1984) identified the following seven attributes:

1. *Humanistic*: individual and society valued over the organization
2. *Holistic*: individual is indivisible
3. *Phenomenological*: importance of the individual's perspective
4. *Teleological*: future orientation and striving for goal attainment
5. *Field-theoretical*: interactional nature of the individual with the social and physical environment
6. *Socially oriented*: individual response to and contribution to society
7. *Operational*: methodology in place

Concepts Translated Into Leader Behaviors

Based on Adlerian concepts, the group leader has to be able to

- establish a working relationship in which the leader and members are equal;

- communicate to the members feelings of mutual trust and respect;
- aid the members in exploring the personal goals, beliefs, feelings, and motives that are determining factors in the development of the members' "style of life";
- assist the members in gaining insight into their fictitious goals and the self-defeating behaviors that impede them from formulating effective life goals;
- help members accept responsibility for their freedom and personal effectiveness so they can develop feelings of self-worth;
- aid members in considering alternative lifestyles and assist them in strengthening their commitment to change;
- help members to enhance their involvement with others and to extend their social interest as this applies to self and others;
- aid members in accepting self with the assets and the liabilities that make up the self;
- assist members in developing a sense of belonging and a sense of community, because their self-meaning is tied closely to their social purpose;
- aid members in exploring alternative behaviors and gaining new insights, and empower them to put these behaviors and insights into action.

Group Stages and Techniques

According to Sonstegard and Bitter (1998), the Adlerian approach to working with groups has four stages:

1. Developing and maintaining the proper therapeutic relationship between leaders and members
2. Assessing the dynamics that operate within individual members
3. Helping the individual to gain insight and self-understanding
4. Assisting the individual to discover new alternatives and make new choices

In each of these stages, certain techniques enhance group members' growth and development. These techniques, however, are not limited to only one stage. Their use throughout the group process is highly effective in bringing forth positive group interaction. The following is a summary of techniques that will aid the Adlerian group leader in enhancing growth and development within the group:

- Model appropriate social skills and show interest to demonstrate acceptance.
- Create contracts to demonstrate the equality of the leader–member relationship.
- Use active listening skills (e.g., restatement, reflection, summarization).
- Employ visual imagery to help members clarify and put into concrete terms some of the absurdities of their thinking and behavior.
- Elicit early recollections to aid members in identifying emotional patterns and feelings and discovering the basis for negatives carried from childhood into adulthood.
- Make use of paradoxical intention by having members attempt to increase debilitating thoughts and behaviors.
- Use confrontation in a constructive fashion, pointing out discrepancies between what group members say and their actions.

■ Assess members' current functioning in work and social relationships.

■ Assess members' goals and how these translate into individual lifestyles.

■ Observe members' interactions, as they may be descriptive of their feelings regarding self and their development of social skills.

■ Observe members' nonverbal behaviors, and do not hesitate to interpret from these observations.

As reported by Milliren et al. (2003), Sharf (1996), and Sweeney (1998), special techniques that have application in an Adlerian group include but are not limited to the following:

The Question
Catching Oneself
Life Style Assessment
Natural and Logical Consequences
Methods of Encouragement
Paradoxical Intention
Acting As If

Each technique is designed to deal with the group stages identified earlier.

Gestalt Theory

Basic Concepts

Gestalt counseling or therapy is rooted in Gestalt psychology, a school of perception that originated in Europe before World War I. Gestalt psychology began with studies of the perceptual field as a whole. Gestaltists then broke down this field into parts (figure and background), identifying the characteristics of each of these parts and their relationships. Using the body of knowledge collected in this academic field, Fritz Perls translated the perceptual approach to psychology into Gestalt therapy, which moved it from the primarily academic realm into the arena of counseling or therapy.

As applied to counseling or therapy, Gestalt theory views the individual (organism) as being fully responsible for determining the essence of his or her being and reality. In this sense, Gestalt theory may be viewed as both phenomenological and existential (Hazler, 2001; Meier & Davis, 2001). Individuals are credited with the ability to find their own way in life and to accept the responsibilities that come from decisions they make. Beyond accepting responsibility for the problems created by their decisions, they must accept the responsibility of dealing effectively with these problems. The major goal of counseling is to aid individuals in attaining greater awareness of their potential, which, in turn, will allow the individuals to exercise their potential in positive growth and change (Seligman, 2001; Shane, 1999).

According to Haley, Sieber, and Maples (2003):

> The process of change in Gestalt counseling and
> psychotherapy consists of the identification and working

through of a variety of blocks or interferences that prevent
the client from achieving a balance. (p. 195)

Contributing to the process of change are what Perls (1969) defined as five lay-
ers of neurosis through which the client passes:

1. *Cliche* layer, in which the individual has no contact with others and interactions are generally routine and superficial
2. *Phony* layer, in which the individual plays a role or a game to avoid contact
   with others
3. *Impasse* layer, in which the individual is "stuck" and unable to change or
   move
4. *Implosive* layer, in which the individual begins to experience himself or
   herself and develop an awareness of who he or she really is but may not act
   on these new perceptions
5. *Explosive* layer, in which the individual becomes alive, authentic, and without pretense and has the motivation to act upon this new awareness

A crucial feature of Gestalt counseling or therapy that is both a valuable asset and
a critical handicap is the open-endedness of the therapeutic approach. Although it
allows for creativity, spontaneity, and inventiveness, it is not necessarily based on a
set of techniques or tools that can be quantified from a "proof of theory" perspective.
Gestalt theory explains motivation as striving toward balance or equilibrium.
This striving is natural and is represented by movement between the polarities of
equilibrium and disequilibrium. According to Polster and Polster (1973), this striving for balance provides the organism with perceptual order, which is best viewed in
terms of a figure set against a background. When the individual perceives a need
(figure), he or she is in a state of disequilibrium. When that need is met, the figure
melds into the background and a new need (figure) takes its place. Therefore, the
individual tends to remain in a constant state of flux.

To further understand the individual, Gestaltists use the principle of holism, the
individual's interdependent combination of body and spirit and his or her relationship to the environment. Gestaltists view the individual as a physical and psychological totality that is unified with the environment. Through the individual's aggressive
capacity, he or she is able to interact with the environment and assimilate from that
environment what is needed for growth and change. Gilliland et al. (1984) commented about the individual's integration of body, spirit, and aggressive capacity:

Connecting these three aspects of personality theory together
presupposes that a person exists in a field that includes the self
and environment. Although the individual and the environment
are separate, the process of interaction between them cannot
be split (holism). Moreover, human aggressive capacity comes
into play at the contact boundary between the organism and the
environment by means of contact or withdrawal (the opposite of
contact). More specifically, when an object has been contacted

or withdrawn from in a way satisfying to the individual, both the object and the need associated with it disappear into the background. The situation is finished; another Gestalt is completed. (p. 96)

These same three aspects (body, spirit, and aggressive capacity) play a role in the development of dysfunctional behavior. Instead of using these aspects for growth, the individual uses them to protect the organism, and in so doing develops defense structures that prevent positive growth and change. Words such as *introjection*, *projection*, *retroflection*, *deflection*, and *dichotomies* describe these nonproductive defensive behaviors, which render the individual's perceptions unclear so that he or she is in danger of erecting rigid, artificial boundaries that do not permit the successful completion of need satisfaction.

Gestaltists believe that to remove these artificial boundaries, counseling or therapy must approach the individual from an experiencing perspective through which the individual can deal with the boundaries that detract from effective functioning. According to Haley et al. (2003), these interventions are behaviors of experimentation that emerge from the cooperative relationship between the client and the counselor or therapist. The interventions are generally labeled "experiments," because they are procedures aimed at discovery rather than exercises in the traditional sense.

The experiments are conducted with a here-and-now orientation that deals with present functioning, as current behavior is more representative of the boundaries than is past behavior. By dealing with behaviors in the here and now, through sensing, feeling, and experiencing the boundaries, the individual is able to move through the impasse and reformulate his or her awareness for more productive results. According to Yontef (1995, p. 280), the purposes of experiments are

- to clarify and sharpen what the client is already aware of and to make new linkages between elements already in awareness,
- to bring into focal awareness that which was previously known only peripherally,
- to bring into awareness that which is needed but systematically kept out of awareness, and
- to bring into awareness the system of control, especially the mechanisms of preventing thoughts or feelings from coming into focal awareness.

To enhance their effectiveness in aiding clients in this experimental process, counselors or therapists can find direction in Naranjo's (1970, pp. 49–50) listing of nine "moral injunctions for the individual," which he stated are implicit in Gestalt counseling:

1. Live now. Be concerned with the present rather than the past.
2. Live here. Deal with what is present rather than with what is absent.
3. Stop imagining. Experience the real.
4. Stop unnecessary thinking. Rather, taste and see.
5. Express rather than manipulate, explain, justify, or judge.

6. Give in to unpleasantness and pain just as to pleasure. Do not restrict your awareness.
7. Accept no *should* or *ought* other than your own. Adore no graven image.
8. Take full responsibility for your actions, feelings, and thoughts.
9. Surrender to being as you are.

Concepts Translated Into Leader Behaviors

Based on Gestalt concepts, the group leader has to be able to

- establish an environment in which leader and members share equally in the process of change;
- allow members to find their own way in life and accept the responsibility that goes with this;
- focus members on their experiences in the present moment (the here and now);
- recognize the blocks and boundaries that impede members' growth, and be willing to bring them to the members' attention;
- aid members in accepting all aspects of themselves, and encourage their sharing of hidden and self-disguised aspects of self;
- assist members in understanding, accepting, and dealing with the concept that they are responsible for their existence;
- confront members with their defensive structures and their unwillingness to take responsibility for self;
- aid members, through exercises, in addressing the unfinished business in their lives;
- help members try out new forms of behavior, to open them up to the full spectrum of their being; and
- help members recognize the splintered parts of self and work toward integrating these parts.

Group Stages and Techniques

Gestalt counseling or therapy does not lend itself well to the traditional concept of group stages. Although certain techniques have special significance in Gestalt counseling or therapy, their use is not limited to one stage. The following is a summary of techniques that will aid the Gestalt group leader in enhancing growth and development within the group:

- Become actively involved with members of the group.
- Demonstrate, through exaggeration, the meanings of gestures, posture, and movement in communication.
- Conduct experiments that will help group members gain greater awareness.
- Demonstrate, through dialogue and exercises, willingness and ability to stay in the here and now.
- Apply active listening skills (e.g., restating, paraphrasing, summarizing).
- Enlist other members of the group in providing feedback.
- Demonstrate intensive interaction with one member as a learning model for all members.

- Use confrontational skills to startle or shock members into greater awareness of their self-defeating behaviors.
- Be a creative agent of change to enhance members' self-awareness.
- Observe and give direct feedback on group members' nonverbal behaviors.

Special techniques (experiments) identified by Baker (2001), Corey (2004), Gladding (2003), and Haley et al. (2003) as having application in a Gestalt group include but are not limited to the following:

Floating Hot Seat	Dream Work
Dual Focused Gestalt Work	Empty Chair or Two Chair Strategy
Playing the Projection	Making the Rounds
Repetition Game	Unfinished Business
Let the Little Child Talk	Fantasy Approaches

Person-Centered Theory

Basic Concepts

Person-centered counseling or therapy arose from the work of Carl Rogers. Based upon its major tenets and belief structures, it may be viewed as both phenomenological (human behavior is based on the individual's perception of reality and the values and attitudes attached to that perception) and holistic (human existence is best understood by viewing individuals as a whole and in relationship to the contexts in which they live their lives). The theory sets forth an optimistic view of human potential. The "organismic valuing process" that Rogers (1959) described is, according to the theory, inborn and provides the individual with the capacity to make wise choices that will maintain and enhance the organism. Rogers contended that people make bad choices—choices that are self-destructive—not because of failure of the organismic valuing process but, rather, because they have subverted this process by accepting (introjecting) the values, beliefs, and experiences of others.

The uniqueness of the individual, which person-centered theory emphasizes, is explained developmentally through the potential that exists within the organism. The organism enters the world with both an organismic valuing process and the tendency toward self-actualization. The infant is able to evaluate what feels good (what actualizes self) and through this process forms a self-concept from experiences, values, meanings, and beliefs that enhance the "I" or "me" of self. With self-concept come perceptions of relationships with others and the values attached to them.

As the organism matures, it identifies the self as an entity separate from others and from the environment. With this awareness, a new need appears—the need for positive regard. This need initially can be fulfilled only through interaction with others and is, fortunately, reciprocal. The need is fulfilled by receiving positive regard from others or by perceiving that one's own behavior has met another's need.

With the emergence of self-awareness and the need for positive regard, the individual becomes concerned with self-regard and seeks experiences that result in positive valuing of the self by others. When a person receives unconditional positive regard from others, the need for positive self-regard is almost automatically fulfilled and no problems are likely to arise. The individual remains congruent and bases his or her behavior on his or her organismic valuing process (Boy & Pine, 1999; Hazler, 2003; Prochaska & Norcross, 1999).

In the course of human development, trouble arises when significant others negatively value some of the individual's positive self-experiences. When this happens, the need for positive regard and the organismic valuing are thrown into conflict and "conditions of worth" develop. To maximize the positive regard received from others and to feel personally worthwhile, the individual is forced to deny or distort the value of some of these experiences. In doing so, the individual becomes incongruent and no longer simply assimilates and symbolizes experiences. The person now denies or distorts experiences that are threatening to the distorted self-concept, and hence to the need for positive self-regard, to support the unrealistic self-structure.

This defensive pattern becomes circular. More and more behavior is based on the need for positive regard rather than on the organismic valuing process, and the person becomes increasingly incongruent, defensive, and rigid, acting compulsively to protect his or her erroneous self-image (Noble, 1977).

Based upon these tenets and beliefs, Rogers (1959, p. 232) identified the following changes that he expected successful counseling or therapy to produce:

1. People come to see themselves differently.
2. People accept themselves and their feelings more fully.
3. People become more self-confident and more self-directing.
4. People become more the person they would like to be.
5. People become more flexible, less rigid, in their perceptions.
6. People adopt more realistic goals for themselves.
7. People behave in a more mature fashion.
8. People change maladjustive behaviors.
9. People become more accepting of others.
10. People become more open to the evidence of what is going on within them and outside of themselves.
11. People change basic personality characteristics in constructive ways.

Successful counseling or therapy, according to Rogers (1959), must include the following "core conditions," which he saw as necessary and sufficient for bringing about personal changes. He believed that if these core conditions were present and if the client were to perceive the existence of these conditions, he or she would change accordingly.

- *Psychological contact*: a relationship between two persons in which impact between the two persons is possible
- *Incongruence*: a condition in which clients are fearful, anxious, or distressed because of differing perceptions of self and their experiences
- *Congruence/genuineness*: a condition describing the counselor's or therapist's ability to be himself or herself

- *Unconditional positive regard*: a condition describing the counselor's or therapist's ability to accept the client without conditions
- *Empathy*: a condition that enables the counselor or therapist to step into the world of the client without being influenced by the client's personal attitudes and values

Concepts Translated Into Leader Behaviors

Based on person-centered concepts, the group leader has to be able to

- establish a facilitative climate within the group, characterized by congruence, unconditional positive regard, and empathic understanding;
- provide an environment in which all group members perceive the constructs of safety and mutual trust;
- establish an environment in which leader and members share equally in the process of change;
- be congruent (genuine) in relationships with members and be able to communicate this to the members;
- have unconditional positive regard for all members and be able to communicate this to the members;
- have empathic understanding and be able to communicate this to the members;
- support members' finding their own way in life and accepting the responsibility that goes with this;
- refrain from giving advice and direction and allow members to positively activate their organismic valuing process; and
- use one's being as a catalyst for change within the group.

Group Stages and Techniques

Person-centered counseling or therapy is not presented in terms of stages or listings of techniques. According to Gilliland et al. (1984):

> Since person-centered counseling is essentially a "being" and a relationship-oriented approach, it is important to note that Rogerian-based strategies for helping people are devoid of techniques that involve doing something to or for the client. There are no steps, techniques, or tools for inducing the client to make measured progress toward some goal; instead the strategies are geared to the experiential relationship. (p. 78)

With this caveat in mind and the knowledge that the core conditions identified earlier have to be met, the person-centered group leader should benefit from the use of

- silence as a way of communicating acceptance and understanding;
- active listening skills (e.g., restatement, paraphrasing, summarizing);
- confrontation to demonstrate congruence and positive regard for group members;
- attending behaviors that allow the leader to focus fully on group members;

- communication skills that allow the leader to verbally and nonverbally communicate his or her depth of empathic understanding for group members;
- self-disclosures, when appropriate, to communicate willingness to be real and to model safety and trust within the group; and
- members' resources to enable and promote self-empowerment.

Rational–Emotive Behavior Therapy (REBT)

Basic Concepts

Rational–emotive behavior therapy (REBT) is a genetic, cognitive, and behavioral approach to human development and counseling or therapy that stems from the work of Albert Ellis. According to Dryden and Ellis (2001), REBT is based on the assumption that humans have a biological tendency to think irrationally or dysfunctionally, as well as rationally or functionally. Even though individuals have the propensity toward growth and actualization, they can readily sabotage their growth by their unrealistic, illogical, and defeatist thinking.

On one hand, they strive to create a happy and more fulfilling life, but on the other hand, they elevate strong goals, desires, and references into absolutistic and unrealistic shoulds, oughts, and musts that lead to a myriad of emotional and/or behavioral problems.

Ellis (1994) stated that these shoulds, oughts, and musts fall under the following three categories:

1. Self-demandingness (we always must perform well and win others' approval)
2. Other-demandingness (we always must be treated fairly, kindly, and with consideration)
3. World-demandingness (we always must live under conditions that are enjoyable, hassle-free, safe, and favorable)

According to DiGiuseppe (1999), emotional distress results not from events and other people but, instead, from dysfunctional thought processes that foster these three demand categories. Central to this theory is the idea that events and other people do not make individuals feel bad or good. It comes from the individual's dysfunctional thought processes such as exaggeration, overgeneralization, oversimplification, illogic, faulty deductions, absolutistic rigid schema, and unvalidated assumptions. Therefore, the best way to reduce emotional distress and resulting behavioral problems is to change the way people think.

According to Ellis and Dryden (1997), the theory of change in REBT involves the following six principles:

1. Acknowledge that a problem exists.
2. Identify any "meta-disturbances" (being disturbed about the original disturbance, i.e., depressed about being depressed).
3. Identify irrational beliefs and understand why the beliefs are irrational.

4. Recognize why rational beliefs would be preferable.
5. Learn how to change irrational beliefs and replace them with rational beliefs.
6. Work on tendencies to think and act rationally

The goal of REBT is to help clients develop a rational philosophy of life that will reduce their emotional distress and self-defeating behavior and result in their ability to be happier and live more meaningfully. According to Vernon (2003), to meet this goal, REBT counselors or therapists aid clients in identifying how they prevent themselves from being happy by focusing on their irrational beliefs that lead to emotional and behavioral disturbances. As reported by Ellis (1994, 1995, 1996), this is accomplished by applying the A–B–C–D–E model. The letters stand for the following:

A = *Activating event*: an external event to which a person is subjected
B = *Belief*: a sequence of thoughts or self-verbalizations in which the person engages in response to the external event
C = *Consequence*: the feelings and behaviors that result from B
D = *Disputing*: the person's attempt to modify the sequence of thoughts or self-verbalizations
E = *Effect*: the presumed affective and behavioral consequences resulting from cognitive disputation

Undergirding this therapeutic approach is the belief that human problems are not based in the actual situation or event (A) that triggers the discomfort (C) but, instead, are based in the thinking, views, beliefs, and attitudes that individuals attach to the situation or event (B). For example, someone who is rejected in attempting to develop a relationship would, according to REBT theory, cognitively process the rejection according to his or her views, beliefs, and attitudes and, based upon that interpretation, react in either a rational or irrational manner.

The person who reacts rationally would interpret the situation as perhaps "too bad" but realize that his or her next attempt could be more successful. The person who reacts irrationally would catastrophize the situation, move beyond it, feel both rejected and rejectable, and come to the conclusion that he or she never will be able to establish a meaningful relationship.

Ellis (1991) contended that people are born with the ability to think and respond both rationally and irrationally. As a result of individuals' interactions with the environment and the significant people who frequent that environment, irrational thinking surfaces as the more consistent mode of operating. This should not be interpreted to mean that external forces exert total control. According to Ellis, individuals, based upon instinctual influences, tend to desire that all things will happen for the best and that they will get whatever they desire. Therefore, according to REBT theory, both internal and external factors influence individuals, whose behaviors are determined more from irrational than rational approaches to problem solving. In Ellis's view, this is the basis for human maladjustment.

Rational–emotive behavior therapy also posits a hopeful view, holding that individuals have a strong growth or actualizing potential that facilitates their seeking counseling or therapy and also provides them with the ability to replace irrational approaches to problem solving with more rational approaches. Once individuals understand how their irrational beliefs, values, and attitudes are causal factors in their emotional and behavioral disturbances, they are both ready and able to dispute (D) these irrational thoughts and use the opportunity to achieve the positive effects (E) that the disputing (D) generates.

In facilitating this change, counselors or therapists operating within the REBT framework are highly active, flexible, somewhat didactic, unconditionally accepting, genuine, and purposely seek to persuade, confront, de-indoctrinate, direct, and lead clients to more rational ways of thinking and behaving. Rational-emotive behavior theory views the client as learner and the counselor or therapist as teacher.

The following statement from Ellis (1982) incorporates the basic tenets of REBT and also provides direction for the group leader who is operating from this theoretical viewpoint:

> In RET group therapy, the therapist not only actively and directively shows members, bringing up their emotional problems, that they are largely creating these problems themselves by devoutly and rigidly inventing and holding on to irrational beliefs, not only vigorously questions and challenges these beliefs and helps rip them up, but he or she also encourages and pushes all the group members to look for and dispute the shoulds, oughts, and musts of the other members and to help them give up their perfectionism and dictatorialness. All group participants are steadily taught to use the scientific method with themselves and others: to phrase logically, to vigorously undermine, and to empirically contradict the disordered disturbance-creating cognitions of the other members. (pp. 384–385)

Concepts Translated Into Leader Behaviors

Based on REBT concepts, the group leader has to be able to

- develop a group climate that is genuine, instructional, didactic, accepting, confrontational, and challenging;
- instruct group members as to the nature of their faulty thinking and the reasons behind their thinking, and provide them with directions for changing;
- separate the behavior of group members from their personhood, and focus on the behaviors reported;
- set aside his or her need for a warm personal relationship with members of the group, as such a relationship may be counterproductive to change and growth;
- confront members with their thinking and resulting behaviors and encourage other members of the group to do the same, to aid in the reeducative process of REBT;

- detect the irrational belief structures of group members and help the group members reach this same understanding;
- dispute the "crooked" thinking of members and teach them ways of disputing or challenging this thinking;
- teach group members the fundamental principles of REBT (the A–B–C–D–E model), which will empower them to strive for greater self-direction;
- provide relevant homework experiences to reinforce and enhance learning and change;
- use principles of contingency management and skill training as viable interventions for growth and change.

Group Stages and Techniques

Rational–emotive behavior therapy is not presented in terms of stages of group development but, instead, in terms of levels of perspectives. According to Gilliland et al. (1984), the techniques that have application in REBT may be viewed from the three perspectives of

1. cognitive–explicatory,
2. evocative–emotive, and
3. behavioristic–active–directive.

Techniques that derive from all three perspectives include

- presentation, instruction, demonstration, and modeling to help members gain an understanding of their behaviors;
- role playing as a form of behavioral rehearsal within the group to aid members' effective operation outside the group;
- distracting methods to get the members involved in activities that will stop them from dealing with their self-defeating thinking and behaving;
- humor directed at members' behaviors so they can begin to see how ridiculous their current ways of thinking and behaving are;
- emotionally charged language, which will have an impact on the members and which they, in turn, can use on themselves;
- shame-attacking exercises, which force group members to place themselves in embarrassing situations and then show that others' reactions are not what the members expected;
- exaggeration to get points across to group members and alert members to their tendencies to exaggerate the end results of their behaviors;
- exhortation and persuasion to convince members to relinquish illogical thinking and acquire more efficient and adaptive ideas.

Special techniques reported by Corey (2004), Gladding (2003), and Vernon (2003) with application to the REBT group include but are not limited to

- cognitive and imaginal disputation or diversion procedures;
- reframing (changing negative thoughts to positive thoughts);

- referenting (changing viewpoints from fragmatic to holistic);
- rational emotive imagery (RIE);
- reinforcement and penalties;
- skills training; and
- analogies, parables, and stories (using verbal images to dramatize rational ideas).

Transactional Analysis

Basic Concepts

The theoretical approaches discussed thus far were developed primarily for individual counseling and therapy. Applications to group work are extensions of this individual frame of reference. Transactional analysis (TA), discussed here, and psychodrama, discussed next, were designed specifically for groups, and their applications are group specific.

Transactional analysis is based on ideas and concepts developed by Eric Berne (1964) and popularized in his book, *Games People Play.* Berne (1966) believed that groups are more efficient than individual counseling or therapy in helping people understand their personal life scripts, and TA has been group oriented since its development. The TA approach is placing a growing emphasis on cultural and intergroup encounters (James, 1994).

Building on the early work of Berne, TA proponents have added structure and concepts that continue to expand this evolving view of human development and change (Dusay & Dusay, 1989; Goulding, 1987; Karpman, 1981; Stewart & Jaines, 1987; Thompson & Rudolph, 1992; Zalcman, 1990). Within TA, the following three schools have emerged:

1. Classical
2. Schiffian (reparenting)
3. Redecisional

Through the efforts of the Gouldings (1979, 1987) and McCormick (1995), the redecisional school has gained prominence. One of the major goals of TA is *individual autonomy*, which is achieved by reversing earlier decisions via the redecisional model. According to TA theory, early decision making sets the parameters for future behavior. The three ego states—parent, adult, child—form early in life, and each carries with it a script on how one is to behave, think, and feel. The developing individual takes in messages, verbal and nonverbal, delivered by the environment and by significant people within that environment, processes those messages, and develops from them a set of scripts that form the framework for the individual's behavior.

Individuals are not passive in this process; they make decisions and develop their own life script. Because the individual is able to decide and, therefore, determine his or her original life script, he or she also can redecide and change the script. Redecision and rescripting are central issues in counseling or therapy.

According to Poidevant and Lewis (1995), TA does not present a set of developmental stages through which individuals proceed. Development of an individual's personality is best understood by analyzing the following key concepts or structures of TA:

- Ego states
- Strokes
- Injunctions
- Decisions
- Script formation
- Life positions

1. *Ego States*

TA theory contends that the *ego states* (parent, adult, child) are the foundation for the personality. From these ego states, individuals build the cognitive, affective, and behavioral dynamics that direct their lives. All three ego states exist in every individual and their operation can be observed in the interaction of individuals with others.

The *parent ego state* consists of two distinct parts:

a. The *nurturing parent*, who functions in a caring role
b. The *critical parent*, who operates as a purveyor of rules, regulations, and wishes aimed at the protection of the individual

The *adult ego state* is the reality-oriented and logical part of the person. It receives and processes information and tries to make the best decisions possible.

The *child ego state* has two facets:

a. The *adapted child* who follows rules and regulations set down by the parent ego state. It complies with parental wishes and is easy to get along with.
b. The *natural child*, who is more spontaneous, curious, playful, and focused on meeting its own needs without regard for others.

As development proceeds, these ego states, although separate and distinct, interplay with one another and, based upon the scripts written for each, form the basis of behavior.

2. *Strokes*

The second key concept of TA, *strokes,* are units of positive or negative attention that stimulate the individual and serve as a motivational force for human interaction. This attention may be positive or negative. The rule seems to be that even negative strokes are better than no strokes at all. Strokes may stem from both internal and external sources, and if strokes are not readily available, the individual may devise "games" and "rackets" (transactions that allow the individual to gain needed strokes) to provide this motivational force. In TA, transactions are generally described in three forms:

a. *complementary* (two persons operating from the same ego state)
b. *crossed* (two persons interacting, but one is operating from an ego state that draws a response from an inappropriate ego state of the other person)
c. *ulterior* (two persons interacting, one from an appropriate ego state and the other from an inappropriate one), in which the message being sent appears to be sent on one level (adult) but is actually transmitted to another level (child).

3., 4., and 5. *Injunctions, Decisions, Script Formation*

These three concepts— *injunctions, decisions,* and *script formation*— are most easily understood in combination.

a. *Injunctions* are parental messages that children receive at an early age. These messages are generally prescriptive in terms of ways of being: "Don't be, don't feel, don't love, don't trust."
b. Upon hearing and processing these messages, the child makes *decisions* regarding them.
c. Based upon these decisions, the child forms a *script* for living his or her life. If the messages are reinforced and repeated, the foundation for this early scripting becomes strong.

6. *Life Positions*

The last of the major concepts, *life positions* represent the resolution of the three-part process of injunctions, decisions, and script formation. Life positions form the framework within which individuals structure and operate the behavioral, cognitive, and affective domains of their lives.

According to Harris (1967), individuals adopt one of the following four life positions:

I'm OK — You're OK.
I'm OK — You're not OK.
I'm not OK — You're OK.
I'm not OK — You're not OK.

Each position characterizes the individual's developmental process and also how he or she interacts with the environment and the people who frequent that environment. The boundaries between the positions are not hard and fast. Even though individuals usually operate more in one position than the others, they can move across all four positions. The life position "I'm OK — You're OK" is considered a "winner's script." The other life positions are viewed as "losers' scripts" and set the stage for maladjustment in later life.

In summary, transactional analysis is based on the philosophy that individuals are inherently okay and have potential and the desire to move toward a positive, growth-oriented position. This potential, however, often is stifled because of early decisions. A redecision process is necessary for individuals to realize their growth potential, and awareness seems to be key to this change process. First, individuals have to become aware of their current scripting and how it impacts on their way of being, and then of their power and ability to change the scripts and create for themselves a more positive and productive way of living.

Concepts Translated Into Leader Behaviors

Based on TA concepts, the group leader has to be able to

- develop a therapeutic contract with the group members that emphasizes equality and identifies the goals to which leader and members mutually agree;
- instruct group members in the specific tenets and specialized terminology of transactional analysis;
- analyze at least four elements in group members' communications: (a) structures, (b) transactions, (c) games, and (d) scripts;
- establish a working partnership with group members in which equality is a key ingredient;
- enhance group members' awareness of their scripts that result from early decisions, and their power and ability to change these scripts;
- provide positive strokes to group members and instruct them in the significance these strokes play in motivating behavior;
- reinforce the redecisions that group members make during the group process, and encourage them to act upon these redecisions;
- function in the cognitive and rational domain of human behaviors, as these are major forces for change in the redecision process;
- challenge group members to change their current patterns of thinking, feeling, and behaving and to move to more growth-producing patterns;
- enhance group members' autonomy to reduce dependence on the leader or on other group members.

Group Stages and Techniques

Although group stages are not specified in transactional analysis, a TA group leader probably would follow a pattern of

1. establishing a facilitative climate;
2. providing instruction in TA concepts;
3. developing contracts that identify goals;
4. working through various analyses of group members' structures, transactions, games, and scripts;
5. terminating with specific directives for action-oriented change.

In each of these stages, the TA group leader would

- use active listening skills to encourage members to participate,
- confront members to challenge them in the redecision process,
- use role play to encourage members to try out their new scripts,

- develop therapeutic contracts to keep members on target in reaching their goals,
- enhance the redecision process by drawing upon members' commitment to change,
- make use of self-scripting to model more positive ways of being, and
- give strokes to motivate members to change.

Corey (2004), Gladding (2003), and Poidevant and Lewis (1995) identified special techniques that have application in a TA-oriented group. These techniques include, but are not limited to the following:

Reparenting
Analysis of Rituals and Pastimes
Life Script Analysis
Game Analysis
Redecision Contracting
Therapeutic Contracting
Closing Escape Hatches
Egograms: Shifting the Energy

Psychodrama

Basic Concepts

Created and developed by Jacob L. Moreno in the 1920s and 1930s (Ohlsen, Horne & Lawe, 1988), psychodrama requires a group member (called the protagonist) to spontaneously act out his or her problems(s) with the assistance of the group leader (called the director) and other members of the group (called auxiliaries, or the audience). This acting-out takes place on a stage and involves a three-step process that includes warm-up (pre-action), action, and integration (Blatner, 1989).

The precursor of psychodrama was the Theater of Spontaneity, which Moreno created in Vienna in 1921 to entertain a variety of audiences. Believing conventional theater to be too structured, Moreno encouraged his young actors to develop improvisational presentations on current issues of the day. Outcomes of these productions, over and above their entertainment value, were cathartic for the actors and the audiences alike.

Moreno moved to New York in 1925, where he began to use spontaneous drama in working with groups of patients in hospitals. In 1936, Moreno opened a sanitarium in Beacon, New York, which included a theater both for treatment through psychodrama and for training in the use of psychodrama as a therapeutic tool (Sharf, 1996).

A basic concept of psychodrama rests in role theory and the relationships that individuals have with others, their views of others, and the psychological distance between individuals based upon both their relationships and their viewpoints. The roles and the interactions that stem from these roles lead to the encounter.

According to Gladding (2003), this encounter is "an existentialist concept that involves total physical and psychological contact between persons on an intense, concrete, and complete basis in the here and now" (p. 424). This encountering, through role-playing, is what rests at the heart of psychodrama. Reexperiencing a troublesome situation in the here and now provides the individual with the opportunity to gain insight by playing someone else, something else, or to play himself or herself. Greenberg (1974) identified the following precepts that undergird this role-play process:

- *Spontaneity*: creative individual responses that provide a degree of "newness" to a past situation
- *Situation or Immediacy*: a present orientation through which past and future concerns or problems can be reexperienced
- *Tele*: a term coined by Moreno to mean "total emotional communication between two or more people"
- *Catharsis*: emotional purging
- *Insight*: new perspectives

In psychodrama, a group member is asked to script and act out a situation, relationship, or other area of concern in front of the other group members. The member selected is the protagonist and, with the assistance of the group leader (director), he or she identifies the situation, relationship, or concern, creates the scenario to be acted out, selects other group members (auxiliaries) to play roles in the scenario, and assigns the rest of the group to serve as the audience.

Once the scenario has been established, the group leader (director) facilitates the first phase, the *warm-up*, of the psychodrama. Its purpose is to make sure that the group leader is ready to lead the group and that the group members (protagonist, auxiliaries, audience) are ready to be led. According to Blatner (1989), the warm-up—done either verbally or through structured activities—is designed to develop the proper frame of mind, for both the leader and the group members, to conduct the psychodrama and to develop trust and spontaneity.

The second phase, *action*, involves the acting out of the group member's (protagonist's) situation, relationship, or other concerns. The group leader (director) aids in setting the scene, assists the other members (auxiliaries) with their roles, encourages role change within the acting-out phase of the scenario, helps the protagonist to expand his or her emotional response pattern, and encourages the protagonist to work through the situation by trying out alternative attitudes, behaviors, and emotional response patterns. As a result of the group leader's directives, the scenario is re-acted several times.

The third phase, *integration*, involves feedback, discussion, and closure. The group (audience and auxiliaries) is encouraged to provide the protagonist with personal, supportive, and constructive affective feedback. The emphasis initially is on the emotional aspects of the enactment. Later in the feedback session, emphasis may be directed to the cognitive aspects of the enactment. The goal of this phase is to provide the protagonist with ways to act differently in the future if similar situations arise (Gladding, 2003).

Concepts Translated Into Leader Behaviors

Based on psychodrama concepts, the group leader has to be able to

- establish a working relationship within the group, based upon equality,
- develop trust among group members,

- develop spontaneity in group members,
- establish a group atmosphere that is accepting and tolerant of change,
- establish a format within the group that allows group members to identify and work on significant issues in their lives,
- encourage group members to risk aspects of self in playing out the psychodrama,
- provide protection for group members from abuse that may arise from playing out the psychodrama,
- utilize his or her creativity as a model for members of the group and encourage group members in their own creative development, and
- utilize his or her knowledge and skill in directing all aspects of the psychodramatic enactment.

Group Stages and Techniques

The group stages for psychodrama, as presented previously, carry with them various directives related to group leader techniques. The following techniques should aid the psychodrama leader in enhancing growth and development as the group moves through the three stages. These techniques are presented from Moreno's (1987) developmental perspective that individuals need approximately 2 years of training and experience in psychodrama prior to taking on the role of director:

- Become comfortable in working effectively with all of the theatrical facets of psychodrama.
- Learn to assess all aspects of the members' behaviors as the psychodrama unfolds.
- Learn which problems, concerns, relationships, and so forth, are best dealt with through psychodrama.
- Develop the ability to actively direct an ongoing emotional drama that could entail, but not be limited to, actor movement, role switching, role creation, and drama reconstruction.
- Learn how to cast various group members effectively in roles that will enhance the ongoing psychodrama process.
- Develop the ability, when indicated by the psychodrama, to effectively weave members of the audience into roles as auxiliaries or alter egos for the protagonist.
- Learn which of the myriad of techniques available within psychodrama are best suited to which types of presenting problems, relationships, and concerns.
- Develop the ability to aid all participants in desensitizing the emotional impact of the psychodrama enactment during closure.

Special techniques identified by Corey (2004), Gladding (2003), and Sharf (1996) that have application in psychodrama groups include, but are not limited to, the following:

Monodrama	The Magic Shop
Role Reversal	The Soliloquy Technique
The Double and Multiple Double	Sculpting
The Mirror Technique	Replay
Act Fulfillment	Future Projection

INTEGRATING THE THEORETICAL APPROACHES

The six theories presented in this chapter offer the group leader options in working with groups. At first glance, each of these approaches seems to represent a unique underpinning for group process, but the six approaches actually have many elements in common, which enhances the possibility for integrating these theories and applying them to the ongoing group process. The following discussion addresses this integrative theme by discussing five factors that are common to all of the approaches: (a) relationship variables, (b) leader role variables, (c) member role variables, (d) process variables, and (e) outcome variables.

Relationship Variables

A working relationship is basic to all six theoretical approaches. Although the terms describing this relationship vary, each approach presents a need for trust, safety, mutual respect, and leader competence, and five of the six approaches present a need for equality in the leader–member interaction. In all six approaches, the working relationship is the foundational building block on which all other aspects of group dynamics rest. Each approach underlines the importance of taking time to build this foundational structure and to ensure that group members understand the nature of this relationship. From the integrative perspective, a working relationship must be established first, regardless of the theoretical positions followed. All other aspects of the group process stem from this relationship.

Leader Role Variables

In all six theoretical positions, the leader's role is an active one. Action-oriented descriptors, such as develop, instruct, analyze, establish, enhance, provide, reinforce, demonstrate, aid, confront, communicate, direct, and observe, guide the leader to take an active role in his or her interaction with the group. (Although some may argue that the person-centered approach does not call for the leader's action, our view is that the person-centered leader does play an active role. He or she must be able to communicate unconditional positive regard and empathy and be congruent in his or her interactions with group members.) Therapeutic conditions are, in themselves, action-oriented, because the leader must demonstrate and communicate them to group members. From the integrative perspective, then, active leader participation is necessary in all six theoretical approaches. The type of action may vary, but action-oriented leadership seems to be a key element in all six approaches.

Member Role Variables

In all of the theoretical perspectives, group members also play an active role. Members must be responsible; committed to change; willing to risk; willing to try out new behaviors; willing to share themselves with others; able to deal with affect, cognitions, and behaviors; willing to do the hard work that change demands; willing to express creativity through role play; and be open to new information, insights, and awareness. In addition, all of the perspectives stress the concept that if change is to occur, members must assume major responsibility for this change. From the integrative perspective, each theoretical approach has the same underlying message with regard to the role of members: If you desire change, you must be willing to take major responsibility for that change and be willing to take the necessary action to make that change possible.

Process Variables

The area that seems to have the most variability across the six theoretical approaches is the process dimension, which encompasses the various experiential activities that take place within groups to attain the desired goals. Even here, however, the six approaches have some similarity. Common to all of the approaches are self-disclosure, role playing, giving and receiving feedback, observing others, using active listening skills, modeling, demonstrating, encountering, and dialoguing. The differences are not as much in terms of process as in the way these processes are applied in each of the six approaches.

For example, in the person-centered approach, giving and receiving feedback is seen as an ongoing means of facilitating group interaction and member growth. From the Gestalt orientation, giving and receiving feedback might be structured to give group members exaggerated exposure to the various affective responses associated with giving and receiving feedback. The group may be directed to engage in this process at a specific time to emphasize a specific point. In psychodrama, giving and receiving feedback centers on the encounter between individuals or with the self acted out in a staged scenario. In psychodrama, all group members participate actively in offering feedback.

From the integrative perspective, the process variable dimension is not nearly as diverse for the six approaches as one might expect. The diversity is not so much in the "what" of process as in the "how" and perhaps the "why" of process. All six approaches provide a process to expand the affective, cognitive, and behavioral realms of group members.

Outcome Variables

The greatest similarity across the theoretical approaches is in intended group outcomes. Common to all six approaches are concepts including increasing awareness, changing dysfunctional behaviors, enhancing self-concept, fostering insight, accepting responsibility, and increasing trust in self and with others. Regardless of theoretical approach, the desired outcomes all center on change. Although the words used to describe this change vary from theory to theory, the end result is to have group members function more effectively in affective, cognitive, and behavioral domains.

From the integrative perspective, although outcome variables for the different perspectives are directed in different areas of positive change—change in the way group members *feel* about themselves and their world, change in the way group members *think* about themselves and their world, and change in the way group members *behave* as a result of changes in the way they feel and think—all have the same end result. The fundamental principles of the six theoretical approaches differ in some ways, but they do not differ fundamentally in terms of outcome variables.

Implementation

We offer the following suggestions to aid group leaders in effectively integrating individual counseling or therapy approaches in working with groups:

- Be familiar with all theoretical approaches, even though most were developed originally for work with the individual. Each will provide insight into human development and change and how to apply this insight in the group setting.
- Attempt to integrate elements of various theoretical approaches in working with groups. An eclectic approach will prove beneficial to you and, consequently, to group members.
- Apply theoretical approaches as they were intended to be used—as facilitative guides to better understand individual dynamics and to assist individuals in the change process. They were not conceived as the true and only way of explaining the human condition.
- Do not rely solely on one approach to the exclusion of the others. Base your approach in working with groups on a broad knowledge base, and take from this base what will make your group work most effective.
- Experiment with many approaches to group work until you find the combination of principles and techniques that best fits your personal philosophy regarding people and your personal style of being with people. The approach you finally develop should be much more a reflection of you than of any single theoretical position.

LEARNING ACTIVITIES

1. As a small-group activity, determine how you would use one of the theories presented in this chapter and its techniques in working with a group of identified at-risk adolescents. Present your conclusions to the class and ask for feedback.
2. As a small-group activity, design a group for adults who have incurred some type of loss. Members of the group will have an opportunity to play the roles designed and also to lead the group. Through various theoretical orientations, demonstrate how the group would be operated. Present your demonstration to the class and ask for feedback.
3. Working alone or with a partner, select one of the theoretical positions presented in this chapter or another theoretical system of your choosing, identify a group

professional within the community who utilizes that theory, and interview this person about his or her use of the theoretical system. If possible, observe this group leader in action with his or her group. Then answer the following questions:

> How is the theoretical system utilized in the group setting?
> What insights did you gain from watching the theoretical system applied in the group setting?
> What insights did you gain from discussing this approach with the group leader?
> Did what happened in the group correspond with what you read in this text? Share your findings with the class.

4. Select a theoretical system not presented in the chapter. Based upon your knowledge of the theoretical system, compare and contrast the system with the six theoretical systems presented with regard to the five following areas:

    1. Relationship variables
    2. Leader role variables
    3. Member role variables
    4. Process variables
    5. Outcome variables

Report your findings to the class. (*Note*: The resources provided earlier in this chapter could assist you in this activity.)

SUMMARY

The questions expressed at the beginning of this chapter by the hypothetical student, Greg, are a legitimate and continual concern of experienced and novice group leaders alike. Group approaches are derived largely from theories and therapies developed for individuals. Because group counseling or therapy has to be based in theory, group leaders must become knowledgeable about the major theories and learn how to integrate and apply them within the group modality. We hope that the discussion of the six theories highlighted in this chapter—Adlerian, Gestalt, person-centered, rational–emotive behavior theory (REBT), transactional analysis (TA), and psychodrama—will aid group leaders in this integration process.

Commonalities among the six approaches in the following five variable dimensions enable leaders to blend these theories in their work with groups:

1. Relationship
2. Leader role
3. Member role
4. Process
5. Outcome

In all six theories, the working relationship is the basis for the group dynamic, and most of the theories advocate equality in leader–member interactions. All six theories propel the leader into an active role, particularly in providing optimum therapeutic conditions. Similarities in member role permeate all the theoretical precepts, and all contend that individuals ultimately have to take responsibility to change whatever they want to change. Although process presents the most diversity of the five dimensions, the differences are more in the "why" and "how" than in the "what" of the process. The theories are similar in the outcome variable: All center on evoking positive change in people.

Group leaders should become familiar with the various theoretical approaches, experiment with different approaches, and strive to find the combination of principles and techniques that work best for them and their groups. The approach developed should reflect their personal philosophy and personal style.

USEFUL WEB SITES

□ American Counseling Association
www.counseling.org
□ American Psychological Association
www.apa.org

REFERENCES

Adler, A. (1938). *Social interest.* London: Faber & Faber.

Baker, F. S. (2001). Healing in psychotherapy: Using energy, touch, and imagery with cancer patients. *Gestalt Review, 4*(4), 267–288.

Bemak, F., & Epp, L. (2001). Countertransference in the development of graduate student group counselors: Recommendations for training. *Journal for Specialists in Group Work, 26*(4), 305–318.

Berne, E. (1964). *Games people play.* New York: Grove Press.

Berne, E. (1966). *Principles of group treatment.* New York: Oxford University Press.

Blatner, A. (1989). Psychodrama. In R. J. Corsini & D. Wedding (Eds.), *Current psychotherapies* (4th ed., pp. 561–571). Itasca, IL: Peacock.

Boy, A., & Pine, G. J. (1999). *A person centered foundation for counseling and psychotherapy* (2nd ed.). Springfield, IL: Charles C Thomas

Bryant-Frank, M. L. (2003). Existential theory. In D. Capuzzi & D. Gross (Eds.), *Counseling and psychotherapy: Theories and interventions* (3rd ed., pp. 136–151). Englewood Cliffs, NJ: Prentice-Hall.

Capuzzi, D., & Gross, D. (2002). *Introduction to group counseling* (3rd ed.). Denver: Love Publishing.

Capuzzi, D., & Gross, D. (2003). *Counseling and psychotherapy: Theories and interventions* (3rd ed.). Englewood Cliffs, NJ: Prentice-Hall.

Corey, G. (2000). *Theory and practice of group counseling* (5th ed.). Pacific Grove, CA: Brooks/Cole.

Corey, G. (2004). *Theory and practice of group counseling* (6th ed.). Pacific Grove, CA: Brooks/Cole.

DiGiuseppe, R. (1999). Rational emotive behavior therapy. In H. T. Prout & D. T. Brown (Eds.), *Counseling and psychotherapy with children and adolescents: Theory and practice for school settings* (pp. 252–293). New York: John Wiley & Sons.

Dryden, W., & Ellis, A. E. (2001). Rational emotive behavior therapy. In K. S Dobson (Ed.), *Handbook of cognitive behavioral therapies* (pp. 295–348). New York: Guilford.

Dusay, J., & Dusay, K. M. (1989). Transactional analysis. In R. Corsini (Ed.), *Current psychotherapies* (4th ed., pp. 374–427). Itasca, IL: Peacock.

Ellis, A. (1982). *Rational emotive therapy and cognitive behavior therapy.* New York: Springer.

Ellis, A. (1991). The philosophical basis of rational-emotive therapy (RET). *Psychotherapy in Private Practice, 8,* 97–106.

Ellis, A. (1994). *Reason and emotion in psychotherapy* (rev. ed.). Secaucus, NJ: Birch Lane Press.

Ellis, A. (1995). Rational emotive behavior therapy. In R. Corsini & D. Wedding (Eds.), *Current psychotherapies* (5th ed., pp. 162–196). Itasca, IL: F. E. Peacock.

Ellis, A. (1996). *Better, deeper, and more enduring brief therapy: The rational emotive behavior therapy approach.* New York: Brunner/Mazel.

Ellis, A. E., & Dryden, W. (1997). *The practice of rational emotive behavior therapy* (2nd ed.). New York: Springer Publishing.

Gazda, G. M., Ginter, E. J., & Horne, A. M. (2001). *Group counseling and group psychotherapy: Theory and practice.* Boston: Allyn & Bacon.

Gilliland, B., James, R., Roberts, G., & Bowman, J. (1984). *Theory and strategies in counseling and psychotherapy.* Englewood Cliffs, NJ: Prentice-Hall.

Gladding, S. T. (1999). *Group work: A counseling specialty* (3rd ed.). New York: Merrill

Gladding, S. T. (2003). *Group work: A counseling specialty* (4th ed.). New York: Merrill.

Glasser, W. (2000). *Reality therapy in action.* New York: HarperCollins.

Goulding, M. (1987). Transactional analysis and redecision therapy. In J. L. Zeig (Ed.), *The evolution of psychotherapy* (pp. 285–299). New York: Brunner/Mazel.

Goulding, M., & Goulding, R. (1979). *Changing lives through redecision therapy.* New York: Brunner/Mazel.

Greenberg, I. A. (1974). Moreno: Psychodrama and the group process. In I. A. Greenberg (Ed.), *Psychodrama: Theory and therapy* (pp. 11–28). New York: Behavioral Publications.

Haley, M., Sieber, C., & Maples, M. F. (2003). Gestalt theory. In D. Capuzzi & D. Gross (Eds.), *Counseling and psychotherapy: Theories and interventions* (3rd ed., pp. 181–211). Englewood Cliffs, NJ: Prentice-Hall.

Harris, T. (1967). *I'm OK—you're OK.* New York: Harper & Row.

Hazler, R. J. (2001). Humanistic theories of counseling. In D. Locke, J. Myers, & E. Herr (Eds.), *The handbook of counseling* (pp. 151–158). Thousand Oaks, CA: Sage Publications.

Hazler, R. J. (2003). Person-centered theory. In D. Capuzzi & D. Gross (Eds.), *Counseling and psychotherapy: Theories and interventions* (3rd ed., pp. 157–180). Englewood Cliffs, NJ: Prentice-Hall.

James, N. (1994). Cultural frame of reference and intergroup encounters: A TA approach. *Transactional Analysis Journal, 24,* 206–210.

Kalodner, C. (2003). Cognitive–behavioral theories. In D. Capuzzi & D. Gross (Eds.), *Counseling and psychotherapy: Theories and interventions* (3rd ed., pp. 212–234). Englewood Cliffs, NJ: Prentice-Hall.

Karpman, S. (1981). The politics of theory. *Transactional Analysis Journal, 11*(1), 68–75.

Lakin, M. (1985). Helping groups in our times. In M. Lakin (Ed.), *The helping group: Therapeutic principles and issues* (pp. 21–28). Reading, MA: Addison-Wesley.

Manaster, G. G., & Corsini, R. J. (1982). *Individual psychology: Theory and practice.* Itasca, IL: F.E. Peacock.

May, R., & Yalom, I. (2000). Existential psychotherapy. In R. J. Corsini & D. Wedding (Eds.), *Current psychotherapies* (6th ed., pp. 273–302). Itasca, IL: F.E. Peacock.

McCormick, P. (1995). Redecisions required for mental health. *Transactional Analysis Journal, 25,* 321–326.

Meier, S. T., & Davis, S. R. (2001). *The elements of counseling* (4th ed.). Belmont, CA: Wadsworth.

Messer, S. B., & Warren, C. S. (2001). Brief psychodynamic therapy. In R. J Corsini (Ed.), *Handbook for innovative therapies* (2nd ed., pp. 67–85). New York: Wiley.

Milliren, A. P., Evans, T. D., & Newbauer, J. F. (2003). Adlerian counseling and psychotherapy. In D. Capuzzi & D. Gross (Eds.), *Counseling and psychotherapy: Theories and interventions* (3rd ed., pp. 91–130). Englewood Cliffs, NJ: Prentice-Hall.

Moreno, Z. T. (1987). Psychodrama, role theory, and the concept of the social atom. In J. K. Zeig (Ed.), *The evolution of psychotherapy* (pp. 341–366). New York: Brunner/Mazel.

Naranjo, C. (1970). Present centeredness techniques, prescriptions and ideals. In J. Fogan & I. Shepherd (Eds.), *Gestalt therapy now* (pp. 45–55). Palo Alto, CA: Science and Behavior Books.

Noble, F. (1977). Procedure for promoting behavior change: Humanistic approach. In G. Blackham (Ed.), *Counseling theory, process and practice* (pp. 165–183). Belmont, CA: Wadsworth.

Ohlsen, M. M., Horne, A. M., & Lawe, C. F. (1988). *Group counseling* (3rd ed.). New York: Holt, Rinehart & Winston.

Perls, F. S. (1969). *Gestalt therapy verbatim.* Moab, UT: Real People Press.

Poidevant, J. M., & Lewis, H. A. (1995). Transactional analysis theory. In D. Capuzzi & D. Gross (Eds.), *Counseling and psychotherapy: Theories and interventions* (pp. 297–324). Englewood Cliffs, NJ: Prentice-Hall.

Polster, E., & Polster, M. (1973). *Gestalt therapy integrated.* New York: Brunner/Mazel.

Prochaska, J. O., & Norcross, H. C. (1999). *Systems of psychotherapy: A transtheoretical analysis* (4th ed.). Pacific Grove, CA: Brooks/Cole

Rogers, C. R. (1959). Significant learning in therapy and in education. *Educational Leadership, 16*(4), 232–242.

Rutan, J. S. (1999). Psychoanalytic group psychotherapy. In J. R. Price & D. R. Hescheles (Eds.), *A guide to starting psychotherapy groups* (pp. 151–166). San Diego: Academic Press.

Seligman, L. (2001). *Systems, strategies, and skills of counseling and psychotherapy.* Upper Saddle River, NJ: Merrill/Prentice Hall.

Shaffer, J. B. P., & Galinsky, M. D. (1989). The Gestalt therapy workshop. In J. B. P. Shaffer & M. D. Galinsky (Eds.), *Methods of group therapy* (pp. 118–140). Englewood Cliffs, NJ: Prentice-Hall.

Shane, P. (1999). Gestalt therapy: The once and future king. In D. Moss (Ed.), *Humanistic and transpersonal psychology: A historical and biographical source book* (pp. 49–65). Westport, CT: Greenwood Press.

Shapiro, J. L. (1978). Major theoretical orientations. In J. L. Shapiro (Ed.), *Methods of group psychotherapy and encounter: A tradition of innovation* (pp. 40–63). Itasca, IL: Peacock.

Sharf, R. S. (1996). *Theories of psychotherapy and counseling: Concepts and cases.* Pacific Grove, CA: Brooks/Cole.

Sonstegard, M. A., & Bitter, J. R. (1998). Adlerian group counseling: Step by step. *Journal of Individual Psychology, 54*(2), 217–250.

Spiegler, M. D., & Guevemont, D. C. (2003). *Contemporary behavior therapy* (4th ed.). Pacific Grove, CA: Brooks/Cole.

Stewart, I., & Jaines, V. S. (1987). *TA today: A new introduction to transactional analysis.* Nottingham, England: Lifespace.

Sweeney, T. J. (1998). *Adlerian counseling: A practitioner's approach* (4th ed.). Philadelphia: Accelerated Development, Taylor and Francis.

Thompson, C. L., & Rudolph, L. B. (1992). *Counseling children.* Pacific Grove, CA: Brooks/Cole.

Vernon, A. (2003). Rational emotive behavior therapy. In D. Capuzzi & D. Gross (Eds.), *Counseling and psychotherapy: Theories and interventions* (3rd ed., pp. 235–254). Englewood Cliffs, NJ: Prentice-Hall.

Walsh, R. A., & McElwain, B. (2002). Existential psychotherapies. In D. J. Cain & J. Seeman (Eds.), *Humanistic psychotherapies: Handbook of research and practice* (pp. 253–278). Washington, DC: American Psychological Association.

Wright, H. (1989). Therapeutic properties of group. In H. Wright (Ed.), *Group work: Perspectives and practice* (pp. 89–99). London: Scutan Press.

Wubolding, R. E. (2001). *Reality therapy for the 21st century.* New York: Brunner/Mazel.

Yalom, I. D. (1995). *The theory and practice of group psychotherapy* (4th ed.). New York: Basic Books.

Yontef, G. (1995). Gestalt therapy. In A. S. Gurman & S. B. Messer (Eds.). *Essential psychotherapies: Theories and practice* (pp. 261–303). New York: Guilford.

Zalcman, M. J. (1990). Game analysis and racket analysis: Overview, critique and future development. *Transactional Analysis Journal, 20,* 4–19.

PART TWO:

Professional Issues

Building upon the foundational information presented in the four chapters of Part One, the chapters in Part Two raise professional issues that counselors and therapists who are interested in group work will have to address as they initiate their study of group work. These issues include the efficacy of group work, evaluating groups, ethical/legal considerations for group work specialists, and diversity issues in group work.

Chapter 5, "The Efficacy of Group Work," takes a hard look at what the research says about the contexts in which group counseling or group therapy does and does not work. The chapter first provides a definition of efficacy and further discusses the professional importance of efficacy questions. This is followed by an explanation of how efficacy is measured in counseling or therapy. Then effective practices in group counseling are analyzed. The discussion turns to the efficacy of group counseling or therapy with select client populations, highlighting what the research shows about effective, ineffective, and harmful interventions with select client populations.

Chapter 6. Evaluating counseling work in groups is vital to ensure that the interventions are effective, do not harm the participants, and are actually therapeutic. Chapter 6, "Approaches to Evaluating Groups," examines this crucial element in counseling regarding how counselors in practice can determine if what they are doing is indeed effective. Evaluative principles are applied to group work, with multiple examples of the quantitative and qualitative measures used to determine efficacy. Several different models illustrate the various ways to evaluate diverse types of groups.

Chapter 7. Ethics is at the heart of the counseling process, especially group counseling, as is an awareness of legal issues. This is the first opportunity that many group members have to be honest and safe as they open themselves up to others. Group leaders are responsible for setting the norms of ethical behavior, for themselves and for the group as a whole. Chapter 7, "Group Work: Ethical/Legal Considerations," presents aspects of the ACA *Code of Ethics* specific to group work, the ASGW *Standards of Best Practice,* an ethical decision-making model, and important legal issues for group work specialists to consider.

Chapter 8. If counseling professionals are to act with integrity and commitment to a changing profession, they must begin to take steps to change the existing mainstream cultural paradigm. Although multicultural knowledge has expanded, it has been directed toward a more general and individual base. Until recently, the area of multicultural group counseling has received little attention in the development of strategic approaches and specific empirical research. Chapter 8, "Diversity Issues in Group Work," presents an overview of factors and cultural considerations important to developing effective multicultural groups. The chapter explores the salient issues surrounding obstacles to achieving this goal and offers strategies for overcoming them, as well as methods of evaluation to help counselors determine their actual effectiveness as leaders of multicultural groups.

The Efficacy of Group Work

Cass Dykeman and Valerie E. Appleton

In professional training, the curriculum usually is determined by an accreditation agency. In counselor preparation the main accreditation agency is the Council for the Accreditation of Counseling and Related Educational Programs (CACREP). In CACREP's accreditation manual (CACREP, 2004), the eight curricular areas designated as the core of the training of any counselor are

1. human growth and development,
2. social and cultural foundations,
3. helping relationships,
4. group work,
5. career and lifestyle development,
6. appraisal,
7. research and program evaluation, and
8. professional orientation.

Of most relevance to readers of this textbook is group work. The other counselor preparation accreditation agency is the Council on Rehabilitation Education (CORE), which accredits rehabilitation counseling programs. Like CACREP, CORE mandates group counseling training (CORE, 2004).

Students in counseling programs often raise the question of whether group counseling or therapy courses should be required. If there is no scientific evidence that group counseling or therapy works, this book and the group counseling or therapy courses required of counseling students seem to be nothing more than "hoops to jump through" that some scholastic bureaucracy imposes on them.

In this chapter we will help readers develop their own answers to the preceding question in four steps. First, we will provide a definition of efficacy and discuss the professional importance of efficacy questions. Second, we will review how efficacy is measured in counseling or therapy. Third, we will detail the scientific knowledge concerning effective practices in group counseling or therapy. Fourth, we will present the scientific knowledge concerning the efficacy of group counseling or therapy with select client populations. Finally, at the end of the chapter, we will discuss the questions about the efficacy of group counseling or therapy that remain unanswered. The term *counseling* is used to refer to both counseling and therapy throughout the remainder of this chapter.

WHAT IS EFFICACY?

The key term in this chapter is *efficacy*. Without a clear understanding of this term, the rest of this chapter is meaningless. In the human services' professions, efficacy refers to "the degree to which desired goals or projected outcomes are achieved" (Barker, 1995, p. 116). A sample group counseling efficacy question one could ask is: To what extent does cognitive group counseling impact people with bulimia? Such a question, however, would be difficult to answer, because each of the two terms in the question (*cognitive group counseling* and *bulimia*) can mean many things. Does the term *bulimic* refer to people with nonpurging bulimia or to those with purging bulimia? When possible, we will consider more fine-grained efficacy questions. In the example of bulimia, then, the question could be: To what extent does challenging shape and weight distortions in a small-group counseling setting decrease the number of eating binges per week in nonpurging bulimic individuals?

THE IMPORTANCE OF EFFICACY QUESTIONS

At first glance, efficacy questions such as the one just posed may seem to be more the domain of researchers than clinicians. But efficacy questions *are* critical to counselors in "the trenches." Specifically, efficacy questions play an important role in the area of ethics, professionalism, and economics.

Ethics

Two ethical considerations for counselors, including those in group counseling, are *nonmaleficence* and *beneficence*.

Nonmaleficence

One of the oldest ethical dictates in health care is, "Above all else, do no harm." This dictate captures the spirit of the moral principle of nonmaleficence, which prohibits counselors from implementing interventions that risk harm to others (Forester-Miller, 2002; Forester-Miller & Davis, 1996). Later in this chapter we review what is known about group counseling "casualties" with the goal of teaching group counselors how to prevent such casualties.

Beneficence

The ethical principle of beneficence carries the imperative that counselors engage in activities that will benefit the client. Thus, counselors must seek out efficacious interventions and avoid or discard interventions that are found to be inefficacious. For instance, a number of rational–emotive therapy psychoeducational programs have been developed for school counselors' use in the classroom. As will be discussed later in this chapter, though, researchers have not found these interventions to be efficacious. Although no evidence suggests that these large-group interventions harm children, they do waste instructional time that could be spent on more fruitful activities.

Professionalism

One behavior that separates a professional from a layperson in any activity is that the professional bases his or her actions upon scientific knowledge rather than on personal preference or whim. The specific term for this professional behavior is *informed practice*. Indeed, the psychologist's code of conduct demands that a clinician's work reflect the pragmatic application of scientific knowledge based upon research (American Psychological Association [APA], 2004). Thus, it is incumbent upon the group counselor to seek out and use such knowledge.

Economics

Spiraling expenses have prompted business and government alike to impose cost-control mechanisms upon the health care system (Budman, Demby, Feldstein, & Gold, 1984; Mone, 1994). The generic term for these mechanisms is *managed care*. The advent of managed health care will force group counselors to demonstrate the cost effectiveness of their group methods (DeLucia-Waack, 1997; Roback, 2000; Scheidlinger, 1995). Thus, efficacy issues are becoming paramount in the practice settings that professional counselors inhabit. These issues are no longer the sole domain of university-based researchers.

HOW EFFICACY IS MEASURED

Wide-ranging research methods are used to study group counseling outcomes. In contrast to individual counseling outcome research, group counseling outcome research involves complex interactions of member, leader, and treatment factors (Stockton & Morran, 1982). To provide a better understanding of how group research is conducted, we will examine two major research methods—quantitative and qualitative—as well as the concepts of reliability and validity.

Quantitative Methods

Quantitative research methods include *correlational*, *causal–comparative*, *true experimental*, *quasi-experimental*, and *action research* (Creswell, 2002). In quantitative studies, outcome is determined through statistical analyses of the numerical data for targeted behaviors. In this frame, group counseling outcomes are those behavioral, role, or process phenomena that can be defined and counted.

Quantitative researchers focus on client and group characteristics that can vary. These characteristics are called *variables*. In quantitative research, there are two types of variables: independent and dependent. The *independent variable* is the component of the group counseling treatment manipulated by the researcher. An example of an independent variable is to introduce a cognitive disputation exercise to a body-image enhancement group (Grant & Cash, 1995).

The variable measured to determine the effects of the independent variable is called the *dependent variable* (Borg & Gall, 1989). In the previous example, a dependent variable might be the pretest-to-posttest score differences on the Private Body Talk Questionnaire (Grant & Cash, 1995).

Also important to quantitative researchers is the issue of *control*, which refers to the researcher's efforts to eliminate the influence of factors other than the independent variable upon the dependent variable. Examples of factors that quantitative researchers usually try to control are age, sex, IQ, socioeconomic status, education, and motivation. The best way to employ control in a study is through the use of a *control group*. In a quantitative study, the control group is matched as closely as possible to the experimental group except that it is not exposed to the independent variable (Reber, 1986).

Qualitative Methods

Qualitative assessment is based on interpretable data generated through *thick description* of client or group phenomena (Guba & Lincoln, 1989; Patton, 1990). Thick description is built through narratives, surveys, interviews, and observations. In this type of research, outcome data can include assessing change in things such as worldview or personal idiosyncrasy.

Yalom (1985) developed his seminal group counseling ideas predominately through thick description. He developed his curative factors theory, for example, from an application of qualitative research methods to group counseling. Interestingly, his qualitative applications spawned a major thrust of quantitative research in group counseling.

Outcome Measurement

One of the most important things a group counseling researcher must determine is whether the tools chosen for studying the behaviors of interest will obtain a measurement that is complete and accurate. To determine accuracy in group measurement, reliability and validity must be considered. In general, *reliability* concerns the consistency of results of a measurement device across observations, and *validity* refers to whether an assessment tool measures what it is supposed to assess.

Reliability

Because quantitative researchers rely on the indirect measurement of targeted features and qualitative researchers rely on narratives rather than numerical data, the two types of researchers can be understood to view reliability quite differently (Martella, Nelson, & Marchand-Martella, 1999). Qualitative researchers view reliability as the match between what they observe happening and the data that are recorded. By contrast, quantitative researchers view reliability as the consistency found across different observations.

Validity

Quantitative and qualitative researchers view the issue of validity differently as well. Quantitative researchers concern themselves with issues of measurement validity. Does a given assessment tool measure what it claims to measure? Quantitative research follows standard procedures for establishing measurement validity. By contrast, qualitative researchers do not rely on empirical means to judge the validity of an assessment tool. Instead, they ask whether the assessment process has "credibility." The assessment has credibility when there is a match between the constructed realities of the participants and the constructed reality of the researcher (Guba & Lincoln, 1989). The methods used to establish credibility are less well developed than are methods for measurement validity. Methods currently used to establish credibility include participants' review of findings and researchers' peer debriefing (Guba & Lincoln, 1989; Patton, 1990).

EFFECTIVE COUNSELOR PRACTICES IN GROUP WORK

The components of effective group counseling have been defined by the Association for Specialists in Group Work (ASGW). ASGW developed 14 specific knowledge and skill competencies for counselors, two of which address research knowledge and skills. These competencies direct students to discover what is efficacious in group counselor practice and apply it (ASGW, 2004). We will review the general group counseling literature and discuss the counseling practices that have been found to be especially effective. The research will be considered in terms of specific factors, nonspecific factors, and group counseling modes.

Specific Factors and Outcome

The term *specific factors,* as used here, refers to a counselor's acts that are unique to a particular theory of counseling. An example is the use of cognitive distortion refutation to combat body imagery problems. Specific factors that are commonly employed in group counseling include *applying structure* and *providing alternatives and instruction.*

Applying Structure

In an analysis of the research literature, Gazda, Horne, and Ginter (2000) found a definite trend toward the use of structured group strategies, which stands in opposition to the traditional unstructured group approach. Structured groups developed as a result of the influence of behavioral counseling and skills training. Rohde and Stockton (1994) reviewed the 40-year controversy over the role and efficacy of structure in therapeutic groups. Early group counseling theorists recommended that group leaders avoid influencing the natural development of group culture. Later, however, group counseling researchers found that the lack of structure actually created the undesired client phenomena of cognitive distortion, interpersonal fear, subjective distress, and premature termination.

Applying structure to groups has been found to be beneficial, but counselors should exercise caution in this regard. All types of structure are not beneficial to all groups. For example, although the application of self-disclosure contracts can increase attraction to a group, it can decrease the members' "mutual liking" (Ribner, 1974). Of note is that the positive impact of structure may be related to clients' ability to engage in risk taking (Evensen & Bednar, 1978). Specifically, higher levels of structure tend to be associated with more negative evaluations of counseling by low risk takers. Also, high levels of structure may result in lower levels of group cohesion (Lee & Bednar, 1977). The practitioner is encouraged to match the techniques utilized with the personalities of the group members.

Providing Alternatives and Instruction

The power of instruction in group counseling lies in the counselor's ability to be clear with clients about the tasks and goals of counseling. The power of providing alternatives to clients is that it often prevents client reactance (Brehm, 1966). The judicious application of instruction and the judicious provision of alternatives have been identified as causal factors of client behavior change with certain populations.

Flowers (1979) discovered that trained group counselors produced more improvement in their clients than did student counselors because they gave less advice and offered more alternatives and instruction in their feedback to group members. Also, student counselors who used alternatives and instruction produced more improvement in their clients than those who did not. The student counselors, however, used these interventions less frequently and produced less client improvement overall. Interestingly, group clients often viewed alternatives and instruction as superior therapeutically but the group counselors often did not, to the detriment of their clients. Flowers's study showed that counselors who are not trained specifically to avoid giving advice may be inclined to do this.

Nonspecific Factors and Outcome

Nonspecific factors of counseling are the change-producing elements in counseling, regardless of theoretical orientation. Gelso and Carter (1994) identified a number of nonspecific factors they believed to be operating in all counseling. The most studied of these factors is *working alliance*. Other nonspecific factors mentioned in the group counseling literature include *curative factors, group development,* and *leadership*.

Working Alliance

Substantial empirical evidence indicates that a working alliance (also called a working relationship) is an important component in all counseling. Actually, working alliance scores are the best known predictor of counseling outcomes (Horvath, 2000). Bordin (1994) defined the working alliance as having three equal and interacting components:

1. *Goal* (collaboration between counselor and client on the goals of counseling)
2. *Task* (collaboration between counselor and client on the tasks of counseling)
3. *Bond* (mutual affective bonding between client and counselor)

Group process stimulates the unfolding of the working alliance in all clients (Glatzer, 1978). For example, a husband-to-therapist working alliance was strongly predictive of the outcome of group treatment for spouse abuse (Brown & O'Leary, 2000).

Curative Factors

Even though working alliance theory has had an enormous impact on individual counseling research, its impact upon group counseling research has been limited. Most of the literature on the nonspecific factors in group counseling has focused on Yalom's (1985) curative factor theory, which postulated that the following 12 curative factors operate in group counseling:

1. Self-understanding
2. Interpersonal learning (input)
3. Interpersonal learning (output)
4. Universality
5. Instillation of hope
6. Altruism
7. Recapitulation of primary family group
8. Catharsis
9. Cohesiveness
10. Existential factors
11. Identification
12. Guidance

Butler and Fuhriman (1983) reviewed 10 years of research on Yalom's curative factors. In the studies they reviewed, clients were asked to rank the 12 factors with regard to their curative value. Butler and Fuhriman's research supported Yalom's own idea of a triad of highly curative factors consisting of

1. self-understanding,
2. catharsis, and
3. interpersonal interaction (input).

More than 10 years later, Shaughnessy and Kivlighan (1995) suggested that the analyses in these early studies were not sufficiently complex. Instead of ranking the clients' views of the 12 factors, Shaughnessy and Kivlighan utilized *cluster analysis* and described three clusters of client responders:

1. Broad-spectrum responders
2. Self-reflective responders
3. Other-directed responders

The broad-spectrum responders, the largest cluster, endorsed all 12 curative factors evenly. The next largest cluster, the self-reflective responders, valued a specific curative factor triad most highly. Based on the results of their analysis, Shaughnessy and Kivlighan recommended that group counselors include a broad range of curative factors in their group counseling, rather than concentrate on a few factors that appeal to a minority of clients.

Group Development

Fundamental to the assessment of group progress and outcome is to understand the stages of group development (Zimpfer, 1984). Most research on group development has been based upon Tuckman's (1965) five-stage theory, which he identified as

1. forming,
2. storming,
3. norming,
4. performing, and
5. adjourning.

Maples (1988) refined Tuckman's work through 5 years of data collection, and from an analysis of her data, she developed a 20-substage model designed as a star. At each stage, or point of the star, Maples offered definitions that can be used in practice to better evaluate clinical progress.

Leadership

Group leadership research fills the counseling literature, as group leadership involves the interaction of so many features of group counseling that it defies any simple definition (Stockton & Morran, 1982). Furthermore, confusion continues to surround leadership functions and their relationship to the therapeutic gains that group members make (Conyne, Harvill, Morganett, Morran, & Hulse-Killacky, 1990). Regardless of the counselor's technique, however, when the counselor's attitudes are acceptable to the client, the client is more likely to report positive therapeutic outcomes (Beutler, Jobe, & Elkins, 1974).

In addition to counselor attitude, the literature has pointed to the following as being important nonspecific leadership factors:

1. *A sense of hope.* Effective leaders were found to project a sense of hope to their clients, manifested in behaviors such as acknowledging the client's

resources and potential to change, conveying a clear and strong belief in the effectiveness of group counseling, and communicating a sense of confidence or personal power (Couch & Childers, 1987). Although the literature indicates that hope is a curative factor in group counseling, it is devoid of strategies for its use.

2. *Leadership style.* Abramowitz, Roback, Abramowitz, and Jackson (1974) found that matching counselor leadership style with client personality promotes positive group counseling outcomes. They described client personality based on Rotter's (1966) research on internal and external locus of control. Clients who were described as having an internally oriented locus of control believe that life events are the result of initiative. By contrast, clients who believe that luck or powerful forces determine life outcomes are described as having an externally oriented locus of control. Abramowitz et al. (1974) found that nondirective techniques were more effective than directive techniques with internally oriented clients. The reverse was true for clients with an external orientation.

3. *Personal characteristics.* Certain personal characteristics may distinguish effective from ineffective group leaders (Combs, Avila, & Purkey, 1978). The literature indicates that effective leaders are more positive than less effective leaders, with effective leaders holding more positive perceptions of clients. Also, effective group counselors display emotionally supportive behaviors (e.g., care, listening, and flexibility) more often than ineffective counselors during group interactions (Stockton, Morran, & Velboff, 1987).

Group Counseling Modes and Outcome

The group counseling literature is replete with reviews of outcome research for different types of groups. These reviews can be digested more easily when the types of groups are categorized into four modes:

1. Task/Work (TASK)
2. Psychoeducational (EDUC)
3. Counseling (COUN)
4. Psychotherapy (THRP)

These are the modes officially recognized by the ASGW (2004).

Task/Work Mode

The TASK classification includes task forces, committees, planning groups, and study circles, all of which are directed at identifying and completing specific goals. Because this is not a therapeutic mode, individuals other than professional counselors usually lead these groups. At times, however, counselors work in a consultant role with these groups. Given the nontherapeutic nature of TASK groups, the literature on these groups will not be reviewed in this chapter. For an excellent review of the TASK literature, see Bettenhausen (1991).

Psychoeducational Mode

The purpose of EDUC groups is to prevent psychological maladjustment (ASGW, 2004). Although EDUC interventions originally were developed for educational settings, the use of EDUC groups has expanded beyond schools and students. EDUC interventions currently are used to educate all types of clients about potential threats (e.g., AIDS), developmental life events (e.g., the empty nest), and life skills (e.g., assertiveness).

Counseling Mode

COUN interventions focus on interpersonal growth and problem solving (ASGW, 2004). Examples of COUN interventions are T-groups, sensitivity groups, and encounter groups. The emphasis in COUN groups is on promoting growth and resolving normative life crises. As such, COUN groups typically do not address remediation of pathology. The American School Counselor Association's (ASCA; 2004a) position statement on group counseling states that this treatment modality is "an integral part of a comprehensive guidance and counseling program" (p. 1).

Psychotherapy Mode

THRP groups are designed to address personal and interpersonal problems of living, remediate perceptual and cognitive distortions or repetitive patterns of dysfunctional behavior, and promote personal and interpersonal growth and development in individuals with severe and/or chronic maladjustment (ASGW, 2004). Budman et al. (1984) provides an excellent example of research on a THRP intervention, in which their psychodynamically oriented group approach was found to be effective in treating clients with severe characterological problems.

GROUP COUNSELING EFFICACY WITH SELECT CLIENT POPULATIONS

Regardless of the mode, group counseling outcomes with specific client populations fall along a single continuum. The main points on this continuum are effective interventions, ineffective interventions, and harmful interventions (see Figure 5.1). We will relay the scientific knowledge on what works, what does not work, and what has been found harmful in reference to specific client populations.

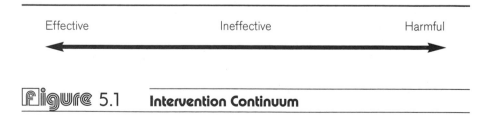

Figure 5.1   Intervention Continuum

Effective Interventions

The literature indicates that group counseling is effective with several different client populations. In general, the reasons that clients enter group counseling fall into three broad categories: mental health problems, physical health problems, and personal growth. The discussion in this section, concerning effective interventions for specific client populations, is structured in accordance with these categories. Drawing on the taxonomic work of Achenbach and McConaughy (1997), we further divided the mental health problems category into two subcategories: internalizing disorders and externalizing disorders. For the present discussion, internalizing disorders are those in which a client's aggression is directed against himself or herself. Externalizing disorders are those in which the client's aggression is directed against others.

Mental Health Problems

Internalizing Disorders

The majority of efficacy studies in the group counseling literature have focused on internalizing disorders. The prototypical disorder of this subcategory is depression.

1. *Depression*

    Researchers have examined group counseling efficacy with depression in pediatric, adult, and geriatric client populations. Beeferman and Orvaschel (1994) reported that the efficacy of group counseling with depressed adolescent clients is well documented in the research literature. They noted that the most effective interventions blend skills training, cognitive restructuring, and a supportive group process.

    In a rare head-to-head comparison study, Reynolds and Coats (1986) compared the effectiveness of cognitive group counseling and group relaxation training for depressed adolescents. They found that the adolescents in both groups moved from moderate depression levels at pretest to nondepression levels at posttest. Cognitive behavioral group therapy continues to be among the most efficacious approaches to acute treatment with adolescents (Clarke, Rohde, Lewinsohn, Hops, & Seeley, 1999).

    The efficacy of group counseling with depressed adult clients is also well established (Vandervoort & Fuhriman, 1991). Scott and Stradling (1991) explored the question of whether an individual approach or a group approach has been more efficacious in cognitive behavioral counseling for depression and found that both approaches have been equally effective. In examining the effectiveness of the social problem-solving approach to depression, Nezu (1986) delineated five separate components: problem orientation (i.e., cognitive and motivation view of problem), problem definition and formulation, generation of alternatives, decision making, and solution implementation and verification. He found that the groups in which this approach was applied showed more improvement than either the unstructured problem-solving groups or the wait-list control groups.

After reviewing the use of group counseling for bipolar depression, Kanas (1993) reported that the research supports group counseling for this client population. Specifically, group counseling helped clients with bipolar depression learn about their disease, gain coping skills, and elicit support on related interpersonal issues. Group counseling also has been discovered to be useful in the pharmacological treatment of bipolar depression. Cerbone, Mayo, Cuthbertson, and O'Connell (1992) reported that their group counseling intervention, which blended EDUC and COUN group approaches, led to greater social functioning and lower relapse rates in this client group.

Depression is the most common mental illness among older adults. Dhooper, Green, Huff, and Austin-Murphy (1993) conducted research to determine whether their Coping Together Group intervention could have an impact on depression in geriatric nursing-home residents. The Coping Together Group program was based upon an amalgam of counseling strategies including reminiscing, problem solving, communication training, and education. At posttesting, depression in members of the Coping Together Groups had decreased significantly compared to depression in members of the control group. Cummings (2003) reported that group counseling was efficacious for depressed assisted-living residents.

2. *Eating disorders*

Professional counselors have made extensive use of group counseling in treating clients with eating disorders. After reviewing 31 studies on group treatment of bulimia, Zimpfer (1990b) reported the following:

> In every group study, regardless of the specific type of treatment, the group intervention was successful on whatever criteria were used. That is to say, binge/purge behavior was reduced or eliminated at a significant level among the participants, and depression was reduced and body image improved. (p. 247)

Specific group treatment approaches for eating disorders mentioned in the literature as effective include cognitive (Levey, McDermott, & Lee, 1989), cognitive and behavioral blend (Davis, Olmstead, & Rockert, 1992), and interpersonal (Agras et al., 1995; Wilfley et al., 1993).

Research also has shown that group counseling is an effective approach to the remediation of distorted body imagery. A study reported in 1995 by Grant and Cash represents a long line of quality studies that have shown cognitive group interventions to be an efficacious treatment for body-image distortion. Foundational to these interventions were the identification, monitoring, and cognitive reconstructing of body-image errors. Other researchers have found that both group cognitive and group behavioral interventions were efficacious with weight-control issues (Lewis, Blair, & Booth, 1992; McNamara, 1989).

3. *Other internalizing disorders*

Researchers have found that group counseling is efficacious with a wide variety of other internalizing disorders. The group outcome studies are usefully divided into two categories of severity: (1) issues of clinical concern, and (2) a diagnosis of mental disorder. The following studies represent the research on group counseling efficacy in these two categories.

Issues of clinical concern: Group counseling is an effective method for addressing issues of clinical concern such as adjustment following divorce (Pedro-Carroll, Alpert-Gillis, & Cowen, 1992; Zimpfer, 1990a), loneliness (Brough, 1994), grief (McCallum & Piper, 1990; Zimpfer, 1991), anxiety (Eayrs, Rowan, & Harvey, 1984; Meichenbaum, Gilmore, & Fedoravicius, 1971; Powell, 1987), and sex abuse trauma (Alexander, Neimeyer, Follette, Moore, & Harter, 1989; Cahill, Llewelyn, & Pearson, 1991; Hiebert-Murphy, De Luca, & Runtz, 1992; Reeker & Ensing, 1998; Silovsky & Hembree-Kigin, 1994; Winick & Levene, 1992).

Issues diagnosed as mental disorders: Among individuals diagnosed with mental disorders, group counseling improves the quality of life and reduces symptoms associated with encopresis (Stark, Owens-Stively, Spirito, Lewis, & Guevremont, 1990), obsessive–compulsive disorders (Krone, Himle, & Nesse, 1991), addictive disorders (McAuliffe, 1990), schizophrenia (McFarlane, Link, Dushay, Marchal, & Crilly, 1995; Svensson, Hansson, & Nyman, 2000), personality disorders (Linehan, Heard, & Armstrong, 1993; Nehls, 1991), posttraumatic stress disorder (Foa, Davidson, & Frances, 1999; Lubin & Johnson, 2000; Lubin, Loris, Burt, & Johnson, 1998), and sexual dysfunctions (Hurlbert, White, Powell, & Apt, 1993).

Among the studies just cited, two of the reports deserve special attention, given their usefulness to practicing group counselors. Pedro-Carroll et al.'s 1992 study on a divorce-adjustment group intervention for children is a good example of efficacy research in an applied setting. In addition, their article describes their protocol in detail, so professional counselors can use the article to replicate this effective intervention at their worksites.

The study by Stark, Owens-Stively, et al. (1990) is a good example of a group behavioral counseling intervention outcome study. The target of this intervention, group work with children and their parents, was retentive encopresis. Although treatment of encopretic children is not discussed widely in the counseling literature, professional counselors who work with children encounter this problem frequently. The researchers provided a clear explication of their treatment steps, as well as an articulate rationale for delivering their intervention in a group setting. They postulated that

> . . . the group format may have enhanced treatment
> effectiveness by providing support to both parents and
> children in complying with the treatment regimen. Often

> parents reported feeling a great deal of relief and support in meeting other families with encopretic children. Further, the children reported enjoying the group and a feeling of relief upon meeting other children with the same problem. The group format may have enhanced the parents' and children's compliance to the treatment protocol because they were required to report back to the group on their success or failure with each aspect of treatment. (p. 669)

As to outcome, the researchers reported that during the intervention phase, soiling was reduced by 83%. Furthermore, at the 6-month follow-up, the average number of soiling incidents per week among the participants had dropped from the baseline of 14 to .021. Efficacy studies with high clinical utility are a gold mine for practicing counselors. Pedro-Carroll et al. (1992) and Stark, Owens-Stively, et al. (1990) represent two of the best examples of this rare research literature genre.

A new area of exploration in group counseling is called *multiple-family group therapy* (MFGT). Conducted with two or more families in the same room, MFGT was found to decrease the stigma associated with mental health services and increase opportunities for engaging at-risk urban children and their families (Stone, McKay, & Stoops, 1996). Thorngren, Christiansen, and Kleist (1998) provided a review of efficacious outcomes of group counseling for culturally diverse clients and for families with schizophrenic members, alcoholism, and affective disorders.

Externalizing Disorders

Illustrative of externalizing disorders are spouse battering and disruptive behavior disorders/delinquency.

1. *Spouse battering*

Following a review of the research literature on group counseling and spouse battering, Tolman and Bennett (1990) reported that most spouse-battering groups utilize a cognitive approach. Their research on these groups showed that "the majority of men stop their physically abusive behavior subsequent to intervention. Percentages of successful outcome ranged from 53% to 85%" (p. 104). Of the programs that Tolman and Bennett reviewed, the most successful of these incorporated cognitive techniques, pro-feminist components, and a highly structured group process. Professional counselors who anticipate working with this population would do well to read this comprehensive review.

Dutton (1986) studied the outcome of a court-mandated group counseling program for wife assault. This COUN program also utilized a cognitive approach, which Dutton defined as follows:

> [It] has as its main objective the decrease or elimination of the use of violence by the husband as a means of resolving

conflict with his wife. A variety of sub-goals exist that includes (a) recognition of one's personal responsibility for the use of violence, (b) termination of externalizing causes of violence to one's wife and minimizing the destructive effects of one's violence, (c) improved ability to detect the warning signs of violence, such as increased arousal or anger, and (d) an expanded behavioral repertoire for dealing with conflict. (p. 164)

The recidivism rate for the clients who completed the program was only 4%. This rate stands in stark contrast to the 40% recidivism rate for the comparison group that did not receive this treatment.

2. *Disruptive behavior disorders and delinquency*

Group counseling has long been the favored approach to working with disruptive and delinquent youth. As early as 1943, Slavson, in his seminal work on group counseling, reported protocols and case studies of group counseling with this population. Strangely, little solid research on group counseling has been conducted with this population.

Braswell (1993) reviewed the available research literature on cognitive interventions with children with disruptive disorders and found that cognitive interventions have produced clinically meaningful and durable treatment effects. The article also described a detailed counseling protocol that Braswell developed. The goal of her cognitive intervention was to change the children's primary response to conflict, instilling in its place a "think first—act later" orientation.

Truax, Wargo, and Volksdorf (1970) examined the impact of a nondirective THRP intervention on institutionalized juvenile delinquents. They found that their twice-weekly, 24-session intervention influenced clients' personality factors positively and decreased the rates of reinstitutionalization.

Smets and Cebula (1987) examined an eclectic five-step group counseling program for adolescent sex offenders. In a detailed report on their intervention, they recounted the behaviors associated with each step, which ranged from "admission of responsibility" (Step 1) to "restitution planning" (Step 5). The structure of the group was such that the group continued until all participants reached Step 5. At the 3-year follow-up assessment, only 1 of the 21 treatment participants had reoffended.

A more recent study reported that a group cognitive–behavioral intervention enhanced coping skills in incarcerated youth (Rohde, Jorgensen, Seeley, & Mace, 2004).

Physical Health Problems

In addition to addressing mental health problems, group counseling interventions have been used with people who have physical health problems. The counseling setting has been both within and outside medical settings with a variety of client populations.

Geriatric Conditions

In groups, participants support one another to increase their levels of exercise, over-all fitness, and consequently their self-efficacy. Adults with chronic diseases, such as heart conditions, achieved greater benefits from group-mediated cognitive behavioral counseling than regular exercise regimes over a 12-month trial (Rejeski et al., 2003).

Among institutionalized older adults, a major presenting problem is confusion, according to McCrone (1991). She commented that the percentage of these adults with confusion can run as high as 70%. In a well-crafted experimental study, she used the term *resocialization* to refer to a "formal group method which encourages interaction among members by introducing a focal stimulus or topic to facilitate reminiscence" (p. 30). She stated that resocialization is thought to remediate both cognitive and social confusion by reinforcing small-group participation and decreasing social isolation. McCrone's positive findings support the efficacy of resocialization as a group treatment modality with confused older adults. Other researchers who have commented on the efficacy of group approaches with institutionalized older adults include Christopher, Loeb, Zaretsky, and Jassani (1988) and Gilewski (1986).

Insomnia

In group counseling interventions applied to insomniacs, Davies (1989) reported success with an approach incorporating both cognitive and behavioral strategies. These strategies included cognitive restructuring, problem solving, anxiety management, and sleep education, and treatment gains were maintained through a 1-year follow-up assessment. In a subsequent study, Davies (1991) examined the interaction of sedative medicines with the same group treatment. He found no difference in treatment efficacy between the group counseling clients who took sedative medicines and the group counseling clients who did not take the medicines.

Kupych-Woloshyn, MacFarlane, and Shapiro (1993) also found a blended approach to be effective in alleviating insomnia. Their clients reported valuing both the educational and the support components of the intervention.

Other Physical Health Conditions

Researchers have found group counseling to be efficacious with a variety of other physical health problems. As a critical component in medical care, group counseling that emphasizes goal setting, planning, and behavior rehearsals is efficacious in managing medical conditions such as asthma, diabetes, and heart failure, which require a change in lifestyle and behaviors to attain optimal control over disease (Schreurs, Colland, Kuijer, de Ridder, & van Elderen, 2003). Group counseling provides ways for patients to adapt and better cope with health problems such as cancer (Harman, 1991), respiratory diseases (Pattison, Rhodes, & Dudley, 1971; Stark, Bowen, Tyc, Evans, & Passero, 1990), and chronic headaches (Kneebone & Martin, 1992). The positive outcomes of group counseling for physical health problems typically include opportunities for self-help, psychoeducational information, acquisition of new skills, socialization, and emotional support (Kurtz, 1997).

From an ethical standpoint, professionals must know whether their services are helpful to clients. Although many clients in medical support groups are shown to improve in emotional function and global satisfaction, we do not know the extent to which the group-based interventions contributed to changes in individual clients (Magen & Glajchen, 1999). In a time of shrinking dollars and increased needs for the psychosocial care of medical patients, this will be a critical area of research.

Personal Growth

Group counseling has been used to help clients optimize their role performance at work and at home. Among the personal growth groups are those involving career development, parent education, bereavement and suicide, and interpersonal relations.

Career Development

The literature on group counseling as a career development intervention extends back to the turn of the 20th century (Gazda et al., 2000). Outlining the research literature on group counseling programs for midlife career changers, Zimpfer and Carr (1989) reported evidence that group counseling helps this population. They noted that successful adult career interventions had a different focus than that of typical youth career development programs and surmised that this difference resulted from the adults' view that changing jobs is a cyclical rather than a linear process. Consequently, for adults, career development components beyond interests and ability require assessment. These components include needs, values, goals, and role salience. In one controlled study for example, women who participated in group counseling to examine career decision making, self-efficacy, and vocational exploration maintained a commitment to these gains over time (Sullivan & Mahalik, 2000).

Baker and Popowicz (1983) conducted a meta-analysis of 18 research studies examining the efficacy of EDUC career interventions with school-aged youth. The settings for these interventions included both small-group counseling and large-group (classroom) counseling. Across the studies, Baker and Popowicz found an average effect size of .50 and noted that such an effect size indicates that a person at the mean of the control group would be expected to rise to the 69th percentile if he or she were to receive the intervention.

Another positive review of the career EDUC research appears in Herr, Cramer, and Niles's (2003) influential text on career counseling. A helpful analysis of career education practices in secondary schools provides a taxonomy defining the dimensions of school-directed programming, including duration of the intervention, pedagogical style, location of the intervention, size of the intervention, and control of the intervention (Dykeman et al., 2001).

Finally, group counseling interventions have been found to increase work performance. For example, Kanas (1991) found that support group activities enhanced the performance of first-year medical residents.

Parent Education

Parents seeking to enhance their parenting skills also have been helped through group counseling. In an excellent review of the research literature, Dembo, Sweitzer, and Lauritzen (1985) examined the differential efficacy of three approaches to parent education EDUC interventions: behavioral, Adlerian, and client-centered. The specific client-centered approach was parent effectiveness training (PET). When they reviewed studies having a single approach, they found that the research literature supported behavioral interventions as being efficacious. By contrast, they found little evidence that the PET interventions were effective. The research findings on Adlerian approaches were mixed. When they reviewed research comparing the three approaches, however, they uncovered no differential effectiveness among the approaches. Other literature reviews also reported finding mixed results among these three approaches (Polster, Dangel, & Rasp, 1987; Todres & Bunston, 1993).

Given the mixed findings of the literature reviews, what is a counselor to do when faced with running a parent education EDUC intervention? A study by Sutton (1992) may provide some clues. Sutton conducted a well-designed study of a parent education EDUC intervention using behavioral principles. The acting-out behavior of children whose parents were in the EDUC group declined significantly. The acting-out behavior of children whose parents were in the control group did not change. Although none of the three approaches (behavioral, Adlerian, or client-centered) offers a 100% guarantee, we think it is justifiable for professional counselors to be asked to conduct such parent education EDUC interventions. Our recommendation to these counselors is to select a program based upon behavioral principles, given the extant positive evidence for this approach in the literature.

Bereavement and Suicide

Group counseling mirrors the benefits of family and community support during times of loss. Of particular concern about death as a result of suicide in families is the increased likelihood of suicide by other family members. An empirical study on approaches to this problem was conducted through the Weill Medical College at Cornell University to determine a method to strengthen coping skills and lessen the distress and anxiety of children bereaved after a parent or sibling committed suicide (Pfeffer, Jiang, Kakuma, Hwang, & Metsch, 2002). The authors documented a manual-based bereavement group intervention for children who suffered the suicide of a parent or a sibling that offers the potential to decrease future morbidity.

Interpersonal Relations

Historically, improving interpersonal relations has been a primary goal in growth-focused group counseling. Indeed, by its very nature, group counseling offers a unique laboratory for developing new interpersonal skills. The research literature documents numerous efficacious group counseling initiatives designed to improve interpersonal skills.

In an outstanding series of studies, Shechtman (1994a) examined the ability of group counseling to improve interpersonal relations among school-aged children. Her counseling protocol (Shechtman, 1994b) included both structured group activities (e.g., therapeutic games) and open-ended group process (e.g., disclosing disturbing feelings and receiving group feedback).

One interesting finding from Shechtman's research was the differential effect of the group counseling treatment between genders. Concerning this effect, "the results suggest that preadolescent girls grow in intimacy in a friendship relationship, whether treated or not, in a somewhat naturalistic developmental fashion. In contrast, only treated boys significantly grow in this domain" (Shechtman, 1994a, p. 833). She emphasized that the development of interpersonal relations skills such as the mutual discussion of feelings and needs is essential to the development of cross-gender attachment.

Shechtman's (1994b) protocol represents an efficacious intervention for professional counselors that is completely consistent with the developmental focus and ethic of the counseling profession. The group counseling literature would benefit from more applied-setting outcome research like the work of Shechtman.

Children are not the only clients who benefit from the experience of counseling groups in promoting interpersonal skills. Adults can grow from these experiences as well. In their classic study of encounter groups, Lieberman, Yalom, and Miles (1973) reported that these groups can promote better interpersonal skills. In this study, Lieberman et al. classified the clients with reference to outcome, labeling those who benefited the most from the group experiences as "high learners." With reference to high learners, they stated:

> [They] changed in their methods of relating to others: They behaved in a more trusting, open, honest manner; they hid less of themselves; they expressed their opinions more forthrightly; they gave feedback to others, and requested it for themselves. They also perceived that adaptive openness is curvilinear; too much as well as too little can jeopardize human relationships. (p. 139)

Despite the benefits of growth-oriented group counseling cited by Lieberman et al. and other researchers, we wonder what the future is for this type of counseling in the current managed-care environment. Will a person have to be labeled dysfunctional in some way to receive group counseling? Will professional counselors have to abandon the growth-promoting segment of their work to earn a place within the health care market?

Multicultural Understanding

Diversity is a critical factor in determining the outcomes of group counseling. Methods for addressing culture, identity, and socialization will influence our discussion of group counseling efficacy. In one study of working women, for example, career self-efficacy and vocational exploration increased only when the group counseling specifically addressed female socialization issues (Sullivan & Mahalik, 2000). In other studies, Native American adolescents (Kim, Omizo, & D'Andrea, 1998) and Hawaiian children (Omizo, Omizo, & Kitaoka, 1998) who participate in culturally focused groups have improved locus of control and increased self-esteem compared to control groups.

Unfortunately, studies such as these are rare in the literature. Empirical studies on group efficacy have to consider the entire spectrum of people served. We recommend that counselors examine the cultural limitations that historically have plagued research on group counseling (Helms, 1990; Merta, 1995; Williams, Frame, & Green, 1999).

Ineffective Interventions

One popular setting for EDUC interventions is the classroom. This type of EDUC intervention is commonly called "large group guidance" (LG-EDUC). Actually, LG-EDUC interventions have long been a staple of professional counselors who work in schools. School counselors have designated LG-EDUC work as essential to their profession. The definition of the role of school counselors published by the ASCA (2004b) specifically designates LG-EDUC as one of the four core activities of a professional school counselor. In this role statement, LG-EDUC is defined as a "planned, developmental, program of guidance activities designed to foster students' academic, career, and personal/social development. It is provided for all students through a collaborative effort by counselors and teachers" (p. 1). Gysbers and Henderson's (2000) influential text on school counseling suggests that LG-EDUC should occupy between 25% and 40% of a school counselor's time.

Several literature reviews support the efficacy of LG-EDUC (e.g., Baker, Swisher, Nadenichek, & Popowicz, 1984; Borders & Drury, 1992; Cartledge & Milburn, 1978; Gerler, 1985; Gerler & Anderson, 1986). These reviews led to including LG-EDUC in the role definitions of many counseling specialties. Except for career development interventions, however, the results of rigorous research studies cast doubt on the efficacy of this intervention. For example, Laconte, Shaw, and Dunn (1993), who used an experimentally rigorous research design to study the impact of an LG-EDUC intervention based on rational–emotive therapy on middle school students, found no significant outcome differences between the students receiving the LG-EDUC intervention and the students who did not receive this intervention.

Wiggins and Wiggins (1992) studied school counselors' ability to improve student self-esteem and classroom behavior, comparing school counselors who used primarily individual counseling to school counselors who used primarily LG-EDUC. They found that student improvement was greater with the individual-counseling-oriented school counselors. Considering their findings, the researchers commented:

> Although counselors have long been urged to do more
> classroom guidance, hard data are difficult to find to support
> this viewpoint; however, assertions that this is the road to take
> are plentiful. (p. 380)

LG-EDUC literature reviews also have raised doubts about the efficacy of LG-EDUC. Strein (1988) reviewed all experimental and quasi-experimental research published on LG-EDUC from 1970 on. He reported that only 103 of the 344 comparisons (29%) reached statistical significance. Moreover, Strein reported that the most rigorous studies showed a strong tendency toward nonsignificant results. In reviewing the school counseling outcome research that appeared from 1988 to 1995, Whiston and Sexton (1998) found five studies addressing the question of whether LG-EDUC impacts student self-esteem, only one of which reported a positive impact.

Gossette and O'Brien (1993) reviewed the research literature on LG-EDUC interventions based on rational–emotive therapy. Like Strein (1988) and Whiston and Sexton (1998), they found dismal support for the efficacy of these interventions. Only 70 of the 278 treatment comparisons they reviewed favored the LG-EDUC intervention. Given these results, Gossette and O'Brien (1993) stated:

> A total of 1,344 children received an average of 10.5 hours of classroom instruction in the philosophy of RET. How have their lives benefited? At best, we must conclude, very little. The justification most commonly cited for classroom intervention was that it would be "preventive," forestalling future maladjustment and presumably facilitating academic performance. Yet no evidence was ever offered to show that the incidence of maladjustment either within the time frame of the intervention, usually about 2–3 months, or even within the school year, was high enough to warrant such an expenditure of school time. (p. 22)

The one notable exception to the long line of LG-EDUC failures is the classroom guidance program called Second Step (Committee for Children, 2004), designed to lessen school violence. In a rigorous research study, Grossman et al. (1997) found that Second Step did reduce physical aggression among second- and third-graders in Washington state. Why Second Step was successful in contrast to the majority of LG-EDUC interventions remains unclear. Our hunch is that this success was the result of the delivery system. Specifically, Second Step was delivered by teachers and was interwoven into the standard curriculum. We believe that this delivery system is optimal for helping students generalize across settings what they are taught in a classroom guidance lesson. The Second Step delivery stands in contrast to the standard LG-EDUC delivery mode of the school counselor delivering intermittent, time-limited instruction.

Despite enthusiastic endorsement by professional associations and influential theorists alike, the utility of LG-EDUC remains a troubling question. Professional counselors must ask themselves: Given the plethora of proven group counseling interventions, what is the justification to engage in interventions such as LG-EDUC, which lack such proven efficacy?

Other than the literature on LG-EDUC, surprisingly little contemporary literature reports ineffective group counseling interventions. Nevertheless, two articles detailing inefficacy merit mentioning. Joanning, Quinn, Thomas, and Mullen (1992) compared three different interventions for adolescent drug abuse: family counseling, adolescent group counseling, and family drug education. The group counseling intervention was a client-centered, process-oriented COUN intervention. The family drug education intervention was an information-only EDUC intervention. The researchers reported that neither the EDUC nor the COUN intervention influenced adolescent drug abuse.

Kneebone and Martin (1992) found that a combined cognitive and behavioral group intervention was efficacious with chronic headache sufferers. When they added a partner involvement (PI) component to this group intervention, however, treatment efficacy was diminished. Kneebone and Martin hypothesized:

> If PI subjects in this study shared responsibility for the program with their partners, they may have considered success to be not just a function of their own efforts. Positive changes in internal locus of control and self-efficacy would have been less likely under such circumstances, and efforts to cope with headache-related stresses would have remained stable or even declined, leading to reduced treatment efficacy. (p. 213)

Kneebone and Martin went on to detail how their findings supported their hypothesis.

On the surface, partner involvement seems like a sound idea. But professional counselors must remain constantly vigilant to the hidden messages contained in their interventions. In particular, counselors must ask whether their actions contain noxious hidden messages. In the case of the PI intervention, the hidden message seems to have been, "Your partner is here because I don't think you can do this on your own." Although this message was wholly unintended, its impact was felt nonetheless.

Harmful Interventions

As we have discussed thus far, group counseling offers the professional counselor a powerful tool to apply to many mental and physical health issues. But any potent therapeutic tool also contains the potential to harm clients (Hadley & Strupp, 1976). Therefore, the potency of group counseling can produce casualties. By "casualty," we mean a client whose lasting deterioration of psychological functioning is directly attributable to a counseling intervention (Crown, 1983).

Bergin (1963) introduced the idea into the research literature that counseling can produce negative as well as positive results for clients. Concerning the production of negative results, Bergin (1966) suggested that counselors should be more cautious and critical of their practices—careful to eliminate ineffective or harmful therapeutic techniques. Later, Bergin and his colleagues examined the research literature on negative effects and reported that the general casualty rate in counseling was somewhere between 9% and 11% (Bergin, 1971; Lambert, Shapiro, & Bergin, 1986).

Group counseling researchers have not ignored the ongoing debate over casualty rates in the general counseling literature. They first directed their attention to personal growth group interventions (e.g., T-groups, encounter groups, and marathon groups). The reported casualty rates for the interventions varied widely (Hartley, Roback, & Abramowitz, 1976; Kaplan, 1982). Careful studies on these group interventions, however, found that casualty rates were no higher than the casualty rate for general counseling (Cooper, 1975; Kaplan, 1982; Lambert et al., 1986; Lieberman et al., 1973).

Although group counseling does not seem to be any more dangerous than other counseling interventions, it still does produce casualties. Thus, in light of the ethical imperative of nonmaleficence, professional counselors must learn how to minimize group counseling casualties, which result from two sources: poor pre-group screening and counselor actions.

Screening and Contraindications

Professional counselors cannot conduct a proper pre-group screening without knowledge of group counseling contraindications. *Contraindication* refers to a client's symptom, condition, or circumstance that warns against taking some course of action (Barker, 1995). Fortunately, group counseling researchers have catalogued a number of contraindications for COUN and THRP interventions. In reference to the COUN and THRP modalities, Toseland and Siporin (1986) detailed three types of contraindications: *practical barriers, specific treatment needs,* and *client personality functioning.* To aid practitioners in screening clients for COUN and THRP group counseling interventions, we will examine these three areas in greater detail.

Practical Barriers

Toseland and Siporin (1986) listed the following practical barriers to prescribing group counseling:

- Lack of clients with similar issues
- Clients' resistance to a group counseling prescription
- Scheduling problems
- Lack of qualified counselors
- Lack of agency or school support

Clients' Treatment Needs

In terms of clients' treatment needs, some clients, such as those in crisis and those with a high potential for suicide, need more immediate one-on-one attention than group counseling can provide (Gazda et al., 2000; Horwitz, 1976; Toseland & Siporin, 1986). Also, some clients may have an authentic need for a private therapeutic setting in which to discuss a highly sensitive issue or critical decision (Toseland & Siporin, 1986).

Clients' Personality Factors

Many personality factors can contraindicate an assignment to group counseling. In their study of group counseling outcomes, Budman, Demby, and Randall (1980) encountered one treatment casualty—a client who had scored high on scales measuring interpersonal sensitivity, paranoid thinking, and psychotic thinking. Similarly, other researchers have commented that strong contraindicators for group counseling include extreme interpersonal sensitivity (Hartley et al., 1976; Lieberman et al., 1973), paranoid thinking (Budman et al., 1980; Crown, 1983; Horwitz, 1976; Toseland & Siporin, 1986), and psychoticism (Gazda et al., 2000; Gurman, 1971; Smets & Cebula, 1987).

Researchers also have consistently indicated that low motivation for change is a strong contraindicator for group counseling (Crown, 1983). Consequently, professional counselors should take care to assess this obvious but often forgotten client characteristic. See Gusella, Butler, Nichols, and Bird (2003) for an excellent discussion of the measurement of this variable for group counseling.

Another obvious client characteristic that group counselors often forget to assess is the client's tolerance for anxiety and frustration. Low tolerance puts a client at risk to become a casualty of group counseling. With reference to this tolerance, Horwitz (1976) commented that

> a group often tends to induce frustration due to competition among members for its time and attention. A common wish is to become the favorite "child." Although support is also an important dimension of the group experience, it may be overshadowed by anxiety in the opening phases of group membership. Patients who deal with heightened tension by engaging in self-destructive actions, who tend to take flight in reaction to anxiety, are best excluded from a group. (p. 506)

One specific type of anxiety that has been mentioned as a contraindicator is acute fear of self-disclosure (Gazda, 1986).

Personality issues that contraindicate group counseling placement include borderline personality disorder (Lambert et al., 1986) and psychopathy (Slavson & Schiffer, 1975). Also, the presence of severe schizophrenia contraindicates group counseling placement (Bergin, 1980; Kanas, 1991; Slavson & Schiffer, 1975; Toseland & Siporin, 1986). Marked emotional lability is an additional contraindicator (Gazda et al., 2000).

Finally, we note two contraindications specific to children and adolescents:

1. Sugar (1993) advised that encounter and marathon group interventions are contraindicated for these populations as these group interventions can present material that is too intense for nascent egos.
2. Baider and De Nour (1989) cautioned that adolescent cancer patients have to be medically stable before they begin any group counseling. They exerted this caution because of their finding that group counseling can strip away denial defense mechanisms that cancer patients who are medically unstable need so they can function adaptively and with hope.

The contraindications for group counseling are summarized as follows:

- Acute self-disclosure fears
- Borderline disorder
- Extreme interpersonal sensitivity
- Low anxiety tolerance
- Low frustration tolerance
- Low motivation for change
- Marked emotional lability

- Paranoia
- Psychopathy
- Psychotic thinking
- Schizophrenia
- Severe depression
- Severe impulse-control problems
- Unstable medical condition

Also, we have found that reviewing case studies can make counseling facts "come alive." Therefore, we recommend the rich descriptions of group counseling casualties by Brandes (1977), Budman et al. (1980), and Kaplan (1982).

Best Practice

Two caveats about our research review on contraindications are as follows:

1. Our discussion pertains solely to the COUN and THRP modalities. The research literature gives us no indication if the contraindications would hold true for EDUC interventions. For example, we know that a COUN group would be contraindicated for a client with extreme fear of self-disclosure. The same client, however, might find an EDUC group helpful (Gazda et al., 2000). Indeed, an EDUC group experience might "set the stage" for an effective COUN intervention or might be in itself a sufficient intervention.

2. Growing evidence indicates that homogeneous EDUC interventions are effective with clients who have borderline personality disorder (see, e.g., Linehan et al., 1993) or schizophrenia (see, e.g., Hayes, Halford, & Varghese, 1995). (The term *homogeneous* denotes groups in which all clients share the same diagnosis. The term *heterogeneous* refers to groups containing clients with a mixture of diagnoses.) Also, in general, treating clients with schizophrenia or borderline personality disorder in homogeneous group settings is gaining in popularity (Hayes, Halford, & Varghese, 1995; Hyde & Goldman, 1992; Kanas, 1993; MacKenzie, 1986; Nehls, 1991; O'Neill & Stockell, 1991).

Given unanswered and conflicting information about contraindicators, what is a counselor to do? We believe the current best practice when screening for group counseling is to consider, but not slavishly apply, the contraindicators listed above. We cannot emphasize enough that counselors best serve clients through a case-by-case application of contraindicators.

Counselor Actions

Although the research on client contraindicators for group counseling is somewhat muddled, the research on counselor actions and group counseling casualties is crystal clear. Counselors' behaviors are a primary source of group counseling casualties

(Cooper, 1975; Hadley & Strupp, 1976; Kaplan, 1982). Hadley and Strupp (1976) discussed two sources of counselor behaviors that can lead to counseling casualties: training/skills deficits and counselor noxious personality traits.

1. *Training/skills issues*

   Deficits in the counselor's skill or knowledge can lead to client casualties. For example, counselors who are unaware of client contraindicators for group counseling will put clients in ill-advised therapeutic situations. Also, counselors may select to work with client populations or employ counseling techniques for which they have had little training. Too, counselors may have the proper skills but apply those skills rigidly regardless of the clinical situation (Crown, 1983). For example, a psychoanalytically oriented counselor may make an accurate transference interpretation to a client during a session. Despite skillful application of this technique, the intervention will fall flat if the client does not have the needed observing ego to use the insight contained in the interpretation. To speak metaphorically, when all that a counselor has in his or her professional toolbox is a hammer, the whole world becomes just a collection of nails. Builders of good counseling experiences possess and use a variety of tools in their work.

2. *Counselor personality issues*

   Hadley and Strupp (1976) detailed the following 12 personality traits that can generate counseling casualties:

   1. Coldness
   2. Obsessiveness
   3. Excessive need to make people change
   4. Excessive unconscious hostility
   5. Seductiveness
   6. Lack of interest or warmth (neglect)
   7. Pessimism
   8. Absence of genuineness
   9. Sadism
   10. Narcissism
   11. Greed
   12. Dearth of self-scrutiny

Combinations of these traits can lead to destructive behaviors by leaders. In their classic examination of group casualties in which they identified five group counseling leadership styles, Lieberman et al. (1973) found that one leadership style produced almost half of the casualties, including the most severe ones. They called this style *aggressive stimulator*. It is characterized by high stimulus input, intrusiveness, confrontation, challenging but demonstrating, and high positive caring (Cooper, 1975; Lieberman et al., 1973). According to Hartley et al. (1976), the critical causal factor of group counseling casualties relates to leadership characteristics.

How can group counselors prevent themselves from producing casualties? Taking a group counseling class is a start, because it helps counselors to build their skills. Roback (2000) emphasized that counselors who practice group work "need to be specifically trained to prevent or reduce nonconstructive confrontation and to identify patients being harmed by it" (p. 120). As for personality traits, access to quality supervision is the key to recognizing and remediating noxious personality traits.

Actually, quality supervision is so important that CACREP standards mandate 1 hour per week of individual supervision for all practicum and internship students. Also, both CACREP and CORE set strict faculty-to-student ratios (1:5) for practicum and internship supervision classes (CACREP, 2004; CORE, 2004).

UNANSWERED QUESTIONS ABOUT EFFECTIVENESS OF GROUP COUNSELING

The research on group counseling casualties has been directed exclusively to the COUN and the THRP types of group counseling interventions. To date, researchers have not addressed the issue of casualties produced by EDUC interventions. Quality research on classroom-level EDUC interventions suggested only that these interventions were ineffective but not harmful. Still, the relationship of harm to other EDUC interventions remains an open question. Specifically, do certain mixes of EDUC interventions and client characteristics produce counseling casualties? If so, what are the contraindicating signs that counselors can look for when screening clients for EDUC interventions?

Another open question concerns how best to compose a group—homogeneously or heterogeneously—with respect to client diagnosis. The traditional thought among group counseling researchers was that with certain diagnoses (e.g., borderline personality disorder and schizophrenia), homogeneous groups are contraindicated. This prohibition existed because of the fear that clients in a diagnostic homogeneous group would actually model and reinforce their pathology. As noted earlier, however, some researchers have had success in working with difficult mental health problems in homogeneous groups (e.g., Kanas, 1993).

Unfortunately, we do not have detailed answers concerning the interaction of *outcome* (effective, ineffective, or harmful), *group composition* (heterogeneous or homogeneous), *group modality* (TASK, EDUC, COUN, or THRP), and *theoretical orientation* (cognitive, behavioral, psychodynamic, or client-centered). Answers concerning these interactions could help professional counselors deliver more effective group counseling services.

Scheidlinger (1995) noted the lack of research on group counseling interventions with children and adolescents. With three exceptions (depression, career development, and sex abuse trauma), the research has reached no consensus about the efficacy of group counseling with any given child or adolescent population. Other researchers have commented on the mixed evidence supporting the efficacy of group counseling with youth (Abramowitz, 1976; Sugar, 1993). Sugar (1993) presented an extensive listing of research needs concerning group counseling with youth, including the differentiation of treatment from maturation effects, the impact of different demographic variables, the impact of working alliance, the identification of family factors, and outcome effects for open versus closed groups. Given the wide application of group methods to children and adolescents, this dearth of research must be remedied if counselors are going to argue for group interventions in a managed-care environment.

LEARNING ACTIVITIES

1. Put a specific group counseling intervention (e.g., behavioral group counseling for adolescent depression) "on trial." Students serving as the defense and prosecution teams will have to conduct research on this approach and present their cases. Classroom discussion prior to this activity can address issues such as: What constitutes admissible evidence (e.g., qualitative research)? Other students can play the roles of the court personnel. A professor with a strong research background can be invited into the class to play the role of judge.

2. Select a client population that you expect to encounter in your internship. Then go to the library and find three journal articles on the efficacy of group counseling with that client population. After reading the articles, answer the following questions:

   a. Is group counseling a useful treatment for this client population?
   b. Are interventions most effective when they are based upon a single theory (e.g., psychodynamic)?
   c. What contraindicators do counselors have to be alert for when considering a group counseling placement for clients from the population you specified?
   d. If time permits, share your findings with the rest of the class.

3. Interview a counselor who has led a number of groups. Ask this person the following questions:

   a. What things that you do in group counseling have you found to be the most helpful to clients?
   b. Can you think of some things you have done that may have slowed a client's progress in group counseling?
   c. Have you found any one counseling theory to be helpful in your group counseling work?
   d. If time permits, share your findings with the rest of the class.

4. The class is divided into three groups: qualitative researchers, quantitative researchers, and consultants. On large pieces of paper (3' by 3' minimum), the two research groups design a brief research proposal exploring the impact of

group counseling with a given client population (30 minutes). Each group of researchers will develop (a) a research question, (b) a measurement tool, and (c) a group counseling intervention. The consultants are to provide support for the groups, making sure that each group considers and represents the features of its assigned method. The groups then present their research proposals to each other, followed by a total class evaluation of the research proposals and a discussion of the specific and nonspecific counseling elements present in each study.

SUMMARY

As with nascent professionals in any field, group counselors are eager to apply their newly learned skills with clients to help heal pain and promote peak performance. The powerful tool of group counseling can, however, cause harm as well as good. Thus, it is critical to first define efficacy as the degree to which the desired project outcome is achieved. Assessing whether and how that outcome was achieved requires measurements, including both qualitative and quantitative research methods. Also covered is the influence on group counseling outcomes of both specific factors (i.e., theory-specific interventions) and nonspecific factors (i.e., pantheoretical interventions). Finally, we detailed the efficacy of group counseling with specific client populations, ranging from children to adults and including both neurosis and psychosis. We also covered the literature to date on interventions that have proven either ineffective or harmful, focusing on some of the ways and reasons why counseling can cause harm to the client and how to avoid that outcome through rigorous training and supervision.

The group counseling literature contains a rich panoply of strategies and techniques available for the asking. Our question to all our readers is: Will you bask in the light shed by research or instead curse in the darkness?

USEFUL WEB SITES

- □ American Psychological Association
  www.apa.org/ethics/code2002.html
- □ American School Counseling Association
  www.schoolcounselor.org/content.asp?contentid=210
  www.schoolcounselor.org/content.asp?contentid=240
- □ Association for Specialists in Group Work
  www.asgw.org/training_standards.htm
- □ Council for Accreditation of Counseling and Related Educational Programs
  www.counseling.org/cacrep/2001standards700.htm
- □ Council on Rehabilitation Education
  www.core-rehab.org/manual/manual.html

REFERENCES

Abramowitz, C. V. (1976). The effectiveness of group psychotherapy of children. *Archives of General Psychiatry, 33,* 320–326.

Abramowitz, C. V., Roback, H. B., Abramowitz, S. I., & Jackson, C. (1974). Differential effectiveness of directive and nondirective group therapies as a function of client internal–external control. *Journal of Consulting and Clinical Psychology, 42,* 849–853.

Achenbach, T. M., & McConaughy, S. H. (1997). *Empirically based assessment of child and adolescent psychopathology: Practical applications.* Thousand Oaks, CA: Sage.

Agras, W. S., Telch, C. F., Arnow, B., Eldredge, K., Detzer, M. J., Henderson, J., & Marnell, M. (1995). Does interpersonal therapy help patients with binge eating disorder who fail to respond to cognitive-behavioral therapy? *Journal of Consulting and Clinical Psychology, 63,* 356–360.

Alexander, P. C., Neimeyer, R. A., Follette, V. M., Moore, M. K., & Harter, S. (1989). A comparison of group treatments of women sexually abused as children. *Journal of Consulting and Clinical Psychology, 57,* 479–483.

American Psychological Association (APA). (2004). *Ethical principles of psychologists and code of conduct.* Retrieved August 1, 2004, from http://www.apa.org/ethics/code2002.html

American School Counselor Association (ASCA). (2004a). *The professional school counselor and group counseling.* Retrieved August 1, 2004, from http://www.schoolcounselor.org/content.asp?contentid=143

American School Counselor Association (ASCA). (2004b). *The role of the professional school counselor.* Retrieved August 1, 2004, from http://www.schoolcounselor.org/content.asp?contentid=240

Association for Specialists in Group Work (ASGW). (2004). *Professional standards for training of group work generalists and of group work specialists.* Retrieved August 1, 2004, from http://www.asgw.org/training_standards.htm

Baider, L., & De Nour, A. K. (1989). Group therapy with adolescent counselor patients. *Journal of Adolescent Health Care, 10,* 35–38.

Baker, S. B., & Popowicz, C. L. (1983). Meta-analysis as a strategy for evaluating effects of career education interventions. *Vocational Guidance Quarterly, 31,* 178–186.

Baker, S. B., Swisher, J. D., Nadenichek, P. E., & Popowicz, C. L. (1984). Measured effects of primary prevention strategies. *Personnel and Guidance Journal, 62,* 459–463.

Barker, R. L. (1995). *The social work dictionary.* Washington, DC: NASW Press.

Beeferman, D., & Orvaschel, H. (1994). Group psychotherapy for depressed adolescents: A critical review. *International Journal of Group Psychotherapy, 44,* 463–473.

Bergin, A. E. (1963). The effects of psychotherapy: Negative results revisited. *Journal of Counseling Psychology, 10,* 244–250.

Bergin, A. E. (1966). Some implications of psychotherapy research for therapeutic practice. *Journal of Abnormal Psychology, 71,* 235–246.

Bergin, A. E. (1971). The evaluation of therapeutic outcomes. In A. E. Bergin & S. L. Garfield (Eds.), *Handbook of psychotherapy and behavior change: An empirical analysis* (pp. 217–170). New York: Wiley.

Bergin, A. E. (1980). Negative effects revisited: A reply. *Professional Psychology, 11,* 93–100.

Bettenhausen, K. L. (1991). Five years of groups research: What we have learned and what needs to be addressed. *Journal of Management, 17,* 345–381.

Beutler, L. E., Jobe, A. M., & Elkins, D. (1974). Outcomes in group psychotherapy: Using persuasion therapy to increase treatment efficacy. *Journal of Consulting and Clinical Psychology, 42,* 547–553.

Borders, L. D., & Drury, S. M. (1992). Comprehensive school counseling programs: A review for policymakers and practitioners. *Journal of Counseling and Development, 70,* 487–501.

Bordin, E. S. (1994). Theory and research on the therapeutic working alliance: New directions. In A. O. Horvath & L. S. Greenberg (Eds.), *The working alliance* (pp. 13–37). New York: Wiley.

Borg, W. R., & Gall, M. D. (1989). *Educational research.* New York: Longman.

Brandes, N. S. (1977). Group therapy is not for every adolescent: Two case illustrations. *International Journal of Group Psychotherapy, 27,* 507–510.

Braswell, L. (1993). Cognitive-behavioral groups for children manifesting ADHD and other disruptive behavior disorders. *Special Services in the Schools, 8,* 91–117.

Brehm, J. W. (1966). *A theory of psychological reactance.* New York: Academic Press.

Brough, M. F. (1994). Alleviation of loneliness: Evaluation of an Adlerian-based group psychotherapy. *Individual Psychology, 50,* 40–51.

Brown, P. D., & O'Leary, K. D. (2000). Therapeutic alliance: Predicting continuance and success in group treatment for spouse abuse. *Journal of Consulting and Clinical Psychology, 68,* 340–345.

Budman, S. H., Demby, A., Feldstein, M., & Gold, M. (1984). The effects of time-limited group psychotherapy: A controlled study. *International Journal of Group Psychotherapy, 34,* 587–603.

Budman, S., Demby, A., & Randall, M. (1980). Short-term group psychotherapy: Who succeeds, who fails? *Group, 4,* 3–16.

Butler, T., & Fuhriman, A. (1983). Curative factors in group therapy: A review of recent literature. *Small Group Behavior, 14,* 131–142.

Cahill, C., Llewelyn, S. P., & Pearson, C. (1991). Treatment of sexual abuse which occurred in childhood: A review. *British Journal of Clinical Psychology, 30,* 1–12.

Cartledge, G., & Milburn, J. F. (1978). The case for teaching social skills in the classroom: A review. *Review of Educational Research, 48,* 133–156.

Cerbone, M. J. A., Mayo, J. A., Cuthbertson, B. A., & O'Connell, R. A. (1992). Group therapy as an adjunct to medication in the management of bipolar affective disorder. *Group, 16,* 174–187.

Christopher, F., Loeb, P., Zaretsky, H., & Jassani, A. (1988). A group psychotherapy intervention to promote the functional independence of older adults in a long term rehabilitation hospital: A preliminary study. *Physical and Occupational Therapy in Geriatrics, 6,* 51–61.

Clarke, G. N., Rohde, P., Lewinsohn, P. M., Hops, H., & Seeley, J. R. (1999). Cognitive–behavioral treatment of adolescent depression: Efficacy of acute group treatment and booster sessions. *Journal of the American Academy of Child and Adolescent Psychiatry 38,* 272–279.

Combs, A. W., Avila, D. L., & Purkey, W. W. (1978). *Helping relationships: Basic concepts for the helping professions.* Boston: Allyn & Bacon.

Committee for Children. (2004). *Second step: A violence prevention curriculum.* Seattle, WA: Author. Retrieved August 1, 2004, from http://www.cfchildren.org/ssf/ssf/ssindex/

Conyne, R. K., Harvill, R. L., Morganett, R. S., Morran, D. K., & Hulse-Killacky, D. (1990). Effective group leadership: Continuing the search for greater clarity and understanding. *Journal for Specialists in Group Work, 15,* 30–36.

Cooper, C. L. (1975). How psychologically dangerous are T-groups and encounter groups? *Human Relations, 28,* 249–260.

Couch, R. D., & Childers, J. H. (1987). Leadership strategies for instilling and maintaining hope in group counseling. *Journal for Specialists in Group Work, 12,* 138–143.

Council for the Accreditation of Counseling and Related Educational Programs (CACREP). (2004). *Accreditation standards and procedures manual.* Retrieved August 1, 2004, from http://www.cacrep.org/2001standards700.htm

Council on Rehabilitation Education (CORE). (2004). *Accreditation manual for rehabilitation counselor education programs.* Retrieved August 1, 2004, from http://www.core-rehab.org/manual/manual.html

Creswell, J. W. (2002). *Research design.* Newbury Park, CA: Sage.

Crown, S. (1983). Contraindications and dangers in psychotherapy. *British Journal of Psychiatry, 143,* 436–441.

Cummings, S. M. (2003). The efficacy of an integrated group treatment program for depressed assisted living residents. *Research on Social Work Practice, 13,* 608–622.

Davies, D. R. (1989). A multiple treatment approach to the group treatment of insomnia: A follow-up study. *Behavioural Psychotherapy, 17,* 323–331.

Davies, D. R. (1991). A comparison of hypnotic and non-hypnotic users in the group psychotherapy of insomnia. *Behavioural Psychotherapy, 19,* 193–204.

Davis, R., Olmstead, M. P., & Rockert, W. (1992). Brief group psychoeducation for bulimia nervosa: II. Prediction of clinical outcome. *International Journal of Eating Disorders, 11,* 205–211.

Dembo, M. H., Sweitzer, M., & Lauritzen, P. (1985). An evaluation of group parent education: Behavioral, PET, and Adlerian programs. *Review of Educational Research, 55,* 155–200.

Dhooper, S. S., Green, S. M., Huff, M. B., & Austin-Murphy, J. (1993). Efficacy of a group approach to reducing depression in nursing home elderly residents. *Journal of Gerontological Social Work, 20,* 87–100.

DeLucia-Waack, J. L. (1997). Measuring the effectiveness of group work: A review and analysis of process and outcomes measures. *Journal for Specialists in Group Work, 22,* 277–293.

Dutton, D. G. (1986). The outcome of court-mandated treatment for wife assault: A quasi-experimental evaluation. *Violence and Victims, 1,* 163–175.

Dykeman, C., Ingram, M., Wood, C., Charles, S., Chen, M., & Herr, E. L. (2001). *The taxonomy of career development interventions that occur in America's secondary schools.* Greensboro, NC: ERIC Digest. ERIC Clearinghouse on Counseling and Student Services. (ERIC Rep. No: EDO-CG-01-04)

Eayrs, C. B., Rowan, D., & Harvey, P. G. (1984). Behavioural group training for anxiety management. *Behavioural Psychotherapy, 12,* 117–129.

Evensen, E. P., & Bednar, R. L. (1978). Effects of specific cognitive and behavioral structure on early group behavior and atmosphere. *Journal of Counseling Psychology, 25,* 66–75.

Flowers, J. V. (1979). The differential outcome effects of simple advice, alternatives and instructions in group psychotherapy. *International Journal of Group Psychotherapy, 29,* 305–316.

Foa, E. B., Davidson, J. R. T., & Frances, A. (1999). Treatment of posttraumatic stress disorder. *Journal of Clinical Psychiatry, 60 (supplement 16),* 4–76.

Forester-Miller, H. (2002). Group counseling: Ethical considerations. In D. Capuzzi & D. R. Gross (Eds.), *Introduction to group counseling* (3rd ed., pp. 185–204). Denver: Love Publishing.

Forester-Miller, H., & Davis, T. E. (1996). *A practitioner's guide to ethical decision making.* Alexandria, VA: American Counseling Association.

Gazda, G. M. (1986). Discussion of "When to recommend group treatment: A review of the clinical and research literature." *International Journal of Group Psychotherapy, 36,* 202–206.

Gazda, G. M., Horne, A., & Ginter, E. (2000). *Group counseling and group psychotherapy.* Boston: Allyn & Bacon.

Gelso, C. J., & Carter, J. A. (1994). Components of the psychotherapy relationship: Their interaction and unfolding during treatment. *Journal of Counseling Psychology, 41,* 296–306.

Gerler, E. R. (1985). Elementary school counseling research and the classroom learning environment. *Elementary School Counseling and Guidance, 20,* 39–48.

Gerler, E. R., & Anderson, R. F. (1986). The effects of classroom guidance on children's success in school. *Journal of Counseling and Development, 65,* 78–81.

Gilewski, M. J. (1986). Group therapy with cognitively impaired older adults. *Clinical Gerontologist, 5,* 281–296.

Glatzer, H. T. (1978). The working alliance in analytic group psychotherapy. *International Journal of Group Psychotherapy, 28,* 147–161.

Gossette, R. L., & O'Brien, R. M. (1993). Efficacy of rational emotive therapy (RET) with children: A critical re-appraisal. *Journal of Behavioural Therapy and Experimental Psychiatry, 24,* 15–25.

Grant, J. R., & Cash, T. F. (1995). Cognitive-behavioral body image therapy: Comparative efficacy of group and modest-contact treatments. *Behavior Therapy, 26,* 69–84.

Grossman, D., Neckerman, H. J., Koepsell, T. D., Liu, P. Y., Asher, K. N., Beland, K., Frey, K., & Rivara, F. P. (1997). The effectiveness of a violence prevention curriculum among children in elementary school. *Journal of the American Medical Association, 277,* 1605–1611.

Guba, E. G., & Lincoln, Y. S. (1989). *Fourth generation evaluation.* Newbury Park, CA: Sage.

Gurman, A. S. (1971). Group marital therapy: Clinical and empirical implications for outcome research. *International Journal of Group Psychotherapy, 21,* 174–189.

Gusella, J., Butler, G., Nichols, L., & Bird, D. (2003). A brief questionnaire to assess readiness to change in adolescents with eating disorders: Its applications to group therapy. *European Eating Disorders Review, 11,* 58–72.

Gysbers, N. C., & Henderson, P. (2000). *Developing and managing your school guidance program.* Alexandria, VA: American Counseling Association.

Hadley, S. W., & Strupp, H. H. (1976). Contemporary views of negative effects in psychotherapy. *Archives of General Psychiatry, 33,* 1291–1302.

Harman, M. J. (1991). The use of group psychotherapy with cancer patients: A review of recent literature. *Journal for Specialists in Group Work, 16,* 56–61.

Hartley, D., Roback, H. B., & Abramowitz, S. I. (1976). Deterioration effects in encounter groups. *American Psychologist, 31,* 247–255.

Hayes, R. L., Halford, W. K., & Varghese, F. N. (1995). Generalization of the effects of activity therapy and social skills training on the social behavior of low functioning schizophrenia patients. *Occupational Therapy in Mental Health, 11,* 3–20.

Helms, J. (1990). Generalizing racial identity interaction theory to groups. In J. Helms (Ed.), *Black and White racial identity: Theory, research, and practice* (pp. 187–204). Westport, CT: Greenwood.

Herr, E. L., Cramer, S. H., & Niles, S. (2003). *Career guidance and counseling through the life span.* Boston: Allyn & Bacon.

Hiebert-Murphy, D., De Luca, R. V., & Runtz, M. (1992). Group treatment for sexually abused girls: Evaluating outcome. *Families in Society, 73,* 205–213.

Horvath, A. O. (2000). The therapeutic relationship: From transference to alliance. *Journal of Clinical Psychology, 56,* 163–173.

Horwitz, L. (1976). Indications and contraindications for group psychotherapy. *Bulletin of the Menninger Clinic, 40,* 505–507.

Hurlbert, D. F., White, L. C., Powell, R. D., & Apt, C. (1993). Orgasm consistency training in the treatment of women reporting hypoactive sexual desire: A comparison of women-only groups and couples-only groups. *Journal of Behavior Therapy and Experimental Psychiatry, 24,* 3–13.

Hyde, A. P., & Goldman, C. R. (1992). Use of multi-modal multiple family group in the comprehensive treatment and rehabilitation of people with schizophrenia. *Psychosocial Rehabilitation Journal, 15,* 77–86.

Joanning, H., Quinn, W., Thomas, F., & Mullen, R. (1992). Treating adolescent drug abuse: A comparison of family systems therapy, group therapy, and family drug education. *Journal of Marital and Family Therapy, 18,* 345–356.

Kanas, N. (1991). University of California, San Francisco: Group therapy research program. In L. E. Beutler & M. Crago (Eds.), *Psychotherapy research* (pp. 305–308). Washington, DC: American Psychological Association.

Kanas, N. (1993). Group psychotherapy with bipolar patients: A review and synthesis. *International Journal of Group Psychotherapy, 43,* 321–333.

Kaplan, R. E. (1982). The dynamics of injury in encounter groups: Power, splitting, and the mismanagement of resistance. *International Journal of Group Psychotherapy, 32,* 163–187.

Kim, B. S. K., Omizo, M. M., & D'Andrea, M. J. (1998). The effects of culturally consonant group counseling on the self-esteem and internal locus of control orientation among Native American adolescents. *Journal for Specialists in Group Work, 23,* 145–163.

Kneebone, I., & Martin, P. R. (1992). Partner involvement in the treatment of chronic headaches. *Behaviour Change, 9,* 201–215.

Krone, K. P., Himle, J. A., & Nesse, R. M. (1991). A standardized behavioral group treatment program for obsessive-compulsive disorder: Preliminary outcomes. *Behaviour Research and Therapy, 29,* 627–631.

Kupych-Woloshyn, N., MacFarlane, J. G., & Shapiro, C. M. (1993). A group approach for the management of insomnia. *Journal of Psychosomatic Research, 37* (Suppl. 1), 39–44.

Kurtz, L. F. (1997). *Self-help and support groups: A handbook for practitioners.* Thousand Oaks, CA: Sage.

Laconte, M. A., Shaw, D., & Dunn, I. (1993). The effects of a rational-emotive affective education program for high-risk middle school students. *Psychology in the Schools, 30,* 274–281.

Lambert, M. J., Shapiro, D. A., & Bergin, A. E. (1986). The effectiveness of psychotherapy. In S. L. Garfield & A. E. Bergin (Eds.), *Handbook of psychotherapy and behavior change* (pp. 157–212). New York: Wiley.

Lee, F., & Bednar, R. L. (1977). Effects of group structure and risk taking deposition on group behavior, attitudes, and atmosphere. *Journal of Counseling Psychology, 24,* 191–199.

Levey, J., McDermott, S., & Lee, C. (1989). Current issues in bulimia nervosa. *Australian Psychologist, 24,* 171–185.

Lewis, V. J., Blair, A. J., & Booth, D. A. (1992). Outcome of group therapy for body-image emotionality and weight-control self-efficacy. *Behavioural Psychotherapy, 20,* 155–165.

Lieberman, M. A., Yalom, I. D., & Miles, M. B. (1973). *Encounter groups: First facts.* New York: Basic Books.

Linehan, M. M., Heard, H. L., & Armstrong, H. E. (1993). Naturalistic follow-up of a behavioral treatment for chronically parasuicidal borderline patients. *Archives of General Psychiatry, 50,* 971–974.

Lubin, H., & Johnson, D. R. (2000). Interactive psychoeducational group therapy in the treatment of authority in combat-related posttraumatic stress disorder. *International Journal of Group Psychotherapy, 50,* 277–296.

Lubin, H., Loris, M., Burt, J., & Johnson, D. R. (1998). Efficacy of psychoeducational group therapy in reducing symptoms of posttraumatic stress disorder among multiply traumatized women. *American Journal of Psychiatry, 155,* 1172–1177.

MacKenzie, K. R. (1986). Commentary: "When to recommend group treatment." *International Journal of Group Psychotherapy, 36,* 207–210.

Magen, R. H., & Glajchen, M. (1999). Cancer support groups: Client outcome and context of group process. *Social Work Practice, 9,* 541–554.

Maples, M. (1988). Group development: Extending Tuckman's theory. *Journal for Specialists in Group Work, 13,* 17–23.

Martella, R., Nelson, J. R., & Marchand-Martella, N. (1999). *Research methods.* Boston: Allyn & Bacon.

McAuliffe, W. E. (1990). A randomized controlled trial of recovery training and self-help for opioid addicts in New England and Hong Kong. *Journal of Psychoactive Drugs, 22,* 197–209.

McCallum, M., & Piper, W. E. (1990). A controlled study of effectiveness and patient suitability for short-term group psychotherapy. *International Journal of Group Psychotherapy, 40,* 431–452.

McCrone, S. H. (1991). Resocialization group treatment with the confused institutionalized elderly. *Western Journal of Nursing Research, 13,* 30–45.

McFarlane, W. R., Link, B., Dushay, R., Marchal, J., & Crilly, J. (1995). Psychoeducational multiple family groups: Four-year relapse outcome in schizophrenia. *Family Process, 34,* 127–144.

McNamara, K. (1989). Group counseling for overweight and depressed college women: A comparative evaluation. *Journal for Specialists in Group Work, 14,* 211–218.

Meichenbaum, D. H., Gilmore, J. B., & Fedoravicius, A. (1971). Group insight versus group desensitization in treating speech anxiety. *Journal of Consulting and Clinical Psychology, 36,* 410–421.

Merta, R. J. (1995). Group work: Multicultural perspectives. In J. G. Ponterotto, J. M. Casas, L. Suzuki, & C. M. Alexander (Eds.), *Handbook of multicultural counseling* (pp. 567–585). Thousand Oaks, CA: Sage.

Mone, L. C. (1994). Managed care cost effectiveness: Fantasy or reality? *International Journal of Group Psychotherapy, 44,* 437–448.

Nehls, N. (1991). Borderline personality disorder and group therapy. *Archives of Psychiatric Nursing, 5,* 137–146.

Nezu, A. M. (1986). Efficacy of social problem-solving therapy approach for unipolar depression. *Journal of Consulting and Clinical Psychology, 54,* 196–202.

Omizo, M. M., Omizo, S. A., & Kitaoka, S. K. (1998). Guided affective and cognitive imagery to enhance self-esteem among Hawaiian children. *Journal of Multicultural Counseling and Development, 26,* 52–62.

O'Neill, M., & Stockell, G. (1991). Worthy of discussion: Collaborative group therapy. *Australian and New Zealand Journal of Family Therapy, 12,* 201–206.

Pattison, E. M., Rhodes, R. J., & Dudley, D. L. (1971). Response to group treatment in patients with severe chronic lung disease. *International Journal of Group Psychotherapy, 21,* 214–225.

Patton, M. Q. (1990). *Qualitative evaluation and research methods.* Newbury Park, CA: Sage.

Pedro-Carroll, J. L., Alpert-Gillis, L. J., & Cowen, E. L. (1992). An evaluation of the efficacy of a preventive intervention for 4th-6th grade urban children of divorce. *Journal of Primary Prevention, 13,* 115–130.

Pfeffer, C. R., Jiang, H., Kakuma, T., Hwang, J., & Metsch, M. (2002). Group intervention for children bereaved by the suicide of a relative. *Journal of the American Academy of Child & Adolescent Psychiatry, 41,* 505–513.

Polster, R. A., Dangel, R. F., & Rasp, R. (1987). Research in behavioral parent training in social work: A review. *Journal of Social Service Research, 10,* 37–51.

Powell, T. J. (1987). Anxiety management groups in clinical practice: A preliminary report. *Behavioural Psychotherapy, 15,* 181–187.

Reber, A. S. (1986). *Dictionary of psychology.* New York: Penguin Books.

Reeker, J., & Ensing, D. (1998). An evaluation of a group treatment for sexually abused young children. *Journal of Child Sexual Abuse, 7,* 65–85.

Rejeski, W. J., Brawley, L. R., Ambrosius, W. T., Brubaker, P. H., Focht, B. C., Foy, C. G., & Fox, L. D. (2003). Older adults with chronic disease: Benefits of group-mediated counseling in the promotion of physically active lifestyles. *Health Psychology, 22,* 414–423.

Reynolds, W. M., & Coats, K. I. (1986). A comparison of cognitive–behavioral therapy and relaxation training for the treatment of depression in adolescents. *Journal of Consulting and Clinical Psychology, 54,* 653–660.

Ribner, N. G. (1974). Effects of explicit group contract on self-disclosure and group cohesiveness. *Journal of Counseling Psychology, 21,* 116–120.

Roback, H. B. (2000). Adverse outcomes in group psychotherapy. *Journal of Psychotherapy Practice & Research, 9,* 113–122.

Rohde, P., Jorgensen, L., Seeley, J., & Mace, D. E. (2004). Pilot evaluation of the Coping Course: A cognitive-behavioral intervention to enhance coping skills in incarcerated youth. *Journal of the American Academy of Child & Adolescent Psychiatry, 43,* 669–677.

Rohde, R. I., & Stockton, R. (1994). Group structure: A review. *Journal of Group Psychotherapy, Psychodrama, and Sociometry, 46,* 151–158.

Rotter, J. B. (1966). Generalized expectancies for internal versus external locus of control reinforcement. *Psychological Monographs, 80* (1, Whole No. 609).

Scheidlinger, S. (1995). The small healing group—A historical overview. *Psychotherapy, 32,* 657–668.

Schreurs, K. M. G., Colland, V. T., Kuijer, R. G., de Ridder, D. T. D., & van Elderen, T. (2003). Development, content, and process evaluation of a short self-management intervention in patients with chronic diseases requiring self-care behaviours. *Patient Education & Counseling, 51,* 133–141.

Scott, M. J., & Stradling, S. G. (1991). The cognitive–behavioural approach with depressed clients. *British Journal of Social Work, 21,* 533–544.

Shaughnessy, P., & Kivlighan, D. M. (1995). Using group participants' perceptions of therapeutic factors to form client typologies. *Small Group Research, 26,* 250–268.

Shechtman, Z. (1994a). The effects of group psychotherapy on close same-gender friendships among boys and girls. *Sex Roles, 30,* 829–834.

Shechtman, Z. (1994b). Group counseling/psychotherapy as a school intervention to enhance close friendships in preadolescence. *International Journal of Group Psychotherapy, 44,* 377–391.

Silovsky, J. F., & Hembree-Kigin, T. L. (1994). Family and group treatment for sexually abused children: A review. *Journal of Child Sexual Abuse, 3,* 1–20.

Slavson, S. R. (1943). *An introduction to group therapy.* New York: Commonwealth Fund.

Slavson, S. R., & Schiffer, M. (1975). *Group psychotherapies for children.* New York: International Universities Press.

Smets, A. C., & Cebula, C. M. (1987). A group treatment program for adolescent sex offenders: Five steps toward resolution. *Child Abuse and Neglect, 11,* 247–254.

Stark, L. J., Bowen, A. M., Tyc, V. L., Evans, S., & Passero, M. A. (1990). A behavioral approach to increasing calorie consumption in children with cystic fibrosis. *Journal of Pediatric Psychology, 15,* 309–326.

Stark, L. J., Owens-Stively, J., Spirito, A., Lewis, A., & Guevremont, D. (1990). Group behavioral treatment of retentive encopresis. *Journal of Pediatric Psychology, 15,* 659–671.

Stockton, R. M., & Morran, D. K. (1982). Review and perspective of critical dimensions in therapeutic small group research. In G. Gazda (Ed.), *Basic approaches to group psychotherapy and group counseling* (pp. 37–83). Springfield, IL: Charles C Thomas.

Stockton, R., Morran, D. K., & Velboff, P. (1987). Leadership of therapeutic small groups. *Journal of Group Psychotherapy, Psychodrama, & Sociometry, 39,* 157–165.

Strein, W. (1988). Classroom-based elementary school affective education program: A critical review. *Psychology in the Schools, 25,* 288–296.

Stone, S., McKay, M. M., & Stoops, C. (1996). Evaluating multiple family groups to address the behavioral difficulties of urban children. *Small Group Research, 27,* 398–415.

Sugar, M. (1993). Research in child and adolescent group psychotherapy. *Journal of Child and Adolescent Group Therapy, 3,* 207–226.

Sullivan, K. R., & Mahalik, J. R. (2000). Increasing career self-efficacy for women: Evaluating a group intervention. *Journal of Counseling & Development, 78,* 54–62.

Sutton, C. (1992). Training parents to manage difficult children: A comparison of methods. *Behavioural Psychotherapy, 20,* 115–139.

Svensson, B., Hansson, L., & Nyman, K. (2000). Stability of outcome in comprehensive, cognitive therapy based treatment programme for long-term mentally ill patients. A 2-year follow-up study. *Journal of Mental Health, 9,* 51–61.

Thorngren, J. M., Christiansen, T. M., & Kleist, D. M. (1998). Multiple-family group treatment: The underexplored therapy. *Family Journal: Counseling and Therapy for Couples and Families, 6,* 125–131.

Todres, R., & Bunston, T. (1993). Parent education: A review of the literature. *Canadian Journal of Community Mental Health, 12,* 225–257.

Tolman, R. M., & Bennett, L. W. (1990). A review of quantitative research on men who batter. *Journal of Interpersonal Violence, 5,* 87–118.

Toseland, R. W., & Siporin, M. (1986). When to recommend group treatment: A review of the clinical and the research literature. *International Journal of Group Psychotherapy, 36,* 171–201.

Truax, C. B., Wargo, D. G., & Volksdorf, N. R. (1970). Antecedents to outcome in group counseling with institutionalized juvenile delinquents. *Journal of Abnormal Psychology, 76,* 235–242.

Tuckman, B. (1965). Developmental sequence in small groups. *Psychological Bulletin, 63,* 384–399.

Vandervoort, D. J., & Fuhriman, A. (1991). The efficacy of group therapy for depression. *Small Group Research, 22,* 320–338.

Whiston, S. C., & Sexton, T. L. (1998). A review of school counseling outcome research: Implications for practice. *Journal of Counseling and Development, 76,* 412–427.

Wiggins, J. D., & Wiggins, M. M. (1992). Elementary students' self-esteem and behavioral rating related to counselor time-task emphases. *School Counselor, 39,* 377–381.

Wilfley, D. E., Agras, W. S., Telch, C. F., Rossiter, E. M., Schneider, J. A., Cole, A. G., Sifford, L., & Raeburn, S. D. (1993). Group cognitive-behavioral therapy and group interpersonal therapy for the nonpurging bulimic: A controlled comparison. *Journal of Consulting and Clinical Psychology, 61,* 296–305.

Williams, C. B., Frame, M. W., & Green, M. (1999). Counseling groups for African American women: A focus on spirituality. *Journal for Specialists in Group Work, 24,* 260–273.

Winick, C., & Levene, A. (1992). Marathon therapy: Treating rape survivors in a therapeutic community. *Journal of Psychoactive Drugs, 24,* 49–56.

Yalom, I. (1985). *The theory and practice of group psychotherapy* (3rd ed.). New York: Basic Books.

Zimpfer, D. G. (1984). Patterns and trends in group work. *Journal for Specialists in Group Work, 9,* 204–208.

Zimpfer, D. G. (1990a). Groups for divorce/separation: A review. *Journal for Specialists in Group Work, 15,* 51–60.

Zimpfer, D. G. (1990b). Group work for bulimia: A review of outcomes. *Journal for Specialists in Group Work, 15,* 239–251.

Zimpfer, D. G. (1991). Groups and grief and survivorship after bereavement: A review. *Journal for Specialists in Group Work, 16,* 46–55.

Zimpfer, D. G., & Carr, J. J. (1989). Groups for midlife career change: A review. *Journal for Specialists in Group Work, 14,* 243–250.

Approaches to Evaluating Groups

Conrad Sieber

hy should group counselors evaluate their groups? Group counselors evaluate their groups to determine whether group goals and objectives, including those of individual participants, have been met. Group counselors need to know if their groups are effective at helping clients achieve their goals and how a group can be improved. It is also important to know if the group was implemented as planned because this affects its outcomes. Thus, evaluation helps group leaders determine the success of their groups. Certainly, success or effectiveness can have many definitions (e.g., skill development, symptom reduction, insight), but once group leaders define these goals there are ways to evaluate the degree to which they have been achieved.

Evaluation is an integral part of the learning, growth, and development process. Psychoeducational, counseling, and therapy groups are formed to promote learning and skill development or to alleviate distressing psychological symptoms. In *psychoeducational groups*, counselors want their clients to learn new skills. *Counseling groups* are designed to foster psychological (i.e., emotional, cognitive, behavioral) and/or social growth. In *therapy groups*, clients commit to an in-depth process of interpersonal contact to help them with serious problems of a personal or relational nature.

EVALUATION PURPOSES AND QUESTIONS

The use of formal evaluation procedures and measurement instruments helps group leaders to systematically organize, categorize, and then review information on group process and outcomes. This improves upon the reliance on the counselor's individual perceptions, which no matter how well developed are limited. As Dwivedi and Mymin (1993) point out, evaluation creates an educational process in which evaluation can improve a counselor's effectiveness by providing constructive and corrective feedback that supports good practice and minimizes poor work.

Groups are formed, led, and attended for a purpose. Group leaders and participants have explicit or implicit goals they want to achieve through group participation. Evaluation helps answer important questions about the extent to which the group meets these goals, as well as associated concerns related to the quality of the group process and the efficacy of various interventions. For instance, did the group help clients develop new skills, grow, or learn to cope better?

Group counselors also want to know if they are effective leaders. They want to know what it is about their methods that are, or are not, supporting the development of the group as an effective place for participants to learn and grow. Counselors can use this information to distinguish between the leadership methods that should be continued and those that should be changed. This information will help them decide whether they have developed the skills necessary to be an effective group leader and, if not, to identify specific skills they need to develop further.

Other relevant evaluation questions address participants' expectations of how groups work and their personal goals. Specific evaluation questions in this area include:

■ What are the participants' personal goals?
■ Are their goals realistic?
■ Do the participants' expectations of how the group works or the potential benefits of participation need to be adjusted to be more realistic?

Thus, participants' expectations, goals, and perceptions can be measured as part of the group evaluation process and used to enhance group and individual outcomes.

Additional questions that counselors often ask include:

■ What should be the duration of the group?
■ Which members benefit most from a specific group, and which seem to have the most difficulties—or even get worse?
■ Why did some group members drop out? Why did others stay? Can I improve retention of group members?

Resource questions also are relevant, especially to administrators and potential participants who want to know if a specific group is a cost-effective way to help people with their needs. An important question about resources is: Should I continue to do this kind of group, or is there a more effective way, given time and resources, to help my clients?

Important for evaluating the efficacy of a specific group are implementation questions such as the following:

■ Did I lead the group as it was planned?
■ Were there barriers that prevented implementation of key components?

■ How can I improve the implementation of key components the next time I lead this group?

The bottom line is that group counselors and participants have important questions that evaluation can answer in an ongoing process of implementation, evaluation, and improvement.

Another interesting thing about engaging in a planned evaluation is the fact that what we measure often leads to change. For instance, behaviorists have discovered that simply asking clients to self-monitor their behavior leads to changes in and of itself. Thus, evaluation, as a form of monitoring and measurement, helps group leaders and participants to focus specifically on what they want to change, whether this involves changing their thinking and behavior or developing new skills. It makes participants aware of those behaviors, thoughts, and feelings that need to be changed and the skills necessary to achieve their personal goals. It also gives participants a tangible way to track progress and to ask for help when they get stuck. For group leaders, evaluation can direct attention to the group process and facilitating a positive climate that fosters learning.

Meaningful evaluation is integrated into group planning and development. It is a systematic way of gathering feedback on group process and the achievement of group goals that can enhance a counselor's efficacy as a group leader. Thus, it is similar to the process we teach participants in group counseling: to learn to give and receive constructive feedback and to use this feedback to improve themselves. In the case of group leaders, the feedback is used to improve their leadership, the group process, and, in turn, group outcomes.

In sum, using evaluation helps to focus leaders and participants on developing effective group processes and working toward their individual and collective goals. Group counselors receive feedback they can use to improve their leadership skills. Engaging in evaluation prompts group leaders and participants to consider how they will define success and what evidence they will gather to measure whether they have achieved their goals. At termination, evaluation information can be used to make decisions about continuing a specific group, making changes to improve it, or deciding that some or all of the participants can best be served in some other way.

EVALUATION METHODS

The goals and objectives established for the group should lead to the outcomes the group is designed to achieve. For evaluation, these outcomes need to be measured in one of the two ways described next.

Quantitative and Qualitative Measures

Group evaluations often make use of both quantitative and qualitative methods (e.g., Balmer, Gikundi, Nasio, Kihuho, & Plummer, 1998). As implied by the term *quantitative*, these measures are designed to quantify the effect of the group experience.

For instance, rating scales can be used to measure the impact of the group on helping participants to decrease symptoms or to develop new skills. This may include quantifying the intensity and frequency of symptoms before, during, and after group participation. Many quantitative psychological tests with application to group counseling are available, including those that are standardized and have empirical evidence of reliability and validity.

Examples of quantitative measures include the following:

- Empirically derived objective tests (e.g., Beck Depression Inventory; MMPI)
- Rating scales to measure attitudes and/or behavior change
- Behavioral observation by a trained observer that uses a structured rating scale or scoring rubric to assess participant behaviors
- Archival data, such as grades and attendance records for school children, or results on previously administered tests from client files

Qualitative methods examine the quality, or subjective experience, of participants, which often is not easy to quantify. Qualitative procedures include asking participants to respond to open-ended questions in their own words, or having an observer take notes while observing the group process. Qualitative methods can be used to track group process, to identify themes raised by participants, and to note the reactions of participants to critical group events. Qualitative methods are often used to understand how participants are using the group and how they are affected by it.

These methods, which emphasize observation and description instead of objective measurement, are often helpful with newly developed groups. For these groups that are not fully defined, evaluation leads to more clearly defining the group structure, strategies, and interventions, as well as the characteristics of participants and their responses (Posavac & Carey, 1997).

Examples of qualitative measures include the following:

- Participant observation in which the group leader or an observer records observations of the group with the goal of accurately describing the group process, critical events, and participant characteristics
- Focus-group methods, utilizing a defined set of questions to interview participants about their group experience
- Open-ended survey questions in which participants write out answers in their own words

Formative and Summative Evaluation

Whenever a group is evaluated, it is important to clarify the purpose of the evaluation. *Formative evaluation* is done to gather ongoing feedback as the group evolves for the purpose of improving and refining the group to improve outcomes. The purpose of *summative evaluation* is to determine if a group has met its goals and should continue. These two primary purposes can lead to gathering different kinds of information or gathering information at different points in the group's life. Sometimes group evaluation is done for both formative and summative reasons.

STRATEGIES FOR EVALUATING GROUPS

The simple evaluation task of describing a group clearly during the planning phase helps leaders clarify the group's purpose and goals, as a basis for judging its success. Information on purpose and goals helps the leader define what will be evaluated. Once these are defined, group leaders can brainstorm the evaluation questions they want to have answered.

At the brainstorming stage, it is important not to worry about how relevant questions can be measured lest this concern limit the identification of important questions to which the leader wants answers. Questions whose answers would be meaningful and useful to the group leader, participants, and/or administrators then can be stated in a way that lends them to evaluation.

Group leaders should also consider methods of evaluating whether the group was implemented and conducted as planned. Many groups are planned to be led in one way, but as the process unfolds, they change. These changes can affect important group processes and, in turn, outcomes. When groups are no longer being delivered as planned, this information should become part of the group evaluation so results can be judged against the way in which the group was actually delivered, not by how it was supposed to be done. Information about implementation can serve as important feedback and prevent misconstruing results because certain group interventions were changed or even abandoned.

EVALUATION MEASURES

There are many variables to measure in the process of evaluating a group. These include measures of

- symptom reduction (e.g., Kruczek & Vitanza, 1999; Lubin, Loris, John, & Johnson, 1998; Morgan & Cummings, 1999; Peterson & Halstead, 1998);
- skill development and behavior change (e.g., McCleary & Ridley, 1999; Wiggins, Singh, Getz, & Hutchins, 1999);
- group process and therapeutic factors (e.g., Holmes & Kivlighan, 2000; Kaminer, Blitz, Burleson, Kadden, & Rounsaville, 1998; Kivlighan, Coleman, & Anderson, 2001; MacNair-Semands & Lese, 2000);
- leadership (e.g., DeLucia-Waack, 1997; Kivlighan & Tarrant, 2001);
- goal attainment (e.g., Macgowan, 2000); and
- client satisfaction (e.g., Mathis, Tanner, & Whinery, 1999).

Measures of Symptom Reduction

For groups designed to help clients with psychological symptoms, many empirically derived measures are available. For instance, in a cognitive therapy group for depressed clients, group counselors could periodically administer a measure of depression, such as the Beck Depression Inventory, to assess the efficacy of the group for reducing depression. The test could be administered prior to the group beginning to measure current levels of depression and then periodically throughout the group, including at termination. Group counselors expect that an effective group for depressed clients would, on the whole, decrease levels of depression over time, and by the end of the group, participants' depression should be measurably lower than at the group's beginning. Clearly, if most clients in a depression group complete the experience just as depressed, or more so, as when they began the group, something would need to be changed.

Other common psychological symptoms that can be measured include anxiety, stress, negative thoughts, and behaviors that contribute to psychological distress including alcohol and drug use.

Measures of Skill Development and Behavior Change

The purpose of psychoeducational groups and some counseling groups is to teach and support clients as they develop important skills and change their behavior. Tests can be developed that measure participants' perceptions of their own skill development and behavior change. Trained observers and group leaders can also use rating scales and observation protocols that evaluate the degree to which participants demonstrate skill development and behavior change.

For instance, in a group for at-risk adolescents, development of communication skills, including active listening, feedback, and conflict management skills, can be measured through student, peer, and/or observer ratings. Prior to the group's beginning, a baseline skill level could be measured for each participant, with follow-up measures to be completed at midgroup and termination. If primary communication skills are not developing by midgroup, the leaders would probably want to consider adjustments to improve the likelihood that the teens will meet the goal of improving their communication skills by the group's termination. If participants in this group show little appreciable improvement in communication skills at termination, the leaders and/or administrator of the program would want to consider significant changes and improvements in the group's methods, a change in the expressed goals of the group, or discontinuation in favor of a more effective method.

Measures of Group Process and Therapeutic Factors

Group counseling interventions are based on a host of assumptions about group process factors that contribute to change and well-being in the participants. Although individual counseling can focus on process, the process is an interpersonal one between a counselor and a client, essentially a dyad. By contrast, group counseling is a more complex interpersonal process involving several other clients and a leader who is attempting to facilitate the development of a working group.

The group research literature (e.g., Yalom, 1995) indicates that unless a constructive group process with significant key characteristics is achieved, the group is likely to be limited in its capacity to achieve its goals for participants. Among these characteristics are group norms that support the development of safety, trust, and belonging that are so important to group functioning. Also, group counselors work toward encouraging active participation by members and, as the group progresses, a greater and greater sense of responsibility on the participants' part for the group's functioning.

Individual counseling cannot offer opportunities for peer learning and observing others with similar concerns. As groups develop from beginning to working and, finally, termination phases, certain key therapeutic factors develop (e.g., see Yalom, 1995). These factors include universality—the understanding that one is not alone with his or her problems; the opportunity to help others; experiencing the social microcosm of the group; and receiving feedback on ways to improve oneself. Because group process development is essential to clients using the group to work on their concerns, finding ways to measure it is necessary.

Likewise, using evaluation to identify key therapeutic factors and to determine whether a group is able to create these factors for its clients is important. Group leaders who want to determine whether they are facilitating the positive development of their group can use measures created for this purpose through research. For instance, Kaminer, Blitz, Burleson, Kadden, and Rounsaville (1998) used the Group Sessions Rating Scale (GSRS), a group therapy process measure, to assess group treatment for teen substance abusers and found it to be effective in the measurement of treatment process.

Getter, Litt, Kadden, and Cooney (1992) also used the GSRS in evaluating two alcoholism after-care treatments, one of which consisted of interactional group therapy, while the other involved coping-skills training. Graduate students rated audiotapes of sessions according to the GSRS. The results showed that therapy groups emphasized interpersonal learning, exploration of feelings, and the here and now. The coping-skills training emphasized education and skill development. Exploring feelings and the here and now correlated negatively with the number of problem-free group members. Education and skills training were associated with fewer members reporting subsequent drinking-related problems. Thus, alcoholics early in their recovery seem to need more help with developing coping skills than with exploring their feelings and developing insight. Using the appropriate intervention at the right time influences treatment outcomes.

Regarding the assessment of therapeutic factors, MacNair-Semands and Lese (2000) studied 15 therapy and support groups in a university counseling center, using the Therapeutic Factors Inventory (TFI). They evaluated the shift in therapeutic factors in groups over time, and the relationship between therapeutic factors and interpersonal problems.

Holmes and Kivlighan (2000) examined the underlying structure of group participants' perceptions of group versus individual therapy process using the Group Counseling Helpful Impacts Scale (Kivlighan, Multon, & Brossart, 1996). Group members' perceptions of helpful factors were highest for Relationship–Climate and Other Versus Self-Focus when compared to individual counseling clients. This four-factor framework—Emotional Awareness–Insight, Relationship–Climate, Other Versus Self-Focus, and Problem Definition–Change—could serve to help group leaders direct their own group process evaluations.

Measures of Leadership

Obviously, a great deal of a group's success has to do with capable leadership. Therefore, identifying the key leadership factors that promote successful groups is important. DeLucia-Waack (1997) reviewed measures appropriate for evaluating group work, including evaluations of leadership behavior. Hamilton et al. (1993) enlisted skilled observers to use the Group Psychotherapy Rating Scale (GPRS) to evaluate the competence and techniques of group psychotherapists. Those authors noted the power of the observers' immediate constructive feedback to the group leaders, who highly valued this input.

Measures of Goal Attainment

Because clients join groups to achieve their goals, evaluating the efficacy of a group in helping clients succeed is just common sense. An intermediate step toward achieving a goal is to apply oneself to the task. In this context, Macgowan (2000) examined the psychometric properties of a measure of client engagement in group work and found the Groupwork Engagement Measure (GEM) to be a promising tool for group workers. Dwivedi and Mymin (1993), who evaluated groups for children and adolescents, advocate rigorous retrospective evaluation of group and individual goals by leaders, including global assessment scales, multidimensional scales, and self-report questionnaires.

Measures of Client Satisfaction

Evaluating client satisfaction is common in counseling and other service professions, and this can be done in several ways. For instance, Mathis, Tanner, and Whinery (1999) asked participants in a divorce-adjustment group to complete a self-report form, rating specific elements of the program. Their results exemplify typical conclusions that can be drawn from client-satisfaction surveys. For instance, they report that 84% of the clients indicated that the orientation helped, and the feature rated most helpful by 42% of the respondents was a parent education video, followed by a brief lecture on grief and adjustment (27%), a judge's comments about mediation and parent responsibilities (21%), and printed material about visitation and divorce (10%). In summary, more than a third of the clients reported that the orientation changed how they approached their case.

Fristad, Gavazi, and Soldano (1998) assessed client satisfaction by collecting 4-month follow-up data from families participating in a six-session group. They reported client satisfaction with the group.

These kinds of self-report, satisfaction surveys do have limitations and leave many unanswered questions. For instance, is satisfaction associated with skill development or symptom reduction? How high does "client satisfaction" have to be to demonstrate the success of a group? For that matter, are clients—who often come to counseling because they misperceive themselves or the world around them—the best judges of what's "good" for them?

When all is said and done, client satisfaction is relevant because, unless they feel some satisfaction by participating, clients are unlikely to continue to attend a group. On the other hand, evaluating client satisfaction alone probably says little about the qualities of leadership and the group factors that promote growth, skill development, and behavior change. Quality group evaluations do not rely solely on client-satisfaction surveys.

EVALUATING A PSYCHOEDUCATIONAL GROUP

The evaluation of a psychoeducational, transition-to-high-school group for at-risk eighth-graders is discussed in this section. Committing to evaluation in the group planning process contributes to the quality of any psychoeducational group, as it focuses the leader on the specific information to be shared and the skills the group is designed to develop. By raising the question of how the group will be evaluated, methods for monitoring implementation of key components and for assessing outcomes are identified. This creates a focus on whether the group is being led as planned and whether participants are progressing toward meeting group goals. Considering evaluation from the planning stages of a psychoeducational group also addresses the realities of cost, quality, and efficiency concerns. Even in nonprofit and school settings, counselors are being held accountable for the efficacy of their practice and its contribution to school/organizational goals, such as decreasing dropout rates and increasing academic performance.

Setting Goals Helps Focus the Evaluation

By clarifying group goals, counselors define outcomes that can be evaluated. Typical goals for adolescent groups, for example, include improving self-understanding, exploring personal identity, learning problem-solving skills, enhancing social skills, developing the ability to relate to authority figures, and learning coping skills to manage the emotional, physical, and behavioral changes inherent in maturation (Ohlsen, 1970). In addition, school administrators are usually concerned with school-related behaviors and how groups will help students improve their academic performance and reduce disruptive behaviors that interfere with the educational process.

Counselors who lead school-based groups must demonstrate the group's relevance to the youth served and its effectiveness in addressing school-related issues. Group counselors can collect information on their group's efficacy and share this information with the school staff as evidence that the group in question works.

Application: Evaluating a Psychoeducational Group for Students Transitioning to High School

To illustrate the evaluation of a psychoeducational group, the information presented so far is applied to a transition-to-high-school group for at-risk eighth-grade students. The group's purpose was to provide important information and referral resources for entering freshman, so they could (a) build skills for working cooperatively with peers, (b) increase their understanding of transition as a process, and (c) receive opportunities to learn coping skills while examining issues of importance to young teens. The students came from primarily Anglo and Latino backgrounds, and some were native Spanish speakers with limited English proficiency. Many of these students, as a result of poverty and/or ethnicity, felt marginalized by the larger community. The students were vulnerable to low self-expectations and often were viewed by others as having limited ability to learn and succeed in school.

During the spring of the eighth-grade year, the at-risk students were recruited from an after-school program for middle school youth. These students were provided with information on the goals and structure of this summer group, which met daily for 5 weeks. The parents also received letters, outlining the purpose and structure of the transition-to-high-school group and the expected benefits for their children. Students who successfully completed the pre-group orientation and whose parents signed a registration form were included in the group.

The group was led by two trainees who were supervised by a psychologist. The transition-to-high-school group was structured as a psychoeducational group with an emphasis on students' learning to work effectively in a culturally diverse peer group similar in demographics to the high school they were entering. A basic tenet of the group was active learning, including the assumption that group members learn from each other and that leaders can learn from students, especially about the ways in which students experience school and being teenagers in today's society. The students were encouraged to become active learners in a number of ways, including support for taking responsibility for the climate and interpersonal process created in the group. Thus, group leaders engaged students in establishing respectful group norms around participation, attendance, feedback, and conflict resolution.

Diversity within the group was addressed directly through learning activities focusing on cultural awareness and provided students the opportunity to talk directly with one another about their experiences of diversity. Unfortunately, this topic rarely, if ever, was addressed in the general education program, so this was often these students' first experience of talking directly and constructively about cultural diversity in a mixed group.

Information and skill-building opportunities through group exercises and information sharing focused on

- team building;
- becoming an active learner;
- learning in a culturally diverse environment;
- communication skills, including giving and receiving feedback;
- conflict resolution;
- understanding transition and change as a process;
- stress-management skills;
- orientation to the high school, key contact persons, student activity opportunities, and academic expectations;

- goal setting;
- exposure to role models from a wide array of careers and jobs based on student interest; and
- health concerns common to at-risk youth including sexuality, STDs, HIV, alcohol, drugs, and tobacco.

Although the coleaders regularly sought verbal feedback from students throughout the life of the group, the major evaluation was completed at the group's last meeting. The evaluation was designed to solicit detailed feedback from students on all educational components of the group, including group exercises and leader-directed information sharing and discussion. Other areas included in the group evaluation were perceptions of the group leaders' helpfulness, the degree to which students enjoyed the group, and whether students would recommend the group to friends. Open-ended questions solicited qualitative feedback, including the students' perceptions of what they had learned, barriers to their participation, and ways by which the leaders could improve the group. Thus, the evaluation solicited students' feedback on their satisfaction with the group and their perceptions of its usefulness in preparing them for high school.

Of course, this approach has limitations. Having yet to experience the transition to high school, the students' judgments about the group's usefulness were based on limited experience. On the other hand, schools far too often fail to take into account feedback from students regarding their educational experiences and teachers.

Several survey items were based on students rating their experiences on 4- or 5-point scales, with 1 being at the low end and 4 or 5 being the top end. For instance, 85% of students enjoyed group participation "most of the time" or "very much," 93% reported that the leaders were "helpful" or "very helpful," and 86% said they "probably would" or "definitely would" recommend this group to their friends.

Each group activity was rated on a 5-point scale, with 1 being "poor," 3 being "okay," and 5 being "excellent." After each item, space was provided for students' comments about the specific activity being evaluated. These responses often give context and depth to quantitative ratings. For instance, when asked what they had learned in the group, students made the following comments:

> "I learned that in high school the most important thing to do is to be yourself."
> "(I learned) to be a team [sic]."
> "That high school can be easy if you do the work."
> "That sexually transmitted diseases are really serious."
> "That you can make more friends if you can be more open-minded and to work together."
> "Not much, but it got rid of my fears."
> "I learned a lot and I think that what I liked the most was all the different topics we talked about."

In reviewing these comments, explicit group goals were stated in the students' own words. For instance, objectives of the transition group included the importance of being oneself, learning to work as part of a team, being open-minded and working together to make friends, that STDs are serious health issues, and alleviating fear about entering high school as a freshman.

Given the previous discussion of the importance of the group process and client engagement through participation, it is helpful to review responses to the question, "Was there anything that got in the way and interfered with your participating more in the group?" Several students responded "no." One student took responsibility for the fact that his absence interfered with his participation, and another student raised a concern about times when other group members were not paying attention. A Spanish-speaking student said, "Yes, because sometimes I was in groups without (Spanish-speaking students) and we had to speak English and I don't know English." Another Spanish speaker said, "Yes, I am very shy with people I don't know."

It was a positive sign that most students did not report major barriers to their participation, although the group leaders should discuss whether there were issues, at times, around students' paying attention. If so, this is something that can be planned for and addressed in future groups. Also, ongoing attention to facilitate the participation of Spanish-speaking students in this diverse group is important. Although one of the coleaders was bilingual, apparently the groupings for class exercises did not always take into account the language needs of these students.

Finally, groups that emphasize participation should address the "shyness" of some participants in group settings. Group leaders can facilitate these students' growth so they will become more active in group participation, which should help them with school in general.

Group leaders generally want to continue to develop their own skills and to improve the quality of their groups. Therefore, responses to the question, "How could the leaders make this group better?" were reviewed carefully. In reviewing qualitative data, attention should be given to individual responses while also tracking the feedback for important themes that summarize the students' input as a whole.

Students made the following suggestions for ways to improve the group:

"Have a more productive first week."
"Control it better."
"More planning would be good and more hands-on stuff."
"Have fun."
"Do more outside activities."
"Explaining more in Spanish and giving more examples" (suggested by a Spanish speaker).

This feedback prompted the group leaders and the supervisor to examine whether this feedback was idiosyncratic to a given student or more generally descriptive of issues that could be addressed in leading future groups. There seemed to be a kernel of truth to the comment regarding the productivity of the first week. Although some of this could be chalked up to a student's possibly not wanting to take the time to hear about group norms and ground rules or become involved with orientation, we also thought the leadership and implementation of activities was uneven as the new group leaders got to know their students and developed a feel for leading this group. Taking into account this feedback and drawing upon their experience of this group, the leaders most likely would plan more effectively in the future for the time the various activities would take and the elements of beginning a new group that require the most attention.

Regarding the "control it better" comment, we again felt there was some merit to this feedback. Given a diverse group composed of at-risk youth with broad interests and learning styles, the leaders faced challenges to their authority and some difficulty with behavioral issues from students who sometimes disrupted the group. Under any circumstances, these challenges would play out. Since this was the first time these leaders led this group, it was anticipated that they would be better prepared in the future to respond to challenges to their authority and to disruptive behavior.

The comment about "more planning" was viewed as similar to the feedback suggesting that the first week be more productive. In an activity-based youth group meeting 4 days per week, there are a multitude of activities and information that is being transmitted. We learned that at times the demands of this schedule can catch up to leaders, especially in the first year, when everything is being planned and implemented for the first time. It is expected that in the future leader time will be freed up by having a base set of activities and information so the leaders will not feel overextended or that they are pressing so hard to keep up with the pace of the group.

The comment "have fun" reminds us that students really want to enjoy the activities in which they participate. We believe that fun and learning can go hand in hand, and thus every effort was made to create an activity-based, interesting group incorporating experiences in which having fun and learning come together. This comment reminded us to continue to take the issue of "having fun" into consideration as we update and improve the group.

The comment about "more outside activities" raised another issue we attempted to balance—the amount of time during summer that is spent inside in a group room and taking the opportunity to hold activities outdoors, with some physical component to them. We did find variance in how much time the students wanted to spend outdoors.

Taken together, the reflections of the group leaders and supervisor and the student comments may be summarized as follows: In the first week, the group activities could have been planned and implemented better to address the needs of the group members more effectively. On the whole, once the group leaders apply this year's experience to improving the group, the students may be expected to find improvement in the implementation, pacing, and mix of activities, and the group leaders will feel less rushed now that they have done much of the preparation involved in leading this group. The group leaders expect to address disruptive behavior more quickly and to feel more confident in responding to challenges to their authority now that they have experience.

In a voluntary summer transition-to-high-school group, it is important to offer a variety of activities and experiences that seek to bring fun and learning together. It is important to recognize that students learn in different ways and, therefore, should be exposed to a variety of methods to facilitate their learning, including experiences that involve physical activity and an opportunity to be outdoors.

This discussion indicates the value of qualitative feedback and the ways in which it can stimulate group leaders to reflect on their perceptions of the group as they consider improvements in both their leadership skills and in the group itself.

From the discussion in this chapter about the broad range of evaluation methods and measures, it should be apparent that evaluation of the transition-to-high-school group had several limitations.

First, evaluation was not integrated into the initial planning process. Therefore, conscious decisions were not made at the outset as to how group goals would be measured and when they would be evaluated. Evaluation took place at the end of the group. It would have been helpful to gather evaluative feedback at various times so this information could be used to make adjustments to improve the likelihood of meeting group goals.

There were also limitations in the measures used. The evaluation surveys were leader-created, self-report rating scales with opportunities for qualitative feedback. No attempt was made to identify reliable and valid tests of the skills being taught or of emotions (such as anxiety) that might interfere with transitioning to high school.

As stated previously, surveys were administered at the end of the group. Thus, the leaders did not identify baseline skill levels, emotions, or attitudes toward the transition to high school using pre-group measures and comparing this to data collected after the group experience. The use of retrospective surveys (i.e., reflecting back on one's experience—in this case, in the transition-to-high-school group) has several limitations based on the idiosyncrasies of an individual's perceptions of the past. Although a primary goal of this group was to facilitate the development of a group process promoting active learning, the evaluation did not include a direct assessment of the group process and the success of the group becoming a "working-stage group."

Finally, responses of the student participants were not compared to results from a similar group of students who did not benefit from this group experience. Comparison groups are important because they help control for the effect of factors other than group participation on the results. Improvements in the evaluation of the transition-to-high-school group for the future would include further clarifying the skills to be learned and seeking reliable and valid measures of these skills. This would hold true also for measuring anticipatory anxiety about entering high school and using some direct assessment of the group process.

Administering measures at key points in the group, including the use of pre-group and post-group skill measures, and early-, mid-, and late-group process assessments, would improve the quality of information gathered. It would make some data accessible in time for leaders to make adjustments in the group as it progressed.

EVALUATING A SUPERVISION AND TRAINING GROUP: AN APPLICATION

The following description of a group evaluation is based on the development and leadership of a supervision and training group for counseling, psychology, social work, and psychiatry trainees in a university counseling center. Although this was not a counseling or therapy group per se, principles of counseling group leadership were used intentionally to enhance this supervision group. Evaluation of this training group took place at the time the group terminated, with an emphasis on assessing group climate, process, leadership, and the skill development of trainees.

Planning a Supervision Group

This training group was developed out of the concern that most supervision groups do not attend to elements of group process and peer learning in a systematic way. Also, supervisors who lead these groups often find themselves in the role of expert and teacher engaging in didactic instruction instead of creating a dynamic learning environment that promotes peer learning. Case presentations in these groups are often unhelpful to students because they focus too much on the student's client instead of the interaction between the client and trainee. Too often, this leads to debating diagnoses and each student sharing their pet, often contradictory, case theories while the presenters find themselves in the position of having to respond to an overwhelming amount of feedback and unsolicited advice.

The group leaders' primary goal was to develop a positive learning environment within which students felt enough trust to be open about their cases and were willing to share their strengths and weaknesses, while also learning from their peers. The leaders wanted to develop a supervision group within which students felt empowered to pursue their development as counselors and therapists in training.

To develop a plan for group process evaluation, it is important to clarify the key elements of the group that affect its processes and their intended effects. The following methods were used to create a constructive group process.

1. The leaders attended to group process with the goal of creating a safe, supportive environment within which students could be constructively challenged to grow as counselors and therapists.
2. The leaders directly addressed the evaluative nature of supervision to help trainees decrease their anxiety about this issue.
3. Each group meeting had a clear beginning, middle, and end, with opportunities for check-in and check-out time for each participant.
4. The group leaders encouraged a high degree of interaction between the trainees and a sense of participant responsibility for development and maintenance of the group. For instance, at the beginning of the group, leaders involved trainees in a discussion of group goals and asked them to agree upon norms for their interactions with one another.
5. After each supervision group meeting, the coleaders met and discussed the group's dynamics and their interactions as coleaders.
6. The leaders facilitated and highlighted opportunities for peer learning.
7. The supervisors demonstrated the attitude that we can all learn from one another's experience. For instance, supervisors shared their work as therapists through videos and discussion of client sessions. Students were given the opportunity to provide feedback to the leaders on these case presentations.

8. Empowerment and shared responsibility for the group was facilitated by providing trainees with opportunities for group leadership through the structuring of group activities such as case presentations, and group time for trainees to share information with one another about their areas of interest and expertise.

The leaders purposefully used principles of time-limited therapy groups. For instance, they provided a focus or theme for each term. The fall term addressed group formation and trainee case presentations in which client conceptualization and treatment planning was discussed.

During winter term, trainees were taught the Interpersonal Process Recall (IPR) method (Griffith & Frieden, 2000; Kagan & Kagan, 1997), which was used to structure case presentations. The IPR process helped students examine the interpersonal process that occurs in counseling and therapy by gaining greater awareness of their communication style, thoughts, and feelings in relationship to their clients. The IPR method, which was used to review video of client sessions, also helped trainees to gain perspective on their own and their client's expectations of one another, unstated agendas, and differing perceptions. During spring term, family genograms were used as a method for participants to explore separation and loss issues as applied to client termination.

Evaluating the Supervision Group

At the last group meeting, participants completed a leader-developed survey to evaluate the group process and its outcomes. Trainees used a 5-point scale, with 1 being "very poor," 3 being "acceptable," and 5 being "excellent," to rate the level of safety, trust, and cohesion in the group and opportunities for group participation (i.e., to express thoughts, ideas, reactions, and feelings openly and honestly). The leaders wanted to assess how effective the group had been in facilitating the development of these key characteristics.

On average, participants gave a 4.6 rating to the items addressing group climate and their engagement in the group. The leaders solicited further information on group climate with an item that asked trainees to rate the degree to which they were treated with sensitivity and respect during case presentations, sharing their family genograms, and providing information about their specific areas of expertise. This was done because an explicit group goal was to improve the experience of group presenters especially during case presentations. On a 5-point scale with 5 being the best possible rating, trainees on average rated this group characteristic 4.7.

In most counseling and therapy groups, feedback is an important tool for learning, and group leaders make every effort to teach participants to give and receive constructive feedback. This was important to the leaders of this group, especially because they had participated in and led supervision groups in which feedback to trainees was often experienced negatively by participants. Thus, participants were asked to rate the degree to which feedback from peers was associated mostly with their behaviors or more with personal criticism. Responses to this survey item revealed that trainees received feedback focused more on their behaviors and actions and little personal criticism.

In a similar vein, the participants were asked to rate the balance between advice-giving and inquiry that facilitated understanding during case presentations. The trainees, on average, indicated that they received mostly questions and understanding from others and little advice-giving. Participants were also positive about the helpfulness of group opportunities for interacting with peers and for receiving peer feedback. On average, they rated this area 4.5.

The evaluation survey also solicited information on specific training components of this supervision group. Participants used a 5-point scale, with 1 being "very unhelpful," 3 being "neutral," and 5 being "very helpful," to rate the helpfulness of using the IPR for case presentations. The trainees, on average, gave a 4.1 rating. Using the same scale to evaluate the helpfulness of using family genograms to examine termination issues, participants, on average, rated this activity 4.5.

This training group had additional unique elements that the leaders wanted to better understand. On a 5-point scale, with 1 being "very negative," 3 being "acceptable," and 5 being "very positive," trainees gave high marks (4.7) to the interdisciplinary nature of the group. The group's lowest rating was reserved for the question: "Was enough attention given to the fact the group had individuals at different developmental levels as therapists?" On a 5-point scale, with 1 meaning "absolutely not," 3 meaning "acceptable," and 5 meaning "absolutely," the trainees gave an average response of 3.2.

Finally, group leaders were interested in getting feedback from group participants on the efficacy of their leadership. The participants gave the leaders high marks for their capacity to work together and lead the group. Using a 5-point scale, with 1 meaning "very poor," 3 meaning "acceptable," and 5 meaning "excellent," participants gave the coleaders an average score of 4.7.

The survey included some open-ended questions to gather qualitative feedback. As discussed, these questions provide the opportunity for more in-depth exploration of participants' experiences and perceptions. In response to the question, "What did you find most helpful about the supervision group?" students gave the following responses:

- Check-in, IPR, case presentations, informal talk, genograms
- Safe place to check in each week, good feedback for case presentations
- Different viewpoints, questions/comments generally helpful, I really liked IPR
- Peer support, different disciplines involved and the individuals involved
- Varied feedback from peers and leaders
- Input from group members and supervisors
- Openness and safety for people to share opinions and varied orientations
- Presenting cases and getting feedback

In response to the question, "What did you find least helpful about the supervision group?" members responded:

- I liked it all; in fact, it was the best part of practicum for me.
- Although IPR was helpful, perhaps a little less time could be spent on it.

- Would have liked more case presentations; video equipment problems.
- Winter term was disappointing.
- Nothing really.
- Variety of levels of experiences—I felt on one hand this was good, but mainly I was on the end of more experience than others.

Finally, in response to a request for other comments, the participants provided the following:

- Use family genograms at beginning of year, focusing on attachment styles to help cohesion of group.
- Check-in sometimes took time away from content but it was good for bonding. It's a hard trade-off, but I think I would advocate a limit on check-in time.
- [The coleaders] work together very well as a team. Complementary duo. Spontaneous, yet respectful. Group supervision felt safe.
- A very important part of my supervision at [this university]. Thank you very much for both of your efforts.
- You two have great energy together. I liked having a male and female combination in the leadership. The humor in the group made it fun. Keep up the good work.

This evaluation helped the leaders determine whether their goals for the group and individual participants had been met. It included identifying areas of strength in the group process, leadership, and content, while also examining survey data for information on problem areas that could be improved in future training groups. Participants rated the group climate highly on the dimensions of safety, trust, and cohesion.

Members also saw plenty of opportunities for participation and engagement. Generally, the themes addressed during each term, including use of the IPR method, were evaluated positively. The coleaders' complementary leadership styles were appreciated, as was their attention to group process and development.

One area that emerged as potentially problematic, at least for some, was the leaders' capacity to respond to the wide variation in the trainees' counseling experience. Planning for future supervision groups should take this feedback into account. Trainees clearly liked the multidisciplinary nature of the group, rating this attribute 4.7 out of 5. They also appreciated efforts to encourage the giving of feedback in a constructive manner. Thus, participants thought feedback focused mostly on actions/behaviors—something that can be changed or improved—versus criticism of the individuals themselves. The participants also reported that their peers did a good job of facilitating the examination of cases through inquiry-focused questions and rarely engaged in advice-giving. As a primary group goal, these principles were emphasized by the group leaders and embedded in the IPR process.

Responses to open-ended questions helped the leaders gain greater understanding for the quantitative ratings the members gave the group. A more experienced group member, while appreciating the diversity of experience among trainees, noted that at times the material was not challenging enough. This issue should be considered in planning future training groups. The participants also commented on training components used in the group (e.g., the IPR method, family genograms, and case presentations), as well as the leaders' efforts to facilitate cohesion, safety, and trust (e.g., check-in, check-out, guidance on giving feedback), and to provide quality leadership. In general, these comments were congruent with the high ratings given to the group as a whole. The evaluation supports the leaders' subjective impression that they had created a valuable supervision group worthy of continuation with some minor fine-tuning.

NEXT STEPS: PLANNING A MORE THOROUGH EVALUATION

As leaders of new groups often find, planning, recruiting members, and delivering a group take a lot of time and energy. In this process, evaluation may not come to mind until near the end of the group. This is what occurred in the applications discussed in this chapter. However, as group leaders gain experience and become more familiar with evaluation methods and instruments, they often refine their assessments to be more inclusive and integrated throughout the life of the group. An improved evaluation of this training group is discussed here with evaluation integrated into the planning, delivery, and review stages.

The group evaluation planning sheet in Figure 6.1 is used to plan for an improved assessment of the counseling training group.

1. The primary purpose of this group is to provide counseling and psychotherapy supervision and training to a multidisciplinary group of trainees. Group goals were to:

   a. Facilitate and capitalize on the group process to create a climate of safety, trust, and engagement that would foster active learning.
   b. Use interventions appropriate to the group's stage of development.
   c. Demystify the expertness of the group leaders by sharing the supervisors' ongoing learning process as therapists through participation in case discussions. Leaders role-model risk taking, giving and receiving feedback, and being active learners.
   d. Share leaders' power within the group by stepping outside the expert role and opening themselves to evaluative feedback.
   e. Support participant engagement, risk taking, and the giving and receiving of feedback and support.
   f. Use the Interpersonal Process Recall (IPR) method for case presentations to focus participants on eliciting and processing information from case presenters instead of advice-giving.

2. The target population consists of social work, psychology, and psychiatry trainees completing masters, doctoral, and medical degrees.

Group Evaluation Planning Sheet

1. Clearly define the group's goals and objectives.

2. Clearly define the client population(s) the group is designed for.

   a. Why is the group being provided to these populations?
   b. How will members benefit from participation?

3. Clearly define the group process, model, and/or psychoeducational techniques to be used.

4. List questions about:

   a. group process, techniques, and psychoeducational strategies
   b. efficacy of implementation
   c. group goals
   d. expected client benefits and outcomes
   e. leadership
   f. retention and early termination/dropouts

5. Given answers to numbers 1–4, what are the specific processes and outcomes that will be evaluated?

6. At what point(s) in the group's life, including the definitive, personal involvement, group involvement, and enhancement stages, will processes and outcomes be measured? (i.e., List below evaluation methods planned for use during each stage of the group's development.)

   a. Definitive
   b. Personal Involvement
   c. Group Involvement
   d. Enhancement and Closure

Figure 6.1   Group Evaluation Planning Sheet

3. Questions about group process:

   a. Were group leaders able to create a group environment characterized by safety, trust, and cohesion?
   b. Did group counseling techniques contribute to the positive evolution of this group so it successfully entered the stage of group involvement?
   c. Did using specific interventions, such as IPR, contribute to the development of a positive learning environment?

      d. Which leader interventions contributed most to development of this group?

4. Questions about outcomes:

      a. Did participants' anxiety decrease from the beginning to the end of the group?

      b. Did participants believe the group helped them to engage in meaningful learning about becoming a counselor or therapist?

      c. Was the group leadership team effective in meeting the group goals?

      d. What were the most valued outcomes by participants and the leaders?

      e. How could the group be improved?

5. Specific processes and outcomes to evaluate:

      a. What expectations do participants have, how accurate are they, and how can they be better aligned with the group process and goals?

      b. How does group cohesion and group development facilitate or interfere with the learning environment and the learning process?

      c. Did the group process evolve to a mature working group, or did it stall at any point? Why or why not?

      d. How effective were the group leaders in facilitating the process goals identified above?

      e. Were the following trainee "symptoms" decreased: anxiety about evaluative nature of supervision process, anxiety and avoidance of sharing perceived "mistakes" made with clients, discomfort with the more social/public nature of group supervision, fear of having one's evolving competence repudiated by the group resulting in shame and humiliation?

      f. Was the group effective in shifting attention away from being evaluated (passive) to engaging in learning (active)?

6. When should evaluations occur?

      a. Pre-group evaluations

         (1) Survey member expectations for the training group, including their assumptions about participant and leader roles.

         (2) Symptoms: Measure the degree of participant anxiety and the focus of anxiety (e.g., being shamed in group, being evaluated negatively by leaders).

         (3) Identify individual participant goals for the training group.

      b. Definitive

         (1) Assess member and leader perceptions of group process at the early phase of group development.

         (2) Assess member perceptions of effective and ineffective leader interventions.

         (3) Assess member engagement in group work.

    c. Group involvement:

        (1) Repeat group process, leader, and participant engagement measures.

        (2) Repeat from pre-group: member goal assessment, symptom/anxiety measures.

    d. Enhancement and closure phase:

        (1) Repeat all measures.

    e. Post-group review:

        (1) Analyze data to answer evaluation questions and to improve future groups.

7. Measures:

    a. Survey of participant goals: Leader-developed survey.

    b. Survey of members' expectations of the group: Leader-developed survey.

    c. Survey of anxiety symptoms: State Trait Anxiety Inventory.

    d. Group process measure that leaders and participants complete: Categories of Good Moments and Elliot's Taxonomy of Helpful Impacts (e.g., see Kivlighan, Multon, & Brossart, 1996).

    e. Survey of member engagement: Group Work Engagement Measure (e.g., see MacGowan, 2000).

LEARNING ACTIVITIES

1. Use the group evaluation planning sheet to plan an evaluation of a group in which the students have participated, helped lead, or would like to develop.
2. In small groups, brainstorm group evaluation questions for a group that the instructor has described to the students.
3. In small groups, discuss methods of measuring evaluation questions students have developed, either from the activity described above or as a result of a class discussion led by the instructor.
4. In small groups, discuss the difference between information gathered from a group leader's ordinary observation of their group and information collected through a planned evaluation.

SUMMARY

Evaluating group work can contribute to improving both the quality and efficiency of these interventions. Two kinds of measurement are used in evaluation: quantitative and qualitative. The literature on group research and evaluation provides models for planning group evaluations. Ideally, evaluation is taken into consideration at the planning stage of the group when leaders consider their questions about group process and outcomes. There are two kinds of evaluation. Formative evaluation provides information that can be used to improve a group. Summative evaluation is used to make decisions about whether a group should be continued.

The literature shows that evaluation of group work has focused on several domains, including symptom reduction, skill development, behavior change, group process and therapeutic factors, leadership, goal attainment, and client satisfaction. A group evaluation planning sheet such as the one in Figure 6.1 can help leaders plan for quality evaluations. This evaluation tool was used to demonstrate the process of improving the evaluation plan for the training group case study. Although leaders may feel too busy with other group planning tasks, developing an evaluation prior to beginning a group is the best way to get useful information.

REFERENCES

Balmer, D. H., Gikundi, E., Nasio, J., Kihuho, F., & Plummer, F. A. (1998). A clinical trial of group counseling for changing high-risk sexual behaviour in men. *Counselling Psychology Quarterly, 11,* 33–43.

DeLucia-Waack, J. L. (1997). Measuring the effectiveness of group work: A review and analysis of process and outcome measures. *Journal for Specialists in Group Work, 22,* 277–293.

Dwivedi, K. N., & Mymin, D. (1993). Evaluation. In K. N. Dwivedi (Ed.), *Group work with children and adolescents: A handbook* (pp. 46–58). London: Kingsley Publishers.

Franko, D. L. (1998). Ready or not? Stages of change as predictors of brief group therapy outcome in bulimia nervosa. *Group, 21,* 39–45.

Fristad, M. A., Gavazi, S. M., & Soldano, K. W. (1998). *Contemporary Family Therapy, 20,* 385–402.

Getter, H., Litt, M. D., Kadden, R. M., & Cooney, N. L. (1992). Measuring treatment process in coping skills and interactional group therapies for alcoholism. *International Journal of Group Psychotherapy, 42*(3), 419–430.

Griffith, B. A., & Frieden, G. (2000). Facilitating reflective thinking in counselor education. *Counseling Education and Supervision, 40*(2), 82–93.

Hamilton, J. D., Courville, T. J., Richman, B., Hanson, P., Swanson, C., & Stafford, J. (1993). Quality assessment and improvement in group psychotherapy. *American Journal of Psychiatry, 150,* 316–320.

Holmes, S. E., & Kivlighan, D. M. (2000). Comparison of therapeutic factors in group and individual treatment processes. *Journal of Counseling Psychology, 47*(4), 478–484.

Kagan, H., & Kagan, N. I. (1997). Interpersonal process recall: Influencing human interaction. In E. E. Watkins, Jr. (Ed.), *Handbook of psychotherapy supervision* (pp. 296–309). New York: John Wiley & Sons.

Kaminer, Y., Blitz, C., Burleson, J. A., Kadden, R. M., & Rounsaville, B. J. (1998). Measuring treatment process in cognitive-behavioral and interactional group therapies for adolescent substance abusers. *Journal of Nervous and Mental Disease, 186,* 407–413.

Kivlighan, D. M., Coleman, M. N., & Anderson, D. C. (2001). Process, outcome, and methodology in group counseling research. In S. D. Brown & R. W. Lent (Eds.), *Handbook of counseling psychology* (3rd ed., pp. 767–796). New York: John Wiley & Sons.

Kivlighan, D. M., Jr., Multon, K. D., & Brossart, D. F. (1996). Helpful impacts in group counseling: Development of a multidimensional rating system. *Journal of Counseling Psychology, 43,* 347–355.

Kivlighan, D. M., & Tarrant, J. M. (2001). Does group climate mediate the group leadership–group member outcome relationship: A test of Yalom's hypotheses about leadership priorities. *Group Dynamics, 5*(3), 220–234.

Kruczek, T., & Vitanza, S. (1999). Treatment effects with an adolescent abuse survivor's group. *Child Abuse & Neglect, 23*, 477–485.

Lubin, H., Loris, M., John, B., & Johnson, D. R. (1998). Efficacy of psychoeducational group therapy in reducing symptoms of posttraumatic stress disorder among multiply traumatized women. *American Journal of Psychiatry, 155*, 1172–1177.

Macgowan, M. J. (2000). Evaluation of a measure of engagement for group work. *Research on Social Work Practice, 10*, 348–361.

MacNair-Semands, R. R., & Lese, K. P. (2000). Interpersonal problems and the perception of therapeutic factors in group therapy. *Small Group Research, 31*, 158–174.

Mathis, R. D., Tanner, Z., & Whinery, F. (1999). Evaluation of participant reactions to premediation group orientation. *Mediation Quarterly, 17*, 153–159.

McCleary, L., & Ridley, T. (1999). Parenting adolescents with ADHD: Evaluation of a psychoeducation group. *Patient Education and Counseling, 38*, 3–10.

Morgan, T., & Cummings, A. L. (1999). Change experienced during group therapy by female survivors of childhood sexual abuse. *Journal of Consulting and Clinical Psychology, 67*, 28–36.

Ohlsen, M. M. (1970). *Group counseling.* New York: Holt, Rinehart and Winston.

Peterson, A. L., & Halstead, T. S. (1998). Group cognitive behavior therapy for depression in a community setting: A clinical replication series. *Behavior Therapy, 29*, 3–18.

Posavac, E. J., & Carey, R. G. (1997). *Program evaluation: Methods and case studies* (5th ed.). Upper Saddle River, NJ: Prentice-Hall.

Wiggins, D. J., Singh, K., Getz, H. G., & Hutchins, D. E. (1999). Effects of brief group intervention for adults with attention deficit/hyperactivity disorder. *Journal of Mental Health Counseling, 21*, 82–92.

Yalom, I. D. (1995). *The theory and practice of group psychotherapy* (4th ed.). New York: Basic Books.

Group Work: Ethical/Legal Considerations

Barbara Richter Herlihy and Lea Flowers

thical values are integral to the practice of group work, and the behaviors of group workers almost always have ethical implications (Association for Specialists in Group Work, 1998a). In this chapter we will explain the ethical responsibilities of group workers and the legal issues that have to be considered when conducting groups.

Group counselors are responsible for protecting the welfare of each individual group member and also for ensuring that the group as a whole functions in a way that benefits everyone involved. All of the major ethical issues that pertain to individual counseling apply to group work as well, and these issues can be more complex in group work because of the significant differences between the two modalities. In addition, ethical issues unique to group work, such as the screening of potential group participants and outside-of-group socializing among members, need to be addressed.

Several features of group work distinguish it from individual counseling:

1. Group members disclose personal information to the counselor and also to other group participants. This changes the nature of confidentiality and affects how the counselor deals with privacy issues.
2. The dynamics of therapeutic change are different in group counseling. In individual counseling the mechanism that fosters growth and change is the relationship between the counselor and client, along with the interventions utilized. By contrast, the effectiveness of

group work results as much from interactions among the members, including feedback and mutual support, as it does from the interventions of the group leader (Welfel, 2002). Thus, the leader must screen and select participants who are compatible and can assist each other in meeting their goals.

3. Counselors have less control over events that occur during and between group sessions than they have in individual counseling situations (Remley & Herlihy, 2005; Welfel, 2002). Group members can respond to each other in some unpredictable ways that the group leader may not be able to anticipate. In addition, if some members of the group interact with each other between sessions, this can have a profound impact on the group's functioning.

4. In an individual counseling relationship, the client has the right to terminate the counseling relationship at any time. Likewise, group participants have the freedom to exit the group at any time, but when group members drop out of an ongoing group, this can have significant effects on other participants and on the functioning of the group as a whole.

5. Research has demonstrated that group counseling is a powerful intervention. Some writers (e.g., Kottler, 1994; Yalom, 1995) have argued that this creates a potential for greater good or greater harm than may be present in individual counseling. Because such powerful forces are generated in groups, leaders have a complex set of responsibilities. They must act ethically and at the same time create an ethical climate in the group (Glass, 1998).

This chapter is organized into three main parts. The first presents a brief overview of ethical codes and other guidelines for group practitioners. The second addresses pre-group issues, examining the ethical considerations that go into preparing to lead a group. Foremost among these issues is the competence of the group leader. Counselors who are thinking about forming and leading a group need to have adequate training, experience, and qualifications, as well as multicultural competence. Counselors need to understand how to avoid malpractice, which is a legal consequence of lacking competence. Careful planning, recruiting members, pre-group screening, and ensuring the informed consent of members also are important steps that need to be completed prior to the formation of a group.

The third part focuses on ethical and legal issues that arise during the life of a group. These issues include dealing with confidentiality and privileged communication, establishing and maintaining boundaries, minimizing risks, dealing with diversity, handling premature withdrawals from the group, and ending a group in an ethically sound manner.

ETHICAL GUIDELINES FOR GROUP WORKERS

All counselors, including group counselors, should be familiar with and adhere to the American Counseling Association (ACA) *Code of Ethics* (2005). The Association for Specialists in Group Work (ASGW) has adopted the ACA code as its sole code of ethics. As Forester-Miller (1998; 2002) explained, ASGW once had its own code, the *Ethical Guidelines for Group Counselors*, but this code was eliminated in 1996 in response to a request from ACA leaders to reduce the number of ethics codes for which counselors were responsible. In 1998, the ASGW published two documents:

1. *Best Practice Guidelines* (ASGW, 1998a), intended to clarify how the ACA code can be applied to group work
2. *Principles for Diversity-Competent Group Workers* (ASGW, 1998b), whose purpose is to help counselors understand how issues of diversity affect all aspects of group work.

These ASGW documents are aspirational; that is, there is no mechanism for enforcing them. Adherence to the ACA *Code of Ethics* is mandatory for all ACA members, including members of ASGW (Cottone & Tarvydas, 2003).

Counselors who are engaged in group work should be fully familiar with the contents of the ACA code and both sets of ASGW guidelines. We also recommend that group workers who conduct psychotherapeutic groups familiarize themselves with the ethical guidelines of the American Group Psychotherapy Association and National Registry of Certified Group Psychotherapists (2002). These codes can be accessed online (see the list of Web sites at the end of the chapter).

PRE-GROUP ISSUES

In the pre-group stage, the competence of the group leader is paramount in planning and recruiting members. Because the counselor is subject to malpractice suits, thorough training in group counseling is essential. Careful planning is necessary if the group is to be successful.

Determining Competence and Avoiding Malpractice

Some experts in group work (e.g., Lakin, 1994) have expressed concern over the casual attitude that some mental health professionals take toward their preparedness to conduct groups. Counselors should not assume that they automatically are qualified to lead all, or even most, types of groups just because they have earned a master's degree or have considerable experience in counseling individuals (Corey & Corey, 2002; Welfel, 2002). Different types of groups require different leader competencies. For instance, a counselor may be well qualified to facilitate a reminiscence group for elderly residents of a nursing home but not at all prepared to lead adolescent groups in a school environment. Or a counselor might be competent to conduct a personal growth group for college students but might be practicing beyond the boundaries of competence by trying to lead process groups in an inpatient setting for clients diagnosed with chronic schizophrenia. Thus, if you are thinking about forming and conducting a group, the first question you should ask yourself is whether you have the competencies you need to lead the group effectively.

Developing competence begins with training. The ASGW's publication, *Professional Standards for the Training of Group Workers* (2000), describes the knowledge and skill objectives that comprise the core competencies in general group work in eight areas:

1. Coursework and experience
2. Knowledge and skills
3. Assessment
4. Planning
5. Implementing interventions
6. Leadership
7. Evaluation
8. Ethics

The standards also specify advanced competencies that are required to lead specialized task and work groups, psychoeducational groups, counseling groups, and psychotherapy groups.

If you are enrolled in, or have graduated from, a counselor education program accredited by the Council for the Accreditation of Counseling and Related Educational Programs (CACREP), you can be assured that your training has met the ASGW standards for content and clinical instruction. Although most graduate counseling programs are not CACREP accredited (Remley & Herlihy, 2005), many nonaccredited programs meet or even exceed the ASGW standards. We recommend that, whatever the accreditation status of your graduate program, you review the ASGW (2000) training standards as part of your planning process to assess your preparedness to lead a group.

You should be aware that achieving professional competence in group work is not a one-time event. Professional growth is a continuous, ongoing, and developmental process (ASGW, 1998a). Therefore, maintaining and increasing your competence as a group worker is a lifelong task. You will have to remain current and continue to work to increase your knowledge and skills in group work by keeping up with your professional reading and seeking continuing education, supervision, and consultation. Joining a peer supervision group can be an excellent way to increase your knowledge and raise your awareness of even minor misjudgments as a group counselor (Gladding, 1995).

Diversity Considerations

Group counselors must understand how issues of diversity affect all aspects of group work. The ASGW publication, *Principles for Diversity-Competent Group Workers* (ASGW, 1998b), provides a thorough description of attitudinal, knowledge, and skills competencies in three domains: self-awareness, awareness of group members' worldviews, and intervention strategies. As a beginning point, you should be aware of how your own cultural background and multiple cultural identities, attitudes, values, and beliefs influence the way you conceptualize and conduct groups.

As you work with diverse group members, you will have to be alert to issues of oppression, bias and prejudice, and discrimination, both within the workings of the group and in the sociopolitical contexts of members' lives. You must be careful not to impose your values on group members or proceed as if all members of your group share your worldview or cultural assumptions. This awareness is particularly important because so many value-laden issues—such as sexuality, religion, divorce, and family of origin—are brought into groups (Remley & Herlihy, 2005).

To be a diversity-competent group worker, you will need to possess relevant knowledge and skills, as well as awareness of self and others. Being able to send and receive both verbal and nonverbal messages accurately and to utilize a variety of methods of group facilitation are among the key skills. Knowledge of the characteristics of different cultural groups, as well as within-group differences, is essential. You will need to understand the barriers that can prevent members of marginalized groups from participating fully in various types of groups and know how to employ institutional intervention skills on behalf of group members. The ASGW *Principles* (1998b) provide a more complete understanding of the specific competencies you will need in order to be a diversity-competent group leader.

Legal Considerations

Our society expects professionals to be competent and enforces these expectations through the courts and licensing boards (Remley & Herlihy, 2005). If a client is harmed by an incompetent counselor, the client can bring a malpractice lawsuit against the counselor.

Although few malpractice suits are filed against counselors (Remley & Herlihy, 2005) and court cases involving group counseling are relatively rare (Paradise & Kirby, 1990), group counselors may be at risk for two reasons:

1. Clients are vulnerable to harm from both the leader and other participants.
2. The powerful nature of the group experience could exacerbate any negative outcomes.

Possibly the greatest area of risk for group counselors is in working with group members who pose a danger to self (may be suicidal) or others (are prone to violent behavior), because of the increased possibility that someone could be harmed.

Malpractice suits by participants in a group try to prove negligence on the part of the leader. To establish negligence, the client has to demonstrate that she or he was harmed or injured by group participation, and that the leader's mistake was what caused the harm. The services the leader provided are measured against the prevailing *standard of care*, defined as the quality of care that other, similarly trained professionals would have provided in this situation (Welfel, 2002).

If a participant is injured and brings suit, the plaintiff will likely try to show that the leader failed to uphold his or her obligation to "protect clients from physical, emotional, or psychological trauma" (ACA, 2005, A.8.b.). Group leaders in these cases might have to demonstrate several points in their defense, including that they could not have reasonably foreseen the harm, that they were adequately trained to lead the group in question, that they provided the plaintiff with fully informed consent regarding the risks, and that they took professionally appropriate precautions against harm or injury. Certainly, these leaders would need an attorney to assist in their defense. Thus, obtaining professional liability insurance is imperative before conducting any kind of group work.

Planning the Group and Recruiting Members

Thorough planning is essential to the success of a group. As you plan for a group, you will have to ask yourself a number of questions, including the following:

- What are the goals and purposes of this group? What is the role of the group members in determining or influencing the group's goals?
- What community needs does this group intend to meet?
- What type of group (task or work, psychoeducational, counseling, psychotherapeutic) is best suited to achieving the group's goals?
- What techniques and leadership style are most appropriate for this group?
- Will I need a coleader?
- What resources do I need to have available for this group to function successfully (e.g., funding, space, privacy, marketing and recruiting members, collaborative arrangements with community agencies and organizations)?
- How will I evaluate the group's success?

In reflecting on the thought and preparation that goes into answering these questions, it will become evident that planning for a group takes considerable time and effort. Nevertheless, experienced group leaders know that thorough planning is well worth the investment, as it increases the odds that the group experience will be successful.

Once planning for a group is complete, the next step is to advertise and recruit members. As Corey (2004) noted, the way the group is announced and advertised will strongly influence who will be attracted to it. Therefore, you will want to give potential members enough information to make clear the group's goals and purposes. You may want to ask other professionals to refer clients whom they think might make good candidates for the group.

When recruiting for groups in school settings, you have to exercise special caution. If you ask teachers to recommend students for possible inclusion in groups for children of divorce, children of alcoholics (COA), children who have suffered abuse, or in groups with similar themes, you might be labeling the students and violating their privacy. Ritchie and Huss (2000) recommend that counselors avoid naming their groups in this way and that counselors invite children to come at their own discretion to discuss their interest in participating.

Screening Potential Members

Screening of potential group members involves deciding both whom to exclude and whom to include. Because not all people can benefit from a group experience and some can even be harmed by participating (Yalom, 1995), these individuals must be identified during screening and directed to individual counseling or other sources of assistance.

The literature suggests that people who generally are not good candidates for group counseling include those who are likely to monopolize group time or dominate the group, have aggressive or hostile interpersonal styles, are suicidal or in severe crisis, are actively psychotic, or have been diagnosed with paranoid, narcissistic, or antisocial personality disorders. Others who are likely to inhibit the development of group cohesion are self-centered people who would be prone to use the group as an audience, and those lacking in ego strength who might display fragmented, acting-out, or bizarre behavior (Corey, 2004). Individuals who are addicted to drugs or alcohol also are poor candidates for most types of groups (Yalom, 1995).

Criteria for inclusion usually depend on the purpose of the group. As a general rule, however, groups are most useful for people whose problems or concerns are interpersonal in nature and who appreciate the commitment they will be making when they join a group (Yalom, 1995).

Ideally, potential members are screened in an individual, face-to-face interview. This allows for a two-way exchange in which the leader can evaluate the prospective member and what the person wants from the group experience, and the candidate can get to know and develop confidence in the leader (Corey, 2004). The leader should ask questions that will elicit the potential member's goals, willingness to share personal information, and commitment to becoming a contributing group member. At the same time, candidates can assess whether this specific group is what they are looking for and whether the leader is someone they think they can trust.

Unfortunately, it is not always possible or feasible to conduct individual screening interviews. Alternative procedures might be to interview prospective members in small groups or individually by phone, or to have them complete a written questionnaire. After all prospective members have been screened, the leader's task is to select the prospective members whose goals seem to be compatible with the purpose of the group and who seem likely to be compatible with each other.

Securing Informed Consent

Informed consent is based on the principle that clients have the right to know what they are getting into before they enter counseling (Remley & Herlihy, 2005). Informed consent is especially important in group work because group counseling involves risks and responsibilities beyond those typically involved in individual counseling (Welfel, 2002). To gain the informed consent of group members, the leader will need to provide them with a considerable amount of information and work to ensure that they understand all the risks and responsibilities of participation.

Securing informed consent is both a pre-group task and an issue that must be revisited during the first session. Here, we will focus on the information that group participants have a right to receive *before* they join a group. The leader can relate this information to prospective members during the screening interview or at a pre-group meeting.

Potential group members usually find it helpful to have information in written form so they can take it home and review it. As part of this written information, the leader must provide prospective members with a professional disclosure statement. According to the ASGW (1998a), this statement should include information on confidentiality and its limits and exceptions (which we will discuss in more detail in the next section) and on the nature, purposes, and goals of the group. The document should describe the roles and responsibilities of the group's members and leader(s) and the services the group can provide. The statement also should tell the members something about the leader, including his or her qualifications to lead this specific group (e.g., degrees earned, licenses, certifications, professional affiliations, relevant experience). It is a good idea to include a brief description of one's theoretical orientation, expressed in everyday language, not in professional jargon.

Prospective members need certain practical information so they can make an informed decision regarding participation. The leader should explain the group's format, procedures, and ground rules. Prospective members will want to know how many weeks the group will run, how frequently it will meet, and how long each session will last. Certainly, they will need to know about any fees involved and what arrangements they can make for payment. If insurance will be billed, potential participants should know what information will be disclosed to third-party payers.

The ASGW (1998a) specifies that certain policies should be discussed as part of the informed consent process, including policies regarding (a) entering and exiting the group, (b) substance use, and (c) documentation of the group. If there will be a coleader, the leader will want to explain the coleader's role and qualifications.

Some topics are best approached as matters for discussion rather than as information to be disseminated. Members may want or need help in developing their personal goals for participating in the group (Corey, 2004), and the leader should be prepared to assist them in this endeavor. The leader may want to talk with candidates regarding ways in which the group process may be congruent or at odds with their cultural beliefs and values. Leaders should discuss the possible impact, in terms of both potential risks and benefits, of participating in the group. Some of the risks that should be explained include the possibilities of scapegoating, undue group pressure or coercion, inappropriate confrontation, or physical harm (Corey & Corey, 2002).

Finally, prospective members should be offered the opportunity to ask questions and explore any concerns they may have. Although these discussions might be time-consuming, research has shown that pre-group preparation of members tends to facilitate positive outcomes in group counseling (Bowman & DeLucia, 1993; Budman, Simeone, Reilly, & Demby, 1994; Burlingame, Fuhriman, & Johnson, 2001).

Child and Adolescent Groups

When a group is going to be composed of minors, informed consent has to be gained in a different way. Legally, the rights of children belong to their parents (Remley & Herlihy, 2005) and have to be exercised through their parents. From a *legal perspective*, then, parents or guardians are the ones who must give their informed consent for their children to participate in the group. From an *ethical perspective*, children and adolescents have the same rights as adults to receive information about a group in which they may be participating. During the screening interview or pre-group meeting, you will want to provide children and adolescents with this information, in language they can understand.

Remley and Herlihy (2005) have offered a model consent form that can be signed by parents or guardians indicating their permission for the child to participate. It is good practice to have the child sign the consent form, too, giving his or her assent to participation.

Mandated Clients and Involuntary Groups

Group counselors sometimes perceive mandated clients as "troublesome" because these clients typically attend the group against their will, with heightened defenses, and with limited motivation to change. Informed consent can be problematic with this population. Ethical guidelines usually require that group members be able to withdraw their consent to participate at any time, without prejudice or penalty. However, freedom to withdraw consent is abridged when counseling is court-ordered, because withdrawal would place clients in a seriously compromised legal position, possibly leading to jail.

The best way to deal with this reality, according to DeJong and Berg (2001), is to present this information in a nonconfrontational but clear manner, making sure that potential group members are aware of the possible consequences of choosing not to participate. It is important to let them know that they do have a choice because they need to feel that, at least in some areas, they do have choices.

GROUP PROCESS ISSUES

Group process issues explored here are confidentiality and privileged communication, managing boundaries, minimizing risks, practicing with sensitivity to diversity, handling premature withdrawal from the group, and termination and follow-up.

Confidentiality and Privileged Communication

One of the key conditions for effective group work is *confidentiality* (Corey & Corey, 2002). Confidentiality builds trust within the group members and develops cohesion among the members as they move through the stages of group development. Group members must have a sense of safety when disclosing issues they have difficulty sharing with others. Thus, the trust and belief that this information will not be disclosed outside the group is the first building block in developing safety and trust in group work.

Group leaders must explain issues of confidentiality to members on an ongoing basis. Conversations regarding confidentiality begin at the screening stage and continue throughout the group process until termination. The group leader is responsible for protecting members' confidentiality. But it is not wise to offer guarantees of confidentiality. The leader's commitment to confidentiality is individual and independent of the group as a whole. Leaders can ensure confidentiality on their own part but cannot guarantee the behavior of the group members (ASGW, 1998a). Leaders cannot promise that leaks of confidentiality will not occur, but they can utilize their skills to empower the members to take ownership of their group's effectiveness by upholding confidentiality and honoring the trust they are building throughout the group process.

Leaders have an ethical responsibility to make members aware of the difficulties involved in enforcing and ensuring confidentiality in a group setting. The ACA *Code of Ethics* (2005) requires counselors to "clearly explain the importance and parameters of confidentiality for the specific group being entered" (B.4.a.) that are inherent in group work. Leaders should provide examples of how confidentiality can be broken, even unintentionally or nonmaliciously. They also should ensure that members clearly understand the potential consequences of intentionally breaching confidentiality (ASGW, 1998a). Because leaders cannot prevent breaches of confidentiality after the group ends, they must address this reality with the group (Gladding, 1995).

Despite a leader's best efforts, confidentiality leaks sometimes do occur, not out of spite or maliciousness of individual group members but more likely out of ignorance. If a breach of confidentiality does occur, the first step on the leader's part is to reflect and assess his or her work in modeling and protecting the confidentiality of the group. Leaders can self-reflect by asking themselves the following questions:

- Have I defined confidentiality clearly, or was I vague in my definition?
- Did I stress the importance of confidentiality in a way that my group members can understand?
- Did I facilitate the group in a way that the members can take ownership of the effectiveness of their group?
- Was I clear that confidentiality cannot be guaranteed?

The second step in handling a confidentiality leak is to bring up the situation in the group for the members to process and collectively develop a resolution. The group leader can model inappropriate breaches of confidentiality in subtle ways. Group leaders should be aware of and maintain confidentiality in all informal conversations with members outside the group. Discussions regarding an absent member should be deferred until that member returns to the group. Coleaders also should be mindful of confidentiality during their conversations when they meet to process and plan group sessions.

Group leaders sometimes want to make audiotapes or videotapes of the group sessions for educational or professional purposes. When this is done, group members must have a clear understanding as to the purpose and use of the recordings and must sign a written informed consent stating that they agree to and understand the intended use of the recording. Members have the right to deny or withdraw consent at any time. If a group has any members who do not wish to be videotaped, the leader could ask them if they would be comfortable with being positioned outside the view of the camera but still participating in the group, because their input in the group process is valued. This compromise might suffice to allow videotaping without the member's feeling uncooperative.

Legal Considerations

The legal counterpart to confidentiality is *privileged communication*. Privileged communication laws protect clients from having their confidential communications with their counselors disclosed in a court of law without their permission. Except for the relatively rare trials involving counselors that take place in federal courts, a state statute must exist for communications between counselors and their clients to be privileged. Although some type of counselor–client privilege existed in 44 of 45 states that licensed counselors in 2000 (Glosoff, Herlihy, & Spence, 2000), the extent to which privilege applies in group counseling varies widely from state to state (Welfel, 2002).

In some states the privileged communication statutes are worded in such a way that courts could conclude that, because a client shared information in the presence of third parties (group members), the information was not truly intended to be confidential (Knapp & VandeCreek, 2003). When such decisions have been appealed, state courts usually have held that statements made in front of third parties are not privileged (Swenson, 1997). There are some exceptions, however. At least four states (California, Illinois, Kentucky, and Minnesota) have specifically established group privilege (Parker, Clevenger, & Sherman, 1997).

As you can see, many complexities are involved in privileged communication as it applies to group counseling. You will have to research the law in your state and keep current with any legislative developments. As part of the informed consent process with group members, leaders will need to explain to each participant that there is no privilege for other group members who will hear what that participant says. Thus, other members could be compelled to testify in a lawsuit. So participants will not be unduly alarmed, the leader should inform them that the probability of this happening is extremely low (Welfel, 2002).

Child and Adolescent Groups

Safeguarding confidentiality in group counseling with children and adolescents is more difficult (Gladding, 1995; Koocher, 2003). When counseling children individually or in a group, two questions that arise constantly are: "Who is my client?" and "Who owns the right to confidentiality?" Legally, group leaders working with children may have to disclose some information to parents if the parents insist. Ethically, however, children and adolescents have a right to privacy and confidentiality just as adults do (Remley & Herlihy, 2005). The mandated breaches of confidentiality intended to protect children from harm, or from harming others, constitute a clear exception (Koocher, 2003).

Group leaders should be aware of the local and state laws regarding confidentiality with minors, because state laws vary with regard to this population. Respecting the rights of the parents while maintaining the trust of minor clients is a delicate balance. To reduce the likelihood that parents will ask what their child has discussed in a group, group leaders are wise to discuss with parents in advance the importance and purpose of confidentiality (Corey & Corey, 2002). A key to working with children and adolescents is to raise the issue of confidentiality limits early and directly, in a manner that fosters the therapeutic alliance (Koocher, 2003).

Maintaining Privacy of Records

The group counselor's obligation to protect clients' privacy and confidentiality extends to the records the counselor keeps. In our experience, many counselors who are diligent about keeping clinical case notes on their work with individual clients are rather lax in documenting their work with groups. Yet, this task is important because special considerations apply to keeping records of group counseling sessions due to the need to respect the confidentiality rights of the individual members.

It is good practice for leaders to make process notes soon after each group session has ended while the memory is still fresh. These notes are valuable in helping leaders do their work effectively. Leaders may want to use notes to keep track of the group's progress through the developmental stages, record any issues of particular attention, document the leader's observations about group dynamics such as the development of trust or cohesion, and describe interventions used and the leader's assessment of their effects. Leaders have to be careful, though, that the group session notes do not make reference to individual group members by name or other identifying information. If the records were ever subpoenaed by an attorney representing a group member and those records were to become public, the leader would be breaching the confidentiality of the other group members named in the records.

Counselors have a responsibility to write case notes for group counseling separately for each individual in the group (Cottone & Tarvydas, 2003). These individual files should not contain any information about other group members. When making notes in an individual client's file regarding that client's participation in a group, the leader should keep in mind that the client is entitled to have access to his or her records. The leader should make these entries accordingly.

If any participants in the group are concurrently participating in individual counseling with another mental health professional, the group leader will have to establish clear guidelines about sharing information with the other counselor. Leaders should consult with the participant's individual counselor only with the participant's permission.

In many institutional settings, clients are concurrently seen in individual counseling, group counseling, occupational or expressive therapy groups, and by a psychiatrist if they are taking psychotropic medications. There should be a clear institutional policy about sharing records, and clients must be informed as to who will be seeing their records and for what purposes.

Mandated Clients and Involuntary Groups

Members of mandatory groups must be informed that their confidentiality cannot be assured, because the group leader usually is required to report to a third party. For this reason, mandated clients should be required to sign a waiver of their privacy rights before they enter a group (Remley & Herlihy, 2005). Leaders who work with involuntary groups must keep in mind that the members deserve a full understanding of the group leader's role and obligations to fulfill any reporting requirements of the court or referring state agency (Adams, 1998).

Managing Boundaries

Helping professionals have debated for decades ethical and legal issues related to the boundaries of the therapeutic relationship. What constitutes appropriate boundaries has been questioned ever since the time of Freud, who emphasized the importance of neutrality, yet analyzed his own daughter (Boller & Lee, 1997). In short, there is no single, correct answer regarding where therapeutic boundaries should be drawn. Boundaries exist along a continuum from very fluid to overly rigid (Marshall, 2000).

Most of what has been written about boundaries relates to counselor behaviors in individual counseling relationships (Marshall, 2000). Boundaries are created with an understanding that counseling is a professional relationship with parameters and certain limits that might not apply to a personal relationship. Clients are in a vulnerable position in the therapeutic relationship; therefore, boundaries serve to protect the structure of the therapeutic relationship (Remley & Herlihy, 2005).

The term "boundary" is interchangeable with other terms such as "dual relationship" or "multiple relationship." In a dual relationship, group leaders take on more than one role simultaneously or sequentially (Herlihy & Corey, 1997) with a member or members. Dual relationships can involve combining the role of counselor with another professional relationship such as teacher, minister, supervisor, employer, or business partner (Smith & Smith, 2001) or combining the leader's role as counselor with a personal relationship such as friend, relative, or, in the worst case, lover.

Avoiding dual relationships is generally difficult, particularly in rural and isolated communities. Do not attempt to make such decisions alone; seek consultation or supervision, as you may be too close to the issue to decide what is just and fair in the situation. Not all dual relationships are considered ethically problematic. However, if there is potential risk of harm, exploitation, or impaired professional judgment, you should not enter into the dual relationship by admitting this individual into your group. If you discover that you have a dual relationship with one of your current group members, it would be wise to openly discuss the problematic issues relating to you having a relationship with this client outside of the counseling context. A referral may be necessary to maintain clear boundaries and your professional integrity.

The ASGW *Best Practice Guidelines* (1998a) address boundary issues only minimally, in the statement that group workers "clearly define and maintain ethical, professional, and social relationship boundaries with group members as appropriate to their role in the organization and the type of group being offered" (B.3.c.). The guidelines do not provide direction as to how group leaders might identify and manage boundary issues.

As mentioned, the ASGW recognizes the commitment of its members to the ethics code of its parent organization, the ACA. Group counselors can find more guidance and a rationale for avoiding dual relationships in the ACA *Code of Ethics* (2005):

> Counselor-client non-professional relationships with clients, former clients, their romantic partners, or their family members should be avoided, except when the interaction is potentially beneficial to the client. (A.5.c.)

Although this standard may seem clear, it has many gray areas with respect to dual relationship issues. Boundary questions can be complex and ambiguous, even for the most seasoned practitioners (Remley & Herlihy, 2005).

The one type of dual relationship that is absolutely prohibited is sexual relationships with current clients (including clients in individual counseling and group members). This prohibition is consistent across codes of ethics in all major helping professions. That is not to say you are being unethical if you find yourself feeling attracted to a group member or if you find an individual in your group to be sexually appealing. If you take steps to actualize your sexual fantasy, however, you have committed an ethical violation.

Although sexual dual relationships are the most obvious boundary issue, group leaders also have to be cognizant of issues associated with nonsexual relationships and boundaries. These include bartering, social relationships with clients and between members, and self-disclosure.

Bartering

When a potential group participant cannot afford to pay the fee, the leader may be tempted to enter into an agreement to receive goods or services in lieu of payment for services. The intent in making such an arrangement might be altruistic, but there are reasons to be cautious.

Two types of bartering arrangements may be especially problematic for group leaders: exchange of services and exchange of goods. In an *exchange of services*, a group participant would provide a service in which he or she has particular expertise, such as plumbing or carpentry. To take an example, it might seem to be a fair trade if you are forming a new group for adolescents and the parent of one of the potential members, who happens to be a plumber, can't afford the fee. Your office needs plumbing repairs, so you barter with the parent to fix your plumbing in exchange for group counseling for her son.

The problem with this arrangement is that the value of services—both those provided by the parent and those provided by the group leader—is subjective. What if you are not satisfied with the plumbing repairs? What if the parent does not think the group was helpful to her son? What if other, paying parents find out that this group member is receiving services based on a bartering arrangement? The very subjective nature of perceptions about fairness and value or quality of work could compromise the therapeutic relationship and create an awkward circumstance that could deter development of the group as a whole.

Bartering for *goods in exchange for counseling services* presents the same problems with perceptions of fairness, value, and quality. The potential problems are described in the ACA *Code of Ethics* (2005), which states that counselors "may barter only if the relationship is not exploitive or harmful and does not place the counselor in an unfair advantage, if the client requests it, and if such arrangements are an accepted practice among professionals in the community" (A.10.d.). The code does not explicitly prohibit bartering arrangements. Instead, it provides guidelines to help the leader determine whether a potential bartering arrangement might be acceptable. Again, if you are faced with a decision on whether to barter, you would do well to seek supervision or consult with professional colleagues, because your needs or desires for the potential services or goods could bias your judgment.

Social Relationships With Clients

In general, group leaders are discouraged from developing friendships with group members and from admitting current friends into their groups (Herlihy & Corey, 1997). A group member who is also a friend could be reticent to fully engage in the group out of fear of jeopardizing the relationship with the leader. Or the opposite could occur: The member who has a "special relationship" with the leader might feel privileged and play out his or her role as the "favorite" during the group sessions. This could easily give rise to feelings of resentment and anger in the other group members who do not have the privilege of friendship with the leader.

Group leaders should be aware that occasionally some members will attempt to insinuate themselves into the role of the leader's "special friend." When leaders find themselves in this situation, they must be careful not to relax their boundaries. Some group members, particularly those who have experienced prior violations of their boundaries or who find themselves unable to accept limits, can be expected to test the boundaries of their relationship with the leader (Haug, 1999). These clients need to feel safe to discuss or even act out their conflicts, and they need to be assured that the group leader will remain committed to appropriate professional boundaries.

Former Clients as Group Members

Sometimes a group leader's prior relationship with a potential group member will be professional rather than personal. For example, you might want to form a group of people who have been your clients in individual counseling. You might see this as a useful progression in that the group setting will allow clients to continue to make therapeutic gains while minimizing their expenses. Problems could arise, however, if your group were composed of some members who had been in individual counseling with you and some who had not. The group members who had all your attention when they were seeing you for individual counseling could easily feel resentful of having to share you with the other members. The members who did not know you before they joined the group might feel jealous of the group members who already have built a relationship with you. These reactions would have to be processed in the group, and this discussion could be therapeutically useful.

To summarize: Admitting a friend of the group leader to a group is quite a different matter than admitting a former client to the group. With a former client, the relationship was professional and had inherent boundaries. By contrast, the relationship with a friend with whom the leader has shared personal experiences is not a professional relationship. In this case, the shifting of roles from a personal relationship to a professional relationship could create many difficulties for the group leader, for the friend who becomes a group member, and possibly for other members of the group (Herlihy & Corey, 1997).

Socializing Among Members

Group leaders have taken varying positions on the question of whether socializing among group members facilitates or hinders the group process (Remley & Herlihy, 2005). This issue is complicated because the leader has limited control over interactions that occur among the members outside of the group. This situation parallels the issue of confidentiality limits, in that the leader cannot offer guarantees that a member will not socialize or converse about group outside of group. Some group leaders set ground rules at the outset to prohibit or discourage members from socializing outside of group time. Group members must understand that the purpose of group is not to make friends (Herlihy & Corey, 1997) but, instead, to normalize and validate each other's experiences and learn adaptive interpersonal skills that will transfer to outside relationships.

Notwithstanding any rules that might be established, socializing can and will occur between and among members outside of group time. If this becomes evident by cliques developing within the group, the leader is responsible for raising the issue for the entire group to process.

It should be noted that socializing among members is not always discouraged. For example, substance abuse groups and support groups actually may encourage members to socialize outside of group time. Members of substance abuse groups typically cling to other members of their group to maintain their sobriety as they develop a new community.

Self-Disclosure

Self-disclosure can be a powerful intervention, and group leaders need to recognize its limits. Hanna, Hanna, and Keys (1999) have suggested that group leaders avoid self-disclosing around issues or incidents that they have not resolved internally. If leaders use their groups to obtain their own therapy, members will be confused, wondering whether the leader is really the leader or a member of the group. The leader must keep in mind that the main purpose of the leader is to facilitate the growth of others, not to work through the leader's own personal issues or problems. The leader should consider joining a group in which he or she does not have the responsibility of leadership if it becomes apparent that a specific issue or theme that arose in the group has tapped into his or her own unfinished business (Herlihy & Corey, 1997). Another obvious rule is to avoid self-disclosing anything the leader does not want repeated (Bernstein, 1996).

Group leaders need to develop guidelines to help them determine appropriate disclosures. A leader self-disclosure can be beneficial to a group when it is used to let members know that the leader can identify with and is personally affected by their struggles (Herlihy & Corey, 1997).

Adolescent Groups

Group leaders must be acutely aware of boundary issues when working with adolescents. Hanna et al. (1999) caution counselors against underestimating the sexual intensity of many adolescents. Sexuality rages in many adolescent boys in particular. It follows that female counselors should be aware that hugs and touching can be highly erotic to many boys even when the counselor does not intend any eroticism. Likewise, male counselors may have to deal with adolescent girls who dress provocatively, seeking approval and validation of their own sexual identities. This behavior should not be ignored but must be handled with extreme sensitivity (Bernstein, 1996).

Legal Considerations

In cases where clients have sued a counselor with whom they have had sexual relationships, the client has an excellent chance of winning the lawsuit (Remley & Herlihy, 2005). Civil suits can be brought on a number of grounds, including malpractice, negligence, assault and battery, intentional infliction of emotional distress, fraudulent misrepresentation, and breach of contract (Jorgenson, 1995). In addition, legislators are becoming so convinced that counselor–client sexual relationships are harmful that these relationships have been criminalized in at least 13 states (Kane, 1994). As you can see, developing a sexual relationship with a client who is a group member is extremely risky in a legal sense, in addition to being wrong from an ethical or a moral perspective.

Legal consequences for most nonsexual dual relationships are much less clear than they are for sexual relationships. Most group leaders, like most counselors who provide individual counseling services, probably cross boundaries occasionally. A "boundary crossing" is a departure from customary practice to benefit a particular client at a particular time. You might, for instance, lend a group member cab fare if the member discovered after a group meeting that he had left his wallet at home. You do not want to be too rigid in maintaining your boundaries, but you should be careful not to let boundary crossings become routine. If a judge or jury could perceive a pattern of blurring your professional boundaries over time, this might be persuasive that you have not been practicing in accordance with professional standards (Herlihy & Corey, 1997; Remley & Herlihy, 2005).

Minimizing Risks

Because groups can be powerful catalysts for change, they involve some risk. The ACA *Code of Ethics* requires counselors to take precautions "to protect clients from physical, emotional, or psychological trauma" in group settings (ACA, 2005, A.8.b.). This standard reflects both the concern that group participants might be harmed and the leader's responsibility to take preventive measures.

The leader's job is not to try to *eliminate* risks, as taking risks is essential to meaningful growth and change. Rather, the leader's responsibility is to *minimize* the inevitable psychological risks inherent in group work (Corey, 2004). To accomplish this, the leader's task is twofold:

1. Leaders must ensure that the group members are aware of the potential risks. This element of informed consent has to be addressed before the group begins, as well as throughout the life of the group, as needed.
2. Leaders must have skills that enable them to manage problems effectively as they arise.

Perhaps the most important discussion a group leader must have with members is to ensure that they understand that they may make some changes in their lives as a result of participating in the group and that, even though these changes may be healthy, other people in their lives might react with resistance or hostility. Thus, there is the risk of putting a strain on relationships. Group members have to understand the possibility that their participation in the group could disrupt their lives, and they must be willing to accept that risk.

The leader's discussion with members or potential members should address some of the group dynamics that could make the group feel unsafe to a member or members. These factors include scapegoating, confrontation, undue pressure or coercion, and, in some groups, the possibility of physical injury resulting from exercises or activities that involve physical contact (Remley & Herlihy, 2005).

1. *Scapegoating*. Occasionally a group will seem to gang up on, or scapegoat, one member and blame that person for difficulties within the group. This person then becomes the "odd person out" toward whom the members' frustrations are channeled. If the leader does not intervene skillfully to deal with this phenomenon, the participant who is the target of the scapegoating may withdraw into silence or quit the group altogether.
2. *Confrontation*. Although confrontation is a valuable tool in group work, it is easily misused. First, leaders have to be comfortable with offering and being the recipient of confrontation. Second, they need to know how to model constructive feedback and appropriate confrontation within the group. Group members who have not learned how to confront others constructively might misuse the technique. Thus, the leader has to be able to intervene when members' confrontations are inappropriate or abrasive.
3. *Undue pressure and coercion*. Group members have the right to be respected within the group and not be subjected to coercion or undue pressure. Group members "may need a certain degree of pressure to challenge them to take the risks involved in becoming fully invested in the group" (Corey, 2004, p. 59), but this can be tricky. At times, they may feel pressure to speak up, to relate something personal, to be honest with the group, or to verbalize their reactions to events occurring in the group. Gentle pressure in these directions can be beneficial to individual members and the group, but it is not appropriate to pressure a member into doing what the group wants or thinks is right when that member truly does not share those wants or desires.

When a participant is being pressured to change in a direction that the participant has not chosen, the leader should intervene (Remley & Herlihy, 2005). Leaders may have to remind the group at times that it is okay for members to "pass" or abstain from certain activities or exercises, or to see things differently than others do. Leaders should keep in mind, too, that members who bend to the social pressure of their peers to change their behavior might attribute some changes they make to external influences rather than to themselves. Leaders must remain sensitive to the individual rights of group members and intervene when these rights are being compromised.

4. *Possibility of physical injury.* Although the odds are remote that a group member might be physically harmed by another group member, the possibility should not be ignored. Some groups present a greater potential for inappropriate acting-out behaviors than do other groups. Examples of groups that carry a greater risk are anger management groups for middle schoolers, therapeutic groups for veterans diagnosed with posttraumatic stress disorder (PTSD), and groups for violent offenders in a prison setting. The leader is responsible for ensuring the safety of group members and for carefully monitoring any members who have known potential for harming others (Remley & Herlihy, 2005).

On a related topic, leaders should keep in mind that individuals can feel violated by physical touching even when no offense was intended. If leaders plan to conduct an activity or an exercise that involves physical contact or touching, they should explain this in the disclosure statement and again before implementing the exercise. Leaders should avoid touching group members in a way that might be considered sexual, offensive, or intrusive, and also be aware of cultural differences in how members perceive touching.

Special cautions apply when working with groups whose members are close peers or workplace associates. Although leaders can monitor group sessions for problems developing, such as estranged work relationships, embarrassment, or loss of prestige, they cannot control what happens when the members leave the safety of the group sessions. Thus, leaders should encourage members to be accountable for their actions in the outside world as well as within the group.

One's skill as a leader is the crucial element in keeping risks within acceptable bounds. It is incumbent on leaders to know their members' limits and respect their requests. Having an invitational style and being skilled at giving feedback that describes (rather than judges) and tentatively suggests (rather than interprets) will do much to help members feel safe to take risks (Corey, 2004). To minimize risk, some writers (e.g., Corey, Corey, & Callanan, 2003; Cottone & Tarvydas, 2003) have suggested having a contract that specifies the responsibilities of the leader and the members. Even with a contract, however, the leader must have the ability to intervene at critical moments to prevent potential harm (Glass, 1998).

At times during the course of a group's life, the needs of a specific member seem to be in conflict with the needs of the group as a whole. In these instances, if the individual member is at risk of being traumatized or harmed, the leader's job is to protect the individual (Cottone & Tarvydas, 2003). At the same time, the leader cannot abdicate responsibility for the group. This is a delicate balance that requires leaders to exercise professional judgment carefully.

A final element of risk addressed here relates to the leader's own values and biases. Leaders might be inclined to give more attention to a member they find likeable or attractive, or to project their own unfinished business onto a member whose concerns trigger countertransference reactions in them, or, as a result of their cultural biases, to treat certain members as if they are thinking and acting as the leader expects them to think and act. Thus, leaders must self-monitor throughout the group process.

Leaders should not try to hide their values, as this actually may do more harm than good in certain situations (Gladding, 1995). Rather, leaders will want to be honest and at the same time work to understand and respect the roles of family and community, religion and spirituality, and ethnicity and culture in the lives of the group members (Remley & Herlihy, 2005).

Practicing With Sensitivity to Diversity

Group counselors historically have not paid substantive or systemic attention to working across ethnically and culturally diverse boundaries and have based their work on predominantly European-American models of counseling (Bemak & Chung, 2004). Until recently, many textbooks on the theory and process of group work relegated discussion of the multicultural aspects of group work to a brief discussion in one of the final chapters (Brinson & Lee, 1997). Given the dramatically changing demographic nature of the U.S. population, today's group workers absolutely have to be culturally competent.

The ASGW formally incorporated multicultural competencies into its *Best Practice Guidelines* in 1998. The guidelines state that group workers are expected to know, understand, and apply the ACA *Code of Ethics*, the ASGW diversity competencies, and the multicultural counseling competencies (Arredondo et al., 1996), among other regulatory documents that influence the practice of group work (A.1.). Diversity is addressed throughout the guidelines (1998a) as follows:

- Group Workers actively assess their knowledge and skills related to the specific group(s) offered. Group Workers assess their values, beliefs and theoretical orientation and how these impact upon the group, particularly when working with a diverse and multicultural population. (A.3.a.)
- Group Workers assess community needs, agency or organization resources, sponsoring organization mission, staff competency, attitudes regarding group work, professional training levels of potential group leaders regarding group work; client attitudes regarding group work, and multicultural and diversity considerations. (A.3.b.)

- Group Workers apply and modify knowledge, skills and techniques appropriate to group type and stage, and to the unique needs of various cultural and ethnic groups. (B.3.a.)
- Group Workers practice with broad sensitivity to client differences including but not limited to ethnic, gender, religious, sexual, psychological maturity, economic class, family history, physical characteristics or limitations, and geographic location. Group Workers continuously seek information regarding the cultural issues of the diverse population with whom they are working both by interaction with participants and from using outside resources. (B.8)

These general guidelines, along with the more detailed and specific guidance given by the ASGW *Principles for Diversity-Competent Group Workers* (1998b), provide a blueprint for assessing one's multicultural competence as a group leader. Inherent in multicultural group work is to foster acceptance, respect, and tolerance for diversity within and among members (Bemak & Chung, 2004). Practicing with sensitivity to diversity may be as simple as adjusting the group's pace for cultural reasons to include members whose worldview may require a slower pace, or selecting an intervention that is drawn from another culture, such as the Cherokee Inner/Outer Circle (Garrett, 2001).

Group leaders will have to be intentional in their approach to addressing diversity issues. Culturally sensitive counselors need to foresee possible conflicts between ethnic and therapeutic values (Shectman, Hiradin, & Zina, 2003). Culture differences must be at the forefront of awareness when implementing a group intervention (Coyne, Wilson, & Tang, 2000).

Cultural awareness includes accepting one's possible limitations in facilitating a group experience with members from a different cultural background. Accepting these limitations might mean that the leader would ask another professional who is a member of a specified cultural group to cofacilitate the group experience.

Some guidelines drawn from various sources (Corey, 2004; Corey & Corey, 2002; Coyne et al., 2000; Remley & Herlihy, 2005) are as follows:

- In designing groups and in orienting members to the group process, be aware of the implications of cultural diversity.
- Take time to reflect on your personal cultural identity, especially as it influences your professional work.
- Think about your needs and behavior styles and the impact these might have on your group participants.
- Assess the group's goodness of fit with community needs.
- Develop the purpose and goals for the group in collaboration with the constituency for which the group is intended.
- Identify techniques and a leadership style appropriate to the type of group for which intervention is planned and the culture in which it is to be implemented.
- Consider the impact of adverse social, environmental, and political factors in designing interventions.

- Be alert to issues of oppression, sexism, racism, and other forms of discrimination as you work with diverse group members.
- Acquire the knowledge and skills you need to work effectively with the diverse members of your group. If you lack some of the needed background, seek consultation, supervision, and further education and training.

Handling Premature Withdrawals From the Group

Whenever group participation is voluntary, members have the freedom to exit the group at any time. This can be problematic because all group members are affected when one participant decides to quit coming to the sessions.

As a foundation, leaders must have clear policies regarding expectations for members' attendance, commitment to remain in the group for a specified number of sessions, leaving a session if unhappy with what is going on in the group, and handling an intended departure from the group before the group ends. These policies should be discussed both in the screening interview and during the group's first session (Corey, 2004).

Even though a leader may be clear about his or her expectations and members may be sincere in their intentions to live up to these expectations, an individual sometimes will want to drop out of the group. If this happens, the trust and cohesion of the group likely will be damaged. For this reason, the leader may be tempted to try to dissuade the individual from exiting the group. If the group is counterproductive for an individual or if the group is not meeting that individual's needs, however, that member certainly has the right to leave.

There is no consensus regarding just how to handle such a situation (Remley & Herlihy, 2005). Generally, it is recommended that the individual who is considering withdrawing be encouraged to bring up the matter for discussion in the group (Corey, 2004; Cottone & Tarvydas, 2003), or at least tell the other members about the decision to exit (Welfel, 2002). The outcome of that discussion might be that the member decides to stay after all. As Welfel noted, "Part of what makes a group beneficial is its power to help clients work through difficult emotions and stick with commitments to others" (p. 184).

A potential problem with this approach, however, is that the individual might feel pressured to stay by the other group members. Statements such as, "The group just won't be the same without you" or "your input is always so insightful" could cause the member who is thinking about leaving to feel guilty for wanting to leave. Leaders have to be careful not to have a hidden agenda—a desire that the person will be persuaded to stay so the group will not be disrupted—as that agenda could affect how they handle the discussion. Careful self-monitoring is crucial here.

This approach could have an advantage, though, in that even if the individual decides to withdraw from the group, both the individual and the other group members are less likely to be left with unfinished business. The individual can achieve a sense of closure by expressing what has made him or her feel uncomfortable or threatened, and the remaining group members won't be left wondering whether they somehow caused the person to depart.

This is a difficult situation for the leader. Ideally, the member who is contemplating dropping out of the group will be willing to talk with the group, or at least with the leader. If the individual still chooses to withdraw, that person should be allowed to leave without being subjected to pressure to remain. One strategy that has been suggested to avoid the problem is to have a trial period, after which members can formally leave the group if they so choose (Cottone & Tarvydas, 2003).

Terminating and Following Up

Although terminating a group usually is not considered as an ethical issue, leaders do have certain ethical responsibilities to fulfill in bringing a group to closure. During the termination phase of a group, three essential leader tasks are to help the participants

1. make meaning of the experience,
2. transfer in-group learnings to their everyday lives, and
3. access further resources if needed.

As the group prepares to end, the leader's work can be challenging. The leader has to deal simultaneously with the difficult emotions that accompany saying good-bye, wrap up any unfinished business, help members personalize what they have learned from the experience, and provide members with suggestions for applying these learnings in their lives after the group ends. The ASGW *Best Practice Guidelines* (1998a) remind counselors of the importance of assisting members to generate meaning from the group experience (B.5).

After the group ends, leaders have two additional responsibilities: evaluation and follow-up. ASGW's *Best Practice Guidelines* (1998a) emphasize the need for evaluation at the conclusion of the group and follow-up contact with members (B.7, C.3). Evaluation is a necessary part of the process of increasing one's competence as a group leader, and the leader must conduct an assessment of the group and use the results to help plan, revise, and improve groups to be conducted in the future.

Leaders have an ethical obligation to make themselves available for follow-up contact with group members as needed (ASGW, 1998a, C.3.b.). Corey (2004) recommends that leaders hold individual follow-up interviews if feasible. Even though these interviews can be brief, they might prove valuable in determining how well the members integrated and transferred their learnings. In addition, the interviews provide an opportunity to discuss referral for further counseling or development—an issue that is best handled on an individual basis.

LEARNING ACTIVITIES

1. Write a brief description of a group you would like to form and lead. Then work in pairs with another student. Student A role-plays a potential member of Student B's group, while Student B conducts a screening interview. Then switch

roles. At the completion of the activity, participate in a class discussion of what you learned about what questions to ask, how to ask them, and how to determine whether an interviewee is a good candidate for the group.

2. Write a professional disclosure statement that is suitable for a group you plan to conduct. Ensure that the statement contains all the necessary elements of informed consent and is written in a style and language appropriate for the intended membership.

3. Research and write a brief report on (a) the laws in your state regarding confidentiality and privileged communication in group counseling, and (b) the provisions in your state's counselor licensure law that pertain to group work. Address methods you plan to use to ensure that you will adhere to these laws in your group work. Working in dyads, critique each other's reports.

4. Develop cultural empathy for diverse group members by drawing a vertical line down the middle of a sheet of paper. On the left side list your characteristics that give you membership in a privileged societal group (e.g., White, male, able-bodied), and on the right side list characteristics that give you membership in a peripheralized group (e.g., Black, gay or lesbian, Jewish). Then, working in dyads, discuss how these characteristics could help and hinder your understanding of the life experiences of diverse group members.

SUMMARY

A myriad of ethical responsibilities affect every aspect of group leaders' work, from the planning stage of a group through termination and follow-up. Helpful written guidelines include the ACA *Code of Ethics* (2005) and three publications of the ASGW: the *Best Practice Guidelines* (1998a), the *Principles for Diversity-Competent Group Workers* (1998b), and the *Professional Standards for the Training of Group Workers* (2000). Although these guidelines are helpful, they cannot substitute for sound, clinical judgment.

The planning phase of a group begins with determining if you have the competencies needed to lead the group in question. Lack of competence can lead to malpractice lawsuits. Other pre-group tasks include addressing a number of planning issues, recruiting and screening potential members, and securing informed consent for prospective members to participate in the group. Groups for children and adolescents and groups for mandated clients have special considerations.

Ethical and legal issues accompanying the life of a group include explaining confidentiality and privileged communication, maintaining privacy of records, managing boundaries, minimizing risks, practicing with sensitivity to diversity, dealing with premature withdrawals, and handling termination and follow-up. Again, groups of minors and mandated clients raise unique ethical and legal considerations.

Taken together, these ethical and legal issues paint a picture of the complexities and ambiguities involved in conducting group work. Ethics committees, licensing boards, and courts of law do not expect leaders to be perfect and never make a mistake. Rather, the expectation is to exercise due diligence—by staying current in your knowledge, keeping careful documentation, seeking consultation and supervision as needed, and using sound professional judgment.

USEFUL WEB SITES

☐ American Counseling Association (ACA) *Code of Ethics*
www.counseling.org
☐ Association for Specialists in Group Work (ASGW)
www.asgw.org
☐ ASGW *Professional Training Standards*
www.asgw.org/training_standards.htm
☐ ASGW *Best Practice Guidelines*
www.asgw.org/best.htm
☐ ASGW *Principles for Diversity-Competent Group Workers*
www.asgw.org/diversity.htm
☐ American Group Psychotherapy Association &
National Registry of Certified Group Psychotherapists
www.groupsinc.org/group/ethicalguide.html

REFERENCES

Adams, J. K. (1998). Court-mandated treatment and required admission of guilt in cases of alleged sexual abuse: Professional, ethical and legal issues. *Issues in Child Abuse Accusations, 99*(3/4), 96–107.

American Counseling Association (ACA). (2005). *Code of ethics.* Alexandria, VA: Author.

American Group Psychotherapy Association and National Registry of Certified Group Psychotherapists. (2002). *Guidelines for ethics.* Washington, DC: Author.

Arredondo, P., Toporek, R., Brown, S. P., Jones, J., Locke, D. C., Sanchez, J., et al. (1996). Operationalization of the multicultural counseling competencies. *Journal of Multicultural Counseling and Development, 24,* 42–78.

Association for Specialists in Group Work (ASGW). (1998a). *Best practice guidelines.* Alexandria, VA: Author.

Association for Specialists in Group Work (ASGW). (1998b). *Principles for diversity-competent group workers.* Alexandria, VA: Author.

Association for Specialists in Group Work (ASGW). (2000). *Professional standards for the training of group workers.* Alexandria, VA: Author.

Bemak, F., & Chung, R. (2004). Teaching multicultural group counseling: Perspectives for a new era. *Journal for Specialists in Group* Work, 29, 31–41.

Bernstein, N. (1996). *Treating the unmanageable adolescent: A guide to oppositional defiant and conduct disorders.* Northvale, NJ: Aronson.

Boller, J., & Lee, S. (1997). Nonsexual touch, self-disclosure, and friendship in the therapeutic setting: A discussion of boundary issues. (ERIC Document Reproduction Service No. ED418352)

Bowman, V. E., & DeLucia, J. L. (1993). Preparation for group therapy: The effects of preparer and modality on group process and individual functioning. *Journal for Specialists in Group Work, 18,* 67–79.

Brinson, J. A., & Lee, C. C. (1997). Culturally responsive group leadership: An integrative model for experienced practitioners. In H. Forrester-Miller & J. A. Kottler (Eds.), *Issues and challenges for group practitioners* (pp. 43–56). Denver: Love Publishing.

Budman, S H., Simeone, P. G., Reilly, R., & Demby, A. (1994). Progress in short-term and time-limited group psychotherapy: Evidence and implications. In A. Fuhriman & G. Burlingame (Eds.), *Handbook of group psychotherapy* (pp. 319–339). New York: Wiley.

Burlingame, G., Fuhriman, A., & Johnson, J. (2001). Cohesion in group therapy. *Psychotherapy: Theory, Research, Practice, Training, 38,* 21–30.

Corey, G. (2004). *Theory and practice of group counseling* (6th ed.). Pacific Grove, CA: Brooks/Cole.

Corey, M. S., & Corey, G. (2002). *Groups: Process and practice* (6th ed.). Pacific Grove, CA: Brooks/Cole.

Corey, G., Corey, M. S., & Callanan, P. (2003). *Issues and ethics in the helping professions* (6th ed.). Pacific Grove, CA: Brooks/Cole.

Cottone, R. R., & Tarvydas, V. M. (2003). *Ethical and professional issues in counseling* (2nd ed.). Upper Saddle River, NJ: Merrill/Prentice Hall.

Coyne, R. K., Wilson, F. R., & Tang, M. (2000). Evolving lessons from group work involvement in China. *Journal for Specialists in Group Work, 25,* 252–268.

DeJong, P., & Berg, I. K. (2001). Co-constructing cooperation with mandated clients. *Social Work, 46,* 4.

Forester-Miller, H. (1998). History of the Association for Specialists in Group Work: Timeline of significant events. *Journal for Specialists in Group Work, 23,* 335–337.

Forester-Miller, H. (2002). Group counseling: Ethical considerations. In D. Capuzzi & D. R. Gross (Eds.), *Introduction to group counseling* (3rd ed., pp. 185–204). Denver: Love Publishing.

Garrett, M. T. (2001). Inner circle/outer circle: A group technique based on Native American healing circles. *Journal for Specialists in Group Work, 26,* 17–30.

Gladding, S. T. (1995). *Group work: A counseling specialty* (3rd ed.). Upper Saddle River, NJ: Merrill/Prentice Hall.

Glass, T. A. (1998). Ethical issues in group work. In R. M. Anderson, T. L. Needels, & H. V. Hall (Eds.), *Avoiding ethical misconduct in psychology specialty areas.* Springfield, IL: Charles C Thomas.

Glosoff, H. L., Herlihy, B., & Spence, E. B. (2000). Privileged communication in the counselor-client relationship. *Journal of Counseling and Development, 78,* 454–462.

Hanna, F., Hanna, C., & Keys, S. (1999). Fifty strategies for counseling defiant, aggressive adolescents: Reaching, acceptance, and relating. *Journal of Counseling and Development, 77,* 395–404.

Haug, I. E. (1999). Boundaries and the use and misuse of power and authority: Ethical complexities for clergy psychotherapists. *Journal of Counseling and Development, 77,* 411–417.

Herlihy, B., & Corey, G. (1997). *Boundary issues in counseling.* Alexandria, VA: American Counseling Association.

Jorgenson, L. M. (1995). Sexual contact in fiduciary relationships. In J. C. Gonsiorek (Ed.), *Breach of trust: Sexual exploitation by health care professionals and clergy* (pp. 237–283). Thousand Oaks, CA: Sage.

Kane, A. W. (1994). The effects of criminalization of sexual misconduct by therapists. In J. C. Gonsiorek (Ed.), *Breach of trust: Sexual exploitation by health care professionals and clergy* (pp. 317–332). Thousand Oaks, CA: Sage.

Knapp, S., & VandeCreek, L. (2003). *A guide to the 2002 revision of the American Psychological Association's ethics code.* Sarasota, FL: Professional Resource Press.

Koocher, G. P. (2003). Ethical issues in psychotherapy with adolescents. *Journal of Clinical Psychology, 59,* 1247–1256.

Kottler, J. A. (1994). *Advanced group leadership.* Pacific Grove, CA: Brooks/Cole.

Lakin, M. (1994). Morality in group and family therapies: Multiperson therapists and the 1992 ethics code. *Professional Psychology: Research and Practice, 25,* 344–348.

Marshall, A. (2000). *Oops, you're stepping on my boundaries.* Paper presented at Annual National Consultation on Career Development, Ottawa, Ontario.

Paradise, L. V., & Kirby, P. C. (1990). Some perspectives on the legal liability of group counseling in private practice. *Journal for Specialists in Group Work, 15,* 114–118.

Parker, J., Clevenger, J. E., & Sherman, J. (1997). The psychotherapist-patient privilege in group therapy. *Journal of Group Psychotherapy, Psychodrama & Sociometry, 49,* 157–160.

Remley, T. P., & Herlihy, B. (2005). *Ethical, legal, and professional issues in counseling* (2nd ed.). Upper Saddle River, NJ: Merrill/Prentice Hall.

Ritchie, M. H., & Huss, S. N. (2000). Recruitment and screening of minors for group counseling. *Journal for Specialists in Group Work, 25,* 146–156.

Shechtman, Z., Hiradin, A., & Zina, S. (2003). The impact of culture on group behavior: A comparison of three ethnic groups. *Journal of Counseling & Development, 81,* 208–216.

Smith, J. A., & Smith, A. H. (2001). Dual relationships and professional integrity: An ethical dilemma case of a family counselor as clergy. *Family Journal, 9,* 438–443.

Swenson, L. C. (1997). *Psychology and the law for the helping professions* (2nd ed.). Pacific Grove, CA: Brooks/Cole.

Welfel, E. R. (2002). *Ethics in counseling and psychotherapy: Standards, research, and emerging issues* (2nd ed.). Pacific Grove, CA: Brooks/Cole.

Yalom, I. (1995). *Theory and practice of group psychotherapy* (4th ed.). New York: Basic Books.

Diversity Issues in Group Work

Deborah J. Rubel

t can be said that all group work issues are related to diversity. The primary question to be answered during group work is: "How can we work together in a way that benefits us all?" (Kline, 2003, p. 7). While the primary concern of individual counseling is the functioning of the individual, the emphasis in group work is facilitating a balance between the needs of the group and the needs of individual group members. This challenge bears great similarity to the task of living and counseling in a pluralistic society, where too often the experiences and needs of some members are devalued or ignored. Changing demographics and the acknowledged priority of developing cultural competence in counselors and group workers places diversity issues as a primary concern of group workers (Bemak & Chi Ying Chung, 2004). This chapter covers key concepts of diversity, presents models for identity development, explores the implications of diversity for counseling, and finally, addresses diversity issues in group work.

DEFINING AND UNDERSTANDING THE CONCEPT OF DIVERSITY

According to U.S. Census Bureau projected estimates, racial and ethnic minority numbers will rise from approximately 30% to near 50% of the population by the year 2050 (U.S. Census Bureau, 2004). The same 2000 census data revealed that approximately 20% of the population is identified as having a disability, and that individuals older than 65 years accounted for nearly 13% of the population. In addition, although the U.S. Census does not address sexual orientation, some estimates indicate that people who identify as gay, lesbian, or bisexual account for between 10% and 15% of the population (Miller, House, & Tyler, 2002). These estimates, coupled with the reality that women, while accounting for the majority of the population, still do not have the requisite status and power in this society (Sue & Sue, 2003), suggest that adapting to an increasingly diverse population is a major issue facing society.

Diversity has the potential to enrich our society but also may result in misunderstanding, conflict, and oppression (Bell, 1997). Although there is an increasing trend toward valuing diversity and promoting the social and economic equality of diverse groups, this exemplar has not been achieved (Sue & Sue, 2003). These inequalities are difficult to discuss because of the strong emotions they generate (Sue & Sue, 2003) and also because of the plethora of terms and concepts that are used to describe diversity and its effects on individuals, groups, and social processes (DeLucia-Waack & Donigian, 2004).

When discussing group and individual differences, two terms that often are used interchangeably are *diversity* and *multiculturalism*. Smith and Kehe (2004) defined diversity as "... aspects of difference among individuals and groups" (p. 329). Bell (1997) suggested that a useful framework in which to explore diversity is membership in a *social identity group*—described as a collection of people who share physical, cultural, or social characteristics within one of the categories of social identity. The social identity group categories generally included in discussions of diversity are race, ethnicity, gender, sexual orientation, socioeconomic status, disability, age, and religion (Bell, 1997; Green & Stiers, 2002).

The term *multicultural* is used more often in relation to differences based strictly on race and ethnicity (Helms & Cook, 1999) or difference based on broader membership in social identity groups (D'Andrea & Daniels, 1995). Smith and Kehe (2004) defined *race* as a categorization of individuals based on skin color and other physical attributes, historical geographic origin, and the perceptions of the dominant group. In comparison, they defined *ethnicity* as identification with a group based on culture, nationalism, citizenship, or the interactions of race, religion, and sociopolitical history. Broader definitions of *multiculturalism* have been criticized for allowing those "... who are uncomfortable with confronting their own biases to avoid dealing with the hard issues related to race and racism" (Sue & Sue, 2003, p. 7). As a result, discussion is sometimes diverted from issues related to race and ethnicity to other diversity issues (Helms & Cook, 1999).

The aim of this chapter is to explore the impact of diversity, including all social identity groups, on the practice of group work. In light of this purpose, the term *diversity* will be used throughout most of the chapter to refer to differences in social identity. The terms *multicultural* and *multiculturalism* will be used when referencing sources that use these terms. Despite the inclusive purpose of this chapter, the reasons for focusing on the impact of race and ethnicity are taken seriously. The intent of this chapter is to focus on diversity issues without losing sight of the significance of race and ethnicity in the dynamics of counseling, group work, and society.

When exploring the impact of diversity upon counseling and group work, the three elements that form an essential framework for understanding are

1. culture and its implications for diverse groups and individuals,

2. the impact of diversity upon individual identity development, and

3. the impact of diversity upon relationships between social identity groups.

These three elements are related to one another, overlap, and interact with each other, and must be understood in the context of how diversity impacts counseling and group work.

Diversity implies, but is not limited to, differences in culture. Smith and Kehe (2004) defined *culture* as the "...characteristic values, behaviors, products, and worldviews of a group of people with a distinct sociohistorical context" (p. 329). On an objective level, cultural differences are exemplified by members of a given cultural group wearing different clothes, eating different foods, and having different customs or traditions (Anderson, 2002). Differences in culture also may mean speaking different languages. Culture also has subtler but crucial dimensions, such as parenting beliefs and practices, family structure, social hierarchy, gender role expectations, use of verbal and nonverbal communication, relationship to time and space, help-seeking behavior, and many other variables (Matsukawa, 2001).

Fundamental differences in language, communication style, beliefs, and values shape individual and group life and affect relationships and communication between groups or individuals of different cultures. While certainly not insurmountable, these differences can be the basis for misunderstanding, mistrust, conflict, and stereotypes that lead to prejudice, discrimination, and, ultimately, systemic oppression (Bell, 1997).

Diversity also affects individual identity formation in profound ways. Tatum (2000) stated, "The concept of identity is a complex one, shaped by individual characteristics, family dynamics, historical factors, and social and political contexts" (p. 9). Sue and Sue (2003), in their conceptualization of three levels of identity, included similar dimensions:

1. The *individual level* of identity is shaped by an individual's unique genetic variation and nonshared experiences.

2. The *group level* of identity is shaped by social identity group membership and interaction.

3. The *universal level* of identity is characterized by shared human experiences such as self-awareness, birth, death, and love.

Even though counseling traditionally has focused on the individual and universal aspects of identity, the group level of identity is central in the discussion of diversity and its impact on counseling and group work.

MODELS OF IDENTITY DEVELOPMENT

A person's sense of self, or identity, begins with the individual characteristics and membership in social identity groups into which that person is born (Tatum, 2000). Throughout life, identity is shaped by reflections from the person's social context, consisting of family, institutions such as schools, churches, and legal systems, and the broader cultural environments of communities, regions, and nations (Harro, 2000). Within these contexts each individual characteristic or group membership is valued differentially. The person internalizes these valuations to some extent as identity.

Identity development affects how people feel about themselves, their social identities, and their cultural context. It affects the way in which they view members of their identity group and those in other groups (Helms & Cook, 1999). In an attempt to simplify the complexities of identity development, theorists have created identity development models. A key assumption behind these models is that individuals have varying degrees of awareness and acceptance of their social identity. Identity development models characterize individuals' level of identification with a social identity group through the behaviors and attitudes they display.

The predominant identity development models describe minority racial, ethnic, and cultural group members' characteristics as they come to terms with their own cultural or racial group membership, the dominant group culture, and the relationship between the groups. Examples of these models are Atkinson, Morten, and Sue's Racial/Cultural Identity Development (R/CID) model (Sue & Sue, 2003), the People of Color Racial Identity model (Helms, 1995), and the Cross model (Cross, 1995).

Sue and Sue (2003) cautioned that racial/cultural identity models "… lack an adequate integration of gender, class, sexual orientation, and other sociodemographic group identities" (p. 233). Hardiman and Jackson (1997) described a generic social identity development model that is inclusive of all target groups within this society. These models and others share a progression from a status of dominant culture acceptance, to minority culture acceptance, and then to a more complex state of minority culture acceptance that allows for connection to, and valuing of, aspects of other cultures including the dominant culture.

Racial/Cultural Identity Development (R/CID) Model

The stages of the R/CID model provide an example of this progression.

1. *Conformity.* This first stage is marked by a strong preference by minority racial and cultural individuals for dominant-culture values over those of their own groups.
2. *Dissonance.* This stage is characterized by conflict between disparate experiences that challenge the individual's valuing of the dominant culture. An individual in this stage is increasingly aware of the presence of racism and discrimination.
3. *Resistance and immersion.* Individuals in this stage endorse minority-held views to the exclusion of dominant-group values and views. They often reject White social values and beliefs and may have a strong desire to combat discrimination against their own group.
4. *Introspection.* In this stage, the individual becomes discontent with the rigid views held during the resistance and immersion stage, reevaluates dominant cultural values, and is confused about how to integrate these values with the minority culture.

5. *Integrative awareness*. Finally, individuals develop an inner sense of security and appreciation of many elements of their own culture, as well as those of the dominant culture. They believe that all cultures have acceptable and unacceptable components and develop a commitment to ending all forms of oppression.

White Racial Identity Model

In addition to identity development models that describe minority-group member experiences, theorists have developed models of dominant-group identity development to describe the psychosocial process of dominant-culture individuals as they become aware of their own cultural identity and the experiences of minority groups and individuals. An example of a dominant-group identity model is Helms's White Racial Identity model (1995), which is based on the assumption that healthy identity development for dominant groups—in this case Whites—involves becoming aware of their privileged status in society and the effect of that status upon other cultural groups.

Helms's model consists of six stages that describe White racial identity ego status from

1. *contact*, in which the White individual is unaware of racism and is content with the racial status quo, to
2. *progressive awareness* of racism,
3. varying *attitudes* toward group identity and
4. *personal responsibility*,
5. *shifting protective strategies* or defenses, and
6. *autonomy*, which finds the White individual having formed a positive, White, nonracist identity, valuing diversity and taking an active stance toward relinquishing White privilege.

A unifying element of these and other identity development models is the assumption that at different stages of development, individuals have differing beliefs and feelings about themselves, the identity group to which they belong, the dominant identity group in their environment, and individuals within those groups. Their level of comfort and acceptance of their social identity group membership, whether agent or target, becomes one of the lenses through which they view others.

Generic Social Identity Model

A factor that complicates understanding the effect of social-group membership on individual identity is the reality that social identity is multilayered. Hardiman and Jackson (1997) suggested that people experience several stages of *social identity development* simultaneously and thus have a blend of social identities, resulting in complex views of themselves and the world. A person might, for example, identify as lesbian, female, Latina, and disabled. She may experience varying levels of identity development with respect to each of her identities and, because of the differing levels, have different feelings about each facet of herself, others who share one or more of the identities, and others who do not share these identities.

Oppression Model

Another concept essential to understanding diversity is its effect on relationships between social identity groups. One way to conceptualize this effect is through the *oppression model* (Bell, 1997). Within each identity group category, specific identities are more esteemed and have more power than others in the context of a given society. For instance, in the United States, heterosexual identity is more valued than gay, lesbian, bisexual, or other sexual minority identities, and as such, heterosexuals have more social power than gays, lesbians, bisexuals, and other sexual minorities. The collection of social identities with more power constitutes what is known as the dominant or *agent group*. In the context of the present-day United States, agent groups include White; heterosexual; male; Christian; physically, emotionally, and intellectually "abled"; high income; and young or middle-aged adults (Bell, 1997; Green & Stiers, 2002).

Target groups are social identity groups that have less power. In the present-day United States, target groups include, but are not limited to, people of color; gay, lesbian, or bisexual; female or transgendered individuals; those with physical, emotional, or intellectual disabilities; people of low socioecomonic status; the elderly; and the very young (Bell, 1997; Green & Stiers, 2002).

According to the oppression model, oppression is a condition in which agent groups systematically devalue the values, beliefs, and experiences of target groups. This devaluation, which can occur covertly or overtly, is perpetuated by a socialization process that occurs at many levels. Although this devaluation is the product of many social and psychological processes, the dynamics can be understood by understanding stereotype, prejudice, discrimination, and privilege.

Stereotype

Stereotypes are negative generalizations about social identity groups and group members. Stereotypes encourage people to attend selectively to negative group attributes, which may or may not exist, forming a simplistic and negative view that denies the complex reality of group identity. Many prejudices are based upon stereotypes.

Prejudice

Prejudices are judgments of social identity groups or group members made without adequate information or contact (Smith & Kehe, 2004). Prejudices may serve the needs of a cultural group by solidifying its identity in contrast to another group or by justifying unequal treatment of other groups (Blumenfeld & Raymond, 2000). This, the active form of prejudice, is called discrimination.

Discrimination

Discrimination is behavior by individuals or institutions of one social identity group that has differential, and often harmful, effects on members of other social identity groups (Pincus, 2000). Discrimination can take different forms. *Individual and institutional discrimination* result from the actions of individuals and institutions and discriminate against target social identity groups and individuals. *Structural discrimination* results from neutral policies, procedures, and practices that unintentionally discriminate against target social identity groups.

Privilege

Privilege, a concept related to structural discrimination, is defined as unearned access to resources that is readily available to members of some social identity groups (Smith & Kehe, 2004). Privilege is much harder to identify and eradicate than is overt discrimination because the key characteristics of privilege are that privileged groups (a) do not have to understand target groups in order to function, and (b) are blinded by their own privilege to the true experience of members of target groups. Like structural discrimination, privilege is an important concept to the helping professions because, though these professions condemn overt prejudice and discrimination, privilege and structural discrimination occur routinely (D'Andrea & Daniels, 1995).

Having less power as a result of social group membership profoundly affects how individuals of target or oppressed groups view themselves, life, and agent groups. While many people rise above oppression and form positive identities and relationships with others, prolonged exposure to oppressive environments may result in internalization of negative cultural messages, called *internalized oppression* (Harro, 2000). Being relegated to a position of less power by those with privilege may compound the painful experience of being discriminated against. The result is that the relationship between groups can be marked by mistrust, hopelessness, anger, and conflict.

HISTORICAL CONTEXT OF MULTICULTURAL COUNSELING

There is consensus that early permutations of counseling were based on the experiences of White European or Euro-American males (Sue & Sue, 2003). According to Jackson (1995), clinical psychology literature did not include multicultural themes until the 1950s. During this early period, the goal of much counseling delivered to minority individuals was their assimilation into the majority culture. Not until the advent of the civil rights movement in the 1960s was significant attention directed to the inadequacy of traditional counseling methods for minority populations. Whereas during the 1960s the focus of multicultural counseling was upon groups defined by race or ethnicity, and in particular African Americans, the 1970s brought a broader focus that included other racial/ethnic groups, as well as women and people with disabilities.

During the 1970s, society in general began to question the merit of assimilation and began to explore pluralism, which allows for the interdependent coexistence of dissimilar cultures within one society. The 1980s and 1990s marked the true prioritization of diversity issues in the counseling profession with unprecedented numbers of publications devoted to the subject (Jackson, 1995).

Despite the prioritization of diversity issues in counseling, the process of examining, evaluating, and renovating a profession is slow work and the profession still has a long way to go toward serving diverse groups equally (Sue & Sue, 2003). Some of the chief concerns regarding counseling that does not fully consider and respect the client's cultural identity are as follows (Neukrug, 1998):

- Incongruent expectations of the counseling process
- The counselor not understanding the impact of social forces such as oppression upon the client
- Interpretation of cultural differences as pathology
- Lack of access to counseling for diverse groups
- The use of assessments that are culturally biased

Furthermore, counselors who are "culturally encapsulated," or expect diverse clients to share their cultural standards, will not be effective in helping the client form relevant goals, will not fully recognize the significance of the client's story, will use interventions and techniques that may be ineffective, or will alienate or harm the client (Neukrug, 1998).

Awareness of these deficiencies has resulted in the emergence of multicultural counseling, which Sue and Sue (2003) defined as

> ... both a helping role and process that uses modalities and defines goals consistent with the life experiences and cultural values of clients, recognizes client identities to include individual, group, and universal dimensions, advocates the use of universal and culture-specific strategies and roles in the healing process, and balances the importance of individualism and collectivism in the assessment, diagnosis, and treatment of client and client systems. (p. 16)

For the purposes of the discussion here, the more inclusive definition of diversity will be considered part of multicultural counseling.

CROSS-CULTURAL COMPETENCIES AND OBJECTIVES

In an effort to provide a conceptual framework that will assist counselors in better serving diverse clients, Sue, Arredondo, and McDavis (1992) extended a call to the profession and proposed what have become the *cross-cultural competencies and objectives*. This model for culturally competent counseling describes three necessary counselor characteristics:

1. Awareness of own assumptions, values, and biases

2. Understanding the worldview of the culturally different client
3. Ability to develop culturally appropriate intervention strategies and techniques

The model further outlined essential counselor beliefs and attitudes, knowledge, and skills in each area. The emphasis in this model of cultural competency is upon counselors' actively seeking understanding of themselves, their clients, and the clients' environments, and combining these understandings to provide counseling interventions and services that fully respect, embrace, and utilize the client's unique life experiences.

Counselor Self-Awareness

Counselors themselves are cultural beings, members of multiple social identity groups, and, as such, have identities, values, beliefs, social norms, and ways of communicating that are based on these contexts. Counselors' views of themselves and others are based on these social contexts, too. Without adequate awareness of the stereotypes, biases, and culturally based reactions that are part of life as cultural beings, counselors unknowingly view culturally different clients' lives, issues, goals, and interactions within the counseling relationship from their own perspective, which may be inaccurate, nonfunctional, and harmful to the client.

Awareness of Client's Worldview

Worldview is a concept related to racial/cultural identity but is more inclusive and can be seen as people's view of themselves in relationship to the world (Sue & Sue, 2003). In comparison to cultural identification, which can be seen as individuals' sense of belonging to a group, worldview is the sum total of their conceptions of the world that guide their meaning-making, decisions, and behavior. To understand a client's worldview is to fully understand their individual, social, and universal context. This context also may consist of dimensions of family, social identity, history, language, and biological, ecological, or environmental factors (Smith & Kehe, 2004).

Being able to discern and understand the subtleties and nuances of worldview comes only through study and direct experiencing of different cultures and their multitude of variations in all aspects of human life. Models such as Kluckhohn and Strodtbeck's (1961) value-orientation model assist counselors in understanding the differences in worldview. This model highlights four areas in which worldviews may differ significantly:

1. Dimensions of experiencing and valuing time
2. Attitudes toward activity
3. Views of social relationship
4. Beliefs regarding the essential nature of people

Worldview also is impacted by the dimensions of locus of control, locus of responsibility, and collectivistic/individualistic views of self-concept (Matsukawa, 2001; Sue & Sue, 2003). Although knowledge of clients' culture is important, counselors should resist the temptation to stereotype clients based on this knowledge. Knowledge of the culture and specific knowledge of the client are both necessary for an accurate understanding.

Culturally Appropriate Counseling Skills

Culturally appropriate counseling interventions take into account several factors related to culture. In addition to ensuring that clients' values and beliefs are respected and their social norms are acknowledged and incorporated to the extent possible, counselors must attend to differences in communication style. Sue and Sue (2003) discussed some elements of communication style that may be relevant to forming culturally appropriate counseling interventions:

- *Proxemics*, a person's culturally influenced sense of personal space
- *Kinesics*, a person's use of movement such as facial expressions, posture, gestures, and eye contact
- *Paralanguage*, the use of voice loudness, pauses, silence, speech rate, and inflection to express differences in meaning

Counselors also may consider whether the client's cultural communication style is low context or high context. *Low-context communication* relies largely on the verbal content of communication. *High-context communication* relies less on verbal content and more on shared understanding, nonverbal language, and paralanguage to convey the full meaning of the message. Culturally appropriate counseling interventions take each of these areas into consideration and may incorporate indigenous or culturally based healing practice if necessary (Sue & Sue, 2003).

DIVERSITY ISSUES IN MULTICULTURAL GROUP WORK

With reference to earlier discussions regarding the great potential of group work to address diversity issues, Merta (1995) lamented, "Despite its auspicious beginning, it appears that the initial promise of group work for the advancement of multicultural counseling has not been fulfilled" (p. 235). More recently, Bemak and Chi Ying Chung (2004) stated, "Historically, group counseling has not paid sustentative or systematic attention to working across ethnically and culturally diverse boundaries." (p. 31). Though group work is commonly assumed to promote collective values more than individual counseling does, in reality current systems of group work continue to express White, Euro-American therapeutic values such as emotional expressiveness, self-disclosure, and open expression and resolution of conflict (Hurdle, 1990).

Realization that group work has not met its potential for benefiting diverse members has resulted in recent attention to these issues both in practice and in training (Bemak & Chi Ying Chung, 2004). A result of this focus has been the development of *Principles for Diversity-Competent Group Workers* by the Association for

Specialists in Group Work (ASGW; 1999). Like the cross-cultural competencies and objectives (Sue, Arredondo, & McDavis, 1992), these diversity principles describe diversity competence in terms of three dimensions:

1. Awareness of self
2. Awareness of group members' worldview
3. Awareness of diversity-appropriate intervention strategies

The principles further describe each of these dimensions in terms of attitudes and beliefs, knowledge, and skills required to achieve competence.

Despite the similarities of the two documents, the diversity issues of group work and individual counseling are distinct from one another. Although many of the same concerns of multicultural counseling also apply to group work, the multilevel nature of group work results in key differences between the theory and the practice of individual counseling and group work (Kline, 2003). Some of the key concepts of group work that must be examined for their applicability to diverse populations include the group as a social microcosm, the therapeutic factors, group cohesion, group development, pre-group planning, and specific skills used during group facilitation.

Groups as a Social Microcosm

A key concept that differentiated group work from individual counseling is the idea of groups as a social microcosm. Yalom (1995) considered it inevitable that the dynamics of groups would mirror the dynamics of the outside social environment and regarded this as a benefit because individuals could learn to deal with these issues in a realistic context. With respect to diversity in groups, this translates into inevitable reenactment of oppression during the group process (Green & Stiers, 2002; Helms & Cook, 1999). Thus, for groups with diverse composition or differences in leader/member social identity, the reenactment of societal dynamics may offer an opportunity to discuss, learn, and heal from oppression, or it may have the potential to propagate and reinforce oppression (Brooks, Gordon, & Meadow, 1998). Without adequate, competent leadership that addresses oppressive dynamics early in the group process, the latter is more likely to occur (Green & Stiers, 2002).

According to Helms and Cook (1999), three main diversity themes typically occur within the dynamics of groups:

1. Power is distributed within the group according to each person's social role in the group. This means that group leaders and group members with powerful roles will tend to have more influence in the group.
2. Power may be distributed according to the numerical representation of social identity groups within the group.
3. Members of agent social identity groups generally have more power than target members.

These themes present themselves in different ways depending on the leader's social identity, diversity in coleadership relationships, and the social identity composition of the group. Understanding the implications of these dynamics is essential in preparing for diverse groups, for recognizing these dynamics, and in preventing harm from occurring to members. Examples of these dynamics include the following:

- Without specific intent otherwise, group leaders who have cultural biases, prejudices, or blind spots will tend to perpetuate these attitudes in the group because the leader generally is the most powerful person in the process (Kline, 2003).
- Agent group members may dominate group interaction. Group norms and process will conform to agent standards, and topics will be those of relevance to agent group members (Han & Vasquez, 2000).
- Members with nonvisible target identities, who hide their identity in many social settings, may hide this identity as well in groups. Although they may do this for safety reasons, the experience parallels the sense of invisibility and powerlessness that the member may have in society at large.
- Members with target identities may be unwilling to discuss their feelings or experiences associated with their status. This dynamic may be related to feeling unsafe or ashamed (Helms & Cook, 1999).
- When target members share their feelings and experiences honestly, agent group members who are uncomfortable with their status may deny, minimize, or openly challenge the reality of such feelings and experiences (Griffin, 1997).
- Agent members may scapegoat target members for resisting dominant group norms or for expressing oppression-related anger, mistrust, or pain. Group leaders may compound this damaging dynamic by labeling a target member too quickly as resistant or problematic (Sue & Sue, 2003).
- Members with target identities may be pressured into roles representative of their identity group or appointed as educator of agent group leaders or members. These roles absolve agent group members and leaders of responsibility for oppressive dynamics in the group and depersonalize target members

Each of these dynamics results in diminishing the target group member's experience and extends to the entire group process. These dynamics are more likely to occur if the group leader is unable to recognize when they are occurring or if the leader is unable to steer the group toward more effective ways of interacting.

Therapeutic Factors

One of the most accepted and well-researched concepts in group work (Helms & Cook, 1999), *therapeutic factors* are elements of group experience from which group members derive benefit. Yalom (1995) has published the most accepted list of therapeutic factors based on research, which includes

- instillation of hope,
- universality,
- imparting information,
- altruism,

- corrective recapitulation of the primary family group,
- development of socializing techniques,
- imitative behavior,
- interpersonal learning,
- catharsis,
- existential factors, and
- group cohesion.

Helms and Cook (1999) have described Yalom's therapeutic factors as a fruitful starting point for exploring diversity-sensitive group intervention, recognizing that his work provides the framework for much of the group counseling conducted today. Helms and Cook indicated that without attention to diversity issues and the differential effects on group members, the therapeutic factors might be counterproductive for some group members. Hurdle (1990) also discussed the implications of diversity on the therapeutic factors. The following discussion summarizes their critiques.

Instillation of Hope

Diverse group members should be exposed to people who are similar in background, either in the group or through information, who have overcome similar challenges and been helped by participating in groups. Group leaders must openly acknowledge the differential limitations to success that society places on some group members.

Universality

Although sharing issues and experiences at the universal level may be helpful, diverse group members may benefit in addition from sharing with others who have similar backgrounds and experiences. Group leaders must be prepared to connect diverse group members who have similar cultural experiences or experiences of oppression while also pointing out universal themes that may unite the group.

Imparting Information

Diverse group members may benefit greatly from receiving information about differing cultural interpretations of behavior, along with information about the group process. Group leaders may have to facilitate information exchanges when members have different communication norms. Leaders also must ensure that didactic group material is relevant to the experiences of diverse group members.

Altruism

Diverse group members may experience validation of their worth as they provide support, advice, and feedback to others. To ensure this, group leaders must be aware that the contributions of diverse group members may be discounted, and the leaders may have to assist group members in seeing the value of all contributions.

Corrective Recapitulation of the Primary Family Group

Although family issues may play a part in any group member's distress, societal dynamics may be even more relevant for diverse group members. Group leaders must be aware of different family structures and exercise caution before interpreting group members' issues as deficits in family relationships.

Development of Socializing Techniques

Definitions of basic social skills are culturally determined. Diverse group members may benefit from learning how to switch cultural styles when necessary. Group leaders must be familiar with a variety of culturally appropriate behaviors and should assist members in determining which are most useful.

Imitative Behavior

Diverse group members may imitate the behavior of group leaders or, in mixed groups, dominant group members. This may be beneficial if the behavior is anti-oppressive and useful to the diverse member. Diverse coleadership relationships that model effective cross-cultural respect and communication may be particularly effective in this case. Imitative behavior will not be beneficial if the group leader demonstrates biased behavior or allows racist, sexist, or other oppressive behavior to continue unchecked.

Interpersonal Learning

Interpersonal learning can be valuable to agent and target group members by uncovering the impact of cultural differences in behavior through the feedback process. Engaging in honest feedback in a diverse group, however, can be anxiety provoking and frustrating. Group leaders must be comfortable with conflict and provide adequate support, structure, and encouragement to group members as they communicate with each other. Leaders also must be cognizant that self-disclosure of personal reactions may be culturally inappropriate for some group members.

Catharsis

Expression of strong emotions may be helpful to some diverse group members. Different cultures view the expression of strong emotions, or catharsis, in varying ways, and group leaders should be aware of these differences, should allow for different modes of expression, and should ensure that the emotional expressions of diverse group members have a reasonable chance of being understood and accepted by other group members.

Existential Factors

Most diverse group members will relate to universal experiences such as interpersonal connections and death, but the existential givens of freedom and responsibility may not be relevant to group members who have experienced chronic oppression. Actually, oppression and related powerlessness may deserve status as an existential condition. Group leaders should not assume that all group members experience existential factors equally.

Group Cohesion

The final therapeutic factor, group cohesion, is one of the most critical to the group process (Yalom, 1995) but also is considered as difficult to achieve in diverse groups

(Brinson & Lee, 1997). Thus the following is a more in-depth discussion of group cohesion and the related element of trust.

Importance of Group Cohesion and Trust

Group cohesion, defined as group members' attraction to the group and other members (Yalom, 1995), is essential for the development of a therapeutic group environment (Brooks, Gordon, & Meadow, 1998). Without group cohesion, group members will not be willing to take the necessary risks to participate in the group and to continue to participate when interaction becomes anxiety provoking or frustrating.

Although trust between group facilitators and group members and between group members is necessary to developing cohesion, diverse group members may have difficulty developing trust, especially with dominant-culture group leaders and members (Brinson & Lee, 1997). When diversity issues affect group members' ability to trust each other or the group leader, communication and understanding are impeded and group cohesion is affected adversely. Then the group's overall functioning toward its goals suffers. As a cautionary note, it is necessary to distinguish between mistrust that is rooted in societal dynamics and suspicions that are rooted in mental disorders (Fenster & Fenster, 1998; Sue & Sue, 2003).

Fenster and Fenster (1998) used the term "good enough basic trust" to describe a condition in which diverse group members feel safe enough to engage in the group process, and they offered several suggestions to the group leader in establishing this level of trust in mixed identity groups:

1. The group leader should be aware of the standard group work practices for developing a safe environment.
2. The group leader must show an eagerness to learn about other cultures, as well as basic knowledge about cultural differences.
3. The leader must model acceptance and respect for diverse identities and experiences.
4. The leader must communicate that the group culture is one in which cultural stereotypes, prejudices, discrimination, and oppressive dynamics will be confronted, discussed, and challenged.
5. The leader also must adequately manage the anxiety level of the group during discussions of diversity-related issues.

In addition, Sue and Sue (2003) discussed factors that influence the perception of dominant-group counselors as trustworthy, and these factors may be relevant to developing trust and cohesion in diverse groups. First, Sue and Sue (2003) place the responsibility of developing trust on the person in power in the relationship, which in a group is usually the leader and and any group members in powerful roles. Sue and Sue also indicated that diverse clients may test dominant-culture counselors for sincerity and openness and indicated that responses that would be perceived as trustworthy include honesty, sincerity, genuineness, and possibly some self-disclosing.

Group Development Stages

Group development theories describe stages, transitions, and issues common to all groups. Group workers who understand group development can better understand the needs of the group and group members during the transitional phases and can gauge the progress of their groups by monitoring the group's development. From the many group development theories, Gross and Capuzzi (2002) created a composite incorporating the main commonalities of many theories. They conceptualized the group development process as having four stages:

1. The definitive stage
2. The personal involvement stage
3. The group involvement stage
4. The enhancement and closure stage

During the definitive stage, leaders set up the group, and members evaluate the group for fit, acceptance, and belonging and begin to make sense of the group's process and structure. During the personal involvement stage, members begin to develop enough trust to engage each other, the group, and the leader in more challenging ways. To enter the group involvement stage, members must have worked through their basic differences and conflicts. During this phase, group members begin to work together toward achieving group and personal goals. Finally, in the enhancement and closure stage, group members consolidate the meaning of their group experiences, plan for life after group, and process the loss of the group.

In groups having a diverse composition, the group may not develop past the early stages without specific attention to differences in culture and issues of diversity (Fenster & Fenster, 1998). Diversity affects each phase of group development, and group leaders should adjust their leadership accordingly (Brinson & Lee, 1997).

Diversity Concerns During the Definitive Stage

Appropriate group composition is essential for diverse groups to progress through the definitive stage and develop the trust necessary to move to more challenging issues (Merta, 1995). In addition to other group screening criteria, potential group members should be evaluated for social identity and levels of identity development and placed in groups whose purpose and composition will allow them to meet their objectives (Anderson, 2002).

During the early definitive group phase, diverse group members may experience anxiety because of unfamiliarity with group work and mistrust of the helping system (Brinson & Lee, 1997). This entry anxiety can be addressed in pre-group interviews by outlining the group's goals, objectives, and process to reduce ambiguity and provide an opportunity for processing anxieties and questions. These issues may be revisited several times during the early definitive phase (Brooks et al., 1998).

Nearly all group members experience some anxiety during the definitive stage, and establishing ground rules and connection between members can lend a sense of safety. A diverse group should acknowledge cultural differences in how members self-disclose and express feelings, and respecting self-determined levels of participation is important. During this formative phase, diverse group members should be encouraged to tell their stories at their own pace, using, if necessary, their primary language or alternative modes of communication.

Throughout this phase, group leaders should check for understanding between group members and encourage members to acknowledge and support each participant's experience (Brinson & Lee, 1997). Culturally appropriate structured activities may ease the diverse group through this early phase, though the activities should not be overused, as they may decrease spontaneity and keep the group at a superficial level (Merta, 1995).

Diversity Concerns During the Personal Involvement Stage

Groups that have developed sufficient trust can move into the personal involvement stage. Because of increased trust, group members may begin to express deeper differences (Kline, 2003). Interactions during this phase are characteristically more challenging, and conflict may arise. Helms and Cook (1999) stated, "Once implicit racial or cultural issues occurring with a group are made explicit, it is likely that related conflicts will also move to the forefront of the group." (p. 242).

In diverse groups, challenge and conflict may center on uncovered power relationships, bias, and feelings related to social identity (Camacho, 2001). Strong leadership is essential during this phase to encourage diverse group members to deal with their differences, maintain a level of safety in the group, set limits on inappropriate or culturally insensitive expressions of anger, guide group members through conflict resolution or management, and help the group make sense of the process (Camacho, 2001; Yalom, 1995).

In addition, group leaders should be aware that many cultural groups view conflict differently (Sue & Sue, 2003). Group leaders should be flexible regarding how conflict is expressed and resolved within the group and be prepared to suggest and negotiate alternative means of resolution. Successful negotiation of culturally based conflict will increase levels of trust within the group.

Diversity Concerns During the Group Involvement Stage

Successful negotiation of the challenging personal involvement stage will result in the diverse group moving to the group involvement stage. Brinson and Lee (1997) described this stage as one of cohesiveness and productivity in which group members can explore significant personal issues in depth and work actively toward the group's goals and objectives. Focusing on these goals, leaders of diverse groups should continue to encourage group members to explore the impact of diversity and culture on personal problem formation, problem resolution, and resiliency.

Some view the social identity development of both target and agent group members as a worthy goal for diverse group experiences (Sue & Sue, 2003). Revisiting diversity themes and issues in the group may be necessary because group development is not a linear process and groups cycle back through phases as new issues come up, and trust has to be rebuilt after addressing challenging issues (Kline, 2003).

Diversity Concerns During the Enhancement and Closure Stage

As groups meet their objectives and begin to draw to a close, they enter the enhancement and closure stage. For all groups, this time is essential for acknowledging member gains in the group, solidifying application of these gains to the outside environment, and bringing the group experience into meaningful perspective.

For members of some social identity groups and cultures, the goal of transferring new behaviors to their everyday lives may be counterproductive, or even dangerous. Group leaders should be aware of the receptiveness of the local community to diversity and should encourage group members to weigh the consequences of trying out new ideas and behaviors in environments that may be less than receptive.

IMPACT OF DIVERSITY UPON THE GROUP LEADERS' ACTIONS

Just as diversity affects the dynamics, development, and impact of groups, it affects group leaders' actions. In critiquing attempts to discuss diversity issues in group work, Brinson and Lee (1997) stated that these attempts generally lack "... clear cut direction for facilitating the group process with clients from diverse cultural backgrounds...." Based on the literature and the preceding conceptualizations of group and social dynamics, the following recommendations are made for the group leader with regard to pre-group planning and the group leadership process.

Pre-Group Planning

Planning is the first step toward conducting any successful group (Kline, 2003), and planning is doubly important for diverse groups. In particular, leaders of diverse groups have to make careful decisions regarding group purposes and goals, group composition and screening, and group duration and settings.

Group Purposes and Goals

Clear purposes and goals are particularly important for diverse groups because they provide the foundation upon which further structure and planning of the group must occur and they must be evaluated for compatibility with group members' diverse worldviews (DeLucia-Waack & Donigian, 2004). In addition, goals that are clear and generally accepted by group members can serve as touchstones for diverse leaders and members as they negotiate culturally compatible processes to achieve those goals. Finally, goals that are clearly understood and accepted by group members may provide a basis for uniting leaders and group members as they take on the challenge of navigating through their differences (Hogan-Garcia, 2003).

The counseling profession typically values individual achievement, emotional independence, and individual responsibility, and these are the values encouraged through traditional group work (Matsukawa, 2001). These values, however, may be inconsistent with the values of some diverse group members. Group leaders should be aware of their own orientation toward these values and remain vigilant in evaluating if diverse group members will benefit from goals based on these values. In addition, two common goals mentioned in multicultural counseling literature are (a) to promote social identity development and (b) to develop bicultural competence, or the ability to function in multiple cultural contexts (Han & Vasquez, 2000; Hurdle, 1990). Group workers should consider these as potential outcome goals for diverse groups.

Group Composition and Screening

Leaders' choices regarding the composition of their groups impact group functioning (Yalom, 1995). In addition to concerns that apply to all groups, a key question for leaders of diverse groups is whether the composition should be homogeneous or heterogeneous (Han & Vasquez, 2000; Merta, 1995). *Homogeneous groups* are composed of group members who share similar characteristics within dimensions such as issues (for example, depression), sociodemographic identity (for example, people with disabilities), or combinations of both. By contrast, *heterogeneous groups* have a more varied composition with respect to these dimensions.

There is a substantial body of literature regarding heterogeneity versus homogeneity in groups. Much of the literature addresses homogeneity/heterogeneity in terms of gender (Schoenholtz-Read, 1996). Han and Vasquez (2000) summarized the potential benefits of homogeneous groups as earlier cohesion, more support, less conflict, better attendance, and faster symptom relief. Gazda, Ginter, and Horne (2001) summarized the potential drawbacks of homogeneous groups as lack of dissent or independent thinking, lack of risk taking, and resistance to leader-suggested changes. Conversely, heterogeneous groups are generally believed to develop cohesiveness more gradually, have a higher probability of conflict, and have higher rates of early termination (Gazda et al., 2001). Group heterogeneity, however, is believed to contribute to greater potential for interpersonal learning through varied feedback, potentially beneficial levels of change-producing anxiety, and a more realistic environment for reality testing (Yalom, 1995).

Leaders' decisions about the composition of their groups should be based upon the purpose and structure of the group and the social identity characteristics of potential group members. Homogeneous groups may be best suited for short-term groups that require quick cohesion. Leaders should consider homogeneous composition for groups whose purpose is to support or develop stronger social identity for target-group populations (Han & Vasquez, 2000). Heterogeneous group composition may be appropriate for groups whose purpose is to develop cross-cultural communication or assertiveness skills and to develop deeper levels of self-understanding and change (Merta, 1995).

When composing a group, the level of identity development of agent and target group members should be considered. For instance, target group members who are in the resistance phase may be limited in their openness to giving and receiving support or seeking connection with agent group members and, as such, may benefit more from homogeneous groups. Target group members who are in stages where they devalue their social identity may benefit more from homogeneous groups in which they will receive support and validation of that identity (Brinson & Lee, 1997). Heterogeneous groups may be less suited for group members for whom the presence of agent group members will prevent their experiencing a sense of safety and trust.

In general, agent group members might benefit more from heterogeneous group composition than target members will (Brown & Mistry, 1994). Nevertheless, target group members who are moving from resistance phases to redefinition phases may benefit greatly from cross-cultural contact.

These important decisions regarding group composition highlight the importance of group leaders' use of adequate screening procedures. Adequate screening is part of the ethical practice that protects group members from harm and ensures group compositions that will increase the chances for beneficial group experiences. Though screening may be minimal for some groups, such as content-oriented psychoeducational groups, and not used at all for others, such as task groups, typical screening procedures for process-oriented psychoeducational groups, counseling groups, and therapy groups may involve personal or group interviews to collect data on presenting concerns, psychosocial history, and past treatment.

Traditional psychosocial intakes, assessments, and diagnosis have been critiqued for ignoring sociocultural dimensions (Anderson, 2002). As such, screening also should involve gathering information about the client's self-identification, cultural background, experiences of oppression, and comfort with other social identity groups. Gathering this information will assist in determining diverse individuals' suitability for group work and the best group composition for their needs.

Pre-Group Orientation

Pre-group orientation may be a critical factor in the success of diverse groups (Brooks et al., 1998; Han & Vasquez, 2000). The screening interview presents an ideal opportunity to begin pre-group orientation. Pre-group preparation involves providing potential group members with information regarding the group's policies, goals, and processes. Although diverse group members may come into the group with many assumptions about group counseling based upon their culture and experiences in society, the potential negative impact of these assumptions can be minimized by providing information and processing anxieties and concerns. For instance, orientation coupled with a clearly communicated commitment from the leader to respect the diverse group member's experiences, feelings, values, and beliefs can alleviate anxieties about being mainstreamed and/or stereotyped (Han & Vasquez, 2000).

Time Considerations and Settings

The natural ebb and flow of relationships and learning rarely match the hectic schedules of professional environments. In diverse groups, however, ample time is needed to build trust, negotiate bicultural group norms, and facilitate understanding between differing group members. Though structure may be important, the temptation to crowd group sessions with topics and content should be resisted. Instead, sessions should be planned and paced so there is adequate time to process communication challenges and strong emotions. Planning for more sessions than is customary, or making sessions longer may be necessary, and leaders may have to justify these departures based upon their diversity-related goals.

The group setting may be significant to the experience of diverse members. Diverse members who are unaccustomed to, or mistrustful of, traditional mental health settings might benefit from having the group located in a safe, familiar setting. If this is not possible, attempts should be made to make the environment safe and comfortable. This includes giving consideration to the arrangement of the room and the social norms of the different members.

Although all needs may not be met, in diverse groups it is important to acknowledge and process the limitations of the setting. Economic factors, too, may affect diverse individuals' access to groups. As such, groups that may benefit underserved populations should be marketed, priced, and located so they are accessible to members of these populations.

Process Goals and Skills

Much of what the group leader does in a group is to encourage facilitative norms or process goals. The process goals of counseling groups are generally emotional expressiveness, self-disclosure, open communication, a here-and-now focus, egalitarian participation, democratic process, personal responsibility, and open expression and resolution of conflict (Kline, 2003). In diverse groups, process goals may have to be adjusted. Helms and Cook (1999) stated that

> the group leader must facilitate the development of a new set of
> norms that recognize cultural and sociopolitical differences in
> group members' socialization while simultaneously uniting
> group members. (p. 226)

This may require that the group leader evaluate the overarching purpose of each process goal and find other ways to meet that goal. For example, leaders who value open communication typically facilitate connection between group members by having the members talk directly to each other about their similar feelings and experiences. If a culturally diverse group member cannot adapt comfortably to this norm, the leader and group members may want to explore alternative means of facilitating connection, such as storytelling, artwork, rituals, or other activities.

Process goals are related directly to the skills group leaders use during sessions. Just as process goals are utilized to advance outcome goals, skills are used to promote process goals. When working with diverse groups, group leaders have three choices regarding the skills they can use (Helms & Cook, 1999; Sue & Sue, 2003):

1. They can use the *generic group skills* that most group workers are taught or skills associated with specific theoretical orientations.
2. They can *adapt specific skills* to be more culturally compatible.
3. They can investigate using *helping skills from other cultures*.

Working with diverse groups does not mean throwing out customary group skills. But skills must be evaluated for use with culturally different clients. Skills that violate cultural norms may have to be adapted or not used at all. Also, using the customary group work skills with diverse groups will be much more useful if the group members are well oriented to the counseling and group work processes. In any case, when using traditional group skills, leaders must be alert to any adverse reactions in diverse group members.

Adapting customary group skills to work with diverse groups can range from using the skill as is but providing context to members about the purpose of the skill or intervention, to incorporating cultural variations. Diverse group members may become comfortable with a customary intervention if they have enough information about its purpose. Providing context also can be useful if group members decide to brainstorm or suggest alternatives that may work better for themselves and the group.

Another alternative is the use of indigenous or culturally based interventions. This may be most helpful in homogeneous groups in which members share a culture and have similar levels of identity development. Heterogeneous groups in which members have expressed openness to experimenting with different cultural activities or forms of communicating also may benefit. Extra care should be taken if the chosen interventions are considered sacred, so important rituals are not trivialized or abused. Research and consultation with culturally knowledgeable community leaders may be necessary to increase the credibility of group leaders (Sue & Sue, 2003).

Group facilitators who want to deal with diversity issues openly and competently in their groups must be prepared to deal with conflict between group members (Camacho, 2001; Merta, 1995; Yalom, 1995). Dealing with conflict effectively in a group—particularly a group with diverse membership—begins with preparing group members before the group begins. Members who anticipate and accept conflict as part of the process will be more apt to participate in resolving the conflict (Kline, 2003).

Group members also should be provided with a tentative framework outlining how the leader will help to resolve conflict. An example of such a framework is Hogan-Garcia's (2003) conflict recovery process. Frameworks such as this one prepare members for the process and lower their anxiety during conflict (Han & Vasquez, 2000). Because group members whose cultures are more collectivistic may view conflict as a breach of the group and may wish to resolve such conflicts in a less confrontational manner, negotiating a process that works for most group members is important (Camacho, 2001).

To maintain a sense of safety during conflict in diverse groups, leaders must maintain their role as leader, be vigilant about setting limits on aggression and blaming, be aware of their own cultural triggers, and maintain a strong boundary between their own issues and the issues of the group. Group leaders also may want to remind the group of the existing purposes, process, and goals so members can focus on commonalities beyond the conflict, adhere to communication guidelines (such as being nonjudgmental or not interrupting), and remain motivated when conflict becomes frustrating (Camacho, 2001).

LEARNING ACTIVITIES

1. Pick one group work theory from this book and one target social identity group that we have discussed. Gather information about values, beliefs, and practices that are central to the group work theory and the cultural group. Identify areas that are compatible and incompatible between the theory and the social identity group. How would group members in conformity, resistance, and redefinition stages of identity development react differently to the theory and practices?

2. Watch the movie *The Color of Fear* (Mun Wah & Hunter, 1994). Keep track of your reactions to the various group members and interactions as the group progresses. If you were the group's leader, how might your reactions affect what you do as a leader? Compare your reactions to the movie to the R/CID, White Identity Development, or the generic social identity development model, whichever is most appropriate for your social identity. What are the implications?

3. Pair up with a classmate. Each of you should pick one of your social identities with which you are comfortable disclosing and discussing. Discuss what it would be like to be a member in a counseling group in which you are the only person, including the leader, with that social identity (gay in an all-heterosexual group, female in an all-male group, hearing in an all-deaf group). Consider and discuss the following:
   a. What would it be like if no one talked about the difference?
   b. What issues would they discuss? What would it be like if the only issues discussed had little to do with you?
   c. Imagine trying to explain this aspect of your identity to the other group members. What would you say?
   d. What would it be like if, when you explained this to the other group members, they didn't believe you or discounted the information you related?

4. Conduct a literature search and find a psychoeducational or counseling group designed for a specific social identity group. What are the goals of the group, and do the goals seem culturally appropriate? How does the design account for the group worker's awareness of self, awareness of group members' worldview, and diversity-appropriate intervention strategies? To what extent does the design account for the identity development levels of group members?

SUMMARY

Diversity is an increasingly important issue in society, affecting individuals' values, beliefs, and views of themselves and others. Models of social group identity development provide a way to understand how people ascribe to the defining characteristics of their social identity groups. Identify is multifaceted and may reflect memberships in many social groups. Identifying with these groups affects the person's self-concept and relationships with others.

The profession of counseling is rooted in Euro-American traditions, and awareness that diverse populations have not received adequate treatment has resulted in a focus on evaluating and adapting counseling theories and techniques. It has also highlighted three essential areas for counselor development. First, counselors must become aware of themselves as cultural beings, acknowledging their biases, stereotypes, and reactions to those who are culturally different. Then counselors must become aware of their culturally different clients' worldviews and how these differences may impact the process of counseling. Finally, culturally competent counselors must be able to evaluate counseling interventions with respect to their clients' different worldviews and must be able to adapt their interventions based on these differences, or to incorporate healing practices that are rooted in the client's own culture.

These concepts regarding cultural competence also apply to groups and group workers. Group workers must be aware that diversity profoundly affects the functioning and leadership of groups. Societal dynamics such as oppression may play out in the group, and these dynamics may be harmful to both target and agent group members. Diversity issues must be considered when assessing the presence of therapeutic factors within groups, especially the factor of cohesion or trust within groups. Similarly, diversity within the group may affect the process of group development and has implications for each of the stages.

Group workers must also consider diversity within a group when planning and screening for their groups. Group composition should be carefully managed so that diverse group members can achieve group goals in a nonhostile environment. Group dimensions such as time allotted for work, location of the group, and arrangement of the room may also become significant for diverse group members. The processes of informed consent and pre-group preparation, while always important, become doubly important when group members are very different in social identity from facilitators or from each other.

In addition to carefully implementing planning and screening processes, group counselors working with diverse populations must evaluate their skills for cultural appropriateness. The customary group interventions should be introduced carefully to diverse groups as they may not be appropriate for all members. Leaders may have to adapt interventions to be compatible with cultural norms or may have to incorporate culturally based interventions or adopt group-related helping skills from other cultures. Conflict resolution skills become very important in group work with diverse members.

USEFUL WEB SITES

- ☐ Counselors for Social Justice
  www.counselorsforsocialjustice.org/
- ☐ Association for Multicultural Counseling and Development
  www.amcd-aca.org/amcd/
- ☐ ASGW *Principles for Diversity-Competent Group Workers*
  www.asgw.org/diversity.htm

☐ Peggy McIntosh's "White Privilege: Unpacking the Invisible Knapsack"
http://seamonkey.ed.asu.edu/~mcisaac/emc598ge/unpacking.html

REFERENCES

Anderson, D. (2002). Multicultural group counseling: Cross-cultural considerations. In D. Cappuzzi & D. Gross (Eds.), *Introduction to group counseling* (3rd ed., pp. 205–235). Denver: Love Publishing.

Association for Specialists in Group Work (ASGW). (1999). Principles for diversity-competent group workers. *Journal for Specialists in Group Work, 24,* 7–14.

Bell, L. (1997). Theoretical foundations for social justice education. In M. Adams, L. Bell, & P. Griffin (Eds.), *Teaching for diversity and social justice* (pp. 3–15). New York: Routledge.

Bemak, F., & Chi Ying Chung, R. C. (2004). Teaching multicultural group counseling: Perspectives for a new era. *The Journal for Specialists in Group Work, 29*(1), 31–41.

Blumenfeld, W., & Raymond, D. (2000). Prejudice and discrimination. In M. Adams, W. Blumenfeld, R. Castaneda, H. Hackman, M. Peters, & X. Zuniga (Eds.), *Readings for diversity and social justice: An anthology on racism, anti-Semitism, sexism, heterosexism, ableism, and classism* (pp. 21–30). New York: Routledge.

Brinson, J., & Lee, C. (1997). Culturally responsive group leadership: An integrative model for experienced practitioners. In H. Forrester-Miller & J. Kottler (Eds.), *Issues and challenges for group practitioners* (pp. 43–56). Denver: Love Publishing.

Brooks, D., Gordon, C., & Meadow, H. (1998). Ethnicity, culture, and group psychotherapy. *Group, 22,* 53–80.

Brown, A., & Mistry, T. (1994). Group work with "mixed membership" groups: Issues of race and gender. *Social Work with Groups, 17,* 5–21.

Camacho, S. (2001). Addressing conflict rooted in diversity: The role of the facilitator. *Social Work with Groups, 24,* 135–153.

Cross, W. (1995). The psychology of nigrescence. In J. Ponterotto, J. Casas, L. Suzuki, & C. Alexander (Eds.), *Handbook of multicultural counseling* (pp. 93–122).Thousand Oaks, CA: Sage Publications.

D'Andrea, M., & Daniels, J. (1995). Promoting multiculturalism and organizational change in the counseling profession. In J. Ponterotto, J. Casas, L. Suzuki, & C. Alexander (Eds.), *Handbook of multicultural counseling* (pp. 17–33). Thousand Oaks, CA: Sage.

DeLucia-Waack, J., & Donigian, J. (2004). *The practice of multicultural group work: Visions and perspectives from the field.* Belmont, CA: Wadsworth.

Fenster, A., & Fenster, J. (1998). Diagnosing deficits in "basic trust" in multiracial and multicultural groups: Individual or social psychopathology? *Group, 22,* 81–93.

Gazda, G., Ginter, E., & Horne, A. (2001). *Group counseling and group psychotherapy: Theory and application.* Boston: Allyn & Bacon.

Green, Z., & Stiers, M. (2002). Multiculturalism and group therapy in the United States: A social constructionist perspective. *Group, 26,* 233–246.

Griffin, P. (1997). Facilitating social justice education courses. In M. Adams, L. Bell, & P. Griffin (Eds.), *Teaching for diversity and social justice* (pp. 279–298). New York: Routledge.

Gross, D., & Capuzzi, D. (2002). Group counseling: Stages and issues. In D. Cappuzzi & D. Gross (Eds.), *Introduction to group counseling* (3rd ed., pp. 37–55). Denver: Love Publishing.

Han, A., & Vasquez, M. (2000). Group intervention and treatment with ethnic minorities. In J. Aponte & J. Wold (Eds.), *Psychological intervention and cultural diversity* (2nd ed., pp. 110–130). Boston: Allyn & Bacon.

Hardiman, R., & Jackson, B. (1997). Conceptual foundations for social justice courses. In M. Adams, L. Bell, & P. Griffin (Eds.), *Teaching for diversity and social justice* (pp. 16–29). New York: Routledge.

Harro, B. (2000). The cyle of socialization. In M. Adams, W. Blumenfeld, R. Castaneda, H. Hackman, M. Peters, & X. Zuniga (Eds.), *Readings for diversity and social justice: An anthology on racism, anti-Semitism, sexism, heterosexism, ableism, and classism* (pp. 15–20). New York: Routledge.

Helms, J. (1995). An update of Helms's white and people of color racial identity models. In J. Ponterotto, J. Casas, L. Suzuki, & C. Alexander (Eds.), *Handbook of multicultural counseling* (pp. 181–198). Thousand Oaks, CA: Sage Publications.

Helms, J., & Cook, D. (1999). *Using race and culture in counseling and psychotherapy: Theory and process.* Boston: Allyn & Bacon.

Hogan-Garcia, M. (2003). *The four skills of cultural diversity competence: A process for understanding and practice* (2nd ed.). Pacific Grove, CA: Brooks/Cole.

Hurdle, D. (1990). The ethnic group experience. *Social Work With Groups, 13,* 59–69.

Jackson, M. (1995). Multicultural counseling: Historical perspectives. In J. Ponterotto, J. Casas, L. Suzuki, & C. Alexander (Eds.), *Handbook of multicultural counseling* (pp. 3–16). Thousand Oaks, CA: Sage Publications.

Kline, W. (2003). *Interactive group counseling and therapy.* Upper Saddle River, NJ: Prentice Hall.

Kluckhohn, F., & Strodtbeck, F. (1961). *Variations in value orientation.* Evanston, IL: Row, Patterson, & Co.

Matsukawa, L. (2001). Group therapy with multiethnic members. In W. Tseng & J. Streltzer (Eds.), *Culture and psychotherapy: A guide to clinical practice* (pp. 243–264). Washington, DC: American Psychiatric Press.

Merta, R. (1995). Group work: Multicultural perspectives. In J. Ponterotto, J. M.Casas, L. Suzuki, & C. Alexander (Eds.), *Handbook of multicultural counseling* (pp. 567–585). Thousand Oaks, CA: Sage Publications.

Miller, J., House, R., & Tyler, V. (2002). Group counseling with gay, lesbian, and bisexual clients. In D. Cappuzzi & D. Gross (Eds.), *Introduction to group counseling* (3rd ed., pp. 469–503). Denver: Love Publishing.

Mun Wah, L. (Producer/Director), & Hunter, M. (Coproducer). (1994). *The color of fear* [Motion Picture]. (Available from Stir Fry Seminars, 2311 8th Street, Berkeley, CA 94710).

Neukrug, E. (1998). *The world of the counselor.* Pacific Grove, CA: Brooks/Cole.

Pincus, F. (2000). Discrimination comes in many forms: Individual, institutional, and structural. In M. Adams, W. Blumenfeld, R. Castaneda, H. Hackman, M. Peters, & X. Zuniga (Eds.), *Readings for diversity and social justice: An anthology on racism, anti-Semitism, sexism, heterosexism, ableism, and classism* (pp. 31–35). New York: Routledge.

Schoenholtz-Read, J. (1996). Sex-role issues: Mixed-gender therapy groups as the treatment of choice. In B. DeChant (Ed.), *Women and group psychotherapy* (pp. 223–241). New York: Guilford Press.

Smith, T., & Kehe, J. (2004). Glossary. In T. Smith (Ed.), *Practicing multiculturalism: Affirming diversity in counseling and psychology* (pp. 325–337). Boston: Pearson Education.

Sue, D., Arredondo, P., & McDavis, R. (1992). Multicultural counseling competencies and standards: A call to the profession. *Journal of Multicultural Counseling & Development, 20,* 64–90.

Sue, D., & Sue, D. (2003). *Counseling the culturally diverse: Theory and practice* (4th ed.). New York: John Wiley and Sons.

Tatum, B. (2000). The complexity of identity: Who am I? In M. Adams, W. Blumenfeld, R. Castaneda, H. Hackman, M. Peters, & X. Zuniga (Eds.), *Readings for diversity and social justice: An anthology on racism, anti-Semitism, sexism, heterosexism, ableism, and classism* (pp. 9–14). New York: Routledge.

U.S. Census Bureau. (2004). *U.S. interim projections by age, sex, race, and Hispanic origin.* Retrieved on August 20, 2004, from http://www.census.gov/ipc/www/usinterimproj/nat projtab01a.xls

Yalom, I. (1995). *The theory and practice of group psychotherapy* (4th ed.). New York: Basic Books.

PART THREE:

Specialty Groups

The three chapters in Part Three of this text provide readers with a comprehensive overview of three of the four group specializations identified by the Association for Specialists in Group Work (ASGW). These chapters present guidelines for conducting each of the three group specialties — task/work groups, guidance/psychoeducational groups, and psychotherapy groups.

Chapter 9, "Task/Work Groups," begins by putting the task/work group specialty under the larger umbrella of contextual group work and defines the special attributes that differentiate a task/work group, including the subtype of teams, from the other types of groups. The chapter gives an overview of the diversity issues associated with this type of group and sets forth two models—the Task Group Performance model and the Balancing Process and Content model (the latter of which is directed specifically to the *meeting* form of task/work groups). ASGW's standards for leaders of task/work groups and leader knowledge and skill competencies are delineated. The chapter addresses how to deal with conflict and challenging members, as well as faulty agendas. Concluding the chapter is a practical example of a task/work group in action.

Chapter 10, "Guidance/Psychoeducational Groups," opens with an overview of the historical development of guidance/psychoeducational groups and their unique value in group counseling. The discussion then turns to the characteristics that differentiate guidance/psychoeducational groups from the other group specializations. The authors take the reader step by step through the phases in implementing a psychoeducational group. The qualities and skills needed for leading this type of group are emphasized. This is followed by examples of guidance groups in three settings—clinical practice, schools, and college campuses, with attention to the diversity inherent in these groups. Ethical considerations are woven throughout. The chapter concludes by presenting, as a practical example, a model of a psychological group—a wellness group for women of color.

Chapter 11. Part Three concludes with chapter 11, "Psychotherapy Groups." After discussing what makes the psychotherapy group different from the other types of groups, the authors use Adlerian, humanistic, and cognitive–behavioral approaches to illustrate a series of therapeutic sessions. ASGW's guidelines for psychotherapy groups are explained, with specific emphasis on the associated core, knowledge, and skill competencies. The authors describe leadership variables, including personal characteristics, as well as how to create the appropriate therapeutic environment and the technical aspects connected with this group specialty. Finally, the authors look at what the future of psychotherapy groups could be like and introduce readers to issues related to managed care, as well as the use of computers and the Internet in psychotherapy groups.

Task/Work Groups

Kurt L. Kraus

> The world is moved not only by the mighty shoves of the heroes, but also by the aggregate of the tiny pushes of each honest worker. —Helen Keller

"Get the job done!"
"Come on—be a team player! We need your help."
"Good groups reach consensus."

These common rallying cries are heard in unlimited settings for limitless ventures. Businesses, schools, faith communities, and clubs create groups to meet a wide demand of varied work and tasks, from decisions to be made, to products to be produced, to performances to be performed.

Small groups that are composed of effective and productive members can complete tasks and accomplish work in ways that individuals cannot. In a special edition of the *Journal for Specialists in Group Work,* dedicated to the teaching of group work, guest editors Conyne and Bemak (2004a) wrote, "While the demand for group work has grown, the need for group work to address modern day concerns and the supply of well-trained group workers are both lagging" (p. 3). Task/work group members form a gestalt; the whole is greater than the sum of its parts.

Consider these examples of task/work groups:

- School kids are celebrating "team spirit" and "group effort," whether it be a soccer team, the debate club, the school orchestra, or collaborative learning groups in science and reading. These are examples of the early emphasis on working together to accomplish common goals.
- The CEO of a Fortune 500-bound company builds her enterprise on the premise that "working together, we can reach our goals." No longer is top-down management the only leadership

style in town. Key terms including *collaboration*, *cooperation*, and *management teams* capture the tenor of the work environment better than hierarchy, seniority, and manpower.

■ The hospital auxiliary and the parent/teacher organization are two enthusiastic organizations whose members are fully invested in the missions of health care and education, respectively. Common to both are ever-changing tasks and a seemingly endless changeover in volunteers and leadership.

The aim of this chapter is to describe the task and work group, a unique specialization within the spectrum of group work. One of four specialty groups identified by the Association for Specialists in Group Work (ASGW; 1991; see also Conyne, Wilson, & Ward, 1997), task/work groups are perhaps least formally investigated and written about of the types of group work (Bettenhausen, 1991; Conyne, Wilson, & Ward, 1997; Hulse-Killacky, Kraus, & Schumacher, 1999; Hulse-Killacky, Killacky, & Donigian, 2001).

As a basis for the subsequent discussion, we will first consider diversity within the context of task/work groups and the concept of working together, which is particularly relevant to task/work groups. This is followed by a presentation of two models for conceptualizing task/work groups—the Task Group Performance model and the Balancing Process and Content model—specifically addressing the subtype of meetings. Then the discussion turns to the special preparation, training, and conduct required of group leaders. The chapter next addresses several problems, conflicts, and challenges encountered in task/work groups. The chapter concludes with an example of a task group—a not-for-profit organization subcommittee whose task is to strategize how to solve the problem of shrinking numbers in the organization.

DIVERSITY ISSUES IN TASK/WORK GROUPS

School teams, clubs, classrooms, businesses, and other types of organizations—wherever task/work groups are present—encounter issues of diversity. This commands our attention from the onset of our exploration of task/work groups (see Wilson, Rapin, & Haley-Banez, 2004). Leaders and members alike bring beliefs, customs (past practices), and expectations that influence their perception of what this group, and the people in it, will be like. As is true in all specializations of group work, leaders of task/work groups must recognize and respect diversity (ASGW, 1989, 1991) and its impact on the group. As an obvious difference, for example, some cultures value individualism; others, collectivism; and others fall somewhere in between (Forsyth, 1999; Greenberg & Baron, 2000).

Whether the diversity is ethnic, political, religious, or geographic, each subculture attaches different values to, and thus creates, different norms, expectations, and methods for functioning within or leading task groups and accomplishing tasks (see Kirchmeyer, 1993; DeLucia-Waack & Donigian, 2004). Differing values create cultural differences (Corey & Corey, 1997). For example, some cultures value cooperation over competition and others value competition over cooperation.

Cultural differences must not be overlooked or misinterpreted (Gladding, 2003), as group leaders or members may inadvertently exclude, misunderstand, neglect, or fail to appreciate others. The leader must be flexible in applying the information in this chapter to diverse task/work groups across a wide spectrum of settings and cultures (see Kirchmeyer, 1993; Reid, 1997; Watson, Johnson, & Merritt, 1998).

THE CONCEPT OF WORKING TOGETHER

Gladding (2003) has asserted, "all task/work groups emphasize accomplishment and efficiency in successfully completing identified work goals (a performance or a finished product) through collaboration" (p. 32). Collaboration—working together—is not always easy. People can recall productive meetings and groups as well as groups in which little was accomplished and that seemed like a waste of time. Further, what is considered a successful group experience by some participants may be perceived by others as wanting (Kraus & Hulse-Killacky, 1996).

This chapter espouses the belief that skilled leadership is a key to the success of task/work groups. Expertise in leading task/work groups can be developed through education and training (see ASGW, 1991; Conyne, Wilson, & Ward, 1997; Gladding, 2003; Johnson & Johnson, 1994; Schindler-Rainman, 1981; Stockton & Toth, 1996).

To understand the unique role that task/work groups play and how they function, one must understand how the task/work group fits into the broader context of group work (see Ward, 2002, and Wilson et al., 2004, for excellent overviews of this context). Greenberg and Baron (2000, p. 252) ask readers to consider two "groups"—one composed of three people waiting in a checkout line at a supermarket; the second, the board of directors of a large corporation. They contend that the latter fits more closely the common definition of a "group," based on the following four criteria:

1. The interaction of members
2. A stable pattern of relationships between them
3. The sharing of common goals
4. Members who perceive themselves as being a group

According to these authors, given that a group meet these four criteria and they form for a special purpose, they can be considered a task group (p. 254).

The concept of *task* can be either ongoing or finite. A board of directors of a company has the *ongoing* task of governing or overseeing the company's financial well-being—how productive and competitive the company is in the marketplace, what it invests in, how it distributes profits, and the like. This task is ongoing, long-term, and may outlast the terms of the members. Boards of directors typically are appointed or elected for a term. The prescribed tenure of office ensures that "fresh blood" will replace old blood in hopes of moving the company progressively forward (Hackman, 1987). Although the membership of the board changes, the task is continuous. The group rather than the task is time limited.

Other task/work groups—a community response group rallying to a cause, a hiring committee—illustrate the *finite* form of a task/work group. These groups consist of a group of people who gather together with a common purpose and endpoint. The task group addresses a specific issue, and once the goal is attained the group dissolves.

The ASGW (1991) defined the specialization of task/work groups as applying principles and processes of group dynamics to improve the practice and accomplishment of identified work goals. Task/work groups differ from counseling and psychotherapy groups primarily in their emphasis on completion of some group goal that is not specific to an individual's growth and development (Dykeman & Appleton, 1998; Gladding, 2003). To differentiate the task/work group from personal-change groups (i.e., psychoeducational group work, counseling and psychotherapy groups), Conyne, Rapin, and Rand (1997) explained that task groups direct their "attention to context and their emphasis on meeting performance goals that are directly connected to the external environment" (p. 117).

This difference—a production agenda instead of a personal-change agenda—can be viewed as task/work groups having *externalized outcomes* rather than internalized outcomes. The externalized product of a task/work group is often the reason for membership, whether the product is a report, a recommendation, a performance, an event, or a project. The range of outcomes of task/work groups is as wide and as diverse as the membership, the settings, and the purposes for which this type of group meets. How group members go about completing the group's tasks is equally varied.

Another aspect of the task/work group that sets it apart from other specializations in group work is how it ends. Once a given task is complete, the group tends to "disband abruptly" (Gladding, 2003, p. 33). This is an important consideration in forming the group and for the life of the group itself. Unlike other groups (e.g., counseling groups), in which members invest personally and rely upon emerging relationships within the group to accomplish personal outcomes, members of task/work groups may see little relevance in attending to any interpersonal relationships in the group. In addition, these task/work groups are often "run" by untrained individuals who may see little relevance in attending to interpersonal relationships in the group. Task/work groups, especially the meeting subtype, are often led by lay volunteers, people with little if any training in group leadership (Dykeman & Appleton, 1998). These lay leaders can easily lead people to conclude, "What's the big deal? Running a group … leading this meeting … facilitating this committee … can't be too challenging." The rich literature on task/work groups bears witness to the contrary: Leading a successful task group is often a complex job (see Bettenhausen, 1991; Fatout & Rose, 1995; Gladding, 2003; Schwarz, 1994; Wheelan, 1999).

THE TEAM

A specialized form of task/work groups is the *team.* Kormanski (1999) differentiated teams from groups:

> Group work ... is a process for bringing individuals together to
> work on shared tasks and to develop supportive relationships....
> All teams are groups; however, the reverse may not be true.
> (p. 6)

Many task/work groups do indeed act like a team. Katzenbach and Smith (1991) described a team's product as dependent upon members' joint efforts and contributions, not unlike the product of other task/work groups. Several attributes of a team, however, set it apart from the broader task/work group. Kormanski continued:

> The team members must have shared goals, be committed to
> work toward those goals, be willing to work interdependently,
> and be accountable to the organization.... A lack of commitment
> to the team efforts creates tension and reduces overall
> effectiveness. (1999, p. 6)

Johnson and Johnson (1994) differentiated task groups and teams in an interesting way. They defined team as

> a set of interpersonal interactions structured to achieve
> established goals. More specifically, a team consists of two
> or more individuals who (1) are aware of their positive
> interdependence as they strive to achieve mutual goals,
> (2) interact as they do so, (3) are aware of who is and is not a
> member of the team, (4) have specific roles or functions to per-
> form, and (5) have a limited life-span on membership. (p. 503)

Teams are highly specialized forms of task/work groups whose function demands additional requirements of its members, leading toward a product, performance, or other outcome that is *unique* to the team itself (e.g., a management plan, a victory, a performance) (Astin, 1987; Cohen & Bailey, 1997). Teams are present in numerous contexts, including sports teams (e.g., Little League, professional teams, intramural athletic teams), leadership teams, managerial teams, production teams, and evaluative teams.

MODELS OF TASK/WORK GROUPS

Two models for conceptualizing task/work groups are described briefly here. The first, the Task Group Performance model (Conyne, Rapin, & Rand, 1997; see also Conyne, Wilson, & Ward, 1997), focuses on the critical choices that leaders make in selecting interventions that promote successful task/work groups. The second model, the Balancing Process and Content model (Hulse-Killacky et al., 2001; see also the Visual Conceptual model, Hulse-Killacky et al., 1999), emphasizes the balance between process and content, a model that will "guide your work as a leader and to enhance the likelihood that your task groups will be both productive and enjoyable" (Hulse-Killacky et al., 2001, p. 27).

Task Group Performance Model

The Task Group Performance model, conceived by Conyne, Rapin, and Rand (1997), is grounded in two principles (p. 120):

1. The open system, in which specific attention is paid to the unique context in which the task/work group is to function
2. A performance-based framework, in which "all task groups are expected to produce something that is tangible through meeting clear performance demands"

The Task Group Performance model focuses on the interventions (actions employed in the leadership of the group) selected by the leader. Interventions are chosen at what the authors call "choice points" (p. 125), which represent critical incidents or moments when the leader is presented with a variety of possibilities or choices, each possibility taking the group in a different direction with potentially different outcomes (see Corey, 2000; Donigian, & Hulse-Killacky, 1999; Donigian & Malnati, 1997; Tyson, Perusse, & Whitledge, 2004). The authors of this model wrote, "Our model is based on the premise that task group leaders must choose from a range of possible intervention options and that informed leader choice is a critical action" (p. 121).

The leaders make choices among the complex interactions of three components (Conyne, Rapin, & Rand, 1997, pp. 121, 131, adapted from Lieberman, Yalom, & Miles, 1973):

1. The *type* of leader intervention (i.e., problem solving or group process)
2. The *level* of leader intervention (i.e., individual, interpersonal, group, or organizational; Cohen & Smith, 1976)
3. The *function* of leader intervention (i.e., caring, meaning, motivation, or managing)

Each intervention the task/work group leader selects will influence how the task group will proceed. The leader's selection is based upon what he or she believes will produce the "greatest possibility for success" (Conyne, Rapin, & Rand, 1997, p. 122). Therefore, the Task Group Performance model attends to the specific context of the group, clarity of the performance demands, and the choices that leaders make in selecting interventions.

Balancing Process and Content Model

Hulse-Killacky et al. (1999) and Hulse-Killacky et al. (2001) developed the Visual Conceptualizations of Meetings, a specialized form of task/work groups.

They espouse that the balance of process and content is vital to the success of the group.

How a task is tackled by a group is considered *process*, and the actual goal of the group is the *content* (Hulse-Killacky et al., 2001). Process and content are intertwined like threads of a string (Kraus & Hulse-Killacky, 1996), the interdependency of the two concepts of which is infinitely complex:

> Too much focus on content obscures attention to human relations issues and the development of cooperation collaboration, and community among all participants. Conversely, too much attention to process, especially process that is not effectively and clearly linked to content, hinders the group's ability to address important task and purpose issues. (Hulse-Killacky et al., 2001, p. 27)

Attaining balance is accomplished by careful attention to the dynamics—what goes on—during the warm-up, action, and closure phases of the task/work group (Hulse-Killacky et al., 1999; Hulse-Killacky et al., 2001).

Warm-Up Phase

The *warm-up phase* is attended to during the formation of the group itself as well as in the early moments of each group session or meeting. Hulse-Killacky et al. (2001) emphasize that the warm-up addresses three questions—two with a process focus and one focused on content: "Who am I? Who am I with you? What do we have to do?" (p. 31). In the warm-up phase, time is dedicated to learning who members are, to purposefully establishing rapport among members, and to creating a direction toward the group's goal. This phase must not be misconstrued as frivolous. Consider Wheelan's (1999) comment:

> Research does not suggest that rock climbing, white-water rafting, blind trust walks, or playing basketball on a donkey increases productivity in any way. These kinds of activities are fun for some people and distasteful to others. (p. 16)

The purpose of any activity must be clear. An effective task/work group builds on members' being knowledgeable of other group members and what each brings to the group.

Action Phase

The *action phase* is the work stage of the task/work group. It is characterized by these focus questions: "Who are we together? What do we have to do to accomplish our goals?" (Hulse-Killacky et al., 2001, p. 61). The answers to these questions are vital to the group's success. Although the task to which members are committed may be concrete, the ways by which members can reach the goal seem unlimited.

Closure Phase

The *closure phase* is dedicated to bringing the group members' experience to an end. Hulse-Killacky et al. (2001, p. 98) identified four themes of the closure phase:

1. Reviewing goal accomplishment
2. Preparing for future activities
3. Reviewing the impact of group relationships on goal accomplishment
4. Expressing appreciation

In effect, closure counters the tendency for task/work groups to finish their task and disband abruptly.

Ingredients for Effective Task Groups

Hulse-Killacky et al. (2001, p. 8) expanded upon the meaning of the following ingredients in effective task groups. Although they are only listed here, many of these concepts are explicated elsewhere in this text. In this model, responsibility for the care of each ingredient is shared, to some extent, between the leader and the members of the task/work group.

- Having a clear purpose
- Balancing process and content issues
- Supporting process and content in all subsystems
- Building a culture that appreciates differences
- Developing an ethic of cooperation, collaboration, and mutual respect
- Addressing conflict
- Exchanging feedback
- Addressing here-and-now issues in the group
- Inviting members to be active resources
- Developing members' ability to be influential
- Practicing effective leadership skills
- Allowing members time to reflect on their work (p. 8)

In this model, attention to balancing process and content in the warm-up, action, and closure phases of a group is critical to the life of the group.

LEADING TASK/WORK GROUPS

The responsibility for successful outcome or productivity from a task/work group lies in large part with the effectiveness of the group's leadership. The group leader has the primary responsibility for motivating members toward reaching its goals (Conyne, 1989; Conyne, Rapin, & Rand, 1997; Corey & Corey, 1997; Wheelan, 1999). Along with this primary task comes the job of attending to group members' needs, wants, and capabilities. Assisting members to make the most effective use of their time and effort falls upon the leader.

The ASGW (1991) has developed standards for leaders of task/work groups. Core coursework, including field experience under supervision, precedes additional training for specialization as a task/work group leader (ASGW, 1991; Conyne, Wilson, & Ward, 1997; Stockton & Toth, 1996). The broader core group leadership competencies are covered elsewhere in the text.

Training Standards for Task/Work Group Leaders

The successful task/work group leader, according to the ASGW *Professional Standards for the Training of Group Workers* (1991), combines specific knowledge and skills built upon a core of competencies applicable to all group workers. A special issue of the *Journal for Specialists in Group Work* ("Teaching," 2004) addresses how people learn to lead task groups (as well as other types of groups).

Conyne, Wilson, and Ward (1997, pp. 126–148) have organized task/work group training standards into five clusters:

1. Teaching the definition of task groups
2. Teaching pre-group preparation
3. Teaching therapeutic dynamics and leader skills
4. Teaching research and evaluation in task groups
5. Teaching ethical practice of task groups

Leadership training specific to task/work groups, we are reminded, is built upon a foundation of core group work skills. We will briefly look at each of the seven knowledge competencies and the eight skill competencies outlined by the ASGW (1991).

Leader Knowledge Competencies

1. *Identify organizational dynamics pertinent to task/work groups.*

    Understanding how an organization functions is imperative to leaders of task/work groups. The organizational dynamics include the qualities that define the structure where the group will take place. As implied, "dynamics" involves the concepts of power, activity, fluidity, and catalyst (Forsyth, 1999, p. 11). If the leader is from within the organization, he or she is aware of the "way things are done here." But as more and more leaders are brought into organizations, either to consult with personnel who will lead task/work groups or to actually facilitate completion of a task, a thorough understanding of the in-house idiosyncrasies is difficult to attain. To maximize the leader's effectiveness, he or she must be able to place the task that lies ahead in an accurate context (Alderfer, 1987; Conyne & Bemak, 2004b; Hackman, 1987; Kirkman & Benson, 2000).

2. *Describe community dynamics pertinent to task/work groups.*

    Like organizations, communities have histories, established norms, and probable or acceptable ways of accomplishing tasks (Cohen & Bailey,

1997; Gladding, 2003; Johnson & Johnson, 1994). Consider a public school district that has limited experience in gathering community input before making decisions. A task/work group leader in this organization might encounter strong resistance at a suggestion that a needs assessment should be completed prior to making any decisions. Or the opposite could be true: In a community where input is the norm, the group might feel uncomfortable in making a unilateral decision. Thus, being prepared to encounter the dynamics of a community, wherever it is, is crucial. (For an intriguing—and fun—cross-cultural metaphor of these concepts, see Kets & DeVries, 1999.)

3. *Identify political dynamics pertinent to task/work groups.*

Political dynamics refer to internal, or within-group, politics and include organizational politics as well. The latter exert influence and expectations for the way a task/work group might function and also for who is appointed to a work group, who leads it, and what outcomes are anticipated and expected (see Schwarz, 1994). One such task/work group may operate under the command of an authoritarian leader in which everything that gets done is by executive fiat. This task group bears little resemblance to the collaborative task/work models advocated in this chapter. Although this scenario is not a rarity, the political dynamics within groups often are not obvious (Lucas, 1999). Perhaps an organization or a larger group operates on covert or silent rules based on seniority or on gender or age bias (Forsyth, 1999; Reed, 1981). The challenges the task/group leader must navigate are difficult when politics interfere with members' attempting to accomplish the group's given task.

4. *Describe standard methodologies appropriate for task/work groups.*

How will "business" be conducted in this group (Conyne, 1989)? What will we do if we encounter challenges or disagreements? What operating rules can we all accept regarding how we communicate with one another in this group? Leaders must have knowledge of models appropriate to the group, as "one size fits all" does not apply to leading task/work groups (see Schwarz, 1994). The communication norms, established in the early stages of a task/work group, are critical to the group's successful development.

5. *Identify specific ethical considerations in working with task/work groups.*

Knowledge of ethics and standards is imperative for group leaders (ASGW, 1989). Because the tasks of work groups are not directed to personal growth, the notion of ethics might not seem like a meaningful consideration. Still, the leader must consider members' expectations in terms of safety, trustworthiness, justice, fairness—all of which have their roots in ethics (Forester-Miller, 2002).

Consider the task/work group whose members wish to work discretely on a project. Perhaps an issue under consideration is highly sensitive or the task facing the group has the potential for angry factions splitting off. Leaders must be sensitive to potential ethical issues including bias, member inclusion or exclusion, scapegoating or blaming, and the complexities of overlapping or dual relationships. Leaders of task/work groups must have a thorough understanding of ethical standards so they can ensure the trust and cooperation that is implicitly required for the group's success.

6. *Identify program development and evaluation models appropriate for task/work groups.*

The professional literature is replete with models for organizational development and models for evaluating groups. With task/work groups, what is evaluated may be the product, the outcome—whatever that may be (Dykeman & Appleton, 1998; Forsyth, 1999). Nevertheless, it is prudent to evaluate other aspects of the group, too (Toseland, Rivas, & Chapman, 1984). Again, the way a group functions has a bearing on the productivity of the group. A group that cannot work together will produce a questionable product (McLeod & Liker, 1992). Also consider that some task groups meet for the purpose of completing more than a single task. In these cases, as the group members learn to function well together, the tasks that lie ahead will be met with more experience and skill.

7. *List consultation principles and approaches appropriate for task/work groups.*

The leader should be aware of consultation principles and know how to implement them effectively in task/work groups. The leader's task in the task/work group is often one of teaching or providing members ways to maximize their own potentials for accomplishment and success (Wheelan, 1999; see also Kormanski, 1999). The effective task/work group leader is able to present strategies that will lead to effective group work, assisting members in working together and, in many cases, working with people outside the group itself.

Leader Skill Competencies

Skills for effective task/work group leadership as recommended by ASGW (1991) are developed through practice and experience, built upon the knowledge competencies described above. Similar to the training of group work specialists covered elsewhere in this text, the task/work group leader will benefit enormously by observing, modeling, coleading, and leading under supervision task/work groups (see Conyne, Wilson, & Ward, 1997; Schindler-Rainman, 1981). The following eight skills (ASGW, 1991) are annotated to provide readers with clear expectations of what skills and behaviors favor their leading effective task/work groups.

1. *Focus and maintain attention on task and work issues.*

Member distractions (e.g., time, responsibilities elsewhere), competing issues and agendas (e.g., within the group or external to it), politics, and other group dynamics all come into play in the task/work group. The skilled leader is able to help members recognize these issues and deal with them productively throughout the life of the group. The leader has to effectively orient members to the task or tasks at hand, to assist them in balancing the demands with other demands, and to remain aware of the delicate balance between productivity and human relationships within the group (see #7 below).

2. *Obtain goal clarity in a task/work group.*

What are we doing here? The clarity of the agenda is paramount in the leadership of task/work groups (Hulse-Killacky et al., 1999; Hulse-Killacky et al., 2001). The answer to "what" is followed by the question of "how." Both must be articulated clearly by the members. Some organizations favor an autocratic, top-down leadership style, in which the goal is simply the will of whomever is in charge. Other models call for mutually agreed-upon goals (see Cohen & Bailey, 1997; Conyne, 1989; Gladding, 2003), including discussion and consensus regarding how the agreed-upon goals will best be achieved.

3. *Conduct a personally selected task/work group model appropriate to the age and clientele of the group leader's specialty area(s) (e.g., school counseling).*

As mentioned, one-size leadership does not fit all. The role of the task/work group leader is dependent on the needs, desires, and abilities of its members, and of the setting. Leaders must develop the skills necessary to implement a successful task/work group model that is a good fit with these requirements. One can envision some groups that require stringent oversight, whereas others are capable of moving forward toward their goals with little intervention whatsoever. Task groups composed of second- and third-grade children cannot be facilitated in the same way as a college team or a community action group. Selecting and applying what will work best in what situation is an important skill for group leaders to develop.

4. *Mobilize energies toward a common goal in task/work groups.*

As stated at the outset, "get the job done" is a rallying cry for many task/work groups. Assisting group members to work together is a crucial leader skill in task/work groups. This skill addresses the end product or outcome for the task/work group while also mobilizing members' energies toward the process of effective task/work groups (see Forester-Miller & Gressard, 1997). Process speaks to the way things are done in groups, so attention to process is critical (Kraus & Hulse-Killacky, 1996).

5. *Implement group decision-making methods in task/work groups.*

Regardless of the desired outcome of a task/work group, its members will not uniformly agree with each other 100% of the time. One of the many benefits of group versus individual effort is the wide variety of approaches, views, suggestions, strategies, and styles that diverse group members bring to a project. The "flip side" is that decisions at times must be made at the expense of someone's ideas. Helping group members deal effectively with decision making is a crucial role of the leader (Toseland et al., 1984). Ensuring that members are heard, valued for their contribution, and appreciated (Hulse-Killacky et al., 2001) are key elements in the decision-making abilities of leaders.

6. *Manage conflict in task/work groups.*

Although conflict is written about frequently with regard to counseling and psychotherapy groups, suggestions on specific ways to address conflict in task/work groups are sparse (see Carroll & Wiggins, 2001; Corey & Corey, 1997; Donigian & Hulse-Killacky, 1999; Kraus, DeEsch, & Geroski, 2001; Yalom, 1995). Understandably, conflict can emerge in task/work groups as either member-to-member or member-to-leader conflict in relation to the task (Kormanski, 1982). One member might not value another member's idea. Or a member might believe that his or her contribution is more valuable than other contributions. Individuals or subgroups that have been silent but have competing agendas can create havoc in the task/work group. Hundreds of variants can derail a group from the tracks of productivity.

Conflicts arising from the task include differing beliefs about how the task should be completed or the steps or sequence toward completing the task (Farmer & Roth, 1998). The leader's ability to recognize conflict as a source of energy that might fuel a successful group is a powerful skill (Kraus et al., 2001). Skilled task/work group leaders have learned how to artfully navigate such challenges. More about this important skill is covered later in the chapter.

7. *Blend the predominant task focus with appropriate attention to human relations factors in task/work groups.*

An underlying factor present when people are working with other people—obvious as it may seem—is how they get along with one another. Relationship factors are complex and are covered thoroughly elsewhere in this text. As Hulse-Killacky et al. (2001) remind us, successful task/work groups require that members

> feel listened to; are accepted for their individuality; have a voice; are part of a climate in which leaders and members acknowledge and appreciate varied perspectives, needs, and concerns; understand and support the purpose of the group; and, have the opportunity to contribute to the accomplishment of particular tasks. (p. 6)

8. *Sense and use larger organizational and political dynamics in task/work groups.*

Knowledge of organizational and political dynamics is crucial, as is development of the leadership skills that address these dynamics. How the leader effectively applies what he or she understands about these often complex dynamics is what actually makes a difference for the group (Forsyth, 1999).

The role and responsibilities of the task/work group leader are complex and demanding. A command of only the basic group work skills is insufficient. Rather, additional knowledge and skill development are essential to competent leadership. Most task/work group leaders whom we will encounter in our lives probably will not have the complete repertoire of expertise outlined here. Predictably, many group tasks will go uncompleted and much work will go unfinished as a result. Emerging specialists in task/work group leadership have the potential to affect group productivity and to achieve the desired group outcomes, as well as the way individuals work together to accomplish their tasks. This also involves knowing how to deal with the inevitable conflicts.

WHEN CONFLICTS ARISE

"I have a better idea."
"If everyone can't get here on time, we'll never finish this project by the deadline!"
"There's no way I'll ever agree to that!"

Although seemingly paradoxical, conflict is important in task/work groups. Conflicts and the effort to work effectively through them are catalysts for sound decision making, establishing trust among members, and unifying often divergent points of view regarding the group process (Fatout & Rose, 1995; Kraus et al., 2001; Wheelan, 1999).

The topic of dealing effectively with challenging group members and conflicts in groups is addressed thoroughly in the literature, particularly for counseling and psychotherapy groups (see Carroll & Wiggins, 2001; Conyne, Wilson, & Ward, 1997; Donigian & Hulse-Killacky, 1999; Napier & Gershenfeld, 1983; Kraus et al., 2001; Yalom, 1995). From this literature, much can be inferred for the leadership of task/work groups. Some unique challenges presented by members in task/work groups are worthy of our consideration in this chapter. Leaders who intervene successfully with difficult members and group conflicts enhance the quality of the group experience and create more pleasant and productive working conditions (Conyne, 1989; Kraus & Hulse-Killacky, 1996; Kormanski, 1982).

The unique functions that task/work groups are often called upon to fulfill raise several challenges. The group typically has a time-limited lifespan: The group forms, performs, and disbands (Gladding, 2003). Because productivity of the membership in a task/work group is often externally driven (Conyne, Rapin, & Rand, 1997; Forsyth, 1999), participants may easily underestimate or overlook the importance of how the group functions (see Greenberg & Baron, 2000) in its effort to reach its goal. Although the eventual aim is to achieve some specific product, the group as a whole might not care about how the members interact to attain that goal or accomplish the group's purpose.

In their task group performance model, Conyne, Rapin, and Rand (1997) emphasize how leaders must promote interdependence between members and their task, and less frequently leaders "may need to gear their interventions to the intrapersonal concerns of a single group member" (p. 123). When the behaviors of individuals create conflict among members, productivity suffers (Fatout & Rose, 1995).

The leader's role in selecting members, which is vital in counseling and psychotherapy groups, is often not feasible for task/work groups. Leaders often have no say in who volunteers for any group project.

Challenging Members

Some participants believe that "too many chefs spoil the broth." Others see some members as less suited or less qualified to participate in or share responsibility for accomplishing the task or tasks that face them. Several typical challenges that members present in task and work groups are discussed in the following pages.

Individualists

As the label suggests, individualists tend to want to do a job themselves. When they become members of task/work groups, they are likely to verbally and/or nonverbally challenge the leader and the other members. For individualists, it's "my way or the highway." The forceful individualist, who has little room for the opinions, suggestions, and efforts of others, can alienate, discourage, and anger other group members. It is easy to see how this can lead to conflict and poor functioning within the task/work group.

Group leaders must apply their knowledge and skills to mitigate challenges to the group. This leader function is delicate and challenging (see Corey & Corey, 1997; Yalom, 1995). One possibility the leader might consider is to intervene by recognizing the individualistic group member, acknowledging his or her contribution to the group. By bringing attention to specific abilities and assets that many group members have to contribute, the individualist may be able to see the strengths and contributions of others in the group. Another possible intervention at the leader's disposal is to rely on the group norm of collaboration and cooperation established early in the development of the group. Norms allow other group members as well as the leader to remind emerging individualists of their initial commitment to the task/work group.

Discontents

Some group members do not like the way things develop and evolve as the group gets under way. For them, the group moves too slowly, discusses things too much, fails to function as it should. Perhaps the discontented member becomes intolerant of the process or the goals of the task group. Or he or she feels left out or unimportant in the group.

The leader must be able to monitor relationships within the group to safeguard members from being inadvertently excluded or catering to the needs of more assertive members at the expense of less assertive ones. The vigilant leader watches for such emerging difficulties. Unlike the individualist, the discontented member has stronger needs for inclusion, direction, and feedback. If their concerns go unaddressed, discontented members may simply stop participating or attending future group meetings. Members who drop out of task/work groups do so for many reasons and, among them, the leader should consider how the dynamics and functioning of the group might contribute to members' discontent and potential dropout.

Saboteurs

As the label implies, the saboteur is a member with a hidden agenda or is otherwise intent on disabling a group. For unknown or overtly seditious reasons, saboteurs are passively or aggressively driven toward rendering the group ineffective. They are invested in disempowering the group in its efforts to attain its goal (Argyris, 1998). These members, who might be labeled as "troublemakers," often hold positions of strength and influence within the group. Their role adds another layer to the group's dynamics and can be challenging to the group's functioning (Nichol, 2000). Again, an axiom applies: "One bad apple spoils the bushel." A lone member can put the group at risk for spoilage.

The saboteur presents a unique challenge for the task/work group leader. For the group to establish itself, to develop a successful method of operation, and to accomplish its agreed-upon task, it must confront the hidden motives of individuals who would thwart the mission of the task/work group. A student sent me a potential remedy, which I appreciate:

> Once I identified this individual's goal as being to go against the grain at every turn, I was able to confront the member in a meaningful and direct way. I said first in private that I was unwilling to have her raise havoc with our group's mission and that although I would try to incorporate her "good suggestions" while keeping us on our original task, I would steer us back whenever I sensed that she was trying to take us off track.

Burned-Outs

Burned-out group members are also uniquely challenging, as they have reached a point where they have nothing left to give. You likely have encountered individuals who seem to volunteer for everything—serving on every committee, championing every cause. They are at risk for burnout. For a multitude of reasons, some group members become overcommitted and, as a result, become unable to accomplish what they set out to do. They fail to complete the tasks to which they were assigned in the group. Although this member's heart might be in the right place, he or she has no energy left to commit to this group.

The leader is faced with the task of helping overcommitted members become aware of their limitations. This can be a difficult message to deliver. The leader does not wish to rob a member—especially one who in the past has volunteered with enthusiasm and productivity—of the opportunity to contribute. Nevertheless, the burned-out group member can create difficulties in the group by failing to do what he or she offered to do.

Super-Members

The super-member resembles the individualist in many ways, but the identifying trait is that super-members offer themselves as the answer to every leader's challenge. The super-member is willing to do anything and everything that has to be done to accomplish the group's objectives. This member is self-sacrificing and appears to be genuinely willing to carry out the project single-handedly. Once the super-member makes himself or herself known to the other group members, some may jump at the chance to let the super-member take over. Busy members often are relieved to leave as much as possible to the super-member.

The leader has to assist super-members in establishing appropriate limits, in strengthening the productivity of the entire group, and in helping the super-members feel fulfilled with their contribution without thinking they have to be solely responsible for the group's success. They have the potential to be valuable members of the group, but care must be taken to shape their behavior before it harms the group dynamics, process, and product.

Faulty Agendas

In addition to challenging members, faulty agendas are responsible for many difficulties that arise in task/work groups (Kormanski, 1982; Kraus & Hulse-Killacky, 1996). Unreasonable tasks, impossible deadlines, and competing agendas are three faulty agendas that are discussed here.

Unreasonable Tasks

Leaders must be sure that the product or outcome of a task/work group is within the abilities of the group members. A group might be guilty of "biting off more than it can chew" for all of the right reasons. Nevertheless, grandiose plans can be destined for failure if the goal exceeds the capabilities of the group. Key questions (see Wheelan, 1999) that the leader should consider include the following:

- What constitutes reasonableness? Is the task(s) that the group is undertaking possible to complete? Will the product or outcome of the task/work group suffice?
- Does the group have adequate resources at its disposal?
- Are the group members willing and able to commit to the time required to complete the proposed task?
- Does the group (e.g., a subcommittee) have authority to undertake this project?

Impossible Deadlines

Can the task/work group do what it sets out to do in the available time? Although deadlines can serve as effective motivators for productive and committed task/work group members (Katzenbach & Smith, 1991; Lucas, 1999), an unreasonable timeline can lead to frustration and anxiety. The resulting product is apt to be less acceptable and will leave the members feeling less successful than they would have, given more time.

Competing Agendas

The last pitfall of a faulty agenda mentioned here is that of competing agendas. Similar to other aspects of organizations, task/work groups face challenges related to resource allocation, human resources, and priorities (Forsyth, 1999). The leader may encounter difficulties in reaching consensus on goals, lack of cooperation and collaboration among members, and other issues stemming from the underlying motives of members. Examples are individuals who cannot seem to stretch their thinking to include others' ideas or possible approaches.

When agendas become competitive—when members cannot agree upon what task to work on first or how to go about reaching one goal when another goal seems equally important—the leader has to involve members in unifying and clarifying the group's agenda. Perhaps this will require prioritizing the otherwise competing agendas. Overlooking the task/work group's agenda, or pretending that it is clear when it is not, confounds group members' ability to work productively together.

EXAMPLE OF A TASK/WORK GROUP IN ACTION

The purpose of the following example, albeit fictional, is to help readers understand how theory may look in practice. Key considerations for each of the six sessions, taken from Hulse-Killacky et al.'s *Model for Task Groups* (2001), are highlighted in the boxes that follow each session.

Recruitment Campaign for New Members

Leaders of a small, not-for-profit national organization became acutely aware that their membership was in decline. Following a prosperous period of growth and expansion that began only 6 years earlier, the organization had lost more than a third of its members. Some of the decline could be attributed to changes in the economy, but most was a mystery.

A committee was formed to study the problem. The committee was comprised of volunteers from the organization's leadership who lived in the local vicinity and were willing and able to meet face to face. They brought enthusiasm and interest in working together to increase their organization's membership rolls. The group leader who was recruited had a thorough understanding of the organization's mission. The task group consisted of 14 members, and the leader and members believed this would be a strong group of people who could work well as a team.

The leader, Maggie, had outstanding group leadership credentials, having earned a graduate degree in counseling and taken several excellent courses in group work according to the ASGW *Professional Standards* (1991; see Conyne, Wilson, &

Ward, 1997). She further prepared for this group by immersing herself in written materials about the organization. She describes her leadership style in the following way:

> I see myself as a facilitator. My approach is to rally the strengths of the group members around a common goal. I like it best when the group itself establishes a clear, doable agenda. I like to think of myself as a consultant of sorts, I suppose. Most of the first meeting, I attempt to have members agree on three elements: What are we going to do here? How are we going to accomplish our task? And third, who are we and what strengths do we bring to offer the group? These three foci seem to mobilize the group, establish a collaborative working climate, and form a strong foundation upon which the group can proceed.

Utilizing the approach set forth in Hulse-Killacky et al.'s book *Making Task Groups Work in Your World* (2001), which attends to the intricate balance of process (i.e., how the group functions) and content (i.e., what the group is working toward achieving) in the task/work group, Maggie believed that the way the members would work together would determine the group's productivity.

The Sessions

The group was conceptualized as having six sessions, described in the following.

Session One

Group members basically fell into one of two categories: the leadership of the organization, which, as a not-for-profit, consisted of stipended, elected individuals who knew one another quite well, plus community members who volunteered to work on the project. The latter people knew each other by name but had not worked with one another previously.

The group members arrived promptly for their first meeting, to which Maggie commented, "I'm so pleased that you're all punctual. This is a great start! I hope we can agree to begin on time and, maybe equally important, end on time, too." This is an example of establishing an important norm early in the life of the group. All of the group members had demonstrated their commitment to the norm simply by being on time. Further, it showed respect for one another, by establishing acceptable behaviors from the start. Maggie reinforced their behaviors and built upon them.

Maggie helped the group members get to know one another, with the goal of warming up to the task by focusing on the participants and how they could work together toward a common goal. She introduced a few brief activities, giving members the opportunity to learn something unique and interesting about each other.

During the final activity, Miguel commented, "I sure hope that this doesn't last too much longer. I can't stand this kind of stuff. After all, we have a job to do. Let's just get to it!" Maggie agreed that Miguel had a good point and asked the members to talk about the value of getting to know one another. Most of the members said it made sense to know the people they were going to be involved with for the next 5 weeks. Although Miguel maintained that he disliked "any group stuff," the consensus was that knowing something about each other would be helpful, that it would make the group's task—deciding how to recruit new members—easier.

For the remainder of the first session, the group worked diligently, under Maggie's direction, to establish two things: (a) a way of working together, fully taking into consideration the unique strengths and styles of the individual members; and (b) an agenda for the rest of the weekly meetings that would culminate in a sound plan to benefit the organization. Ultimately, the product of the task group was to design and present to the rest of the organization's leadership a plan for recruiting new members and retaining current members.

In the final moments of the first session, Maggie reviewed what she had observed. She reestablished what the group members had agreed upon and reminded them of the norms (e.g., to arrive and depart at the agreed-upon time, treat each other with respect and honesty, and work together toward the common goal while being aware that effective decision making, compromise, collaboration, and problem solving are essential). Maggie considered the first meeting successful.

Highlights From Session One

- Balancing process and content issues
- Developing an ethic (and norm) of cooperation, collaboration, and mutual respect
- Building a culture that appreciates difference
- Recognizing a clear purpose

Session Two

Promptly at 7:00 p.m. all of the group members arrived for the second meeting—everyone except Stanley, that is. The members' being on time and having completed their homework tasks pleased Maggie, and she told them so. The only mentions of Stanley's absence were a couple of comments about hoping he was all right. At 7:45 in walked Stanley, apologizing for being late and complaining about the traffic "even at this hour." He proceeded to quickly insert himself in the ensuing discussion, offering many points that had been made in his absence.

Maggie noticed that several of the members were aloof, at best, following Stanley's late arrival and apology. At an appropriate moment, she commented, "I'm noticing that a few of you have fallen silent and have become rather disengaged from our discussion tonight. Is there something we can do?"

This created the opportunity for members to comment on how they were feeling about Stanley's late arrival. One member, Julie, commented to Maggie about how worried she'd been that something had happened to Stanley: "It might seem irrational, but I was worried. I pictured his car broken down."

Maggie interrupted and asked Julie to tell Stanley directly what she was feeling rather than talking to her. Julie appeared startled. Then Maggie said, "Remember— last week we spoke about talking directly to one another, to be honest, and to work together in a way that would be productive? This," she reminded the group, "is one of those moments."

Julie took a deep breath and told Stanley that she was worried and frustrated that he was so cavalier about arriving late. Stanley again apologized: "Julie, I really am sorry. I didn't mean to arrive late. I'll leave home earlier next week."

To the surprise of many, the group quickly began to discuss the idea of contacting the people whose membership in the organization had lapsed. Resolving this minor conflict gave rise to a greater sense that the group could be honest and use the conflict to progress toward its goal. Maggie had a feeling that this group was going to accomplish a lot.

Notice how Maggie's intervention—paying attention to interpersonal relationships—benefited the group. Had she not brought the frustration to the foreground, Julie likely would have harbored some resentment toward Stanley, which might have lessened the effectiveness of the group in some way. The leader was astute. The silence, the disengagement—these clues prompted her to pay attention to what was happening in the moment. Though this was a task/work group and the goal for this group was not personal growth, the human dynamics were better addressed than ignored.

Highlights From Session Two

- Exchanging feedback
- Addressing here-and-now issues in the group

Session Three

By now, the group had generated several popular plans. One subcommittee had conducted a thorough needs assessment, another had collected data on membership trends of other similar organizations, and yet another had completed cost projections for the possible plans. The group had established a unique identity—one of shared purpose, of one goal. The interpersonal relationships were professional, and often the group members could be seen laughing together, despite the seriousness of their task. Maggie's presence had become less noticeable, and to this she commented:

> I watch now, but I need to say less. The norms that the group adopted, and tested, over the last sessions seem to work. I'm on the lookout for potential problems. I keep the group focused on the time remaining, and on the task ahead. I'm thrilled that the group members are working so well together. I guess I take on a bit of coach role, too. "Keep up the good work" is nice to hear.

By now, the group was very productive. In the closing moments of the session, it was agreed that during the next session each of the subcommittees would make a brief presentation to the others and that they would begin to pull together a final proposal for recruiting and retaining members.

Highlights From Session Three

- Inviting members to be active resources
- Supporting process and content in all subsystems

Session Four

Just when things were going so smoothly, one member called prior to the meeting and said she was no longer able to arrange childcare and would have to drop out of the group. Also, Marcus, who had emerged as a strong leader, called and said he was unable to attend tonight. Two other members simply did not show up. Maggie described the remaining members as "angry and disappointed.... No one knew what we should do. It was interesting—they really didn't want my opinion either! Seemed like they thought, 'We were doing fine, so we'll figure this out.'"

The group members who were angry seemed to take it out initially on each other. One lamented, "What are we going to do now?" Several wanted to "just forget it."

Maggie listened as they vented their feelings. She supported and assisted them in voicing everything they were frustrated and angry about. After a few energy-filled moments, the venting lessened and one or two members began to turn to Maggie for direction.

"I was torn," Maggie stated. "I wanted to have the solution, but I didn't. There they were, the vital members of the group, and they needed a plan." One member suggested a strategy for dealing with the sudden change. Open discussion followed, and Maggie encouraged the members to speak, to offer their feedback to others, and to come to consensus. She facilitated the discussion by keeping the members focused on an effective strategy that would allow them to reach their goal. Maggie reminded them that only two group meetings remained.

Once they reached a decision, the members spent their remaining time that evening accomplishing the components of the agenda that still were possible, given the absence of the four members. Also, the group members talked about what they thought would work best, given that only two meetings remained—an adjustment to the agenda to reach their goal. Before the members left that evening, Maggie asked them to talk about how they wanted to begin next week's meeting, especially if any of the four absent members would return. Considering that the initial response had been to give up altogether, the group accomplished a significant amount of work in this session.

Highlights From Session Four

- Addressing conflict
- Practicing effective leadership skills

Session Five

Marcus returned, and so did two other members. One had called Maggie the day after the third session, explaining that she had attended a surprise birthday party— and she was the guest of honor! The other member told the group that he was sick with the flu and felt badly about not calling to tell them he was unable to attend. Surprising to several members, the group reconnected quickly. Maggie allowed time for the group to explain what had been decided last week. The group was careful to allot time to ensure the previously absent members' input into the changes in the plans. The group was back on track. The next session would be the last one. Maggie worked diligently to bring the members back to the task at hand. She found her role particularly busy:

> It surprised me at first that those members who were here last week weren't at the throats of the ones who were absent. But once my shock dissipated, I had to pay attention to some of the anxiety that arose. A few members seemed to lose perspective tonight. One or two seemed to need others' reassurance that the project could be completed on time. I was really glad to see that the reassurance was there, and it wasn't from me.

Toward the end of the evening, Maggie asked the members to carefully review each subcommittee's plans. The members voiced their opinions. Some agreed readily, while others were less amiable. By the end of the session, though, all 14 members of the group agreed on the strategy they believed would be most beneficial to the organization. Plans were initiated for the coming week's final session, when they would prepare a presentation for the organization.

Highlight From Session Five

- Developing member ability to be influential

Session Six

The final meeting went smoothly. Maggie paid particular attention to what the group had accomplished. She talked about how effectively they engaged in their work together. During the evening, as the group put together the presentation, many of the members reflected on some moment or event over the past 5 weeks. Some of the reflections were humorous, some related to the task itself (the content), and some related to the process. Maggie encouraged the members to talk about what they thought they did well and also what they thought they could have done differently, given the opportunity. Overall, the group came to the end with two outcomes: (a) the presentation itself, and (b) positive thoughts and feelings about their accomplishment.

Highlights From Session Six

(the final meeting)

■ Allowing members time to reflect on their work
■ Validating the collective effort of the task group; including eliciting feedback on the process, strengths and weaknesses of this group, directions for future initiatives

---

What to Learn From This

Some tasks are complex, and others are easy. Some require individual effort, and others benefit from a group of people. We are paid for some tasks, and others are freebies. Some are fun, some not. Work is like that, too. Although "work" evokes different images, work, for many, is what gives meaning to life, and for others it is what provides the resources (e.g., money) that allow us to really live. Society indeed is moving toward accomplishing numerous tasks through group efforts (ASGW, 1991). Because so much is accomplished through this specialized form of the task/work group, it is imperative that we learn more about this type of group, how to conduct these groups, and to consult more effectively with individuals who lead task/work groups.

LEARNING ACTIVITIES

1. Take a careful look specifically at your group work curriculum. Identify strengths and areas in which improvements seem necessary in your learning to facilitate task/work groups. Then, in keeping with Killacky and Hulse-Killacky's model in *Group Work Is Not Just for the Group Class Anymore: Teaching Generic Group Competency Skills Across the Counselor Education Curriculum* (2004), identify how your educational program has modeled and demonstrated task/work group competence. Discuss what you find.

2. Make a two-column list. On the left side, list as many things as you can that you would like to have present in a task group, of which you were a member, to help you be most effective. On the right side, list things that would turn you off. Consider what a leader's role in these two lists might be. Exchange your list with that of a class member. How do your lists compare? How are they similar? Different? How does this activity help you understand more about membership in a task/work group? Discuss with your partner how becoming aware of these

pluses and minuses could impact your leadership of a task/work group.

3. Put on your creative thinking cap for this exercise. There is a student parking crisis on campus. Consider that the parking fees are unreasonably high, that most parking spaces are gone by 7:55 a.m., and that the campus commuter bus system is inconvenient and "never comes close to fitting my class schedule." In small groups of four or five members each, imagine that prior to this "meeting" each of your group members were individually asked to generate one suggestion that would remedy the student parking crisis on campus. The group's task is to evaluate each of the individual plans, prioritize them, and send a single recommendation to the parking administration office for consideration. How should the group go about this task? Pay particular attention to what feelings emerge, what suggestions are made, who takes what role, and why.

4. Ask yourself what the members of this group experienced. Consider issues of balancing process and content; who, if anyone, emerged or was "appointed" to be the leader, and how he or she fulfilled that role. Finally, as a group, discuss what this exercise made you aware of in terms of task/work groups.

5. Check your local newspaper for a public meeting that you can attend to observe. Look for a local school board meeting, a city planning committee meeting, or perhaps a committee meeting on campus. Attend the meeting and observe this task/work group. Write two one-page summaries—one briefly summarizing the content (e.g., what was discussed, what was accomplished), and the second, the process (e.g., who did what, how members worked together). Pay particular attention to issues of leadership, membership, balance, and other concepts unique to task/work groups covered in this chapter. Discuss your observations with others.

SUMMARY

Much of society is adopting a group orientation in task and work groups. Concepts of consensus, collaboration, and teamwork are finding their way into business, politics, and social circles. Successful task/work groups do not spring forth without considerable effort. The effectiveness of task/work groups is grounded firmly in group dynamics, "the interactions fostered through the relationships of members and leaders in connection with the complexities of the task involved" (Gladding, 2003, p. 32).

Awareness of diversity in task/work groups is essential, as individuals across a wide variety of settings, representing all types of diversity, find themselves working in groups (Brinson & Lee, 1997). Leaders must give every consideration to incorporating multicultural competence into their group work efforts.

According to Wheelan (1999), members need meaningful tasks and goals, new learning, access to technical and human resources necessary to accomplish the task, and physical space where their work can be conducted. Members and leaders of task/work groups must invest in the accomplishment of their agreed-upon goal. The outcome of a successful task/work group is greater than the product or performance it produces. It is also an outcome of people working together toward a common goal.

The chapter includes numerous typecastings of challenging if not difficult members of groups. These characterizations are intended to alert future group leaders so that once real characters are encountered they are neither surprised nor caught unaware. In a similar fashion, a number of faulty agendas are presented. These are commonly encountered pitfalls. Unreasonable deadlines or impossible completion dates have the potential to render even the most enthusiastic and committed task/work group members discouraged and hopeless.

Watching members succeed while leading through empowering is a great experience. Task groups require every leadership skill to be carefully applied. Leading effective task/work groups can be exhilarating and rewarding.

USEFUL WEB SITES

- ☐ Association for Specialists in Group Work
  www.asgw.org
- ☐ Presbyterian Council of Canada: *Goal Oriented Planning Check Sheet*
  www.telusplanet.net/public/pdcoutts/leadership/checklist.htm
- ☐ The University of Edinburgh Master of Engineering: *Leadership Attitudes*
  www.see.ed.ac.uk/~gerard/MENG/ME96/Documents/Styles/group.html
- ☐ White Stag: *Leadership Development By Design*
  www.whitestag.org/resources/sb207.htm
- ☐ North Dakota State University Extension Service: *Leadership Development Within Groups*
  www.ext.nodak.edu/extpubs/yf/leaddev/he497w.htm
- ☐ *Outdoor Action Guide to Group Dynamics and Leadership* from Princeton University
  www.princeton.edu/~oa/manual/sect9.html

REFERENCES

Alderfer, C. P. (1987). An intergroup perspective on group dynamics. In J. W. Lorsch, *Handbook of organizational behavior* (pp. 190–222). Englewood Cliffs, NJ: Prentice-Hall.

Argyris, C. (1998, May/June). Empowerment: The emperor's new clothes. *Harvard Business Review,* pp. 98–105.

Association for Specialists in Group Work (ASGW). (1989). *Ethical standards for group counselors.* Alexandria, VA: Author.

Association for Specialists in Group Work (ASGW). (1991). *Professional standards for the training of group workers.* Alexandria, VA: Author.

Astin, A. W. (1987). Competition or cooperation? Teaching teamwork as a basic skill. *Change, 19* (5), 12–19.

Bettenhausen, K. L. (1991). Five years of group research: What we have learned and what needs to be addressed. *Journal of Management, 17,* 345–381.

Brinson, J. A., & Lee, C. C. (1997). Culturally responsive group leadership: An integrative model for experienced practitioners. In H. Forester-Miller & J. A. Kottler, *Issues and challenges for group practitioners* (pp. 43–56). Denver: Love Publishing.

Carroll, M. R., & Wiggins, J. D. (2001). *Elements of group counseling: Back to the basics* (3rd ed.). Denver: Love Publishing.

Cohen, S. G., & Bailey, D. E. (1997). What makes teams work: Group effectiveness research from the shop floor to the executive suite. *Journal of Management, 23,* 239–290.

Cohen, A. M., & Smith, R. D. (1976). *The critical incident in growth groups: Theory and technique.* La Jolla, CA: University Association.

Conyne, R. K. (1989). *How personal growth and task groups work* (Sage human service guides: v. 55). Newbury Park, CA: Sage.

Conyne, R. K., & Bemak, F. (2004a). Guest editor's introduction: Preface. *Journal for Specialists in Group Work, 29,* 3–5.

Conyne, R. K., & Bemak, F. (2004b). Teaching group work from an ecological perspective. *Journal for Specialists in Group Work, 29,* 7–18.

Conyne, R. K., Rapin, L. S., & Rand, J. M. (1997). A model for leading task groups. In H. Forester-Miller & J. A. Kottler (Eds.), *Issues and challenges for group practitioners* (pp. 117–132). Denver: Love Publishing.

Conyne, R. K., Wilson, F. R., & Ward, D. E. (1997). *Comprehensive group work: What it means & how to teach it.* Alexandria, VA: American Counseling Association.

Corey, G. (2000). *Theory & practice of group counseling* (5th ed.). Belmont, CA: Wadsworth.

Corey, M. S., & Corey, G. (1997). *Groups: Process and practice* (5th ed.). Pacific Grove, CA: Brooks/Cole.

DeLucia-Waack, J., & Donigian, J. (2004). *The practice of multicultural group work.* Belmont, CA: Wadsworth.

Donigian, J., & Hulse-Killacky, D. (1999). *Critical incidents in group therapy* (2nd ed.). Belmont, CA: Wadsworth.

Donigian, J., & Malnati, R. (1997). *Systemic group therapy: A triadic model.* Pacific Grove, CA: Brooks/Cole.

Dykeman, C., & Appleton, V. E. (1998). Group counseling: The efficacy of group work. In D. Capuzzi & D. R. Gross (Eds.), *Introduction to group counseling* (2nd ed., pp. 101–129). Denver: Love Publishing.

Farmer, S. M., & Roth, J. (1998). Conflict-handling behavior in work groups: Effects of group structure, decision processes, and time. *Small Group Research, 29*(6), 669–713.

Fatout, M., & Rose, S. R. (1995). *Task groups in the social services* (Sage sourcebooks for the human services series: vol. 30). Newbury Park, CA: Sage.

Forester-Miller, H. (2002). Group counseling: Ethical considerations. In D. Capuzzi & D. R. Gross (Eds.), *Introduction to group counseling* (3rd ed., pp. 185–204). Denver: Love Publishing.

Forester-Miller, H., & Gressard, C. F. (1997). The Tao of group work. In H. Forester-Miller & J. A. Kottler, *Issues and challenges for group practitioners* (pp. 117–132). Denver: Love Publishing.

Forsyth, D. R. (1999). *Group dynamics* (2nd ed.). Belmont, CA: Wadsworth.

Gladding, S. T. (2003). *Group work: A counseling specialty* (4th ed.). Upper Saddle River, NJ: Merrill Prentice-Hall.

Greenberg, J., & Baron, R. A. (2000). *Behavior in organizations: Understanding and managing the human side of work.* Englewood Cliffs, NJ: Prentice-Hall.

Hackman, J. R. (1987). The design of work teams. In J. W. Lorsch, *Handbook of organizational behavior* (pp. 315–342). Englewood Cliffs, NJ: Prentice-Hall.

Hulse-Killacky, D., Killacky, J., & Donigian, J. (2001). *Making task groups work in your world.* Upper Saddle River, NJ: Prentice-Hall.

Hulse-Killacky, D., Kraus, K. L., & Schumacher, R. A. (1999). Visual conceptualizations of meetings: A group work design. *Journal for Specialists in Group Work, 24,* 113–124.

Johnson, D. W., & Johnson, F. P. (1994). *Joining together: Group theory and group skills* (5th ed.). Boston: Allyn & Bacon.

Katzenbach, J. R., & Smith, D. K. (1991, March-April). The discipline of teams: What makes the difference between a team that performs and one that doesn't? *Harvard Business Review,* pp. 111–120.

Kets, F. R., & DeVries, K. (1999, Winter). High-performance teams: Lessons from the Pygmies. *Organizational Dynamics, 27,* 66–77.

Killacky, J., & Hulse-Killacky, D. (2004). Group work is not just for the group class anymore: Teaching generic group competency skills across the counselor education curriculum. *Journal for Specialists in Group Work, 29,* 87–96.

Kirchmeyer, C. (1993). Multicultural task groups. *Small Group Research, 24,* 127–149.

Kirkman, B. L., & Benson, R. (2000, Winter). Powering up teams. *Organizational Dynamics, 28,* 48–66.

Kormanski, C. (1982). Leadership strategies for managing conflict. *Journal for Specialists in Group Work, 7,* 112–118.

Kormanski, C. (1999). *The team: Explorations in group process.* Denver: Love.

Kraus, K. L., DeEsch, J. D., & Geroski, A. (2001). Stop avoiding challenging situations in group counseling. *Journal for Specialist in Group Work, 26,* 31–47.

Kraus, K., & Hulse-Killacky, D. (1996). Balancing process and content in groups: A metaphor. *Journal for Specialists in Group Work, 21,* 90–93.

Lieberman, M. A., Yalom, I. D., & Miles, M. B. (1973). *Encounter groups: First facts.* New York: Basic Books.

Lucas, J. W. (1999). Behavioral and emotional outcomes of leadership in task groups. *Social Forces, 78* (2), 747–779.

McLeod, P. L., & Liker, J. K. (1992). Process feedback in task groups: An application of goal setting. *Journal of Applied Behavioral Sciences, 28,* 74–98.

Napier, R. W., & Gershenfeld, M. K. (1983). *Making groups work: A guide for group leaders.* Boston: Houghton Mifflin.

Nichol, B. L. (2000, February/March). Top ten reasons teams become dysfunctional. *National Public Accountant, 45,* 12–15.

Reed, B. G. (1981). Gender issues in training group leaders. *Journal for Specialists in Group Work, 6,* 161–170.

Reid, K. E. (1997). *Social work practice with groups: A clinical perspective* (2nd ed.). Pacific Grove, CA: Brooks/Cole.

Schindler-Rainman, E. (1981). Training task-group leaders. *Journal for Specialists in Group Work, 6,* 171–174.

Schwarz, R. M. (1994). *The skilled facilitator: Practical wisdom for developing effective groups.* San Francisco: Jossey-Bass.

Stockton, R., & Toth, P. (1996). Teaching group counselors: Recommendations for maximizing preservice instruction. *Journal for Specialists in Group Work, 21,* 274–283.

Teaching group work [Special issue]. (2004, March). *Journal for Specialists in Group Work, 29*(1).

Toseland, R. W., Rivas, F., & Chapman, D. (1984). An evaluation of decision-making methods in task groups. *Social Work, 29,* 339–349.

Tyson, L. E., Perusse, R., & Whitledge, J. (2004). *Critical incidents in group counseling.* Alexandria, VA: American Counseling Association.

Ward, D. E. (2002). Prime times for group work. *Journal for Specialists in Group Work, 27,* 251–253.

Watson, W. E., Johnson, L., & Merritt, D. (1998). Team orientation, self-exploration, and diversity in task groups. *Group & Organization Management, 23,* 161–189.

Wheelan, S. A. (1999). *Creating effective teams: A guide for members and leaders.* Thousand Oakes, CA: Sage.

Wilson, F. R., Rapin, L. S., & Haley-Banez, L. (2004). How teaching group work can be guided by foundational documents: Best practice guidelines, diversity principles, training standards. *Journal for Specialists in Group Work, 29,* 19–29.

Yalom, I. D. (1995). *The theory and practice of group psychotherapy* (4th ed.). New York: Basic Books.

Guidance/ Psychoeducational Groups

Lisa Langfuss Aasheim and Susan H. Niemann

sychoeducational/guidance groups are structured therapeutic groups that emphasize learning more about a problem or issue and/or developing new life skills for the purpose of prevention, growth, or remediation. As directive, short-term, counseling interventions gain favor over open-ended, long-term approaches, the former groups are becoming increasingly popular. Originally developed for use in educational settings, time-limited groups that focus on learning and doing as avenues of change are finding utility in a variety of clinical and community settings.

In 2000, the Association for Specialists in Group Work (ASGW) revised and adopted its standards for training group workers. The guidance/psychoeducational group, the topic of this chapter, differs from the other specializations in its focusing on growth through knowledge and skill building. The term *guidance* is usually associated with groups conducted in school settings, and *psychoeducation* is often broadly applied to groups in educational, community, and clinical settings.

Compared to most counseling or therapy groups, psychoeducational groups are more structured, issue specific, and leader directed. In addition to emphasizing education and skills training, these groups may stress self-awareness and self-empowerment. Although members may compare stories, share anecdotes, or offer suggestions in regard to specific issues, the emphasis is not on deep self-disclosure or member interactions. A fundamental task of the psychoeducational group leader is to keep the group focused on established group goals while effectively balancing content and process.

Psychoeducational groups require a structured group design, the dissemination of relevant new material, meaningful experiential activities, and opportunities for processing. Among several types of psychoeducational groups are school counseling groups addressing responsible sexual behavior, substance use, healthy choices, or conflict resolution, led by a school counselor. Likewise, groups are offered by career counselors addressing stress management, diversity awareness, anger management, and career readiness. Other examples of psychoeducational groups are groups emphasizing healthy lifestyle choices for seniors and groups presenting effective parenting strategies for parents of adolescents, offered by agency counselors.

THE CASE FOR PSYCHOEDUCATIONAL GROUPS

Psychoeducational groups are ideally suited to the current emphasis on short-term treatment modalities. In essence, a well-planned and executed psychoeducational group combines some of the therapeutic aspects of traditional group counseling with the goal-directed emphasis of psychoeducation. Common goals for participants in psychoeducational groups include learning new information, developing new or increased skills, finding more effective ways of communicating or relating, increasing self-management abilities, and developing personal insights (Brown, 1998).

Psychoeducational group work is firmly rooted in the history of the counseling profession. From the early part of the 20th century, the guidance movement emphasized teaching clients to make better choices, working with populations that needed direction and support. A physician, Joseph Pratt, often is credited with beginning the group movement in the early 1900s. He offered psychoeducational groups to tuberculosis patients; these groups included a presentation of didactic material followed by patients' telling their own stories and processing the information (McWhirter, 1995). At the turn of the century, schools began to offer vocational and moral guidance in group settings. Although school guidance groups often were directive in nature and offered little opportunity for reflective discussion, they established the importance of education in group settings. Today, psychoeducational groups emphasize raising client awareness and helping individuals make sound decisions concerning important issues in their lives (Neukrug, 1999).

Psychoeducational groups are becoming uniquely independent therapeutic entities that do more than simply supplement individual counseling (Conyne & Bemak, 2004). And they are therapeutic without being "therapy." These groups stress learning but may incorporate emotional, behavioral, and spiritual elements of change, depending upon the group's purpose and structure. A psychoeducational approach to group work is consistent with the wellness model of counseling, focusing on prevention, personal responsibility, and empowerment. Either as a primary focus of treatment or as an adjunct to individual or family counseling, these groups can provide effective and appropriate interventions for several important reasons:

1. Knowledge is empowering. Increasingly, counselors are incorporating more psychoeducation into all treatment modalities, recognizing that group

members who are well informed about the options associated with their challenges are better prepared to make healthy choices. In the group setting, participants learn from the group leader and from one another. In addition, they have opportunities to build skills and to practice new behaviors through learning exercises such as role play and directed group activities.

2. Group members benefit from the universality inherent in an issue-specific group. From the beginning, clients experience the cohesion of sharing similar concerns or challenges. A sense of common purpose helps maintain the group's focus, allowing for maximum member benefit from the experience.

3. In many cases, psychoeducational groups are appropriate from a multicultural perspective. Individuals from some cultures may not be interested in openly sharing feelings or sensitive information about themselves and/or their family. Groups that encourage self-disclosure, identify and work through resistances, or explore past relationships are rooted in value systems that are not universally shared across cultures. By contrast, psychoeducational groups offer specific and concrete interventions that emphasize learning and developing adaptive skills in a way that respects the participants' desire for privacy or less verbal learning styles. Also, the structured nature of psychoeducational groups may prove attractive to members from nonmajority cultures who are more comfortable viewing the group leader as a coach or teacher.

4. Psychoeducational groups can attract clients who otherwise would not be drawn to counseling. For many, a group that emphasizes learning new and useful skills is likely to be far less threatening than a group designed to explore personal issues and interactions. Mental health counseling in general and group counseling in particular may be associated with stigma, and individuals who are looking to address a specific area of growth or remediation may feel more at home in a group that emphasizes learning. Few are wary of education as a purpose of the group.

   Sometimes, participating in a psychoeducational group helps people recognize the need for further counseling. A positive experience in a group, coupled with referrals from a skilled leader, can lead to clients' exploring additional counseling.

5. Because the format allows for more members, psychoeducational groups are often more cost-effective than smaller counseling groups. Because of the structured nature of the group, member interaction is less crucial and effective groups can be conducted with a varying number of participants.

6. Psychoeducational groups provide short-term, specific interventions. Clients who participate fully will enjoy concrete, immediate results. Although open-ended groups are appropriate for some populations, clients are increasingly drawn to time-limited options, particularly when they are looking to address specific challenges or areas of growth. In a time of increasing dependence on managed care, short-term, issue-specific groups are becoming increasingly popular as a treatment modality (Rice, 1995).

7. The psychoeducational format allows for more open and inclusive group membership. Screening is still important, but the inclusion criteria may be

broad, allowing for more individuals to participate. Many psychoeducational groups are open to all who are interested in the topic or issue to be addressed, provided that they have no characteristics that would place them or other group members at risk.

8. Psychoeducational groups are less dependent upon the relationships among group members and upon elements of group process that often take several sessions to develop. Instead, goals and objectives are made clear from the beginning. Members who receive appropriate pre-group information and preparation will understand the intent and nature of the group, allowing for a more focused intervention from the first session.

9. The psychoeducational group is an ideal format for addressing adjustment and growth issues from a wellness perspective. The psychoeducational group leader offers an intervention that emphasizes the decision-making capabilities of group members. Members are given opportunities to learn new strategies and practice new skills, with each member ultimately responsible for applying this new knowledge outside of the group setting.

CHARACTERISTICS OF EFFECTIVE PSYCHOEDUCATIONAL GROUPS

Brown (1998) has classified psychoeducational groups by their primary purpose: education, skills training, or self-understanding/self-knowledge.

1. *Education groups* have as a primary purpose the learning of new material through lecture, discussion, observation, or participation. The emphasis is primarily cognitive, with the leader acting as a teacher, disseminating new information as ideas, concepts, or facts.

2. *Skills-training groups* have a strong experiential component. Participants are challenged to practice new skills in the group setting while the leader models the desired skills and structures the experiences to emphasize mastery. Feedback is included as a component of the training.

3. *Self-understanding/self-knowledge* groups may resemble counseling groups, but they differ by de-emphasizing self-disclosure, working through resistances, or exploring past relationships. The understanding and knowledge gained are expected to reassure the members, give them feedback on the impact of their behavior on others, or build self-confidence.

Although categorizing groups by primary purpose is helpful, most psychoeducational groups contain elements of all of the above. In addition, these groups often provide support to members, through interactions both with the leader and with one another. Rivera et al. (2004) emphasized other related purposes of psychoeducational groups—specifically, prevention, examination of personal beliefs and attitudes, and integration of information with life experiences.

Effective psychoeducational groups differ from simple informational work-shops in that groups are tailored to meet the needs of the members, both in design and as an evolving entity. Rather than one-size-fits-all presentations, psychoeducational groups are specific to a given population at a given time. Although they are structured in nature, effective groups are designed to allow for flexibility.

Basic Group Traits

Psychoeducational groups range in size from 5 to 50 or more members. To aid in processing exercises or fostering discussions, larger groups may have to be broken into subgroups. The length and duration of groups can vary widely, depending upon the group design and composition. The time allotted to each session also often varies with the group's composition. For example, children often benefit from shorter sessions that meet more frequently. Generally, weekly group sessions last from 1 to 2 hours. The number of sessions often depends upon the scope of the group or on institutional or other external time constraints. Most psychoeducational groups meet from 4 to 12 sessions. Groups emphasizing skill development or self-knowledge and support may benefit from more sessions than groups with a primarily educational focus.

Incorporating Learning Principles

The most important component of psychoeducational groups is *learning*. Counselors who lead these groups should understand some of the important principles of learning so they can plan activities, develop attainable goals and objectives, and tailor the group to meet the needs of the participants.

In designing learning activities for the group, general characteristics of the members should be kept in mind. Age, developmental level, education, and cultural factors all influence preferred learning modalities. Varying teaching strategies is also advisable, as some members may be primarily auditory in their learning while others absorb information visually or kinesthetically.

Ability to learn is also affected by *motivation*. This is a complex concept affected by many factors, but, essentially, group members are most motivated to learn and participate when the group offers something of value to them. In counseling or psychotherapy groups, the attractiveness of the group to its members is often described as *cohesion*, an essential component of group process that develops over time. Conversely, in a psychoeducational group, interactions among members are directed and purpose specific. Generally, interpersonal communication within the group is a method of learning rather than a group goal. It falls upon the leader to manage content and process in a manner that attracts and motivates group members.

Another factor affecting learning is *anxiety*. Members who are anxious or nervous about participating in the group are often too focused on their own internal dialogues to gain maximally from the experience. All group work involves taking risks and self-disclosing, and members may feel vulnerable, especially in groups that tackle sensitive topics or work on overcoming real or perceived personal deficits.

Effective group leaders address and normalize anxiety from the beginning and incorporate strategies for offering encouragement and support to members.

The following strategies or approaches are recommended to incorporate learning principles into psychoeducational group work:

1. *Develop goals and objectives that are specific, realistic, clearly articulated, and appropriately challenging* (Bridbord, DeLucia-Waack, Jones, & Gerrity, 2004). Leaders should consider the impact of the group intervention on members' lives and evaluate their own expectations of how participants will change or grow following the group's completion. While goals may be broad, objectives should articulate specific learning or behavioral changes. For example, if the goal of a group is to help women increase their self-esteem, objectives might include reframing criticism, countering negative self-talk, engaging in daily self-affirmations, and identifying self-denigrating behaviors. This is accompanied by work aimed at replacing these behaviors with positive activities.

2. *Consider the developmental level of group members.* With children, it is important to choose learning activities that approximate their reading or processing levels. Adolescents may greet activities geared toward grade-school children with disdain. Likewise, educational factors including reading level and appropriate content must be considered in learning activities for adults.

3. *Incorporate culturally meaningful learning activities.* As with all counseling interventions, group leaders must develop an understanding of and communicate respect for diversity and cultural differences. Learning materials should be culturally appropriate. Counselors are urged to consult when working with diverse cultures, especially with cultures outside their own. When a group is culturally homogeneous, culture-specific learning activities can be incorporated into the group design.

   For example, an anger-management group serving a primarily Hispanic male population should address cultural issues such as gender-role socialization, and learning examples should incorporate Hispanic individuals, families, and customs as revealed by group members. Group leaders must be familiar with, and abide by, the *Principles for Diversity-Competent Group Workers* endorsed by the ASGW (1999) because all group work contains some multicultural aspects (Wilson, Rapin, & Haley-Banez, 2004).

4. *Vary methods of instruction to accommodate different learning styles.* As a general rule, leaders should keep in mind that few members will attentively absorb more than 15 minutes' worth of content lecture, and that members who learn primarily through visual or kinesthetic pathways may be limited in the amount of information they can hear and process at one time. Visual strategies, such as incorporating video or other visual images, are often helpful as auxiliary teaching methods. Activities involving movement help kinesthetic learners master new material.

5. *Incorporate active and/or discovery teaching methods.* Hands-on activities and activities that allow members to reach conclusions during the group session are likely to create more lasting impressions. Directed learning exercises that promote active participation and interaction are powerful teaching tools. Educational games often are applicable to group settings and may provide an effective balance between content and process.

6. *Tie content to relevant examples or stories.* The best teachers are often described as the best storytellers. In relating didactic material, real-life examples are often helpful. Depending on the purpose and structure of the group, some leaders use self-disclosure. In this way, the leader serves as a model for the participants and gains credibility as someone who understands their challenges. This teaching technique is most common in groups that incorporate support and psychoeducation, such as a group on parenting skills led by a counselor who is also a parent.

7. *When teaching behavioral skills, break the overall task into small stages or component parts.* These should be taught systematically, from the simple to the more complex. McWhirter (1995) recommended the following strategy for teaching behavioral skills:

    a. *Instruction* (teach, using oral instruction and providing rationale)
    b. *Modeling* (show, by demonstrating the skill via videotape, leader, or another member)
    c. *Role play* (practice, in which the group member is encouraged to imitate and use the skill)
    d. *Feedback* (reinforce, through leader encouragement and coaching)
    e. *Homework* (apply, by asking students to perform the newly acquired skill outside the group)

8. *Give opportunities for feedback and be willing to adapt to members' learning needs.* Although it is critical to develop a structured plan for a psychoeducational group, an effective leader will solicit formal and informal feedback throughout the group and make changes when necessary.

PLANNING AND IMPLEMENTING A PSYCHOEDUCATIONAL GROUP

To be meaningful and effective, psychoeducational groups must be well crafted, with a predetermined plan and clearly articulated goals and objectives. Furr (2000) described a model of structured group design having two phases of development. The first phase, the *conceptual phase*, has three steps: (a) statement of purpose, (b) establishing goals, and (c) setting objectives. The second phase, the *operational phase*, also has three steps: (d) selecting content, (e) designing experiential activities, and (f) evaluating effectiveness. In this model, group design begins with a broad conceptual idea and moves toward specific content and exercises. In structuring the group, each step is derived from the preceding step.

Step 1: Statement of Purpose

A statement of purpose is an explicit statement of the reason for a group's existence. Ideas about psychoeducational groups often evolve from clinical practice, as counselors notice similarities in clients' problems or recognize that a number of clients could benefit from learning certain skills. Ideas for groups also may arise from community needs, such as a public outcry for more anger-management groups or groups for male batterers. School counselors often find that several students share a need for addressing a certain issue and would benefit from a structured group approach. A college counselor may find that many students could benefit from a group on how to develop time-management skills.

At the conceptual level, the leader has to determine the theoretical perspective of the group. Some groups work best from an insight-oriented perspective; others are more behavioral in nature. The group may be conceptualized as primarily educational or skills based, or focused on self-awareness, or some combination of these. In addition, the leader must become familiar with the topic and investigate which theoretical approaches have been most effective.

Step 2: Establishing Goals

Goals indicate how a participant may change as a result of group involvement. The leader must specify the type of change expected from the members, and the goals have to be consistent with the theoretical approach selected in the statement of purpose. Goals are often expressed as specific areas of mastery, so success can be evaluated. For example, a group whose statement of purpose is to help college students gain time-management skills may establish several group goals, such as (a) learning to structure daily activities, (b) developing strategies to combat procrastination, and (c) prioritizing responsibilities. The goals of the group should be reasonable and attainable, given the characteristics of the members and the time frame. In addition, the goals should be culturally appropriate for the target population.

Step 3: Setting Objectives

Furr (2000) described goals as the compass setting the direction for the group, and objectives as providing the road map on how to get there. Objectives specify, generally in behavioral terms, the steps needed to reach each group goal. Each goal involves a number of objectives, the completion of which signals successful mastery of the goal. For example, in addressing the goal of structuring daily activities, objectives might include the following:

1. Purchase a notebook to leave at the side of the bed.
2. Before going to bed, make a list of the next day's expected tasks, including the approximate time needed for each.
3. When you get up in the morning, review the upcoming day's activities.
4. Before going to bed that night, check off completed tasks against the length of time you took for each and write the next day's list.

Group members who complete the objectives will gain insight into how they use their time and be more capable of realistically structuring the day's activities.

Step 4: Selecting Content

Group content may be organized into three categories: didactic, experiential, and process.

1. *Didactic material* is often presented first, incorporating teaching strategies that are mindful of members' developmental level and attention span.
2. *Experiential learning* allows the material to be understood on a personal level. Experiential activities should be chosen to reinforce didactic content in a way that is consistent with the group's theoretical orientation.
3, The goal of the *process* component is to help members connect the didactic and experiential components of the group. Participants may have to clarify the conclusions they derived from the experience or examine questions that arose from the experience. Members who are able to link their experiences with didactic material will be more likely to generalize their learning to a broader life context. Processing may include discussing what happened in the activity; participants' reactions to the activity; what thoughts, feelings, and insights were generated; and how these insights can be applied outside the group.

Step 5: Designing Activities

To be effective, group activities must be tailored to address group goals and objectives. When choosing activities, the primary theoretical orientation of the group should be considered As examples: Groups with the goal of behavioral change might include exercises such as role-play and relaxation techniques; groups emphasizing cognitive change might use activities on identifying and changing self-talk; groups with goals reflecting insight and greater self-understanding might employ activities that link affective, cognitive, and/or behavioral domains. Activities should be designed to be brief and simple to implement and require active participation. Some examples that may be effective in psychoeducational groups include

- self-assessment exercises, designed to increase self-knowledge;
- group games, designed to promote cooperative learning;
- cognitive restructuring, skills-building activities that stress changing self-talk or disputing irrational beliefs;
- role-playing to facilitate behavioral change;
- imagery, used to promote interpersonal awareness and visualization of options;
- creative arts, such as music, visual arts, and drama, to allow for emotional expression and interpersonal learning;
- relaxation techniques, mindfulness activities, and other body-awareness exercises;
- homework or out-of-group exercises.

Step 6: Evaluating Effectiveness

Psychoeducational groups address specific concerns through education, skill building, and member processing. Leaders should evaluate the effectiveness of their intervention through a combination of process and outcome methods. The *process evaluation* involves soliciting and incorporating feedback during each session and incorporating changes when necessary. Many leaders incorporate process evaluation informally, and some solicit written feedback following each session.

Leaders also should conduct an *outcome evaluation* of the group. Two ways to evaluate the success of the group are to (a) measure goal attainment, and (b) assess members' satisfaction with the group experience.

Measuring *goal attainment* involves giving the members a pretest before the group experience, followed by a posttest after group has ended. For example, if the group targeted test anxiety, the participants' responses to questions such as, "When I see the questions on the test, my mind goes blank," should improve on average after completion of the group.

In the other method of outcome assessment, *member satisfaction*, participants report their subjective reaction to the group. They may evaluate the leader's style, content of the group, and group activities. Though group satisfaction itself is not sufficient to create change, it is a facilitative condition for nurturing change, and this feedback is helpful to the group leader.

LEADING A PSYCHOEDUCATIONAL GROUP

Effectively leading a psychoeducational group requires careful planning and intentional implementation. The leader should have all of the qualities and skills of an effective counseling group leader and in addition be prepared to lead a large group in directed activities. The following are guidelines for effective leadership:

1. *Have a clear understanding of the needs of the group members.* Some group leaders start with a needs assessment regarding the population they wish to serve. In a clinical setting, this may begin with informal feedback from colleagues that a number of female clients might benefit from a women's empowerment group. Before planning the group, it is helpful to get an idea of the interest in the proposed intervention, including the elements that potential participants would find most desirable. Because psychoeducational groups are highly structured, a good fit between the leader's group goals and the goals of individual members is particularly important.

2. *Make sure that group members are clearly informed about the scope and nature of the group.* Written informed consent, including a description of group goals and activities, is recommended. In addition, a thorough discussion of the limitations and guidelines for confidentiality must be discussed in detail with potential group members.

3. *Use stage-appropriate interventions.* Initial group activities should be non-threatening. More intensive activities are most effective during the group's

working stage, when members' trust and group cohesion are high. Closure activities should address cognitive learning and skill building, as well as the participants' feelings associated with the group's conclusion (e.g., "I'm glad I learned some new skills"; "I'll miss this group and wish we could keep meeting").

Jones and Robinson (2000) have provided a model to ensure that the timing of group activities is stage appropriate, especially regarding intensity of the activity. They suggest the following steps for counselors to take in choosing activities:

a. Brainstorm group activities appropriate for the group theme.
b. Assess the intensity of each activity.
c. Choose activities for the early stages of the group.
d. Choose activities for the middle stages of the group.
e. Choose activities for the ending stage of the group.

Leaders should not assume that they will avoid storming (conflict) in psychoeducational groups. Although member interaction will be more focused and goal directed than in counseling groups, members will form relationships and may experience conflict or resistance. Storming may be subtle and may be seen in the form of challenges to the leader or member tardiness or absenteeism. Primarily didactic psychoeducational groups may experience no discernable storming at all. Regardless of group structure, though, soliciting and incorporating members' feedback throughout the life of the group often reduces or eliminates problematic leader challenge.

4. *Be mindful of therapeutic factors as they unfold within the group setting.* One study found that adolescents in a psychoeducational group did not differ significantly from those in a counseling group regarding their attribution of therapeutic factors in play. Both groups identified interpersonal learning, catharsis, and the development of socializing skills as most significant (Schectman, Bar-El, & Hadar, 1995). This suggests that even structured groups allow for the development of important relationships among members. The therapeutic factors that are most likely to appear are universality, altruism, imitative behavior, and imparting of information (Brown, 1998).When personal issues or problems are addressed, instillation of hope provides an impetus for members to continue to work toward their goals. In groups that emphasize social skills training, socializing techniques and interpersonal learning become important therapeutic factors.

5. *Take on the role of therapeutic mentor.* Psychoeducational group leadership integrates counseling and teaching strategies, providing a structured intervention that allows for personal reflection and meaning-making. The therapeutic mentor demonstrates mastery of knowledge and skills, as well as the ability to individualize instruction to group members. Mentoring implies modeling, guidance, and patience with members as they learn new information and incorporate new behaviors. Group leaders play a key role

in demonstrating desired behaviors, and group members inevitably will learn new skills by observing an effective leader (Riva & Korinek, 2004).

PSYCHOEDUCATIONAL GROUPS IN CLINICAL PRACTICE

Increasingly, psychoeducational groups are finding popularity in clinical practice as counselors and other mental health professionals identify common needs among clients or community members. These groups often address skill building and personal growth issues. Some groups address developmental issues, such as marital enhancement (Durana, 1996), parenting skills (Nicholson, Anderson, Fox, & Brenner, 2002), and self-esteem or friendship skills in children (Schectman, 2002). Others may address difficult life transitions, illness, and mental health issues such as dementia (Cheston, Jones, & Gilliard, 2003) or giving care to a family member with schizophrenia (McDonell, Short, Berry, & Dyck, 2003).

More clinicians are using the structured group model to address serious mental health issues. For example, Reiss and Rutan (1992) suggest time-limited, structured groups as an intervention with clients who have eating disorders. They note that although long-term psychotherapeutic groups may be helpful in providing insight and long-term change, improvements are difficult to quantify, the group may not address crucial behavioral changes, and many clients drop out early without improvement. Time-limited groups provide an entrance into treatment for the new client, an adjunct to individual counseling, or an introduction to open-ended group counseling.

Olson and McEwen (2004) utilize bibliotherapy to help educate and provide counsel to grieving prisoners. Nerenberg (2000) suggests that sexual addicts in a residential setting also benefit from psychoeducation and cites the importance of utilizing a didactic approach to impart information to addicted clients. Fristad, Goldberg-Arnold, and Gavazzi (2002) introduce multifamily psychoeducational groups for families with children who have been diagnosed with bipolar disorder. The goal of this group is to help improve coping skills, communication, and problem-solving strategies within the family system.

Psychoeducational groups are being used increasingly with people who have psychiatric diagnoses including bipolar disorder (Bauer & McBride, 1996) and schizophrenia (Gallagher & Nazarian, 1995). The emphasis of these groups is on participants' learning and practicing adaptive skills that allow for their maximum independence, including compliance with medication, confronting and refuting paranoid ideations, self-care and vocational skills, anger management, and conflict resolution. Family psychoeducation often is provided with a goal of reducing the level of expressed emotion (a climate of criticism and emotional overinvolvement) in the family (Fristad, Arnett, & Gavazzi, 1998). Structured family groups also may include help with educational planning, vocational training, financial planning, and day-to-day management of the illness (Lundwall, 1996). Psychoeducational groups, too, have helped foster parents deal with the emotional issues and problem behaviors of children who have been sexually abused (Barth, Yeaton, & Winterfelt, 1994).

Didactic group interventions frequently are used to help people with other types of disabilities gain adaptive or vocational skills. Williams (1989) used a group approach to teach social skills to children with autism. Through activities such as recreational games, role-playing exercises, and modeling, in addition to direct instruction, group leaders have taught members interpersonal skills including eye contact, appropriate body language, voice tone, greeting and saying good-bye, managing temper, and increasing flexibility in interactions with others. Psychoeducational groups also have been effective in helping students with learning disabilities make the transition from one learning environment to the next (Milsom, Akos, & Thompson, 2004).

Couples counselors have described the usefulness of psychoeducational groups in preventive or enrichment contexts, as an adjunct to marital or family counseling, or as the focus of counseling. Worthington and Drinkard (2000) described a novel six-step group method for promoting marital reconciliation between partners whose relationship is marred by mutual hurts and offenses, incorporating the visual image of a bridge with six "planks," or steps. Each plank is named, and a picture is given to each partner. Partners learn and practice each plank toward building their reconciliation before moving to the next step. The planks are as follows:

1. Decide whether to reconcile
2, Softness
3. Forgive
4. Reverse the negative cascade
5. Deal with failures in trustworthiness
6. Actively build love

Each step is associated with a series of structured self-assessments and group process tasks.

GUIDANCE GROUPS IN SCHOOLS

Group work provides an essential component of comprehensive guidance programs in educational settings. School-based intervention programs often rely heavily upon psychoeducational or guidance groups, as school counselors are faced with the dilemma of addressing the emotional needs of large numbers of students. Children and adolescents learn well in social settings, and a group approach provides an ideal intervention for a myriad of prevention and adjustment issues. A primary responsibility of school counselors is to promote a positive emotional and academic climate for the school at the systemic level.

In addressing schoolwide wellness, counselors may use large- and small-group interventions to address issues such as encouraging academic excellence, preventing substance abuse, enhancing self-esteem, promoting conflict resolution, and facilitating future planning. In broad systemic approaches, parents may be incorporated into after-hours preventive groups that address active parenting. Even as systemic issues are addressed, counselors are expected to identify individual students with specific mental health concerns, address these concerns, and determine the need for outside referral and intervention. In some cases, clinical counselors may conduct psychoeducational groups in school settings as part of programs to address community needs or concerns.

An example of a preventive group is one to teach children sexual-abuse prevention skills (Hazzard, 1993). Using the *Feelings Yes, Feelings No* curriculum developed by the National Film Board of Canada (1985) and comic books on sexual abuse, counselors provided an in-school series of psychoeducational groups to elementary school children. The groups incorporated 15-minute videotapes, discussions, role plays, and activities.

Children with social–emotional problems may benefit from a group experience, either as a preventive strategy for students at risk or as an adjunct to community clinical intervention. Childhood depression, for example, is a serious and debilitating condition, and depressive disorders in adolescents can lead to suicide. Sommers-Flanagan, Barrett-Hakanson, Clarke, and Sommers-Flanagan (2000) described a group model for middle school students with mild to moderate depressive symptoms at risk for depression. Drawing from a cognitive–behavioral theoretical base, this model emphasizes social and coping skills. The 12-week structured group incorporates group discussion, role play, activities and exercises, and take-home assignments, and addresses coping and social skills to combat depressive symptoms. In the psychoeducational group cited by Sommers-Flanagan et al., the students learned to recognize their negative focus and how to replace it with a positive focus, how to use relaxation techniques to combat tension and anxiety, and became aware of the social effects of irritating habits versus attempts to be friendly.

In promoting systemwide academic mastery, school counselors may conduct classroom guidance groups emphasizing academic or career goals. These groups are generally didactic in nature and may incorporate the classroom teacher as a co-leader. Counselors who conduct these groups have to master classroom management techniques and understand the age-related, large-group behaviors of children and adolescents. Conducting classroom guidance groups can be challenging for counselors who do not have teaching experience, as these groups often demand leadership skills and group techniques related more to teaching than to counseling.

PSYCHOEDUCATIONAL GROUPS ON COLLEGE CAMPUSES

Demands for more services attuned to counseling and crisis management, career development, special student needs, and concerns about student retention have led to a proliferation of psychoeducational groups in college counseling centers (McWhirter, 1995). College campuses are ideal settings for groups, as many students are young adults living away from home for the first time with accompanying academic and interpersonal challenges.

Student affairs professionals often promote student development through group work for a variety of reasons (Taub, 1998):

- Student development groups are economical.
- Student groups can provide an intensity of focus on the developmental issue of concern.
- Group settings provide a natural mode for many of the strategies in student development.
- Peer-group affiliations are important in the traditional-age college population.

With large numbers of young adults to draw from, campus groups can address specific adjustment issues. For example, a group model for helping college students overcome shyness—a personality trait that can negatively impact the social and emotional well-being of college students—has been detailed. The model includes a variety of techniques for helping shy students learn assertive behaviors such as initiating and maintaining conversations (Martin & Thomas, 2000). McWhirter (1995) described several psychoeducational groups conducted during a single semester at a large university in the Midwest, including a group for achieving academic success, a resource group for students with disabilities, a loneliness group, and a number of self-awareness groups dealing with women's experiences, making peace with food, men's issues, personal growth, self-discovery through imagery, stress management, and assertiveness training.

Career groups can help university students become more aware of careers they might wish to pursue and more decisive about occupational choices they might make. In Career and Self-Exploration (CASE) groups, students listen to brief lectures on specific topics such as self-disclosure, self-esteem, trust, and communication skills, combined with small-group discussions designed to facilitate evaluation of career options (McWhirter, Nichols, & Banks, 1984).

CONSIDERATIONS OF DIVERSITY

A large university with many international students offered group counseling to help these students adapt to life in the United States. This group was not able to maintain enough members to continue, despite the concerns of school officials that many international students were struggling academically and emotionally. The dean responsible for international student affairs explained that most students were not receptive to suggestions that they seek counseling and had no interest in discussing personal issues.

An astute counselor intern redesigned the group, calling it a Seminar for Success, an eight-session group including topics such as learning about the city and accessing community and university resources, as well as time-management and study skills needed for academic success. The group became popular with students from a variety of cultures and was frequently recommended by international students who had completed the group.

Group goals must be congruent with the values of group members. Sometimes a group is designed to target a specific population without considering whether that population sees a need to make a change. The group may focus on teaching behavior-change skills without examining the values associated with the behavior. Unless participants see the group goals as congruent with their own values, they will not commit to the change process. For example, a group addressing job-seeking skills may stress the importance of making eye contact—in direct conflict with cultural group values (Furr, 2000).

ETHICAL CONSIDERATIONS

As with all group work, leaders of psychoeducational groups must follow relevant ethical guidelines, including informed consent, screening, confidentiality, avoiding dual relationships, and providing appropriate referrals. A few ethical considerations warrant further discussion.

Leaders of certain kinds of psychoeducational groups may not be given the opportunity to screen members with the same level of scrutiny as leaders of counseling or psychotherapy groups. Brown (1998) thinks that screening members to determine their suitability has limited application, in part because leaders may not be in a position to determine who would benefit from the group. Notwithstanding this drawback, leaders have a responsibility to inform potential members about the nature of the group, including criteria for exclusion. For example, couples who are having severe marital problems may not benefit from, and actually may create discord in, a group emphasizing marital enrichment through better communication. Leaders have a responsibility to articulate group goals clearly to interested couples and suggest alternatives to those who need more intensive counseling interventions.

Confidentiality is more of a concern for group counseling/psychotherapy than for psychoeducational groups, as the latter groups usually do not touch upon issues requiring privacy (Brown, 1998). It is important, however, to emphasize to all members the need for confidentiality regarding individual disclosure. What may seem like innocuous information to one member may be regarded by another as highly sensitive. Discussing confidentiality is especially important in psychoeducational groups, because members may assume that the group resembles a classroom or workshop format in which information is shared freely. Issues of trust and safety are especially important in groups that introduce experiential exercises involving self-disclosure.

In a variety of settings, psychoeducational groups provide an adjunct to clinical interventions such as individual or family counseling. In these cases, potential group participants should discuss with their other counselors their intended group involvement. As with all group work, leaders should inquire about any other mental health services they are receiving and inform potential clients of the need to coordinate interventions.

Because group participation may trigger sensitive personal issues for members, leaders must be prepared with referral resources for the group as a whole and for any members who appear to be experiencing distress in the group. A psychoeducational group intervention may not provide an appropriate level of therapeutic intervention for serious clinical issues, and counselors must be aware of the scope of their expertise and of the clinical utility of their interventions.

AN EXAMPLE: A WELLNESS GROUP FOR WOMEN OF COLOR

The group model presented here has been adapted from a group designed and implemented by Cynthia Kline Buras (1999), a counseling graduate student at Our Lady of Holy Cross College in New Orleans, Louisiana, under the supervision of Susan Niemann.

Originally conceived as a group emphasizing nutrition and exercise, this structured, time-limited group evolved after the leader met with her population and conducted an assessment of interests and needs. The participants were a group of young African American mothers living in a government-subsidized housing area in a suburban region of New Orleans. After interviewing the women, the leader expanded and altered the group to incorporate physical, emotional, and spiritual aspects of wellness.

Although many psychoeducational groups are directed to a single aspect of wellness, this group was conceptualized as a broad-based overview of topics these women chose as meaningful in their lives. A general goal of the intervention was to expose members to a positive experience with counseling, as many of the participants had previous experiences with mental health interventions as agents of control or punishment. Most held negative views of mental health workers as being out of touch with their emotional concerns.

The original group met for 2 hours over 12 weeks in a recreational facility at the participants' place of residence and incorporated several topics, including parenting skills and job-search strategies. At the conclusion, the women overwhelmingly rated the group as highly beneficial, reporting that it significantly increased their knowledge regarding health and nutrition. The members named the session addressing spirituality as the most personally meaningful and helpful. Attendance was excellent, and all members expressed a desire to become part of similar groups in their communities.

This group emphasized some of the important multicultural considerations of planning and implementing psychoeducational groups. The group leader and the supervisor, both majority-culture women, were challenged to provide a culturally appropriate intervention to a group of historically marginalized women, regarding both ethnicity and socioeconomic status. The leader and the supervisor took great care to listen to the concerns of the participants during the planning and implementation stages. These meetings led to the development of group content as well as addressing practical concerns, such as providing childcare during group time. The pre-group meetings also allowed the counselor to gather pre-test data and to screen and pre-train potential members.

The following is a six-session model of this psychoeducational group, with an overall goal of increasing wellness through awareness and lifestyle changes. Each session was designed to last 2 hours.

Session One: Introductions and Overview of Wellness and Lifestyle

Objectives: Upon completing Session One, participants will be able to

- clearly articulate group guidelines and goals;
- comprehend a definition of wellness;
- identify feelings, thoughts, and behaviors that contribute to or hinder personal wellness;
- explain the relationship between positive self-concept and wellness; and
- learn a strategy for relaxation.

The initial session was a time of orientation to the group culture. The leader reviewed and emphasized the ground rules and provided reassurance regarding the voluntary nature of participation and the ongoing openness to feedback from group members. The leader also addressed questions regarding housekeeping items such as access to phones, breaks, bathrooms, and starting/stopping times.

As an ice-breaker exercise, modeled by the leader, group members were asked to state their first name, followed by an adjective best describing themselves, or giving the origin or reason behind their first name. This exercise encourages members of a new group to learn the names of all the members and contributes to group cohesion.

Next the leader introduced the psychoeducational content of the group and read aloud and distributed handouts of the following definition of wellness:

Wellness

Wellness is a choice—

A decision you make to move toward optimal health.

Wellness is a way of life—

A lifestyle you design to achieve your highest potential for well-being.

Wellness is a process—

Developing awareness that there is no end point, but that health and happiness are possible in each moment, here and now.

Wellness is an efficient channeling of energy—

Energy received from the environment, transformed within you, and sent on to affect the world outside.

Wellness is the integration of body, mind, and spirit—

The appreciation that everything you do, think, feel, and believe has an impact upon your state of health.

Wellness is a loving acceptance of yourself.

The leader facilitated a group discussion addressing the members' reactions to the reading, highlighting the portions they found most personally relevant. She asked the members to state the behaviors in their lives that they considered as contributing to their wellness and those that hindered their wellness. The leader provided an overview of group content to be addressed in the coming sessions, including stress reduction, good nutrition, exercise, positive body image, and spirituality.

To emphasize the relationship between wellness and self-concept, the leader read the poem "Phenomenal Woman" by Maya Angelou (1995). The members discussed how the poem's author achieved wellness through her strong, confident self-image.

During the last 15 minutes of the first session, the leader introduced a relaxation strategy, emphasizing the link between physical and emotional wellness. The leader demonstrated nonimpact exercises, including head and shoulder rolls, and the members followed her lead. She also led them through a series of simple stretching exercises and encouraged them to practice these relaxation exercises during the coming week.

As the leader demonstrated, it is important to bring closure to each psychoeducational group session by summarizing the group's goals, asking for feedback, and introducing the topic for the next session. The initial session ended with a discussion of members' current feelings and their feedback concerning the first session. The leader gave an overview of the content to be addressed in the next session and reminded the members to bring their group folders each week.

Session Two: Reducing the Stress in Our Bodies

Objectives: Upon completing Session Two, participants will be able to

- discuss the relationship between stress and wellness,
- identify their own physical cues that they are under stress, and
- learn three strategies for lowering their stress levels.

The second session began with the leader's briefly reviewing the previous week's learning, followed by an introduction of the topic for Session Two. The group leader identified and discussed the internal body cues of excessive stress and assisted the participants in identifying their personal body cues, such as sweaty palms, increased heart rate, muscle tension, or headaches. She taught and demonstrated three behavioral stress-reduction strategies:

1. Slow deep breathing
2. Backward counting
3. Pleasant visual imagery

After the group practiced these strategies, the leader introduced the topic of time management as a way to reduce stress. She asked the members to note during the coming week when they would feel stress in their bodies and to check their bodies periodically for signs of stress. The members also were to note what strategies they used to lower their stress and if these were helpful. In addition, the participants were asked to bring a healthy recipe to the next session, which would have the theme of nutrition.

Session Three: Learning a Healthier Way to Eat

Objectives: Upon completing Session Three, participants will be able to

- discuss the relationship between food and health,
- learn to make healthier food decisions using the Food Guide Pyramid,
- learn techniques for cooking with less fat and sugar, and
- incorporate strategies for improving family nutrition.

By the third week, the participants were familiar with the group's culture and arrived ready and eager to engage in the activities. During Session Three the leader provided basic information about nutrition, including the Recommended Daily Allowances (RDA) as set forth by the Committee on Dietary Allowances (1989) and the Food Guide Pyramid. The leader provided handouts and gave examples of foods that make up a healthy diet. Members were asked to discuss their own diets and how they made decisions on what to eat and to feed their families.

The group discussed the challenges of maintaining healthy eating habits, and the participants brainstormed how they might incorporate healthier foods into their family's diet. Activities included a recipe swap, in which participants exchanged recipes they brought to the group, and a discussion of strategies for preparing their favorite foods in healthier ways. The members also were given coupons for healthy foods and copies of simple, healthy recipes and were asked to incorporate some of the week's suggestions about healthier eating into their cooking and shopping routines over the next week.

Session Four: Moving More and Feeling Better

Objectives: Upon completing Session Four, participants will be able to

- discuss the benefits of regular exercise;
- explain how exercise can reduce stress, increase energy, and contribute to cardio-vascular health;
- discuss the relationship between body shape and exercise; and
- incorporate strategies for including exercise as a lifestyle.

Session Four emphasized the role of exercise in overall wellness. The leader provided information about exercise and distributed handouts about the importance of combining exercise with a balanced diet. The members discussed ways by which they might incorporate exercise into their lives and exchanged ideas on healthy exercise options, such as walking groups. The group leader modeled and led members in stretching and marching-in-place activities. The members were encouraged to obtain medical advice before embarking on exercise programs on their own.

Building on Session Three, Session Four emphasized the importance of better eating habits and regular exercise. Members were challenged to add mild exercise to their daily routines at least three times over the next week and to note how they felt on the days they exercised. At this point, the leader addressed group closure, reminding the members that just two sessions remained.

Session Five: Learning to Love Our Beautiful Selves

Objectives: Upon completing Session Five, participants will be able to

- explain the connection between appearance and self-esteem,
- identify negative self-talk about their appearance and replace these with affirmations,
- demonstrate how self-care can improve body image and self-esteem, and
- learn strategies for maximizing personal attractiveness.

During the fifth session, the group focused on how women perceive their physical appearance and how this affects wellness. First, the members watched a short session of a taped television segment of a newsmagazine depicting majority and minority women discussing body image. The videotape suggested that while majority-culture women are more concerned with thinness, minority-culture women, and African American women in particular, also are concerned with their bodies and their appearance.

The leader led the members in a discussion about their feelings about themselves and their bodies and how incorporating a positive self-concept, along with incorporating strategies for healthy living, could improve their emotional and physical wellness. The leader explained and gave examples of negative self-talk, how to reframe negative self-talk into affirmations, and asked the participants to identify some of the negative self-messages they gave themselves about their appearance. The participants practiced responding to negative self-talk with affirmations and encouragement.

In the last hour of Session Five, an outside participant—a beauty consultant of the nonmajority culture—dispensed advice about maintaining style on a budget. The group members received samples of healthy beauty products donated by area vendors. The members were encouraged to find time over the next week to engage in self-care activities to help them feel more confident about their appearance.

Session Six: Embracing Our Higher Power

Objectives: Upon completing Session Six, participants will be able to

- articulate a greater awareness about the role of spirituality in their lives,

- understand the relationship between spirituality and wellness, and
- integrate the components of wellness discussed over the last 6 weeks into a unified goal of healthier living.

During the final session, the leader introduced the concept of spirituality as a component of wellness. Spirituality was addressed not only as church membership but as a broad relationship with one's higher power. Members were asked about the role of spirituality, a higher power, and church in their lives, and what their beliefs have meant to them during stressful times. Accompanied by tranquil music, each member completed a fill-in-the-blank letter to her higher power. These letters were too personal for some members to talk about, but others shared some of their insights or feelings.

The last half of the final session was devoted to integrating the six sessions and to saying good-bye. The members were asked to articulate how they would continue to incorporate the components of wellness into their lifestyles after the group ended. The leader invited their feedback, in both written and verbal form, about which elements of the group were most helpful and which might be improved upon. Finally, the members were asked to share their hopes and dreams for themselves and for one another. In saying good-bye, leader and members gave one another "gifts" by completing the sentence, "My greatest wish for you is that____."

LEARNING ACTIVITIES

1. In small groups, identify through discussion at least five common needs of the clients they anticipate or are working with at present. Develop a list of psychoeducational group topics addressing each of these needs.
2. Create a psychoeducational group curriculum, addressing the client population, the goals of the group, and logistical matters, and include a detailed curriculum of each group's topics and activities.
3. As a small-group activity, utilize the curriculum you developed in the prior activity in "practice groups" with your peers. Select and practice facilitating one activity from the curriculum and gather feedback at the conclusion of the practice group.
4. Provide a detailed summary of your practice activity, addressing the strengths of the activity and the needs for improvement, efficacy toward meeting the desired goal, and ease of implementation. Include the feedback from the practice group.

SUMMARY

Psychoeducational groups are structured therapeutic groups that emphasize learning or developing skills for the purpose of prevention, growth, or remediation. Psychoeducational groups are becoming increasingly popular as both primary and supplemental interventions in a variety of settings. Effective psychoeducational groups are highly organized and time limited, and they integrate principles of learning with traditional group intervention strategies. Compared to counseling groups and other types of group work, psychoeducational groups are highly cognitive, involve fewer sessions, include more members, do not emphasize catharsis or deep personal disclosure, have predefined goals for members, incorporate specific activities with desired outcomes, and limit group content to predetermined topics.

Leaders of psychoeducational groups must be knowledgeable and skilled regarding group leadership and teaching strategies. At their most effective, these groups integrate the best elements of counseling and teaching and provide effective and powerful interventions for many clinical and adjustment issues. These groups have proven to be effective in treating a variety of issues, including eating disorders, substance abuse, and depression. Clients who benefit from psychoeducational groups find their emphasis on knowledge and skill building to be empowering, either as a primary source of help or as an adjunct to individual or other counseling interventions. These groups are popular in primary, secondary, and postsecondary education settings, where they often provide an important component of comprehensive guidance programs.

Ethical considerations in implementing psychoeducational groups include informed consent, screening, confidentiality, and coordinating services with other mental health professionals. Group leaders must be able to recognize and refer emotional issues outside of the scope of the group, to ensure that members will receive services appropriate to their mental health challenges. Group leaders also must ensure that their group interventions are culturally responsive, consistent with the cultural considerations of the populations they serve, and emphasize cultural enhancement whenever possible.

USEFUL WEB SITES

□ Association for Specialists in Group Work
  www.asgw.org
□ American Group Psychotherapy Association
  www.agpa.org
□ *Group Psychotherapy for Psychological Trauma*
  www.agpa.org/pubs/GC_0801_trauma.html
□ Psychoeducational Counseling Services
  www.psychoeducation.com/psychoeducation.htm
□ Resource Site for Group Practitioners
  www.psyctc.org/mirrors/asgw/resource.htm
□ New York State Office of Mental Health
  www.omh.state.ny.us/omhweb/ebp/Family_psychoEducation.htm
□ Article: "Content and Curriculum in Psychoeducation Groups for Families of Persons With Severe Mental Illness"
  http://ps.psychiatryonline.org/cgi/content/full/49/6/816

REFERENCES

Association for Specialists in Group Work (ASGW). (1999). Principles for diversity-competent group workers. *Journal for Specialists in Group Work, 24*, 7–14.

Association for Specialists in Group Work (ASGW). (2000). ASGW professional standards for the training of group workers. *Journal for Specialists in Group Work, 25*, 327–342.

Angelou, M. (1995). Phenomenal woman. *Ebony, 51*, 189.

Barth, R. P., Yeaton, J., & Winterfelt, N. (1994). Psychoeducational groups with foster parents of sexually abused children. *Child and Adolescent Social Work Journal, 11*, 405–424.

Bauer, M., & McBride, L. (1996). *Structured group psychotherapy for bipolar disorder: The life goals program.* New York: Springer.

Bridbord, K., DeLucia-Waack, J. L., Jones, E., & Gerrity, D. A. (2004). The nonsignificant impact of an agenda setting treatment for groups: Implications for future research and practice. *Journal for Specialists in Group Work, 29*, 301–315.

Brown, N. W. (1998). *Psychoeducational groups.* Philadelphia: Accelerated Development.

Buras, C. K. (1999). *A total wellness group for single mothers with dependent children.* Unpublished master's thesis, Our Lady of Holy Cross College, New Orleans, LA.

Cheston, R., Jones, K., & Gilliard, J. (2003). Group psychotherapy and people with dementia. *Aging & Mental Health, 7*, 452–461.

Committee on Dietary Allowances. (1989). *Recommended dietary allowances, 10th edition.* Washington, DC: National Academy Press.

Conyne, R. K., & Bemak, F. (2004). Teaching group work from an ecological perspective. *Journal for Specialists in Group Work, 29*, 7–18.

Durana, C. (1996). A longitudinal evaluation of the pairs psychoeducational program for couples. *Family Therapy, 23*, 11–36.

Fristad, M. A., Arnett, M. M., & Gavazzi, S. M. (1998). The impact of psychoeducational workshops on families of mood-disordered children. *Family Therapy, 25*, 151–159.

Fristad, M.A., Goldberg-Arnold, J.S., & Gavazzi, S.M. (2002). Multifamily psychoeducation groups (MFPG) for families of children with bipolar disorder. *Bipolar Disorders, 4*, 254–262.

Furr, S. R. (2000). Structuring the group experience: A format for designing psychoeducational groups. *Journal for Specialists in Group Work, 25*, 29–49.

Gallagher, R., & Nazarian, J. (1995). A comprehensive cognitive-behavioral/educational program for schizophrenic patients. *Bulletin of the Menninger Clinic, 59*, 357–371.

Hazzard, A. (1993). Psychoeducational groups to teach children sexual abuse prevention skills. *Journal of Child and Adolescent Group Therapy, 3*, 13–23

Jones, K. D., & Robinson, E. H. (2000). Psychoeducational groups: A model for choosing topics and exercises appropriate to group stage. *Journal for Specialists in Group Work, 25*, 356–365.

Lundwall, R. A. (1996). How psychoeducational support groups can provide multidiscipline services to families of people with mental illness. *Psychiatric Rehabilitation Journal, 20*, 64–71.

Martin, V., & Thomas, M. C. (2000). A model psychoeducation group for shy college students. *Journal for Specialists in Group Work, 25*, 79–88.

McDonell, M. G., Short, R. A., Berry, C. M., & Dyck, D. G. (2003). Burden in schizophrenia caregivers: Impact of family psychoeducation and awareness of patient suicidality. *Family Process, 42*, 91–103.

McWhirter, J. J. (1995). Emotional education for university students. *Journal of College Student Psychotherapy, 10*, 27–38.

McWhirter, J. J., Nichols, E., & Banks, N, M. (1984). Career awareness and self-exploration (CASE) groups: A self-assessment model for career decision making. *Personnel and Guidance Journal, 62*, 367–389.

Milsom, A., Akos, P., & Thompson, M. (2004). A psychoeducational group approach to postsecondary transition planning for students with learning disabilities. *Journal for Specialists in Group Work, 29*, 395–411.

National Film Board of Canada. (1985). *Feelings yes, feelings no.* Evanston: Perennial Education.

Nerenberg, A. (2000). The value of group psychotherapy for sexual addicts in a residential setting. *Sexual Addiction & Compulsivity, 7,* 197–209.

Neukrug, E. (1999). *The world of the counselor: An introduction to the counseling profession.* Pacific Grove, CA: Brooks/Cole.

Nicholson, B., Anderson, M., Fox, R., & Brenner, V. (2002). One family at a time: A prevention program for at-risk parents. *Journal of Counseling & Development, 80,* 362–371.

Olson, M. J., & McEwen, M. A. (2004). Grief counseling groups in a medium-security prison. *Journal for Specialists in Group Work, 29,* 225–236.

Reiss, H., & Rutan, J. S. (1992). Group therapy for eating disorders: A step-wise approach. *Group, 16,* 79–83.

Rice, A. (1995). Structured groups for the treatment of depression. In K. R. MacKensie (Ed.), *Effective use of group therapy in managed care* (pp. 61–96). Washington, DC: American Psychiatric Press.

Riva, M. T., & Korinek, L. (2004). Teaching group work: Modeling group leader and member behaviors in the classroom to demonstrate group therapy. *Journal for Specialists in Group Work, 29,* 55–63.

Rivera, E., Wilbur, M., Roberts-Wilbur, J., Phan, L., Garrett, M. T., & Betz, R. L. (2004). Supervising and training psychoeducational group leaders. *Journal for Specialists in Group Work, 29,* 377–394.

Schectman, Z. (2002). Child group psychotherapy in the school at the threshold of a new millennium. *Journal of Counseling & Development, 80,* 293–299.

Schectman, Z., Bar-El, O., & Hadar, E. (1995). Therapeutic factors and psychoeducational groups for adolescents: A comparison. *Journal for Specialists in Group Work, 22,* 203–213.

Sommers-Flanagan, R., Barrett-Hakanson, T., Clarke, C., & Sommers-Flanagan, J. (2000). A psychoeducational school-based coping and social skills group for depressed students. *Journal for Specialists in Group Work, 25,* 170–190.

Taub, D. J. (1998). Promoting student development through psychoeducational groups: A perspective on the goals and process matrix. *Journal for Specialists in Group Work, 23,* 196–201.

Williams, T. I. (1989). A social skills group for autistic children. *Journal for Autism and Developmental Disorders, 19,* 143–155.

Wilson, F. R., Rapin, L. S., & Haley-Banez, L. (2004). How teaching group work can be guided by foundational documents: Best practice guidelines, diversity principles, training standards. *Journal for Specialists in Group Work, 29,* 19–29.

Worthington, E. L., & Drinkard, D. T. (2000). Promoting reconciliation through psychoeducation and therapeutic interventions. *Journal of Marital and Family Therapy, 26,* 93–101.

Psychotherapy Groups

Jonathan W. Carrier and Melinda Haley

t is widely held that the end of World War II and the subsequent influx of "psychiatric casualties" led to the widespread group practices we see today (Scheidlinger, 1994), although there has been some disagreement over its exact point of origin. Much of this debate has been definitional in nature. Earlier groups, such as Joseph Hersey Pratt's 1905 "class method" for treatment of individuals with tuberculosis (intended to save time in teaching patients hygiene practices), were found to have a psychotherapeutic effect, although this was not the initial purpose (Brown & Srebalus, 2003; Gazda, Ginter, & Horne, 2001; Hadden, 1955).

Other early practitioners, such as E.W. Lazell and L.C. Marsh, also provided what many would consider to be group psychotherapeutic intervention. While Lazell's group procedures consisted mainly of lectures, Marsh utilized group discussions, music, art, and dance in his efforts to aid individuals residing in mental hospitals (Gazda, 1982; Gazda et al., 2001). It was Marsh who uttered the famous statement, "By the crowd they have been broken; by the crowd they shall be healed" (Gazda, 1982).

Slavson (1959) argued that group psychotherapy was not actually being practiced before 1930, because these groups did not meet his criteria of small group size, permissive group leadership, grouping clients on related diagnostic criteria, and freedom and spontaneity of group members' actions. Slavson's criteria seem to follow what might be expected of some modalities of modern-day group psychotherapies.

More recently, group psychotherapy has been defined as "any intervention designed to alleviate psychological distress, reduce maladaptive behavior, or enhance adaptive behavior through counseling, structured or unstructured interaction, a training program, or a predetermined treatment plan" (Dagley, Gazda,

Eppinger, & Stuwart, 1994, p. 340). Many theorists and practitioners, however, state that this definition also meets the criteria for group counseling, which many hold to be separate from group psychotherapy.

Gazda (1982) suggested that the definitional problems stem from using the terms *group psychotherapy*, *group therapy*, and *group counseling* interchangeably. In many instances, the term *group therapy*, or *group counseling*, is a colloquial version of group psychotherapy. According to Gazda, although the term *group therapy* may include group procedures such as psychotherapy, it also may incorporate elements such as physical therapy, recreational therapy, psychoeducational activities, and counseling. Group psychotherapy, therefore, may be looked upon as a specialized type of group therapy.

Possibly, no professional consensus for a steadfast definition of psychotherapy will be forthcoming. Naturally, how counselors view psychotherapy groups depends on the theoretical model to which those counselors subscribe (Engler & Goleman, 1992). Therefore, the criteria of Slavson (1959) and Dagley et al. (1994) are applicable to qualifying certain psychotherapeutic groups, yet they leave much to be desired for some groups and exclude others that might fit different practitioners' ideas of the psychotherapeutic framework. Theorists and practitioners might find it easier to define the psychotherapeutic group according to several primary attributes that differentiate it from other types of therapy groups than to subscribe to a mutually inclusive or exclusive set of characteristics. To further delineate and refine the definition of group psychotherapy, we will address the specific characteristics that set psychotherapy groups apart from other types of counseling groups.

WHAT IS DIFFERENT ABOUT THERAPEUTIC GROUPS?

Regardless of the many differing opinions concerning the definition of group psychotherapy, a review of the literature reveals a distinct set of criteria that distinguish it from other forms of group work. According to Brown and Srebalus (2003) and Roberts (1998), for example, in a psychotherapy group—more so than in any other group—a match must be made between and among counselor, group members, theory base, developmental level of the group, and the issue at hand. Group psychotherapy can be used in almost every setting, with most categories of mental illness, and with a wide range of age groups—which sets it further apart from other, more limited forms of group therapy (Brabender, 2002; Kottler, 2001; Schmidt, 2003). Above all, most theorists agree that psychotherapeutic groups have a diagnostic foundation, the opportunity for transference, and a goal of effecting change or growth in the individual or group.

Diagnostic Foundation

In the strictest sense of the definition of psychotherapy, the culmination of therapy is to have an effect on, or produce growth within, the client. Nevertheless, the literature and the various therapeutic models blur what is considered to be counseling and what is considered to be psychotherapy (Schmidt, 2003). Some theorists proclaim that there is no difference, while others declare that there are profound differences. For the purpose of this chapter, we will present psychotherapy in its purest form, which requires a diagnostic basis for the foundation of the group (Gazda et al., 2001; Kottler, 2001; Nystul, 2003).

For example, a homogeneous psychotherapeutic group experience might have as a goal changes in the behavior or cognitions in a group whose members are experiencing anxiety, a phobia, an eating disorder, or an adjustment disorder (Brown & Srebalus, 2003). This psychotherapeutic group would not deal with issues relating to transitional events, or with issues relating to specific problems. Instead, psychotherapy groups seek to remediate basic personality, emotional, behavioral, or interpersonal maladjustments (Capuzzi & Gross, 2002; Roberts, 1998). Psychotherapy works toward lasting personality change and, ultimately, self-actualization. According to Slavson (1974), the goal of psychotherapy is to resolve inner malformation of the personality from which maladjustments flow.

Transference

Weinberg (1984) defined *transference* as the client's carrying forth expectations, impressions, and feelings from a past person to the therapist. Although transference can occur in almost any situation, it is most likely to happen within psychotherapy and especially within the group experience. It is important to note that transference also may occur between group members.

One therapeutic benefit of the psychotherapy group is that the group itself can become symbolic to a group member's family of origin and may even become a microcosm of society itself (Brown & Srebalus, 2003; Kottler, 2001). In this way, analogies related to intrafamilial relationships develop and relational patterns of members in the real world can be re-created within the group context. When this happens, the counselor can help group members examine their current behavior and thought patterns and analogize it to past experience (Mullan & Rosenbaum, 1962). In this manner, psychotherapy often links past experience to current action, thoughts, philosophies, or phobias and seeks to mitigate a change in the group member's distorted worldview, behavioral patterns, cognitions, or self-talk.

Change

Again, the aim of a psychotherapy group is to influence change in the group members. Roberts (1998) defined psychotherapy as a method for understanding why, what, and how a person responds to life's challenges. The ultimate goal is to change the "why" and "what," because these things often have not been adaptive.

The focus is on changing or refining ingrained personality traits, behavioral patterns, or cognitive miscues that are disabling the client or group member from functioning effectively in the world (Capuzzi & Gross, 2002; Slavson, 1974; Weinberg, 1984). Therefore, the aim is not to educate the client as it would be in a guidance/psychoeducational group or to develop teamwork or group skills in completing a project as would be found in a task/work group. The goal of psychotherapy groups is to achieve actual change in basic personality structure and clients' way of living and behaving in their world.

GROUP THERAPY MODELS

As new theories of personality and treatment methods have unfolded, most practitioners have found application to group work. Today, psychoanalytic, humanistic, Adlerian, transactional analytical, cognitive–behavioral, and Gestalt psychotherapies (as well as a myriad of others) all can be used effectively in a variety of group settings. We have chosen to discuss three psychotherapeutic modalities that encapsulate a wide array of techniques and principles evident in many of today's group psychotherapies.

The Adlerian Modality

Founded in the 1920s by Alfred Adler, individual or Adlerian psychology is based on the notion that each person possesses what Adler called "social interest," the innate human potential to cooperate with others in achieving personal and societal goals (Schultz & Schultz, 1996). Adler used "collective therapy" with children and families in Vienna as early as 1920, making him one of the pioneers of group work (Dreikurs, 1932). Because Adlerians believe that the most important life problems are social, the individual must be considered within the social context. Based on this theoretical cornerstone, tenets of Adlerian psychotherapy became widespread throughout group work in the early 1960s (Corsini, 1988).

Adlerian group process is characterized by a deliberate attempt to reorient faulty living patterns and instill a better understanding of the principles that stimulate useful interactions and cooperation. Sonstegard (1998) described reorientation as "a change in a group member's attitude toward a present life situation and the problems that must be faced" (p. 221). This concept is central to Adlerian psychotherapeutic group work and emphasizes reorientation of the individual's self and worldviews.

Adlerian group psychotherapy can be useful with many client populations, particularly those experiencing life difficulties that stem from feelings of inferiority or personal inadequacy. According to Adlerian theory, failing to compensate for feelings of inferiority may give rise to an inferiority complex, which can render the individual incapable of coping with life's problems (Schultz & Schultz, 1996). In Adlerian group psychotherapy, clients are asked to rely on the creative power of the self to aid themselves and the other group members in overcoming their difficulties. The main goal of Adlerian group psychotherapists is to help group members tap into this creative power and, in so doing, overcome feelings of inferiority and solve their difficulties.

Critics of Adlerian group psychotherapy maintain that its theory and application are too scripted and lacking in scope for widespread use with the array of difficulties that clients present (e.g., Schultz & Schultz, 1996). Although little research has been done on the efficacy of Adlerian group psychotherapy or its application to various presenting problems, this does not speak for or against the argument. In Adler's defense, few psychiatric impairments or life difficulties cannot be aided by Adlerian psychotherapy's attention to alleviating feelings of inferiority and improving self-concept (Yalom, 1995).

The Humanistic Modality

Although many psychotherapeutic modalities have integrated humanistic principles into their techniques, the theorist Abraham Maslow and the theorist–practitioner Carl Rogers may be credited with founding this school of thought. At the center of humanistic psychotherapy is the concept of *self-actualization*, the full development of one's abilities and the realization of one's potentials (Maslow, 1970). Humanistic psychotherapies are applicable to almost any pathology because, according to Maslow, self-actualized individuals are free of neuroses and are better able to cope with life difficulties.

According to humanistic theory, individuals move naturally toward actualization and have psychological difficulty when they find themselves pursuing a path in their lives that is nonactualizing (Hazler, 2003). The goal of humanistic psychotherapies, then, is to aid the client in attaining congruence, or bringing their lives in line with their self-actualizing goals. This goal is accomplished in part through *unconditional positive regard*, a nonjudgmental, warm, and empathetic attitude modeled by the psychotherapist, which humanistic psychotherapists believe is necessary for client growth to take place. Humanistic psychotherapy is applicable to group work because, as members learn and exhibit unconditional positive regard for other members, a safe environment emerges that is conducive to growth (Schultz & Schultz, 1996).

Detractors of humanistic psychotherapy say that its treatment of human nature and psychopathology is too simplistic to be of much use in the field of psychotherapy. Other critics claim that humanistic psychotherapy does not lend itself to curing neuroses, anxiety, or depression, that it is aimed more at clients of normal to average mental health. A humanistic psychotherapist's response might be that neuroses such as anxiety and depression are a direct result of incongruencies in the individual's path to self-actualization and, therefore, are well within the realm of humanistically oriented psychotherapy.

The Cognitive–Behavioral Modality

Cognitive–behavioral psychotherapy is a somewhat generic term used to describe a set of principles and techniques that embody elements of both cognitive and behavioral theories. A relatively recent development in traditional behavior therapy, cognitive–behavior therapy arose as some behavioral practitioners began to realize that the range of human psychopathology encompasses far more than phobias and simple behavioral deficits (Schultz & Schultz, 1996). Cognitive–behavioral psychotherapists hold a very different view of human nature than do the other psychotherapeutic modalities.

According to Kalodner (2003), cognitive–behavioral psychotherapists view human nature as an amalgam of stimulus–response patterns that the individual has learned over life. This stimulus–response pattern can be quite different for each individual, as no two individuals view the same experience in exactly the same way. Therefore, cognitive–behaviorists do not subscribe to the concept of an all-encompassing "human nature," instead viewing human nature in a wholly individual sense.

Adherents of this theory hold that psychopathology is learned through a maladaptive set of stimulus–response patterns. The goal of cognitive–behavioral psychotherapy, then, is to break this pattern of maladaptive responses through both cognitive and behavioral interventions. Depending on the pathology, cognitive or behavioral techniques may be relied on individually or in conjunction if necessary. According to Hollon and Kendall (1979), for behavioral excesses or deficits, behavioral psychotherapy may be used; for cognitive excesses or deficits, cognitive psychotherapy may be used; and for behavioral and cognitive excesses or deficits, cognitive–behavioral psychotherapy should be used.

Behavioral interventions rely on techniques including positive and negative reinforcement, extinction, shaping, and stimulus control to change specific behaviors (Brabender, 2002; Gazda et al., 2001; Lacey, 2004). By comparison, cognitive interventions use techniques to break thought distortions such as all-or-nothing thinking, disqualifying the positive, and catastrophizing, all of which inhibit personal growth (Kalodner, 2003). Together, these techniques are formidable and have been proven to be easily within the scope of individual or group psychotherapy.

The marriage of cognitive and behavioral theories has been able to overcome many of the limitations of either therapy alone (Kalodner, 2003). Detractors, however, criticize cognitive–behaviorism's lack of recognition of unconscious motivators in human behavior, arguing that humans are born with predispositions toward certain types of behavior that cannot be broken through cognitive–behavioral techniques alone. Cognitive–behaviorism has also garnered criticism for its here-and-now approach to treatment from theorists who insist that emphasis on the past is a necessary component of treatment.

AN EXAMPLE: PSYCHOTHERAPY SESSIONS

Six group psychotherapy sessions will be briefly outlined to illustrate some of the nuances of group psychotherapy as different from group counseling and group psychoeducation. The theoretical framework will be eclectic, pulling aspects from the Adlerian, humanistic, and cognitive–behavioral theories just introduced. The primary theme of the group is anxiety.

Session One

The first session of group psychotherapy resembles the initial session of most group modalities. The theme is one of introduction, education, and reassurance. The psychotherapist introduces the group topic—in this case, anxiety—and informs the group of the nature of the topic, his or her experience with applying group psychotherapy to this topical area of anxiety, and the eventual goals for the group pertaining to the topic. Ground rules for the group are established, informed consents are signed, and group members' expectations for the group are discussed. Toward the end of the session, the psychotherapist describes some of the techniques he or she will utilize (wholly at the psychotherapist's discretion) in dealing with anxiety, after which questions and concerns from group members are addressed.

Session Two

At the beginning of the second session (and each session thereafter), the psychotherapist briefly addresses any questions or concerns about the group that clients may have thought of during the past week. After this, the psychotherapist allots a set amount of time (perhaps 3–5 minutes per person) for each member to discuss his or her personal experience with the topic of anxiety and his or her goals pertaining to the topic. When members are self-disclosing and vocalizing in these sessions, the psychotherapist likely will utilize humanistic techniques such as reflection and empathy in response to clients' individual experiences, in an effort to join and create rapport with each group member. Although this is not necessarily the time for confrontation or psychotherapeutic intervention, as members are merely expressing their personal experiences, the psychotherapist is garnering useful information for future exercises and interventions.

During each member's recounting of anxiety-related experiences, the psychotherapist notes fallacious thinking and discrepancies in logic. For example, a group member states, "I become really anxious when I want to ask someone out for a date, because I'm sure I'll be turned down." At this point, the psychotherapist points this out to the group as an example of an irrational thought (a well-known cognitive technique). The psychotherapist expounds on the topic of irrational thinking and how it may exacerbate anxiety. Then the psychotherapist asks each member to recount to the group an example of his or her own irrational thinking.

The psychotherapist closes the session with a homework assignment relating to the theme of the session. Group members are asked to write down five examples of irrational thinking they engaged in during the week and bring it in for discussion for the third session. At the end of this session (and all others), the psychotherapist closes with a brief question-and-answer period.

Session Three

After a brief question-and-answer period, a fourth to a third of this session is spent discussing the homework assignment of the previous week. Then the psychotherapist introduces a behavioral intervention—deep-muscle relaxation (or another systematic relaxation technique)—for members to utilize during periods of high anxiety. Group members spend the rest of this session practicing this technique and discussing its application. At the end of the session, questions and concerns are fielded and homework is assigned: Practice relaxation for 15–30 minutes each day until the next group meeting.

Session Four

The fourth session opens in the usual manner with a brief question-and-answer period, then moves to a discussion of the week's homework assignment. As with any discussion of assigned homework, the psychotherapist is aware of difficulties that members may have had with the homework and addresses these expeditiously. This is of paramount importance because the homework is based on interventions applied during the group for treating the group topic—in this case, anxiety. If difficulties are not addressed and discussed, group members may not master these interventions, which would inhibit the psychotherapy.

After addressing the difficulties, the psychotherapist asks group members to provide examples of when they might use this tool to help them alleviate anxiety. The psychotherapist then asks the members to imagine a time when they were anxious and then to utilize their newly learned relaxation technique to extinguish this anxiety. The members should practice until the end of the session, at which time questions and concerns are addressed. As homework, members are asked to apply the relaxation technique they practiced in the group to a real-life anxiety-provoking situation and report the results during next week's session.

Session Five

The fifth session follows the format of the previous three sessions—briefly addressing questions before jumping into a discussion of the week's homework. Members are asked to recount their experiences in applying the relaxation technique to real-life situations. These self-reports are discussed thoroughly, which takes up half the session. Afterward, the psychotherapist reminds the group members of the topic for the second week—illogical and irrational thinking—and asks them to imagine another anxiety-provoking situation.

The members are asked to question themselves, before entering into the relaxation technique, whether they considered that illogical or irrational thinking might be causing their feelings of anxiety. If they recognize that their anxiety is caused by irrational thinking, its power over them is reduced, which makes relaxation that much easier. The group members practice this technique until the end of the session, when the usual procedure to end the week's group is followed. As fifth-week homework, the members are asked to try to recognize irrational thinking and relaxation in their responses to anxiety-provoking situations during the coming week.

Session Six

The beginning of the sixth session follows the pattern of the previous sessions. Questions are addressed, followed by discussion of the homework, which takes up the first half of the session. In this final session, the remaining time is used to address issues surrounding closure of the group. Feedback on the efficacy of the group is elicited from the members, and concerns for the future discussed. Finally, remaining questions and concerns are considered. As with any mental health group, the leader makes any necessary referrals and instates follow-up procedures.

ASGW STANDARDS APPLIED TO PSYCHOTHERAPY GROUPS

Although the Association for Specialists in Group Work (ASGW) has been referred to throughout this text, it merits review and special attention in this chapter in relation to its salience for psychotherapy groups. Founded in 1973, the ASGW was drafted to address the multiple needs for consistency in the quality of group work provided to clients, for universal and methodical training in support of the practitioners who offered it, and the need to promote research in group work both nationally and internationally (Capuzzi & Gross, 2002). In 1974, the ASGW became a division of the American Counseling Association (ACA) and currently has 1200 members (ASGW, n.d.).

In 1983, the ASGW published its *Training Standards for Group Counselors,* which established 9 knowledge and 17 skill competencies. A counselor must master these before being considered qualified to lead a group (ASGW, 2000; Brown & Srebalus, 2003; Dykeman & Appleton, 2002). These standards were revised, and the 1990 revision emphasized

> (a) the articulation of the term, group work, to capture the variety of ways in which counselors work with groups, (b) differentiation of core training, deemed essential for all counselors, from specialization training required of those intending to engage in group work as part of their professional practice, and (c) the differentiation among four distinct group work specializations: task and work group facilitation, group psychoeducation, group counseling, and group psychotherapy. (ASGW, 2000)

In 2000, the ASGW *Professional Standards for the Training of Group Workers* was revised, with further emphasis upon receiving feedback from public discussion and scholarly debate over principles and practices. Additional importance was placed upon the distinction between core group training requirements and training in the specializations, which culminated with the ASGW's seeking to delineate more concretely the definitions between the group work specializations while applying universal training standards across the entire group work spectrum. Thus, a single set of guidelines was created, with supplemental material for each specialization as it may apply to each type of group (ASGW, 2000; Gladding, 2003).

Core Competencies

Core competencies were developed in alignment with the standards set by the Council for Accreditation of Counseling and Related Educational Programs

(CACREP; ASGW, 2000). The emphasis has been placed upon the mastery of basic knowledge and skills as they apply to all group situations. The ASGW specifically states, "Mastery of basic knowledge and skill in group work provides a foundation which specialty training can extend but does not qualify one to independently practice any group work specialty" (ASGW, 2000).

Beyond the competencies needed for group work, each group specialization now has its own competency and skill requirements specific to that specialization (i.e., psychoeducational, task, counseling, or psychotherapy). A summary of the core competencies for psychotherapy groups follows (ASGW, 2000; Gladding, 2003):

- The application of principles and theories of normal and abnormal human development and functioning, in general as well as specifically, to the intended population.
- The application of these principles through group-based cognitive, affective, behavioral, or systemic intervention strategies, along with an understanding of how these theories and interventions apply specifically to groups.
- The application of interventions that address personal and interpersonal problems of living, remediate perceptual and cognitive distortions or repetitive patterns of dysfunctional behavior, and promote personal and interpersonal growth and development.

Knowledge Competencies

Accompanying the core competencies for group work are knowledge competencies for each type of group. Examples of some of the knowledge competencies for psychotherapy groups are (ASGW, 2000; Gladding, 2003) as follows:

- *Knowledge of the theories of group work.* This knowledge includes an understanding of the commonalities and differences of each theory applied to psychotherapy groups.
- *Knowledge of the research literature pertinent to psychotherapy groups.* Knowledge of the specific ethical considerations involved in group work in general, and those that apply to specific populations in particular.
- *Knowledge of the different stages within groups.* How they develop and what therapeutic benefit are derived from each.
- *Knowledge of what is efficacious in group work.* This includes, but is not limited to, knowledge of which theories work best with which client population or issue. And knowledge is needed for what is contraindicated for the same.
- *Knowledge of assessment, diagnosis, psychopathology, and personality theory* as these apply to groups.

In addition, the knowledge competency for psychotherapy groups includes course mastery, which is inclusive of, but not limited to, classes in abnormal human development, family pathology and family therapy, diagnosis and treatment planning of mental disorders, assessment tools, and theory and practice of group psychotherapy. This includes a minimum of 45 supervised hours conducting a group within the student's proposed client population and setting.

Skill Competencies

The ASGW has defined skill competencies for all group work and for each specialization. According to the ASGW (2000) and Gladding (2003), these skills-based criteria are broken down into competencies in these specific areas:

- *Assessment*: includes the assessment of group members, their social systems, group process and efficacy, diagnostic criteria, and the ability to demonstrate mastery of these skills and techniques.
- *Intervention*: includes the skills needed to plan appropriate and efficacious group interventions with the ability to implement them in the most effective and therapeutic manner and the ability to make accurate behavior assessments upon which these interventions apply.
- *Leadership and coleadership*: includes knowledge of leadership styles and the purpose and practice for each.
- *Attending behaviors*: includes the skill and ability to engage each group member, use empathetic understanding, provide an atmosphere of safety, be able to clarify, summarize, impart information and feedback, and identify and acknowledge group member behavior.

For more specific and comprehensive information regarding the ASGW core, skill, and knowledge competencies, the student is advised to explore the ASGW Web site at www.asgw.org.

LEADERSHIP VARIABLES

What determines an effective group experience? Many factors interact to determine the outcome of a group experience (Brown & Srebalus, 2003). These factors often are explicitly under the group leader's control or direction. Some of the variables are obvious and are covered by the ASGW in the knowledge, skill, and core competencies. The group counseling literature is saturated with discussions about presence, personal power, courage, and inventiveness (Capuzzi & Gross, 2002; Corey, 2004). The text you are now reading is replete with techniques and concerns about group process and effectiveness. But some considerations when evaluating whether a group experience will be effective may not be so obvious. These include the personal characteristics of the group leader, the counselor's belief in the group process, the therapeutic environment the counselor provides, and, of course, how the counselor uses his or her knowledge of theory and group process.

Personal Characteristics

One could say that a psychotherapeutic group is only as good as its leader. Using the analogy of a painting to describe the group therapeutic process, the leader would be seen as the framework upon which the group canvas is laid. While the members themselves do the painting and artwork, the leader provides the structure and boundaries that contain the experience. Without the framework the leader provides, the therapeutic process cannot be fulfilled.

Effective group leaders have specific personal characteristics that further the group process (Capuzzi & Gross, 2002; Gladding, 2003). The group counselor's personality has a profound impact upon the group experience (Corey, 2004; Forester-Miller & Kottler, 1997; Kottler & Brown, 2000; Levine, 1979; Naar, 1982). This is especially true in the early stages of the group, as members tend to rally around the leader, who becomes an interpersonal anchor around which the group can coalesce and establish a sense of group cohesion (Spitz, 1996). Extensive lists have been published on this topic, and the factors we find most relevant are the following.

Willingness to Confront Oneself

Willingness to confront oneself entails asking hard questions: Who am I? As a person? As the group leader? Effective leaders are aware of all the facets of their personality, values, and beliefs, and use their interpersonal style to enhance the group process. Once psychotherapists have achieved this knowledge of self, they display courage in exploring their own weaknesses (Corey, 2001; Corey & Corey, 2002; Forester-Miller & Kottler, 1997; Spitz, 1996). This includes having the courage to face mistakes, admit to fears, act upon hunches or hypotheses, feel genuine emotion, be able to examine one's own life and values, and model positive behaviors (Gazda et al., 2001; Nystul, 2003; Posthuma, 1999).

Authenticity

Successful group leaders are genuine with group members and do not hide behind the cloak of professionalism, stereotyped images of what they think a counselor is or should be, or the "psychotherapist" title. Rather, they accept the same risks and vulnerabilities as other group members (Capuzzi & Gross, 2005; Kottler, 2001; Naar, 1982). This also means being able to be emotionally present with group members. Group leaders cannot be truly empathetic unless they are in touch both with their own emotions and the emotions of other group members (Corey & Corey, 2002).

Self-Care

If one takes to heart the adage that a client is bound by the limits of his or her counselor, the group counselor's own mental health is imperative. Because group needs come first, good leaders know how to take care of their own mental health requirements without imposing upon the group to provide the context for doing so. Leaders of groups, or any psychotherapeutic counselor, should seek personal counseling when needed (Forester-Miller & Kottler, 1997). And leaders should not be afraid to get professional support, supervision, or evaluation when indicated (Alonso & Swiller, 1993; Forester-Miller & Kottler, 1997).

Self-Awareness

Along with good mental health, effective leaders are self-aware. Effective counselors have an identity; they know who they are, what they are capable of becoming, what they want out of life, and what is essential (Corey, 2001). This also means knowing one's power and how to use it for the benefit of the group. The leader must show confidence in himself or herself as an effectual human being and show his or her authentic self to group members (Corey, 2001).

Leaders, too, must be aware of their interpersonal style of relating (Levine, 1979; Nyman & Daugherty, 2001). Does the leader need to be the center of attention? Does the leader need to always feel accepted? Does the leader need to be the "authority?" Is the leader uncomfortable in confrontational situations? The group leader must be aware of his or her true self, including personal biases, preferences, and prejudices, so as not to project these onto the group members or let them influence the group process (Capuzzi & Gross, 2005; Moursund, 1993). The counselor must be comfortable with himself or herself and have self-respect, affirmative self-beliefs, and projected positive self-worth (Capuzzi & Gross, 2002; Corey, 2001).

Faith and Enthusiasm

One of the most important individual traits that directly influence the group outcome is the level of personal faith and enthusiasm the group leader brings to the group process (Posthuma, 1999). If the group leader does not believe in the group process, group members likely will not either, and the opportunity for therapeutic benefit may be lost (Gazda et al., 2001). Corey and Corey (2002) further posit that group leaders who do not genuinely believe in the value of psychotherapeutic work and who engage in it only for power or money are behaving unethically.

Group psychotherapy works to a certain extent because the group leader and the group members alike believe in the group's power to effect change. Faith in the efficacy of treatment is the major reason, perhaps the only reason, why it works (Mullan & Rosenbaum, 1962). The faith of the group transcends from the faith of the leader. Along with this faith in group process, an effective leader expresses faith in the group members' abilities to achieve their goals and effect change and also believes strongly that the group is the best vehicle to effect that change (Moursund, 1993; Mullan & Rosenbaum, 1962).

The Therapeutic Environment

Another leadership variable that contributes to the success or failure of any group experience is the ability to create an environment in which the psychotherapeutic process can take place. Obviously, if the atmosphere is hostile and uncomfortable, psychotherapeutic work is impeded because the essential elements of trust and safety are missing. It is the leader's role to provide the climate, or arena, in which members can safely explore their feelings, thoughts, and behavior patterns, arrive at solutions to their problems, and achieve personal growth. In the absence of this atmosphere, psychotherapeutic, self-curative activities will not take place (Brabender, 2002; Corey, 2001).

Ensuring a Safe Environment

The leader ensures a safe environment by providing structure, boundaries, and group interactive guidelines (Kottler, 2001). There is a fine line between respecting individual autonomy and establishing overall safety of the group (Clark, 2002; Roberts, 1998; Steiner & Johnson, 2003). The counselor can provide safety by modeling congruent behavior, demonstrating personal boundaries and effective modes of confrontation, and being honest and authentic (Gladding, 2003; Greenberg, 2003; Pan, 2004). Because group members "follow the leader," it is imperative that the counselor model positive behavior (Forester-Miller & Kottler, 1997; Moursund, 1993).

Setting Rules and Norms

If the counselor leading the group will prescribe any group rules, prohibitions, or restrictions, he or she has to be exceedingly clear about these at the beginning of the group process. Effective group leaders keep rules to a minimum and empower the group by letting the members develop their own rules and norms (Gazda et al., 2001; Pan, 2004). While group members should be encouraged to develop their own rules, it is the leader's role to make sure that these rules and norms will not hinder the therapeutic process.

Setting Goals

Effective group leaders encourage members to set group and individual goals, and to make sure that these goals are actually set, to avoid aimless wandering without purpose or direction. The group psychotherapist must ensure that these goals are realistic and obtainable. Once the goals are in place, the group leader must keep the group focused (Greenberg, 2003; Spitz, 1996). The leader can help group members structure goals and expectations to provide optimum benefit and maximum use of peer support and individual learning (Meuser, Clower, & Padin-Rivera, 1998).

An Atmosphere of Respect

The leader should provide an atmosphere in which each group member can feel important, respected, and worthwhile, and that he or she is a contributing member of the group (Clark, 2002; Vernon, 2002). In that way, the group leader helps to mold and develop individual and group esteem and integrity (Levine, 1979; Mullan & Rosenbaum, 1962). The leader does this by setting clear boundaries regarding relational issues.

Positive Interchange

The group leader must be ready to confront any member who is attacking or abusing another, including possible termination of the offending member (Alonso & Swiller, 1993; Clark, 2002; Gazda et al., 2001). Alonso and Swiller (1993) go so far as to proclaim that the competence of the group leader is the best defense against member-to-member abuse and exploitation. This is a weighty responsibility, and the group leader must be able to deal with this issue effectively to ensure the viability of the group process. As part of this responsibility, the leader must be able to discern when a member is being destructive to the group process and when he or she is being resistant, uncooperative, or defensive, the latter of which signal psychotherapeutic intervention, not dismissal from the group.

The psychotherapist leading the group must go beyond intervening in conflicts to promote positive interchange among group members (Gladding, 2003; Pan, 2004). An effective leader understands that members move at differing paces. Again, the leader should model behavior and interactional techniques that will encourage group members to talk with one another in a nonhostile, noncoercive way (Alonso & Swiller, 1993; Kottler & Brown, 2000; Moursund, 1993; Naar, 1982).

Integration of Technical Knowledge and Theories

Personal characteristics and a positive therapeutic environment are two requisites for an effective group. An additional leadership variable relates to how the group leader integrates technical knowledge and theories learned in training.

Use of Knowledge

It is not just *what* the psychotherapeutic group leader knows but *how* he or she uses that knowledge that is important. It is not enough to know which theories apply to groups. The leader must understand which theories work best for which populations and which therapeutic issues. And it is just as important to know in which populations or issues those theories would be contraindicated (Levine, 1979; Steiner & Johnson, 2003).

Application of Theories

An effective leader of a psychotherapeutic group applies theory and modality to the group and not vice versa (Brown & Srebalus, 2003; Roberts, 1998). It is also essential that the group leader interject his or her personal style into whatever theory he or she uses. The wooden application of theory straight out of a textbook is unlikely to be effective and probably will be perceived as stilted and phony (Moursund, 1993). The successful psychotherapy group leader is flexible and considers each group unique in its own way. This type of leader will mold his or her role to the needs of the group (Levine, 1979).

Selecting Group Members

To attain the best possible group membership, the leader must understand group dynamics. Baruch Levine (1979) makes a strong case, stating emphatically, "No single activity on the part of the group therapist can influence the nature and destiny of a therapy group as much as the selection and matching of people for membership" (p. 12). The interpersonal qualities of each member, as well as those of the leader, are the determinants of how far the group can grow (Schmidt, 2003). Each member's limitations and growth potential must be carefully determined and weighed to provide the best possible group composition for therapeutic gain (Brown & Srebalus, 2003). It has been found, for example, that similarities among group members are conducive to interpersonal attraction and mutual support, whereas differences among group members are conducive to confrontation and change (Levine, 1979). Therefore, when selecting group members, the leader should have a working knowledge of what he or she wants to accomplish.

Interventions

The leader must have a thorough understanding of what occurs in each stage of group development and which interventions are prudent for each stage. Interventions should be timed in a stage-specific context (Brown & Srebalus, 2003; Gazda et al., 2001). For example, using an anxiety-provoking exercise during the group cohesion stage would be detrimental to the group process. Effective leaders further understand what the likely outcomes of their interventions will be and know what interventions will facilitate group goals.

A Facilitative Style

One other leadership variable that must be considered is leadership style. The leader's style affects how a group is composed, how it proceeds, and whether the psychotherapist leading the group is seen as a "technical expert" or as a "model-setting participant" (Spitz, 1996; Vernon, 2002). These two approaches are very different, and group leaders should understand the applications for each approach.

Technical Expert Style

In the role of *technical expert*, a leader imparts knowledge of the psychological process, asks probing questions, and uses specific therapeutic techniques such as guided imagery, hypnotherapy, making the rounds, psychodrama, sculpting, and bibliotherapy (Moursund, 1993). This approach is directive. An image that comes to mind with this approach is the group leader as conductor of an orchestra and the group members playing the instruments and parts. The group makes the music and the leader directs the score.

Model-Setting Participant Style

In some ways, the technical assistant approach utilizes some of the approaches of the model-setting participant style, in processing of information, being responsive to members and assisting them as they work through their issues, helping members deal with each other honestly, authentically, and with respect, and helping members reach their full growth potential. The model-setting approach, however, is participatory rather than directive (Moursund, 1993). The leader's ability to serve as a role model for members aids considerably in facilitating insight and interpersonal learning (Johnson & Johnson, 2003).

CACREP Requirements

Many leadership variables influence the group process. It is not enough for students of psychotherapy groups to understand terminology, strategies, interventions, and theories. Students must develop a deep understanding of how these tools are applied and for what reasons, and this comes together through experience and trial and error. For this reason, CACREP and ASGW mandate 10 to 20 clock hours of observation or participation within a group experience, as well as 45 to 60 clock hours in supervised practice conducting a counseling group (ASGW, 2000).

THE FUTURE OF PSYCHOTHERAPEUTIC GROUPS

At the dawn of the 21st century, the mental health profession is experiencing both excitement and apprehension. New technologies ushered in by the computer age are aiding the counseling profession, while at the same time managed care is profoundly restricting it.

Managed Care

> The director of a managed care company died and went to heaven. At the Pearly Gates, St. Peter met the director and said,
>
> "We have good news, and we have bad news."
> "What's the good news?" the director asked.
> "You can come in," replied St. Peter
> "And the bad news?"
> "You can stay for only two days!"
>
> — Anonymous (in Hoyt, 1992)

Nothing has affected the future of group psychotherapy as much as the development of the managed care system, the genesis of which is rooted in the staggering costs of health care for consumers and employers. During the 1990s, approximately 85% of businesses that had 1,000 employees or more turned to managed care for a solution to rising health care costs (Fields, 1995; Hoyt, 1992; Kuettel & Masi, 1998).

In the wake of this development, managed care has had a profound impact on the mental health professions, especially on actual clinical practice parameters and mental health service delivery (Gazda et al., 2001; Glosoff, 2005). This has come mainly through the cost-containment practices of setting session limits, limiting provider availability to clients, and mandating which DSM diagnostic procedures are included (Durham, 1998; Fields, 1995).

Types of Managed Care

Most people do not realize the broad spectrum of companies that provide managed care. A sampling follows

Health Maintenance Organizations (HMOs)

The best known of the managed care facilitators are HMOs. The counselors on staff work for the HMO. The stated goals of HMOs are to monitor, control, and contain the costs of medical and mental health services while maintaining the quality of care (Kuettel & Masi, 1998; Nystul, 2003).

Employee Assistant Programs (EAPs)

Employers pay EAPs flat fees to provide free short-term counseling. Currently, more than 20,000 companies in the United States provide services to their employees through EAPs. These companies boast multilingual therapists and provide services to a broader-based client population than most. Advocates of EAPs have stated that EAPs have opened up the world of psychotherapy to a diverse range of races, income levels, and geographic locales (Kuettel & Masi, 1998).

Preferred Provider Organizations (PPOs)

PPOs have a list of preferred providers that offer therapy for a set fee. For the client to be covered by insurance, he or she must see a counselor on the preferred provider list (Engler & Goleman, 1992).

Managed Mental Health Care (MMHCs)

MMHCs oversee provider networks. Any counselor who works for a MMHC must adhere to the clinical guidelines and procedures of the MMHC, accept a set fee for services, and obtain clients from the network (Nystul, 2003; Spitz, 1996).

At some time during a counselor's career, he or she will be involved in some capacity with managed care. Currently, more than 100 million people are enrolled in the managed health care system, and enrollment continues to grow as other options dwindle (Hoyt, 1992; Shescher & Comarow, 1999).

Impacts of Managed Care

Managed care companies have many similarities, and to simplify the following discussion, we will limit ourselves to these commonalities. When we have to be specific, we will use the HMOs as an example, as it is the most well-known form of managed care.

Group Psychotherapy

A positive effect of managed care for counselors who use group psychotherapy is that the need for these skills will be in high demand as the managed care industry grows (Spitz, 1996). The appeal for group therapy in the managed care setting is obvious. It offers access and affordability to more clients than individual psychotherapy does, and the higher patient-to-staff ratio requires fewer mental health personnel, which reduces employment costs for the HMO (Alonso & Swiller, 1993; Meuser et al., 1998; Spitz, 1996). Daniel Goleman (1993) emphatically stated that "the effect of HMOs on psychotherapy practice has been a veritable renaissance and proliferation of group therapies" (p. 31). Because only 3% of HMO funding goes toward mental health at present, group therapy will continue to proliferate (Fields, 1995).

Although this is good news for those who wish to practice group psychotherapy, some things have to be considered when practicing in the managed care setting. First, managed care companies require a verifiable diagnosis based on DSM criteria. This can lead to a multitude of ethical problems, which will be discussed at the end of this section. Problems can arise for the group counselor when this requires the counselor to include clients whose diagnosis is compatible with the group therapy being offered, yet the client does not have the interpersonal skills necessary to be successful within this therapeutic modality. Pressure is often applied for the counselor to accept the client into the group regardless (Spitz, 1996).

Another concern is that, based upon time limitations, most group experiences are homogeneous, which, while not bad in itself, limits the options that accompany a heterogeneous group (Sonstegard, 1998). Group members will have more similarities than differences, and this can shape and limit the group experience. At times a heterogeneous group would be more prudent and efficacious but, as a result of session limits, it cannot be offered as an option because these groups take more time (Spitz, 1996). Group psychotherapy as offered under managed care also will not address counselors' character or personality refinement as a goal but instead will focus on client strengths and resources (Spitz, 1996).

Brief Therapy

Increasingly, brief therapies are being advocated for individual and psychotherapy groups (Gazda et al., 2001; Kottler & Brown, 2000). Brief therapy is goal specific and symptom focused, prescribes a limited number of sessions, is episodic, uses a psychodynamic theory as its framework, is effective for a wide range of issues and populations, and has documentable treatment plans that lend themselves to scientific study (Consumer Reports On Health, 1993; Corey, 2001; Engler & Goleman, 1992; Fields, 1995; Messer & Wachtel, 1997; Roberts, 1998; Spitz, 1996; Tuttle & Woods, 1997). These group experiences will be homogenous rather than heterogeneous (Spitz, 1996).

When talking about managed care and brief therapy, Fields (1995) states that managed care "assumes that psychotherapy is a process that occurs in pieces over time" (p. 344). Daniel Goleman (1993), an advocate for HMOs and managed care, says, "HMOs are not the perfect solution, but quality HMOs are making valuable contributions by developing effective brief therapies and providing mental health services to many patients who would otherwise go without" (p. 40). According to Goleman, the focus of brief therapy under the managed care model is

1. amelioration of distress,
2. reduction of symptomatic discomfort,
3. reestablishment of emotional equilibrium,
4. defining and utilizing resources,
5. increasing understanding, and
6. increasing coping skills.

Pharmacotherapy

Drug therapy, too, has seen a substantial increase in practice under managed care. Although medications sometimes are used in conjunction with individual or group psychotherapy, managed care providers increasingly are turning to drug therapy as a preferred method of treatment (Clay, 2000). Obvious concerns have arisen as a result of this trend, one of which is that many HMO consumers are being treated with potent drugs in nonpsychiatric settings (Fields, 1995). One study on HMO enrollees who used antipsychotic drugs found that the dosage levels administered put HMO clients at risk for tardive dyskinesia, a devastating disfiguring and disabling condition characterized by abnormal and involuntary bodily movements (Fields, 1995). If this trend intensifies, it may have an impact on counselors who wish to practice group psychotherapy under the managed care system.

Effects on the Counseling Profession

One might ask what the overall effect of managed care has been on psychotherapeutic group counseling and the mental health industry. Daniels (2001) states:

> During informal conversations with colleagues who are mental health practitioners, there is a fairly predictable response to the term managed care. Almost imperceptibly, their bodies tense and they pull back ever so slightly. On a more noticeable level, there may be a rolling of the eyes and a look crossing their faces that can best be described as repulsion. The verbal reaction that follows is always negative, often with a horror story about ethical violations allegedly perpetrated by the managed care organization. (p. 119)

Clearly, from Daniels's (2001) statement, managed care has garnered few friends in the mental health industry. This stems in a large part from the ethical ramifications that managed care has had on the practice of mental health, along with a number of other factors.

One effect has been that managed care has drastically reduced the income potential of counselors who offer individual and group psychotherapy (Gazda et al., 2001). As Kuettel and Masi (1998) put it, "Gone are the days when insurance companies blindly paid high hourly rates for treatment with questionable outcomes" (p. 105). These authors also cited a survey in which 60% of psychologists in the San Francisco area stated that their income had declined because of managed care and 44% said they were considering leaving the field of mental health altogether. Paradoxically, managed care has been the catalyst for the increased use of group psychotherapy and has caused the use of group therapy as a field of counseling to explode.

Another effect has been that, because managed care follows the medical model, anyone wishing to provide services must provide documentable diagnoses. If a client wants insurance coverage, whatever the issue, it must be called a disorder. This creates the terminology of "patient" instead of the term preferred by the counseling profession—"client." The mandate of a DSM diagnosis before services are rendered also applies what could be a misappropriate label to a client's insurance record. This could have long-term repercussions in many areas, including employment opportunities and future insurance coverage (Engler & Goleman, 1992; Spitz, 1996).

A serious effect of managed care on group practice is that anyone working for the managed care system will be faced with enormous caseloads without the authority or with limited control to specify treatment modalities or to authorize additional sessions. The counselor is essentially an employee of the insurance provider and must follow its edicts (Fields, 1995; Spitz, 1996). In the United States, although there is approximately one mental health professional available for every 1,000 Americans, HMOs designate one mental health care professional for every 5,000 to 6,000 members (Kuettel & Masi, 1998). To receive services, the client first must pass through a "gatekeeper," usually a primary care physician who then makes a referral to the mental health professional or, in many cases, treats the mental health issue on his or her own (Spitz, 1996).

Ethical Considerations Under Managed Care

Ethical concerns associated with managed care are vast—too extensive to be covered adequately here. The following will give the reader some idea of what these concerns entail:

- Managed care limits the choices of clients and counselors in the areas of therapy modality, length of treatment, and counselor selection (Engler & Goleman, 1992; Fields, 1995).
- Managed care limits confidentiality because of the large number of people who have access to case files (case managers, gatekeepers, primary care physicians, etc.; Engler & Goleman, 1992; Fields, 1995; Spitz, 1996).
- Managed care in essence is ethically flawed, as it is based on cost containment and cost effectiveness rather than clinical effectiveness. What is not medically necessary will not likely be provided (Browers, 2005; Fields, 1995; Granello & Witmer, 1998).
- The client has a fundamental inability or difficulty to obtain services when needed (Tuttle & Woods, 1997). A survey of 17 HMOs showed the average wait for an urgent mental health appointment was 1.9 days, a nonurgent appointment was 16.9 days, and a follow-up appointment was 11.1 days, and the client also has limited access to specialty care (Fields, 1995). In addition, in a survey done by the Henry J. Kaiser Family Foundation, 9 in every 10 doctors surveyed reported that within the last 2 years they had patients who had been denied services under managed care, and 18% of their client caseload was denied weekly (Abate, 1999).
- HMOs provide incentive for primary care providers to limit referrals for care. Counselors in the managed care system are placed in the ethically precarious position of being responsible both for providing care and for limiting the amount of care provided (Fields, 1995).
- Counselors must follow the guidelines of their managed care company, which may contradict the ACA *Code of Ethics* (Fields, 1995; Goleman, 1993).
- Because of limited options for consumers of managed care, some counselors feel compelled to "up-code" a client's diagnosis to obtain extended treatment or even basic mental health services for the client under managed care. Giving a client a more serious diagnosis than what is warranted is unethical and also illegal, yet some counselors do just that so their clients can get services (Abate, 1999; Hoyt, 1992).

Those who are interested in working with managed care companies would be well advised to obtain a copy of the company policies and compare these to the ACA *Code of Ethics*. This is the only way to ascertain the differences in practice parameters and thereby be reasonably informed as to what ethical concerns may become evident.

Computers and the Internet

Among the most spirited debates in the mental health fields are those revolving around the role of information technology—specifically the Internet (Amig, 2001). Some professionals hold that, if handled responsibly, the Internet could be the most productive innovation in the behavioral health field in recent memory (Amig, 2001). Others, however, maintain that the Internet threatens the trustworthiness and integrity of the field (Amig, 2001). Regardless of how practitioners feel about it, one thing is certain: Thanks to the computer age, a plethora of technological computer and Internet aids are available to psychotherapists.

Interactive Computer Programs

Computer programs now help counselors in training, research, network building, diagnosis, assessment, and treatment planning (Haley, 2005). One current interactive program even simulates the counselor/client therapeutic relationship (Hohenshil, 2000; Sampson, 2000). Students can go online and access counseling and psychology journal articles through the American Psychological Association (APA), the ACA, or through their local college library.

This innovation benefits counselors who offer group psychotherapy because research articles on efficacy, treatment modalities, populations that are contraindicated, and so forth are literally at the student's or counselor's fingertips. In addition, the Association for Counselor Education and Supervision (ACES) has adopted 12 technology competencies, as well as a set of guidelines for Online Instruction in Counselor Education (Hohenshil, 2000). Clearly, use of the Internet for education and training is expected to increase in the future.

Cyber-Counseling

With expanded access to the Internet, many counselors are providing services on the World Wide Web (www), listed as cybertherapy, e-therapy, webcounseling, and online-therapy. The National Board of Certified Counselors (NBCC) defines Internet counseling as

> the practice of professional counseling and information delivery
> that occurs when clients and counselors are in separate or
> remote locations and utilize electronic means to communicate
> over the Internet. (Bowman & Bowman, 1998, p. 431)

Internet counseling does not pertain only to individuals; group psychotherapy is offered through bulletin boards, chat rooms, and e-mail (Haley, 2005).

The use of Web sites to promote counseling has been prolific. In one 1997 informal study done on Internet counseling, researchers found 3,764 Web sites with the term "counseling" in the title. One month later, this list had grown by 6%, and 3 months after that by 15%. According to projections, the number of sites related to Internet counseling is expected to double each year (Bowman & Bowman, 1998).

Although Internet counseling has reached thousands of people who have never engaged in face-to-face therapy, one drawback of this method is the inability of the consumer to verify the credentials of the person providing the service, and currently there is no efficient way to regulate this growing therapy modality (Haley, 2005; Wylie, 2000). The NBCC has developed a code of ethics to help regulate counseling services offered on the Web (Haley, 2005; Hohenshil, 2000). It can be accessed at www.nbcc.org.

Students who are planning to incorporate group psychotherapy into their practice are on the edge of an exciting but uncertain time. One thing is certain: In the foreseeable future, counselors who are proficient in providing group psychotherapy will be in high demand as a result of the changes that managed care has brought to the mental health field. In addition, new technological advances will give group psychotherapists enhanced access to resources, research, and communication, and they will, therefore, be better equipped to serve clients. If the ACES technological guidelines are used, many future counselors of group psychotherapy will have well-developed technological skills to lead the profession deeper into the technological age.

LEARNING ACTIVITIES

1. Participate in a group of six to eight in a course-long psychotherapy group. Each student will act as the group psychotherapy leader for 1 to 2 weeks, depending on the duration of the course. This should be done under supervision so students will benefit from the knowledge of a professional practicing in the field and be covered legally.
2. Participate in a group of four to six in 1-hour role plays. Each student will function as the group psychotherapy leader for 10 minutes while the others role-play members in a specific topic group (such as anxiety or grief).
3. Participate in a group of four to six in 1-hour specific-modality role plays. This activity is similar to the activity in #2, except the acting group psychotherapist may utilize techniques from only a singular modality (such as Gestalt, behavioral, or Adlerian) for the 10 minutes.
4. Observe or sit in on a minimum of two live (not videotaped) group psychotherapy sessions. Report back, in written form, a summary of the sessions, what worked and what didn't work, and how you would have changed the session.

SUMMARY

Mental health professionals historically have used the terms *group therapy, group counseling*, and *group psychotherapy* interchangeably. This has led to confusion as to exactly what group psychotherapy entails. The major differences between psychotherapy groups and other group forms are that

1. psychotherapy groups require a diagnostic basis for the foundation of the group,
2. transference is more likely to occur in group psychotherapy, and
3. group psychotherapy requires actual change in group members.

Although these foundations may occur in other forms of group work, they are foundational to group psychotherapy.

The process of a psychotherapeutic group can be largely impacted by its group leader. Some personal characteristics of effective group leaders are self-awareness, willingness to engage in self-confrontation, authenticity, self-care, and faith in group process. The role of an effective group leader also involves creating a suitable environment that will facilitate members' growth and change. Effective group environments are safe, include suitable rules and norms, engender an atmosphere of respect, and allow for confrontation.

Finally, group psychotherapists must have current technical knowledge. At the dawn of the 21st century, the psychotherapy group leader is faced with a mixed bag of forces that both inhibit and enable various aspects of group work. Managed care legislation has resulted in more group psychotherapy but at the same time has increased ethical concerns including, but not limited to, type and length of treatment, greater threats to confidentiality, difficulty in obtaining needed treatment, and managed care guidelines that at times contradict professional ethical guidelines.

Computers and the Internet also have positive and negative effects on group professionals. Interactive computer programs have allowed students of group methods more access to a wide array of training methods and research. Online counseling has enabled individuals to tap into previously unobtainable resources. This type of psychotherapy is fraught with ethical dangers, as there currently is no efficient way for consumers to verify the credentials of online group professionals or for legislators to regulate this growing modality. We hope that with new legislation and professional attention, online psychotherapy will reach the same levels of professionalism and efficacy that are found in today's face-to-face work.

REFERENCES

Abate, T. (1999). Effects of managed care. *San Francisco Chronicle*. Retrieved October 1, 2000, from http://www.sfgate.com/cgibin/article.cgi?file=/chronicle/archive

Alonso, A., & Swiller, H. (1993). *Group therapy in clinical practice*. Washington, DC: American Psychiatric Press.

Amig, S. (2001). Internet dilemmas. *Behavioral Health Management, 21*, 48.

Association for Specialists in Group Work (ASGW). (n.d.). *ASGW*. Retrieved July 18, 2005, from http://www.asgw.org/about.htm

Association for Specialists in Group Work (ASGW). (2000). *Professional standards for the training of group workers*. Retrieved July 18, 2005, from http://www.asgw.org/training_standards.htm

Brabender, V. (2002). *Introduction to group therapy*. New York: John Wiley & Sons.

Bowman, R., & Bowman, V. (1998). Life on the electronic frontier: The application of technology to group work. *Journal for Specialists in Group Work, 23*(4), 428–445.

Browers, R. T. (2005). Counseling in mental health and private practice settings. In D. Capuzzi & D. R. Gross (Eds.), *Introduction to the counseling profession* (4th ed., pp. 357–379). Boston: Allyn & Bacon.

Brown, D., & Srebalus, D. J. (2003). *Introduction to the counseling profession* (3rd ed.). Boston: Allyn & Bacon.

Capuzzi, D., & Gross, D. R. (2002). *Introduction to group counseling* (3rd ed.). Denver: Love Publishing.

Capuzzi, D., & Gross, D. R. (2005). *Introduction to the counseling profession* (4th ed.). Boston: Allyn & Bacon.

Clark, A. J. (2002). Scapegoating: Dynamics and interventions in group counseling. *Journal of Counseling and Development, 80*(3), 271–277.

Clay, R. (2000). Psychotherapy is cost effective. *Monitor on Psychology, 31*(1). Retrieved October 1, 2000, from http://www.apa.org/monitor/jan00/pr2.html

Consumer Reports on Health. (1993). Brief psychotherapy: Can it replace years on the couch? *Consumers Union of U.S., 5*(4), 40.

Corey, G. (2001). *Theory and practice of counseling and psychotherapy* (6th ed.). Belmont, CA: Wadsworth.

Corey, G. (2004). *Theory and practice of group counseling* (6th ed.). Belmont, CA: Wadsworth.

Corey, M. S., & Corey, G. (2002). *Groups: Process and practice* (6th ed.). Wadsworth Publishing.

Corsini, R. J. (1988). Adlerian groups. In S. Long (Ed.), *Six group therapies*. New York: Plenum Press.

Dagley, J. C., Gazda, G. M., Eppinger, S. J., & Stuwart, E. A. (1994). Group psychotherapy research with children, preadolescents, and adolescents. In A. Fuhriman & G. M. Burlingame (Eds.), *Handbook of group psychotherapy* (pp. 340–370). New York: Wiley.

Daniels, J. A. (2001). Managed care, ethics, and counseling. *Journal of Counseling and Development, 79*, 119–122.

Dreikurs, R. (1932). Early experiments with group psychotherapy. *American Journal of Psychotherapy, 13,* 882–891.

Durham, M. L. (1998). Mental health and managed care. *Annual Review Public Health, 19*, 493–505.

Dykeman, C., & Appleton, V. E. (2002). Group counseling: The efficacy of group work. In D. Capuzzi & D. R. Gross (Eds.), *Introduction to group counseling* (3rd ed., pp. 119–154). Denver: Love.

Engler, J., & Goleman, D. (1992). *The consumer's guide to psychotherapy*. New York: Simon and Schuster.

Fields, H. (1995). Managed mental health care: Changing the future of mental health treatment. American Health Lawyers Association, *Journal of Health Law, 28*(6), 344.

Forester-Miller, H., & Kottler, J. A. (1997). *Issues and challenges for group practitioners*. Denver: Love.

Gazda, G. M. (1982). *Basic approaches to group psychotherapy and group counseling* (3rd ed.). Springfield, IL: Charles C Thomas.

Gazda, G. M., Ginter, E. J., & Horne, A. M. (2001). *Group counseling and group psychotherapy: Theory and application*. Boston: Allyn & Bacon.

Gladding, S. (2003). *Group work: A counseling specialty* (4th ed.). Upper Saddle River, NJ: Prentice-Hall.

Glosoff, H. L. (2005). The counseling profession: A historical perspective (pp. 3–55). In D. Capuzzi & D. R. Gross (Eds.), *Introduction to the counseling profession* (4th ed.). Boston: Allyn & Bacon.

Goleman, D. (1993, May 10). Mental health professionals worry over coming change in health care. *New York Times,* p. A16, col. 4.

Granello, P. F., & Witmer, J. M. (1998). Standards of care: Potential implications for the counseling profession. *Journal of Counseling and Development, 76*(4), 371–380.

Greenberg, K. R. (2003). *Group counseling in K–12 schools: A handbook for school counselors*. Boston: Allyn & Bacon.

Hadden, S. B. (1955). Historic background of group psychotherapy. *International Journal of Group Psychotherapy, 5*, 62.

Haley, M. (2005). Technology in counseling. In D. Capuzzi & D. R. Gross (Eds.), *Introduction to the counseling profession* (4th ed., pp. 123–152). Boston: Allyn & Bacon.

Hazler, R. J. (2003). Person-centered theory. In D. Cappuzzi & D. R. Gross (Eds.), *Counseling and psychotherapy* (3rd ed., pp. 157–180). Upper Saddle River, NJ: Prentice Hall.

Hohenshil, T. H. (2000). High tech counseling. *Journal of Counseling and Development, 78*(3), 365–368.

Hollon, S. D., & Kendall, P. C. (1979). *Cognitive–behavioral interventions: Theory, research, and procedures*. New York: Academic Press.

Hoyt, M. F. (1992). *Brief therapy and managed care*. San Francisco: Jossey-Bass Publishers.

Johnson, D., & Johnson, F. (2003). *Joining together: Group theory and group skills* (8th ed.). Boston: Allyn & Bacon.

Kalodner, C. R. (2003). Cognitive–behavioral theories. In D. Capuzzi & D. R. Gross (Eds.), *Counseling and psychotherapy* (3rd ed., pp. 212–234). Upper Saddle River, NJ: Prentice Hall.

Kottler, J. (2001). *Learning group leadership: An experiential approach*. Boston: Allyn & Bacon.

Kottler, J., & Brown, R. (2000). *Introduction to therapeutic counseling: Voices from the field* (4th ed.). Redmond, CA: Brooks/Cole.

Kuettel, R. M., & Masi, D. S. W. (1998). *Shrink to fit: Answers to your questions about therapy*. Deerfield Beach, FL: Health Communications.

Lacey, T. (2004). Group therapy and CBT. *Counselling and Psychotherapy Journal, 15*, 34–36.

Levine, B. (1979). *Group psychotherapy: Practice and development*. Englewood Cliffs, NJ: Prentice-Hall.

Maslow, A. H. (1970). *Motivation and personality* (2nd ed.). New York: Harper & Row.

Messer, S. B., & Wachtel, P. L. (1997). *Theories of psychotherapy: Origins and evolution*. Washington, DC: American Psychological Association.

Meuser, T. M., Clower, M. W., & Padin-Rivera, E. (1998). Group psychotherapy: Ideas for the managed care environment. In Hartman-Stein, P.E. (Ed.), *Innovative behavioral healthcare for older adults*. San Francisco: Jossey-Bass Publishers.

Moursund, J. (1993). *The process of counseling and therapy*. Englewood Cliffs, NJ: Prentice-Hall.

Mullan, H., & Rosenbaum, M. (1962). *Group psychotherapy: Theory and practice*. New York: Free Press of Glencoe.

Naar, R. (1982). *A primer of group psychotherapy*. New York: Human Sciences Press.

Nyman, S. J., & Daugherty, T. K. (2001). Congruence of counselor self-disclosure and perceived effectiveness. *Journal of Psychology, 135*(3), 269–276.

Nystul, M. (2003). *Introduction to counseling: An art and science perspective* (2nd ed.). Boston: Allyn & Bacon.

Pan, P. (2004). Members' perceptions of leader behaviors, group experiences, and therapeutic factors in group counseling. *Small Group Research, 35*(2), 174–185.

Posthuma, B. W. (1999). *Small groups in counseling and therapy* (3rd ed.). Boston: Allyn & Bacon.

Roberts, F. (1998). *The therapy sourcebook*. Los Angeles: Lowell House.

Sampson, J. P. (2000). Using the Internet to enhance testing in counseling. *Journal of Counseling and Development, 78*(3), 348–356.

Schmidt, J. J. (2003). *Counseling in schools: Essential services and comprehensive programs* (4th ed.) Boston: Allyn & Bacon.

Schultz, D. P., & Schultz, S. E. (1996). *A history of modern psychology* (6th ed.). New York: Harcourt Brace.

Scheidlinger, S. (1994). An overview of nine decades of group psychotherapy. *Hospital and Community Psychiatry, 45,* 217–225.

Shescher, M. W., & Comarow, D. D. (1999). *Talking about therapy*. Westport, CT: Bergin and Garvey.

Slavson, S. R. (1959). Parallelisms in the development of group psychotherapy. *International Journal of Group Psychotherapy, 9*, 451.

Slavson, S. R. (1974). In DeSchill, S. (Ed.), *The challenge for group psychotherapy: Present and future*. New York: International University Press.

Sonstegard, M. A. (1998). The theory and practice of Adlerian group counseling and psychotherapy. *Journal of Individual Psychology, 54*, 217–250.

Spitz, H. I. (1996). *Group psychotherapy and managed mental health care: A clinical guide for providers*. New York: Brunner/Mazel Publishers.

Steiner, M., & Johnson, M. (2003). Using restorative practices in group treatment. *Children and Youth 12*(1), 53–58.

Tuttle, G. M., & Woods, D. R. (1997). *The managed care answer book*. Bristol, PA: Brunner/Mazel.

Vernon, A. (2002). Experiencing loss: Practical guidelines for group counseling. *Counseling and Human Development, 34*(8), 1–16.

Weinberg, G. (1984). *The heart of psychotherapy: A journey into the mind and office of the therapist at work*. New York: St. Martin's Press.

Wylie, M. (2000, Sept. 3). Just relax on the cyber couch. Portland, OR: *Oregonian Newspaper,* p. L15.

Yalom, I. D. (1995). *The theory and practice of group psychotherapy* (4th ed.). New York: Basic Books.

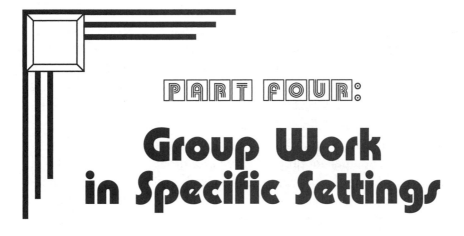

PART FOUR:

Group Work in Specific Settings

The chapters in Part Four address group work in specific settings. Examples of the training in specializations that counselor education departments and programs offer to graduate students are the special groups unique to schools, community and mental health centers, and rehabilitation settings. The specifics of group work in each of the settings, and their differences, are discussed and described.

Chapter 12, "Groups in Schools," points out the characteristics of these groups, as contrasted to groups in other settings. Although the goal of helping participants achieve healthy psychological functioning is still important, groups in the school setting have a primary goal of helping students to become effective learners despite the issues for which group counseling may be needed. The chapter further delineates the types and formats of group work in schools at each level—elementary, middle, and high—as well as issues associated with efficacy, ethics, and diversity.

Chapter 13, "Groups in Mental Health Settings," introduces readers to the scope of group work as it is applied in various mental health environments. This group work encompasses a wide array of services in both private and public sectors. As a result of market forces and shortfalls of the mental health care system, group work in these settings is complex, challenging, and often difficult. To capture some of the details of group planning and implementation, this chapter presents examples of three specific types of outpatient groups: a women's group, a couples group, and a group addressing the eating disorder of bulimia nervosa. For each group, the conceptual framework, limitations and ethical considerations, goals, screening and orientation, stages, referral, evaluation, and follow-up are discussed.

Chapter 14, "Groups in Rehabilitation Settings," concludes Part Four. For illustrative purposes, the discussion centers on three specific types of groups in which rehabilitation counselors are likely to be engaged: job clubs, offender and mandated population groups, and groups in hospital/medical settings. The same parameters used in chapters 12 and 13 are applied: Make the discussion relevant and concrete for readers who anticipate practicing group work in settings like these.

Groups in Schools

Tamara E. Davis

roup work in schools—an effective way to work with youth today—differs from group work with youth in other settings. The American School Counselor Association (ASCA; 2002) posited that:

> Group counseling, which involves a number of students working on shared tasks and developing supportive relationships in a group setting, is an efficient and positive way of dealing with students' developmental problems and situational concerns. (p. 1)

To understand group counseling within the context of this chapter, a few things should be noted:

1. Group work in schools may be conducted in a large-group format, also known as *classroom guidance*, as well as small-group counseling sessions with groups of six to eight students. In this chapter, the discussion will pertain only to small-group counseling sessions, as large-group sessions (i.e., classes) tend to be more instructional in nature than other types of group counseling.
2. Group work in schools also may extend to providing groups for parents and teachers. Facilitating parenting education and giving support to teachers is an important function of group leaders in schools. Because the majority of time spent in group work in schools involves group counseling with students, however, this discussion will focus primarily on group counseling with students in a school setting and will be referred to interchangeably as *group counseling* and *group work*.
3. Various school personnel—school psychologists, student assistance program (SAP) counselors, community health liaisons—facilitate

small-group sessions in schools. Rainey, Hensley, and Crutchfield (1997) suggested having cofacilitators for middle and elementary school students, utilizing SAP counselors and school counselors collaboratively. The primary school personnel responsible for group counseling, however, is the school counselor or school counseling department. According to the ASCA (2002), the professional school counselor is trained to "...facilitate many groups, as well as train others as group facilitators" (p. 2). Therefore, this discussion relates primarily to the group leader as a school counselor who has been trained to conduct small-group counseling sessions in schools.

Group counseling is considered a direct service provided by school counselors. After surveying 80 school counselors, Burnham and Jackson (2000) found that 90% of those counselors conducted small-group counseling and that, further, the counselors who conducted small-group counseling spent 10%–23% of their entire counseling time conducting small groups. In the same study, two problems emerged (p. 46):

1. The groups often included too many students (more than six to eight).
2. The groups were held on an irregular basis.

Because of the inconsistency in school schedules and unexpected interruptions, groups are often postponed and rescheduled, which interferes with the consistency of the group process. This differs from small groups in other settings, in which the group schedule is set and rarely is changed.

Although the overall goal of helping participants achieve healthy psychological functioning is still primary, the school setting requires that group work focus on helping students become effective learners despite the issues that bring them to group counseling. For example, when a student is mourning the death of a close family member, he or she understandably may have difficulty concentrating on schoolwork. The purpose of this student's participating in small-group counseling is twofold:

1. To help the student work through the grieving process in a healthy manner
2. To provide support within the school setting so the child can concentrate on academic demands

The dual obligation to the participant—first as a person but also as a student—differentiates school counseling from other types of counseling.

Another obvious difference is that counselors who conduct group work in schools have a readily accessible population because of compulsory school attendance laws. In other counseling settings, it often is a challenge to get group members to attend the scheduled group sessions. This is not as much of an issue in the school setting, where, as long as the student attends school, he or she is also present for group sessions. Therefore, group leaders in schools generally do not have the task of recruiting and securing group members—an obvious benefit of working in the school setting.

This chapter covers the types of group work in schools at each level—elementary school, middle school, and high school. The advantages as well as challenges in group work with these students in schools are explored, backed by a review of research on the efficacy of group counseling in schools. The chapter also addresses ethical and cultural considerations. Finally, two examples of groups are presented— one for elementary and one for secondary—along with sample activities and guidelines for planning and conducting the groups.

TYPES OF GROUPS

School groups typically are formed to address a specific need or issue that emerges within the school setting. Groups may be

1. *remedial* (with the goal of improving specific skills),
2. *supportive* (providing emotional or psychological support for student experiences), or
3. *psychoeducational* (based on common issues that occur at certain stages of development).

Table 12.1 gives examples of types of groups in each of these categories.

Some small groups are also preventive—teaching life skills or strategies to handle life circumstances—although these topics, such as conflict resolution, tend to be covered more frequently in large-group settings.

Although the listing in Table 12.1 is not exhaustive, it represents the range of topics that may be appropriate for small-group counseling in schools. Notice that some of the groups appear in two or more categories and may serve multiple purposes. For example, a middle-school female may decide to participate in a group that deals with female adolescent issues and, while in the group, might have problems with her parents and need the support of other group members. Also included are examples of groups for teachers and parents. Although most of the group work conducted in schools is with the students, counselors also may offer group counseling sessions for parents and/or teachers to address concerns or situations that affect students.

In addition to the various types of groups, the structure of groups in schools may have different formats. For instance, small groups may be open or closed.

1. An *open group* is one that is scheduled at a specific time, and any student with parental permission (if under the age of 18) may participate. Open groups often are conducted during "free times" (such as lunch time or before/after school) so students will have the freedom to attend if they choose. The group leader usually facilitates a discussion on a topic generated by the group. These groups probably are most similar to group work with youth in other settings. Open groups tend to be popular at middle school and high school levels because of the difficulty of attending group sessions every week as a result of scheduling conflicts with class attendance.
2. The *closed group* is one in which only selected students are invited to participate. In this format, the participants may share a common issue, such as "changing families" or "social skills." Closed groups tend to be more

Table 12.1 Types of Groups and Possible Topics for Each

Remedial	Supportive	Psychoeducational
Study skills	Changing families	Peer relationships
Assertiveness skills	Grief/loss	Girls' issues/boys' issues
Building self-concept	New students	Dating relationships
Social skills/friendship skills	Bullying (victims or perpetrators)	Understanding parents
Test-taking skills	ADHD	Decision making
Anger management	Diversity/multicultural issues	Self-concept
Stress management	Substance use or abuse (self or family member)	Understanding your teenager (group for parents)
Behavior management	Teenage pregnancy	College/career issues
Attention issues	Gender-specific issues	
Working with challenging students (group for teachers)	Students with common medical problems (e.g., eating disorders, physical challenges, etc.)	
	Adoptive or foster children	
	Homeless students	
	Students who are retained	
	Children of incarcerated parents	

structured and have specific goals, and the group leader's role may be more directive than in an open group.

Students who participate in open groups usually decide to do so themselves, whereas students in closed groups may be referred by parents or teachers, in addition to self-referral. Also, open groups tend to be offered on an ongoing basis, perhaps even throughout the school year, whereas closed groups have a limited time to meet, such as a grading period or an 8-week period.

GROUP WORK IN ELEMENTARY, MIDDLE, AND HIGH SCHOOLS

Group counseling services differ across school levels and also from school to school, depending on the school's counseling program and the emphasis on group counseling services, as well as school district policies. Still, group counseling in schools shares some advantages and challenges at each level, influenced by the students' developmental age, the school day schedule, and the topics to be addressed at each level. Table 12.2 lists some of the possible group counseling topics that could be explored at each level. Notice that each of the levels incorporates topics from the previous level. This is indicative of the developmental scope of school counseling programs and the need to cover the needs of students at each level.

Relevant research will be presented for each level. In general, only a moderate amount of research explores the efficacy of small-group counseling in schools, and the research that is available is often more descriptive than empirical. A recent shift toward results-based accountability practices in school counseling (ASCA, 2003) may contribute extensively to research related to the efficacy of group counseling in schools.

Group Counseling in Elementary Schools

Group counseling at the elementary school level is a logical and efficient way to provide counseling services for students. Because schedules usually are more flexible in elementary schools than in middle and secondary schools, school counselors are able to offer groups on a variety of topics (see Table 12.2), and they have more options in terms of time available for group sessions.

Table 12.2 Examples of Possible Group Topics at Each Level

Elementary School	Middle School (+ all of those in elementary school)	High School (+ all of those in elementary and middle school)
Study skills	Transitions	Dating relationships
Assertiveness skills	Career exploration	Understanding parents
Changing families	Diversity	Decision making
Grief/loss	Substance use/abuse	College and career planning
Self-concept	Children of incarcerated parents (also in elementary)	Time management
Anger management	Children of alcoholics (also in elementary)	Sexuality (depending on school policy)
Behavior management	Gender-specific issues	Community service
Attention issues	Body image	Stress management
Bullying/victims of bullying	Peer relationships/peer pressure	

Although group counseling does not take the place of individual counseling, students often move naturally from receiving individual counseling services that address specific issues to receiving group counseling in which they gain support from other students in similar circumstances. For example, after a student who is experiencing a parental divorce receives individual counseling, he or she might be invited to participate in a group on "Changing Families."

Research has indicated that group counseling with elementary school students is an effective way to provide counseling services around a variety of issues. Webb and Myrick (2003) conducted a 6-week group intervention program with elementary students with attention deficit hyperactivity disorder (ADHD). Survey results from the students and teachers supported the need and usefulness of the program, and a longer intervention (12 weeks) resulted in significant improvement in how students and teachers rated its success.

Similarly, group counseling interventions have been used with students who have behavioral adjustment problems. Nelson and Dykeman (1996) used group counseling to help a group of elementary students identify social problems, initiate goal-setting, generate solutions, analyze consequences of the solutions, and evaluate the success of the solutions. Teachers of students who participated in the group noted marked improvement in the behavior of the group participants, whereas the behavior of students in the control group showed no such adjustment.

In a meta-analysis of effective group counseling sessions with elementary students, Whiston and Sexton (1998) found support for the use of groups to develop social skills (Ciechalski & Schmidt, 1995; Utay & Lampe, 1995) and positively address family problems, such as divorce (Richardson & Rosen, 1999; Sanders & Riester, 1996; Stolberg & Mahler, 1994). In addition, Riddle, Bergin, and Douzenis (1997) found that a group counseling intervention was effective in raising the self-concept of children of alcoholics. Further, the group participants demonstrated significant improvements in self-perception of their academic and personal lives.

Several resources are available focusing on developing life skills (Greenberg, 2003; Morganett, 1994) and addressing a variety of topics that pertain to elementary school students. Other resources (see DeLucia-Waack & Gerrity, 2001) provide the protocol or model for conducting small groups based on life events such as parental divorce.

One of the positive features of group counseling in elementary schools is that it lacks the stigma that often accompanies receiving counseling services in other settings. Students in an elementary school typically are involved in small-group counseling of some sort at some point in their elementary school experience. Many of these students enjoy the small-group setting rather than being one of many in a large classroom.

Group Counseling in Middle Schools

Group counseling at the middle school level tends to be more challenging than group counseling at the elementary level because of the schedule of the school day. When students are taken from class to participate in small groups, both teachers and students may feel stressed because of academic instruction or classwork that is missed. As one strategy, school counselors often try to vary the block or period that students miss each week to participate in the group. Therefore, students might miss second period one week, third period the next week, and so on, to participate in a small group. Although this is a viable solution for some students, it brings up the issue of having students make up what they miss while they are attending the group session. Successful group intervention places the responsibility on students to make sure they do not lag in their academic progress, and students may not accept this responsibility.

Despite the obvious challenges to small-group counseling in middle schools, few would deny that providing support and guidance to students at this level is important. Developmental changes (physically, emotionally, mentally, cognitively) during the middle school years can wreak havoc on students' self-concept, peer relationships, and decision-making ability. Therefore, small-group counseling may be even more important at this level than either of the other two levels.

Even though the structure of the middle school day may not allow abundant opportunities for group counseling, small groups may be conducted at obvious times. For example, lunch blocks usually vary but do give students 30–45 minutes of free time (outside-of-class time). Also, there may be a planning period or a homework period that students possibly could miss from time to time without interfering with their academic progress. A final option would be to offer groups either before or after school.

Once the scheduling challenge has been resolved, conducting small groups at the middle school level is a feasible and necessary counseling service. Group counseling with adolescents is an effective way to bring together students with common issues and provide effective services in a timely way (Prout & Prout, 1998).

A review of the literature reveals curricula that can be used for conducting small groups with specific populations in middle school. Arman (2002) offered a 6-week curriculum that provided support for middle school students with mild disabilities. Although the results of the support group were not measured, the curriculum provides a template for recruiting group members, starting the group, and conducting the sessions. Sonnenblick (1997) offered a less structured group approach, conducting group work as a club to promote belonging for at-risk middle school girls. Activities of the club included community service and recreational events that required responsibility for self and a commitment to serving others. Greif (1999) described a collaborative program involving counselors, middle and high school students, and teachers in an anger management program with themes related to the students' anger—exploring the basis of their anger, assessing the anger, and receiving strategies to address anger issues. Several books and curricula address adolescent issues through group counseling (e.g., Greenberg, 2003; Smead, 2000; Walker & Waterman, 2001).

Research regarding the efficacy of group counseling in schools has indicated positive results with middle school students. Cook and Kaffenberger (2003) implemented a solution-focused counseling and study skills program with 35 middle school (seventh- and eighth-grade) students. The results showed that 75% of the students who participated made some or significant changes in grade point average, thereby reducing the number of students who had to repeat a course or be retained.

Kellner and Bry (1999) implemented an anger management program for emotionally disturbed adolescents and achieved positive results, including a decrease in the incidence of participants' physical aggression.

Much of the research involves participants from grades 7–12 and therefore pertains to adolescents in both middle school and high school. Therefore, studies that have been conducted with middle school students are often applicable and relevant for high school group counseling. The secondary group that is presented later in this chapter is an example of group work that can be used with adolescents in both middle school and high school.

Group Counseling in High Schools

In high school, block scheduling, high-stakes testing, and the emphasis on time on task make it more difficult to schedule groups. Because of the pressure for achievement in the academic program, teachers and administrators are reluctant to have students miss instructional time. Still, high school students have specific issues that group counseling can serve.

When students reach the high school level, their developmental needs shift somewhat. Career and college issues begin to move to the forefront, and counseling services can facilitate the decision making of adolescents as they approach adulthood. Also, group counseling may explore the topics suggested in Table 12.2. Issues surrounding dating, graduation, and changing family relationships often emerge as critical during this time.

Even though group counseling services are necessary, the tendency is to offer fewer or no group counseling services at this vulnerable time in the students' lives. The issues mentioned earlier, such as time constraints and academic demands—not to mention counselors' time and availability—may dissuade school counselors from conducting groups. To aid counselors in implementing group counseling at the secondary level, Ripley and Goodnough (2001) offered strategies including developing awareness about group counseling, revealing how group counseling can support the academic curriculum, and giving students easier access to group services.

The high school setting offers greater opportunities for open, unstructured groups on a variety of topics. Drop-in, small-group counseling sessions during lunch, free periods, or before and after school make the open format more attractive than closed groups. Some might argue that this does not constitute "true counseling," but in the school setting it enables students to explore and share their thoughts and feelings about their lives and life events. Structured groups may have a common theme such as relationship or family issues. Groups that support the academic progress of students should be a priority, as students are beginning to consider their life after high school.

The research generally falls into two categories: (a) curricula for group counseling on certain topics, and (b) efficacy research of group counseling practices. Muller and Hartman (1998) provided a template for conducting small-group counseling for sexual-minority youth. At the high school level, issues such as homophobia, harassment, and general misconceptions about being gay, lesbian, bisexual, or transgender

(GLBT) can be a major source of stress for high school students. Some conservative school districts have policies prohibiting discussions about sexual preference, and this illustrates another difference between small-group counseling in schools and in other settings. In a private or agency counseling setting, counselors have the freedom to conduct small-group counseling on sensitive issues such as those that GLBT youth might encounter.

School counselors must consider the policies of the school district prior to considering small-group counseling on volatile issues such as sexual behavior and sexuality. School counselors may be able to address these issues within groups that are not formed around these issues as a specific topic, but as part of a discussion of broader issues, such as relationships and dating.

Efficacy studies of group counseling with high school students have been positive. Zinck and Littrell (2000) found that a 10-week group counseling program with 35 high school girls identified as at risk resulted in positive individual change in the group participants. Follow-up interviews with the participants indicated continued progress toward the goals established in the group sessions.

Another study that supports action research with high school students in group counseling was conducted by Bauer, Sapp, and Johnson (1999). The researchers implemented two 9-week group counseling interventions with rural at-risk high school students (as defined by academic and behavior problems) to improve self-concept, behavior, and academic achievement. The results indicated that the groups that received cognitive–behavioral interventions showed significant improvements in self-esteem and academic self-concept.

ADVANTAGES AND CHALLENGES OF GROUP COUNSELING IN SCHOOLS

While group counseling in schools has been shown to offer benefits to students, teachers, and parents, there are challenges in this setting that may not be present in other counseling settings. Table 12.3 sets out the advantages and challenges for group work in schools, which are discussed further in the following sections.

Advantages

Providing group counseling services in schools fills a critical need to address the developmental issues of youth in today's schools. Although school counselors are not therapists, they are mental health professionals who work in the school setting. Therefore, group counseling represents a resource for students, parents, and teachers to provide essential services.

The school is a natural setting where group participants are readily available to partake in group counseling services, with parental consent if under the age of 18. Again, group counseling in schools is not therapy, but counseling professionals have the knowledge and training to identify situations and issues of concern. If

Table 12.3 Advantages and Limitations of Group Counseling in Schools

Advantages	Challenges
Provides a resource to support students, parents, and teachers	Handling a large number of referrals—more students might be referred for groups than can possibly be seen on a weekly basis
Gives students the opportunity to share experiences in a safe setting ("I'm not alone")	Students might feel ostracized when participating in a counseling group
Is a more efficient way to serve a greater number of students	Scheduling challenges
Increased likelihood of behavior change as a result of peer influence	Missed class time and teacher resistance could create stress

more extensive intervention is indicated, the school counselor has an ethical obligation to refer the student, parent, or teacher to outside mental health resources.

Another benefit of group counseling in schools is that schools are a safe environment in which students can express their thoughts and feelings and practice behaviors before trying them out in their everyday lives outside of school. Despite this advantage, many schools today are overcrowded, and class size continues to increase. Often, students feel intimidated or are afraid to express their feelings because they want to fit in with their peer group. Small-group counseling gives students a safe venue in which to express their thoughts, feelings, and concerns within a circle of fewer students who share similar ideas. The connection of participants in small groups in schools often carries over into the larger environment. Facilitating participants' transfer of skills or behaviors learned within the small group to the world outside of the group is a goal of small-group counseling.

Schools have a shared responsibility for the development of thousands of students, and school counselors face quite a challenge in making counseling services available to those students. ASCA's (2002) position is that "small- and large-group approaches are the preferred medium of delivery for developmental guidance and counseling activities, in terms of efficiency as well as effectiveness" (p. 1). If a counselor can gather a group of students around a common theme, issue, or concern, these students' individual needs can be met through group counseling. This is not to deny the importance and efficacy of individual counseling, but the reality is that group work in schools is often a more realistic, implementable way to meet the developmental needs of students. In short, it is an efficient way to serve larger numbers of students.

A final benefit of group counseling in schools is the potential influence of the peer group in the school setting. In group work with youth in other settings, they most likely go to a specific place at a specific time. Group counseling in schools offers participants the opportunity to interact during the group sessions and also to influence each other during the remainder of the school day.

Especially at the higher levels, students are more responsive to information and feedback from their peers than from adults. Group members might keep each other "in check" in terms of individual or group goals. In addition, groups in schools often provide the opportunity to utilize members as role models. Securing peer role models is relatively simple because a population of students is readily available from which to participate in group counseling and from which to draw role models.

> School counselors help foster peer interaction and the positive results of peer modeling by providing opportunities for students to observe each other responding to relevant and challenging situations. (Davis, 2005, p. 71)

Group work has proven to be a useful component of counseling in schools. Some challenges, however, are unique to group work in the school setting. Although some of these have been mentioned already, we should consider them more closely so we will be better able to face them effectively.

Limitations

The limitations of group work in schools seem to center for the most part on the issue of time. Because participation in group counseling is not mandatory, it often is not recognized as a priority. For example, if Rosa is a member of a "Celebrating Diversity" small group but she is failing English and math, teachers will be hesitant to release her from class to participate in the group. This is a consideration that is not present in other group work settings. The group leader must develop strategies to provide counseling services that do not impede the academic progress of students.

Also, faculty, administration, and parents must be informed of the goals and benefits of group counseling. In Rosa's case, issues surrounding English as a second language (ESL) and acculturation into the mainstream culture may be contributing to her academic failures. Through group counseling, perhaps Rosa's problems can be addressed in a small group of students with similar multicultural concerns while developing individual goals and identifying support resources for her and the other students with similar issues.

Another challenge is the actual scheduling of the groups. Again, this differs from group work with youth in other settings, in which a group time can be readily scheduled over a long term. Because of the nature of schools, daily schedules are interrupted, students are tested throughout the school year, and other similar circumstances vie for time, resulting in inconsistent counseling services.

The school schedule is not the only interference. Sometimes the school counselor's schedule is interrupted by unplanned crisis events or situations. These challenges demand flexibility on the part of counselors. Alternating blocks or times when groups meet, making up group sessions within the same week, and consulting the school calendar before scheduling groups may avoid some of these issues.

As mentioned, participation in group counseling in schools is not mandatory, and, ethically, students are given the option to terminate counseling services at any time. Sometimes, particularly with older students, being referred for group counseling or being part of a small group results in the student feeling ostracized. This is not a problem at the elementary level, when most students anticipate the opportunity to receive special attention in small group. Adolescents, however, usually do not want to be singled out from their peer group and they shy away from activities that brand them as different or unique. Therefore, school counselors and other personnel who serve as group leaders should promote group counseling services in a way that is supportive and attractive to adolescents. Soliciting membership for groups may require creativity in showing that groups can be fun and helpful in a variety of ways.

A final limitation of group work in schools is actually both an advantage and a challenge: Group counseling in schools is a reasonable and relatively easy counseling service to offer because of the large pool of potential group members—the entire student population! However, this also presents a challenge in trying to meet the needs of all students through group counseling. The number of referrals can be overwhelming, especially for small groups focusing on academic issues such as time management, study skills, test-taking skills, and homework. As a result, group counseling may be initiated only to address the most immediate issues, often in the remedial category or in crisis situations, such as the sudden death of a student or teacher.

Because of the advantages that offset the limitations, groups in school represent a vital part of any school program at any level. The skills and information gleaned from participating in small-group counseling in school can lay the foundation for developing other life skills, academic skills, and personal and professional goals.

ETHICAL CONSIDERATIONS FOR GROUPS IN SCHOOLS

The ASCA addresses group work in schools in its *Ethical Standards for School Counselors* (2004). The standards (A.6.a) emphasize the necessity of screening group participants prior to beginning group work and of protecting group participants from harm. Another critical area addressed is consent for a student's participation in group counseling. The protocol for acquiring consent varies from school to school, but most would agree that parental consent for a minor child to participate in counseling services is imperative for two reasons:

1. Because students are being taken out of class, parental support for group participation is necessary.
2. When parents consent to group participation, the group leader should involve parents in the goals that the individual is working on in the group. (Students who are 18 may consent for services themselves.)

Confidentiality

The largest ethical concern for group work in schools is confidentiality. Because the group membership involves children and adolescents, it is difficult to be sure that confidentiality will be maintained. Consider the following example:

An elementary counselor is conducting a social skills small group of fifth-grade students. The group has met four times, each time including a review of the rules of confidentiality. One afternoon, two group members came to the counselor and reported that they heard a third group member telling a student (not in the group) what one of the other members had said about a family situation during group. The counselor thanked the students for sharing and assured them that she would address this breach. She then sent for the student who allegedly broke confidentiality. The student acknowledged that she had repeated this group member's disclosure outside of the group and said she "forgot" about the rules of confidentiality. She apologized for doing so and agreed that she should apologize to the group member and to the group as a whole for breaking the rules of confidentiality.

The member whose confidentiality had been breached was upset but did forgive the other member. After allowing the two students to talk, the counselor asked the student who had breached confidentiality to leave. The counselor found that even though the student whose confidentiality had been broken had agreed to forgive the other student, she was hurt and angry. She indicated that although she had agreed to forgive the other student, she did not think she could share openly in the group any more.

When the group met the following week, group members showed animosity toward the one who had broken confidentiality. The group tried to process the negative feelings and reached a resolution, but the group leader realized that the trust and cohesion of the group probably would not be regained. Further, group goals were not achieved. The school counselor decided to terminate the group after two more sessions, because the violation of confidentiality ultimately halted the group process and progress.

The structure of the school day gives students opportunities for free time in which to interact—lunch, recess, between classes, bus stops. The open nature of counseling in schools can lead to the accidental breaching of confidentiality. The ASCA *Ethical Standards* (2004) require that

> the professional school counselor establishes clear expectations in the group setting and clearly states that confidentiality in group counseling cannot be guaranteed. (A.6.c)

School counselors and other group work leaders in the school must emphasize the importance of confidentiality and provide concrete examples of when and how a breach might occur. Within the group, the leader should introduce the topic of how a breach of confidentiality might be handled in the group and the consequences for breaches.

Record Keeping

Another ethical consideration that is somewhat different for group work in schools is record-keeping. Typically in mental health settings, group leaders keep detailed notes of individual group members' progress, as well as group progress. Schools have no ethical obligation to keep records of the students' participation in a group. Although group members ethically are required to be involved in counseling plans, records of their attendance, participation, and progress in the group are not mandated. Many group leaders in schools do keep informal notes about individual students in groups, but these notes are for informational use only and would be exposed only if subpoenaed in court. The ethical standard that addresses record-keeping (ASCA, 2004) states that

> the professional school counselor follows up with group members and documents proceedings as appropriate. (A.6.d)

This standard gives group leaders in schools flexibility in documentation pertaining to the group, its members, and the impacts of group counseling.

As in any setting, school counselors and other personnel who conduct group work have an ethical obligation to act in the best interest of the client—in this case, the student. When ethical dilemmas or situations arise, group leaders must follow the protocol of the school district, as well as that of applicable professional organizations, to make informed decisions.

APPROACHES TO GROUP WORK IN SCHOOLS: WHAT WORKS?

Group work in the school setting imposes restrictions that result in some counseling approaches being more useful than others. Because group counseling in schools is not therapeutic counseling, it is difficult to engage students in a long-term, intensive analysis of the issues being explored. Therefore, approaches that adhere to specific strategies that are time efficient and action oriented may be more appropriate for group work in the school setting because they parallel the pace and structure of other school events.

Solution-Focused Brief Counseling (SFBC)

Some evidence indicates that solution-focused brief counseling (SFBC) approaches to group counseling are effective in the school setting. Arman (2002) provided a model for a brief counseling intervention to develop resilience in students with mild disabilities, noting that the need for a time-sensitive intervention would be beneficial for the students and the counselors alike. LaFountain, Garner, and Eliason (1996) explored the use of solution-focused techniques in small-group counseling with elementary, middle, and high school students. The results indicated that students who received solution-focused group counseling had higher levels of self-esteem, higher self-perception scores, and a greater ability to cope than a control group of students who did not receive solution-focused counseling. Some evidence also points to SFBC as an effective approach when working with parenting groups (Gingerich & Wabeke, 2001).

Activity-Oriented Group Counseling

Activity-oriented group counseling may be more effective than discussion-oriented group counseling. Page and Chandler (1994) found that a structured group with planned activities had a more positive effect on improving the self-concept of ninth-grade at-risk students than did an open discussion group with little or no structure.

It is reasonable to assume that school-age students respond more positively to action-oriented approaches because of their level of development. Hands-on, experiential techniques that actively involve group participants may be more engaging and, therefore, have a greater impact on students than less active group approaches. As an example, Utay and Lampe (1995) successfully used a cognitive–behavioral group counseling game to improve the social skills of children with learning disabilities.

Utilizing action-oriented techniques such as playing games and role playing lend themselves more readily to some group topics than others. For example, a middle school group called "Girl Power" may benefit from group discussions, whereas a group on "Behavior Management" might revolve around activities that allow participants to practice self-control and new behaviors.

Research supports the claim that short-term, action-oriented approaches lend themselves naturally to the time constraints of the school setting. Therefore, they may be the most appropriate approach for group work in schools.

CULTURAL CONSIDERATIONS FOR GROUP WORK IN SCHOOLS

Diversity is a consideration in every facet of our society, and schools are no exception. Just as the changing demographics indicate a huge influx of diverse ethnic groups into communities, the schools must develop more programs to support the cultural needs of a diverse mix of students. Group counseling with themes of culture and diversity are an effective way to foster tolerance for diversity and improve acculturation to the mainstream culture. Although there is an assumption that culture refers only to race and ethnicity, many different cultures in schools deserve attention—the gang culture, the sports culture, GLBT youth, and gender-specific cultures, as examples.

Research supports a mixed composition of students in group counseling to promote understanding of cultural differences. Stroh and Sink (2002) stated:

> Diversity is integral to the group counseling process. Heterogeneous group membership not only reflects more accurately the diversity of persons in the school, community, and world, but it also provides the expanded opportunities for learning through varied interpersonal interactions. (pp. 76–77)

The school is a setting where interaction between various cultures is a natural occurrence, and counseling services, including group counseling, must embrace those differences and promote tolerance and acceptance among students and faculty. Research also advocates for homogeneous groups of students from similar cultural backgrounds (Bradley, 2001; Perrone & Sedlacek, 2000). Group work with students who share common concerns and cultural experiences is a catalyst for identifying sources of support within the school setting, and group leaders must be culturally responsive to the needs of students. Although this is true of group work in other counseling settings, too, schools are an agency in which the interaction of cultural groups should be particularly encouraged and the uniqueness of cultures should be celebrated.

Next we will explore two groups that might be offered in a school setting—one for elementary students and one for secondary students. The group curricula are not offered in their entirety, but the framework for conducting the group can be built upon to develop a comprehensive group around the topic.

It should be noted that both groups are examples of structured, closed groups. Open groups would be facilitated differently with a more flexible focus, as in experiential or therapeutic groups. For consistency, the term *group leader* will be used to refer to the school counselor or other trained personnel within the school who might conduct the group, and the term *group participants* refers to the students in the group.

AN ELEMENTARY SCHOOL GROUP: STUDY SUPERSTARS

In schools, one of the most popular types of group work is offered to students who are academically challenged. Group counseling sessions with a goal of improving academic achievement reinforce the school counselor's role in promoting students' academic success. Study-skills groups typically are task oriented, especially for elementary students, and are structured by the group leader to foster individual goal setting as well as working toward a group goal. Also, emphasis is placed on improving work habits to increase academic performance. Groups that focus on improving academic skills typically involve collaboration with teachers and parents to assess the effectiveness of the group intervention.

At the elementary level, each group should include up to six participants, with a difference of no more than one grade level between members. Developmentally, having more than six members can present problems in attending to individual needs and can be overwhelming for the group leader. The students participate in group work for eight sessions (one 9-weeek grading period).

Purpose

The purpose of the group is to work with students in the third and fourth grades who demonstrate difficulty in completing academic tasks and whose work is consistently below grade level. Outcomes for this group will be (1) an increase in the completion of student work, and (2) improvement in grades in the core subjects (English, math, science, and social studies).

Conceptual Framework

The group is task oriented and falls under the *remedial* category discussed earlier in the chapter. The theoretical approaches used include behavioral (goal setting and reinforcement of positive behaviors) and solution focused (looking for exceptions to failure).

Group Goals

As a result of this group, participants will

- identify a personal learning style that works best,
- identify impediments to work completion,
- develop strategies for studying for success,
- establish weekly goals for completing work,
- improve grades during the grading period in which the group occurs, and
- practice habits that will lead to greater academic success in core areas.

Pre-Group Screening and Orientation to Group

Group members are referred by teachers and parents. In an initial meeting with the individual participants, the group leader informs them of their referral to the group and explains the goals, process, and desired results of group counseling. The emphasis is on the shared issues for the participants so each student will understand that this is not an isolated problem. Rules of confidentiality are explained and students are given the choice to participate or not. Group schedules are explained, along with a general overview of the types of activities that will be introduced.

A pre-group survey is given to each student. The survey contains the following items:

> - List three strategies you use to try to complete your work.
>
> - In what subject(s) do you believe you can improve your grades?
>
> - On a scale of 1 to 5 (with 1 being not good and 5 being the best), how would you rate yourself as a student?   1   2   3   4   5

At the end of the screening, if the students assent to participating in the group, send home a permission slip for the parent/guardian to sign and return (see Sample 12.1).

Possible Challenges, Limitations, and Ethical Considerations

Parental consent for small-group counseling is required because the participants involved are minors (see Sample 12.1). Further, parent participation in the group

Sample 12.1   Parental Consent for Group Counseling

Dear Parent/Guardian:

As part of a comprehensive school counseling program, students are often invited to participate in small-group counseling sessions. Your child has been invited to join a Study Skills group that is starting this month. The group offers an opportunity for your child to recognize his/her own learning style, to set personal goals, to make the most of classroom time, to improve study habits, and to learn time-management skills. The goal of the group is to improve work habits and grades in the next grading period.

This group will meet weekly for eight sessions and for half an hour each session. The time that the Study Skills group will meet will be coordinated with the teacher so your child will not miss valuable class time.

Please give your permission by signing the form below, and return the form to the Counseling Office as soon as possible. Your signed permission is necessary before your child can participate in the group. If you have questions, please contact me at 123-456-7890. I look forward to working with you and your child.

Sincerely,
[Name]
Group Leader

Student _____ Teacher _____

- -

_____ I give permission for my child, _____, to participate in the group.

_____ I do not give permission for my child, _____, to participate in the group.

_____
(Parent/Guardian signature & date)

process can help the child reinforce concepts learned in the group and perhaps institute a similar behavior plan for schoolwork at home. Sometimes this is a challenge because parents' work schedules or other life activities may take priority over the student's academic progress, but parent support and participation have been shown to improve students' chances for completing the group successfully.

The Study Superstars group poses a particular challenge because poor study skills may be ingrained in a child's work habits by third or fourth grade. Also, some students may not aspire to improve their grades because they have come to accept their less-than-adequate performance. Thus, in the midst of providing tangible and useful study skills, group leaders must work to improve students' self-concept as related to academic performance.

Another challenge of the group may be for participants to show marked academic improvement at the end of the group. The group leader will have to review participants' grades prior to the group and again after the group intervention.

Also, time poses a challenge because, to maximize effectiveness, the group leader should consult with the teacher of each group participant at least weekly to note any change in participants' work habits. Because of the popularity of academic-focused small groups in schools, school counselors often find themselves running multiple small groups simultaneously, which makes monitoring individual students' progress a time challenge.

Group Sessions by Stages

The possible course of this preadolescent group is presented according to the definitive, personal involvement, group involvement, and enhancement and closure stages proposed by Capuzzi and Gross in chapter 2.

Definitive Stage

Activity: "Getting to Know You"
Theme: Who I Am, Why I'm Here, and What I Want to Improve
Purpose: Participants will get to know each other and share common concerns about study skills and work habits.

1. Remind participants about the rules of confidentiality and that they were invited to this group because they have something in common. Invite them to guess the common issue or theme of the group.
2. Ask participants to come up with an animal whose name starts with the first letter of their own name (e.g., Bobcat Brittany, Kangaroo Kevin).
3. When participants say their names, ask them to suggest one thing they would like to work on in the Study Superstars group and one thing that gets in the way of their being successful in school.
4. As the students respond, make a list on the board or chart and, after all the participants have identified their goal, ask the group as a whole to add others to the list.
5. Distribute a folder to each child, which they may decorate if they wish, and ask them to write their individual goal on the inside of the folder. Tell them that each week they will evaluate how things are going and come up with strategies for achieving the goal.
6. Finally, ask the group to come up with a group goal that everyone can work on (Example: "By the end of the group, everyone will have improved their grades in at least two subjects."). Decide on a reward if the group achieves its goal.

Personal Involvement Stage

Activity: "What Kind of Learner Am I?"
Theme: Learning Style
Purpose: Participants will identify their personal learning style and commit to try a new strategy based on their identified learning style.

1. Ask students to complete the page given in Sample 12.2, explaining the answer key as needed.
2. Ask the participants to count how many A, V, and K responses they had. The one circled most often is indicative of their primary learning style.
3. Discuss what it means to be an auditory learner, a visual learner, or a kinesthetic learner.
4. Once the students have identified their learning style, have them each come up with one strategy they could use in their schoolwork based on their primary learning style.

Sample 12.2 Learning Style Activity

Circle the answers that are most true for you:

Answer key:

A = Auditory (hearing)
V = Visual (seeing)
K = Kinesthetic (doing)

1. I do better on my schoolwork when I work . . .
   (A) alone   (V) with others

2. I understand my schoolwork better when . . .
   (A) my teacher reads   (V) I read it myself   (K) I can make a
      it aloud   model of it

3. When I do a book report, I would rather . . .
   (V) read it or watch   (A) listen to it on tape (K) create a project
      a movie of it   about it

4. When I try to memorize something, I . . .
   (A) say it over and over (V) read it over and over (K) write it over
                                                          and over

5. I find it easier to learn when I . . .
   (K) do it   (A) say it   (V) see it

5. Ask the students to write this strategy in their folders and set an individual goal to try out this strategy before next week's group.

Note: It is important that the group leader consult with the teacher during the time between groups to see if the students are actually employing the new strategies in the classroom.

> *Activity*: "What Do I Do With My Time?"
> *Theme*: Time Management
> *Purpose*: Participants will discover how they use their time and identify patterns of time management that affect school performance.

1. Give each student a chart that lists each school day, along with a block for each hour of the day.
2. Ask the members to fill in the chart with their activities and daily schedules.
3. Have the participants calculate how much time they spend doing schoolwork (both in school and at home).
4. Ask the students if they can identify "extra" time in their day that they could devote to schoolwork or school projects.
5. Have the students write the specific times they will devote to schoolwork.
6. Make a copy for the group leader and a copy for the teacher. Allow the students to take the schedule home to show their parents/guardians.

> *Homework*: The participants should be prepared to report if they adhered to their schedule and why or why not.

Group Involvement Stage

> *Activity*: "What Works for Me?"
> *Theme*: Recognizing Success Factors
> *Purpose*: Participants will learn strategies that others use to be successful.

1. Ask the participants how they did on last week's goal. If any were not successful, have the group generate new strategies for the participant to try.
2. Give the students a piece of paper and ask them to draw a line down the middle of the page. On one side, have them write or draw a picture of themselves being successful at something (does not have to be school related). For example, a student might draw a picture of kicking a goal in soccer or helping with a chore at home.
3. Ask the students to share their "success stories." As they do this, discuss how the students might use the same strategies for school that they use for their success in other situations.
4. Have the students draw a picture, on the other side of the paper, of themselves being successful in schoolwork. Ask them: What would that look like and feel like?
5. Encourage the students to use the strategies of other group members if they think that will help them to be successful.

Group Challenge: Ask participants to commit to a group goal such as: "Each member of the group will complete all in-class and homework assignments during the next week." Decide on the group reward if the group meets the goal.

Enhancement and Closure

Activity: "You Did It!"
Theme: Identifying Academic Success and Challenge
Purpose: Participants will be reinforced for successful study strategies and celebrate individual and group successes.

1. Have the participants review their progress over the past sessions and share things in which they have improved (or not improved).
2. Ask the participants to review their time-management schedules and determine if they are adhering to the time they allotted for schoolwork and homework.
3. If all participants have improved, acknowledge each member and identify the strategies that seemed to work for them.
4. Have the students each go around and compliment another group member on one way they have seen that person improve. (Peer reinforcement of strategies enhances the likelihood of students' success.)
5. Review the group goal and decide on the reward for the final group celebration.

Strategies to Evaluate the Group

During the last group session, the group leader gives a post-group survey to the participants (see Sample 12.3). The leader compares the results of the pre- and post-group survey and notes (1) any new strategies that the participants used, and (2) any change in the student's academic self-concept on the scale. A change in grades can be assessed by reviewing grades prior to the group and grades after the group intervention. In some schools, an "interim" grading report is issued, and this could be utilized mid-group to see if students are making academic progress. Midterm grades can indicate whether individual goals should be adjusted or determine if group interventions should be altered.

Follow-Up and Referral

The group leader should follow up with the participants within 2 weeks after the group has terminated. The sessions can be conducted with individual students and/or the entire group, as deemed appropriate. Also, follow-up consultation with the teachers of the group participants is crucial to see if the students are continuing to progress or if any students need a "booster group" to address their regression in academic performance. The leader should follow up with parents, either in writing or through personal communication, to reinforce the need for parents to work with their children to maintain and improve academic performance.

Because of the academic focus of the group, outside referral to mental health counseling agencies probably will not be necessary. However, if the group leader

Sample 12.3   Post-Group Survey

■ List three strategies you use to try to complete your work:

1.

2.

3.

■ In what subject(s) did you improve your grades?
■ On a scale of 1 to 5 (with 1 being not good and 5 being the best), how would you
rate yourself as a student?

1   2   3   4   5

---

observes that a participant is not making progress or is not motivated to improve his
or her work habits, the leader may want to consider setting up a conference with the
teachers and parents to assess possible reasons for this lack of progress.

If a participant is not improving despite his or her obvious efforts to do so, the
group leader may want to consider collaborating with the teacher and parents to
determine if the problem is the result of a learning disability. This may point to a
possible referral of the child for special education testing. Through observation and
appropriate monitoring, the group leader is in a position to assess progress and make
informed decisions in the best interest of the child.

A SECONDARY SCHOOL GROUP:
THE RESILIENCE GROUP

The Resilience Group falls under the psychoeducational category of group counseling and addresses personal and social issues of middle school students. In particular,
the group is offered to students who (a) already have overcome great difficulty and
adversity in their lives, or (b) students who seem to be at risk for difficulty dealing
with adversity. The group meets for 8 weeks for 45 minutes each session. Because
most middle school and high school students have block scheduling or change
classes after a certain time period, the group sessions alternate time slots each week
to prevent students from missing the same class every week. This group is applicable to middle and high school students.

Purpose

The purpose of the Resilience Group is to increase participants' awareness of the
attributes and characteristics of resilience as well as to develop tools to handle life's

challenges. Expected outcomes include having participants identify internal assets and external resources that they can rely on when they encounter a difficult situation in their lives. The goal is for participants to realize that much of their future and destiny is a matter of personal control. Finally, it is hoped that group members will include the group leader in their support system and as a resource when needed.

Conceptual Framework

The Resilience Group is heavily based in reality therapy/choice theory, and the activities ask participants to explore their past reality (the "real" world) and focus on the choices they make that will impact their future. The emphasis on awareness of internal assets is solution focused in that participants understand how their attributes may be applied to other situations. For example, if a student identifies patience as a characteristic he or she possesses in dealing with a sibling, the student might apply the same patience in a situation in which something at school or home is not going as planned. Transferring successful coping skills to other challenging situations is characteristic of solution-focused counseling.

Group Goals

In this group, participants will

- understand that many of the "bad" things that have happened to them have been out of their control;
- identify the internal assets that they possess that help them deal with adversity;
- identify the external resources (i.e., people) they can turn to when they need support;
- create a Life Book that they will use to document their thoughts and feelings in the group, along with activities from the group; and
- develop a general sense of hopefulness for the future and a feeling of control over what happens in their lives.

Pre-Group Screening and Orientation to the Group

Participants for the group may be referred by teachers and/or parents, or students may self-refer. In individual pre-group screening meetings, the group leader informs the student about the group process and the group activities that will be conducted. The leader notes that to maximize success and benefit from the group, the student has to be willing to share some of his or her past, as well as some of the present and future. Although group members are not forced to share openly in the group, sharing does foster a sense of cohesion. The rules of confidentiality are heavily emphasized, as the life events that are shared could be sensitive and painful. Therefore, the group leader may want to have the group participants sign a form indicating that they understand the rules of confidentiality and agree to abide by those rules.

During screening and orientation, the student receives a permission slip to take home for parental consent. In addition, the student receives the evaluation form shown in Sample 12.4.

⒮⒜⒨⒫⒧⒠ 12.4   Pre-Group / Post-Group Evaluation

1. When something bad happens to you, name three ways you handle it.

   _____

   _____

   _____

2. When you need to talk to someone about a problem, how many people can you think of that you could talk to? (Circle one)

   1 or 2   3–5   5–10   10+

3. On a scale of 1–5 (with 5 being the best, 3 being pretty good, and 1 being the worst), how do you think you handle things when they don't go the way you would like?

   1   2   3   4   5

Possible Challenges, Limitations, and Ethical Considerations

As always, confidentiality in groups in schools is a concern, and in this group it is crucial. If students start sharing things about their personal lives outside of the group, confidentiality becomes even more paramount. Students often disclose information that might be perceived as gossip or that others might use to tease or harass them. Developmentally, students in middle and high school might be tempted to spread rumors or gossip about information they hear in the group. Therefore, the group leader must emphasize confidentiality within the group from the beginning. In addition to signing the statement regarding confidentiality, group participants should discuss and decide what the consequences will be for breaching confidentiality. The seriousness of a breach cannot receive too much emphasis.

Another challenge could arise in soliciting membership for the group. Adolescents might perceive participation in small-group counseling as not "cool," so group leaders might have to do some outreach to secure members. This is a bit different from group work in other settings, where youth may come to the group as a demand of parents or a mandate from the court. Schools do not have mandatory participation requirements, so students cannot be forced into group counseling. The group leader should consider how to market the group in a way that is attractive to adolescents.

Group Sessions by Stages

The definitive, personal involvement, group involvement, and enhancement and closure stages of group work proposed by Capuzzi and Gross in chapter 2 are reviewed in light of the target population in the school setting.

Definitive Stage

Activity: "What's Your Story?" (Davis, 1997)
Theme: We All Have a Story to Tell
Purpose: To define "resilience" (the ability to bounce back or overcome) and identify times in the past when group participants have had to be resilient.

1. In the first session, introduce an ice-breaker activity that allows participants to become familiar with each other. Distribute the blank books (hardbound books with blank pages) and tell the participants that they will be telling the story of their life and writing the story of their future in these Life Books.
2. On a sheet of scratch paper, have the students list significant life events that have happened from their birth to the present. They may include any events—happy or sad.
3. Ask the members to transfer this information to the "What's Your Story?" paper (see Sample 12.5 for the format) on the top of the lifeline, labeled "Life Events."
4. Once all the life events have been listed, discuss with the members how they would feel if that event had happened to them and who or what could control whether that event happened. *The goal is to have students see that some of the adverse events in their life have been out of their control.*
5. Have the students list their feelings and control responses on the bottom of the lifeline, labeled "Feelings/Control."

Sample 12.5 Format for Lifeline

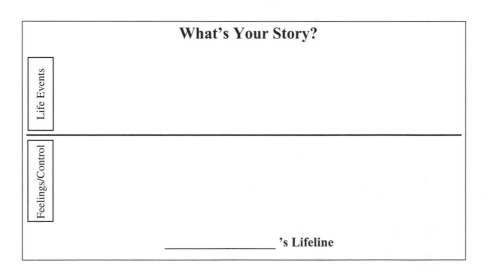

What's Your Story?

Life Events

Feelings/Control

_____ 's Lifeline

6. Encourage the group members to share as much as they would like. Members may want to share only one event or all of them.

Processing:

- What kinds of feelings do you have when you reflect on things that have happened in your life so far?
- What events do you have in common with other group members? What events are different?
- If you listed anything you could have controlled, what would you have done differently to change things?

Follow-Up: Let the students know that they will see this sheet again, but at that time it will be related to their future.

Personal Involvement Stage

Activity: "I'm a Survivor"
Theme: Strengths and Talents
Purpose: To help participants identify their internal resources that will help them deal with adversity.

1. Ask students to list on a page in their Life Books the things they would consider to be their strengths or talents.
2. Have the participants share times when these strengths and/or talents have helped them overcome a difficult situation.

Activity: "Who Can I Turn To?"
Theme: Identifying External Assets
Purpose: Participants will identify people on whom they can rely when they have a problem or when they need support.

Have the participants list the following categories down the left-hand side of a page of the Life Book:

Friends	Sports Heroes
Family Members	Community Members
Teachers	Church Members
Coaches	

1. Discuss what it means to "influence" someone and the difference between someone who is important and someone who is influential.
2. Discuss the categories and ask students to brainstorm a list of people they consider to be important in their lives.
3. Have the students write how the people they identified either influenced them or their behavior (this could be either positive or negative influence).
4. Discuss when the identified people would be those to whom the students would turn during difficult times: "Under what circumstances/situations would you turn to someone on your list?" "Under what circumstances/situations would you *not* turn to this person?"

Group Involvement Stage

Activity: "Sharing Our Stories"
Theme: Sharing Life Books and Compliments
Purpose: To have group members share experiences with the purpose of normalizing adversity and recognizing resilience in each other.

1. Have the group members share their Life Books and identify one thing in each other that will help get them through life's challenges.
2. Ask each participant to write his or her name at the top of a page of the Life Book. Then have them pass around the Life Books so each group member has an opportunity to write something they have learned about the person that will help them deal with challenging times in their lives.
3. When the original owner of the book gets the book back, have the students read the things that group members wrote about them and respond to the comments if they wish.

Enhancement and Closure

Activity: "My Future Lifeline"
Theme: Forging Toward the Future and Choosing Your Journey
Purpose: To give group participants a sense of hopefulness about the future and help them understand their ability to choose their futures.

1. On a sheet of scratch paper, have participants brainstorm what they would like to have happen in their lives from today until the "end of your story." Ask the students to be specific (age, place, event, etc.).
2. Ask each participant to transfer this information to the lifeline (see Sample 12.5), on the top part labeled "Life Events."
3. Once all the life events have been listed, go back and discuss how the participants would feel if that event would have happened to them and who or what would control whether the event would happen at all. *The goal is to have the participants recognize that they have some control over what happens in their lives.*
4. Have the students list their feelings and control responses on the "Feelings/ Control" part of the lifeline (the bottom) in Sample 12.5.
5. Discuss what the student will have to do to achieve the future event. Include the reality of events (such as "become a professional basketball player") as well as the details about what will be required to make each event happen. Emphasize the importance of what students can do *now* to promote success in the future. For example, it will be difficult to go to college if a student doesn't do well academically throughout school.
6. Have the participants compare their "Future Lifeline" with the one they completed in the first session. Ask: "What do you notice about the control of these events in your future?"
7. Guide group participants in recognizing that they have hope for their future and that they have control over what happens to them in many circumstances in

their lives. Help the students realize that whatever has happened in the past, "you have choices for your future!"

8. Let the participants know that they may take their Life Books home. Encourage them to share their books with their families and significant others.

Strategies to Evaluate the Group

A post-group survey consisting of the same questions as the pre-group survey should be given to assess the effect of the group intervention. A comparison of pre-group and post-group results should indicate the progress of each member in the group. Other types of evaluation include observation of students' relationships and reactions to events at home and at school.

Follow-Up and Referral

Follow-ups with students should be frequent, even if these are only a brief check-in to assess the student's level of functioning. A group follow-up is appropriate if the group had developed cohesion to an extent at which the group wanted to maintain contact as support for each other. Follow-ups with teachers and with parents could include asking them for feedback in terms of how students are handling difficulties or adversity at school and at home. If these reports indicate that the students seem able to deal with the anxiety and stresses of student life, the group leader can feel confident that the group was helpful.

It should be noted that when group members reveal life events from the past, bringing them to the surface might uncover a traumatic or emotional experience that is beyond the group leader's scope of training. In these cases, the school counselor or group leader shouldn't hesitate to refer the student for outside mental health counseling.

CONCLUSION

The two examples of small-group counseling presented in this chapter are illustrative of the numerous group topics that can be addressed in schools. These samples offer a template for developing other themes in group counseling designed to meet students' needs in a comprehensive and meaningful way.

LEARNING ACTIVITIES

1. With a partner, develop a plan for overcoming challenges such as those mentioned in this chapter. How can group work in schools help to overcome these obstacles?
2. Participate in a group of four members. Choose a school level and pick a group topic that might be developmentally relevant to that age group. List goals for the group, suggest activities that might be used, and identify a way to evaluate the group's success.

3. Referrals to outside mental health agencies are often necessary for group counselors in schools. Identify some ways by which school counselors and other group leaders in the school might connect with outside counselors to enhance the cooperative relationship between schools and community agencies.
4. School counselors must connect with parents in acquiring permission to work with their children in small groups. Pair up with a partner and create a brochure advertising group counseling services to parents and soliciting their support for group work in schools.

SUMMARY

Schools are an ideal venue for group counseling. Themes may be academic, personal/social, or career related, and the format may be remedial, supportive, or psychoeducational. Although some issues are common across school levels, group counseling differs in some ways from elementary school to middle school to high school. Considerations such as the developmental level of students and the impact of family situations change between and within levels.

Ethical considerations for group work in schools include consideration of state and local school board policy. Consent for services and rules of confidentiality vary from school to school. To make informed decisions, group leaders in school settings must be well versed in the ethical and legal requirements of working with youth in schools. Multicultural considerations for group work in schools are similar to diversity issues in agency or mental health group work, although in group work these issues may occur more naturally in schools because the population is readily available and required to interact regularly. As concerns or issues emerge around diversity, group work is a viable option for working with youth in schools.

The chapter presents templates for two actual group curricula that might be used at the elementary and secondary levels. The group sessions are considered by developmental level, with suggested themes and activities. These examples illustrate topics among the many that may be addressed in group work in school settings and the format for conducting these groups in schools.

The possibilities for group intervention and group work in schools are limited only by ethical and legal constraints. The efficacy of group counseling in schools at all levels is supported by research.

USEFUL WEB SITES

☐ American School Counselor Association
www.schoolcounselor.org
☐ Games for Groups
www.gamesforgroups.com
☐ Youth Light, Inc.
www.youthlight.com

☐ Childswork / Childsplay
www.childswork.com

REFERENCES

American School Counselor Association (ASCA). (2002). *Position statement: Group counseling.* Alexandria, VA: Author.

American School Counselor Association (ASCA). (2003). *The ASCA national model: A framework for school counseling programs.* Alexandria, VA: Author.

American School Counselor Association (ASCA). (2004). *Ethical standards for school counselors.* Alexandria, VA: Author

Arman, J. F. (2002). A brief group counseling model to increase resiliency of students with mild disabilities. *Journal of Humanistic Counseling, 41*(2),120–128.

Bauer, S. R., Sapp, M., & Johnson, D. (1999). Group counseling strategies for rural at-risk high school students. *High School Journal, 83,* 41–50.

Bradley, C. (2001). A counseling group for African-American adolescent males. *Professional School Counseling, 4,* 370–373.

Burnham, J. J., & Jackson, C. M. (2000). School counselor roles: Discrepancies between actual practice and existing models. *Professional School Counseling, 4,* 41–49.

Ciechalski, J. C., & Schmidt, M. W. (1995). The effects of social skills training on students with exceptionalities. *Elementary School Guidance & Counseling, 29,* 217–222.

Cook, J. B., & Kaffenberger, C. J. (2003). Solution shop: A solution-focused counseling and study skills program for middle school. *Professional School Counseling, 7,* 116–123.

Davis, T. E. (1997). Telling life stories and creating lifebooks: A counseling technique for fostering resilience in children. *Dissertation Abstracts International, 58*(11A).

Davis, T. E. (2005). *Exploring school counseling: Professional practices & perspectives.* Boston: Houghton Mifflin/Lahaska Press.

DeLucia-Waack, J., & Gerrity, D. (2001). Effective group work for elementary school age children whose parents are divorcing. *Family Journal: Counseling and Therapy for Couples and Families, 9,* 273–284.

Gingerich, W. J., & Wabeke, T. (2001). A solution-focused approach to mental health intervention in school settings. *Children & Schools, 23*(1), 33–47.

Greenberg, K. R. (2003). *Group counseling in K-12 schools: A handbook for school counselors.* Boston: Allyn & Bacon.

Greif, A. (1999). *Unscrewing yourself: One approach to anger management groupwork with adolescents.* Boulder, CO: Association for Experiential Education. (ERIC Document Reproduction Service No. ED 443607)

Kellner, M. H., & Bry, B. H. (1999). The effects of anger management groups in a day school for emotionally disturbed adolescents. *Adolescence, 34,* 645–651.

LaFountain, R. M., Garner, N. E., & Eliason, G. T. (1996). Solution-focused counseling groups: A key for school counselors. *School Counselor, 43*(4), 256–267.

Morganett, R. S. (1994). *Skills for living: Group counseling activities for elementary students.* Champaign, IL: Research Press.

Muller, L. E., & Hartman, J. (1998). Group counseling for sexual minority youth. *Professional School Counseling, 1*(3), 38–41.

Nelson, J. R., & Dykeman, C. (1996). The effects of a group counseling intervention on students with behavioral adjustment problems. *Elementary School Guidance & Counseling, 31,* 21–33.

Page, R. C., & Chandler, J. (1994). Effects of group counseling on ninth grade at-risk students. *Journal of Mental Health Counseling, 16*(3), 340–351.

Perrone, K. M., & Sedlacek, W. E. (2000). A comparison of group cohesiveness and client satisfaction in homogeneous and heterogeneous groups. *Journal for Specialists in Group Work, 25,* 243–251.

Prout, S. M., & Prout, H. T. (1998). A meta-analysis of school-based studies of counseling and psychotherapy: An update. *Journal of School Psychology, 36,* 121–136.

Rainey, L. M., Hensley, F. A., & Crutchfield, L. B. (1997). Implementation of support groups in elementary and middle school student assistance programs. *Professional School Counseling, 1,* 36–40.

Richardson, C. D., & Rosen, L. A. (1999). School-based interventions for children of divorce. *Professional School Counseling, 3,* 21–26.

Riddle, J., Bergin, J. J., & Douzenis, C. (1997). Effects of group counseling on the self-concept of children of alcoholics. *Elementary School Guidance and Counseling, 31,* 192–203.

Ripley, V. V., & Goodnough, G. E. (2001). Planning and implementing group counseling in high school. *Professional School Counseling, 5*(1), 62–65.

Sanders, D. R., & Riester, A. E. (1996). School-based counseling groups for children of divorce: Effects on the self-concepts of 5th grade children. *Journal of Child and Adolescent Group Therapy, 6,* 147–156.

Smead, R. (2000). *Skills for living: Group counseling activities for young adolescents* (vol. 2). Champaign, IL: Research Press.

Sonnenblick, M. D. (1997). The GALSS club: Promoting belonging among at-risk adolescent girls. *School Counselor, 44,* 243–245.

Stolberg, A. L., & Mahler, J. (1994). Enhancing treatment gains in a school-based intervention for children of divorce through skill training, parental involvement, and transfer procedures. *Journal of Counseling and Clinical Psychology, 62,* 147–156.

Stroh, H. R., & Sink, C. A. (2002). Applying APA's learner-centered principles to school-based group counseling. *Professional School Counseling, 6*(1), 71–78.

Utay, J. M., & Lampe, R. E. (1995). Use of a group counseling game to enhance social skills of children with learning disabilities. *Journal for Specialists in Group Work, 20,* 114–120.

Walker, E., & Waterman, J. (2001). *Helping at-risk students: A group counseling approach for grades 6-9.* New York: Guilford Press.

Webb, L. D., & Myrick, R. D. (2003). A group counseling intervention for children with attention deficit hyperactivity disorder. *Professional School Counseling, 7,* 108–115.

Whiston, S. C., & Sexton, T. L. (1998). A review of school counseling outcome research: Implications for practice. *Journal of Counseling and Development, 76,* 412–426.

Zinck, K., & Littrell, J. M. (2000). Action research shows group counseling effective with at-risk adolescent girls. *Professional School Counseling, 4,* 50–59.

Groups in Mental Health Settings

Mark D. Stauffer, Dale Elizabeth Pehrsson, and Cynthia A. Briggs

66 ental health settings" is a catch-all phrase encompassing an array of environments. Mental health can be divided into two broad sectors: public and private. In the public sector, city, county, state, and federal agencies provide services from public monetary funding. In the United States, public payers provide for more than half of mental health spending (e.g., Medicaid, Medicare; U.S. Department of Health and Human Services [USDHHS], 1999). Private institutions generally are nongovernmental for-profit or not-for-profit agencies.

Another framework (USDHHS, 1999) places mental health settings into four sectors:

1. The *mental health* sector, with its sole purpose to provide mental health services
2. The *general medical and primary care sector*, which offers a wide range of health-related services that include mental health
3. The *human services sector*, which consists of social welfare settings (e.g., educational, religious, charitable groups, and criminal justice)
4. The voluntary support network, which refers to self-help and support networks, groups, and organizations

In all, group counseling may occur in psychiatric hospitals, general hospitals with psychiatric units, outpatient clinics, residential treatment facilities, day treatment centers, drug rehabilitation programs, group homes, nonprofit community-based agencies, and private practice settings.

THE MENTAL HEALTH SYSTEM: THEN AND NOW

The delivery of mental health services in the United States shifted in the 1960s with evolving ideas related to mental health and the burgeoning of psychopharmacology. This change brought about the Community Mental Health Centers (CMHC) Act of 1963, which called for community-based mental health services (Borenstein, 2001). Community mental health services were expected to replace the prevailing system, which relied upon large state institutions whose treatment and "warehousing" of patients came under scrutiny.

After enactment of the CMHC law, many people diagnosed with chronic mental illness were released from these institutions with the idea that community mental health centers would provide services to individuals in their own communities. For psychiatric care, patients would be transferred from state to regional hospitals and receive both state and federal funding. Over decades, this eventually meant the closure of 115 of 350 long-term mental health hospitals (Barrett, Greene, & Mariani, 2004).

Financial funding from sources such as Medicaid, Medicare, and Social Security was anticipated to subsidize community mental health services, but from the beginning, community-based service providers have been drastically under-funded (Borenstein, 2001). What emerged was a patchwork of services that is often criticized for lacking a unified set of guiding principles. Currently, in most states, community health services are spread thin and are in fluctuation.

The U.S. Department of Health and Human Services (1999) stated that:

> While this hybrid system serves a range of functions for many people, it has not successfully addressed the problem that people with the most complex needs and the fewest financial resources often find it difficult to use. (Ch. 2, p. 1)

For example, all too often, responsibility for care of chronic mental illness has been transferred from the mental health agencies to institutions in criminal penitentiary systems. The number of mentally ill people in U.S. jails and prisons grew to 283,000 in 1999 as the number of patients in state and county mental hospitals declined from 600,000 in 1950 to 72,000 in 1994 (Borenstein, 2001, p.1).

The World Health Organization (WHO; 2004) noted that "cost-effective treatments exist for most disorders and, if correctly applied, could enable most of those affected to become functioning members of society" (p. 1). Barrett et al. (2004) commented, "To be blunt, Americans are living with first-rate medicine and a third-rate health care system" (p. 1). Often, the ideal of group counseling and psychotherapy butts against market forces and the shortfalls of our mental health care system. Our health system leaves nearly 44 million people without medical and mental health coverage (Barrett et al., 2004). There are "(1) pressures to maintain high levels of consumer satisfaction, (2) provide rapid stabilization of functioning and effective relapse prevention interventions, and (3) include all patients in active treatment" (Chambliss & Oxman, 2003, p. 3).

In addition, public and private sector agencies are being pressured to cut costs, sometimes by limiting services rather than denying coverage. Therefore, in many sectors, the desirability of group counseling has increased with the argument that group modalities should be emphasized when they are as effective as individual modalities because they are less expensive. Short-term and brief modalities of group therapy also have been advocated because of financial concerns. Group therapist expert Irvin Yalom offered these words of caution related to short-term therapy as a means of cutting costs:

> It all sounds absolutely wonderful except that it is not in touch with reality. The kinds of issues that we deal with are issues that people are struggling with for 10 or 20 years and change happens slowly. Psychotherapy is a form of education and education is not something that can be crammed into a course. I think the idea that you have to do therapy in some mechanistic way following some sort of manual is exactly the opposite of what you actually want to do—which is to form an authentic relationship, let the relationship unfold, and as the patient begins to develop trust in this relationship, change will occur simultaneously to that. There are certain things that can't be rushed. (in Duffrene, 2004)

Considering the limited resources, a movement toward funding only "evidenced-based" mental health practices is gaining ground (Barrett et al., 2004; Geddes, Reynolds, Streiner, & Szatmari, 1997). Thus, some theoretical orientations and counseling practices that are more difficult to research are being deemphasized. Despite existing problems, this de facto system of mental health services allows for the inclusion of preventive and alternative therapies and a focus on well-being. In addition, it creates many new venues for individual and group counseling. Group counseling and therapy has expanded and has taken many new forms.

The idealized group experience, group leadership, and group dynamic is quite different from the common experience of group workers. For example, in a common ideal of group counseling, the group meets on a regular basis at a specific time with all members present—ideally 4 to 10 persons. In reality, group counselors in mental health settings regularly adjust to dropouts, latecomers, and absentees—not to mention attracting enough members to start a group or to keep a group viable. Concerns and challenges such as these need not hinder the benefits of group counseling, though. As one group counselor commented, "These 'less than perfect' group meetings can also bring new possibilities" (Rose, 2004, p. 42).

When dealing with clients who have severe disorders, counselors attempt to maintain or improve a baseline of mental health. Significant distress and impairment in functioning (e.g., social, physical, and occupational) are the most basic markers of disorders (American Psychiatric Association [APA], 2000). Because of fiscal constraints, community mental health centers and psychiatric hospitals see rapid turnover and admit fewer patients compared to the past, which results in attending to only the most severe cases. For this reason, inpatient groups have become more heterogeneous and rarely consist of individuals who all share the same disorder. High turnover means that groups are in constant fluctuation, and this poses challenges for group leaders, who must be flexible, innovative, and creative. A further byproduct of shrinking inpatient services is that outpatient groups consist of clients with more severe clinical features (Chambliss & Oxman, 2003).

Outpatient groups often are geared toward alleviating specific mental health problems. Abuse, anxiety, depression, divorce, substance abuse, pain relief for cancer, or anorexia may be the focus of a group. Here, a challenge is that those with one clinical diagnosis are more likely to have co-occurring disorders than their nonclinical counterparts (D.A.T.A, 2004). For example, those diagnosed with schizophrenia tend to have relatively high rates of substance abuse disorders. Furthermore, dual-diagnosis clients often experience less optimal outcomes than their single-diagnosis counterparts (Tsuang & Fong, 2004).

Though clients tend to seek counseling when problems arise, not all group counseling is focused on pathology. Groups also give attention to well-being, with themes such as improving relationships, parenting, assertiveness, and skill building. Whatever the group format, the positive elements of strength and interpersonal resources can be emphasized.

Multicultural counseling and research in group work is beginning to inform the counseling profession (see chapter 8). Recognizing the changing demographics and the diversity of the populations that counselors serve, movement in the field is now informally, and often formally (e.g., ACA *Code of Ethics*), requiring group workers to be culturally competent.

Some populations greatly benefit from specific types of groups. For example, adolescent clients may have an affinity for member-directed group work because of the importance of peer affiliation at that developmental level (Aronson, 2004). Other individuals may not benefit from group experience during a certain time. It is safe to say that every group is right for some and not for all. When screening, however, the group facilitator is more likely to be involved in a process of deselecting rather than selecting group participants. Group composition, screening, and counseling practices should factor-in the diversity of the group and the needs of the individual.

Support groups are another common intervention. These groups are often member-centered and are facilitated by a trained group leader or counselor. Alongside support groups, self-help groups are generally operated by their members and may be organized and sponsored by a mental health professional or agency. Kessler, Mickelson, and Zhoa (1997) estimated that 10 million Americans attend self-help groups each year and found that one third of support groups were substance-related. Another study found that many professionals view self-help groups in negative and unsupportive ways (Salzer, Rappaport, & Segre, 2001), even though these groups potentially expand the resources available to persons in need and can have a supportive effect to counseling. Because professional and self-help groups differ in their operation and theoretical underpinnings, beginning counselors might gain from studying these differences and visiting some of the groups, to develop a better understanding of this resource base.

Group work in mental health settings also includes work with couples and families. Some of the first to benefit from multiple-family groups were families with schizophrenic members (Lurie & Harold, 1967). Multiple-family groups have come to be regarded as a viable form of group counseling (Meezan & O'Keefe, 1998; O'Shea & Phelps, 1985; Thorngren & Kleist, 2002). These groups tackle a variety of issues such as parenting, substance-abusing teens, family enrichment, and adjustment after divorce. Couples groups also can be valuable. They often focus on relationship enrichment, marital discord, divorce adjustment, and parenting in blended families. With changing family systems and mounting pressures on the modern family, group counseling can be an effective resource in a community.

This chapter offers a foundational introduction to the vast scope of groups as they are applied in mental health settings. To capture some of the more specific details of group planning and implementation, we present examples of three outpatient groups: (a) a women's group composed of members working with anxiety and depression, (b) a couples-oriented group for building healthy relationships, and (c) a group for women battling the eating disorder of bulimia nervosa.

A GROUP FOR ADULT WOMEN LIVING WITH DEPRESSION AND ANXIETY

A group of women sat waiting for the first session of an anxiety and depression group to begin.

Angie looked at her fingers guiltily. Despite her best efforts, she had bitten down to the quick of her exposed and raw nailbeds. She did feel good, though, about keeping her appointment for the "class to help me with my nerves."

Across the waiting room, Susan leaned against a wall, restless and fidgeting nervously. Thoughts raced through her mind as she wondered, "How has life come to this?"

As Kat hunched in a chair near the exit, her stomach churned with hunger. She had virtually stopped eating a month ago. What little she did eat she vomited. Kat read books and watched television many hours a day to stop worrying about everything. She often drank wine to forget and to sleep.

Tricia sat in a corner chair wracked with guilt, believing she was failing her struggling family. "This is a waste of time and money," she thought, while considering her family needs. Yet she lacked the energy to move. She felt exhausted all the time.

Keely sat in a corner opposite Tricia with reddened eyes, trying to hold back tears. She cried easily and too often. Life overwhelmed her. She no longer felt connected to friends and family. Although her involvement in her church had been substantial and important to her, more recently she felt isolated and detached from everyone and everything.

Each of these women was entering counseling with different lived experiences and backgrounds, though they shared the commonality of depression and anxiety. They all suffered from the day-to-day fallout of living with severe disorders. For some of these women, medication helped somewhat, yet group counseling became attractive when their symptoms persisted and also because medical practitioners suggested that they participate in a group.

Conceptual Framework

Mental health agencies develop groups and treatment interventions to deal efficiently with specific disorders and issues (WHO, 2001). It may be most appropriate to compose groups of similar or "like clients" when clients are likely to do better with those who have similar life and treatment experiences (MacKenzie, 1990). Thus, benefits accrue to running a "women only" group. Women communicate, deal with stress, react to therapy, and have ways of being and knowing that differ from the ways of men (Acierno, Kilpatrick, Resnick, Saunders, & Best, 1999). Women may be able to speak more freely without mixed-gender group dynamics, which may perpetuate entrenched and oppressive behaviors (Ivey, Pedersen, & Ivey, 2001). In short, common bonds lend support to the healing and learning.

Yalom (1995) suggested that group process enhances the transfer of new behavior to real life by providing a microcosm for becoming and transforming oneself. Though the group is homogeneous as it relates to gender and shared pathology, a heterogeneous mix is preferred in terms of age, life experiences, issues, and cultures, because it provides opportunities for clients to learn and grow from one another's experiences. Clients' issues differ because of their varying backgrounds, which can be a source of strength to others. But commonalities, too, may be explored in group. For example, no matter what the ethnicity of a client, the Ameri-centric culture is one of high demands and high stress. In any case, group leaders should take care that the differences within the group do not impede group cohesion.

Clinicians who work with women who have anxiety and depression should be well informed about women's issues, especially as these relate to clients' culture, family, and profession. Again, the needs of women are unique and often differ from those of men (USDHHS Report, 2004). In examining how depression relates to gender, research indicates that women are particularly vulnerable to depression. An estimated 1 in 7 women will suffer from depression during her lifetime (National Alliance of Mental Illness [NAMI], 2004). In terms of anxiety, depression, and suicide, women are three times more likely than their male counterparts to engage in nonfatal suicidal behavior (suicidal gestures or overtures with no or low intention to inflict damage). For these reasons, learning healthy coping strategies is essential (Canetto, 1997). The National Institute on Mental Health (NIMH) Web site (www.nimh.nih.gov) contains valuable current information related to the impact of biological, reproductive, genetic, and psychosocial factors of women's depression.

Women develop depression as a reaction to stressful events at a rate three times higher than their male counterparts (Maciejewski, Prigerson, & Mazure, 2001). Early sexual and physical abuse adds to the risk, as does domestic violence. The statistics for women who have been raped, abused, or assaulted in the U.S. culture are staggering (see NAMI, 2004; NIMH, 1999). Many women live much of their lives in fear, a major stressor that impacts their wellness and depression rates. Depression sometimes is accompanied by somatization, weight changes, anger, irritability, and anxiety. When depression is untreated, women are at risk for health complications and their careers may suffer (NIMH, 1999). Issues of shame, grief, and loss, often related to trauma, also must be discussed in a sheltered yet structured setting. A safe, supportive environment is essential for the group to process experiences and develop effective coping strategies (Yalom, 1995).

According to NIMH (1999), the treatment of choice for depression is a combination of medication and psychotherapy. Synthesized approaches combining medication/medical management and psychodynamic and cognitive behavioral interventions are effective. Therefore, outpatient group work focusing on management and on preventing the exacerbation of symptoms is well suited to group counseling in mental health settings.

Purpose of the Group

An anxiety and depression group requires a master treatment plan outlining specific goals, objectives, and measurable outcome criteria. This group is designed to help clients

- reduce negative symptoms and live successfully;
- cope with specific symptoms related to anxiety and depression;
- identify and develop support systems and processes;
- make behavioral, cognitive, and emotional adjustments that decrease the intensity of symptoms; and
- feel supported by healthy communication among people who share common but also unique lived experiences.

Finally, the group creates a therapeutic opportunity in the form of a supportive microcosm for sharing concerns, information, support, and behavioral interventions.

Group Goals

Goals for dealing with depression and anxiety revolve around symptom prevention, management, and alleviation. The following goals can be met by providing psychoeducation and supportive learning experiences within the context of a group.

1. *Self-monitoring*: Clients can learn to self-monitor signs and symptoms of depression and anxiety and can learn and reinforce effective re-patterning of less functional behavior.
2. *Decreasing negative thinking*: Critical to the process is to replace catastrophic and nonproductive thinking and emotions related to cognitions with positive and realistic thoughts.

3. *Self-care*: Clients learn and practice relaxation techniques, anxiety-reduction practices, how to recognize oppressive environments, and how to manage stress.

4. *Support*: Through the group process and trust, these women get a chance to be heard in a way that might not have occurred in their lives and within their social environments.

5. *Emotional catharsis*: In the group, clients have the opportunity to express deep and complex emotions in a safe environment.

6. *Normalization*: Hearing the stories of trauma, stress, depression, and anxiety from others has a normalizing and leveling effect. Group members begin to see that they are not so odd or different from others and that many others are dealing with similar issues.

7. *Communication*: The group offers an opportunity for clients to practice positive and assertive communication, which is directly applicable to their getting what they need in the outside world.

Pre-Group Screening and Orientation

Although clients at first may appear to have the same diagnosis and presenting symptoms, many confounding variables and cultural influences can impact the group's process. Clinicians screen clients to discover what is not apparent in case paperwork. The evaluation and screening of clients for possible inclusion in the group should be systematic. This is particularly germane when the group is time-limited and topic-specific.

Screening for women's groups has important implications for planning treatment, making intervention choices, and following up. For example, an important clinical issue that often surfaces through interview is a client's earlier traumatic experience, such as physical or sexual abuse. This is especially relevant when dealing with women in therapeutic settings because depression and anxiety often develop in the aftermath of abusive and other traumatic experiences (Acierno et al., 1999; Canetto, 1997; NAMI, 2004).

Screening for a group of this nature should evaluate client fitted-ness and willingness to engage in self-discovery, trust building, and sharing with others. Participants should demonstrate a commitment to the process and agree to respect the confidentiality of group members. Clients have to be functional enough to participate as active members who are willing to support, communicate, and cooperate with group members to meet group, individual, agency, and therapist goals.

Although diagnostic, behavioral, and therapeutic issues occur on a continuum, these issues should not vary so much that they do not allow clients to establish a connectedness with one another. Depending on the quantity and complexity of the goals, the individual screenings should assess the applicants' historical, medical, and social–cultural backgrounds and individual goals and readiness for this group. The screening should include an orientation to the group process, therapeutic expectations, prospective risks, and commitments. When working in conjunction with medical personnel, confidentiality and related parameters are imperative. Coordinating the treatment information and communications can become more challenging when multiple practitioners are providing care (see Salvendy, 1993, for more information on group selection and orientation).

Group membership varies, but generally a group composite should total between five and eight members. Sessions should last 90–120 minutes and be held weekly for 8 to 12 weeks, to allow for development, growth, and synthesis of new information and behaviors.

Potential Challenges, Restrictions, and Ethical Considerations

A group takes on its own life. Some events are foreseeable and some are surprising. Clients who are in treatment for depression and anxiety are at risk for escalation of symptoms culminating in crisis events including anxiety–panic attacks and suicidality. These potential risks invariably accompany women's groups dealing with depression. The group process can be stressful for some, with the associated potential for dysfunctional behavior. Counselors should have systems in place to reduce these elements of risk.

Group leaders should be mindful of the barriers that can restrict successful group interventions, including the client's ability to be financially, emotionally, and physically present for the group. The needs of members as they relate to childcare must be considered. The leader can assist clients in planning for childcare and timing the sessions to accommodate group members whenever possible.

Group Sessions by Stages

The possible course of a women's depression and anxiety outpatient group is presented here. The progression follows the definitive, personal involvement, group involvement, and enhancement and closure stages of group work proposed by Capuzzi and Gross in chapter 2.

Definitive Stage

In the beginning stage of group therapy, the members often have questions about what is going to happen in this group and how they will fit in. This is the stage when the "getting to know you" dynamics take place and parameters of the process are outlined. Establishing basic and solid trust, clarifying, and engaging of self and with others are essential at this early stage. The members begin to accept their responsibility in the group process, and self-awareness begins to emerge. The members start to lose the sense of loneliness and isolation that often accompanies depression and anxiety. This is the time when the group members discuss and agree upon the goals of the group.

This stage is particularly challenging for individuals who live with anxiety and depressive symptoms. Establishing clear guidelines and distributing informational packets can ease the anxiety of these clients when they are exposed to new and often threatening situations. Group counselors should be particularly mindful that the woman may be experiencing enormous stress and vulnerability in entering a group counseling process, and that these symptoms may intensify. The leader may also want to allow for a follow-up telephone conversation or electronic contacts such as email, as the client's ability to "hear" may be impeded.

Personal Involvement Stage

At the personal involvement stage, group processes are mobilized at a more in-depth level. The initial trust and sharing becomes richer as the group members get to know one another in a way they may not have experienced before in their lives. This may involve corrective emotional experiences that can be very healing.

The group begins to model and provide feedback, and the direction moves away from the leader, who assumes more of a facilitative role. During this stage, the sharing of common experiences related to group members' lives and the impact of their disorders is powerful.

Group Involvement Stage

Once alliance and trust have been established and the group members feel valued and heard, they begin to mobilize resources and look toward solutions. They become unstuck as they engage and learn from one another. The group members pull each other forward. They, along with the leader, examine the patterns of behavior and dysfunction that impede healthy living. They challenge one another in respectful ways.

This stage is uncomfortable for some, but not too threatening in a safe and supportive environment. Family, cultural, career, and social systems are explored in regard to their influence on the disorder and the symptoms. The group members also are examining these factors in terms of the support they can bring to bear. They address grief, loss, hope, and the reality and conditions of their lives.

Enhancement and Closure Stage

During the enhancement and closure stage, group members ready themselves for saying good-bye. Bargaining to continue the group is an issue that frequently emerges during the latter stages of group work. In preparing for termination, the group and the therapist deal with issues of closure, continuance of support, referral, and development of other resources. The group manages the anxiety that often is present when the group nears its end. Moreover, termination is an issue that does not begin in the late stages of therapy. Prepared therapists deal with these issues early on, instituting them in the screening process by disclosing the risks and expectations of the group process.

Relationships end, but the leader's modeling of healthy termination and closure strategies can have a lifelong impact on members' functioning, setting boundaries, and engaging in healthy relationships. It is essential for the leader to assist them in fostering healthy connections, developing resources, and gaining support practices that will give them balance and avoid additional stress.

Strategies to Evaluate the Group

The evaluation is determined by the nature and goals of the group. Depression and anxiety groups in an outpatient setting are diagnosis-specific, well-defined, time-limited, short-term, and goal-focused. Evaluation of the group should include issues such as clients' satisfaction, the minimizing of dysfunctional symptomology, and the learning of positive behaviors and coping strategies. This information can be gathered in several ways—from clinical data indicating therapeutic improvement, counselor and client surveys, self-reports, and pre- and posttreatment questionnaires and evaluations. These measures yield information about the integration of client gains in lifestyle.

Follow-Up and Referral

Because women have unique issues and deal with life in complex ways, prevention and ongoing support related to depression and anxiety must be woven into the termination plans. Therapists must have a working knowledge of community issues, and wise group leaders will cultivate women's resources and community contacts and referrals to help clients deal with the pressures of society, specifically as these pressures relate to gender. Access to resources is critical to their sustained recovery.

In addition, the therapist must understand the individual needs of clients from social, cultural, and familial perspectives. No two women are the same, though some overlying issues have an impact on all women. How each woman deals with the complexities of her life varies, just as the effects of oppression and anxiety vary.

Medical and wellness referrals should be part of the follow-up, because women have a biological and physical propensity for recurring bouts of depression. Support groups and possible career development and education are other possible components to be woven into the referral process.

It is useful for group leaders to incorporate follow-up timetables with clients in planning long-term strategies for their wellness. Finally, the group counselor should examine with these women cyclical trends and issues such as employment, reproduction, menopausal issues, and care of elderly family members.

A HEALTHY RELATIONSHIPS GROUP

Purpose

A vital component of mental health and development rests in relatedness to others (Cusinato & L'Abate, 2003; Vygotsky, 1978; Waring, Chamberlaine, Carver, Stalker, & Schaefer, 1995). A group enhances what is already natural to humans—relationships. Notwithstanding cultural differences, human life is wrapped in relationships. We are interdependent even when we are unaware of this need and lack intentionality in our ties to others. Like an iceberg in which 90% of the mass is under water, the vast majority of our connections go unnoticed, below the surface of ordinary consciousness.

This example centers on the specific relationship between couples. The high divorce rates are cited as a consequence of living in our high-paced, modern society. At some point—maybe it's the 100th verbal battle, or another day living under the same roof without talking, or some indefinable barrier stifling intimacy—couples look to counseling for solutions. The group offers one venue for couples searching for answers, and group counselors work under the assumption that couples can learn to cultivate healthier relationships.

The purpose of a relationship-enrichment group is to promote satisfying relationships and prevent problems in the future. A primary expected outcome is increased intimacy and relational satisfaction. Participation is expected to increase couples' awareness of the essential components of the relationship and to increase the skill base that is vital to maintaining healthy relationships. The group also has a role as a support resource.

Conceptual Framework

Research suggests that it is not the quantity but the quality of relationships that encourages well-being and satisfaction with life. The presence of just one confidant may be more important than a number of people in a person's social network (Seligman, 1999). This is not to lessen the impact of environment. Many relational problems arise because the current social environment lacks opportunities for creating close ties. Moreover, environment affects the systems that support healthy relationships. For example, poverty and the lack of associated community resources that are vital to mental health (e.g., other families, churches, community agencies) often affect couples and families negatively (Browning, 2002; Dodge, Pettit, & Bates, 1994; McLeod & Shanahan, 1993).

At the core of helping is relationship (Bordin, 1994; Egan, 2001; Rogers, 1957). The group model presented here is intended to enhance the quality of relationships by examining adaptive processes and, to a lesser extent, life events and social/cultural influences, through the use of a genogram. The proposed psychoeducation group brings awareness and effort to the relationship process and is based on a therapeutic alliance, which is believed to be a significant extratherapeutic factor in individual and group counseling alike (Glueckauf et al., 2002).

Relationship-enrichment groups have been carried out under a wide range of theoretical modalities and have been shown to improve relationships. In a literature review of research on relationship-enrichment education groups, Fagan, Patterson, and Rector (2002) asserted that relationship education produces significant outcomes. The following are emphasized in groups suggesting the influence of systemic and cognitive–behavioral orientations:

- Self-regulation
- Awareness of intimacy and other vital relationship components
- Conflict resolution
- Problem solving
- Improving communication skills
- Increasing positive-to-negative ratios of interaction
- Engaging in pleasant activities
- Exploring family context through genograms

First- and Second-Order Change

First-order change occurs when a specific problem is settled (e.g., making up after a specific verbal confrontation). Second-order change occurs when the way the system operates is changed (Gladding, 1998); for example, the fighting couple adopts and integrates a new way to communicate.

Self-Regulation

Even when working on skill development, the goal is to produce second-order change, and conducting a relationship-enrichment group within a framework of self-regulation may produce the most lasting results (see Halford, Wilson, Lizzio, & Moore, 2002). For example, teaching self-regulation along with communication techniques can help participants learn to self-regulate around issues of communication in the future. Self-regulation is a self-directed process guiding behaviors, cognitions, and emotions toward goal attainment (Zimmerman, 2002). Self-regulation means that members are helped to learn independently so they are better able to personally manage problems in the future. Zimmerman listed three general phases of self-regulation:

1. Forethought phase
2. Performance phase
3. Self-reflection phase

Halford, Sanders, and Behrens (1994) proposed that self-regulation of relationship has four phases:

1. Self-appraisal
2. Self-directed goal setting
3. Self-implementation of change
4. Self-evaluation

As with the therapeutic alliance, goals play a vital part in self-regulation:

> Effective goal setting requires that people set a long-term goal, break it into short-term, attainable sub-goals, monitor progress and assess capabilities, adjust the strategy and goal as needed, and set a new goal when the present one is attained. (Schunk, 2001)

Intimacy

Another important concept emphasized in this type of group is intimacy, a multidimensional aspect of relationship. Enhancing intimacy in romantic and platonic relationships has a positive effect on physical and mental well-being and on overall satisfaction with the relationship (Gulledge, Gulledge, & Stahmann, 2003; Prager, 1995). Various components of intimacy have been discussed in the research literature (Dorian & Cordova, 2004; Hatfield & Rapson, 1993; Hook, Gerstein, Detterich, & Gridley, 2003):

- Closeness
- The ability to self-disclose without punishment

- Connectedness
- Self- and other-validation
- Physical affection
- Bonding

Individuals experience intimacy differently. Further, some studies suggest gender differences in the way intimacy is experienced (Hook et al., 2003). The group outlined here builds on strengths found in different experiences of intimacy and allows participants to assess, explore, share, and learn from others.

With many relationships, fighting and distressful behaviors are the impetus for involvement in counseling, because discord and distress have many negative consequences. Research by Gottman and Levenson (2000) suggested that the presence of negative reciprocity and negative affect during conflict correlates with early divorce.

Time-Outs and Repair Attempts

Time-outs and *repair attempts* are used in teaching, personalizing, and having members practice how to disrupt negative interaction.

1. *Time-outs.* Even though time-outs are best known as a behavioral technique used with children, adults can learn to stop unwanted behavior by self-imposing a break, self-soothing, and returning with an attitude conducive to teamwork. This technique should be used in a highly structured manner and is best when developed by participants for personal fit.
2. *Repair attempts* (Gottman, 1999; Tabares, Driver, & Gottman, 2004). Repair attempts are communication efforts to stop negative reciprocity by emphasizing teamwork, compromise, and personal responsibility in the middle of an argument. For example, one partner may attempt repair by saying, "I see that I'm responsible for some of the problem," or "We've worked through problems like this before, so let's start over and tackle this together." As a resource, Gottman (1999) created a repair checklist that is useful for the group's exercise.

Communication and Problem Solving

Couples intuitively believe that communication and problem solving are central to a good relationship (Halford, 2001; Sullivan & Anderson, 2002). In accord with these intuitions, research suggests that effective communication is a marker of a healthy relationship (Gottman, 1994; Weiss & Heyman, 1997). Communication exercises teach active listening and dialogue that emphasizes reflection, empathy, warmth, and other skills including summarization and concreteness.

Problem solving is most effective when the communication is constructive rather than defense-provoking (Floyd, 2004). Effective problem solving occurs in the presence of hearing and understanding, teamwork, brainstorming, opening possibilities, and collaboration.

Accentuating the Positive

Even though decreasing negative affect and reciprocity is one change agent, many counselor interventions focus on the negative aspects of relationship (see Rugel, 1997) at the expense of more strength-based interventions. Increasing positive affect outside of conflictual contexts is just as important as stopping harmful behaviors in making lasting changes for partners (Driver & Gottman, 2004; Gottman, 1999).

Assessing and implementing strategies for positive connection is part of the group process. Learning and acting on ways people feel loved and engaging partners in planning pleasant activities are two fundamental ways to achieve this. One woman took this principle to heart and had a favorite meal delivered to her husband during his lunch break. It was the talk of his crew, and he felt special—which resulted in some associated and unexpected shifts in the counseling group. Shifting the emphasis from problems to positive interactions and intimate encounters fosters revitalized relationships and educates participants on the importance of proactive relationship building (Fredrickson, 2001).

Group Goals

The goals of this couples group are

1. to practice and integrate communications skills including reflective listening and empathy;
2. to learn more about the building blocks of relationship, the reality of relationship, and intimacy as an ongoing process requiring effort;
3. to practice setting aside time weekly for pleasant and rewarding activities;
4. to increase self-confidence and efficacy in relationship; and
5. to practice and integrate useful skills such as time-outs and problem-solving techniques.

Pre-Group Screening and Orientation to the Group

During the orientation with participants prior to group participation, issues of professional disclosure, confidentiality, expectations, client rights and responsibilities, counselor responsibilities, and agency concerns related to the group are discussed (Association of Specialists in Group Work [ASGW], 1998). These issues from the initial orientation are repeated at the first session of the group.

A relationship-enrichment group is designed for adults of diverse backgrounds, skills, and abilities. Referrals might come from an agency that is already providing counseling services to couples. In these cases, the group leader should obtain a release of information and contact these service providers to make sure that group participation is in the client's best interests. The costs to the couple in time and money to participate in both group and couples counseling should be considered.

If domestic violence is a concern, the group leader should consider exclusion and referral. The pre-screening should probe for legal issues involved in a couple's efforts to find counseling, as couples group work may be effective only after counseling and group work dealing specifically with domestic violence has been seriously engaged. Also, the group leader should consider excluding couples who have moderate to severe problems related to substance disorders if concurrent treatment is not in progress.

Couples groups can range from 10 to 20 participants. Groups of this size will be effective as long as assistants are added as needed to help with break-off groups and activities.

Possible Challenges, Limitations, and Ethical Considerations

A basic challenge of the group is to promote an idea of relationships that addresses the needs and realities of everyone who is participating so the members can relate to the various lived experiences within the group. This may require the consistent use of reframing. This educational component validates the many differences in the range of possible relationships

Therapeutic leverage and participants' motivation may be additional considerations in a larger group, in which less time is spent on an individual and dyad level. One study (Simons & Harris, 1997) elicited some of the reasons that 640 respondents chose not to attend premarital education:

- Marital privacy
- Lack of interest
- Lack of relationship problems
- No need for counseling
- Did not want to discuss personal issues

These same items may be present as challenges in the couples group.

In a psychoeducational couples group, the level of personal and intimate sharing is monitored for levels of self-disclosure because the size and context of the group may not be as supportive as therapeutic groups are. Sometimes this creates an environment in which couples can remain on the surface of current problems. Also, the larger groups may not afford as much attention to couples and individuals as smaller groups or couples therapy could. The amount of time given to this group (8 to 10 weeks) is only a booster to the longer process of relationship enrichment.

Breakups sometimes occur during the course of the group, and this challenges the individuals who are breaking up to be brave and the group to be supportive of these members whether they choose to stay or to leave. In a break-up situation, the group leader should consider the ramifications of both partners' staying in the group. The leader would be wise, going into the group, to have a clearly stated policy related to relationship endings.

Finally, in an effort to maintain a confidential space, group participants should be asked not to get together outside of the group and discuss the group but, instead, to wait until after the last session. The leader must inform members about the limitations to confidentiality in groups, and especially that a counselor cannot enforce confidential communication by group members.

Group Sessions by Stages

The possible course of a couples group is presented here. The progression follows the definitive, personal involvement, group involvement, and enhancement and closure stages of group work proposed by Capuzzi and Gross in chapter 2.

Definitive Stage

Purpose: To make introductions and set the ground rules for the group, including a review of clients' rights and responsibilities. The leader discusses safe sharing, which may take the form of icebreakers related to healthy relationships. The leader presents an overview of some of the most important information so the group members can set goals jointly with the group leader.

Activities: The leader encourages participants' sharing what they believe are the qualities and components of a healthy relationship. The leader comments on societal myths about relationships (e.g., heterosexual marriage is the most important type of relationship, or happy relationships are always exciting).

Personal Involvement Stage

Purpose: To begin the assessment of current relationships and start to formulate goals. It also is important to expand and reframe the meanings of relationship, discuss barriers to relationship, and enhance member rapport through sharing. This is a time to begin creating personalized homework.

Activities: A primary goal at this stage is to expand the notion and meaning of relationship, to create leverage for personal motivation. Highlights might be the following:

1. *Reframing relationship as teamwork* is essential, to redirect the propensity of individuals to point to their partners as the source of the relationship problems.
2. *Phases of relationship* must be understood so participants know there are ebbs and flows and what to expect and gain from different phases of intimacy.
3. The leader can *expand the meaning of relationship* to encompass spiritual, physical, emotional, relational, and other aspects of oneself.
4. Emphasizing that *little things count* in a relationship helps create space for incorporating strategies to meet newly forming goals.
5. *Personal responsibility* is highlighted, followed by a discussion of how individuals may look with magical eyes at relationships to solve personal problems, to fill a sense of emptiness, to provide care that one should give to oneself, to obtain a sense of self-worth, or to gain external validation.
6. The importance of *self-regulation* is discussed as an important learning tool. This includes self-appraisal, self-directed goal setting, self-implementation of change, and self-evaluation (Halford et al., 1994).

Group Involvement Stage

Purpose: To teach, over several sessions, the concept of self-efficacy in relationship. The group involvement stage also should continue to build on skills and enhance participants' motivation and understanding through involvement. This should advance a supportive effect.

Activities: At the beginning of each group, the group leader leads a discussion of the successes and roadblocks to integrating the material and skills learned in the group and introduces new skill-building techniques and reviews those covered previously. The leader incorporates assessment tools and examines personal strategies and their implementation. As participants practice the time-outs, repair attempts, communication exercises, and other self-created enrichment techniques, the leader provides a framework for different ways to evaluate their attempts to improve their relationships.

Enhancement and Closure Stage

Purpose: To provide an overview and initiate closure by emphasizing the important gains the group has made and real steps that the participants have made in improving their relationships. The leader builds in time to discuss other resources and future possibilities for continued work in the realm of relationship.

Activities: The participants evaluate the usefulness of techniques and goals they have implemented over the duration of the group. Their individual sharing about what they have gotten out of the group is followed by eliciting some of their ideas for post-group growth and continued pursuit of relationship enrichment. Finally, a sharing of sentiments for and about the group precedes the leader's awarding a certificate of accomplishment to each participant for completing this group.

Strategies to Evaluate the Group

Self-evaluation has been a component of this group. If handled appropriately and in an ethical manner, psychological measures can be administered and introduced into the group process to bring awareness and provide for such evaluation. Moreover, a group leader may want to evaluate the effectiveness of any group format that is used more than once or on a continual basis. There are several scales that can help a group leader evaluate the effectiveness of a relationship-enhancement group. One example is the Dyadic Adjustment Scale (DAS), which has four subscales: Dyadic Consensus, Dyadic Satisfaction, Dyadic Cohesion, and Affectional Expressions (see Sabourin, Valois, & Lussier, 2005; Spanier, 1976). Other measures that may be helpful are Hendrick's (1988) Relationship Assessment Scale and the Relationship Rating Form (Davis, 1987), which assesses seven global aspects of friend and romantic relationships (i.e. viability, intimacy, care, passion, satisfaction, commitment, and conflict/ambivalence).

Follow-Up and Referral

The group leader may want to encourage couples to take a further step toward healthy relationships by enrolling in a therapeutic group for couples. The leader may see a need to refer others to individual and couples counseling. The group leader can present options for continual growth by providing a variety of resources, including books for continued study and practice on issues covered in the group.

A SPECIALIZED GROUP FOR WOMEN WITH BULIMIA NERVOSA

Purpose

Over the past two decades, the rate of bulimia nervosa (BN) has increased dramatically (Valbak, 2001). Approximately 90% of BN occurs in women, and 5% of women overall meet the diagnostic criteria for the disease. As the long-term mortality rate for women with BN sits at 10%, we must increase our knowledge of effective treatment options (Sonnenberg & Chen, 2003).

Because clients with BN do not necessarily display significant weight loss, they often are harder to diagnose if they are not willing to talk about their binging and purging behaviors. Some physical signs of BN are dehydration from electrolyte imbalance (which can result in heart problems and death), inflammation of the esophagus, tooth and gum problems, and irregular bowel movements or constipation. Emotionally, clients with BN can suffer from depression, shame, guilt, low self-esteem, estrangement from family and friends, and perfectionism. These emotional factors also may be rooted in the causes of BN (see http://www.helpguide.org/mental/bulimia.htm).

Various treatment modalities are used with BN clients, though group treatment is preferred for several reasons (Gerlinghoff, Gross, & Backmund, 2003; Lenihan & Sanders, 1984):

1. In this age of managed care, long-term inpatient treatment for eating disorders has been shortened by as much as 85% (Wiseman, Sunday, Klapper, Klein, & Halmi, 2002). Long the preferred treatment modality, inpatient care is no longer a financially viable option for many clients with BN.
2. The demand for resources addressing treatment for BN is high, and group treatment is one way to meet the needs of many clients at once without taxing clinical resources excessively (McKisack & Waller, 1997).
3. Feminist theorists assert that BN results from a relational disconnect, and group therapy is an effective means for women to reconnect with one another in an authentic way (Tantillo, 2000).

Notwithstanding these indications for group treatment, studies indicate that the dropout rate for group treatment is higher than for individual treatment (29.3% and 15.3%, respectively) (Chen et al., 2003). Few studies, however, have been conducted to determine what factors specifically predict success in treatment. Furthermore, success rates for group and individual treatment seem to be comparable (Chen et al., 2003). As the need for BN treatment groups grows, additional research on group efficacy is essential.

Conceptual Framework

Group treatment for clients with BN has been approached from nearly every possible theoretical framework, including psychoanalytic, supportive, feminist, cognitive–behavioral, and eclectic. Traditionally, it was assumed that treatment had to be long-term and intensive to maximize positive results. For example, the duration of psychoanalytic groups can range from 1 to nearly 5 years, at considerable expense to the client (Valbak, 2001). As mentioned, though, the group duration is shortened considerably in managed care. Cognitive–behavioral group therapy (CBTG) is the most researched modality for treating BN and currently is the treatment of choice (Lundgren, Danoff-Burg, & Anderson, 2004; McKisack & Waller, 1997). This treatment is relatively short-term—averaging 14 weeks and meeting approximately 2½ hours per week. Some research has shown that additional weeks of treatment, or increasing time spent in therapy each week, may further improve the treatment outcomes, including a decrease in symptoms (McKisack & Waller, 1997).

Feminist theorists assert that the use of CBTG, a separation–individuation approach, may not be the most effective treatment for women with BN. Feminist theorists perceive the presence of BN to be a result of broader societal factors—namely, a male-oriented society that focuses on individuation, competition, and autonomy over community and intimacy (Black, 2003). Thus, focusing solely on eating behaviors will not lead to lasting change for clients. Instead, feminist theorists focus on relationship building within the group setting. In this way, clients can heal their perceived disconnect from others (Tantillo, 2000). The goal is to create a curative culture rather than merely to reduce the symptoms (Black, 2003).

In the discussion here, we take an eclectic approach, incorporating elements of both CBTG and feminist theory techniques. Group leaders should keep in mind that factors such as empathy, positive regard, validation, and genuine human contact are essential to the success of group treatment (Lenihan & Sanders, 1984; McKisack & Waller, 1997). Further, we recommend that this group have two leaders. Some studies have shown a female/male pairing to be the most effective (Lenihan & Sanders, 1984).

Group Goals

One of the obvious, most immediate goals is to reduce symptoms and thereby improve physical and mental health. Because much of BN and the binge/purge cycle exists in secrecy, participants can use the group to increase accountability for their behaviors. More broadly, participants can use the group experience to enhance authenticity, reconnect with their feelings, and learn self-care (Tantillo, 2000). Over the course of treatment, clients will learn the following skills (Tantillo, 2000; Wiseman et al., 2002):

- Building awareness of patterns of food consumption
- Identifying interpersonal patterns
- Fostering intimacy
- Increasing self-awareness
- Evaluating strengths and maladaptive behaviors
- Problem solving
- Assertiveness
- Reworking cognitive distortions

Pre-Group Screening and Orientation to the Group

Each prospective group member must meet individually with the group leader prior to beginning treatment—perhaps for an additional or more sessions if warranted (Lenihan & Sanders, 1984). These pre-group sessions are necessary for several reasons (Lenihan & Sanders, 1984):

1. The group leader should determine whether the prospective client will benefit from treatment and will not hinder the treatment of others.
2. The prospective group member may have a co-current diagnosis (e.g., personality disorder, addiction, suicidality) that requires more intense immediate care.
3. Motivation for change can be assessed, and additional individual sessions can be used to build and enhance motivation if the potential member is in the pre-contemplation or contemplation stages of change (Gerlinghoff et al., 2003).
4. Prospective members can be acclimated to group norms, including confidentiality, commitment to attendance, and commitment to personal change (Lenihan & Sanders, 1984).

Possible Challenges, Limitations, and Ethical Considerations

In spite of the clear benefits that can accrue to group treatment for women with BN, the following caveats have to be kept in mind:

1. Clients with BN are more likely to drop out of group treatment than individual treatment (Chen et al., 2003). Generally, clients with eating disorders have created an interpersonal culture of silence, avoidance, and secrecy, and, as a result, struggle to achieve intimacy in the group setting.
2. The overall dropout rate for BN treatment is quite high (McKisack & Waller, 1997). This may stem in part from insufficient assessment of motivation and motivation building during the initial screening period.
3. Clients with co-current diagnoses, especially personality disorders, may be disruptive to the group process, may require more intensive treatment, or

may drop out of treatment prematurely. All of these effects can be minimized in thorough pre-group screening, assessment, and referral.

Group Sessions by Stages

The possible course of a treatment group for individuals with bulimia is presented here. The progression follows the definitive, personal involvement, group involvement, and enhancement and closure stages of group work proposed by Capuzzi and Gross in chapter 2.

Definitive Stage

This initial stage in the BN treatment group involves establishing and maintaining task focus and group cohesion (Tantillo, 2000). The group leaders facilitate this process by validating the group members' strengths and abilities, modeling empathy, positively reinforcing risk taking, and encouraging open dialogue among group members (Tantillo, 2000). Lenihan and Sanders (1984) also emphasize the importance of appropriate confrontation and direct communication with clients early on. Empathy alone may generate disrespect from group members.

The primary activity during this stage is for each member to establish a food diary, in which they are to monitor their intake and relationship with food throughout each day (Lenihan & Sanders, 1984; Tantillo, 2000). The diary will be a group tool throughout treatment. As a note of caution, though, group leaders should not overemphasize food as the primary focus of conversation. The group members will benefit more from a balanced discussion, including relational issues.

Personal Involvement Stage

During this stage, group members begin to evaluate their own internal processes in relation both to food and to other group members. A primary goal of this stage is to stabilize self-concept (Gerlinghoff et al., 2003). This is accomplished as the participants experience and process the inevitable disconnect they will feel from other group members and the group leader. Throughout this process, members are encouraged to practice self-empathy rather than resorting to internal shaming (Tantillo, 2000).

The group leaders and group members practice providing feedback to one another regarding observed relational patterns (Tantillo, 2000). The emphasis is on accuracy in expression of emotions and acknowledgement of personal responsibility. Clients also are given time to openly acknowledge their accomplishments to the group. Additional skill development might include relaxation and assertiveness training (Lenihan & Sanders, 1984).

Group Involvement Stage

Central to this stage is the extension of personal skills into the group process (Gerlinghoff et al., 2003). Now that a safe and validating environment has been established, the group members are more ready to examine interpersonal differences, to address the tension that might exist between leaders and group member expectations, and to attend to perception differences between members (Tantillo, 2000).

At this point, clients are encouraged to compare their interactions within the group with their familial, peer, and professional relationships and note similarities in maladjusted patterns (Tantillo, 2000). As intimacy grows, leaders might consider engaging group members in creative therapies such as art, music, or dance therapy (Gerlinghoff et al., 2003). Furthermore, family patterns of behavior may be analyzed by creating a genogram (Lenihan & Sanders, 1984).

Enhancement and Closure Stage

The focus of this final stage is on reviewing personal accomplishments, celebrating achievements, and processing the impending loss of the group. The group has become a laboratory for exploring the disconnect/connect cycle of relationships, and detachment from the group can be a powerful learning tool for group members (Tantillo, 2000). The group members review their food diaries, noting progress and change in their binge/purge behaviors and in their relationship to food as a whole.

Group leaders may want to incorporate career counseling as a tool at this stage (Sonnenberg & Chen, 2003). Often clients experience a loss of identity along with the loss of their disordered eating patterns. Thus, establishing the possibilities of new academic or professional roles may relieve anxiety. This activity also serves to engender hope.

Strategies to Evaluate the Group

Studies have found that mean posttreatment binge abstinence rates range from 50% to 70%, and purge abstinence rates average 35%–50%. Overall, reduction in binging ranges from 70% to 94%, and reduction in purging ranges from 75% to 94% (Lundgren et al., 2004). Clearly, although the results are far from perfect, quantitative evidence indicates substantial benefits from treatment.

To monitor ongoing client status, follow-up contact at 3, 6, and 12 months will yield useful information for evaluation. Surveys evaluating what components of treatment were most helpful or effective are particularly informative (McKisack & Waller, 1997).

Referral and Follow-Up

Once group treatment is over, some clients may find it necessary to continue with therapy at a less intense level than individual counseling. In these instances, Lenihan & Sanders (1984) encourage individual group members to continue with group treatment. As stated, some research shows that longer treatment may increase the overall efficacy of group therapy. In addition to follow-up group work, clients may be encouraged to seek ongoing individual counseling and medication management, particularly to address depressive or anxious symptoms (McKisack & Waller, 1997).

LEARNING ACTIVITIES

1. Take part in a group of three in which each participant assumes a different role. The goal of this activity is to develop an initial relationship in which the group leader is building trust, gathering information, and assessing client fit related to pre-screening women clients for possible participation in an anxiety/depression group. One participant acts as the counselor, building rapport and working on informational gathering skills. The second student acts as the client, working from a contrived scenario related to anxiety and depressive features. The third participant serves as timekeeper and observer. After 15 minutes of role play, the observer provides a 5-minute feedback session. The roles rotate until everyone has taken each role.

2. Participate in a triad in which two of the three participants role-play a couple learning reflection, summarization, and empathy. Participant #3, acting as counselor, provides an emotion chart and walks the clients through the following procedure, in which one participant is the speaker and the second takes the role of listener.

    a. In discussing a problem, the speaker says only one sentence, or two sentences at the most, at a time.
    b. After each sentence, the listener tries to repeat exactly, not paraphrase, what has just been said.
    c. After everything has been expressed, the listener summarizes what he or she has heard and asks, "Is there anything more?"
    d. After summarization, the listener makes empathic statements, without adding any content, and while using a feelings chart, says, "From what I heard, do you feel_____?"
    e. After the listener has run out of imaginable feelings, he or she asks, "Is there anything more?"

    Adhere rightly to the reflection, and when it veers off, the role of the counselor is to kindly and in inventive ways encourage the role players to stick to the structure. Afterward, the counselor provides positive client feedback and probes into whether the participants felt like they had been heard.

    Rotate the roles. After role playing, you should be able to apply this technique with couples in relationship groups.

3. Take 15 minutes to free-write about one of the topics highlighted in this chapter. Acknowledge any bias, discomfort, or concern you would have in working with any of these populations. Process how you might authentically empathize with clients in the group setting.

SUMMARY

Group work is a vital and effective mode of counseling in mental health settings. Group counseling is now being emphasized by our mental health system, especially as the financial strains and the costs of care increase. Ideal group rarely fits the reality of group work. Though it is hard to reflect the variety of issues and diversity of clientele that are present in group counseling, three prototypic groups can be used to represent how group work in a mental health setting might appear: a women's group related to disordered eating (i.e., bulimia nervosa), a women's group focused on depression (representing the realm of mood disorders), and a mixed-gender relationship enhancement group to portray what might likely be offered in settings that serve couples and families. Each of these groups has its unique challenges and benefits. Each group has its own conceptual framework, group goals, developmental stages, and other important issues such as pre-group screening, potential challenges and limitations, and ethical considerations so that counselors new to mental health settings may better understand how to operationalize group theory and implement appropriate intervention strategies.

USEFUL WEB SITES

- ☐ The National GAINS Center for persons with co-occurring disorders
  www.gainsctr.com
- ☐ Helpguide, a project of the Rotary Club of Santa Monica and the Center for Healthy Aging
  www.helpguide.org/mental/bulimia.htm
- ☐ National Alliance of Mental Illness (NAMI)
  http://web.nami.org
- ☐ National Institute of Mental Health (NIMH)
  www.nimh.nih.gov
- ☐ Peer-to-Peer Resource Center
  www.peersupport.org
- ☐ USDHHS Centers for Disease Control and Prevention
  www.cdc.gov
- ☐ USDHHS SAMHSA's National Mental Health Information Center
  www.mentalhealth.org
- ☐ World Health Organization
  www.who.int

REFERENCES

Acierno, R., Kilpatrick, D. G., Resnick, H. S., Saunders, B. E., & Best, C. L. (1999). Risk factors for rape, physical assault, and posttraumatic stress disorders in women: Examination of differential multivariate relationships. *Journal of Anxiety Disorders, 13*, 541–563.

American Psychiatric Association. (2000). *Diagnostic and statistical manual of mental disorders* (4th ed. rev.). Washington DC: Author.

Aronson, S. M. (2004). Where the wild things are: The power and challenge of adolescent group work. *Mount Sinai Journal of Medicine, 71*(3), 174–181.

Association for Specialists in Group Work (ASGW). (1998). *Best practices.* Retrieved December 8, 2004, from http://www.asgw.org/best.htm

Barrett, K., Greene, R., & Mariani, M. (2004). A case of neglect: Why health care is getting worse, even though medicine is getting better (Government Performance Project, State Health Care, *Congressional Quarterly*, Inc. From Governing's February 2004 issue. Retrieved Sept 6, 2004, from http://www.governing.com/gpp/2004/intro.htm

Black, C. (2003). Creating curative communities: Feminist group work with women with eating issues. *Australian Social Work, 56,* 127–140.

Bordin, E. S. (1994). Theory and research on the therapeutic working alliance: New directions. In A. O. Horvath & L. S. Greenberg (Eds.), *The working alliance: Theory, research, and practice* (pp. 13–37). New York: John Wiley & Sons.

Borenstein, D. (2001). From the president: Shame on government. *Psychiatric News.* American Psychiatric Association. Retrieved Sept 1, 2004, from www.psych.org/pnews/01-02-02/pres2a.html

Browning, C. R. (2002). The span of collective efficacy: Extending social disorganization theory to partner violence. *Journal of Marriage & Family, 64,* 4.

Canetto, S. S. (1997). Meanings of gender and suicidal behavior during adolescence. *Suicide & Life Threatening Behavior, 27,* 339–351.

Chambliss, C., & Oxman, E. (2003). Customizing group therapy. Laurel, MD (ERIC Document Reproduction Service No. ED479320).

Chen, E., Touyz, S. W., Beumont, P. J. V., Fairburn, C. G., Griffiths, R., Butow, P., Russell, J., Schotte, D. E., Gertler, R., & Basten, C. (2003). Comparison of group and individual cognitive–behavioral therapy for patients with bulimia nervosa. *International Journal of Eating Disorders, 33,* 241–254.

Cusinato, M., & L'Abate, L. (2003). Evaluation of a structured psychoeducational intervention with couples: The Dyadic Relationships Test (DRT). *American Journal of Family Therapy, 31*(2), 79–90.

D.A.T.A. (2004, August). Pharmacological treatment of alcohol abuse/dependence with psychiatric comorbidity. *Brown University Digest of Addiction Theory & Application, 23*(8), 1–4.

Davis, K. E., & Latty-Mann, H. (1987). Lovestyles and relationship quality: A contribution to validation. *Journal of Social and Personal Relations, 4*(4), 409–428.

Dodge, K. A., Pettit, G. S., & Bates, J. E. (1994). Socialization mediators of the relation between socioeconomic status and child conduct problems. *Child Development, 65,* 649–665.

Dorian, M., & Cordova, J. V. (2004). Coding intimacy in couple's interactions. In P. K. Kerig & D. H. Baucom (Eds.), *Couple observational coding systems* (pp. 243–256). Mahwah, NJ: Lawrence Erlbaum.

Driver, J. L., & Gottman, J. M. (2004). Turning toward versus turning away: A coding system of daily interactions. In P. K. Kerig & D. H. Baucom (Eds.), *Couple observational coding systems* (pp. 209–225). Mahwah, NJ: Lawrence Erlbaum.

Duffrene, A. (2004, July). Dr Irvin Yalom. *Counselling & Psychotherapy Journal, 15*(6), 8–11.

Egan, G. (2001). *The skilled helper: A problem-management approach to helping* (7th ed.). Pacific Grove, CA: Brooks/Cole.

Fagan, P. F., Patterson, R. W., & Rector, R. E. (2002). Marriage and welfare reform: The overwhelming evidence that marriage education works. *Heritage Foundation Backgrounder.* Washington, DC: Heritage Foundation.

Floyd, F. J. (2004). Communication skills test (CST): Observational system for couples' problem-solving skills. In P. K. Kerig & D. H. Baucom (Eds.), *Couple observational coding systems* (pp. 143–158). Mahwah, NJ: Lawrence Erlbaum.

Fredrickson, B. L. (2001). The role of positive emotions in positive psychology: The broaden-and-build theory of positive emotions. *American Psychologist, 56*(3), 218–226.

Geddes, J., Reynolds, S., Streiner, D., & Szatmari, P. (1997). Evidence based practice in mental health. *British Medical Journal, 315,* 1483–1484.

Gerlinghoff, M., Gross, G., & Backmund, H. (2003). Eating disorder therapy concepts with a preventive goal. *European Child & Adolescent Psychiatry, 12,* 72–77.

Gladding, S. T. (1998). *Family therapy: History, theory, and practice* (2nd ed.). Upper Saddle River, NJ: Merrill/Prentice Hall.

Glueckauf, R. L., Liss, H. J., McQuillen, D. E., Webb, P. M., Dairaghi, J., & Carter, C. B. (2002). Therapeutic alliance in family therapy for adolescents with epilepsy: An exploratory study. *American Journal of Family Therapy, 30*(2), 125–140.

Gottman, J. M. (1994). *What predicts divorce? The relationship between marital processes and marital outcomes.* Hillsdale, NJ: Erlbaum.

Gottman, J. M. (1999). *The marriage clinic: A scientifically based marital therapy.* New York: Norton.

Gottman, J. M., & Levenson, R. W. (2000). The timing of divorce: Predicting when a couple will divorce over a 14-year period. *Journal of Marriage and the Family, 62,* 737–745.

Gulledge, A. K., Gulledge, M. H., & Stahmann, R. F. (2003). Romantic physical affection types and relationship satisfaction. *American Journal of Family Therapy, 31*(4), 233–242.

Halford, W. K. (2001). *Brief couple therapy: Helping partners help themselves.* New York: Guilford.

Halford, W. K., Sanders, M. R., & Behrens, B. C. (1994). Self-regulation in behavioral couples therapy. *Behavior Therapy, 25*(3), 431–452.

Halford, W. K., Wilson, K. L., Lizzio, A., & Moore, E. (2002). Does working at a relationship work? Relationship self-regulation and relationship outcomes. In P. Noller & J. A. Feeney (Eds.), *Understanding marriage: Developments in the study of couple interaction* (pp. 493–518). Cambridge, MA: Cambridge University Press.

Hatfield, E., & Rapson, R. L. (1993). *Love, sex, and intimacy: Their psychology, biology, and history.* New York: HarperCollins.

Hendrick, S. S. (1988). A generic measure of relationship satisfaction. *Journal of Marriage and Family, 50,* 93–98.

Hook, M. K., Gerstein, L. H., Detterich, L., & Gridley, B. (2003). How close are we? Measuring intimacy and examining gender differences. *Journal of Counseling & Development, 1*(4), 462–472.

Ivey, A. E., Pedersen, P. B., & Ivey, M. B. (2001). *Intentional group counseling; A microskills approach.* Belmont, CA: Wadsworth.

Kessler, R., Mickelson, K., & Zhoa, S. (1997). Patterns and correlates of self-help group membership in the United States. *Social Policy, 27*(3), 27–47.

Lenihan, G. O., & Sanders, C. D. (1984). Guidelines for group therapy with eating disorder victims. *Journal of Counseling & Development, 63,* 252–254.

Lundgren, J. D., Danoff-Burg, S., & Anderson, D. A. (2004). Cognitive–behavioral therapy for bulimia nervosa: An empirical analysis of clinical significance. *International Journal of Eating Disorders, 35,* 262–274.

Lurie, A., & Harold, R. (1967). *Multiple group counseling with discharged schizophrenic adolescents and their parents.* Laurel, MD (ERIC Document Reproduction Service No. ED027550).

Maciejewski, P. K., Prigerson, H. G., & Mazure, C. M. (2001). Sex differences in event-related risk for major depression. *Psychological Medicine, 157,* 897–903.

MacKenzie, H. R. (1990). *Introduction to time limited group psychotherapy.* Washington, DC: American Psychiatric Press.

McKisack, C., & Waller, G. (1997). Factors influencing the outcome of group psychotherapy for bulimia nervosa. *International Journal of Eating Disorders, 22,* 1–13.

McLeod, J. D., & Shanahan, M. J. (1993). Poverty, parenting, and children's mental health. *American Sociological Review, 58,* 351–366.

Meezan, W., & O'Keefe, M. (1998). Evaluating the effectiveness of multifamily group therapy in child abuse and neglect. *Research on Social Work Practice, 8,* 330–353.

National Alliance of Mental Illness (NAMI). (2004). *Helpline fact sheet: Women and depression.* Retrieved on Dec. 9, 2004, from http://web.nami.org/helpline/women.html

National Institute of Mental Health. (1999). *Anxiety disorders.* Retrieved Nov. 1, 2004, from http://www.nimh.nih.gov/publicat/anxiety.cfm#anx9

O'Shea, M. D., & Phelps, R. (1985). Multiple family therapy: Current status and critical appraisal. *Family Process, 24,* 555–582.

Prager, K. J. (1995). *The psychology of intimacy.* New York: Guilford.

Rogers, C. R. (1957). The necessary and sufficient conditions of therapeutic personality change. *Journal of Consulting Psychology, 21,* 95–103.

Rose, C. (2004). The less-than-perfect group. *Counselling & Psychotherapy Journal, 15*(5), 40–43.

Rugel, R. P. (1997). *Husband-focused marital therapy: An approach to dealing with marital distress.* Springfield, IL: Thompson.

Sabourin, S., Valois, P., & Lussier, Y. (2005). Development and validation of a brief version of the dyadic adjustment scale with a nonparametric item analysis model. *Psychological Assessment, 17*(1), 15–27.

Salvendy, J. T. (1993). Selection and preparation of patients and organization of the group. In H. I. Kaplin & B. J. Saddock (Eds.), *Comprehensive group psychotherapy* (3rd ed.). Baltimore: Williams & Wilkins.

Salzer, M. S., Rappaport, J., & Segre, L. (2001). Professional support of self-help groups. *Journal of Community & Applied Social Psychology, 11*(1), 1–11.

Schunk, D. H. (2001). Self-regulation through goal setting. *ERIC/CASS Digest.* Greensboro, NC: ERIC Clearinghouse on Counseling and Student Services. (ED462671)

Seligman, C. K. (1999). *Life-span and human development* (3rd ed.). Pacific Grove, CA: Brooks/ Cole.

Simons, M., & Harris, R. (1997). Non-participation in adult education: A case study of pre-marriage education programmes. *New Zealand Journal of Adult Learning, 25*(2), 31–52.

Sonnenberg, S. L., & Chen, C. P. (2003). Using career development theories in the treatment of clients with eating disorders. *Counselling Psychology Quarterly, 16,* 173–185.

Spanier, G. B. (1976). Measuring dyadic adjustment: New scales for assessing the quality of marriage and similar dyads. *Journal of Marriage and Family, 48,* 15–27.

Sullivan, K. T., & Anderson, C. (2002). Recruitment of engaged couples for premarital counseling: An empirical examination of the importance of program characteristics and topics to potential participants. *Family Journal: Counseling and Therapy for Couples and Families, 10*(4), 388–397.

Tabares, A. A., Driver, J. L., & Gottman, J. M. (2004). Repair attempts observational coding system: Measuring de-escalation of negative affect during marital conflict. In P. K. Kerig & D. H. Baucom (Eds.), *Couple observational coding systems* (pp. 227–243). Mahwah, NJ: Lawrence Erlbaum.

Tantillo, M. (2000). Short-term relational group therapy for women with bulimia nervosa. *Eating Disorders, 8,* 99–121.

Thorngren, J. M., & Kleist, D. M. (2002). Multiple family group therapy: An interpersonal/postmodern approach. *Family Journal: Counseling and Therapy for Couples and Families, 10*(2), 167–176.

Tsuang, J., & Fong, T. W. (2004). Treatment of patients with schizophrenia and substance abuse disorders. *Current Pharmaceutical Design, 10*(18), 2249–2252.

U.S. Department of Health and Human Services (USDHHS). (1999). *Mental health: A report of the Surgeon General.* Rockville, MD: Author.

U.S. Department of Health and Human Services (USDHHS). (2004, October). *Substance abuse and mental health services administration report.* Retrieved October 15, 2004, from http://www.mentalhealth.org/highlights/ october2004/Domestic/default.asp

Valbak, K. (2001). Good outcome for bulimic patients in a long-term group analysis: A single-group study. *European Eating Disorders Review, 9,* 19–32.

Vygotsky, L. S. (1978). *Mind in society.* Cambridge, MA: Harvard University Press.

Waring, E. M., Chamberlaine, C. H., Carver, C. M., Stalker, C.A., & Schaefer, B. (1995). A pilot study of marital therapy as a treatment for depression. *American Journal of Family Therapy, 23*(1), 3–10.

Weiss, R. L., & Heyman, R. E. (1997). Couple interaction. In W. K. Halford & H. J. Markman (Eds.), *Clinical handbook of marriage and couples intervention* (pp. 13–41). New York: Wiley.

Wiseman, C. V., Sunday, S. R., Klapper, F., Klein, M., & Halmi, K. A. (2002). Short-term group CBT versus psycho-education on an inpatient eating disorder unit. *Eating Disorders, 10*, 313–320.

World Health Organization (WHO). (2001). *World Health Report. Mental health: New understanding, new hope.* Retrieved Nov. 1, 2004, from http://www.who.int/whr/2001/chapter2/en/

World Health Organization (WHO). (2004). *Mental health: The bare facts.* Retrieved on Sept. 5, 2004, from http://www.who.int/mental_health/en/

Yalom, I. D. (1995). *The theory and practice of group psychotherapy* (4th ed.). New York: Basic Books.

Zimmerman, B. J. (2002). Becoming a self-regulated learner: An overview. *Theory into Practice, 41*(2), 64–70.

14

Groups in Rehabilitation Settings

Malachy Bishop and Debra A. Harley

Group counseling has become an increasingly important and prevalent modality in rehabilitation counseling. The ultimate goal of rehabilitation counseling is to improve the quality of life of people with disabilities (Bishop & Feist-Price, 2002; Livneh, 2001) by assisting those who have physical, mental, developmental, cognitive, and emotional disabilities in reaching their personal, career, and independent living goals.

At the origin of the profession in the early 20th century, rehabilitation counselors were employed primarily in public vocational rehabilitation settings, but in the last 30 years, they have applied their skills in an ever increasing range of settings. Currently, rehabilitation counselors work in independent living centers, private and nonprofit community-based rehabilitation settings, hospitals and clinics, mental health organizations, employee assistance programs (EAPs), school-transition programs, forensic settings, employer-based disability prevention and management programs (Leahy, 2004), geriatric rehabilitation settings, substance abuse treatment facilities, and correctional facilities. Across these settings, group counseling has made significant strides toward achieving the stature of long-respected individual treatment models for delivering mental health services, vocational counseling, and counseling toward psychosocial adaptation to disabilities (Ward, 2004).

ADVANTAGES OF GROUPS IN REHABILITATION

Group counseling in rehabilitation counseling settings offers a number of advantages over individual counseling (Thomas,

Thoreson, Parker, & Butler, 1998). Some of these advantages reflect economic benefits in terms of both time and money. Clearly, if counselors can see more clients in less time by utilizing the group approach, they can make more efficient use of their own time and the clients' economic resources. More important, however, are the significant therapeutic benefits that accrue when the group counseling approach is applied in the context of rehabilitation settings.

The group approach offers individuals who have disability-related barriers the opportunity to learn that their questions and concerns, problems, impediments, and hopes and fears are not unique, and this normalizing perspective can be highly therapeutic. Group settings afford clients the opportunities suggested by Thomas et al. (1998):

- To learn and practice new ways of relating effectively to others
- To gain vocational and disability- or illness-related information
- To take risks in a supportive environment
- To develop social support, insight, and self-confidence as a result

In addition, group counseling gives counselors the opportunity to provide information efficiently; to teach vocational, functional, social, and coping skills; and to observe and provide feedback on social interactions.

Types of Groups Typically Used in Rehabilitation

Group work in rehabilitation settings takes many forms (e.g., psychoeducational, psychotherapy, self-help, support groups), occurs across numerous settings (e.g., vocational, correctional, medical), and involves working with people who have different disabilities across age, gender, and culturally diverse groups. Livneh, Wilson, and Pullo (2002) suggested that among the many group formats utilized in rehabilitation counseling, four types dominate the field:

1. Psychoeducational or educational groups
2. Social support groups
3. Psychotherapeutic groups
4. Coping and skill-training groups

Psychoeducational groups, sometimes referred to as "educational" or "guidance" groups, emphasize using educational and developmental methods to impart information and facilitate growth and change (Association for Specialists in Group Work [ASGW], 2000; Brown, 1997). The primary goal in psychoeducational group work is "to prevent future development of debilitating dysfunction while strengthening coping skills and self-esteem" (Conyne, 1996, p. 157). The focus of psychoeducational groups in rehabilitation settings is on imparting factual information about disability or illness to participants. Examples include groups in which participants with diabetes learn to monitor and control their condition and groups for people who have incurred a recent spinal cord injury to learn self-care and mobility skills.

Social support groups allow participants with disabilities to receive support from peers in a forum designed to foster the sharing of ideas, information, concerns, and problem-solving methods. Among the many possible support groups are those for people with cancer, multiple sclerosis, and traumatic brain injury.

Psychotherapeutic groups emphasize the affective domain. These groups promote increased self-understanding by directly addressing emotional issues such as anxiety, depression, anger, and changes in identity.

Finally, *coping and skill-training groups* tend to have a cognitive–behavioral orientation. In these groups participants learn skills and coping mechanisms for dealing with the personal, social, and environmental impacts of disability or chronic illness (Livneh et al., 2002).

For the purpose of this chapter, we discuss three specific types of groups in which rehabilitation counselors in various settings are likely to be engaged: job clubs, offender and mandated population groups, and groups in hospitals/medical settings. The specific advantages, limitations, associated research, challenges, and ethical considerations are described in the context of each group modality. This selection of groups represents different foci and different skill and knowledge requirements and reflects the increasing diversity found in rehabilitation counseling.

A JOB CLUB AND GROUP-BASED EMPLOYMENT COUNSELING

Purpose

Helping individuals with disabilities to achieve successful employment outcomes is frequently the primary focus of rehabilitation counselors. A disability or chronic illness, either congenital or having a later onset, influences the individual's ability to attain and maintain employment in a number of ways. Identified barriers to employment for people with congenital disabilities include low expectations by parents and educators during the individual's childhood and adolescence. As a result of lower expectations with regard to adult work, particularly in home and school environments, individuals with developmental disabilities have limited opportunities to develop the social and work skills that are critical to success in employment, as well as limited opportunities for career exploration. This leads to restricted awareness of the diversity of career opportunities. For those with later-onset disability or illness, the barriers to maintaining employment may include the need for work modifications, changes in work productivity, altered relationships with employers and co-workers, and, frequently, job loss.

For most people, seeking employment is challenging at best. It involves learning (frequently by trial and error) and effectively executing complex job-seeking skills and tasks while attempting to navigate various employers' expectations and other complex social processes. This requires patience, commitment, organization, and emotional fortitude. For many people with disabilities, this process becomes even more challenging because of the functional limitations associated with the disability and, further, by negative or uninformed attitudes of employers and coworkers.

Rehabilitation counselors in a variety of settings often are involved in helping individuals with disabilities navigate the employment-seeking process. The job club is an efficient, and generally successful, approach to job-seeking for people with disabilities. This approach offers members support, as well as opportunities to observe and learn from the experiences of others. "In addition, it shows group members how to engage in mutual support endeavors, confront similar problems, share resources, and offer peer support" (Livneh et al., 2002, p. 457).

Significant research supports the efficacy of the job club approach. Early research with this model suggested that job club participants were more likely to find employment, more quickly, and at a higher rate of pay than those involved in traditional, individual placement approaches (Azrin & Philips, 1979). Similarly supportive research has been consistently reported regarding the efficacy of this approach with people having a wide range of disabilities (Black, Tsuhako, & McDougall, 1998; McWhirter & McWhirter, 1996; Rutman, 1994) as well as recipients of welfare (Brooks, Nackerud, & Risler, 2001). According to Gilbride and Stensrud (2003), the job club remains a widely used approach in rehabilitation, and the majority of state rehabilitation agencies have indicated that they use this approach.

It should be noted that the job club represents a specific and detailed framework for job seeking. The purpose of the discussion in this chapter is to provide an overview of the job club approach. Readers who are interested in developing a job club are referred to Azrin and Besalel (1980) for more detailed coverage.

Conceptual Framework

A job club is an intensive, highly structured, short-term behavioral group approach to vocational counseling. This group-based job search strategy was developed by Azrin and associates (Azrin & Besalel, 1980; Azrin, Flores, & Kaplan, 1975; Azrin & Philips, 1979) in the 1970s and has been used continuously since then with demonstrated efficacy. Emphasis is placed on the development of interpersonal skills, job-seeking skills, and personal responsibility, in the context of a highly structured and supportive group process. The job club is essentially an open group, in which new members can be enrolled continually. Azrin and Besalel recommend a maximum of 20 members at any time.

The job club represents a behavioral approach to group employment-seeking skills training. The counselor's style is characterized by "adherence to standardized procedures; a directive manner; an emphasis on using positive statements and constant encouragement; an approach to learning by using small steps at a time, following highly structured training procedures; and an emphasis on final outcome" (Azrin & Besalel, 1980, p. 8). When applied to job search skills, the behavioral approach focuses on observable behavior rather than the mental processes that accompany the behavior. The group is outcome-oriented rather than process-oriented. Instead of goals such as job readiness, willingness to work, or developing appropriate attitudes toward or aptitudes for work, the primary objective is to help the group members find jobs.

To achieve this goal, the job club identifies the steps involved in attaining a job and then arranges and teaches these in a standardized and consistent manner for each group member. Azrin and Besalel (1980) identified more than 30 procedures and activities for use with this approach, including practice with standard scripts and forms, support from other group members, assigning partnerships among members, emphasizing personal skills, identifying job leads, interview training, developing resumes, and completing daily progress charts (Azrin & Besalel, 1980; Livneh et al., 2002). Although the job club approach has been modified for use in different settings and agencies, a typical job club includes the following components (Brooks et al., 2001):

1. Team building and personal encouragement of members by the counselor
2. Clear articulation of the goals of the job club (to identify a career goal and find satisfying employment)
3. Training in how to obtain occupational information and learning about career fields
4. Developing a script of what to say to potential employers, both by phone and in person
5. Practicing how to effectively counter employers' reasons for not hiring the applicant
6. Education about appropriate grooming and appearance
7. Learning how to network and to identify members of one's social circle as potential job leads
8. Preparing answers for anticipated interview questions
9. Reducing interview stress and overcoming barriers to employment
10. Preparing a resume
11. Completing job application forms

Group Goals

The stated goal of the job club is to help the individual members "obtain a job of the highest feasible quality within the shortest feasible time period" (Azrin & Besalel, 1980). The job club approach involves coordinating the activities of each individual in the context of a group of job seekers working together to promote the success of the participants under the supervision, instruction, and encouragement of a skilled leader. Every job seeker is seen as employable, regardless of disability, educational background, or employment outlook. The group leader assumes that employment is possible—that a job exists for everyone—and views his or her task as helping the job seeker to find that job.

Pre-Group Screening and Orientation to the Group

Each prospective participant in the job club must attend an orientation meeting prior to participating. Azrin and Besalel (1980) suggested that this may be accomplished in either a group or an individual format, depending on the time available to the counselor. Regardless of format, during this session the counselor orients the potential participants to the details of the program, addressing issues such as cost of the program, the group leader's commitment to finding each member a job, expectations of the participants, benefits of the group approach, potential impact of employment on any benefits the participant is currently receiving, and transportation or scheduling issues.

The job club approach represents an intensive commitment. Job clubs typically meet daily for 2 to 2½ hours per day (Gilbride & Stensrud, 2003). Members have to understand and be able to commit to the various requirements in terms of time and effort.

Possible Challenges, Limitations, and Ethical Considerations

Even though the job club is an effective, economical, and efficient approach to job-seeking, group leaders must be aware of the potential limitations and challenges associated with this approach. When the group member's goal is to attain employment, the participant and the group leader must decide which of the various forms and levels of employment counseling are most appropriate. Because rehabilitation counselors work with people who have a wide range of disabilities and differing levels of severity and psychosocial impact, no single method of employment counseling is appropriate for everyone.

An important consideration is the level of support and information the participant will require. If the person is capable of completing most of the work of locating, applying for, and interviewing for jobs, the counselor generally plays a supportive role and offers information and other assistance when required. In other cases, when the client has more limited awareness of, or experience with, work and the job-seeking process, the counselor has to take significantly more responsibility in the job-finding tasks and work more intensively with the client on developing work skills.

In deciding whether the job club is the most appropriate approach to employment counseling for an individual client, the counselor should assess the client's level of understanding of work and job seeking. Although it is beneficial to have a range of experience within the job club, extreme differences between members may affect the progress and coherence of the group and its membership. The counselor also should assess the client's comfort with a group approach, as a group is not appropriate for everyone. Therefore, group leaders should describe the experience, expectations, and makeup of the group, and assess the client's concerns. Although entering a group situation may engender responses ranging from uncomfortable to frightening, and some level of concern is to be expected, counselors must assess whether the client's concerns, fears, or expectations are such that they may have negative consequences for the client or the group as a whole.

Group Sessions by Stages

The definitive, personal involvement, group involvement, and enhancement and closure stages of group work proposed by Capuzzi and Gross in chapter 2 are reviewed with respect to the job club.

Definitive Stage

The job club gets off to a quick start, and even in this initial stage involves intensive activity at a relatively fast pace. Azrin and Besalel (1980) have developed a highly structured format for the job club and its progress, including what the first session should include. Essentially, the members receive information about the group and take part in a number of orienting activities. These activities include completing a written agreement of responsibilities between the group leader and each member of the group, followed by member introductions. The activities consist of information provided by the counselor alternating with individual, partner, and group exercises. Typical exercises include identifying job leads, role-playing the process of making employer contacts, making employer contacts over the telephone, and rehearsing responses to employment interview questions.

Personal Involvement Stage

One of the most important elements of the job club is the opportunity for members to learn from and with each other, to cooperate and assist each other in the job-seeking process. These benefits begin to emerge in the personal involvement stage, as the participants begin to engage in member-to-member interactions through the cooperative activities. The group leader promotes personal involvement by allowing and encouraging this interaction, observing members' interactions as they grow more comfortable with the group and become more committed.

Because much of the work after the initial meeting is done independently (e.g., searching for job leads), the group leader must alternate group activities with individual activities. Further, because of the intensive and relatively directive nature of the job club, the leader must remain vigilant in maintaining the rules and promoting members' progress. Activities at this stage include role play and rehearsal and the continued use of group education alternating with individual or partnered job-seeking activities.

Group Involvement Stage

Although the purpose of the job club is for individual members to achieve success in the workplace, effectiveness of the group depends on the cooperative efforts of the members. As members' personal comfort and confidence with the group and their own role increase, they will realize the benefits of cooperation and shared efforts. At this stage the group members increasingly take on responsibility for the group's progress. As new members join, more experienced members welcome and assist them. The leader, though always actively involved, particularly seeks to facilitate and encourage these leadership behaviors of the members.

Enhancement and Closure Stage

Given the open nature of the typical job club, closure is generally an individual rather than a group effort. In the case of the job club, though, closure typically means employment and the realization of the exiting member's vocational goals. The importance of formally recognizing this success is vital to the job club for a number of reasons:

1. It encourages the members that they can reach their goal.

2. It recognizes and rewards the successful efforts and hard work of the member and marks the member's achievement in leaving the group.

3. The member who leaves to begin employment becomes a potential resource for employment for the other members. For this reason, Azrin and Besalel (1980) developed a formal method for maintaining contact with members of the group who are successful in finding employment.

Strategies to Evaluate the Group

Obviously, with the job club approach, the primary measure of success is the members' attaining employment. As described above, research evaluating the effectiveness of this approach has generally been very positive. Even though employment is the primary goal of the job club, other potential benefits to participation may guide additional approaches to evaluation.

In today's labor market it is unusual for anyone to remain in the same job for the course of a career. It is far more likely that people will change jobs several times during their lives. Among the reasons the job club plays such an appropriate and important role in rehabilitation counseling is not just that the members get a job but that they *learn how to get a job*. If the job club is successful in this goal, the benefits to the members are significant and long lasting.

Follow-Up and Referral

As noted, the job club might not be appropriate for some job seekers, and this may not become apparent until after the person has started to participate in the group. If a group leader determines that a member is inappropriate for the job club, the reasons should be discussed with the member to reach a decision on a different approach.

Following up with previous members is crucial. Azrin and Besalel (1980) suggested keeping a list of successful members and contacting them at regular intervals. If for no other reason, they represent potential resources for current job-seeking members. Further, former members are encouraged to return as needed. The job club is described as a resource continually available to its members.

Regardless of the reason for leaving the club—including either dropping out or successfully attaining a job—Azrin and Besalel (1980) emphasize that the "job club perspective is to continue to assist the job seeker whenever help is needed" (p. 91). Further, they suggested that returning job club members usually require less assistance and remain for a shorter time than new members.

GROUPS WITH OFFENDER AND MANDATED POPULATIONS

Purpose

Offender populations include incarcerated and mandated clients. For purposes of this chapter, the term *offenders* refers to individuals convicted of a crime and includes both incarcerated (i.e., housed in a secure correctional environment) and nonincarcerated (on parole, probation, etc.) individuals. *Mandated clients* are those who are required to attend treatment services by a governing agency (e.g., a department of corrections, the judicial system, parole/probation officers; Morgan, 2004). A large number of offenders have disabilities, are in need of rehabilitation services, and are being overlooked (Harley, 1996; Van Steele & Moberg, 2004). Since the 1980s the number of adults in the correctional population has been increasing. In 2003, 6.9 million people were on probation, in jail or prison, or on parole at year's end (3.2% of all U.S. adult residents, or one in every 32 adults; Bureau of Justice Statistics, 2005a). More specifically, as of December 31, 2001, there were an estimated 5.6 million adults who had ever served time in state or federal prison, including 4.3 million former prisoners and 1.3 million adults in prison. Nearly a third of former prisoners were still under correctional supervision, including 731,000 on parole, 437,000 on probation, and 166,000 in local jails. In 2001, an estimated 2.7 percent of adults in the United States had served time in prison, up from 1.8 percent in 1991 and 1.3 percent in 1974. The prevalence of imprisonment in 2001 was higher for Black males (16.6%) and Hispanic males (7.7%) than for White males (2.6%). Likewise, the rate was higher for Black females (1.7%) and Hispanic females (0.7%) than for White females (0.3%; Bureau of Justice Statistics, 2005b). In addition, the Bureau of Justice Statistics (2005b) reported that nearly two-thirds of the 3.8 million increase in the number of adults ever incarcerated between 1974 and 2001 occurred as a result of an increase in first incarceration rates; one-third occurred as a result of an increase in the number of residents age 18 and older.

An estimated 28% of incarcerated juveniles have disabilities, and 10% of adults in state facilities (Bureau of Justice Statistics, 2005a; Scarborough, Glaser, Calhoun, Stefurak, & Petrocelli, 2004). Included in the offender population are those with disabilities including mental retardation, learning disabilities, chemical dependency, mental illness, and various physical disabilities, and they are integrated into the general prison population with little or no accommodation for their disability (Van Steele & Moberg, 2004).

Even though the offender population consists of those who are adjudicated and incarcerated for a variety of offenses, they have in common a cluster of characteristics specific to them. Overwhelmingly, incarcerated offenders have a low level of educational attainment, lack vocational skills, have higher than average rates of unemployment, have mild mental retardation or learning disabilities, are alcohol and/or drug dependent, and have some form of serious emotional disturbance (Condelli, Bradigan, & Holanchock, 1997; Rutherford, Bullis, Anderson, & Griller-Clark, 2002; Van Steele & Moberg, 2004).

Offender and mandated clients frequently resist the therapeutic process and may actively avoid engaging in treatment or rehabilitation (Morgan, 2004; Riordan & Martin, 1993). Nationally, 10% of offender populations report a mental condition and nearly 38% of alcohol-dependent offenders reported having a mental disorder (Maruschak & Beck, 2001). Nevertheless, approximately 20% of incarcerated offenders participate in group treatment programs (Morgan, Winterowd, &

Ferrell, 1999). In efforts to involve offenders in treatment or rehabilitation groups, counselors should take into consideration the unique nature of this population because its members present problems that are not typical of therapy groups in other settings (Morgan, Winterowd, & Ferrell, 1999; Van Steele & Moberg, 2004). Typically, offenders are a disenfranchised group, represent a captive audience (involuntary), exhibit chronic/repetitive behaviors (offenses), and have a host of psychosocial adjustment issues (especially adult offenders). Among the specific types of adult offenders targeted for treatment in groups are those serving time for sex offenses and individuals found guilty of driving under the influence, shoplifting, domestic violence, and substance abuse (Gladding, 1999).

Relevant Research

Research examining the success of group work with offender populations in general has been mixed, but some consensus indicates that group psychotherapy and group counseling approaches are far more effective than individual treatment for sex offenders (DeAngelis, 1992), juvenile offenders (Claypoole, Moody, & Peace, 2000; Leone, Quinn, & Osher, 2002), and female inmates (American Correctional Association, 1993: Champion, 1996).

Group work and counseling services have been an important component of rehabilitation for offender populations in correctional settings, resulting in positive treatment gains across a range of outcome variables (Morgan & Flora, 2002; Winterowd, Morgan, & Ferrell, 2001). Research indicates the following benefits of group counseling with offender populations:

1. Groups provide an outlet for offenders to talk out their thoughts and feelings about their past criminal activity as well as their relationships with family friends, fellow offenders, and prison staff. The group may be a place for offenders to learn how to share or release pent-up thoughts and feelings in socially and therapeutically appropriate ways without hurting themselves or others in the process (Winterowd et al., 2001).
2. Groups offer offenders the opportunity to learn healthier attitudes and behaviors (Scott, 1993); new ways of thinking, feeling, and behaving; and more about their relationships in the here and now (Gendreau, 1996).
3. The group experience reinforces social and conventional rules in every context and helps offenders to understand that their actions have consequences for others (Winterowd et al., 2001).
4. Groups offer offenders a forum for developing strategies on how to resolve conflicts and transfer this knowledge into their daily lives (Morgan, 2004).
5. Groups often facilitate institutional adjustment (i.e., coping with and adjusting to incarceration) (Winterowd et al., 2001).
6. The use of moral dilemma discussions as a group intervention influences offenders' institutional post-release behaviors positively (Claypoole et al., 2000; Gibbs, Potter, Goldstein, & Brendtro, 1996; Leeman, Gibbs, & Fuller, 1993).

Conceptual Framework

Of the primary types of groups, three are highly applicable to work with offender and mandated clients: psychoeducational groups, counseling groups, and psychotherapy groups (Morgan, 2004). The following discussion describes the application of each with offender and mandated clients.

Psychoeducational Groups

The ultimate aim of psychoeducational groups with offender and mandated clients is to foster cognitive changes that may reduce the likelihood of criminal behaviors in the future (Morgan, 2004). Psychoeducational groups offer concrete functional outcomes (Morgan, 2004; Shields, 1986) including

- less defensiveness compared to the more ambiguous group counseling and group psychotherapy models;
- less of a need to test the group, the therapeutic boundaries, or the therapist;
- fewer hidden agendas; and
- heightened direction and focus in early group sessions, less prevalent in other types of group work.

In psychoeducational groups with offenders, out-of-group homework exercises yield the greatest improved outcomes, compared to groups not utilizing such exercises (Morgan & Flora, 2002). But offenders often resist completing work outside of group sessions (Morgan, Winterowd, & Fuqua, 1999). Thus, counselors/therapists will have to provide a clear and logical rationale for this intervention and promptly address any lack of client compliance with assigned homework (Morgan, 2004).

Group Counseling

Group counseling is basically preventive, with an educational, vocational, social, or personal focus aimed at promoting growth (ASGW, 2000; Gladding, 1999). Examples of counseling groups with offenders and mandated clients include an institutional adjustment group, support groups, interpersonal-communication/relationship-building groups, and a vocational group. According to Morgan (2004), an institutional adjustment group is aimed specifically at assisting offenders to function at the highest possible level within the correctional environment, rather than remediation.

Many offenders have made poor life decisions, and group counseling can help these clients achieve an optimal level of functioning within the penitentiary setting and after release into society. The goals of group counseling with offender populations (Morgan, 2004) are for members to

1. increase self-awareness;
2. identify attitudes, choices, and behaviors that led to problematic behavior; and
3. promote prosocial decision making and behavior.

The group focuses on strategies for reducing recidivism, fostering prosocial integration back into society, cognitive restructuring, addressing criminogenic needs, and supplementing other rehabilitative programs such as substance abuse, vocational, educational, and leisure programs (Champion, 1996; Claypoole et al., 2000; Morgan, 2004; Morgan, Winterowd, & Ferrell, 1999).

Group Psychotherapy

Group psychotherapy with offenders and mandated clients is directed to the remediation of problematic behaviors and personality restructuring (ASGW, 2000; Gazda, Ginter, & Horne, 2001). Group psychotherapy is "a dynamic interpersonal process focusing on conscious and hidden patterns of thought (e.g., unconscious) and behavior that are relatively pervasive in the member's life" (Gazda et al., 2001, p. 15). The goal of psychotherapy groups for offender or mandated populations is to reduce their harmful behaviors and antisocial acts in the future. The focus of group psychotherapy is on the here and now of dysfunctional interactions as they occur within the group, with the aim of using these interactions to facilitate greater self-awareness and behavioral change. The end result of group psychotherapy is to assist the offender in reducing dysfunctional symptoms and developing adaptive coping skills.

Group Goals

Generally, groups with offender and mandated clients are designed to

- provide clients with opportunities to learn more about themselves (Morgan, 2004);
- increase awareness of values and opinions (Scott, 1993);
- improve relationships with others (Gendreau, 1996);
- modify antisocial behaviors and attitudes;
- change lifestyle issues such as substance abuse, career development, and leisure interests (Gendreau, 1996);
- increase social support; and
- effectively express feelings and emotions (Olson & McEwen, 2004).

Thus, the focus on development of a healthier lifestyle seems essential to rehabilitation (Winterowd et al., 2001). The ultimate outcome of an intervention is to either stop or alter a behavior.

Winterowd et al. (2001, pp. 411–414) identified eight overarching goals reported by group counselors working with incarcerated offenders. These goals include the following:

1. *Self-exploration and learning within a supportive group environment:* Focuses on group members learning personal awareness through expression of in-depth issues and learning relational and coping skills within a cohesive and supportive group environment
2. *Group relationship building:* Focuses on the development of interpersonal relationships in group as well as group relationship dynamics
3. *Substance abuse:* Focuses on substance abuse issues as well as the importance of reducing addictive behaviors
4. *Learning healthier attitudes and behaviors:* Focuses on the acquisition of behavioral skills (social skills training, conflict resolution, impulse/anger management) and insight (personal growth, self-esteem enhancement)

5. *Conformity:* Focuses on addressing recidivism issues and institutional compliance

6. *Prosocial behavior:* Focuses on improving relationships and preparing for life outside prison

7. *Lifestyle:* Focuses on addressing career issues, diet, stress management, and the development of leisure activities

8. *Institutional adjustment:* Focuses on inmates' need to deal with prison life, including relationships with prison staff and inmates; managing stress, anger, and crises; and dealing with existential issues of incarceration

Each of these goals is applicable to general group work; however, specific factors (e.g., prosocial behavior modification, conformity issues, and institutional adjustment issues) are unique to group work with offender and mandated populations (Morgan, 2004). Morgan stressed that these group goals are consistent with the criminogenic needs of offenders as found by researchers (e.g., Andrews & Bonta, 1994; Andrews, Bonya, & Hoge, 1990). Each of these goals is reported to be critical to the effectiveness of treatment programming with offenders (Gendreau, 1996).

Pre-Group Screening and Orientation to the Group

Pre-group screening interviews are recommended to counter the manipulation and resistance associated with offender and mandated clients and to facilitate the client's development of therapeutic goals (Morgan & Winterowd, 2002; Morgan, Winterowd, & Ferrell, 1999). As mentioned earlier, offender and mandated clients tend to be resistant to group participation. In addition, some group members enter treatment without identified therapeutic goals (Morgan, 2004). Thus, pre-screening identifies the appropriateness of individuals for placement in a group while also addressing group cohesion.

Orientation to the group for offender populations involves several steps, as outlined by Morgan (2004):

Step 1:   *Orient members to the group's focus.* The group members and therapist are clear about the purpose and goals of the group. In addition, the leader explains the rules for group participation.

Step 2:   *Review members' valued therapeutic factors.* Offenders and mandated clients may be presenting with needs that the group leader does not recognize. Thus, the leader must provide opportunities for members to talk about the purpose of the group for them and their direction in life (either in a prison environment or in society).

Step 3:   *Establish a therapeutic environment.* The leader must teach group members appropriate group behavior by having them direct comments to other group members rather than just to the leader. Trust and authenticity usually are demonstrated through appropriate self-disclosure and restraint.

Possible Challenges, Limitations, and Ethical Considerations

In examining the literature on adult offenders, Zimpfer (1992) identified the low level of trust and high level of anger, frustration, and sense of deprivation as potentially problematic for group leaders. Morgan (2004) identified several additional characteristics that may present challenges to group leaders:

1. Some members are described as "religious converts" (e.g., members who will no longer engage in antisocial or criminal acts because they have found or renewed their faith in God).
2. Some members see themselves as "a helper member" (e.g., members who avoid the therapeutic process by assuming a helper role for those they see as less fortunate in the group rather than seeking help for themselves).
3. Some members see themselves as the "superior member" (e.g., entrenched in narcissism, using the helper role to avoid self-exploration).
4. Some members fall into the category of "the involuntary member" with no therapeutic goals or expectation of benefit from group experience.

The group leader must take care to consider the unique ethical implications of working with offender populations, because conducting groups in this context creates a number of potentially problematic dynamics. For one thing, when members feel pressured or forced to participate in counseling without their acquiescence, it is likely to affect their relationship with the group leader. Also, group leaders should examine their own feelings about the reason group members have been incarcerated or treatment in the group has been mandated and be cognizant of the impact of these feelings on the development of the counseling relationship.

Group leaders further must be aware of the potential power that group members may perceive them as having—and indeed have, when their assessments, reports, or perceptions of progress may have a direct bearing on the participant's situation. To better prepare counselors for the complex ethical and professional issues involved, additional training is recommended in the use of group skills, as well as in managing security and safety issues when conducting groups in correctional settings and with offender and mandated populations (Winterowd et al., 2001).

Group Sessions by Stages for Offender Populations

In outlining the developmental stages of groups for offender and mandated populations, we will follow the sequence presented in chapter 2: definitive stage, personal involvement stage, group involvement stage, and enhancement and closure stage. Although the development of each offender and mandated group is unique, each progresses in approximately the same manner as described in the group counseling literature.

Definitive Stage

Assuming that the appropriate foundational steps (described in chapter 2) have been taken in establishing the group, the role of the leader in this stage is to explain the rules and the consequences of breaking the rules. Given the mandated or otherwise not-entirely-voluntary nature of participation, the leader must be very clear about both the rules and the consequences of breaking them. The leader then engages members in activities aimed at acquainting them with each other and attempts to draw from the participants their goals and expectations for the group. The leader attempts to model behaviors expected of the group members.

The group members typically are involved with evaluating the leader in terms of skills, ability, and capacity to understand and trust offender members, and evaluating the other members in terms of their commitment, safety, confidentiality, observation of rules, and any use of intimidation to control or manipulate participants. Members define the group experience in terms of their life experiences while living on the outside and while incarcerated. A major goal is trust building.

Personal Involvement Stage

At this stage the leader's role is to foster interpersonal interactions, openness and sharing of information, and working through power struggles in an environment in which power is considered the definitive representation of status. Members may openly challenge other members, the leader, and the organizational structure of the prison environment and those in authority as they strive to find their place in the group. Members may resist integrating the feedback they receive when they perceive the suggested changes as being too weak for them to survive in the prison environment. Over time, however, group members generally become more willing to share themselves with others and take a more active role in the group process.

The leader demonstrates awareness of the emotional makeup of the group and encourages affective expression. He or she works to provide an environment conducive to privacy and safety within the regulations of the prison or environment and is aware of and may seek to highlight the impact of the prison environment on the offenders' behaviors. The leader allows members to move through this stage at their own pace.

Group Involvement Stage

During the group involvement stage, offender populations move toward more cooperation and cohesion while decreasing conflict and confrontation. With the leader's encouragement, members become more confident in themselves and their ability to relate effectively in the group environment. The members focus more on developing self-adjustment skills that will help them avoid recidivism. Finally, members increasingly are observed to support other members and work within the organizational structure to effect change. The leader functions more in a helping capacity to enhance the development of individual members and the group as a whole in improving the quality of life in prison.

Enhancement and Closure Stage

In this final stage, the group members must evaluate their success and prepare for the group to come to an end. The members evaluate the amount of progress they have made during the life of the group. This is a period during which members share their concerns about what will happen when they make the transition to life outside of prison. Leaders can use this period of evaluation to assist members in evaluating their growth and development. Leaders may explore with members the various options facing individual members, explore previous and ineffective responses, and reinforce new learning and the capacity to make more effective choices.

As members start to deal with the loss that group closure will bring, the leader should encourage consideration of alternatives to the group that they might engage in to gain the positive support the group provided. The leader facilitates closure by initiating structured ways of saying good-bye for those who will not only leave the group but also will leave prison. Finally, the leader explains and encourages members to take advantage of follow-up procedures and transition services that will assist them when they leave prison.

Strategies to Evaluate the Group

A number of important questions remain with regard to evaluating the efficacy of groups for offenders and mandated clients. Evaluating the success of these groups represents a complex endeavor, partly because members, leaders, and facilities may have different goals for the group and different ideas about "success," and partly because of the mandated nature of the members' participation. Morgan (2004) identified several strategies that should be considered and implemented in evaluating groups for offender populations.

1. Group research should investigate the efficacy of differing theoretical approaches, strategies, and dynamics in group work with offenders.
2. Group treatment outcome studies with offender populations must incorporate measures to accurately assess client progress, intergroup relations as a measure of therapeutic progress and institutional behavior, and postrelease follow-up.
3. Too much emphasis has been placed on the effectiveness of group therapy in reducing recidivism. Recidivism may not be an appropriate measure of effectiveness of group treatment, especially since rehabilitation programs are more comprehensive in nature with the inclusion of more than one treatment modality. Thus, the evaluation of programs should be specific to the goals and aims of the group.

Follow-Up and Referral

Follow-up with offender populations is guided by logistics (e.g., members who are incarcerated, are on probation, or who have been paroled). The ability to follow up with offender populations is much easier if they are a captive audience (e.g., incarcerated). Once they are paroled or on probation, it becomes more difficult to locate them and track their progress. The type of facility (minimum versus maximum security) also may influence follow-up with offender populations. For example, incarcerated inmates in minimum-security correctional environments may have opportunities to slowly make a transition back to society by spending some time in the "middle ground" between full incarceration and freedom (e.g., work- and study-release status) (Vernick & Reardon, 2001). Probation and parole officers can play an important role in the follow-up when group participation is a condition of the offenders' probation or parole requirements.

The referral procedure of offender populations to groups depends in part upon the type of offender (e.g., violent, nonviolent, juvenile), severity of the offense, and logistics. For example, drug offenders may be required to attend groups as part of their sentencing in drug court, while other offenders are prohibited from group activities and placed in solitary confinement because of their offense. In addition, the referral process should be sensitive to gender and cultural needs and perceptions regarding various components of the correctional system.

GROUPS IN HOSPITALS AND MEDICAL SETTINGS

Groups became a frequent mode of therapy within hospital settings in the 1980s and have become the most consistently used format for therapeutic change ("New Model Proposed," 1982; Satterley, 1995). Today, groups in inpatient facilities are common, although inpatient groups have their own theoretical framework (Emer, 2004). Group counseling in hospital/medical settings may involve working with individuals who have recent-onset disabilities, chronic illnesses such as diabetes, mental illness and psychiatric disorders, terminal diagnoses, and life-threatening disorders including cancer, AIDS, and others. Group approaches are used in medical and health care settings because they are time- and cost-efficient (Spira, 1997).

The flexibility of group formats can be applied to a wide array of issues specific to a medical condition or unique to a given population. Specific group formats used in medical and health care settings include social support, educational, psychoeducational, counseling, and task groups (Elliott, Rivera, & Tucker, 2004). Elliott et al. advocate the therapeutic properties of groups in addressing the many issues accompanying various health-related problems.

Patients with chronic or terminal illnesses find group counseling beneficial in adjusting to psychosocial problems that can exacerbate their medical condition. Among the advantages for this population are the following:

- Group counseling "has been effective in assisting patients with chronic illnesses gain information, receive social support, develop individual meaning for their illness, and acquire skills and adaptive behaviors with which to cope with their disease" (McRae & Smith, 1998, p. 148).
- Groups offer members a sense of belonging and a forum in which they can express their emotions. Realizing the counterproductivity of suppressed emotions and fears, patients find a sense of freedom in their expression and the knowledge that they are not alone (Roberts, Kiselica, & Fredrickson, 2002).

- Groups help members by instilling a sense of hope and optimism, offering members opportunities to help and assist others, and to learn from others about coping with their health (Elliott et al., 2004; Yalom, 1995).

Purpose

Groups with patients in medical and health care settings may serve a number of separate or conjoint purposes. Generally, these groups are designed to

- assist patients with coping and psychosocial adjustment to illness;
- provide education and information about effective medical and functional management of the chronic illness, condition, or disability with which the members are living; and
- develop an atmosphere of support and communication among those who share the experience of living with a disability or illness and its psychosocial effects.

Relevant Research

As suggested above, research concerning the benefits and efficacy of group counseling in hospitals and medical settings has generally been very supportive. Because of limitations of space and the significant body of literature associated with relevant research, only a few representative findings are described briefly here. Among the benefits reported, group counseling of different types in hospital and medical settings has been shown to improve psychosocial adaptation, reduce psychological distress, improve illness self-management and self-efficacy, and promote improved compliance with treatment.

Group counseling has been reported to provide an efficient means of delivering counseling services to older people with chronic illnesses and encourage the development of supportive relationships between and among members (Corey & Corey, 1982). Also, groups of elderly patients with diabetes have been shown to improve compliance with diet plans and to lower peak blood glucose levels (Robison, 1993).

Structured groups for gay men newly diagnosed with HIV/AIDS have been reported to counter social isolation and provide solidarity for the group members. These groups may focus on living with the disease instead of dying from it, revealing sexuality and health issues to the family, and deflecting social condemnation (Smiley, 2004).

A growing body of empirical evidence suggests that groups for women with breast cancer are successful at improving members' psychosocial, social, and physiological well-being (Cope, 1995; Fawzy et al., 1993; Gore-Felton & Spiegel, 1999; Richardson, Shelton, Krailo, & Levine, 1990; Spiegel, 1993). For example, patients who participated in group therapy had significantly higher levels of personal control (e.g., they felt events were contingent on their behavior instead of feeling that events were externally controlled) compared to patients who received only standard medical care (Bloom, Ross, & Burnell, 1978). Further, women patients with breast cancer who participated in group counseling experienced less distress and less pain than those who received standard care (Goodwin et al., 2001). In addition, short-term group counseling has been effective in reducing physical symptoms, and participants who attended more sessions realized a greater benefit (Kashner, Rost, Cohen, Anderson, & Smith, 1995).

Conceptual Framework

Patients with chronic or terminal illness, especially upon receiving a serious medical diagnosis, experience psychological, emotional, and spiritual distress from the impact of the news. The effects can be pervasive, impinging on all aspects of their life. Common reactions include anxiety about pain and discomfort, fear and uncertainty about the future, and depression. Although individuals dealing with an illness or medical crisis may not fully regain their previous level of functioning, they can utilize coping strategies to improve their quality of life. Roberts et al. (2002) suggested that

> what is needed to facilitate this process are counseling
> professionals to address the myriad of medical crises and
> medical professionals willing to enter into collegial relationships
> with counselors to foster a more holistic therapeutic encounter
> with the client. (p. 422)

Group counseling is an effective approach to addressing issues related to medical illnesses in that it often negates the social isolation the clients experience and allows them to experience positive affirmation.

The *educational group* is the most commonly used modality of group counseling in the medical/hospital setting. The purpose of an educational group in this setting is to disseminate specific information to participants. Educational groups often are part of interdisciplinary treatment programs (e.g., pain management) that may include counselors, nurses, psychologists, nutritionists, pharmacists, and physical and occupational therapists.

Educational groups are commonly used for several reasons (Elliot et al., 2004):

1. A health care professional can disseminate valuable medical information to several patients at once.
2. Patients may benefit from contact with others who have experienced similar injuries or medical conditions.
3. Family members may also observe, participate, and establish contact with other patients and caregivers.

According to Johansson, Dahl, Jannert, Melin, and Anderson (1998), educational groups can effectively augment interdisciplinary treatment programs and, over time, participants show significant improvements in activity levels, physical fitness, and occupational training, and have lower levels of medication use, sick leave, and distress compared to patients who do not participate in group sessions. In another example of the effectiveness of the educational group approach, participation in an educational group resulted in reducing personal distress more effectively than peer discussion groups among women with breast cancer (Helgeson, Cohen, Schulz, & Yasko, 1999; 2001).

Overwhelmingly, educational groups are open in nature, with meetings lasting from one to many sessions (Spira, 1997). Closed groups are used to limit the number of participants or in situations when the group deals with sensitive materials and subject matter (e.g., HIV/AIDS). Self-disclosure is voluntary, and as self-disclosure increases, concern for confidentiality increases as well. "Ideally, the focus of the group is on the exchange of educational information" (Elliot et al., 2004, p. 341).

Group Goals

The goals of groups for patients with medical illnesses depend on the type of group (e.g., support) and its purpose (e.g., acceptance of an illness, preparing to die). Nevertheless, several general goals in medical settings are applicable across various types of groups (Gore-Felton & Spiegel, 1999, pp. 277–279):

1. *Social support*: Allows patients to validate and normalize disease-related feelings and experiences; empowers patients to develop effective coping strategies
2. *Expression of emotion*: Encourages open expression of emotion and assertiveness in assuming control over the course of treatment, life decisions, and relationship
3. *Detoxifying dying*: Explores fears associated with the process of dying to reduce the anxiety aroused by the threat of death
4. *Reordering life priorities*: Helps patients to think about what is really important to them and allows them to take control of the aspects of their lives they can influence while grieving and relinquishing the parts over which they have no control
5. *Family support*: Assists patients in recognizing needs that family members are not meeting and helps the patient communicate these needs to establish closer and more meaningful relationships between patients and family members
6. *Effective communication with physicians*: Provides mutual encouragement to get questions answered, to participate actively in treatment decisions, and to consider alternatives carefully
7. *Symptom management*: Promotes effective coping, both behavioral and psychological, to manage external and internal stressors that can strain individual resources. Coping behaviors are problem focused (e.g., changing the source of the stress) and emotion focused (e.g., regulating stressful emotions).

Although each of these goals is applicable to groups in general, these group goals in hospital/medical settings are effective in helping patients with medical crises reduce their anxiety related to psychosocial adjustment to illness, death and dying, strengthen interpersonal relationships, and improve their quality of life. For patients who endure the necessary traditional medical interventions for illness, it is important to note the evidence indicating that group psychotherapy is an effective adjunct to treatment (Gore-Felton & Spiegel, 1999; Ward, 2004).

Pre-Group Screening and Orientation to the Group

Because of the considerable variance in the nature, size, focus, and form of group counseling in medical and hospital settings, conducting pre-group screening and orientation will vary considerably as well. The general considerations are discussed in this section. According to Huebner (2004), fundamental guidelines in group formation are the following:

- Groups should not be fewer than 4 or 5 members or more than 12 members.
- Meeting rooms should be large enough for members to see each other and participate in group activities.
- Meetings typically range from 90 minutes to 3 hours, guided by the group composition.
- Frequency of the meetings is guided by the population involved.

As examples, in a longer-term outpatient support group, weekly or even monthly meetings may be appropriate, while in an inpatient, acute rehabilitation setting where patients are in the hospital or facility for a short time, meetings may occur more frequently.

Prior to consenting to participate, members should be made aware of the nature and purpose of the group. Group leaders should identify whether the purpose will be primarily educational, or to develop social support, or to foster coping strategies, and so on. The potential members should be made aware of the expectations and potential risks involved in participation. To the extent possible, based on variables such as time since diagnosis and response to diagnosis, age of the potential participant, and type of illness or disability, group leaders should attempt to select members whose needs and goals are compatible with goals of the group, who will not impede the group process, and whose well-being will not be jeopardized by the group experience (Commission on Rehabilitation Counselor Certification, 2002).

Possible Challenges, Limitations, and Ethical Considerations

The most appropriate type of group in terms of format, theoretical approach, and specific methods applied in hospital-based groups will be determined to some extent by the constraints of the environment and the needs of the members (Huebner, 2004). Based on the population, the availability to patients of alternative counseling modalities (e.g., individual counseling), and the financial and physical constraints of the hospital or other facility, group leaders may be involved with groups characterized by rapid turnover of members and significant variation in terms of the interests and needs, ages, and level and type of illness or disability of the members. Group leaders may be faced with decisions concerning the format, open or closed nature of the group, and content, or these decisions may be made for them by the hospital or agency hosting the group.

Group leaders must consider the barriers and limitations to full participation of the members based on illness- or disability-related variables. Factors such as cognitive and physical limitations, communication barriers, limitations in mobility, and the potential effects of treatment on attention and energy level must be considered when planning interventions, activities, and the group's time and space parameters.

Group Sessions by Stages

The stages of groups for clients in hospital/medical settings are outlined following the sequence presented in chapter 2: the definitive stage, personal involvement stage, group involvement stage, and enhancement and closure stage.

Definitive Stage

Initially, the group members are likely to have questions and concerns about the nature and purpose of the group and their participation in it. Depending on the group's purpose, members may be encouraged to discuss their own experiences with the illness or disability, significant disability-related problems, or questions they may have about their experience.

> Using methods such as reflection, clarification, self-disclosure, positive reinforcement, role playing, and establishing a relaxed atmosphere, group leaders encourage participants to develop mutual trust, openness, involvement, personal awareness and responsibility, and commitment. (Livneh et al., 2002, p. 441)

Personal Involvement Stage

The typical personal involvement stage is characterized by a deeper level of personal sharing and exploration; an awareness, through this sharing, of the similarities and commonalities of the current experience; and increased willingness to express oneself. Leadership at this stage begins to take a less directive form and involves providing encouragement, linking shared experiences, and proposing and maintaining themes or topics for the meetings.

Group Involvement Stage

As the group members become increasingly comfortable with the process and the experience of sharing and working together with the other members, their attention is likely to shift from sharing problems and issues to discussing solutions and resources. At this stage, the leader plays a critical role in providing information and resources about methods of coping, problem solving about and planning for the future, and, in some cases, community, social, and/or family reintegration. Specific topics that leaders may encourage members to consider include the impact of disability- or illness-related changes on familial, social, and work roles; the realization of increased dependence on others or on accommodations; and coping with the emotional impact of living with a chronic or permanent condition.

Enhancement and Closure Stage

The degree to which group members experience a sense of loss of the group's support—whether that support comes primarily in the form of education or social support—depends to a great extent on the purpose and nature of the group. In the case of psychoeducational groups, which are highly structured and where group cohesion is typically lower than in more support-based groups, members may experience little or no sense of loss. The same may be true to some extent for groups conducted in acute rehabilitation settings over a short period of time. In other cases, however, the loss of the group's support may be significant. This may be particularly true for group members who are, at the same time, experiencing loss of function or other significant life changes as a result of illness or the onset of disability.

As the group nears closure, grieving a loss of function may produce more anger or dependency than might be typical (Huebner, 2004). Counselors should evaluate the members in this regard well before the group actually ends and assess the need for ongoing services and the development of longer-term supports.

Strategies to Evaluate the Group

Evaluation of groups in hospital/medical settings depends on the nature of the group. In psychoeducational groups, evaluation is likely to be based on the development of new skills, such as self-management, illness monitoring, improved mobility, or behavior change such as increased awareness of lifestyle on disease management and subsequent adaptive changes. In support groups or groups aimed at helping people cope with the emotional and psychosocial impact of illness or disability, evaluation of the group's effectiveness may be based on reduction of depression or anxiety, enhanced feelings of self-efficacy or confidence, or more concrete goal attainment, such as the member's return to work or other pre-illness activities.

Follow-Up and Referral

Given the significant changes that are likely to occur simultaneously with group participation, careful attention must be paid to both follow-up and referral. Counselors should make clear to members the availability of returning to the group, or participating in new groups, or other means of continued access to support. Ethically, rehabilitation counselors are bound to be knowledgeable about referral resources and to suggest appropriate alternatives. Members must be informed that further support, if not currently required, will be available in the future. Hosaka et al. (2001) reported that "booster sessions" may be necessary to help participants who live with a chronic health condition. These booster sessions may be particularly important for those who have difficulty maintaining health-promoting behaviors (Roffman et al., 1998).

LEARNING ACTIVITIES

1. Arrange and conduct an interview with a counselor/therapist who specializes in group counseling with patients/clients in medical crisis (e.g., diagnosis of cancer, AIDS, diabetes) to learn more about group counseling in medical or health care settings. Give a brief presentation to the class on what you learned from this activity.
2. In a small group, take turns role playing a counseling group meeting for a specific offender population (e.g., women, juveniles) with a focus on a specific issue (e.g., grief, sexual abuse).

3. In a small group, discuss your feelings, concerns, and fears about conducting a group with people who were recently diagnosed with a chronic illness or recent onset of a significant disability. What common concerns are expressed? How might these feelings and concerns affect a group leader's ability to develop an effective counseling relationship?

4. In a small group, discuss your feelings, concerns, and fears about conducting a group for offenders. Are different kinds of offenses more or less problematic for different people? What common concerns are expressed? How might your own values, experiences, and ideas about offenders and their offenses affect your ability to develop an effective counseling relationship? Are there some groups that you think you would not be comfortable or effective in serving?

SUMMARY

Group counseling is increasingly gaining acceptance as a critical component of rehabilitation counseling. Rehabilitation counselors today are more likely than ever before to be engaged in conducting groups, regardless of their professional practice setting. This increased professional use of group counseling is reflected in the professions' Scope of Practice statement and its standards for educational preparation (CORE, 2004), as well as in several studies of how rehabilitation counselors spend their professional time (e.g., Leahy, Chan, & Saunders, 2001). The most recent revision of the *Code of Professional Ethics for Rehabilitation Counselors* includes a section dedicated to the ethical practice of group work in rehabilitation counseling (Commission on Rehabilitation Counselor Certification, 2002).

As the profession of rehabilitation counseling continues to experience growth and expansion into new and different areas of focus and professional practice, skill in conducting group counseling will become even more critical. Opportunities to conduct group counseling in rehabilitation settings will increasingly occur across the range of professional settings (e.g., vocational, educational, correctional, medical) and will involve working with people from diverse backgrounds with respect to cultural, disability, age, and gender characteristics.

There are three specific types of groups or group settings in which rehabilitation counselors are increasingly likely to be engaged. The job club and related employment-focused group frameworks offer an efficient and effective approach to assisting persons with disabilities in attaining employment. Outside of the traditional vocational rehabilitation settings, rehabilitation counselors are increasingly likely to be engaged in group counseling with offender and mandated clients or in hospital or medical settings. Across the range of professional settings in which rehabilitation counselors are employed, they will increasingly be responsible for conducting psychoeducational groups, counseling groups, and psychotherapy groups aimed at assisting persons with disabilities to achieve their goals and fulfill their potential. Rehabilitation counseling is a process in which counselors will need to continuously expand their skills and expertise, and group work with offender populations is one such area.

USEFUL WEB SITES

- ☐ American Rehabilitation Counseling Association
  www.arcaweb.org
- ☐ Careers in Vocational Rehabilitation
  www.rehabjobs.org/
- ☐ U.S. Department of Justice
  www.usdoj.gov
- ☐ Federal Bureau of Prisons
  www.bop.gov
- ☐ Commission on Rehabilitation Counselor Certification
  www.crccertification.com
- ☐ Council on Rehabilitation Education
  www.core-rehab.org
- ☐ National Council on Disability
  www.ncd.gov
- ☐ National Council on Rehabilitation Education
  www.rehabeducators.org/
- ☐ National Institutes of Health
  www.nih.gov
- ☐ National Institute of Mental Health
  www.nimh.nih.gov/
- ☐ National Rehabilitation Association
  www.nationalrehab.org/website/index.html
- ☐ National Rehabilitation Counseling Association
  http://nrca-net.org
- ☐ U.S. Sentencing Commission
  www.ussc.gov

REFERENCES

American Correctional Association. (1993). *Female offenders: Meeting needs of a neglected population*. Laurel, MD: Author.

Andrews, D. A., & Bonta, J. (1994). *The psychology of crime*. Cincinnati, OH: Anderson.

Andrews, D. A., Bonta, J., & Hoge, R. D. (1990). Classification for effective rehabilitation: Rediscovering psychology. *Criminal Justice and Behavior, 17*, 19–52.

Association for Specialists in Group Work (ASGW). (2000, January). *Professional standards for training of group workers*. Retrieved from http://asgw.educ.kent.edu/training_standards.htm

Azrin, N. H., & Besalel, V. A. (1980). *Job club counselors manual: A behavioral approach to vocational counseling*. Baltimore: University Park Press.

Azrin, N. H., Flores, T., & Kaplan, S. (1975). Job-finding club: A group-assisted program for obtaining employment. *Behavior and Research and Therapy, 13*, 17–27.

Azrin, N. H., & Phillips, R. (1979). The job club method for the job handicapped: A comparative outcome study. *Rehabilitation Counseling Bulletin, 23,* 144–155.

Bishop, M., & Feist-Price, S. (2002). Quality of life assessment in the rehabilitation counseling relationship: Strategies and measures. *Journal of Applied Rehabilitation Counseling, 33*(1), 35–47.

Black, R. S., Tsuhako, K., & McDougall, D. (1998). Job club intervention to improve interviewing skills of young adults with cognitive disabilities. *Journal for Vocational Special Needs Education, 20*(2), 33–38.

Bloom, J. R., Ross, R. D., & Burnell, G. (1978). The effect of social support on patient adjustment after breast surgery. *Patient Counseling Health Education, 1*, 50–59.

Brooks, F., Nackerud, L., & Risler, E. (2001). Evaluation of a job-finding club for TANF recipients: Psychosocial impacts. *Research on Social Work Practice, 11*(1), 79–93.

Brown, B. M. (1997, March). Psychoeducational group work. *Counseling and Human Development, 29*, 1–16.

Bureau of Justice Statistics. (2005a). Correction statistics. *Sourcebook of criminal justice statistics*. Retrieved June 15, 2005, from http://www.ojp.usdoj.gov/bjs/correct.htm

Bureau of Justice Statistics. (2005b). Criminal offenders statistics. *Sourcebook of criminal justice statistics*. Retrieved June 15, 2005, from http://www.ojp.usdoj.gov.bjs/crimoff.htm

Champion, D. J. (1996). *Probation, parole and community corrections* (2nd ed.). Upper Saddle River, NJ: Prentice Hall.

Claypoole, S. D., Moody, E. E., & Peace, S. D. (2000). Moral dilemma discussions: An effective group intervention for juvenile offenders. *Journal for Specialists in Group Work, 25*, 394–411.

Commission on Rehabilitation Counselor Certification. (2002). *Code of professional ethics for rehabilitation counselors*. Rolling Meadows, IL: Author.

Condelli, W. S., Bradigan, B., & Holanchock, H. (1997). Intermediate care programs to reduce risk and better manage inmates with psychiatric disorders. *Behavioral Sciences and the Law, 15*, 459–467.

Conyne, R. K. (1996). The Association for Specialists in Group Work training standards: Some considerations and suggestions for training. *Journal for Specialists in Group Work, 21*, 155–162.

Cope, C. G. (1995). Functions of a breast cancer support group as perceived by the participants: An ethnographic study. *Cancer Nursing, 18*, 472–478.

Corey, G., & Corey, M. (1982). *Group counseling: Process and practice*. Monterey, CA: Brooks/Cole.

Council on Rehabilitation Education (CORE). (2004). *Accreditation manual*. Retrieved August 2004, from http://www.core-rehab.org//index.html

DeAngelis, T. (1992, November). Best psychological treatment for many men: Group therapy. *APA Monitor, 23*, 31.

Delbecq, A. L., Van de Ven, A. H., & Gustafson, D. H. (1975). *Group techniques for program planning: A guide to nominal group and delphi processes*. Glenview, IL: Scott, Foresman.

Elliott, T., Rivera, P., & Tucker, E. (2004). Groups in behavioral health and medical settings. In J. L. DeLucia-Waack, D. Gerrity, C. Kalodner, & M. Riva (Eds.), *Handbook of group counseling and psychotherapy* (pp. 338–350). New York: Sage.

Emer, D. (2004). The use of groups in inpatient facilities: Needs, focus, successes, and remaining dilemmas. In J. L. DeLucia-Waak, D. A. Gerrity, C. R. Kalodner, & M. T. Riva (Eds.), *Handbook of group counseling and psychotherapy* (pp. 351–365). Thousand Oaks, CA: Sage.

Fawzy, F. I., Fawzy, N. W., Hyun, C. S., Elashoff, R., Guthrie, D., Fahey, J. L., & Morton, D. L. (1993). Malignant melanoma. Effects of an early structured psychiatric intervention, coping, and affective state on recurrence and survival 6 years later. *Archives of General Psychiatry, 50*, 681–689.

Gazda, G. M., Ginter, E. J., & Horne, A. M. (2001). *Group counseling and group psychotherapy: Theory and application*. Boston: Allyn & Bacon.

Gendreau, P. (1996). Offender rehabilitation: What we know and what needs to be done. *Criminal Justice and Behavior, 23*, 144–161.

Gibbs, J. C., Potter, G. B., Goldstein, A. P., & Brendtro, L. K. (1996, Winter). Frontiers in psychoeducation: The EQUIP model with antisocial youth. *Reclaiming Children and Youth*, 22–28.

Gilbride, D., & Stensrud, R. (2003). Job placement and employer consulting: Services and strategies. In E. M. Szymanski & R. M. Parker (Eds.), *Work and disability: Issues and strategies in career development and job placement* (2nd ed., pp. 407–440). Austin, TX: ProEd.

Gladding, S. T. (1999). *Group work: A counseling specialty* (3rd ed.). Upper Saddle River, NJ: Merrill.

Goodwin, P. J., Leszcz, M., Ennis, M., Koopmans, J. M., Chochinov, H., Navarro, M., Speca, M., & Hunter, J. (2001). The effect of group psychosocial support on survival in metastatic breast cancer. *New England Journal of Medicine, 345*, 1719–1726.

Gore-Felton, C., & Spiegel, D. (1999). Enhancing women's lives: The role of support groups among breast cancer patients. *Journal for Specialists in Group Work, 24*, 274–287.

Harley, D. A. (1996). Vocational rehabilitation services for an offender population. *Journal of Rehabilitation, 62*, 45–48.

Helgeson, V., Cohen, S., Schulz, R., & Yasko, J. (1999). Education and peer discussion group interventions and adjustment to breast cancer. *Archives of General Psychiatry, 56*, 340–347.

Helgeson, V., Cohen, S., Schulz, R., & Yasko, J. (2001). Long-term effects of educational and peer discussion group interventions on adjustment to breast cancer. *Health Psychology, 20*, 387–392.

Hosaka, T., Sugiyama, Y., Hirai, K., Okuyama, T., Sugawara, Y., & Nakamura Y. (2001). Effects of a modified group intervention with early-stage breast cancer patients. *General Hospital Psychiatry, 23*, 145–151.

Huebner, R. A. (2004). Group procedures. In F. Chan, N. L. Berven, & K. R. Thomas (Eds.), *Counseling theories and techniques for rehabilitation health professionals* (pp. 244–263). New York: Springer.

Johansson, C., Dahl, J., Jannert, M., Melin, L., & Anderson, G. (1998). Effects of a cognitive–behavioral pain management program. *Behavior Research and Therapy, 36*, 915–930.

Kashner, T. M., Rost, K., Cohen, B., Anderson, M., & Smith, G. (1995). Enhancing the health of somatization disorder patients: Effectiveness of short-term group therapy. *Psychosomatics, 36*, 462–470.

Leahy, M. J. (2004). Qualified providers. In T. F. Riggar & D. R. Maki (Eds.), *Handbook of rehabilitation counseling* (pp. 142–158). New York: Springer Publishing Company.

Leahy, M. J., Chan, F., & Saunders, J. (2001). *An analysis of job functions and knowledge requirements of certified rehabilitation counselors in the 21st century.* Chicago: Foundation for Rehabilitation Education and Research.

Leeman, L. W., Gibbs, J. C., & Fuller, D. (1993). Evaluation of a multi-component treatment program for juvenile delinquents. *Aggressive Behavior, 19*, 281–292.

Leone, P. E., Quinn, M., & Osher, D. (2002). *Collaboration in the juvenile justice system and youth-serving agencies: Improving prevention, providing more efficient services, and reducing recidivism for youth with disabilities.* Washington, DC: Office of Juvenile Justice and Delinquency Prevention.

Livneh, H. (2001). Psychosocial adaptation to chronic illness and disability: A conceptual framework. *Rehabilitation Counseling Bulletin, 44*(3), 151–160.

Livneh, H., Wilson, L. M., & Pullo, R. E. (2002). Group counseling for people with physical disabilities. In D. Capuzzi & D. R. Gross (Eds.), *Introduction to group counseling* (3rd ed., pp. 435–468). Denver: Love Publishing.

Maruschak, L. M., & Beck, A. J. (2001). *Bureau of justice statistics special report: Medical problems of inmates, 1997.* Washington, DC: U.S. Department of Justice, Office of Justice Programs.

McRae, C., & Smith, C. H. (1998). Chronic illness: Promoting the adjustment process. In S. Roth-Roemer, S. R. Kurpius, & C. Carmin (Eds.), *The emerging role of counseling in health care* (pp. 137–156). New York: Norton.

McWhirter, P. T., & McWhirter, J. J. (1996). Transition-to-work group: University students with learning disabilities. *Journal for Specialists in Group Work, 21,* 144–148.

Morgan, R. D. (2004). Groups with offenders and mandated clients. In J. L. DeLucia-Waak, D. A. Gerrity, C. R. Kalodner, & M. T. Riva (Eds.), *Handbook of group counseling and psychotherapy* (pp. 388–400). Thousand Oaks, CA: Sage.

Morgan, R. D., & Flora, D. B. (2002). Group psychotherapy with incarcerated offenders: A research synthesis. *Group Dynamics: Theory, Research, and Practice, 6,* 203–218.

Morgan, R. D., & Winterowd, C. L. (2002). Interpersonal process-oriented group psychotherapy with offender populations. *International Journal of Offender Therapy and Comparative Criminology, 46,* 466–482.

Morgan, R. D., Winterowd, C. L., & Ferrell, S. W. (1999). A national survey of group psychotherapy services in correctional facilities. *Professional Psychology: Research and Practice, 30,* 600–606.

Morgan, R. D., Winterowd, C. L., & Fuqua, D. R. (1999). The efficacy of an integrated theoretical approach to group psychotherapy for male inmates. *Journal of Contemporary Psychology, 29,* 203–222.

New model proposed for inpatient group therapy. (1982, March 19). *Psychiatric News, 9,* 32–34.

Olson, M. J., & McEwen, M. A. (2004). Grief counseling in a medium-security prison. *Journal for Specialists in Group Work, 29,* 225–236.

Richardson, J. L., Shelton, D. R., Krailo, M., & Levine, A. M. (1990). The effect of compliance with treatment on survival among patients with hematologic malignancies. *Journal of Clinical Oncology, 8,* 356–364.

Riordan, R. J., & Martin, M. H. (1993). Mental health counseling and the mandated client. *Journal of Mental Health Counseling, 15,* 373–383.

Roberts, S. A., Kiselica, M. S., & Fredrickson, S. A. (2002). Quality of life of persons with medical illnesses: Counseling's holistic contribution. *Journal of Counseling & Development, 80,* 422–432.

Robison, F. F. (1993). A training and support group for elderly diabetics: Description and evaluation. *Journal for Specialists in Group Work, 18,* 127–136.

Roffman, R. A., Stephens, R. S., Curtain, L., Gordon, J., Craver, J., Stern, M., Beadnell, B., & Downey, L. (1998). Relapse prevention as an intervention model for HIV risk reduction in gay and bisexual men. *AIDS Education and Prevention, 10,* 1–18.

Rutman, I. (1994). How psychiatric disability expresses itself as a barrier to employment. *Psychosocial Rehabilitation Journal, 17*(3), 17–35.

Rutherford, R. B., Bullis, M., Anderson, C. W., & Griller-Clark, H. M. (2002). *Youth with disabilities in the corrections systems: Prevalence rates and identification issues.* Washington, DC: Office of Juvenile Justice and Delinquency Prevention.

Satterley, J. A. (1995). Needed: A fresh start for psychiatric inpatient groups. *Social Work With Groups, 17,* 71–81.

Scarborough, Z. Y., Glaser, B. A., Calhoun, G. B., Stefurak, T., & Petrocelli, J. V. (2004). Cluster-derived groupings of the behavior assessment system for children among male juvenile offenders. *Journal of Offender Rehabilitation, 39,* 1–17.

Scott, E. M. (1993). Prison group therapy with mentally and emotionally disturbed offenders. *International Journal of Offender Therapy and Comparative Criminology, 37,* 131–145.

Shields, S. A. (1986). Busted and branded: Group work with substance abusing adolescents in schools. *Social Work With Groups, 9,* 61–81.

Smiley, K. A. (2004). A structured group for gay men newly diagnosed with HIV/AIDS. *Journal for Specialists in Group Work, 29,* 207–224.

Spiegel, D. (1993). Psychosocial intervention in cancer. *Journal of the National Cancer Institute, 85,* 1198–1205.

Spira, J. L. (1997). *Group therapy for medically ill patients.* New York: Guilford.

Thomas, K. R., Thoreson, R. W., Parker, R. M., & Butler, A. J. (1998). Theoretical foundations of the counseling function. In R. M. Parker & E. M. Szymanski (Eds.), *Rehabilitation counseling: Basics and beyond* (3rd ed., pp. 225–268). Austin, TX: ProEd.

Van Steele, K. R., & Moberg, D. P. (2004). Outcome data for MICA clients after participation in an institutional therapeutic community. *Journal of Offender Rehabilitation, 39,* 37–62.

Vernick, S. H., & Reardon, R. C. (2001). Career development programs in corrections. *Journal of Career Development, 27,* 265–277.

Ward, D. E. (2004). The evidence mounts: Group work is effective. *Journal for Specialists in Group Work, 29,* 155–157.

Winterowd, C. L., Morgan, R. D., & Ferrell, S. W. (2001). Principle components analysis of important goals for group work with male inmates. *Journal for Specialists in Group Work, 26,* 406–417.

Yalom, I. (1995). *The theory and practice of group psychotherapy* (4th ed.). New York: Basic Books.

Zimpfer, D. (1992). Group work with adult offenders: An overview. *Journal for Specialists in Group Work, 17,* 54–61.

PART FIVE:

Group Work With Specific Populations

Part Five of this text, "Group Work With Specific Populations," provides a combination of background information and practical techniques for working with specific populations—people dealing with loss, those who have addictions, elderly people, and gay, lesbian, and bisexual people. These chapters provide group work specialists with the background they need to practice effectively with these populations. As with the chapters in Part Four, these include session overviews and examples for working with these specific populations.

Chapter 15, "Group Work: Loss," addresses life's losses within a group setting where members can share common problems, provide mutual aid, and develop coping skills. The chapter provides both background information and practical guidelines for leading theme-focused groups on the topic of loss. The chapter covers the mourning, feelings associated with loss, the purpose of loss-and-support groups, types of loss groups, age-specific variations, and the application of brief counseling or therapy related to loss.

Chapter 16, "Group Work: Addictions," imparts information on the topics of physiological, psychological/cognitive, and sociological factors affecting groups, with emphasis on group processes with chemically dependent populations. Substances of abuse are categorized and discussed, with model groups for women and for adolescents. The chapter blends the empirical view with pragmatic, implementable information.

Chapter 17, "Group Work: Elderly People and Their Caregivers," presents a history of group work with older adults, explains the types of groups, and explores considerations in a diverse group. The chapter presents two models—one a life-review group and the second a brief-solution-focused group or elderly people who are facing a move. Each session is described in detail. The chapter explains how technological advances—particularly eGroups—can be of benefit to older people.

Chapter 18. Part Five of this text concludes with chapter 18, "Group Work: Gay, Lesbian, and Bisexual Clients." The chapter first provides culture-specific information, then addresses language variables, affirmative counseling, and general group approaches. Like the previous chapters, this one turns to the specifics and provides concrete examples and models that the practitioner can apply in specific groups for working with gay, lesbian, and bisexual clients.

As the chapters in Part Five indicate, the effective use of group approaches is based upon a combination of knowledge and skills and the ability to apply this information to specific groups. These chapters are particularly helpful for group leaders who plan to practice in any of these specialties.

Group Work: Loss

Ann Vernon

Although we typically equate loss with death, loss is considered more accurately within the broader context of someone or something close to us being no longer present (Locke, 1994). Loss is inescapable, and it is tied intricately to change and growth, loss and gain (Parkes, 2001). A major loss entails "something in a person's life in which the person was emotionally invested" (Harvey, 2002, p. 5), which Harvey differentiated from minor losses that occur daily (such as losing an umbrella) and are not associated with emotional attachment. Weiss (2001) identified three types of major loss:

1. Losses of important relationships
2. Losses that damage our self-esteem
3. Losses resulting from victimization

Loss is multifaceted. It is associated with homelessness (Harvey, 2002), mental illness (Morse, 2000), terminal illness (Ellis, 2000), dementia (Quinn, 2002), aging (Harvey, 2002), chronic illness (Thompson & Kyle, 2000), infertility (Abbey, 2000), miscarriage (Auz & Andrews, 2002; Midland, 2002), violence and war (Harvey, 2002), relationship infidelity (Boekhout, Hendrick, & Hendrick, 2000), and close interpersonal relationships (Hobfoll, Ennis, & Kay, 2000). Viorst (1986) noted that losses also can consist of loss of expectations, abilities, power, and freedom.

Rando (2000) distinguished between *physical loss*, which is the loss of something tangible, and *psychosocial* or *symbolic loss*, which is the loss of something intangible such as the loss of health resulting from a chronic illness. Schlossberg and Robinson (1996) discussed loss associated with non-events—the dreams that are never realized or the events that are reasonable to expect but never happen. Morales (1997) described the concept of *silent loss*, such as the loss of a pet, which sometimes is not formally recognized in society.

Boss (1999) identified another type of loss, *ambiguous loss*, when a family member is either physically or psychologically absent, and maintained that of all the losses experienced in personal relationships, "ambiguous loss is the most devastating because it remains unclear, indeterminate" (p. 6). Boss identified child abduction, soldiers missing in action, incarceration, and adoption as examples of ambiguous loss in which the individual is physically absent but psychologically present, and Alzheimers disease, addictions, and chronic mental illnesses as examples of losses in which the person is physically present but psychologically absent. According to Boss, ambiguous losses are not ritualized or officially documented. Yet another type of loss, *nonfinite* loss, refers to "losses that are contingent on development; the passage of time; and lack of synchrony with hopes, wishes, ideals, and expectations" (Bruce & Schultz, 2001, p. 7).

Harvey (2000) maintained that "life is full of losses, small and large, sustainable and sometimes insuperable and incalculable in their impacts" (p. 1). According to Harvey and Miller (2000), positive outcomes such as changes in self-perceptions, social relationships, and life perspective are frequent results of a loss. Losses are necessary, according to Viorst (1986), because "we grow by losing and leaving and letting go" (p. 16).

Thus, whether the loss involves a dream, an ideal, a job, a home or possessions, an absent family member, an ability, a friendship, or one's health, looks, or status, losses are inevitable. As Harvey (2000) noted, we are affected by a sense of personal loss from youth to death and concluded that "loss is such a fundamental part of our lives that it beckons us to begin negotiating it early in life" (Harvey, 2002, p. 297).

As a result of loss, one's attitudes, values, beliefs, and perceptions are altered (Becvar, 2001). Adapting to loss and using it as a vehicle for change and growth require an adjustment to new patterns, relationships, roles, and events (Volkan & Zintl, 1993). Any loss entails a transition, which impacts roles, relationships, and routines and also one's assessment of self (Schlossberg, 1989). The impact of a loss depends on whether the loss is temporary or permanent, the nature of the loss and how it occurred, previous history of significant losses, the individual's psychological make-up, other life stressors, and whether the loss is visible or invisible (Locke, 1994; Rosoff, 1994). From another viewpoint, the extent of a support system, the current lifestyle and circumstances, and philosophical and spiritual beliefs determine the impact of the loss (Roos, 2002).

Another factor in understanding the impact of loss relates to the nature of *primary loss* and *secondary loss* (Rando, 2000). A secondary loss is a physical or psychosocial loss that coincides with or develops as a result of the initial loss. For example, if an older person has to move to a new home because he or she could not manage the steps, the loss is a secondary one. Rando emphasized that the ripple effects from the primary loss must be taken into consideration. Before we can fully comprehend the impact of a loss, we must understand the relationship between attachment and loss (Harvey, 2000; Worden, 2002).

Becvar (2001), Walter (2003), and Harvey (2002) all cited John Bowlby's pioneering research on attachment and loss, which proposed that attachments come from a need for security and safety, with the goal of maintaining an affectional bond.

When this bond is threatened, grieflike behavior ensues. According to this theory, the greater the attachment or dependency (for safety or security), the greater the sense of loss.

How we experience loss is "as individualized as our fingerprints, marked by our past history of losses and by the particulars of the relationship" (Volkan and Zintl, 1993, p. 12). Despite the variability, every loss involves, first, accepting the reality of the loss, followed by a period of letting go of the loss and working through the pain, then a transition and adjustment period involving adaptation to the new reality, and finally a new beginning (Rando, 2000; Straub, 2001; Worden, 2002). Bozarth (1986) described this process as "going through a little death. In time, one comes out on the other side, a bit worn, perhaps, but in many ways brand new" (p. 90).

Although grieving a loss is a natural and necessary process, Harvey (2000) noted that some people have difficulty transforming losses into something positive and growing from them. Harvey and Miller (2000) cited several factors that can influence growth and vulnerability, including

- an individual's coping style,
- an optimistic versus a pessimistic outlook on life,
- a strong sense of self,
- perceptions of control, and
- the extent of preexisting vulnerabilities.

Given that people experience a plethora of types of loss and react in a multitude of ways, counselors can play a key role in offering support and intervention, especially with the decline of the family and religious institutions. One of the most effective approaches is group work (Harvey, 2000; Harvey & Miller, 2000; Lehmann, Jimerson, & Gaasch, 2001; Straub, 2001; Walter, 2003).

The topics of this chapter include the bereavement process, feelings associated with loss, the format and purpose of loss groups, and considerations in conducting these groups. Two specific examples of loss groups are offered, followed by age-specific variations with children and adolescents, and concluding with applications of brief counseling to loss.

BEREAVEMENT, GRIEF, AND MOURNING

The terms *bereavement*, *grief*, and *mourning* have been used interchangeably in the literature (Harvey, 2002), although some experts offer distinctions. Stroebe, Hansson, Stroebe, and Schut (2001) described bereavement as "the objective situation of having lost someone significant" (p. 6), noting that the usual reaction to bereavement is grief. Rando (2000) explained grief as the "process of experiencing the psychological, behavioral, social, and physical reactions to the perception of loss" (p. 60), and mourning as the conscious and unconscious processes and courses of action that help the individual break the ties with the loved one or object, adapt to the loss, and learn to adapt to the new reality. According to Rando, grief is the beginning of mourning, but because it relates only to the reactions and perceptions of loss, the mourning process is what helps the individual readjust, adapt, and integrate.

Volkan and Zintl (1993) defined mourning as "the psychological response to any loss or change, the negotiations we make to adjust our inner world to reality" (p. 2), and grief as the wide range of emotions and behaviors that accompany mourning. They stressed the importance of completing the mourning process, noting that if we are unable to mourn, "we stay in the thrall of old issues, dreams, and relationships, out of step with the present because we are still dancing to tunes from the past" (p. 3). The mourning process, we should point out, is influenced by culture, traditions, and customs (Becvar, 2001; Churn, 2003; Parkes, 2001).

Rando (2000) identified six "R" steps in mourning:

1. Recognizing the loss, which involves acknowledging the loss and understanding it
2. Reacting to the separation: experiencing the pain; feeling, identifying, accepting, and expressing the psychological reactions to the loss; and identifying and mourning the secondary losses
3. Recollecting and reexperiencing the deceased or lost object and the relationship by reviewing and remembering realistically and reviving and reexperiencing the feeling
4. Relinquishing old attachments and assumptions
5. Readjusting and adapting to the new reality without forgetting the old
6. Reinvesting

Worden (1996, 2002) named four similar basic tasks of mourning:

1. Accepting the reality of the loss
2. Experiencing the pain of grief
3. Adjusting to a new "environment"
4. Withdrawing from the lost relationship and investing emotional energy elsewhere

Although many experts contend that there is a general progression from one task to the next, mourning is also a fluid process that varies from person to person. The phases or tasks overlap, and individuals pass back and forth through them (Stroebe et al., 2001). Mourning must be looked at in context, taking into account the individual's beliefs and coping skills, and noting that the process might have no fixed endpoint (Becvar, 2001). Harvey (2000) concurred, noting that some people are so overwhelmed by a key loss that they never complete the mourning process. Stroebe et al. (2001) suggested that rather than "getting over" their loss and returning to normal, individuals adapt and adjust to the changes but may never resolve or complete their grief (p. 9).

Accepting the Reality of the Loss

Whether the loss involves control, self-esteem, ability to function, relocation, or personal autonomy, the first task of mourning is to accept the reality of the loss

(Worden, 2002). This is often difficult, and denial is common—denying the facts of the loss, denying the meaning of the loss by making it seem less significant than it really was, selectively forgetting by blocking out the reality of a person or an event, or denying that the loss is irreversible (Worden, 2002). Although the denial functions as a buffer by allowing the mourner to absorb the reality of the loss over time and not become overwhelmed (Straub, 2001), working through it is essential before a person can experience the pain of grief (Crenshaw, 1999).

After a loss, it is common to "retreat psychologically" (Staudacher, 1991, p. 5) as a way of managing pain and anxiety. When they are numb and dazed, it is not unusual for people to deny that the loss actually occurred (Nolen-Hoeksema & Larson, 1999). Although periods of disbelief are common, the reality of the loss ultimately must be acknowledged.

Experiencing the Pain of Grief

"Grief happens at its own pace" (Straub, 2001, p. 77). Although not everyone experiences the same intensity of pain or feels it in the same way, no one can lose someone or something without some pain. Grief is a profound experience related to the pain of detachment, and the acute grieving phase may last several months (Schuchter & Zisook, 1993). Pain that is not acknowledged and worked through impacts physical and mental well-being (Worden, 2002).

Grief is a highly individualized process that differs from person to person and is influenced by a multitude of variables, including age and culture (Silverman, 2000; Stroebe et al., 2001). According to Schuchter and Zisook (1993), there is little agreement regarding the time period for normal grief. They contended that in the case of loss involving death, many people maintain a "timeless" emotional involvement with the deceased that does not necessarily imply an unhealthy adaptation (p. 25). According to those researchers, some aspects of grief will continue for several years after the loss or never will be totally resolved.

Although grieving is a normal, healthy process that is a necessary part of healing, society is often uncomfortable with grieving and may send the subtle message that "you don't need to grieve; you're only feeling sorry for yourself" (Worden, 1991, p. 13). This may lead to denying the need to grieve, manifested by repressing feelings or thinking only pleasant things about the loss as a way to protect oneself from the discomfort.

The pressure for people to "get over" grief also may be based on an oversimplified view of what loss is. Loss is not a simple event, and everything that is lost is not relegated to one period of time. Instead, a sequence of new losses and relegations can span many years or a lifetime (Klass, Silverman, & Nickman, 1996). O'Connor (1995) emphasized the importance of grieving, noting that people who choose not to grieve "remain locked in a shell of unresponsiveness, refusing to feel, and resisting the pain and tests of life" (p. 181).

Acknowledging and Resolving Conflicting Feelings

Loss almost always entails a mixture of intense feelings that must be acknowledged and resolved before grief can be resolved (Crenshaw, 1999; Worden, 2002). This crucial step is difficult for children, and many adults also find it difficult to recognize and express their own negative feelings (Crenshaw, 1999). Nevertheless, helping mourners identify, accept, and achieve a realistic balance between positive and negative feelings is necessary before they can let go and move to the next task—adjusting to a new environment.

Adjusting to a New Environment

Depending on the extent of attachment to the person or object of loss, adjusting to a new environment means different things and may be multifaceted. Death of a spouse, for example, may mean loss of a companion, a sexual partner, a financial provider, a helpmate—depending on the roles this person played (Auz & Andrews, 2002; Walter, 2003). In the case of diagnosis of a terminal illness, critical adjustments have to be made to accommodate new medications, limited physical stamina, probable loss of employment at some point, and reactions of family and friends.

The process of developing new skills and assuming new roles is often accompanied by feelings of resentment or anxiety. Depending on the nature of the loss, many people are faced with the challenge of forming a new identity or finding a new direction in life. Loss can threaten fundamental life values and beliefs (Worden, 2002).

Adjusting to a new environment implies accommodation to the reality. The primary task is to break old habits and adjust to the new reality with new patterns and interactions, which Attig (2002) described as involving emotional, behavioral, physical, social, and intellectual change. This task is not easy, and when people are unable to adapt to a loss, they may promote their own helplessness, withdraw, or be unable to develop coping skills for the new environment. These nonadaptations make the outcome of mourning more difficult.

Withdrawing and Reinvesting Emotional Energy

The task of withdrawing and reinvesting one's emotional energy requires withdrawing from the person or object of loss and moving on to another relationship or situation. For many people, particularly after loss from death or divorce, this is associated with a fear of reinvesting their emotions in another relationship and risking another loss (Worden, 2002). With other types of loss as well, a person has to successfully work through the withdrawal stage to live fully in the here and now. As Straub (2001) noted, "Your life may never be the same again, but it doesn't have to be. If you have hope, then love, peace, and happiness will return" (p. 81).

The prospect of moving on may create ambivalence, and people often are tempted to hold onto the past attachment rather than work through the feelings associated with the new reality (Worden, 2002). It is easy to get stuck at this point because it is so painful to give up the past reality.

Mourning can be a long-term process, and it is impossible to set a date by which it should be accomplished (Worden, 2002). The acute grieving is over only when the tasks of mourning are completed and the person can regain interest in life, feel more hopeful, and adapt to new roles.

FEELINGS ASSOCIATED WITH LOSS

Following many types of loss, people experience a sense of unreality and numbness that helps them temporarily disregard the loss (Bruce & Schultz, 2001; Straub, 2001; Worden, 2002). But accepting the loss is important, and people must be encouraged to talk about it and to identify and express their feelings. The feelings commonly associated with loss are anger, guilt, sadness, anxiety, loneliness, helplessness, frustration, and depression (O'Connor, 1995; Straub, 2001; Worden, 2002). Worden pointed out that the person also may feel emancipated and relieved, particularly if the loss was associated with the deceased's long illness or a negative situation.

Although the feelings mentioned are typical, all people do not express their feelings in the same way (Staudacher, 1991). The expressions of loss are somewhat dependent on cultural and religious beliefs, as well as on gender. Staudacher emphasized that men in Western cultures are expected to be strong and not to openly express their feelings. Men may be more reluctant to seek help and support, instead feeling responsible for resolving their own grief. Men in these cultures also are expected to be more in control, able to bear the pain, and be more concerned with thinking than feeling. The reality remains, however, that they probably have the common feelings associated with loss even though they might not express their feelings in the same way.

Anger

"Anger is the shadow of grief" (Straub, 2001, p. 83) and is linked to a loss of power and control (Staudacher, 1991). Although feeling angry over a loss is normal, many people have trouble admitting this anger because they feel ashamed (Locke, 1994) or are frightened by it. Part of the anger stems from frustration about not being able to change the reality or be in control (Straub, 2001; Worden, 2002). In the case of the death of a partner, survivors may be angry particularly because they may be left with many new responsibilities, limited finances, and necessary painful changes. At the same time, they may feel guilty because they know their mate suffered and did not want to die. In such instances, they may turn their anger inward and experience it as depression. Rando (2000) stressed the importance of talking through the guilt and acknowledging the anger so it can be set aside.

With some types of loss, the anger may be more clearly directed toward the person or the situation causing the anger—at the ex-mate in the case of divorce, at the employer in the case of job termination or loss of job status, at the doctor who cannot find the cure for a terminal illness, or at the adolescent who was driving while intoxicated (Locke, 1994; Rando, 2000). Sometimes, however, identifying the anger or determining the target is more difficult, as in life transitions. In these situations the anger may be displaced to other people who look younger or have more physical stamina, or the anger may be turned inward, resulting in depression at one's personal loss (Rando, 2000).

Guilt

Guilt plays a major role in most types of loss and can take various forms—survivor guilt ("Why him and not me?") (Schuchter & Zisook, 1993, p. 28), guilt related to responsibility for the loss (Straub, 2001), and guilt over betrayal. Helplessness often accompanies guilt and leaves people feeling like they are not in control of the situation. In the case of death, Walter (2003) proposed that "guilt is an important aspect of most adverse grief responses because the survivor's belief that the death was somehow his or her fault can be a way of coping with the grief" (p. 26). Harvey (2000), however, pointed out that people need to realize they cannot always prevent bad things from happening. At times, guilt stems from conscious or unconscious feelings of hostility toward the deceased (Worden, 2002).

Guilt arises from many sources and can be considered along a continuum (Roos, 2002). There is guilt based on *rational* considerations, such as a mother feeling guilty about having a child with fetal alcohol syndrome, and *irrational* guilt, such as blaming oneself for an accidental injury or illness. Straub (2001) distinguished between *normal guilt* and *neurotic guilt* by explaining that normal guilt is what we feel when we have done something or neglected to do something, as contrasted to neurotic guilt, which is guilt out of proportion to the actual involvement in the situation. A lot of guilt is irrational, and counselors should help people test the reality of their "if only" statements (Worden, 2002). Guilt slows recovery, and those who are convinced that the loss was their fault must work on forgiveness (O'Connor, 1995). They also may have to reconcile with the reality that they cannot change the situation.

Sadness

"Sadness is the most common feeling found in the bereaved" (Worden, 2002, p. 11). Sadness is associated with all types of loss (Emswiler & Emswiler, 2000). The sadness may be accompanied by tears and an awareness of how much someone or something is missed and generally is in direct proportion to the strength of attachment and the meaning attributed to the person or situation (Nolen-Hoeksema & Larson, 1999; Worden, 2002). Bozarth (1986) differentiated sadness and depression, noting that sadness is highly focused in relation to the loss, whereas depression is a more general state.

Counseling professionals can support people who have experienced losses by encouraging them to express their feelings, legitimizing and normalizing these feelings, and helping them understand the meaning of the loss. Counselors also can convey the expectation that even though the situation is difficult, the person will be able to tolerate it and at some future time will have less pain and more pleasure.

Anxiety and Helplessness

Anxiety often develops after a loss, stemming from fear of the unknown, having to learn new skills (Payne, Horn, & Relf, 1999), and being unable to perceive how one will manage without the support of a partner or the security of a familiar situation or way of being (Worden, 2002). Anxiety also is related to a heightened sense of one's own vulnerability (Emswiler & Emswiler, 2000).

Individuals may need help in identifying the uncertainties they feel and the sources of their anxiety, as well as to recognize ways they managed situations prior to the loss and how, with some adjustment, they will be able to do so again. In the case of death or disability, survivors may become increasingly anxious about their own death or disability and must be able to articulate these fears. The anxiety will lessen as people accept their anxiety and recognize that it is a normal part of grieving (Straub, 2001).

Frustration

Frustration results "when the bereaved is deprived of the things that heretofore have been expected, needed, and cherished, and when there is no hope of retrieving these resources" (Sanders, 1989, p. 66). Accompanying the frustration is a sense of disappointment and emptiness that things will not be the same again. Regardless of the type of loss, people become frustrated in their attempts to adjust to new situations. Although some frustration is natural, counselors should help individuals deal with their expectation that things shouldn't be frustrating or require adaptation.

Depression

Depression is another necessary feeling in the grief process (Rando, 2000). Often, depression is connected to what is lost from the past, what one misses in the present, and the losses one anticipates for the future. Common symptoms that accompany depression are sleep difficulties, weight loss or gain, social withdrawal, apathy, feelings of despair, physical aches and pains, and feelings of being overwhelmed and out of control (Matsakis, 1999; O'Connor, 1995). Counselors should encourage people to express their feelings and identify and mourn the actual loss as well as the symbolic losses (such as opportunities, meaning, beliefs, hopes, and expectations) (O'Connor, 1995; Rando, 1993).

Viorst (1986) maintained that even though loss involves a great deal of pain,

> throughout our life we grow by giving up. We give up some of
> our deepest attachments to others. We give up certain cher-
> ished parts of ourselves.... Passionate investment leaves us vul-
> nerable to loss. (p. 16)

Looking at loss as it relates to growth and change can facilitate the healing process.

FORMAT OF LOSS GROUPS

Any type of loss disrupts familiar patterns and relationships. The losses we encounter throughout our lives have consequences for our self-esteem, general sense of well-being, and emotional integrity. Whether the change is dreaded or welcomed, accidental or planned, it requires adjustment. This often results in anxiety or ambivalence.

Many of the needs resulting from a loss can be addressed effectively within a group setting. In recent years there has been a steady increase in group work for various types of bereavement (Cox, Bendiksen, & Stevenson, 2002; Lehmann et al., 2001; Nolen-Hoeksema & Larson, 1999; Powell, 2002; Straub, 2001; Walter, 2003). Loss groups can be conducted in several different formats (Straub, 2001), two of which are as follows:

1. *Self-help support groups*, which usually center on a common theme, such as death of a child, widowhood, or losing a loved one by suicide. Members gain support from each other, validate reactions, and provide reassurance that the mourners will ultimately resolve their grief. This type of group may not have a group leader, but if there is, he or she may be a volunteer or a trained layperson. Many different dynamics can occur in loss groups, and if there is no group leader to resolve these dynamics, the group may not be as productive (Jacobs, Masson, & Harvill, 2002).

2. *Support groups run by a leader* whose goal is to create a safe environment in which members can share. In this type of group, the leader invites members to share concerns and ideas, and works to establish trust, commitment, and caring among members (Jacobs et al., 2002).

In addition, there are counseling groups that have a designated leader and are more structured than self-help or support groups. These leaders usually are professionals with counseling degrees, although they also may be trained volunteers (Straub, 2001).

Regardless of the type of group, all loss groups allow people to share common problems, fears, sorrows, and coping strategies, and thereby help people develop new social support systems (Janowiak, Mei-Tal, & Drapkin, 1995; Powell, 2002). In addition to helping members learn more about different styles of grieving and validating their experience (Becvar, 2001), groups provide emotional and educational support, which has a direct relationship to problem solving. In addition to receiving encouragement and relief, learning about resources, and mastering burdens, group members benefit from the opportunity to help others gain strength.

> The group format is touted as the treatment of choice because it creates community, puts the locus of control on the individual, and emphasizes interaction and growth—all essential ingredients in bereavement. (Zimpfer, 1991, p. 47)

Further, group participation helps individuals cope with the pain as well as maintain attention to the reality of the loss, and prevents them from delaying or distorting the mourning process (Janowiak et al., 1995).

PURPOSES OF LOSS GROUPS

Zimpfer (1989) identified five purposes for loss groups: support, sharing of feelings, developing coping skills, gathering information and education, and considering existential issues. These are discussed in the following pages.

Support

Perhaps the most important function of groups is to provide the support that comes from meeting with others who share a similar experience (Cox et al., 2002; Perschy, 1997; Powell, 2002; Straub, 2001). Following a loss, people frequently feel a sense of isolation because they are reluctant to divulge their feelings to people in their usual support system. They may feel a need to protect others from the pain or may think others won't understand because they haven't had the same experience. Meeting with people who have had a similar experience helps them feel less alone and can create a bonding as group members share reactions they all readily understand (Silverman, 2000).

Members' support comes through encouragement (Auz & Andrews, 2002) and helping others mobilize their inner resources to work through the pain and get on with life and living (Straub, 2001; Walter, 2003). They also can participate in rituals and share memories (Cox et al., 2002). In the group setting, members feel safe to bring up issues without avoidance, disapproval, or patronization.

Sharing Feelings

Among the many negative feelings that surface after a loss are anger, anxiety, guilt, helplessness, shock, relief, numbness (Worden, 2002), denial and betrayal (Straub, 2001), shame (Christ, 2000), hopelessness (Fogarty, 2000), depression (Rando, 2000; Silverman, 2000), and loneliness (Silverman, 2000). Within the group setting, negative feelings can be ventilated, enabling members to develop more stability and make clearer decisions (Moore & Freeman, 1995; Powell, 2002).

Group leaders must help members understand that their feelings are normal in this circumstance. This point is extremely important because many people believe that they shouldn't feel the way they do or that they shouldn't express their feelings—they should "be strong" for others. Worden (2002) stressed that, although there is nothing pathological about any of these feelings, if they remain for a long period with excessive intensity, this may be an indication of more complicated grief.

Developing Coping Skills

The coping skills needed to survive a loss vary greatly depending on the loss. In most cases, however, how well and how quickly one adjusts after a loss relates to finances, social and family relationships, independence and dependence, employment, disfiguration or physical stamina, and issues of day-to-day living.

Because the coping skills needed are so varied, each group member likely will have some of the skills but not others. Group members who have dealt successfully with at least one of the problems can relate their experiences and offer suggestions. Hearing that others have dealt successfully with a similar concern restores a sense of control and instills a more positive outlook (Moore & Freeman, 1995).

Gathering Information and Education

Again, depending on the type of loss, group members may have to be assured about the normalcy of their reactions and feelings (Middleton, Raphael, Martinek, & Misso, 1993; Straub, 2001), as well as issues connected with the loss—how to get help with finances following the death of a spouse, how to cope with the loss of physical function following injuries incurred in an auto accident, what to do with one's time following retirement, how to manage routine tasks if in a wheelchair, or where to look for a new job.

Many times, people have to learn new behaviors. Group members can play a significant role in providing knowledge, modeling, and assurance in these areas, making others' adjustment easier by relaying information on how to proceed and what to expect (Powell, 2002). The group leader and resource personnel also may be good sources of information because they can be more objective and draw from their experiences in previous leadership roles (Perschy, 1997).

Existential Considerations

Whether the loss involves death, dismemberment, serious illness, or change in status, loss often leads to the realization that the present is temporary. People begin to see that ultimately they have the responsibility for their own lives and happiness. This realization brings several results—recognizing the importance of living each day to the fullest, clarifying what is important and meaningful in life, and learning the importance of not leaving things unsaid (Locke, 1994; Nolen-Hoeksema & Larson, 1999).

A group leader can facilitate discussion about the nature of loss, the meaning of the loss, and how it affects one's future. Dealing with these existential issues can help members grapple with their present losses and with their future impacts. Understanding these issues can lead to positive growth and change.

LEADERSHIP AND MEMBERSHIP CONSIDERATIONS

Members of all loss groups share the common experience of some sort of loss for which they are seeking emotional relief and a supportive atmosphere where they can discuss problems and seek solutions. Because group members most likely are at different points in grieving their loss, modeling is an important learning tool as participants share their feelings and describe how they are coping. Modeling is just one of the considerations in conducting loss groups. Additional leadership and membership issues also must be addressed.

Leadership

Facilitating a loss group is an intense process (Price, Dinas, Dunn, & Winterowd, 1995). Leaders may experience their own unresolved grief issues or overidentify with group members' situations. Thus, coleadership is suggested for this type of group, so the leaders can give each other feedback and support (Janowiak et al., 1995).

Group leadership may be facilitative or instructional.

1. *Instructional leadership*. In groups that are basically informational, the leader tends to be more instructional. He or she will have expertise or experience in the specific area of loss and can dispense appropriate information, as well as structure discussion or activities around predetermined topics (Zimpfer, 1989).
2. *Facilitative leadership*. The goal of facilitative leaders is to encourage people to share their feelings and skills that enable them to cope more effectively with the loss. Leaders are less likely to provide information. These groups typically do not have as much structure, and they do not have a predetermined agenda. Topics for discussion emerge from the group members, and the leader facilitates the exchange (Zimpfer, 1989).

Because people who are experiencing loss need information and support, both styles of leadership are often found in groups, with the dual focus of helping participants take control of their lives through problem solving and emotional support. Regardless of style, the leader has to actively set the tone for mutually sharing and exploring feelings.

Leaders should model respect, acceptance, nonjudgmental attitudes, and encouragement (Nolen-Hoeksema & Larson, 1999). Group leaders also must work actively to remain open to the members' losses, avoiding the tendency to placate or protect. They must be skilled in dealing with communication barriers and problematic behaviors such as monopolizing. Also essential to good leaders are flexibility and sensitivity (Nolen-Hoeksema & Larson, 1999).

Empathy is another essential leadership trait. Larson (1993) discussed empathy as "the bridge between altruism and helping" (p. 15), the ability to feel and be sympathetically aroused by someone else's distress. Empathy is what transforms altruism into "caring action" (p. 15). Conveying empathy encourages further disclosure, exploration, and release of feelings.

The group leader also can encourage mourners to reminisce. Reminiscing is vital to the grieving process and can be facilitated through photos, scrapbooks, and other mementos. Telling the story of the loss helps to relieve the pain and provides necessary catharsis. Group members often feel uplifted and relieved after shedding this emotional burden (Price et al., 1995).

Group leaders should continue to help members acknowledge the truth of their loss. Avoiding the reality will prolong the grief process, and grief could be incomplete (Worden, 2002).

Membership

Membership in loss groups may be open or closed (Price et al., 1995). In a closed group the same members attend for a series of sessions, which usually results in more cohesiveness. Open groups continue indefinitely, with members rotating in and out depending on their needs (Jacobs et al., 2002). Open membership may offer more opportunities for modeling and sharing because of the wide range in the stages of grief represented as new members join and others leave.

Individuals may be recommended for a loss group by a physician, a religious leader, a hospice organization, or a mental health clinic. Other members are self-referred. It is advisable to screen potential group members individually to explain the purpose of the group, ascertain the individual's type of loss and expectations for the group, and determine whether group or individual counseling or therapy would be most appropriate (Janowiak et al., 1995; Price et al., 1995).

Most experts recommend a heterogeneous group and indicate that this may not be much of an issue in any case because of the natural bonding in these groups based on the mutual need for support (Nahmani, Neeman, & Nir, 1989). Although participants in loss groups tend to be at different stages of grief, bereaved individuals generally are relieved to find a safe place to share their feelings, and the group experience lessens their sense of alienation (Price et al., 1995).

EXAMPLE: A LOSS GROUP DEALING WITH DEATH OF A PARTNER

Although all loss involves some feelings and stages in common, group members gain the most benefit from a group that addresses their specific kind of loss. This example group is designed for those who have lost a partner to death.

Of all losses, the death of a partner is the number-one stressor (Holmes & Rahe, 1967). The actual experience of losing a spouse varies depending on the circumstances under which the spouse died, the age and gender of the people involved, and the stage in the family's life cycle during which the death occurred (Becvar, 2001). The closeness of the bond contributes to the depth and extent of the grieving process (Harvey, 2002).

Actually, the death of a spouse results in numerous losses, as the couple may have shared confidences, parenting and household responsibilities, advising one another in financial matters and career issues, and serving as links to each other's extended family (Becvar, 2001). Because of the numerous roles that spouses fill for each other, the survivor experiences an increasing sense of loss that is "intensified because the grief is not only for the person who has died, but for the connection to the spouse, as well as for the bereaved person's plans, hopes, and dreams for a future with the spouse" (Walter, 2003, p. 13).

Following the loss of a spouse, relationships with friends, family, and social networks change considerably. Widows and widowers are particularly vulnerable, and loss groups represent an excellent approach with this population, as the small-group format can lessen the intense social isolation and help participants move forward as they share their pain with others who have experienced a similar loss (Walter, 2003).

Nolen-Hoeksema and Larson (1999) cited three important functions of support groups for those who have lost a partner:

1. *Instrumental support*: helping with the funeral, household tasks, and so on
2. *Emotional support*: helping the mourners accept the reality of the death
3. *Validational support*: helping the mourners know what to expect during the period of grief and reassuring them that what they are experiencing is normal

The group format encourages members to cope with their pain in an atmosphere where they are understood by others, combating the social isolation and supporting members as they face the many changes that the death of a spouse brings (Walter, 2003). In a group format, members "can struggle together with the common feelings related to being cheated out of a long and happy marriage" (Harvey, 2002, p. 269).

Specific Issues

In addition to providing a place for catharsis and for normalizing and dealing with the feelings of anger, guilt, anxiety, helplessness, sadness, and depression, this loss group can address the following specific issues:

1. *Loneliness and aloneness.* After the death of a partner, the mourner loses the daily intimacies of having someone special with whom to share significant events and the sense of being the most important person in someone else's life (Walter, 2003). The struggle with loneliness includes a shift in identity from "we" to "I" (p. 14) and taking responsibility for oneself. Even though the intensity of a relationship with the deceased usually diminishes over time, the relationship does not disappear entirely (Shapiro, 1994). Facing the reality of being single rather than part of a couple is also a difficult transition, as is the realization that part of the mourner's "history" died with the partner (Staudacher, 1991; Stroebe & Stroebe, 1993).

2. *Sense of deprivation.* The sense of deprivation following the death of a partner is particularly acute (Sanders, 1989). Widowers and widows may feel deprived financially, socially, sexually, physically, and emotionally, in any combination. Redefining one's roles becomes a major task that is frequently painful and frustrating. To fill roles the partner had assumed or to learn the skills needed to fill those roles often seems overwhelming (Staudacher, 1991). Survivors with children have an even greater sense of deprivation as they struggle with their own issues of grief compounded by those of their children.

3. *Freedom and growth.* Despite the negative impact of loss, mourners find an awareness of freedom and the potential for change. Losses are linked to gains; loss can result in "creative transformations" (Viorst, 1986, p. 326).

Helping group members recognize the strength that comes from facing and surviving loss and coping effectively with adversity is an important step in recovery. Encouraging participants to look at the potentials of independence and freedom is also essential. Frequently, participants come to appreciate the freedom of not having to adhere to a schedule, prepare meals, watch certain shows on television, or do things to please a partner. Creating and choosing new and different ways to meet one's needs results in greater awareness of who one is and what one enjoys. This growth results in a positive change in self-esteem (Lopata, 1996).

4. *Identity and change.* A spouse often represented the other's main source of identity (Becvar, 2001), so following his or her death, the survivor may engage in major introspection and struggle with his or her identity: "What is my identity without the person I love most?" (Klass et al., 1996, p. 181). In addition, the survivor often has to learn new behaviors that result in personal change—learning to cook and care for a house and children, handling repairs and financial responsibilities, and making decisions alone (Becvar, 2001; Walter, 2003). A major lifestyle change, such as relocating or starting a job, also may accompany loss. Even though these changes can be positive, stress and readjustment are to be expected. The occasion of death can be used as a turning point in one's life (Harvey, 2000).

5. *New relationships.* Forming a new relationship may signify readiness to put aside the past and move ahead, but this change is often difficult (Becvar, 2001). Widows and widowers often feel as if they would betray their marriage or diminish their love for the deceased mate if they were to enter into a new relationship (Yalom, 1995). Many widows and widowers consider their spouses irreplaceable and think they would be betraying their ties with the deceased partner if they were to become involved with someone else (Becvar, 2001).

Group leaders should be sensitive to these issues but at the same time encourage participants to address the fallacy of the "perfect marriage" or the notion that they would be discounting the significance of the previous relationship if they were to form a new one. At the same time, the leader should point out the importance of completing the necessary tasks of grieving before forming another relationship.

Leader Techniques

Unless it is a self-help support group, a loss group typically spans 8 to 12 weeks, with each weekly session ranging from 1 to 2 hours (Corey & Corey, 1997; Perschy, 1997). A group has between 8 and 12 members, who may be referred or who join voluntarily. They likely will be in varying stages of the grief process. Sessions may be facilitated by either a coleader team or by one leader, though the coleadership model is encouraged.

Widows and widowers frequently want human contact because of their recent loss and, therefore, tend to be open from the beginning (Leick & Davidsen-Nielsen, 1991). This sense of openness frequently results in spontaneous sharing and has implications for the amount of structure imposed on the group.

According to Nolen-Hoeksema and Larson (1999), participants in a loss group should have the opportunity to

- share what bothers them instead of holding it in and trying to "be strong";
- gain insight into their experience by asking questions and listening to others relate similar circumstances;
- receive support for the way they are handling their lives; and
- receive advice and help with decision making on issues such as finances, how to carry out responsibilities the deceased partner formerly handled, how to deal with friends, children, and relatives, and how to manage and settle an estate.

The Sessions

The following is a sample progression for a loss-of-partner closed group that meets once a week (2-hour sessions) for 8 weeks. This outline is only one of several group approaches that could be used to deal with loss of this nature.

Session One

The group members introduce themselves, and the leader (or coleaders) facilitates a discussion on the group's purpose, soliciting participants' hopes and expectations and emphasizing confidentiality. The leader reassures the participants that the group will provide a safe atmosphere for them to talk about painful issues and that a goal will be to help members move ahead despite the pain. During this first session, the members each are invited to describe their situation involving the loss of their partner.

Because the participants usually are eager to relate their story to others who have gone through a similar experience, the leader typically does not have to introduce any more structure during this initial session. The sharing of experiences most likely will evoke a good deal of emotion, so the group leader will want to monitor the process closely and intervene if a member becomes too emotional, checking to see if the speaker should stop talking and receive other support or referral. At the end of the first session, and depending on the group's openness, the leader may want to ask the participants to bring scrapbooks, photos, or similar mementos to the next session.

Session Two

The leader begins Session Two with a brief go-around in which members are invited to express their reactions to the first group session and thoughts they have had during the past week related to this experience or to their loss in general. If group members brought scrapbooks or photos to the session, these can be used to stimulate further discussion. Whether the discussion is more open-ended or is introduced by sharing the mementos, the focus may be on memories, what participants miss most (and least) about the deceased partner, and what has changed in their life as a result of the death. The group leader encourages expression of feelings and helps members recognize the commonality of their experiences.

Session Three

To introduce the third session, the leader invites group members to talk about how they are dealing with being alone and lonely. Depending on the nature of the discussion, the leader may introduce the theme of deprivations during this session. If the group is cohesive and the sharing is spontaneous and open, a simple invitation may be sufficient to start participants talking about ways in which they feel deprived. If this is not the case, a structured activity such as the following could be introduced.

Activity: Give each member an index card and ask the group members to write the word "deprivation" across the top. Next, briefly discuss the concept of deprivation and brainstorm as a group the different kinds of deprivation that widows and widowers might experience. Afterward, invite group members to write on their cards three types of deprivation they have experienced following the loss, when they experienced these, and how they feel about these deprivations. Depending on the group's cohesiveness, participants can share some of the ideas on their card with a partner or with the entire group. Debriefing should center on the participants' feelings and how they have dealt with deprivation.

Session Four

The first three sessions were directed largely toward the past, offering the group members an opportunity to share common feelings, concerns, and experiences during this important stage in the grief process. Likewise, looking to the future and entering the healing and renewal phase are important. As a transition, the leader might introduce the topic of freedom and growth.

Generally, by this session, little structure is needed because the participants have developed trust and rapport based on their common experiences with loss (Price et al., 1995). If necessary to stimulate discussion, the leader might introduce the following activity:

Activity: On separate sheets of chart paper, write the following:

"What I can do or am learning to do now that I didn't or couldn't do before" and "Freedoms or new experiences I have now that I didn't have before"

Then invite group members to randomly share their thoughts on these two topics and write their responses on the appropriate chart. After all responses have been recorded, invite discussion about what it has been like for them to learn new things or experience new freedoms. In debriefing this activity, help the participants realize that growth comes through pain and that the loss actually can offer each of them an opportunity to become a more fully developed person.

Session Five

The theme of the fifth session is also change and growth, but with more emphasis on the pragmatics of change. Because a partner assumes so many roles and responsibilities, the survivor may have to learn new behaviors to carry out these functions. By this stage, group cohesiveness probably will allow the participants to openly share information and advice on their new roles and responsibilities, such as finances, childcare, household responsibilities, settling an estate, or disposing of personal effects. The group leader may want to provide information on community resources relative to these concerns.

Session Six

As widows and widowers work through the stages of grief, their perspective on life changes and new relationships may be a good topic to explore. If group sharing is spontaneous and open, the leader may simply invite participants to share their reactions, feelings, and experiences about this topic. Or the leader could introduce the subject through the following activity.

Activity: Give each member an index card and ask the group members to select one of three future periods—a month from now, 6 months from now, or a year from now. After identifying the time period, the participants are to project what their life might be like in relation to (a) where they might be living, (b) how they might be spending their time, (c) who they might be spending their time with, and (d) what kinds of feelings they might have about these changes.

Have each participant write the time period and their responses on the card. Then invite them to share their responses, focusing on their feelings concerning change and new relationships. Specific issues might include guilt about getting involved with another person, how to enter the single world, how society views new relationships, how new relationships may be a way of avoiding grief, and anxiety about change in general.

Session Seven

The leader may use this session to encourage the group participants to continue exploring issues and feelings carried over from the previous session. Because members enter the group at different places in the grieving process, they are ready to make changes and enter into new relationships at different points. Encouraging discussion about anxieties and concerns may offer them the opportunity to clarify issues and support one another in these transitions.

During this session the group might wish to discuss the meaning of life in general. Marriage may have provided some members a basic sense of purpose. The loss in these cases may necessitate an examination of their personal identity and life purpose. Straub (2001) suggested a structured exercise in which participants are asked to think about how they would like to be remembered, and Corey (1996) suggested writing an obituary and sharing it with the group as a good way to think about their own lives. Prior to completing this exercise, it might be helpful for group members to talk with a partner or the entire group about dreams or desires they might have set aside during their marriage and whether those dreams still have a place in their present life.

Session Eight

In this last session, the leader encourages group members to deal with what they have left unsaid or unasked and what regrets they expect to have after the group is over. This process could be loosely structured by inviting members to express an appreciation and a regret about what the group has meant to them. An activity such as this evokes powerful feelings and reinforces the idea that support from others is vital. The leader may want to encourage post-termination meetings for periodic support.

EXAMPLE: A LOSS GROUP DEALING WITH LIFE TRANSITIONS

Loss as a result of death is acknowledged and ritualized, unlike the loss that can accompany life transitions. Transitions are events, such as retiring or moving, or nonevents, such as not having children or not getting promoted (Schlossberg, 2004). Actually, life is a series of transitions: from dependence to independence, from childhood to adulthood, from being single to being married, from work to retirement, from life to death. Transitions also may be prompted by illness, promotion, birth of a child, job relocation, or unemployment.

Transitions can take the form of subtle changes such as the loss of career aspirations or events that never occurred to obvious life changes such as marriage or bereavement (Schlossberg, Waters, & Goodman, 1995). The changes may be major or minor, anticipated or unexpected, but, regardless, they influence an individual's roles, relationships, routines, and assumptions (Schlossberg et al., 1995).

Transitions, then, are the changes—gains as well as losses—that affect everyone and necessitate adjustment. Bridges (2001) distinguished between change and transition by noting that transition is "the way we all come to terms with change" (p. 3) and defined transition as "the process of letting go of the way things used to be and then taking hold of the way they subsequently become" (p. 2). According to Bridges (2001), transitions may be *reactive*, triggered by an external event such as death, or they may be *developmental*, such as the transition to midlife. Regardless of the type of transition, it involves a three-phase process:

1. An ending
2. A neutral zone in which things may be chaotic but also potentially creative
3. A new beginning

Even though we face transitions regularly, we do not receive any training or preparation for dealing with them (Schlossberg, 1989). We may assume that some transitions, such as retirement, are easy (Schlossberg, 2004), but in reality people frequently approach transitions feeling anxious, upset, or overwhelmed.

Transitions can be linked to growth because moving from disorientation to orientation marks a turning point involving various degrees of transformation (Merriam & Clark, 1991). Bridges (1980) contended that

> every transition begins with an ending. We have to let go of the old thing before we can pick up the new, not just outwardly, but inwardly, where we keep our connections to the people and places that act as definitions of who we are. (p. 11)

People often make external changes before they recognize that they have not yet dealt with the endings. Not until the endings have been resolved can a person move to the second phase of transition, which Bridges identified as the "lostness and emptiness" (p. 17), and continue to the third stage, a new beginning.

Categories of Transitions

Schlossberg (1989) proposed four categories of transitions:

1. *Elected transitions* are social milestones, such as marriage, having a child, and retirement; and individual choices, such as choosing a new job and moving to a different city.
2. *Surprise transitions* are those that are not anticipated. These unanticipated events could be good or bad, such as winning the lottery or being fired from a job.
3. *Nonevents* are those events that we expect to happen but never do—for example, never becoming pregnant or never being promoted after years of hard work.
4. *Sleeper transitions* are those that involve a gradual process rather than a significant identifiable beginning, such as gradually becoming more addicted to alcohol or gaining weight.

Regardless of the category, the impact of the transition relates to whether it was gradual or sudden, permanent or temporary, reversible or irreversible, voluntary or involuntary. The impact of the transition also depends on how it affects relationships, routines, roles, and assumptions (Schlossberg, 1989, 2004).

Transitions often begin with a marker event (Merriam & Clark, 1991), but Schlossberg (1989) suggested that even though the onset may be linked to one identifiable event, transitions take time. Depending on the situation, several months to several years may pass before a major transition is completed, and there may be surprises, both positive and negative, along the way (Schlossberg, 2004). Schlossberg (1989) identified three stages of the transition:

1. Preoccupation with the change
2. Disruption as the old roles and routines are replaced with new ones
3. Completion of the transition, when the individual has accommodated to the new way of life

Hudson (1991) contended that life is a Ferris wheel with ups and downs that are repeated as we continue to change with each transition. He maintained that we go through periods of stability followed by periods of transition, and he rejected the notion that life exists as a sequence of events within a timetable and with predictable outcomes.

Tasks of Transitions

Golan (1986) proposed that, to deal successfully with transition, people need to accomplish material (instrumental) tasks and psychosocial (affective) tasks.

The *material tasks* include

- recognizing the need to do something about the old situation;
- exploring solutions, looking at options, weighing alternatives;
- making a choice and taking on the new role; and
- functioning under the new circumstances.

The *psychosocial tasks* involve

- dealing with the loss and the lack of security;
- coping with anxiety, frustration, pressure, ambivalence;
- handling the stress of taking on the new role or adjusting to the new situation;
- adapting to shifts in status or position, which may result in feelings of inferiority, lack of satisfaction, or lack of appreciation from others; and
- learning to live with the different reality, which may involve adjusting to new standards and levels of satisfaction.

Although the span from age 60 to 65 is generally considered as the transition period to late adulthood, this transition may start before age 60 as individuals realize they now have lived longer than they will likely live in the future (Browers, 1991; Levinson & Levinson, 1996). At this point, people begin to think more about what their life includes and its meaning.

Although the transition to late adult years is part of the normal life cycle changes, this stage differs from earlier life cycle changes because it involves continuously adapting to decreasing abilities and increasing dependence (Browers, 1991). The multiple physical and emotional adjustments that accompany this period present a challenge to which individuals respond in different ways depending on their life experiences and personalities.

The following areas are among those that may be of concern:

- Declining health and limited physical stamina
- Adjusting to retirement
- Role shifts/identity issues
- Changes in living conditions/arrangements
- Changes in looks/physical appearance
- Financial security after employment

■ Finding a new balance with society and self
■ Establishing new relationships

Group work to help people deal with transitions has expanded tremendously over the past several years. In the group setting, members can receive social support and factual information and can take part in emotional interactions, all of which can help them deal more effectively with the problems they may face during transition periods (Hudson, 1991; Worden, 2002).

The Sessions

The possible group format suggested below is for a 6-week group sequence, each weekly session lasting 1½ –2 hours.

Session One

The group leader begins by welcoming the participants and explaining that this group will explore issues surrounding the loss experienced in the transition to late adult years. The leader explains the ground rules and issues of confidentiality. Because the group members may not be in crisis, as with the death of a partner, they may not show as much spontaneity and bonding. If that is the case, the leader should instill more structure to facilitate discussion. After group members introduce themselves, the following activity is suggested

Activity: Give each member a sheet of paper divided into four squares. In the first square, the participants are to identify a positive aspect about this transition and, in the second square, a negative aspect. In the third space, they are to describe why they chose to participate in the group and what they hope to get out of it and, in the last square, something about themselves that others can't tell by looking at them. After exchanging their responses with a partner, have the partners introduce each other to the group by telling one thing they've learned about the other person related to this transition to late adult years.

Then lead a discussion of the entire group about the positive and negative words the participants wrote in squares one and two, to elicit the range of topics that might be brought up in subsequent sessions. Record the responses on a chart. End the session with a discussion of hopes and expectations for the group and for themselves, recorded in the last two squares.

Session Two

The leader posts the list of positive and negative aspects of the transition that were generated during the first session. Group members are invited to identify the negative issue that poses the greatest problem for them and to discuss this issue with a partner.

After allowing time for discussion, the leader distributes the following questions and has the partners analyze their related feelings:

■ Does this area of concern represent an ending?

- If so, is this ending positive or negative?
- If this does represent an ending, is it voluntary or involuntary?
- Is it a myth or a tradition (such as not being as sexual during this period of life or having to retire at a certain age)?

The leader encourages sharing in the total group and challenges participants to look at what will change, how much control they have over this change, and how endings also signify beginnings.

Session Three

In this session the leader challenges participants to think about the losses connected with their transition and to identify their feelings associated with these losses. To stimulate discussion, the leader reads the following quote:

"One cannot deal with loss without recognizing what is lost."
—Klass et al. (1996)

Next, the leader writes the following categories on the top of a chart, invites participants to brainstorm the actual and possible losses in each area, and records their responses on the chart.

- Physical health
- Emotional/mental health
- Relationships
- Work
- Housing
- Roles
- Appearance
- Social roles
- Finances

After the lists have been generated, the leader invites discussion about how the members have dealt with or will deal with the actual losses and what information, resources, and support they need to deal effectively with the possible losses.

Session Four

As a follow-up to the previous session, the leader focuses on the members' feelings associated with the losses. By this time, the group most likely is cohesive and members will discuss their feelings openly. If the leader senses that more structure is needed to inspire a discussion of feelings, he or she can invite members to pick one of the nine categories identified in Session Three and write down several feelings describing their reactions to the loss, which then can be shared with the total group.

Some of the members may relate negative feelings typically associated with loss, such as anger, guilt, depression, sadness, frustration, anxiety, and helplessness. Others may express relief, anticipation, or other positive feelings because the transition involves giving up some responsibilities, simplifying their lifestyle, embracing new challenges, or moving to a new location. Hearing both the positive and negative sides helps participants clarify their personal feelings and, perhaps, develop a different perspective.

At this point, the leader may introduce a discussion about where feelings come from, drawing from rational–emotive behavior therapy (Ellis & Dryden, 1997), to show group members that feelings derive from thoughts about the event. To begin the discussion, the leader might point out that negative feelings associated with loss and change are the result of thinking that the event is awful, that it shouldn't happen, that it is impossible to accept, or that it somehow implies that older adults are not as worthwhile. Providing a specific example, such as the following, can be useful:

Event:	Retiring from a job
Feeling:	Depressed, anxious
Thoughts:	I'll be lonely.
	How will I meet people if I'm not working?
	I won't feel productive and worthwhile if I don't work.
	Who will I be without my job status and identity?
	What will I do with my time?

The intensity of the depressed and anxious feelings could be diminished if the person were to think:

How do I know I'll be lonely? Aren't there other ways to meet people besides at work? Aren't there other ways besides my former job to feel productive and worthwhile?

Lots of other people seem to like retirement, so isn't it possible that I will also?

Helping group members understand where their feelings come from may give them a better sense of control and a different perspective.

Session Five

This session looks at change. To introduce the concept, the leader distributes the following piece for members to read:

To everything there is a season, and a time to every purpose under the heaven;
A time to be born, and a time to die;
A time to plant, and a time to pluck up that which is planted;
A time to kill, and a time to heal;
A time to break down, and a time to build up;
A time to weep, and a time to laugh;
A time to mourn, and a time to dance;
A time to cast away stones, and a time to gather stones together;
A time to embrace, and a time to refrain from embracing;
A time to seek, and a time to lose;
A time to keep, and a time to cast away;
A time to rend, and a time to sew;

A time to keep silence, and a time to speak;
A time to love, and a time to hate;
A time for war, and a time for peace. (Ecclesiastes, 3:1-8, in Golan, 1986, p. viii)

After the participants have finished reading, the leader gives each a sheet of paper with the following written across the top:

It's a time in my life to _____.

The leader allows several minutes for the participants to complete the sentence as many times as they can and then invites discussion, highlighting the concept of endings and beginnings.

Session Six

The final session is actually a continuation of the fifth session, with emphasis on the individual's ability to take charge of the transition. The leader refers to the instrumental and psychosocial tasks involved in transitions (Golan, 1986). The instrumental tasks involve recognizing the need to do something about the old situation, exploring alternatives and solutions, choosing to function differently, and making the change. The psychosocial tasks entail dealing with the loss, coping with the feelings, handling the stress of change, adapting to change, and learning to live with the different reality.

To facilitate discussion of these tasks and how they relate to the group members' situations, the leader might divide the group in half, giving one half a sheet that lists the instrumental tasks and the other half a sheet that lists the psychosocial tasks. The leader instructs each group to discuss how these tasks relate to the life changes the group members have made or anticipate making and then to summarize the issues and present them to the total group. Each participant could be invited to identify one task that he or she would like to work on and to discuss with a partner strategies for doing this.

In closing the session, the leader encourages members to relate something they have learned from participating in the group and how this knowledge will help them handle the transition.

LOSS: AGE-SPECIFIC VARIATIONS IN CHILDREN AND ADOLESCENTS

Children process information differently than adults do. Group leaders must be aware that although children have many of the same feelings as adults concerning loss, they may not be able to articulate those feelings as effectively (Emswiler & Emswiler, 2000). Instead, they may reflect their feelings through misbehavior or in causal reaction (Worden, 2002).

Adolescents may express themselves behaviorally rather than emotionally or cognitively, sometimes engaging in risky behaviors such as driving fast, engaging in reckless sexual activity, or using drugs and alcohol to escape from the pain (Emswiler & Emswiler, 2000). Adolescents are already involved in a time of loss as they relinquish their childhood, a distinct group with specific developmental needs, which complicates the grieving process for them (Lenhardt & McCourt, 2000).

Loss From Death

Understanding the way children comprehend death and how this affects their mourning is a major task for counselors (Worden, 1996). Children under age 2 have little conception of death, although they may react with confusion and separation anxiety (Emswiler & Emswiler, 2000). Because they sense that something is gone, sleep disturbances or changes in eating and bladder habits may develop. Between ages 2 and 6, children are likely to see death as reversible and assume that the dead person will return (Jackson & Colwell, 2002). Because of their egocentric and concrete thinking, they may think the loss resulted from something they did (Becvar, 2001; Crenshaw, 1999; Emswiler & Emswiler, 2000; Tollerud & McFarland, 2004). They may express concern for the physical well-being of the person who died, because they don't understand the reality of the death.

Also, young children might misperceive the euphemisms of adults. Because children are literal thinkers, they might become fearful about taking a nap because they were told that the person who died was "taking a long nap" or "sleeping peacefully" (Jackson & Colwell, 2002).

Between the ages of 6 and 9, children better understand the finality of death, although they do not comprehend their vulnerability to death (Emswiler & Emswiler, 2000). They tend to believe death happens only to older people, and some children think it is contagious. Many children think of death as something physical, like a spirit, a ghost, or a monster (Tollerud & McFarland, 2004), or they may think the death was a punishment for their bad behavior (Emswiler & Emswiler, 2000).

Between ages 10 and 13, children are beginning to think more abstractly. Although they understand that death is irreversible and inevitable, they struggle with why it happens. They also consider how death affects relationships (Emswiler & Emswiler, 2000).

By the time they reach adolescence, teens think more abstractly and understand death cognitively, seeing it as a natural, universal process (Jackson & Colwell, 2002; Lehmann et al., 2001). At the same time, younger teens are self-absorbed and focus on the present, therefore viewing death as something remote, something that couldn't happen to them (Goldman, 2000). At this age, adolescents struggle with the existential question of why bad things happen to good people (Emswiler & Emswiler, 2000).

Tollerud and McFarland (2004) cited benefits of group counseling for grieving children and adolescents, noting that it is most beneficial when children are in different stages of the grieving process because the early- and middle-stage participants can learn effective coping skills when they hear how children in later stages have survived. In conducting group sessions with children who have experienced a loss through death, the leader should use concrete techniques incorporating fairy tales, role playing, storytelling, art and music activities, photographs, bibliotherapy, and puppetry to deal with the children's fears, anger, sadness, and guilt (Charkow, 1998; Cox et al., 2002; Crenshaw, 1999; Tollerud & McFarland, 2004).

Because many children have not had a chance to say good-bye to the deceased, they can be encouraged to write a letter, make a tape, draw a picture, or use imagery to mentally tell the person things that were left unsaid. Children also may need facts about what happens during a funeral, how the body is prepared for burial, and so forth. Information of this sort can help alleviate fear and anxiety (Jackson & Colwell, 2002).

Life Transitions

Like adults, children go through many chronological transitions, including starting school, entering middle school or high school, becoming an adolescent, and leaving home after graduation. They also experience marker events, such as moving, changing schools, and parental divorce and remarriage. The usefulness of group work to facilitate these transitions is well documented (Costa & Stiltner, 1994; Perschy, 1997; Vernon & Clemente, 2005).

In groups for children experiencing life transitions, the leader has to provide adequate structure and use concrete illustrations and activities to help the children understand the concepts. Preschoolers, for example, need a lot of play activities to help them deal with separation anxiety and to gain control of the transition of starting school. Older students may benefit from bibliotherapy, journaling, role playing, or structured activities and games geared to the specific transition issues.

For children who have experienced loss as a result of death and those who have experienced (or anticipate experiencing) loss as a result of a life transition, groups can facilitate the grieving process. When designing loss groups for children and adolescents, developmental issues should be considered along with the feelings, adjustments, and meaning of the specific loss (Kandt, 1994; Vernon, 2004).

APPLICATION OF BRIEF COUNSELING OR THERAPY

Since the 1970s, counselors have focused increasingly on approaches to speed client change (Littrell, Malia, & Vanderwood, 1995). Brief counseling or therapy embraces several assumptions about how meaningful change can occur in a shorter time span than with traditional approaches. These assumptions, which can be readily applied to groups, include the following:

1. Time will not be spent searching for an underlying, deeper problem. The problem the client presents in counseling or therapy is the problem (Nichols & Schwartz, 1998).
2. Clients often have the resources to resolve their problems themselves (deShazer, 1991; Littrell & Zinck, 2004).

3. A small change may be sufficient to interrupt clients' recurring patterns and help them act with more intention to incorporate new responses to life (deShazer, 1991; Murphy, 1997).

Despite the adjective *brief,* Littrell et al. (1995) noted that brief counseling or therapy is not always short term. Some forms of brief counseling or therapy involve 15 or more sessions, and others are only single sessions. Because the client is considered to be the expert on attaining goals he or she has set, the amount of time allotted to the group is based largely on the client's self-assessment.

Brief therapy or counseling focuses on the exceptions—on times when the problems are *not* occurring (Littrell & Zinck, 2004; Murphy, 1997). Brief therapy also emphasizes what can be done to change the situation in the present and the future. Clients develop specific goals and steps to achieve them and also identify areas of their competence, interest, and skill (Nichols & Schwartz, 1998).

Elements of Brief Therapy

At first glance, it might seem that loss issues cannot be addressed effectively through brief counseling or therapeutic approaches. Whether these approaches can be effective depends, to some extent, on the nature of the loss. With most loss issues, however, elements of brief therapy or counseling could be applicable for the following reasons:

1. The focus is on making a small change that will interrupt a pattern and thereby bring about new responses. This strategy is particularly helpful in dealing with depression, which is prevalent in most forms of loss. Taking the initiative to change something helps the client get unstuck (Littrell & Zinck, 2004).
2. In brief therapy, clients are encouraged to look at exceptions, as well as strengths and areas of competence. Because negative experiences are associated with many issues of loss, clients frequently become more discouraged the more they talk about the problem. Focusing on the positive is an effective way for clients to feel more hopeful (Littrell & Zinck, 2004).
3. With the brief therapy approach, it is assumed that clients possess the resources to address the problem. This is an empowering concept, and within the group setting, empowered group members can help others access their own solutions.

Limitations of Brief Therapy

Limitations of brief counseling or therapy applied to issues of loss include the following:

1. For many types of loss, "telling your story" is an important part of adjusting to the loss. In many of these cases, reviewing the past by sharing memories is helpful (Lehmann et al., 2001; Worden, 2002). Brief approaches may not allow enough time for this type of catharsis.

2. Dealing with feelings is central to grief work (Straub, 2001; Walter, 2003). Although clients tend to become more overwhelmed, depressed, or angry as they talk about loss issues, it is important for them to express their feelings and have them acknowledged. If the counselor or therapist moves too quickly into the goal and the exceptions, the brief counseling or therapy approach may have limited value.

Many of the needs resulting from a loss can be addressed within a group setting, which allows participants to share common problems, provide mutual aid, and develop coping skills. The leader can play an important informational and educational role, in addition to facilitating the discussion and introducing helpful activities. The leader should model respect, acceptance, nonjudgmental attitudes, and encouragement and should be empathetic. Finally, the leader should encourage group members to reminisce and to acknowledge the truth of the loss.

LEARNING ACTIVITIES

1. Divide a card into four sections and respond to each of the following: (a) identify a loss you have experienced and are willing to discuss in a small group, (b) identify a feeling you recall experiencing as a result of this loss, (c) list ways in which you grew or changed as a result of this loss, and (d) describe how you coped with the loss. Then discuss in a triad to the responses to these questions.
2. With a partner, identify an ambiguous loss or a loss associated with a nonevent. One partner plays the role of the counselor who helps the other address the issues, then the two of you switch roles. Analyze the counseling skills that were most helpful, how you felt discussing these issues, and how you felt in the counselor role.
3. In a small group and with one of the following assigned types of loss—nonevent, ambiguous, loss associated with abilities, or loss associated with separation/departure of loved ones—design two group counseling sessions that would help clients address the issues associated with the designated type of loss.
4. In a group divided by children and adolescents and further subdivided into a triad within one of these two groups, brainstorm various types of loss associated with the specific age group and design a group counseling session to help children or adolescents deal with this specific type of loss.

SUMMARY

Throughout the life cycle we are faced with losses that Viorst (1986) described as necessary and having "subsequent gains" (p. 366). If we fail to mourn, we will express grief in a delayed or distorted way. Mourning involves accepting the reality of the loss, experiencing the pain of grief, acknowledging and resolving conflicting feelings, adjusting to a new environment, and withdrawing and reinvesting emotional energy. In dealing with loss, people need support on some level, and group counseling is an effective way to help mourners of all ages in the adjustment and grieving process (Cox et al., 2002; Crenshaw, 1999; Nolen-Hoeksema & Larson, 1999; Powell, 2002; Straub, 2001).

Many of the needs resulting from a loss can be addressed within a group setting, which allows people to share common problems, receive mutual aid, and develop coping skills. The leader can play an important informational and educational role, in addition to facilitating the discussion and introducing helpful activities. The leader should model respect, acceptance, a nonjudgmental attitude, as well as offering encouragement and being empathetic. The leader also should encourage group members to reminisce and to acknowledge the reality of the loss.

Death of a partner is the number-one stressor of all losses because of the close bonds established in that form of relationship. The survivor faces loneliness and a sense of deprivation, but at the same time the possibility of freedom and growth, change, and new relationships.

Another form of loss results from life transitions signified by developmental passages or marker events. To adjust to these losses, individuals have to accomplish material (or instrumental) tasks and psychosocial (or affective) tasks. The transition to the late adult years involves potentially difficult losses because people are faced with adapting to diminishing abilities and relinquishing social roles.

Young children and adolescents experience loss differently than adults, according to their developmental stage. Therefore, counseling professionals have to recognize how children interpret loss and adapt procedures accordingly. Brief counseling applications are particularly appropriate since children's sense of time is more immediate. In working with children, the group leader incorporates games, role playing, puppetry, and similar activities to help the children deal with their fears surrounding loss, felt most strongly as a result of death, divorce, or separation of parents.

USEFUL WEB SITES

- ☐ Northern County Psychiatric Associates
  www.ncpamd.com/bereavement.htm
- ☐ National Mental Health Association
  www.nmha.org
- ☐ Bridges Center for the Alliance of Community Hospices and Palliative Care Services
  www.hospices.org/bridges.htm
- ☐ Grief Healing
  www.griefhealing.com/index.htm
- ☐ Dr. John Grohol's Psych Central
  http://psychcentral.com/resources/Grief_and_Loss/Support_Groups/
- ☐ Wendt Center for Loss and Healing
  www.wendtcenter.org

□ Family Caregivers Online
www.familycaregiversonline.com
□ Healing After Loss.Org
www.healingafterloss.org
□ AARP's grief and loss resources
www.aarp.org/griefandloss
□ Sedona Training Associates
www.sedona.com/html/grief.aspx
□ GriefShare
www.griefshare.org

REFERENCES

Abbey, A. (2000). Adjusting to infertility. In J. H. Harvey & E. D. Miller (Eds.), *Loss and trauma: General and close relationship perspectives* (pp. 183–204). Philadelphia: Taylor & Francis.

Attig, T. (2002). Relearning the world: Always complicated, sometimes more than others. In G. R. Cox, R. A. Bendiksen, & R. G. Stevenson (Eds.), *Complicated grieving and bereavement: Understanding and treating people experiencing loss* (pp. 7–19). Amityville, NY: Baywood.

Auz, M. M., & Andrews, M. L. (2002). *Handbook for those who grieve: What you should know and what you can do during times of loss.* Chicago: Loyola Press.

Becvar, D. S. (2001). *In the presence of grief: Helping family members resolve death, dying, and bereavement issues.* New York: Guilford.

Boekhout, B., Hendrick, S. S., & Hendrick, C. (2000). The loss of loved ones: The impact of relationship infidelity. In J. H. Harvey & E. D. Miller (Eds.), *Loss and trauma: General and close relationship perspectives* (pp. 358–372). Philadelphia: Taylor & Francis.

Boss, P. (1999). *Ambiguous loss: Learning to live with unresolved grief.* Cambridge, MA: Harvard University Press.

Bozarth, A. R. (1986). *Life is goodbye, life is hello: Grieving well through all kinds of loss.* Center City, MN: Hazelden.

Bridges, W. (1980). *Transitions.* Reading, MA: Addison-Wesley.

Bridges, W. (2001). *The way of transition: Embracing life's most difficult moments.* Cambridge, MA: Perseus Publishing.

Browers, R. (1991). Retirement and aging: A lifelong view. *Counseling and Human Development, 24,* 1–12.

Bruce, E. J., & Schultz, C. L. (2001). *Nonfinite loss and grief: A psychoeducational approach.* Baltimore: Brooks Publishing.

Charkow, W. B. (1998). Inviting children to grieve. *Professional School Counseling, 2*(2), 117–127.

Christ, G. H. (2000). *Healing children's grief.* New York: Oxford University Press.

Churn, A. (2003). *The end is just the beginning: Lessons in grieving for African Americans.* New York: Broadway Books.

Corey, G. (1996). *Theory and practice of counseling and psychotherapy.* Pacific Grove, CA: Brooks/Cole Publishing.

Corey, M. S., & Corey, G. (1997). *Groups: Process and practice.* Pacific Grove, CA: Brooks/Cole.

Costa, L., & Stiltner, B. (1994). Why do the good things always end and the bad things go on forever: A family change counseling group. *School Counselor, 41,* 300–304.

Cox, G. R., Bendiksen, R. A., & Stevenson, R. G. (Eds.) (2002). *Complicated grieving and bereavement: Understanding and treating people experiencing loss.* Amityville, NY: Baywood.

Crenshaw, D. A. (1999). *Bereavement: Counseling the grieving through the life cycle.* New York: Crossroad Publishing.

deShazer, S. (1991). *Putting difference to work.* New York: Norton.

Ellis, C. (2000). Negotiating terminal illness: Communication, collusion, and coalition in caregiving. In J. H. Harvey & E. D. Miller (Eds.), *Loss and trauma: General and close relationship perspectives* (pp. 286–304). Philadelphia: Taylor & Francis.

Ellis, A., & Dryden, W. (1997). *The practice of rational emotive behavior therapy.* New York: Springer Publishing.

Emswiler, M. A., & Emswiler, J. P. (2000). *Guiding your child through grief.* New York: Bantam.

Fogarty, J. A. (2000). *The magical thoughts of grieving children: Treating children with complicated mourning and advice for parents.* Amityville, NY: Baywood Publishing.

Golan, N. (1986). *The perilous bridge: Helping clients through mid-life transitions.* New York: Free Press.

Goldman, L. (2000). *Life and loss: A guide to help grieving children* (2nd ed.). Ann Arbor, MI: Sheridan Books.

Harvey, J. H. (2000). *Give sorrow words: Perspectives on loss and trauma.* Philadelphia: Brunner/Mazel.

Harvey, J. H. (2002). *Perspectives on loss and trauma: Assaults on the self.* Thousand Oaks, CA: Sage.

Harvey, J. H., & Miller, E. D. (2000). *Loss and trauma.* Philadelphia: Brunner-Routledge.

Hobfoll, S. E., Ennis, N., & Kay, J. (2000). Loss, resources, and resiliency in close interpersonal relationships. In J. H. Harvey & E. D. Miller (Eds.), *Loss and trauma: General and close relationship perspectives* (pp. 267–283). Philadelphia: Taylor & Francis.

Holmes, T. H., & Rahe, R. H. (1967). Social readjustment rating scale. *Journal of Psychosomatic Research, 11,* 213–218.

Hudson, F. M. (1991). *The adult years: Mastering the art of self-renewal.* San Francisco: Jossey-Bass.

Jackson, M., & Colwell, J. (2002). *A teacher's handbook of death.* Philadelphia: Jessica Kingsley.

Jacobs, E., Masson, R. L., & Harvill, R. L. (2002). *Group counseling: Strategies and skills* (4th ed.). Pacific Grove, CA: Brooks/Cole.

Janowiak, S., Mei-Tal, R., & Drapkin, R. G. (1995). Living with loss: A group for bereaved college students. *Death Studies, 19,* 55–63.

Kandt, V. E. (1994). Adolescent bereavement: Turning a fragile time into acceptance and peace. *School Counselor, 41,* 203–211.

Klass, D., Silverman, P. R., & Nickman, S. L. (1996). *Continuing bonds: New understandings of grief.* Washington, DC: Taylor & Francis.

Larson, D. G. (1993). *The helper's journey: Working with people facing grief, loss, and life-threatening illness.* Champaign, IL: Research Press.

Lehmann, L., Jimerson, S.R., & Gaasch, A. (2001). *Mourning child grief support group curriculum: Middle childhood edition.* Philadelphia: Taylor & Francis.

Leick, N., & Davidsen-Nielsen, M. (1991). *Healing pain: Attachment, loss and grief therapy.* New York: Tavistock/Routledge.

Lenhardt, A. M. C., & McCourt, B. (2000). Adolescent unresolved grief in response to the death of a mother. *Professional School of Counseling, 3*(3), 189–196.

Levinson, D. J., & Levinson, J. D. (1996). *The seasons of a woman's life.* New York: Knopf.

Littrell, J. M., Malia, J. A., & Vanderwood, M. (1995). Single session brief counseling in a high school. *Journal of Counseling and Development, 73,* 451–458.

Littrell, J. M., & Zinck, K. (2004). Brief counseling with children and adolescents: Interactive, culturally responsive, and action-based. In A. Vernon (Ed.), *Counseling children and adolescents* (3rd ed., pp. 137–162). Denver: Love Publishing.

Locke, S. A. (1994). *Coping with loss: A guide for caregivers.* Springfield, IL: Charles C Thomas.

Lopata, H. (1996). Widowhood and husband sanctification. In D. Klass, P. Silverman, & S. Nickman (Eds.), *Continuing bonds* (pp. 149–162). Philadelphia: Taylor & Harris.

Matsakis, A. (1999). *Survivor guilt: A self-help guide*. Oakland, CA: New Harbinger.

Merriam, S. B., & Clark, M. C. (1991). *Lifelines: Patterns of work, love, and learning in adulthood*. San Francisco: Jossey-Bass.

Midland, D. L. (2002). Miscarriage in the emergency room: Meeting parents' needs. In G. R. Cox, R. A. Bendiksen, & R. G. Stevenson (Eds.), *Complicated grieving and bereavement: Understanding and treating people experiencing loss* (pp. 219–226). Amityville, NY: Baywood.

Middleton, W., Raphael, B., Martinek, N., & Misso, V. (1993). Pathological grief reactions. In M. S. Stroebe, W. Stroebe, & R. O. Hansson (Eds.), *Handbook of bereavement: Theory, research, and intervention* (pp. 44–63). New York: Cambridge University Press.

Moore, M. M., & Freeman, S. J. (1995). Counseling survivors of suicide: Implications for group postvention. *Journal for Specialists in Group Work, 20,* 40–47.

Morales, P. C. (1997). Grieving in silence: The loss of companion in modern society. *Journal of Personal and Interpersonal Loss, 2,* 243–254.

Morse, G. A. (2000). On being homeless and mentally ill: A multitude of losses and the possibility of recovery. In J. H. Harvey & E. D. Miller (Eds.), *Loss and trauma: General and close relationship perspectives* (pp. 249–262). Philadelphia: Taylor & Francis.

Murphy, J. J. (1997). *Solution-focused counseling in middle and high schools*. Alexandria, VA: American Counseling Association.

Nahmani, N., Neeman, E., & Nir, C. (1989). Parental bereavement: The motivation to participate in support groups and its consequences. *Social Work With Groups, 12,* 89–98.

Nichols, M. P., & Schwartz, R. C. (1998). *Family therapy: Concepts and methods*. Needham Heights, MA: A Viacom Company.

Nolen-Hoeksema, S., & Larson, J. (1999). *Coping with loss*. Mahwah, NJ: Lawrence Erlbaum.

O'Connor, N. (1995). *Letting go with love: The grieving process*. Tucson, AZ: La Mariposa Press.

Parkes, C. M. (2001). *Bereavement: Studies of grief in adult life*. Philadelphia: Taylor & Francis.

Payne, S., Horn, S., & Relf, M. (1999). *Loss and bereavement*. Philadelphia: Open University Press.

Perschy, M. K. (1997). *Helping teens work through grief*. Washington, DC: Taylor & Francis.

Powell, J. (2002). Grieving in the context of a community of differently-abled people. In G. R. Cox, R. A. Bendiksen, & R. G. Stevenson (Eds.), *Complicated grieving and bereavement: Understanding and treating people experiencing loss* (pp. 119–136). Amityville, NY: Baywood.

Price, G. E., Dinas, P., Dunn, C., & Winterowd, C. (1995). Group work with clients experiencing grieving: Moving from theory to practice. *Journal for Specialists in Group Work, 20,* 159–167.

Quinn, C. A. (2002). Dementia: A cause of complicated grieving. In G. R. Cox, R. A. Bendiksen, & R. G. Stevenson (Eds.), *Complicated grieving and bereavement: Understanding and treating people experiencing loss* (pp. 153–162). Amityville, NY: Baywood.

Rando, T. A. (1993). *Treatment of complicated mourning*. Champaign, IL: Research Press.

Rando, T. A. (2000). *Clinical dimensions of anticipatory mourning: Theory and practice in working with the dying, their loved ones, and their caregivers*. Champaign, IL: Research Press.

Roos, S. (2002). *Chronic sorrow: A living loss*. New York: Brunner-Routledge.

Rosoff, B. D. (1994). *The worst loss*. New York: Henry Holt.

Sanders, C. M. (1989). *Grief: The mourning after*. New York: Wiley.

Schlossberg, N. K. (1989). *Overwhelmed: Coping with life's ups and downs*. Lexington, MA: Lexington Books.

Schlossberg, N. K. (2004). *Retire smart retire happy: Finding your true path in life*. Washington, DC: American Psychological Association.

Schlossberg, N. K., & Robinson, S. P. (1996). *Going to plan B: How you can cope, regroup, and start your life on a new path*. New York: Simon & Schuster.

Schlossberg, N. K., Waters, E. B., & Goodman, J. (1995). *Counseling adults in transition: Linking practice with theory* (2nd ed.). New York: Springer.

Schuchter, S. R., & Zisook, S. (1993). The course of normal grief. In M. S. Stroebe, W. Stroebe, & R. O. Hansson (Eds.), *Handbook of bereavement: Theory, research, and intervention* (pp. 23–43). New York: Cambridge University Press.

Shapiro, E. R. (1994). *Grief as a family process*. New York: Guilford Press.

Silverman, P. R. (2000). *Never too young to know: Death in children's lives*. New York: Oxford University Press.

Staudacher, C. (1991). *Men and grief*. Oakland, CA: New Harbinger Publications.

Straub, S. H. (2001). *Death without notice*. Amityville, NY: Baywood.

Stroebe, M. S., Hansson, R. O., Stroebe, W., & Schut, H. (Eds.) (2001). *Handbook of bereavement research: Consequences, coping, and care*. Washington, DC: American Psychological Association.

Stroebe, M., & Stroebe, W. (1993). The mortality of bereavement: A review. In M. S. Stroebe, W. Stroebe, & R. O. Hansson (Eds.), *Handbook of bereavement: Theory, research, and intervention* (pp. 175–195). New York: Cambridge University Press.

Thompson, S. C., & Kyle, D. J. (2000). The role of perceived control in coping with the losses associated with chronic illness. In J. H. Harvey & E. D. Miller (Eds.), *Loss and trauma: General and close relationship perspectives* (pp. 131–142). Philadelphia: Taylor & Francis.

Tollerud, T., & McFarland, W. (2004). Counseling children and adolescents with special needs. In A. Vernon (Ed.), *Counseling children and adolescents* (pp. 257–309). Denver: Love.

Vernon, A. (2004). Working with children, adolescents, and their parents: Practical application of developmental theory. In A. Vernon (Ed.), *Counseling children and adolescents* (pp. 1–34). Denver: Love Publishing.

Vernon, A., & Clemente, R. (2005). *Assessment and intervention with children and adolescents: Developmental and multicultural approaches*. Alexandria, VA: American Counseling Association.

Viorst, J. (1986). *Necessary losses*. New York: Simon & Schuster.

Volkan, V. D., & Zintl, E. (1993). *Life after loss*. New York: Scribner's.

Walter, C. A. (2003). *The loss of a life partner: Narratives of the bereaved*. New York: Columbia University Press.

Weiss, R. S. (2001). Grief, bonds, and relationships. In M. Stroebe, R. Hansson, W. Stroebe, & H. Schut (Eds.), *Handbook of bereavement research: Consequences, coping, and care* (pp. 47–62). Washington, DC: American Psychological Association.

Worden, J. W. (1991). *Grief counseling and grief therapy: A handbook for the mental health practitioner*. New York: Springer.

Worden, J. W. (1996). *Children and grief: When a parent dies*. New York: Guilford.

Worden, J. W. (2002). *Grief counseling and grief therapy: A handbook for the mental health practitioner* (3rd ed.). New York: Springer.

Yalom, I. D. (1995). *The theory and practice of group psychotherapy*. New York: Basic Books.

Zimpfer, D. G. (1989). Groups for persons who have cancer. *Journal for Specialists in Group Work, 14*(2), 98–104.

Zimpfer, D. G. (1991). Groups for grief and survivorship after bereavement: A review. *Journal for Specialists in Group Work, 16*(1), 46–55.

Group Work: Addictions

Abbé Finn

The problems associated with addictions pose serious public health concerns. Consider the following:

- Substance abuse is the most common disorder encountered by physicians (American Medical Association [AMA], 1993), accounting for 30% to 50% of all psychiatric emergencies (Evans & Sullivan, 1990).
- An estimated 60% of hospitalizations are related to chemical abuse (Ciraulo, Shader, Ciraulo, Greenblat, & von Moltke, 1994).
- 640,000 drug-related emergency room admissions were recorded in 2001 (Office of National Drug Control Policy [ONDCP], 2003).
- 60% of men and 30% of women who regularly consume alcohol will have at least one medical or legal complication (American Psychiatric Association [APA], 2000).
- Substance abuse contributes to 56% of domestic violence cases reported to authorities (Gentillelo, Donovan, Dunn, & Rivara, 1995), and the illicit use of drugs increases the risk of death for the woman in the home by 28 times (National Foundation for Brain Research, 1992).
- Half of all murderers are under the influence of drugs at the time they commit the homicide (National Foundation for Brain Research, 1992).
- The overall cost of drug abuse amounted to $160.7 billion in 2000 (ONDCP, 2003).
- It is estimated that 4.8 million adults (18 years and older) and 1.1 million young people (ages 12 to 17 years old) are in need of drug treatment (Substance Abuse and Mental Health Services Administration [SAMHSA], 2001), which leaves a large number of people without services who are in need of care.

- A quarter of the people who commit suicide were alcoholics (Hyman & Cassem, 1995).
- In approximately 675,000 cases of child abuse, substance abuse by their caregivers played a significant part (Bays, 1990; Evans, 1998).

Because of the widespread nature of problems with addictions, most mental health professionals will encounter clients who have been affected by addiction disorders. Clinicians working in outpatient settings can expect that 15% to 20% of their clients will have a history of substance abuse and 8% to 10% will currently have an abuse problem (Fleming & Barry, 1992). Therefore, mental health professionals must have a working knowledge of the models for understanding addictions, the problems associated with addictions, and various treatments for addictive behaviors.

DEFINING ADDICTION

Many substances to which people become addicted are legal and used in social settings. *The Diagnostic and Statistical Manual of Mental Disorders* (*DSM-IV-TR*; APA, 2000) defines a client as being substance-dependent if he or she meets three or more of the following criteria during the previous 12-month period:

1. Demonstrating an increase or decrease in tolerance
2. Showing symptoms of withdrawal or using the substance to relieve or avoid symptoms of withdrawal
3. Using more of the substance or increasing the frequency of use
4. Having a strong desire to stop using and/or repeated unsuccessful attempts to stop
5. Spending more time than intended obtaining, using, or recovering from use
6. Avoiding or failing to meet social, family, occupational, or recreational activities because of use
7. Continued use in spite of the likelihood of negative physical or psychological consequences

The *DSM-IV-TR* further differentiates substance dependence from substance abuse. Substance dependence is the more serious diagnosis. To meet the criteria for substance abuse, the person must not have met the criteria for substance dependence. The following are the criteria of substance abuse:

1. Significant degree of impairment or distress within the past 12 months
2. Recurrent failure to meet family, occupational, or school responsibilities due to use
3. Recurrent use under hazardous conditions
4. Persistent use in spite of negative consequences to health, family, social interactions, work or school performance

Whenever people turn to mental health professionals for help with their addiction problem, they are in crisis (Schneider & Schneider, 1996). Whether the person is abusing drugs or alcohol, is addicted to gambling, or is engaging in compulsive sexual activities, the dynamics are similar. The person feels out of control and unable to stop and persists in the behavior while suffering dire consequences. Clients describe "hitting rock bottom" and feeling "sick and tired of feeling sick and tired" as a motivation for entering treatment.

MODELS FOR UNDERSTANDING ADDICTIONS AND COMPULSIVE BEHAVIORS

Although the concept of addictions was originally developed to explain compulsive and habitual use of alcohol and narcotics, it currently is used to explain many additional behaviors including abuse of prescription medications, cigarette smoking, gambling, overeating or undereating, compulsive exercising, compulsive spending, and compulsive sexual behavior (Buchanan, 1994; Carnes, 1992; McCormick & Ramirez, 1988; McGurrin, 1994; Schneider & Schneider, 1996; Swisher, 1995; Walters, 1999). Activities that once were considered "bad habits" or "immoral" are now considered by many to be the manifestation of a disease known as addiction (Erickson, 1998), although recognizing addiction as a disease is hotly contested (Doweiko, 2002; Peele, 1989; Walters, 1999).

Because many aspects of addictive behavior patterns mirror each other and respond to similar interventions, they will be included in this chapter. These client behavior patterns include ("Treatment," 1995)

- the apparent inability to control their behavior,
- increased level of use, and
- continuing the behavior in spite of numerous negative consequences.

Several models attempt to define and explain addictive behavior, including the moral weakness model, the medical model, the sociocultural models, and the biopsychosocial model. These models provide a framework upon which the problem is viewed, treated, and prevented, as well as how the outcome is predicted and relapse is prevented (Erickson, 1998; Johnson, 2003).

The Moral Weakness Model

The first model to be applied was the moral weakness model. From this perspective, the addict is viewed as having a character disorder, lacking the moral fortitude to do the right thing—to abstain from the problem behavior. From this perspective, addicts can be cured if they control their urges. Addicts are considered sinful and morally weak. Consequently, they are likely to feel ashamed and keep the problem a secret from others.

When these people have sought help, they most likely turned to their religious and moral leaders. Religions that forbade gambling, sexual relations outside of marriage, and the use of substances such as alcohol have used the pulpit as a platform to warn their congregations of the moral risks. According to this model, the person only has to have will power and moral strength. If the person does relapse after a period of sobriety, the cause is considered to be a spiritual deficiency. This conceptualization of alcoholism, in combination with the medical model, was the foundation for forming Alcoholics Anonymous (AA) (Miller & Kurtz, 1994).

The Medical Model

The birth and development of the medical model is credited to the work of Jellinek (1952, 1960), who has profoundly influenced the treatment of addictions. Jellinek specifically addressed alcoholism, which he characterized as a sequence leading from loss of control, to increased severity of symptoms, and finally to death if untreated. Jellinek proposed the following specific stages of alcoholism along a continuum—pre-alcoholic, prodromal, crucial, and chronic, described as follows:

1. *Pre-alcoholic stage*, characterized by the use of alcohol to relieve social stress and pressures.
2. *Prodromal stage*, marked by blackouts, preoccupation with obtaining and using the substance, shame about using the substance, concealing the use, and feelings of guilt about behavior while under the influence.
3. *Crucial stage*, characterized by physical dependence. The alcoholic suffers from malnutrition as a result of poor diet. In addition, there are psychological characteristics including loss of control over the substance use, loss of self-esteem, abandonment of other activities that interfere with the use of alcohol, and heightened self-pity.
4. *Chronic stage*, characterized by lowering of moral and social standards, use of other drugs when alcohol is unavailable, and the development of persistent tremors.

As a result of Jellinek's work, the American Medical Association (AMA) recognized alcoholism as a disease in 1956.

Conceptualizing alcoholism as a disease opened the door for systematic investigation of the problem (Doweiko, 2002; Johnson, 2003) and made treatment available to many people by allowing medical insurance to reimburse for treatment. It also reduced the stigma attached to the diagnosis of substance abuse. In 1960, Jellinek developed a diagnostic framework that classified alcoholics into four subgroups. These were not discrete, and as the disease progressed, the person could move from one category to the next.

Since the 1960s, the medical community and contemporary society at large have moved away from the moral model toward the medical model (Erickson, 1998). In the first edition of the *Diagnostic and Statistical Manual of Mental Disorders* (*DSM-I*; APA, 1952), addiction came under the classification of *sociopathic personality disturbance*, which connotes a lack of moral character. The second edition of the *DSM* (APA, 1968) recognized alcoholism and drug dependence as a distinct medical diagnosis. This demonstrates how well accepted among the medical community this conceptualization of the disease had become. According to the fourth edition and text revision, the current *DSM-IV-TR* (APA, 2000), the presence of four or more of the following signs indicate a diagnosis of addiction:

- Preoccupation
- Increase in use
- Increased tolerance
- Symptoms of physical or emotional withdrawal
- Use to avoid or control withdrawal symptoms
- Unsuccessful attempts to cut back
- Use of the substance at unsafe or inappropriate times
- Restriction of previous activities (social, occupational, and recreational) in favor of participation in addiction behavior
- Persistent use in spite of negative consequences

These diagnostic criteria encompass several domains, taking into account psychological characteristics, behavior, physical symptoms, and negative impact on relationships.

The *genetic model* for understanding addictions is a subcategory of the medical model. The genetic model proposes that people become addicted to substances because of a genetic predisposition. This is not a new observation. The ancient Roman philosopher Plutarch proclaimed, "Drunks beget drunkards" (in Anthenelli & Schuckit, 1992, p. 39). As a result of observations such as this, studies on twins, adoption, and the clustering of alcoholism within families have explored the possible genetic link (Anthenelli & Schuckit, 1992; Barondes, 1999; Pickins & Svikis, 1991). The implication is that if some people are predisposed to alcoholism and other addictions, they should be targets of prevention efforts.

One conclusion from the investigations is that males seem to inherit the risk at a higher rate than females, and biological children of alcoholics are at a significantly higher risk for addiction than children adopted into alcoholic homes (Anthenelli & Schuckit, 1992; Goodwin, 1989). Although these findings support the genetic model, they do not explain why some children in a family are vulnerable while the majority of the children (66%) do not become alcoholics (Anthenelli & Schuckit, 1992; Searles, 1991). Social learning and social norms are thought to play a role in addictions.

Sociocultural Models

The sociocultural models of addiction encompass the concepts of family systems, peer pressure, cultural norms, and modeling theories. These models explain the addictive process from the perspective of forces in the environment that either encourage or inhibit the development of addictive behaviors.

Systems Theory

The *systems theory* proposes that roles and scripts in the family channel people toward certain behaviors and beliefs. The family system has a primary role of maintaining homeostasis, and any change to a member of the system impacts all other members of the system (Erickson, 1998). When a member of the family system becomes addicted, the role of the entire system is directed to maintaining the addiction, and the well-being of the individuals within the system becomes secondary (Steinglass, 1987).

Sociocultural Theory

The *sociocultural theory* assumes that the decision to use or not to use substances rests with the community or social group in which they reside. Pihl (1999) proposed five levels of cultural background that impact an individual's chemical use:

1. The individual's cultural history and general cultural environment
2. Community standards
3. Subcultures within the community
4. Family environment and peer influences
5. Prevailing community attitudes regarding substance use

Biopsychosocial Model

The biopsychosocial model for understanding addictions integrates elements of the medical model, sociocultural models, and psychological models. It holds that addiction is a result of a combination of factors including genetic predisposition, exposure, individual reaction to the substance or behavior, social factors, learning, and environmental influences (Erickson, 1998; Anthenelli & Schuckit, 1992). According to this model, these factors are reciprocally interactive and may function to promote or inhibit the development of an addiction (Anthenelli & Schuckit, 1992). For example, a genetic predisposition may team up with the social influence of a college binge-drinking culture, accompanied by the psychological desire to feel more relaxed in social settings, which results in alcohol abuse. From the perspective of this model, no single factor is responsible for the addiction; instead, it is a cumulative interactive effect (Erickson, 1998).

SUBSTANCES OF ABUSE

Humans have used psychoactive substances since prehistoric times, and they are present in every culture (Stevens-Smith, 1998). There was a time when beer and wine were safer to drink than water (McAnally, 1996). Psychoactive substances cross the blood–brain barrier and cause chemical changes in the brain. These substances are used to relieve pain, stimulate the mind and body, relax the mind and body, give pleasure, cause hallucinations, offer escape, and achieve intoxication

(Porter, 1998). They are classified according to their effect on the body and the mind. The categories are stimulants, depressants, cannabinols, hallucinogens, and inhalants (Porter, 1998).

Stimulants

The category of stimulants encompasses legal substances such as caffeine, nicotine, and Ritalin, as well as illegal substances such as cocaine, methamphetamines, and other amphetamines. It is a mistake to assume that a substance is safe because it is legal or "natural." For example, tobacco is both legal and natural, but cigarette smoking leads to 434,000 deaths in the United States each year (Centers for Disease Control, 2000) making it the deadliest addictive substance used.

Depressants

The category of depressants includes alcohol, benzodiazepines, barbiturates, and opiates.

1. *Alcohol* accounts for 100,000 deaths yearly in the United States (Porter, 1998). It accounts for 10% of all deaths in the United States, reducing the life expectancy of an alcoholic by 15 years (Goldberg, 2006).

2. *Benzodiazepines*

   Benzodiazepines are sold under the trade names of Valium, Librium, Rohypnol, Halcion, and Xanax. They frequently are prescribed to treat anxiety and insomnia. People become addicted to benzodiazepines by escalating their use beyond the prescribed amount, continuing to take the medication for an extended period, using the medication without a prescription to control withdrawal symptoms of other drugs, or to achieve intoxication in combination with other drugs (APA, 1990; Longo & Johnson, 2000).

3. *Barbiturates*

   The most commonly used barbiturates are phenobarbital, sodium pentothal, and Nembutal. Barbiturates potentiate alcohol and benzodiazepines; therefore, when taken in combination, the effects of the drugs are heightened and the risk of overdose increases (Porter, 1998). This lethal combination was responsible for the demise of the famed actress Marilyn Monroe.

4. *Opiates*

   Opiates are legally prescribed primarily to manage pain. This group includes codeine, morphine, and Demerol. Tolerance can develop quickly. Heroin is used illegally as a recreational drug. After years of stable-use figures, the use of heroin has increased by younger users (Hopfer, Mikulich, & Crowley, 2000). The purer forms of heroine now available can be inhaled through the nose rather than injected. Heroin overdose accounts for half of the deaths by drug-induced overdose (Epstein & Gfroerer, 1997).

Cannabinols

Cannabinols include marijuana and hashish, in which the active ingredient is tetrahydrocannabinol (THC). The strength of marijuana has increased exponentially because of selective plant production propagation (Porter, 1998). Marijuana is the most frequently used illegal drug with 12.1 million users (SAMHSA, 2002); 21.5% of high school seniors reported using within the past month (National Institute on Drug Abuse [NIDA], 2002).

The drug impacts perception and reaction time and impairs the ability to operate vehicles. Use is also associated with reduction of motivation and achievement (Fisher & Harrison, 2000). Damage to the brain, reproductive system, and lungs has been noted with long-term use (Zimmer & Morgan, 1997).

Hallucinogens

Frequently used by young people, drugs in the category of hallucinogens include LSD, PCP, MDA (Ecstasy), and Psilocybin (hallucinogenic mushrooms). These drugs change the state of consciousness to the extent that the person becomes temporarily psychotic, experiencing visual, auditory, and tactile hallucinations. When individuals are experiencing these altered perceptions and thought processes, they are vulnerable to self-harm. Some people reexperience the hallucinations months later, known as "flashbacks." This category of drug is not thought to be addictive (Fisher & Harrison, 2000).

Inhalants and Volatile Hydrocarbons

The final category of abused substances consists of inhalants and volatile hydrocarbons. Many inhalants are substances that were not intended to be ingested by humans. These are mostly legal household products and are inhaled—in slang, "huffing" or "sniffing." This route to intoxication usually is chosen by preadolescents, adolescents, and people of low socioeconomic status (Doweiko, 2002; Fisher & Harrison, 2000; Porter, 1998). In the NIDA 2002 Monitoring the Future Study, 11.7% of participating high school seniors reported use of inhalants (NIDA, 2002).

In contrast to chemical propellants and other household cleaning materials, nitrous oxide and ether are intended for use with humans as anesthetics. When inhaled, they may cause sudden loss of consciousness resulting in accidents and injuries and respiratory arrest leading to sudden death. They also may bring on hallucinations, euphoria, brain damage, liver failure, and lung damage (Fisher & Harrison, 2000; Johnson, 2003). Nitrous oxide sometimes is sold in balloons to young people at teen rock concerts known as "raves" (Schwartz, 1989). Others inhale the chemical from whipped cream canisters. Often parents are unaware that their child has been abusing inhalants until tragic consequences ensue.

OTHER ADDICTIONS

Additional compulsive behaviors can cause serious social, economic, medical, and family problems. These behaviors, which have the commonality of being outside the client's ability for self-control, include pathologic gambling, sexual compulsions, and food addictions. Many other behaviors have been described as addictive, but discussion of all of the possible addictions is well beyond the scope of this chapter. All of these behaviors, however, follow similar patterns of addictive development.

Gambling

People have been gambling for at least the past 6,000 years. Governments have utilized games of chance to raise revenues since the third Crusade in 1190. When the United States was colonized, the Puritans outlawed gambling because it was considered immoral, but politicians have not been able to resist the temptation to legalize gambling because it provides an opportunity to raise money without raising taxes. Land-based and riverboat gambling has proliferated throughout the United States (McCormick & Ramirez, 1988; McGurrin, 1994), with a corresponding increase in the number of people reporting problems with pathological gambling (Politzer & Hudac, 1992).

Pathological gambling ranks second to the abusive use of alcohol. An estimated 2% to 5% of adults in the United States are pathologic or problem gamblers (*Prevention Researcher*, 1999). The pathological gambler is characterized as a person who continues wagering in spite of negative consequences and apparently is unable to stop even when highly motivated to do so (Politzer and Hudac, 1992).

Several personality profiles are common to pathologic gamblers:

- *Avoidant personality*. Gamblers with avoidant personality wager to escape, repress, or deny anxiety. They may suffer from posttraumatic stress disorder.
- *Undersocialized personality*. People with the undersocialized personality style seek validation through external sources. They tend to be impulsive, verbal, charismatic, suspicious, and manipulative, and they rely on projection and rationalization as self-defenses.
- *Narcissistic personality*. Gamblers with a narcissistic personality are boastful, exploitative charmers who overlook their losses and focus only on their wins. They act as if their dreams were reality and as if they are entitled to be the center of attention at all times. They employ the self-defense mechanisms of exhibitionism, projection, splitting, and tantrums. They are easily bored, have a superior attitude, and act as if they know a secret no one else knows.
- *Angry–aggressive personality*. Gamblers exhibiting the angry–aggressive personality style have a history of threatening and harming others. They are likely to see danger when others do not. They may view their losses as proof of a conspiracy against them. They also display elements of grandiosity.

Many, but not all, gamblers manifest these various personality styles (McCormick & Ramirez, 1988). In general, gamblers have above-average intelligence, are friendly, charming, adept at reading others, hard working, and successful. Often they have been successful athletes and are highly competitive (Politzer & Hudac, 1992).

Gaudia (1992) documented three stages in the development of pathological gambling:

1. People in the first phase look like essentially normal gamblers. They enjoy wagering and winning, but they do not quit when they are winning. When they lose, they attribute the loss to outside forces. These two characteristics differentiate normal gamblers from potentially pathologic gamblers.

2. The second stage is marked by increasing losses and increased importance of gambling to the gamblers. They begin to identify themselves as "high-rollers." Casinos reinforce this identity by granting frequent gamblers extra privileges, special treatment, and added benefits. Gambling becomes a point of pride and part of their identity. These gamblers are obsessed with recapturing their losses. They also feel increased physical and psychological tension when anticipating gambling. When they gamble, they experience high excitement and pleasure (McGurrin, 1992). They become more and more risky with their wagering.

3. In the third stage, known as "the desperate phase," the gamblers become secretive and deceitful about their gambling and their debts. The pleasure has gone out of gaming and is supplanted by desperation, depression, and recklessness (Gaudia, 1992). Gamblers in this stage are facing overwhelming pressure from family, employers, law enforcement, and friends to stop gambling, but they do not seem to know any way to escape their losses except through gambling. At this point, the gambler may foster thoughts of suicide (Fisher & Harrison, 2000).

Sex Addiction

Historically, compulsive sexual behavior was considered pathological only if it was same sex or if a female was engaging in promiscuous behavior (Logan, 1992). Pathological sexual addictions include preoccupation with pornography, solicitation of prostitutes, numerous affairs outside of marriage (Fisher & Harrison, 2000), and the newest manifestation of this disorder, consisting of multiple liaisons over the Internet known as *cybersex*. These "cyber-relationships" can be highly damaging to primary relationships because so much time and energy are transferred from real to the imagined relationships, resulting in the partner feeling neglected and ignored.

Sexual addictions can result in job loss, termination of relationships, arrest, and public humiliation (Fisher & Harrison, 2000). After surveying 76 sex addicts and 74 partners of addicts, Schneider and Schneider (1996) concluded that this group was highly educated and had a high incidence of other addictive behaviors (81%) in their family of origin. This included substance dependence of at least one parent (36%), sexual addiction (36%), eating disorders (30%), compulsive work patterns (38%), and gambling (7%). In addition, 52% of the men and 39% of the women reported a history of childhood sexual abuse.

Swisher (1995) surveyed 248 counselor–members of the American Mental Health Counseling Association (AMHCA) and the International Association for Addictions and Offender Counselors (IAAOC). The researcher concluded that the most common sex addict is a heterosexual male who was physically or sexually abused as a child and had at least one parent with a substance-dependence problem. Of the survey respondents, 88% believed that sexual addictions are misdiagnosed.

Carnes (1992) delineated three levels of addictions, described in the following paragraphs.

Level One

Level One addicts frequently masturbate, have sexual relations with prostitutes, spend a great deal of time and money on pornography, may have frequent casual sexual affairs, and usually are in denial regarding their problem. What differentiates Level One sexual addicts from the general population is their desperation and the amount of time they spend ruminating on and anticipating their sexual behavior.

Level Two

Level Two addicts engage in higher-risk behaviors—exhibitionism, voyeurism, obscene phone calls, and sending pornographic e-mails. Their behavior targets victims and is illegal. Level Two sex addicts may rationalize their behavior but know that it is illegal and may bring about their ruination if discovered. They persist in the behavior despite real or imagined consequences.

Level Three

Level Three sex addicts engage in violent criminal activity, committing acts of rape, child sexual abuse, incest, and child pornography. Most Level Three addicts engage in all three levels of behavior. Some addicts abstain from sexual behavior only to incur a relapse and go on a sexual deviance binge. Like the other two levels, Level Three is characterized by shame, secrecy, and the inability to control their behavior.

Food Addictions

Consuming food for reasons other than purely nutritional purposes is common. As with the other addictive disorders, the behavior is essentially normal at early stages. There is a range of behavior in which some activities are considered normal and outside of that range the behavior is considered abnormal. The various forms of food addictions include compulsive consumption of food leading to chronic obesity, bulimia (binging and purging), and anorexia (fasting and compulsive exercise) (Fisher & Harrison, 2000).

As with other forms of addiction, the thoughts of food addicts are consumed with the object of their addiction. They spend most of their free time thinking about food, diet, drugs (laxatives, purgatives, and amphetamines), and exercising to obtain an imagined ideal physical image (Barry, 1992). People with food addictions have a distorted self-image and an abnormal relationship with food (Fisher & Harrison, 2000).

People with eating disorders share many behaviors in common with people who have other addictions. They are secretive, feel that they are out of control, are in denial, and continue the behavior in spite of negative physical, social, and emotional consequences (Barry, 1992). While most people who are addicted to drugs and alcohol are men, 95% of those with food addictions are women (APA, 2000).

TREATMENT MODALITIES OF ADDICTIONS

The many interventions for addictions range from a single conversation with a professional to inpatient treatment. Outcome measures for these various treatment modalities likewise give a full spectrum of results. Some research indicates that a single informative discussion with a health care professional has a positive result in some cases. In the majority of cases, however, more intensive intervention is required (Carmack, Owens, & Dewey, 1987). Interventions range from the least restrictive, bibliotherapy, to the most restrictive, inpatient residential treatment on a locked ward (Manfrin, 1998).

Participation in a support group is a common thread running through all treatments. Examples of these support groups are AA, Narcotics Anonymous (NA), Cocaine Anonymous (CA), Overeaters Anonymous (OA), and Gamblers Anonymous (GA).

Inpatient Programs

Most inpatient programs are based upon the Minnesota model, which combines the expertise of physicians, recovering addicts, counselors, psychologists, nurses, and social workers in treating substance abuse. The three phases of treatment are

1. detoxification,
2. rehabilitation, and
3. aftercare.

When people enter an inpatient treatment program, they usually undergo assessments including medical, psychiatric, psychological, social, and family appraisal. Based upon the assessment, the treatment plan may consist of detoxification, family counseling, psychoeducation, individual counseling, medication, family counseling, and/or group counseling. Not all treatment facilities have the resources to detoxify patients, in which case the patient might be admitted to a medical hospital until withdrawal symptoms have passed. Although, with the traditional Minnesota model, patients remained as inpatients from 21 to 28 days (Manfrin, 1998), the 28-day stay has become rare. Now, most treatment plans emphasize outpatient treatment. Patients are admitted to hospitals only if the outpatient plan fails, if they require medical intervention for detoxification, or in cases of a complex dual diagnosis (Hayashida et al., 1989; Weiss, 1994).

Balancing the decision to enter an inpatient program versus an outpatient program can rest on financial factors, availability of childcare, or the decision of a managed care agency rather than the needs of the client (Kinney & West, 1996). Because the cost of inpatient treatment is ten times higher than outpatient treatment of addictions, mental health professionals must justify the more expensive and restrictive inpatient treatment (Stevens-Smith, 1998). A follow-up study 6 months after intervention showed no differences in maintaining abstinence between people who had received inpatient versus outpatient treatment (Hayashida et al., 1989).

Partial Hospitalization and Intensive Outpatient Programs (IOP)

Along the continuum of care, partial hospitalization and intensive outpatient programs (IOP) are a step down from inpatient treatment. As the title implies, both are rigorous interventions for substance abuse. Clients receive the same kind of treatment that they would have received in inpatient treatment except detoxification. The clients attend meetings three to five times a week. Clients in partial hospitalization programs may attend all-day sessions in the hospital and then go home overnight. They also may attend meetings every evening.

These models have distinct advantages. In addition to saving money over inpatient programs, they afford clients an opportunity to continue caring for their families and earning a living while obtaining treatment (Kinney & West, 1996). By making these treatment options available to clients, people who could not enter treatment because of work or family responsibilities have avenues to recovery (Manfrin, 1998). This is particularly true for women who once were excluded from treatment because of lack of childcare for the duration of the 28-day treatment (Morgan & Kinney, 1996; Schliebner & Peregoy, 1998). Outpatient programs have the additional advantage of clients' being able to maintain contact with family members and friends who can provide emotional support. The shadow side of this treatment is that clients may relapse while in treatment because of their access to drugs and the increased pressures of living at home. Outpatient programs incorporate drug screening as part of their routine for early identification of clients who have relapsed (Washton, 1992).

Support Groups

The first effective intervention for treating alcoholism consisted of support groups (Fisher & Harrison, 2000). In 1935 the self-help organization known as AA was born (AA, 1976). At this time, as mentioned, alcoholism was considered a symptom of moral failure.

Two alcoholics, Bill W. and Dr. Bob, who had failed at all other interventions, were the founders of Alcoholics Anonymous. Thus, the organization was founded by alcoholics for alcoholics. AA was influenced by a spiritual awakening in an alcoholic friend of Bill W. who belonged to an evangelical organization known as the Oxford Group. The friend spoke to Bill W. about his spiritual awakening and his subsequent sobriety. Profoundly influenced by this encounter, Bill W. also became sober. He credited his recovery to the spiritual nature of the encounter and the power of conversation between alcoholics.

While out of town, Bill W. met another alcoholic named Dr. Bob. Bill W. spoke with Dr. Bob face to face about his addiction and recovery. When Dr. Bob subsequently became sober, the two men decided to share the word and thereby strengthen their own recovery.

From these encounters, the essential components of AA, which include sharing personal experiences, recognizing alcoholism as a disease, requesting spiritual intervention, and engaging in conversation to help other alcoholics achieve sobriety, were formed. The goal of AA is to abstain from alcohol entirely (Nace, 1992).

AA groups are autonomous and may be very different from each other (Doweiko, 2002), but commonalities (Roots & Aanes, 1992) are as follows:

- Members share their experiences.
- The format is educational, not psychotherapeutic.
- Each group is autonomous.
- Each member is encouraged to take responsibility for his or her actions.
- The purpose is to help alcoholics achieve and maintain sobriety.
- Membership is anonymous and voluntary.
- The goal is a change in lifestyle.

The AA sessions begin with some type of ritual, usually repeating the Serenity Prayer or the AA Preamble. New members are introduced, and members celebrating anniversaries of sobriety are recognized (Fisher & Harrison, 2000). The AA program for recovery is based on the 12 steps and the 12 traditions. Because most inpatient, outpatient, relapse prevention, and aftercare treatment programs include some variation on the Twelve-Steps program, all drug rehabilitation counselors should be familiar with these steps. For this purpose, the 12 steps are reproduced below:

1. We admitted that we are powerless over alcohol—that our lives have become unmanageable.
2. We came to believe that a power greater than ourselves could restore us to sanity.
3. We made a decision to turn our will and our lives over to the care of God as we understood Him.
4. We made a searching and fearless moral inventory of ourselves.
5. We admitted to God, to ourselves, and to another human being the exact nature of our wrongs.
6. We're entirely ready to have God remove all these defects of character.
7. We humbly ask him to remove our shortcomings.
8. We made a list of all persons we had harmed, and became willing to make amends to them all.
9. We made amends to such people wherever possible, except when to do so would injure them or others.

10. We continued to take personal inventory and when we were wrong, promptly admitted it.

11. We sought, through prayer and meditation, to improve our conscious contact with God as we understood Him, praying only for knowledge of His will for us and the power to carry that out.

12. Having had a spiritual awakening as the result of these steps, we tried to carry this message to alcoholics, and to practice these principles in all our affairs. (AA, 1981)

New AA members are encouraged to find another addict with some accumulated time in sobriety to act as a sponsor. This is a casual relationship without the boundary restrictions between professionals and clients. If addicts are tempted to relapse, they are encouraged to contact their sponsor (Nace, 1992).

AA meetings are of different types. Some meetings are called "open" because anyone may attend, and others are known as "closed meetings" because they are intended only for addicts (Fisher & Harrison, 2000). In some meetings, the speaker is an addict who tells his or her story to the group. In discussion meetings, someone leads a discussion about a specific aspect of recovery. In "step meetings," a specific step is described, means for completing that step are explored, and ramifications and the impact of that step are investigated (Nace, 1992).

Most treatment plans include participation in some type of support group (Manfrin, 1998; Nace, 1992). Many recovering addicts credit their success to participating in a support group, although there is remarkably little quality outcome research on the effectiveness of support groups (Nace, 1992). Nevertheless, participation in a support group is widely associated with stable social relationships, steady employment, and sobriety (Emerick, 1987). Khantzian (1999) concluded that the power of AA rests with the group's maintaining cohesion, positive peer pressure, emotional support, and positive problem solving.

Group Counseling

In contrast to AA and similar support groups, which are led from within by recovering addicts, therapeutic groups are led by mental health professionals. Group counseling has been credited as the best treatment for most clients with addiction problems (Golden, Khantzian, & McAuliffe, 1994; Golden & McAuliffe, 1999; Matano & Yalom, 1991; Stevens-Smith, 1998). This is true regardless of the theoretical conceptualization of the etiology or type of addiction (Golden & McAuliffe, 1999). Some believe that group counseling is best used in conjunction with other treatment modalities (Doweiko, 2002).

Among the advantages of group counseling for the treatment of addictions are the following:

1. Groups represent a powerful way to harness positive peer pressure to achieve treatment goals. Members identify with each other's problems and are in a position to confront and challenge the denial associated with

addictions (Galanter, Castaneda, & Franco, 1998; Golden & McAuliffe, 1999; Matano & Yalom, 1991; Washton, 1992).

2. The group reduces the sense of isolation that many recovering addicts feel. This is particularly important because many addicts report that they began using drugs to reduce their anxiety in social situations.

3. Clients in recovery are admonished to stop spending time with their acquaintances who are addicts and to make friends with people who are abstinent. The group members provide a ready-made circle of friends to replace their addicted friends. The group also provides an opportunity to heal the guilt, shame, stigma, and isolation associated with having addictions.

Because most groups for the treatment of addictions have members in various stages of recovery, the members who are further along in the process act as role models and guides for the newer members. The members with long-term recovery counteract the myth that addictions are hopeless. Yalom (1985) identified seven factors that create the therapeutic environment in group counseling:

1. Instilling hope
2. Recognizing the universality of their problems
3. Gaining information
4. Caring for each other
5. Creating a healthy family environment
6. Improving social skills
7. Modeling healthy behavior

The therapeutic group for addictions incorporates all of these factors. The group also provides novel solutions for meeting the demands of recovery. Group members remind participants that recovery from addiction is a life-long journey and addiction may manifest itself in many ways such as alcoholism, gambling, eating disorders, drug addiction, compulsive spending, and compulsive work (Golden & McAuliffe, 1999; Washton, 1992).

In addition, treatment in the group format is much less expensive than individual treatment (Washton, 1992). Therefore, group treatment is often the treatment of choice when addressing addictions in today's culture of managed care with the cost benefit as a driving force in the selection of treatment modalities (Manfrin, 1998; Stevens-Smith, 1998).

Structure of the Group and Group Rules

The structure of the group is determined before clients are enrolled for membership (Yalom, 1985). Establishing firm boundaries and educating the participants about the ground rules increases the likelihood that their goals will be met. The rules address issues including attendance, abstinence from the source of addiction, confidentiality, and conduct during the sessions.

When new members enter a group, they are oriented to know what to expect, which promotes a feeling of safety (Golden & McAuliffe, 1999). With closed groups it is possible to include the group members in creating the group rules (Stevens-Smith, 1998). This is more problematic with open groups, in which new members enter throughout the life of the group. When group members participate in making the rules, compliance and group cohesion are strengthened.

Group Size and Format

Washton (1992) has recommended a group size of 8 to 12 members. Yalom (1985) advocated groups between 5 and 10 members. Once group membership falls below five members, the quality of the group interactions diminishes (Washton, 1992; Yalom, 1985). Groups also may be organized to include members with diverse characteristics, or they may be homogeneous with members who are similar to each other along a certain dimension.

Groups can be open to new members on a rolling basis, or membership may be closed to new members once the group has been formed. These closed groups meet for a predetermined number of sessions. Because groups addressing addictions have a high dropout rate, a closed group might disappear because of attrition. Therefore, closed groups might be impractical except in restricted settings such as prisons or long-term hospital care facilities where the participants are required to attend (Washton, 1992; Yalom, 1985).

In open groups, members may counteract the negative dynamics by encouraging attendance through peer pressure. For example, if some members miss sessions, other members may phone them or go to the members' home to check on them. In open groups, new members benefit from the experiences of others who are further along in the recovery process. These more seasoned members act as role models for members who are less familiar with the recovery process (Golden et al., 1994). In addition, the success of other members allays the myth that nothing can be done to help addicts (Washton, 1992).

Homogeneity Versus Heterogeneity in Groups

Members are more likely to benefit from group treatment if they have some characteristics in common with other group members. Therefore, a group with just one woman in a group of men is not desirable, nor is one cocaine addict in a group of alcoholics, or one older adult in a group of adolescents. Group leaders should avoid attempting to include someone who is not homogeneous with other members of the group (Washton, 1992).

At the same time, groups should have some diversity. In most circumstances, the diversity should be with regard to gender, ethnicity, substances used, education, and occupation. Diversity facilitates admission of new members into the group because they may identify with one or more of the current members. Furthermore, groups that reflect the many faces of people with addictions points out the universality of the problems associated with addiction (Washton, 1992). Because most addicts are polysubstance abusers, it doesn't make sense to separate clients into separate groups according to their drug of choice (Rawson, 1990). Finally, heterogeneous groups are more dynamic than groups in which everyone seems to be the same.

Some programs use the heterogeneous group format in the initial phases of treatment and then break the group into more homogeneous subgroups to address specific issues coexisting with the addictions. For example, there may be smaller specialty groups for women who have addiction problems as well as issues associated with childhood sexual trauma (Rawson, 1990). Women who were abused by males might feel uncomfortable disclosing their experiences, memories, and emotions in a group with male participants (Washton, 1992).

If new treatment issues emerge during the recovery process, the group composition might have to be adjusted or a member might have to be transferred to another plan or group. There may be specialty groups to address problems associated with specific substances, such as cocaine (Rawson, 1990), or for certain occupational groups such as nurses, physicians, dentists, and pharmacists, because their professional status sometimes brings about specific problems as a result of their access to narcotics and other drugs.

There is little agreement regarding the most desirable balance between homogeneity and heterogeneity. After exhaustive consideration, Yalom (1985) proposed that diverse groups are ideal as long as members are able to attain cohesion and compatibility.

Leadership

In the case of addiction groups, coleadership is generally advisable. The group benefits from multiple perspectives and sharing the high stress of leading a substance abuse group. The leaders also can be positive role models for working together. Effective coleadership has the same requirements as a good marriage. The coleaders must agree on fundamental principles, theoretical orientation, and the group process, have mutual respect, be compatible and cooperative, and share program coordination. Their skills must complement each other. The group leaders should coordinate their efforts by meeting regularly outside of the session to discuss the group members, their progress or lack of progress, and possible interventions (Washton, 1992).

The shadow side of coleadership is that group members sometimes attempt to split the leadership. To counteract this possibility, the coleaders must engage in regular and open communication between themselves and remain vigilant to signs that members are playing one leader against the other. Leaders must confront these issues as they arise in group counseling (Matano & Yalom, 1991).

A great deal of debate continues to surround the issue of how the leaders' gender impacts the therapeutic progress and outcome of the group (James & Gilliland, 2000; Threadcraft & Wilcoxon, 1993). Generally, it is advocated that groups dealing with gender-sensitive issues have leaders of the same gender as the group participants. Although the conventional wisdom holds that women should lead groups designed for females who were subjected to sexual abuse, little evidence is available to support this claim. In one study, women were randomly assigned to either a male–female counselor dyad or a female co-counselor-led group, and there were no significant differences in the outcomes (NeSmith, Wilcoxon, & Satcher, 2000).

GROUPS DESIGNED FOR WOMEN

As a population, women tend to be among the hidden faces of addicts (Cohen, 2000). Many women who are addicted to substances are in their childbearing years and potentially can deliver children with symptoms of fetal exposure to drugs. Fetal alcohol syndrome is the primary cause of mental retardation in the United States and is completely preventable (Santrock, 1999). For reasons such as these, groups designed particularly for women are preferable.

Unique Needs of Women

When women abuse drugs, they suffer physical consequences sooner then their male counterparts. Female alcoholics suffer gastrointestinal hemorrhages and cirrhosis of the liver after fewer years of use than men. There is also a link between breast cancer and alcohol consumption. Female substance abusers are likely to live with men who are also addicts. These woman get less social support for maintaining recovery than men who enter treatment. They also are more likely to be survivors of sexual abuse (Liebschutz, Mulvey, & Samet, 1997) and physical abuse (Blume, 1992; Windle, Windle, Scheidt, & Miller, 1995). Addiction in women also is accompanied frequently by depression, low self-esteem, and posttraumatic stress disorder (Blume, 1992; Doweiko, 2002).

There are not enough treatment facilities with programs focusing singularly on the special needs of addicted women. This impacts the outcome of women's treatment programs because women who have been sexually abused are likely to drop out of treatment unless they can participate in all-female groups (Doweiko, 2002). Further, women in alcohol treatment programs drop out much more often than their male counterparts.

Families of Group Members

Parenting skills are often the focus of discussion in groups addressing women's interests (Burman, 1992) because divorced and single women in substance abuse treatment often have children (Blume, 1992; Doweiko, 2002). This is particularly important because many women addicts are themselves children of addicts and, therefore, have few natural role models for adequate parenting skills (Blume, 1992). Groups that address women's family issues focus on self-disclosure regarding sexual and physical abuse, self-esteem, problem solving, empowerment, and parenting skills (Burman, 1992).

A GROUP DESIGNED FOR ADOLESCENTS

Adolescents with addiction problems tend to have several characteristics in common with other substance abusers. Many adolescent substance abusers are survivors of child abuse (Fuller & Cabanaugh, 1995) or have witnessed violence (Kilpatrick et al., 2000). They are likely to come from families that either use substances or have a casual attitude about using substances (Liddle & Rowe, 2002). These adolescents also are characterized by a higher incidence of family conflict preceding the adolescent's substance use (Perkins, 2002; Stanton & Todd, 1982). Their parents tend to have poorer relationships with each other and with the children (Hogan, 2000). In addition to the increased conflict, these families have a lack of cohesion and the parents are less involved with their children's lives (Brook, Brook, Gordon, Whiteman, & Cohen, 1990).

Characteristics of Group Members

Drug-abusing adolescents are inclined to have a pattern of drug use including frequent intoxication, impulsivity, polysubstance abuse, and encounters with the criminal justice system (Doweiko, 2002; Johnston, O'Malley, & Bachman, 2000). The age of first use of mood-altering substances is estimated to be about age 12 (Hogan, 2000), and peer pressure plays a strong role in the decision to use. Alcohol continues to be the drug of choice, with an estimated 30% to 40% of high school seniors reporting heavy alcohol use and 10% meeting the diagnostic criteria for alcohol abuse (DeBellis et al., 2000).

   When children begin to use drugs at an early age, they suffer from the combined effects of educational deficit (from attending school while intoxicated or truancy from school), lack of social skills, increased impulsivity, and loss of ambition, and they have a foreshortened future. Because their bodies are still developing, adolescents are far more vulnerable than adults to the damaging physiological effects of drug use (DeBellis et al., 2000). The still-developing adolescent brain may be up to four or five times more vulnerable than the adult brain to the toxic effects of alcohol (Wuethrich, 2001).

Group Leader Skills

When adolescents enter group treatment, they bring with them unique qualities and special needs. Group leaders must understand childhood and adolescent physical and emotional developmental needs (Doweiko, 2002; Rose, 1998) and the addiction process (LeCoq & Capuzzi, 1984). If possible, in ethnically diverse groups one of the coleaders should represent minority group members, as adolescents are more likely to establish a strong therapeutic bond with counselors with whom they can identify.

The Sessions

The sessions begin with get-acquainted activities, with the goal of increasing a sense of community and honest interactions. The group members develop their own group rules, which increases their sense of ownership and identification with the group. Other group sessions revolve around education regarding birth control and methods for preventing sexually transmitted diseases (Doweiko, 2002). This is particularly important because many drug-abusing adolescents have a history of unprotected sex, including some trading of sex for drugs. Adolescent drug rehabilitation group members may benefit from educational assessment and remediation, as well as career counseling. Other sessions may emphasize self-disclosure, drug refusal strategies, social skills, and leisure activities (Johnson, 2003). Some groups address coexisting psychiatric disorders (Rose, 1998).

Although the reasons adolescents use drugs parallel the motivations for adult use at times, some motivations are unique to young people. According to Hogan (2000), these include needs

- to feel grown-up,
- to rebel against their parents and the adult world,
- to have a sense of belonging,
- to conform to a risk-taking peer group,
- to achieve a relaxed emotional state, and
- to satisfy a sense of adventure.

These motivating factors for use and abuse are the focus of group sessions.

Family Group Counseling

Because adolescents usually live within a family milieu, the most successful drug rehabilitation interventions incorporate family counseling (Rose, 1998). Family group counseling requires special skills and involves unique counseling concerns because the members are related and interact at many levels at once. Also, the unequal distribution of power within a family unit influences the interactions. In family and multifamily group counseling sessions, topics might include family members' patterns of substance use, deemphasis on guilt, an emphasis on honest communication, fostering of self-responsibility, ventilation of feelings, and education regarding the addiction process (Johnson, 2003).

There is debate regarding the necessity for drug intervention with most adolescents who abuse substances because statistics show that most grow out of this problem behavior (Evans & Sullivan, 1990). Many, however, do not, and some die prematurely as a direct result of their substance abuse. In addition to the immediate benefits of early intervention, the skills learned during the group involvement can be applied to successfully solve problems in other domains throughout their lives.

PREVENTING RELAPSE

"Relapse" means that the person returns to the abusing activity during or after treatment. Historically, as many as half of the individuals leaving treatment will be abstinent two years later (Hoffman & Harrison, 1988). Other studies variably predict that one third will remain abstinent, another third will have reduced their use but continue to use at some level, and the remaining third will stay the same or get worse (Miller & Hester, 1980). Because the rate of relapse is so high under any study, preventing relapse is a logical topic in recovery groups (Doweiko, 2002), analogous to inoculating clients to reduce the risk of contracting a disease.

The causes of relapse are associated with several variables (Daley & Marlatt, 1992) including

- lack of social support,
- negative or positive mood,
- behavioral characteristics such as impulsivity or poor social skills,
- coexisting psychiatric disorders, and
- low school or vocational expectations.

Chiauzzi (1990) identified four factors that contribute to relapse:

1. *Personality traits* including compulsive behavior, difficulty adapting to change, passive–aggressive behavior, a tendency to blame others, antisocial personality traits, impulsivity, and refusing to ask for help.
2. *Tendency to substitute addictions.* An apparently recovering cocaine addict, for example, might begin spending all night at a casino. Recovering clients describe this behavior as "changing cabins on the Titanic."
3. *Restricted view of the recovery process.* Instead of changing their personal perspective and lifestyle, individuals focus on changing one single characteristic while keeping other aspects of their life intact. These people follow the treatment in a superficial manner but avoid insight and self-awareness. Recovering addicts refer to this as "talking the talk." They say they want to keep throwing darts at the bar where they used to drink with their friends. True recovery requires changing their recreational activities as part of their lifestyle change. This is important because while using the substance, their leisure time was consumed with acquiring and using the objects of their addiction. This is true for gamblers, drug addicts, alcoholics, and people with compulsive sexual behaviors.
4. *Failure to attend to warning signs.* These people don't recognize the seemingly meaningless decisions that put them on the slippery slope of relapse. For example, they fail to connect their decision in the morning to put extra cash in their wallet with their choice later in the day to go down the street to buy the drugs.

The same factors that created the addiction can be a powerful force in triggering relapse. For example, a deficit in social support may take the form of a spouse who continues to drink alcohol and attempts to sabotage the other's abstinence. People have reported that their spouses say things such as, "I liked you better when you were drinking." And because peer pressure is one of the primary causes for starting drug use in the first place (Doweiko, 2002), that same pressure can be influential in adolescents' relapsing.

Group members might be asked to complete checklists to help them identify the risk factors associated with relapse. These instruments include the Inventory of

Drinking Situations (Annis, 1982), the Inventory of Drug Taking Situations (Annis, 1985), and the Substance Abuse Problem Checklist (Carroll, 1983).

To maintain recovery, clients must learn to manage their cravings and at the same time learn to deflect the social pressure to use. Recovering addicts often discover that it is difficult to get away from drug dealers. To the dealers, recovery is bad for business, and they will go to any length to keep their addicts using, even going to recovering addicts' homes and giving away drugs. Clearly, recovery programs should teach their clients how to decline offers and assert themselves. Role plays and discussions regarding resolution of hypothetical scenarios are appropriate activities during group counseling sessions.

A Group Emphasizing Relapse Prevention

The following presents an example of a six-session group for women in recovery. The emphasis of this group is on preventing relapse.

Session 1: Getting to Know Each Other

During the first session the coleaders introduce themselves, explain the purpose of the group, establish ground rules, and ask each member to introduce herself. The introduction includes an explanation of treatment for this addiction. Each member is asked to sketch a road map of her life and share this information with other group members. The session closes with members' discussing what they gained from the activity.

Session 2: Education Regarding Causes of Relapse

At the beginning of the second session, each member is invited to offer her reactions to Session 1 and evaluate the ground rules established in the first session. Each member completes the Substance Abuse Problem Checklist (Carroll, 1983). The members share specific relapse vulnerabilities with the group. The session closes with a discussion of ways to avoid these situations and conditions.

Session 3: Relationship Problems

The coleaders initiate a discussion of the impact of relationships on relapse. Members are encouraged to relate their experiences in past relationships and link these relationships to their increase or decrease in drug use. Each member is asked to list the qualities of her ideal partner and to list the characteristics of her current partner or a partner from the past. She is asked to compare these two lists and share her insights with the group. The session closes with a discussion of what the members gained from the activity.

Session 4: Environmental Support

Each member is asked to make a list of the people in her life who (a) support her recovery, (b) are neutral to her recovery, and (c) jeopardize her recovery. The members each share their lists, and the leaders facilitate a total group discussion of the activity, emphasizing what each member learned about herself and others and what she gained from the activity.

Session 5: Self-Esteem

The co-leaders initiate a discussion of the risks posed by low self-esteem. Each member is asked to explore the negative messages she sends to herself. The members share these negative messages with the group. Each group member is asked to "make the rounds," telling each member of the group what she admires in that member. This is followed by a total group discussion in which members share what they gained from this activity.

Session 6: Termination

Each member is asked to explore what she has learned from the group experience and to list things she will say to herself or do when she is tempted to relapse. The members share and evaluate these plans with other members of the group. The leaders encourage each member to say good-bye to other group members, and to continue in some type of support group after this group ends.

LEARNING ACTIVITIES

1. As a participant in a group, design an outpatient treatment program to meet the needs of both males and females with an identified addiction. Have each group emphasize how the needs differ depending on the gender of the group members. Have each group report to the entire class.
2. Role-play a scenario in which a drug dealer approaches a recovering addict. In one scenario the addict is successful in maintaining abstinence. In the second scenario the client relapses. Discuss the differences between the scenarios. What factors played a part in the relapse? What direction does this give you in working with groups of addicted persons?
3. As a group participant, design a group model for quitting smoking. Describe the population (male, female, young, old, etc.), and be specific about the interventions to be used. Have each group report back to the entire class.
4. Based on what we know about addictions, discuss the following question: Why do you think prevention programs such as "Just Say No" don't work? In the discussion, stress (a) the model this approach represents, (b) what seems to be lacking in this approach, and (c) how it might be changed to be more effective.

SUMMARY

Although the most commonly thought of addictions are to substances such as alcohol, drugs, or tobacco, individuals become addicted to many things, including gambling, food, spending money, or sex. With all of these addictions, groups are a potent treatment modality, sometimes alone but often in conjunction with medical care or other psychological assistance. Models for understanding addictions include the moral weakness model, the medical model, the sociocultural models, and the biopsychosocial model.

Group leaders working with those addicted to substances should understand the difference between substance abuse and substance dependence so that clients can obtain the appropriate level of intervention. Substance dependence is the more severe diagnosis of addiction. Substance dependence interferes with every domain of people's lives. To meet the diagnosis of substance abuse, the person must never have met the criteria of substance dependence (APA, 2000).

Many different types of substances are abused, classified into stimulants, depressants, cannabinols, hallucinogens, and inhalants. Each carries different risks. For example, stimulant use can lead to premature death from strokes and heart attacks. Use of depressants can also lead to early death due to medical complications and increased risk of accidents. People who use cannabinols may experience the loss of motivation as well as health risks. Use of hallucinogens may result in an increased risk of self-harm and psychosis. Inhalants can lead to brain damage, liver failure, and death.

Treatment modalities include inpatient, partial hospitalization, and intensive outpatient treatment, support groups, and group counseling. In this chapter we focus on the importance of the group structure, formation of group rules, closed versus open groups, and homogeneous versus heterogeneous groups, and factors related to leadership are explored. Two specific group sessions are outlined, one designed to meet the special needs of women addicts in treatment and another to prevent relapse.

Overcoming an addiction is a lifelong endeavor, and relapse is common. With some groups, dropout rates are high, and group leaders must be prepared to cope with the changing composition of groups. Even with these limitations, groups are often the best approach to dealing with addictions, as the success of Alcoholics Anonymous and other member-directed groups has shown. The leadership of an experienced, well-trained counselor should further increase the chances that those who are suffering from addictions will be able to overcome these compulsions and go on to live healthy, prosperous lives.

USEFUL WEB SITES

☐ Alcoholism Treatments
  www.alcoholism.about.com
  www.alcoholics-anonymous.org
  www.niaaa.nih.gov/
  www.alcoholism-cer.com
  www.soberrecovery.com
☐ Addictions and Women
  www.womo.com
  www.epiphanyhouse.org/resources/articles/signs.html
☐ Addiction Recovery Groups
  www.healthyplace.com/Communities/Addictions/site/comm_calender.htm

□ Adolescents and Addictions
   www.oaklawn.org/services/addi.php
□ Gambling Recovery
   http://au.groups.yahoo.com/group/escapefromgambling
   www.tgsrm.org/Gambling.html
   www.lifespan.org/Services/MentalHealth/RIH/Gambling/tx/group.htm
□ Inhalant Abuse
   www.inhalants.org/important_news.htm
   www.whitehousedrugpolicy.gov/drugfact/inhalants/
   www.health.org/govpubs/phd631/
   www.drugabuse.gov/drugpages/inhalants.html
□ Sexual Addictions
   www.cybersexualaddiction.com
   www.sexaa.org

REFERENCES

Alcoholics Anonymous (AA). (1976). *Alcoholics Anonymous* (3rd ed.). New York: Alcoholics Anonymous World Service.

Alcoholics Anonymous (AA). (1981). *Twelve steps and twelve traditions.* New York: Alcoholics Anonymous World Services.

American Medical Association (AMA). (1993). *Factors contributing to the health care cost problem.* Chicago: Author.

American Psychiatric Association (APA). (1952). *The diagnostic and statistical manual of mental disorders.* Washington, DC: Author.

American Psychiatric Association (APA). (1968). *The diagnostic and statistical manual of mental disorders* (2nd ed.). Washington, DC: Author.

American Psychiatric Association (APA). (1990). *Benzodiazepine dependence, toxicity, and abuse.* Washington, DC: Author.

American Psychiatric Association (APA). (2000). *The diagnostic and statistical manual of mental disorders* (4th ed., text rev.). Washington, DC: Author.

Annis, H. (1982). *Inventory of drinking situations.* Toronto: Addiction Research Foundation.

Annis, H. (1985). *Inventory of drug taking situations.* Toronto: Addiction Research Foundation.

Anthenelli, R., & Schuckit, M. (1992). Genetics. In J. Lowinson, P. Ruiz, R. Millman, & J. Langrod (Eds.), *Substance abuse: A comprehensive textbook* (2nd ed., pp. 39–50). Baltimore: Williams & Wilkins.

Barondes, S. (1999). An agenda for psychiatric genetics. *Archives of General Psychiatry, 56,* 549–552.

Barry, K. (1992). Eating disorders. In M. Fleming & K. Barry (Eds.), *Addictive disorders* (pp. 303–314). St. Louis: Mosby Yearbook.

Bays, J. (1990). Substance abuse and child abuse. *Pediatric Clinics of North America, 37,* 881–903.

Blume, S. (1992). Alcohol and other drug problems in women. In J. Lowinson, P. Ruiz, R. Millman, & J. Langrod. *Substance abuse: A comprehensive textbook* (2nd ed., pp. 794–807). Baltimore: Williams & Wilkins

Brook, J., Brook, D., Gordon, A., Whiteman, M., & Cohen, P. (1990). The psychosocial etiology of adolescent drug use: A family-interaction approach. *Genetic Social and General Psychology Monographs, 116*(2), 111–267.

Buchanan, L. (1994). Helping people with eating disorders: Research and practice. In J. Lewis (Ed.), *Addictions: Concepts and strategies for treatment* (pp. 123–142). Gaithersburg, MD: Aspen Publishers.

Burman, S. (1992). A model for women's alcohols/drug treatment. *Alcoholism Treatment Quarterly, 9*(2), 87–99.

Carmack, M. A., Owens, R. G., & Dewey, M. E. (1987). The effects of minimal interventions by general practitioners on long-term benzodiazepine use. *Journal of Royal College of General Practitioners, 39*(327), 408–411.

Carnes, P. (1992). *Out of the shadows: Understanding sexual addictions* (2nd ed.). Center City, MN: Hazeldon.

Carroll, J. (1983). *Substance abuse problem checklist.* Eagleville, PA: Eaglesville Hospital.

Centers for Disease Control. (2000). *Tobacco information and prevention source.* Atlanta: Author.

Chiauzzi, E. (1990). Breaking the pattern that leads to relapse. *Psychology Today, 23*(12), 18–19.

Ciraulo, D. A., Shader, R. I., Ciraulo, A., Greenblat, D. J., & von Moltke, L. L. (1994). Alcoholism and its treatment. In R. I. Shader (Ed.), *Manual of psychiatric therapeutics* (2nd ed., pp. 181–192). Boston: Little Brown.

Cohen, M. (2000). *Counseling addicted women.* Thousand Oaks, CA: Sage Publications.

Daley, D., & Marlatt, G. A. (1992). In J. Lowinson, P. Ruiz, R. Millman, & J. Langrod. *Substance abuse: A comprehensive textbook* (2nd ed., pp. 533–542). Baltimore: Williams & Wilkins.

DeBellis, M. D., Clark, D., Beers, S., Soloff, P., Boring, A., Hall, J., Kersh, A., & Keshavan, M. (2000). Hippocampal volume in adolescent-onset alcohol use disorders. *American Journal of Psychiatry, 157,* 737–744.

Doweiko, H. (2002). *Concepts of chemical addictions* (5th ed.) Pacific Grove, CA: Brooks/Cole.

Emerick, C. (1987). Alcoholics Anonymous: Affiliation process and effectiveness as treatment. *Alcoholism, 11,* 416–423.

Epstein, J., & Gfroerer, J. (1997). *Heroine abuse in the United States.* Rockville, MD: SAMHSA.

Erickson, S. (1998). Etiological theories of substance abuse. In P. Stevens-Smith & R. Smith (Eds.), *Substance abuse counseling: Theory and practice* (pp. 25–64). Upper Saddle River, NJ: Prentice-Hall.

Evans, W. (1998). Assessment and diagnosis of the substance use disorders. *Journal of Counseling & Development, 76,* 325–333.

Evans, K, & Sullivan, J. M (1990). *Dual diagnosis.* New York: Guilford Press.

Fisher, G., & Harrison, T. (2000). *Substance abuse: Information for school counselors, social workers, therapists, and counselors* (2nd ed.). Boston: Allyn & Bacon.

Fleming, M., & Barry, K. L. (1992). Clinical overview of alcohol and drug disorders. In M. Fleming & K. L. Barry (Eds.), *Addictive disorders* (pp. 3–21). St. Louis: Mosby–Year Book.

Fuller, P., & Cabanaugh, R. (1995). Basic assessment and screening for substance abuse in the pediatrician's office. *Pediatric Clinics of North America, 42,* 295–307.

Galanter, M., Castaneda, R., & Franco, H. (1998). Group therapy, self help groups, and network therapy. In R. Frances & S. Miller (Eds.), *Clinical textbook of addictive disorders* (2nd ed., pp. 221–246). New York: Guilford Press.

Gaudia, R. (1992). Compulsive gambling: Reframing issues of control. In E. M. Freeman (Ed.), *The addiction process: Effective social work approaches* (pp. 237–248). White Plains, NY: Longman.

Gentillelo, L. N., Donovan, D. M., Dunn, C. W., & Rivara, F. P. (1995). Alcohol interventions in trauma centers: Current practice and future directions. *Journal of the American Medical Association, 274,* 1043–1048.

Goldberg, R. (2006). Alcohol. *Drugs across the spectrum* (5th ed.). Belmont, CA: Thomson Wadsworth.

Golden, S., Khantzian, E., & McAuliffe, W. (1994). Group therapy. In M. Galanter & H. Kleber (Eds.), *Textbook of substance abuse treatment* (pp. 303–314). Washington, DC: American Psychiatric Press.

Golden, S., & McAuliffe, W. (1999). Group therapy for psychoactive substance use disorders. In E. J. Khantzian (Ed.), *Treating addictions as a human process* (pp. 601–614). North Bergen, NJ: Jason Aronson.

Goodwin, D., W. (1989). The gene for alcoholism. *Journal of Studies on Alcohol, 50,* 397–398.

Hayashida, M., Alterman,, A. I., McLallan, A. T., O'Brien, C. P., Purtell, J. J., Volpicelli, J. R., Raphaelson, A. H., & Hall, C. P. (1989). Comparative effectiveness of inpatient and outpatient detoxification of patients with mild-to-moderate alcohol withdrawal syndrome. *New England Journal of Medicine, 320,* 358–365.

Hoffman, N., & Harrison, P. (1988). CATOR 1986 report: Findings two years after treatment. St. Paul, MN: Author.

Hogan, M. (2000). Diagnosis and treatment of teen drug use. *Medical Clinics of North America, 84,* 927–966.

Hopfer, C., Mikulich, S., & Crowley, T. (2000). Heroin use among adolescents in treatment for substance use disorders. *Journal of American Academy of Child and Adolescent Psychiatry, 39,* 1316–1323.

Hyman, S. E., & Cassem, N. H. (1995). Alcoholism. In E. Rubenstein & D. D. Federman (Eds.), *Scientific American medicine* (pp. 1–12). New York: Scientific American Press.

James, R., & Gilliland, B. E. (2000). Sexual assault. *Crisis intervention strategies* (3rd ed., pp. 229–282). Pacific Grove, CA: Brooks/Cole Publishing.

Jellinek, E. M. (1952). Phases of alcohol addiction. *Quarterly Journal of Studies on Alcoholism, 13,* 673–674.

Jellinek, E. M. (1960). *The disease concept of alcoholism.* New Haven, CT: College and University Press.

Johnson, S. (2003). *Therapist's guide to substance abuse intervention.* Boston: Academic Press.

Johnston, L. D., O'Malley, P. M., & Bachman, J. G. (1996). *National survey results on drug use from the monitoring the future study, 1975–1995.* Rockville, MD: U.S. Department of Health and Human Services.

Johnston, L. D., O'Malley, P. M., & Bachman, J. G. (2000). *National survey results on drug use from the monitoring the future study, 1975–1999.* Rockville, MD: U.S. Department of Health and Human Services.

Khantzian, E. (1999). Alcoholics Anonymous—cult or corrective? *Treating addictions as a human process* (pp. 431–450). Northvale, NJ: Jason Aronson.

Kilpatrick, D., Acierno, R., Saunders, B., Resnick, H., Best, C., & Schnurr, P. (2000). Risk factors for adolescent substance abuse dependence: Data from a national sample. *Journal of Consulting and Clinical Psychology, (68)*1, 19–30.

Kinney, J., & West, D. (1996). Substance use treatment. In J. Kinney (Ed.). *Clinical manual of substance abuse* (pp. 74–98). St. Louis: Mosby.

LeCoq, L., & Capuzzi, D. (1984). Preventing adolescent drug abuse. *Journal of Humanistic Education and Development, 22,* 155–169.

Liebschutz, J. M., Mulvey, K. P., & Samet, J. H. (1997). Victimization among substance abusing women. *Archives of Internal Medicine, 157,* 1093–1097.

Liddle, H., & Rowe, C. (2002). Multidimensional family therapy for adolescent drug abuse: Making the case for a developmental-contextual, family-based intervention. In D. Brook & H. Spitz (Eds.), *The group therapy of substance abuse* (pp. 275–293). New York: Haworth Medical Press.

Logan, S. M. L. (1992). Overcoming sex and love addiction: An expanded perspective. In E. M. Freeman (Ed.), *The addictive process: Effective social work approaches* (pp. 207–222). White Plains, NY: Longman.

Longo, L., & Johnson, B. (2000). Addiction: Part I. *American Family Physician, 61,* 2121–2128.

Manfrin, C. (1998). Treatment settings. In P. Stevens-Smith & R. Smith (Eds.), *Substance abuse counseling* (pp. 135–165). Upper Saddle River, NJ: Merrill.

Matano, R. A., & Yalom, I. D. (1991). Approaches to chemical dependency: Chemical dependency and group therapy—a synthesis. *International Journal of Group Psychotherapy, 41,* 269–293.

McAnally, B. (1996). Chemistry of alcoholic beverages. In J. C. Garriott (Ed.), *Medicolegal aspects of alcohol* (3rd ed., pp. 146–150). Tucson, AZ: Lawyers and Judges Publishing Co.

McCormick, R., & Ramirez, L. (1988). Pathological gambling. In J. G. Howells (Ed.), *Modern perspectives in psychosocial pathology* (pp.135–157). New York: Brunner/Mazel.

McGurrin, M. (1992). *Pathological gambling: Conceptual, diagnostic, and treatment issues.* Sarasota, FL: Professional Resources Press.

McGurrin, M. (1994). Diagnosis and treatment of pathological gambling. In J. Lewis (Ed.), *Addictions: Concepts and strategies for treatment* (pp. 123–142). Gaithersburg, MD: Aspen.

Miller, W. R., & Hester, R. K. (1980). Treating problem drinkers: Modern approaches. In W. R. Miller (Ed.), *The addictive behaviors: Treatment of alcoholism, drug abuse, smoking, and obesity* (pp. 11–141). New York: Pergamon Press.

Miller, W. R., & Kurtz, E. (1994). Models of alcoholism used in treatment: Contrasting AA with other perspective with which it is often confused. *Journal of Studies on Alcohol, 55,* 159–166.

Morgan, S., & Kinney, J. (1996). Women. In J. Kinney (Ed.), *Clinical manual of substance abuse* (pp. 318–332). St. Louis: Mosby.

Nace, E. (1992). Alcoholics Anonymous. In J. Lowinson, P. Ruiz, R. Millman, & J. Langrod (Eds.), *Substance abuse: A comprehensive textbook* (2nd ed., pp. 486–495). Baltimore: Williams & Wilkins.

National Foundation for Brain Research. (1992). *The cost of disorders of the brain.* Washington, DC: Author.

National Institute on Drug Abuse (NIDA). (2002). Monitoring the future 2002 data from in-school surveys of 8th, 10th, and 12th grade students. Retrieved June 16, 2005, from http//monitor ingthefuture.org/data/02data.html#2002data-drugs

NeSmith, C., Wilcoxon, S. A., & Satcher, J. (2000). Male leadership in an addicted women's group. *Journal of Addictions & Offender Counseling, 20*(2), 75–84.

Office of National Drug Control Policy (ONDCP). (2003, February). *The President's National Drug Control Strategy.* Retrieved July 26, 2005, from http://www.whitehousedrugpolicy.gov/publications/policy/ndcs03/index.html

Peele, S. (1989). *Diseasing of America: Addiction treatment out of control.* Lexington, MA: Lexington Books.

Perkins, R. (2002). Adolescent treatment. In R. R. Perkinson (Ed.), *Chemical dependency counseling: A practical guide* (2nd ed., pp. 177–186). Thousand Oaks, CA: Sage.

Pickins, R. W., & Svikis, D. S. (1991). Genetic contributions to alcoholism diagnosis. *Alcohol Health & Research World, 15*(4), 272–277.

Pihl, R. (1999). Substance abuse; Etiological considerations. In T. Millon, P. Blaney, & R. Davis (Eds.), *Oxford textbook of psychopathology.* New York: Oxford University Press.

Politzer, R., & Hudac, C. (1992). Gambling disorders. In M. Fleming, & K. Barry (Eds.), *Addictive disorders* (pp. 352–365). St. Louis: Mosby Year Book

Porter, J. (1998). Major drugs of abuse and their addictive properties. In P. Stevens-Smith & R. Smith (Eds.), *Substance abuse counseling* (pp. 65–96). Upper Saddle River, NJ: Merrill.

Prevention Researcher. (1999). *Adolescent compulsive and problem gamblers* [On-line]. Available: http://www.tproneline.org/v6n1abst.htm

Priyadarsini, S. (1986). Gender role dynamics in an alcohol therapy group. *Alcohol interventions: Historical and sociocultural approaches* (pp. 179–196). New York: Haworth Press.

Rawson, R. (1990). Cut the crack. *Policy Review, 51,* 10–24.

Roots, L.E., & Aanes, D. L. (1992). A conceptual framework for understanding self help groups. *Hospital and Community Psychiatry, 43,* 379–381.

Rose, S. (1998). Mental health and substance abuse. In *Group work with children and adolescents: Prevention and intervention in school and community systems* (pp. 124–140). London: Sage.

Santrock, J. (1999). Prenatal development and birth. In *Life-span development* (7th ed., pp. 89–117). Dubuque, IA: W. C. Brown & Benchmark.

Schliebner, C., & Peregoy, J. (1998). Working with selected populations: Treatment issues and characteristics. In P. Stevens-Smith, & R. Smith (Eds.), *Substance abuse counseling* (pp.193–217). Upper Saddle River, NJ: Merrill.

Schneider, J., & Schneider, B. (1996). Couple recovery from sexual addiction/coaddiction: Results of a survey of 88 marriages. *Sexual Addiction & Compulsivity, 3*(2), 111–126.

Schwartz, R. (1989). When to suspect inhalant abuse. *Patient Care, 23* (10), 39–50.

Searles, J. S. (1991). The genetics of alcoholism: Impact on family and sociological models of addictions. *Family Dynamics of Addictions Quarterly, 1*(1), 3–21.

Stanton, M.D., & Todd, C. (1982). *The family therapy of drug abuse and addiction.* New York: Guilford Press.

Steinglass, P. (1987). *The alcoholic family.* New York: Basic Books.

Stevens-Smith, P. (1998). Introduction to substance abuse counseling. In P. Stevens-Smith & R. Smith (Eds.), *Substance abuse counseling* (pp. 1–24). Upper Saddle River, NJ: Merrill.

Substance Abuse and Mental Health Services Administration (SAMHSA). (2001). National Survey of Substance Abuse Treatment Services. Retrieved June 13, 2005, from http://www.dasis.samhsa.gov.nssats 2000report.pdf

Substance Abuse and Mental Health Services Administration (SAMHSA). (2002). *Results from the 2001 Household Survey on Drug Abuse.* Retrieved June 15, 2005, from www.oas.samhsa.gov/nhsda/2k1nhsda/vol1/toc.htm

Swisher, S. (1995). Therapeutic interventions recommended for treatment of sexual addiction/compulsivity. *Sexual Addiction & Compulsivity, 2*(1), 31–39.

Threadcraft, H., & Wilcoxon, S. (1993). Mixed gender group co-leadership in group counseling female survivors of childhood sexual victimization. *Journal for Specialists in Group Work, 18*, 40–44.

Treatment of drug abuse and addictions–Part 1. (1995). *Harvard Mental Health Letter, 12*(2), 1–4.

Walters, G. (1999). *The addiction concept: Working hypothesis or self-fulfilling prophesy?* Boston: Allyn & Bacon.

Washton, A.M. (1992). Structured outpatient group therapy with alcohol and substance abusers. In J. Lowinson, P. Ruiz, R. Millman, & J. Langrod (Eds.), *Substance abuse: A comprehensive textbook* (2nd ed., pp. 39–50). Baltimore: Williams & Wilkins.

Weiss, R. (1994). Inpatient treatment. In M. Galanter, & H. Kleber (Eds.), *Textbook of substance abuse treatment* (pp. 359–368). Washington, DC: American Psychiatric Press.

Windle, M., Windle, R. C., Scheidt, D. M., & Miller, G. B. (1995). Physical and sexual abuse and associated mental disorders among alcoholic inpatients. *American Journal of Psychiatry, 152*, 1322–1328.

Wuethrich, B. (2001). Getting stupid. *Discover, 22* (3), 56–63.

Yalom, I. (1985). The therapeutic factors in group therapy. *Theory and practice of group psychotherapy* (3rd ed., pp. 3–19). New York: Basic Books.

Zimmer, L., & Morgan, J. (1997). *Marijuana myths, marijuana facts.* New York: Lindesmith Center.

Group Work: Elderly People and Their Caregivers

M. Carolyn Thomas and Virginia Martin

At the beginning of the 20th century, people 65 years of age and older represented about 4% (slightly more than 3 million people) of the U.S. population (Administration on Aging, n.d.). Little interest in this age group was evident among mental health professionals, partly because the elderly population was so small (Gladding, 1991) but also because of prevailing negative societal attitudes toward aging. Robert Butler, founding director of the National Institute on Aging, coined the term *ageism* to describe prejudice and discrimination against the aging population (Dickman, 1979). At that time, Butler described life for many older Americans as "a tragedy, a period of quiet despair, deprivation, desolation and muted rage" (Butler, 1975, p. 2).

Now, during this first decade of the 21st century, the picture is drastically changing. By 2002, the number of older Americans had increased elevenfold to 35.6 million, and the percentage of Americans older than age 65 had more than tripled (Administration on Aging, n.d.). Ageism hasn't disappeared, but mental health professionals now recognize the developmental significance of later life.

Psychologist Erik Erikson (1963) pointed out that old age is a time when people struggle to find meaning in the life they have lived, a sense of ego integrity, and satisfaction with a life well spent. Both individual and group counseling can help older people and their caregivers find meaning during this often difficult stage of development.

The period of life designated as "old age" may span 30 years or more and presents diverse counseling challenges. The issues of a vigorous, active, and involved person dealing with the transition from work to retirement, role loss, and related identity problems are very different from the issues of a declining older person who is coping with loneliness, alienation, and fear resulting from multiple losses including the deaths of cohorts, impaired health, and loss of autonomy.

Changing the traditional negative focus from assessing and remedying the limitations of older people to a more positive emphasis on wellness, planning for successful adaptations, and empowerment is necessary to realize the developmental goal for everyone to reach their full potential. In addition, technology is becoming an empowerment instrument that is effectively reducing the social isolation of older people (Thomas, Martin, Alexander, Cooley, & Loague, 2003). Consequently, counselors are challenged to revise their attitudes about aging and to promote a community for the elderly population based on a fulfillment model. Although traditional group counseling has been effective in meeting many of the diverse needs of the older population, group counselors are further challenged to create innovative uses of technology in helping older people to connect, build community, and expand their social support network (Martin, Thomas, Alexander, & Loague, 2004).

HISTORY OF GROUP WORK WITH OLDER PEOPLE

Group work with the elderly seems to have emerged in the 1950s with the early reality orientation and remotivation groups being conducted by nursing staff or assistants in institutions. Early psychotherapy groups for older persons were also conducted, primarily with mentally ill patients in hospitals, but they were facilitated by health professionals with more training than nursing aides. Reminiscing groups, begun in the 1970s, moved groups for older people out of institutions and into the community. Once the settings and professionals conducting the groups became more diverse, the types and numbers of groups quickly proliferated.

Although *psychotherapy groups* for senile psychiatric patients were first described by Silver (1950), Linden (1953) is most often considered the pioneer of these groups. Kaplan's (1953) book about a social program for older people and Kubie and Landau's (1953) book on group work with the aged strengthened the emphasis on psychotherapeutic groups for this population. Shere (1964) later described group work with the very old, and Yalom and Terrazas (1968) wrote about their work with psychotic elderly patients.

Remotivation groups were initially used by Dorothy Smith, a hospital volunteer, with mentally ill patients. In 1956, she trained a large number of Pennsylvania State Hospital staff members in remotivation therapy. After the American Psychiatric Association formed a Remotivation Advisory Committee to encourage the use of remotivation therapy, training spread throughout the country. By 1967, 15,000 nurses and aides at 250 mental hospitals had been trained (Dennis, 1986).

The earliest *reality orientation groups* were conducted in a Topeka, Kansas, Veterans Administration Hospital as a pilot program, where Dr. James Folsom trained nursing assistants to help patients take more responsibility for their own care. Based on Folsom's work in Topeka and other work at the Mental Health Institute in Mt. Pleasant, Iowa, Folsom and Lucille Taulbee finalized the reality orientation group model at the Tuscaloosa, Alabama, Veterans Administration Hospital (Donahue, 1986; Folsom, 1968).

The 1970s

In the 1970s, *reminiscing groups* were developed from individual reminiscing and life review therapy, in which the focus was changed from offering groups for mentally ill geriatric patients in hospitals to providing help for a more diverse older population in all settings. Prior to 1960, R. G. Havighurst and others advised older people to avoid reminiscing, but by 1972 Havighurst was reporting its benefits (Havighurst & Glasser, 1972). Robert Butler (1963) is generally considered the pioneer of this change, even though his early article on *life review therapy* did not mention reminiscing in groups. Priscilla Ebersole, a psychiatric nurse, reportedly adapted Butler's life review to include reminiscing and began conducting reminiscing groups in 1970 (Burnside, 1978; Ebersole, 1978b). Butler and Lewis later advocated group life review in all settings (Butler & Lewis, 1977; Lewis & Butler, 1974).

Although the four distinct types of groups for the elderly discussed in the following pages had emerged by the late 1970s, little had been written about their use. Butler and Lewis (1977) suggested that much more group therapy was being conducted with elderly people in and out of hospitals than was reflected in the literature. Irene Burnside (1978) also lamented the paucity of literature about group work with the elderly, noting that groups were indeed being conducted by professionals other than nurses and in settings other than institutions.

Nurses were the first to publish reports about their group work, but few such reports are found in the proceedings of national or international gerontology meetings of the 1970s. Gwen Marram's (1973) book on group work for nurses contains only a brief description of groups for the elderly population. The Lewis and Butler (1974) article on psychosocial approaches for the aged also includes a small section on groups, but publications describing the groups undoubtedly being conducted for the elderly by a variety of professionals in every helping discipline and in many settings did not appear in significant numbers until the 1980s.

The 1980s

Irene Burnside (1978, 1986) combined the efforts and expertise of many professionals in the first comprehensive nursing text on group techniques for the elderly. She and her colleagues fully described the planning and implementation of reality orientation, remotivation, reminiscing, and psychotherapy groups, as well as numerous topic- and member-specific groups. The 1980s heralded the proliferation of group work for the elderly in the counseling profession, including an increase in numbers and types of groups outside the institutional setting. Capuzzi and Gross (1980) encouraged counselors to consider using the types of groups described by Burnside, and Kaminsky (1984) edited a book on the uses of reminiscence in working with older adults. Descriptions of groups for the elderly population using the arts, groups designed to help aging people with specific concerns, and groups for caregivers of elderly people appeared in counseling journals in increasing numbers (Bledsoe & Lutz-Ponder, 1986; Burke, 1986; Capuzzi & Gossman, 1982; Cohen, 1983; Hammond & Bonney, 1983; Hawkins, 1983; Malde, 1988; Mardoyan & Weis, 1981; Zimpfer, 1987).

The 1990s

By the 1990s, work with older people and their caregivers had become a major focus in the counseling profession, as evidenced by publication of several special counseling journal issues dedicated to the topic. All of these special issues included articles on groups. Myers (1990) edited a special issue of the *Journal of Mental Health Counseling* on techniques for counseling older adults, including articles on group work. Waters (1990a) edited a special issue of *Generations* in which Capuzzi, Gross, and Friel (1990) described trends in group work with elders. Gladding and Thomas (1991) edited a special issue of the *Journal for Specialists in Group Work* focusing on group work with aging people and their caregivers. In addition, Chandras (1992) edited a special section of *Counselor Education and Supervision* in which Thomas and Martin (1992) described training considerations for group counselors of older people and their caregivers.

Books by Nancy Schlossberg, Elinor Waters, and Jane Goodman provide further evidence that the counseling profession is now emphasizing using individual and group counseling strategies to address the developmental, social, economic, and emotional needs of older people. In advocating groups to empower older adults, Waters and Goodman (1990) described appropriate groups for older people as antidotes for loneliness, laboratories for teaching social skills, opportunities for catharsis, networks for accessing resources and developing plans of action, and sources of inspiration. Schlossberg, Waters, and Goodman (1995) provided additional information on using groups to counsel adults in transition, thoroughly describing the types of groups that are appropriate for older people and their caregivers, steps in organizing groups, and considerations for accommodating cultural diversity.

The 1990s also witnessed the publication of several group counseling texts that include chapters dedicated to groups for elderly people and their caregivers (Capuzzi & Gross, 1998; Corey & Corey, 1997; Gazda, 1989; Gladding, 1991). Including this topic in group counseling training texts validates the elderly as an important population on which to focus group counseling efforts.

NBCC and CACREP Standards

Specific competencies for group counselors were added to the training standards for gerontological counselors in the 1990s. Myers and Sweeney (1990) incorporated group counseling competencies in their *Gerontological Competencies for Counselors and Human Development Specialists,* which became the foundation of the 1990 national *certified gerontological counselor specialty* of the National Board for Certified Counselors (NBCC; 1990). The NBCC dropped this specialty in 1999 for lack of applicants, and it was not included in the 2001 NBCC specialties (NBCC, 2001). Myers, however, was instrumental in advocating and building the gerontological counseling specialty standards of the Council for the Accreditation of Counseling and Related Educational Programs (CACREP, 1994). CACREP retained standards for community counseling programs with a specialization in gerontological counseling (CACREP, 2001).

In 1975, Salisbury reported that counseling the elderly was a neglected area in counselor education in the United States, with only 18 programs offering relevant coursework. By 1988, more than half of the country's counselor education programs offered a gerontological counseling focus area, and nine offered a specialization in this area. Although availability of gerontological counseling certification remains low, an evident increased emphasis on group work training with the elderly paralleled the emergence of counselor training for working with older persons (Myers, 1989).

Trends

Trends in the emergence of group work with older people can be described as progressing from isolated groups for institutionalized people conducted by nurses or other medical personnel to widespread groups conducted by all helping professionals in a variety of settings. Reminiscing treatment helped move groups from the hospitals into the community, which led to a proliferation in the types and topics of groups. As the gerontological counseling specialty emerged, and as group work became an increasingly important counseling strategy with the elderly, goals changed from treating severe disorders to facilitating healthy development, making transitions, finding meaning, and increasing empowerment for older adults and their familial and professional caregivers. The pairing of changed attitudes about counseling older people with emerging technological possibilities promises to create an exciting new history for counselors who are developing innovative group formats for the elderly.

TYPES OF GROUPS

Several types of groups for the elderly and their caregivers can be categorized based on topics, goals, settings, member capabilities, and counselor competencies. The most commonly cited categorization consists of (a) reality orientation, (b) remotivation, (c) reminiscing and life review, and (d) psychotherapy groups (Burnside, 1986; Capuzzi et al., 1990; Thomas & Martin, 1992). Additional categories of groups include topic- and theme-focused groups, groups for caregivers, and brief solution-focused groups.

Reality Orientation Groups

Reality orientation groups are designed to help regressed elderly people who have dementia become more accurately oriented in time, place, and person. These groups help confused older persons correct misperceptions about their environment. Generally consisting of four or fewer members, these groups typically meet daily for periods of 30 to 40 minutes and utilize informational props.

When first implemented, reality orientation groups met in hospitals or other inpatient facilities and all institutional staff members were trained to continually reinforce reality orientation. Later, outpatient or daycare groups were found to be effective, too, particularly when family members and other caregivers were trained to reinforce the techniques used in the groups. The recommended schedules for meals, dates, weather, events, and other information can be displayed on boards in daycare facilities or on calendars in homes as well as in institutions. Family members and paraprofessional caregivers can learn the same simple techniques and exercises that institutional staff members use, such as waking people by calling their name.

Remotivation Groups

The primary goals of remotivation therapy groups are to stimulate involvement in life for those who have lost interest in the present and future, increase their communication and interaction with others, and help them progress toward resocialization. The groups historically met in classroom-type settings in hospitals and extended-care facilities for 30 minutes to an hour three or four times a week for approximately 12 sessions, but variations of this organization have also proved to be effective (Dennis, 1986). Recommended membership usually consists of no more than 15 members who are oriented to time, place, and person.

The discussion focuses on nonproblem topics such as vacations, gardening, sports, pets, transportation, holidays, hobbies, families, or any other topic that might interest group members from diverse backgrounds. Burnside (1986) criticized the traditional remotivation group as being too rigid and as disallowing feelings, leader spontaneity, touching, work-related topics, or refreshments. Group counselors conducting remotivation groups today would undoubtedly agree with Burnside. They generally are more flexible and extend the groups outside institutional settings to intermediate-care facilities, boarding houses, and community outpatient programs. This change in setting and membership probably has influenced the groups to decrease the classroom orientation, depend on process as well as on information, include work-focused topics, and allow discussion of feelings.

Whether the traditional or the altered remotivation model is followed, the typical session covers one of the chosen topics and follows a five-step sequence of

1. creating a climate of acceptance through greetings, introductions, or other brief rapport-building exercises;
2. building a bridge to reality by encouraging members who are not sight-impaired to read aloud articles about the topic;
3. developing a sense of sharing the world we all live in by using visual aids, props, and questions directly related to the topic;
4. encouraging an appreciation of the world of work and how it relates to our own work; and

5. providing a climate of appreciation by encouraging the members to express pleasure that the group has met and to plan the next meeting.

Reminiscing and Life Review Groups

Reminiscing and *life review* are generally considered to be synonymous, defined as a naturally occurring, universal process whereby experiences and unresolved conflicts are revived, surveyed, and reintegrated into people's views of their lives (Butler, 1963). Perhaps reminiscing, or retrieving memories from the past, is a part of life review, which adds working through unresolved conflicts and reintegrating the remembered experiences into a more meaningful view of one's life. Regardless, both result in a deepened sense of identity and connectedness with the world (Kaminsky, 1984). Reminiscing groups of six to eight members meet for 1 hour once or twice a week for 6 to 12 weeks. These groups originated in long-term care facilities but quickly became popular in independent environments, community settings, and nutrition centers.

Leaders of life review groups need more advanced skills in group process than do leaders of reality orientation groups or remotivation groups. Group members are assumed to be more functional than members of the first two categories, but some counselors have suggested that reminiscing also can be helpful for people who have diminishing short-term memory. A modified version of reminiscing can be used with families to help members of different generations understand central family values, behaviors, and themes, and resolve learned repeated patterns that create problems, as well as to heal family wounds and build or strengthen supportive relationships.

Psychotherapy Groups

Psychotherapy groups help older people in institutional or community centers manage life stresses and new or ongoing unresolved, serious personal problems. Members typically have deep feelings of fear, loneliness, or anxiety that may be caused or exacerbated by aging (Capuzzi et al., 1990). Forming relatively small groups of six to eight members is recommended. These groups may be conducted in institutional settings, outpatient mental health centers, or other treatment centers. Burnside (1986) noted differences between psychotherapy groups for younger and older members. In groups for elderly people, counselors often share more personal information, more physical contact is evident, silence may be tolerated more readily, greater emphasis is placed on reminiscence and life review, and the themes of loss, intergenerational conflicts, and struggling to adapt are more common. Counselors are advised to screen potential members carefully, assessing their competencies to process conflict and emotional issues. Group psychotherapists are advised to have gerontological training in addition to graduate counseling credentials.

Topic- and Theme-Focused Groups

Support groups for older people and groups with a specific focus have proliferated with the increase in these types of groups for other populations. These groups target issues often shared by aging persons, such as health, retirement, loss, sexuality, career transitions, and spirituality. Skill-building groups help increase assertiveness, social skills, independent living competencies, and intrafamily communication skills. Counselors with specialties in psychodrama, music, art, dance, or scribotherapy may incorporate these techniques into their groups.

Leaders of intergenerational groups with older people mentoring younger people who may be at risk need basic knowledge about developmental tasks over the lifespan. Most topic- and theme-focused groups can be offered in a variety of settings. The size, composition, duration, and frequency of the group depend upon the group goals and member competencies.

Groups for Caregivers

Caregiver groups typically have been designed for family members, but groups for professionals working with older people are also receiving limited attention. Because families assume more than 80% of the care for their older members, providing family members with support and information is crucial in improving the environment and quality of life for the entire family. The goals of caregiver groups for family members (Hinkle, 1991; Myers, Poidevant, & Dean, 1991) are to help members

1. plan safe care for the older relative;
2. obtain social support from other caregivers who understand the issues they face;
3. learn skills for dealing with the older person;
4. improve conflict-management skills for use with professionals and other family members; and
5. find new ways to cope with changed roles, added responsibilities, and intensified stressors.

Because family members often have unrealistic expectations of older persons, group counseling can provide the psychoeducational forum through which they can realign their expectations with the older family member's functional level (Burnside, 1986).

Professionals, too, need opportunities for catharsis and support. The relationships between committed professionals and their older patients or clients may be different from the relationships between family members and their older relatives, but the bonds are often similarly strong. Like family members, nonfamilial caregivers experience loss, guilt, stress, anger, depression, conflicts about care, burnout, and isolation. They have similar needs for networking, education, conflict resolution, and healing opportunities.

Membership in groups for caregivers varies with the goals of the group. For example, family members of persons with Alzheimer's disease may be assigned to groups based on the stage of the disease. Psychoeducational groups may have more members than groups for people who are learning to deal with family conflicts about care. Professional caregiver groups are often small, ongoing, and open to new members.

Brief Solution-Focused Groups

Solution-focused groups may be either ongoing or time limited (Coe & Zimpfer, 1996), but most solution-focused or solution-oriented groups are discussed in terms of brief counseling. Brief solution-focused groups do not necessarily constitute a distinct type of group, but they may use approaches different from any of the previously described types of group, particularly topic- or theme-focused groups.

Because groups develop sequentially or cyclically over time through identifiable stages of growth (Donigian & Malnati, 1997), the term *brief group counseling* may seem to be an oxymoron or a paradox to many group leaders. As the number of sessions increases, a greater sense of safety emerges, and what and how members disclose may change as a result (Donigian & Malnati, 1997). The healing capacity of groups depends upon the trust, cohesion, and congruence that increase as a group progresses through the stages of development (Yalom, 1985).

The number of group meetings required for a specific group to achieve a significant healing potential depends upon many variables (Posthuma, 1996). Regardless of the group development model used, the healing capacity of groups is most often described as occurring after the transition or conflict stage. Unless the group regresses to an earlier stage for some reason, the healing capacity is thought to increase as group development progresses.

The time it takes for healing to take place might vary according to the therapeutic factor being tracked. For instance, the educational goal of sharing information about the progression of Alzheimer's disease, or of accessing resources for the older group members, may be achieved in one or a few sessions. But developing social skills, experiencing the group as a family, or learning new behaviors to use in resolving family conflicts may occur only after trust and cohesion develop, usually following several meetings. Reality testing depends upon self-disclosure, and self-disclosure depends upon trust (Yalom, 1985). Because group leaders are acutely aware of this relationship between healing and group development over time, they may fail to tap the benefits of problem-solving or solution-focused groups.

Coe and Zimpfer (1996) and LaFountain and Garner (1996, 1997) countered that solution-focused groups are not merely content related, that, as in longer-term groups, process plays an important role. They identified stages of development and listed clear benefits in their solution-focused groups. Even Yalom (1985) suggested the need to sometimes regard the life of a group as a single session. He encouraged group leaders to strive to offer something useful to as many patients as possible, regardless of the number of group sessions. When the life of the group is to be only one or a few sessions, he advised counselors to avoid conflict, provide no time for issues to develop and be resolved, establish a set sequence of events, give direct support to members, and maintain moderate group structure. Hinkle (1991) recommended problem-solving approaches with caregivers of patients with Alzheimer's disease, noting that these approaches enhance family relationships when families must make difficult decisions about an older family member.

Brief solution-focused groups generally meet from one to six times. The emphasis is on members' competencies rather than deficits and on strengths rather than weaknesses. When issues about aging are discussed, the focus is on possibilities instead of limitations. The time focus is the future rather than the past or present (O'Hanlon & Weiner-Davis, 1989). Group leaders help members change the discussions from how errors are made to how to make corrections. The goals of brief counseling are to empower the members; mobilize potentialities; reframe problems in solvable, autonomous terms; identify styles of cooperation; and create expectations of change (Talmon, 1990). Advocates of brief counseling basically recommend that counselors minimize talk about problems or complaints of the past and present and maximize talk about solutions for the future (de Shazer, 1988; Walter & Peller, 1992).

Solution-focused principles can be used in a myriad of topic-specific or caregiver groups. Family members can learn to draw on their strengths and manage difficult situations with an older relative. Older persons who have lost a spouse can learn to live independently and build a new supportive network. These brief groups can serve as adjuncts to other groups designed for catharsis, ongoing support, and other long-term treatment effects. The briefer solution-focused groups may be offered concurrently with, before, or after other types of groups.

Littrell, Malia, and Vanderwood (1995) urged strong cautions for counselors who plan to lead brief groups. They advised counselors not to focus prematurely on one concern to the exclusion of other, more serious concerns. When brief solution-focused counseling is offered as an adjunct treatment, sequencing is important. For example, when an older person has lost a spouse, grieving should not be ignored. Learning to live independently is important, but a group or other form of help to process the loss should accompany or precede the solution-focused group. Littrell and colleagues also urged counselors to remember that a brief group treatment approach is only one tool and is not appropriate in many situations. Counselors should resist using brief groups when long-term treatment is indicated, regardless of demanding client loads, third-party restrictions, or administrative demands.

eGroups: A Future Reality

Encouraged by Thomas et al. (2003), the eGroup is a recent forum for older persons who are homebound or separated from friends, relatives, and other potential group members. Although these groups are not discussed in the current literature, they have the potential of emerging into several different types of technology-based groups. Thomas et al. (2003) suggested the following as possible types of eGroups:

- Life review groups using eMemories and eStories
- Career development and retirement planning groups
- Bereavement groups
- Various types of support groups
- Family discussion groups

Kennedy (2004) has recommended several kinds of intergenerational groups conducted in community centers, and these intergenerational mentoring groups, child-rearing skills groups, and interest sharing groups could be adapted as eGroups.

Thomas and Martin (2004) also described intergenerational career development exercises that could be used as eGroup activities.

When considering eGroups for older people, counselors first must dispel the myth that technology has escaped older people, leaving them behind and increasing their isolation. By 2002, nearly half of North Americans over the age of 58 were using computers, and most of these users were self-taught (SeniorJournal.com, 2003). Senior citizens are leading other populations in the growth of Internet use (Heineman & Kim, 2003). Certainly, many older people do not have access to technology and may have to acquire the skills requisite for eGroups, but counselors can be advocates for providing user-friendly centers, training "tech pals" who understand the needs of older people, and convincing agencies and educational institutions to become invested in technology offerings for the population of older people (Thomas et al., 2003).

Leaders of eGroups also must consider some basic group organization decisions and ethical concerns. Counselors must adhere to the *Ethical Standards for Internet Online Counseling* (American Counseling Association [ACA], 1999). Issues such as confidentiality, security of the counselor's site, records of electronic communications, and electronic transfer of information are all serious concerns and special challenges for eGroup leaders. Until the practice of eGroups builds a successful history and ethical and logistical concerns are thoroughly resolved, we make five strong recommendations for organizing and conducting eGroups of any kind.

1. Potential group members should be referred directly by a qualified counselor rather than recruited indirectly from an Internet advertisement.
2. The eGroup leader should conduct a thorough, face-to-face screening with the potential eGroup member. If the eGroup counselor practices in a location too far from the member to conduct the screening, the counselor can provide specific screening guidelines for a counselor in the potential member's community to conduct the screening.
3. If the eGroup counselor finds the skills and equipment of the potential member to be insufficient for participation in the group, the counselor should identify and provide a "tech pal" or other technological assistance.
4. When the member's personal, economic, physical, or technological limitations make it difficult to maintain confidentiality, the eGroups should be limited to types of groups aimed more at relieving isolation than groups dealing with deep personal issues.
5. The eGroup counselor should identify a backup counselor accessible to each group member in case a referral for a nongroup-related concern is indicated. Until professional practices based on sound and ethical judgment are tested and proven ethical, the eGroup leader must exercise caution in developing new online group counseling approaches.

The potential for eGroups seems limited only by creativity. Techniques for older people with limited equipment and skills might employ e-mail, instant messaging, and protected chat room dialogues. Older people with advanced skills and access to more sophisticated equipment may utilize word processing with picture and document attachments and multimedia applications. Web cameras with sound capabilities provide the closest approximation to a traditional group (Thomas et al., 2003).

If the barriers of acquiring technology equipment and skills are overcome and ethical challenges are met, the advantages of eGroups for older people are numerous. Older persons isolated in small communities can be connected with cohorts in other geographic areas. The ability to share can increase their knowledge of resources, access to services, and meaningful communication with friends and family. In addition to the known advantages of group counseling, eGroups can build a supportive and healing community for older people who otherwise would be more isolated. This can produce the feeling of personal control that is so important for the empowerment and psychological and physical well-being of older people (Kampfe, 1995).

CONSIDERATIONS OF DIVERSITY

Even though older people share many characteristics related to their developmental stage, diversity in this population mirrors the diversity of the worlds in which they live. Culture consists of far more than racial or ethnic background, language, and socioeconomic status (Corey & Corey, 1997). Pedersen (1990) recommended that "culture" be broadly defined to encompass many relevant variables. Placing everyone from Spanish-speaking countries within one culture ignores the rich differences between Cubans, Mexicans, Guatemalans, Panamanians, and Venezuelans, not to mention the differences among several subcultures within those groups. Likewise, narrowly including all individuals from African backgrounds in one culture limits appreciation of the differences between people from the French, Dutch, British, or American Caribbean islands, as well as regional cultural differences among African Americans.

Gillies and James (1994) encouraged professionals who work with older people, particularly those using reminiscing therapy, to pay close attention to the total experiences of the older person. Historical events, social movements, political and technological changes, and economic conditions that older persons have experienced have molded their values, beliefs, behaviors, and feelings. Younger counselors should listen to older clients' stories to gain an understanding of the social and cultural contexts in which their values and behaviors were formed. Gillies and James (1994) approached counselors' needs for specific cultural information by dividing the 20th century into decades and listing the important historical events that occurred in several different countries. This chronological approach gives professionals an index to culture-changing events.

Group work with older people often presents a cultural challenge to counselors that is beyond the traditional scope of multicultural considerations. Older group members have lived through a history of which many counselors are aware only from books and other media. Many of these elderly people have come from countries and cultures that have been partly or wholly forgotten and lost in their American acculturation. In addition, the world is becoming smaller and the activities and focus of mental health professionals are expanding to address international issues beyond the diversity challenges within U.S. borders. The older population is growing all over the world, and the cultural challenge to counselors is far greater than attending to specific populations or special interest groups.

To meet the challenge of group work with a diversity of older people, counselors have to learn the history that formed the culture of their clients, understand the political, religious, and economic forces that molded their differences, and recognize the clients' strengths and values. Among the many paths to learn about diversity, probably the most important is to listen to the stories of older people, because these stories are the living histories and the primary sources for understanding cultural diversity.

A LIFE REVIEW GROUP: MY LIFE QUILT

The following is a model for a life review group for older members. The structure and process are explained, along with leader skills, group goals, potential outcomes, membership, screening, settings, length, frequency, duration, size, and mobility.

A life review group is a reminiscing experience that helps older adults identify their life accomplishments, resolve conflicts in a nonthreatening atmosphere, and recapture meaning (Hayden & Thomas, 1990; Lewis & Butler, 1986). The group is characterized by progressively returning to the consciousness of past experiences, which often results in a restored sense of resolution, balance, and wholeness (Butler, 1963; Ellison, 1981). Participants complete a developmental task of their life stage by taking stock of their lives and evaluating their goals, accomplishments, failures, and regrets (Kiernat, 1986).

Essentially, counselors introduce open-ended topics such as a happy time, a sad time, school days, courting, holidays, family, cooking, tools, or toys. Usually, a different topic is introduced at each session, and the older participants informally relate remembrances about the topic. Their stories become the bits and pieces that eventually converge into a meaningful, personal pattern.

At first the stories seem disconnected, and no orderly progression of memories is discernible. The stories are not organized into coherent narratives. The reminiscing process, however, is ongoing, repetitive, and progressive, illuminating both conscious and unconscious material. Central values and attitudes become evident as new stories emerge and participants become more open in expressing feelings with the story content. Each new story can be seen to represent a piece of a person's life. When the pieces are put together, the person's life can be symbolically envisioned as a quilt made up of important story pieces. Perceptive group counselors can use the group process to help older participants stitch their stories together in new ways to discover central themes and find the wholeness and harmony important in their search for meaning.

Pitfalls and Leader Skills

The major pitfall the leader of a life review or reminiscing group may encounter is to allow this group to evolve into an overly structured series of stories, in which the participants simply complete the exercise with little or no interaction, expression of feelings, identification with other members, or introspection. Other common pitfalls include allowing competition between stories, oversocializing or subgrouping, isolating members, and planning too much for a single group session (Hayden & Thomas, 1990). Finally, failing to perceive and respond appropriately to any depression and anxiety that emerges from bringing memories to the surface can impede group progress (Ellison, 1981).

Leader skills that contribute to the success of life review groups include the ability to detect central themes in the stories; understand participants' cultural histories; facilitate the developmental accomplishments of older persons; promote interaction, sharing, and the building of community; help members from diverse populations identify with one another; and use humor in the therapeutic process. Leaders of life review groups are cautioned to avoid behaviors that group members could interpret as being condescending, authoritarian, stereotyping, or impatient with members' limitations. Some researchers have recommended the use of mixed-gender cofacilitators, because male and female leaders tend to elicit different memories (e.g., Ebersole, 1978a). A skilled facilitator of either gender, however, may be sensitive to this tendency and able to counteract the gender effect.

Group Goals and Potential Outcomes

Typical goals of a life review group (Hayden & Thomas, 1990; Thomas, 1991; Thomas & Martin, 1997) are to

1. renew meaning in life by reviewing life experiences;
2. discover central themes in previously disconnected parts of life;
3. create a sense of community and belonging by sharing common concerns, experiences, and losses;
4. restore and maintain social interaction and a support network;
5. decrease isolation;
6. develop new ways of coping;
7. resolve previous life-stage issues in a nonthreatening atmosphere to increase hope, wisdom, and ego integrity;
8. find order and affirmation in life patterns; and
9. discover the importance of one's uniqueness.

Additional positive outcomes and specific effects of life review groups emerge as the groups progress. Members are helped to transcend difficult times and accept being older when they see how they navigated difficult times in the past. They discover wells of strength and courage and learn how to tap that strength to survive their final stage of life. They find moments of closeness with other group members when they have lost a great deal, and they experience unconditional love. They enjoy the therapeutic effects of humor by relating funny stories and lessons from mischievous escapades. They often are able to recover and heal lost relationships, make new friends, and learn to like themselves better. They are stimulated to continue growing and learning. They reap the benefits of helping and supporting others. And they realize their roles as culture bearers from one generation to the next and discover the need to keep alive the values and ways of the past.

Membership, Screening, and Settings

Life review groups are appropriate for nutrition sites, domiciliary centers, adult day-care centers, long-term care facilities, community agencies, and religious institutions. Membership should be voluntary, and recruiting is best accomplished through personal group or individual presentations by the leader. The group description and goals should be presented concisely and clearly in both written and verbal communications, emphasizing the positive aspects. Brief videos or role plays may be used to demonstrate the group process to potential members. Selecting members in residential, daycare, or nutrition centers should be the result of collaborative efforts with the program's staff.

The membership of these groups is homogeneous in that all participants are older, but the group may be heterogeneous with respect to cultural diversity. Depending upon the group leader's skills, cultural diversity can contribute significantly to the group's success, accomplishment of goals, community building, and depth of interaction. Ebersole (1978a) recommended that groups be composed of equal numbers of male and female participants, although some articles describe success with single-gender reminiscing groups (Creanza & McWhirter, 1994) and with mixed groups without an emphasis on equal numbers of men and women (Waters, 1990b).

Some leaders choose to implement a group screening process during the first session. Individual screening is often preferred, however, because many older people have little or no experience with therapeutic groups and may be more comfortable expressing their fears and asking questions in an individual screening session. Ebersole (1978a) recommended individual screening that allows participants to know who the other participants are and planning a group of compatible members.

Screening also provides the opportunity for the leader to assess for special needs and provide a barrier-free setting for the participants. Members should be oriented in time and place, and they should be free from severe emotional, cognitive, or physical impairments that would significantly interfere with their ability to interact in a group. Finally, members should not be overly medicated or in crisis.

Length, Frequency, and Duration of Groups

Most reminiscing and life review groups meet for 1 to 1½ hours once or twice a week for 10 to 12 weeks. Some leaders advocate reminiscing groups of much longer duration (20 weeks or more), arguing that adaptation to growing older, developing wisdom, and maintaining integrity take longer than a few weeks. Ebersole (1978a) described ongoing reminiscing groups that meet for a year or longer.

Increased illness in the fall and winter seasons often results in more absenteeism, which has led some group leaders to plan the groups for spring and summer (Kiernat, 1986). Others argue that because activities are restricted in the colder months, fall and winter groups are needed more than ever. The duration of these groups may be longer to compensate for the irregular attendance. Mid- or late-morning meetings usually are preferred to afternoon sessions (Kiernat, 1986). Consistency is important, so groups should meet at the same time and place, giving members something definite to anticipate.

Group Size and Mobility

The recommended group size varies from five to nine members. Most leaders planning these groups prefer smaller groups of five or six members. Larger groups may be manageable, but the session length and membership may require adjustments to accommodate the larger group. When members have moderately impaired cognitive function, the size of the group and length of the sessions probably should be reduced.

Most groups are time limited and are closed to new members. Long-term ongoing groups are generally open, and the process and timing for adding new members are determined cooperatively by group members and group leaders.

Selecting Topics for Life Review

Topics for individual sessions can be chosen by the leader or chosen cooperatively by the leader and participants. Groups may choose themes that follow a life span or chronological order or may select random topics with no apparent pattern. Some group leaders stipulate that only positive topics or themes are appropriate, whereas other counselors argue that including some losses, unresolved conflicts, and regrets is necessary for adequate life review. Burnside (1995) distinguished between reminiscing and life review by identifying reminiscence as including only positive memories and life review as integrating both positive and negative memories.

In selecting session themes, we propose the following guidelines:

1. Include topics that elicit memories about both positive and negative experiences and feelings. Merely reminiscing about happy times reduces the potential for increasing the ego integrity achievable from a more complete life review.
2. Sequence the themes by beginning with stimulants for positive memories, following with topics about conflicts, regrets, or unhappy times after trust is established, and ending with topics that integrate both positive and negative memories.
3. Seek a balance between more open-ended topics, which elicit broad discussions of memories, and highly specific topics. For instance, asking members to share memories about open-ended topics such as "a very happy time" or "an unhappy time" usually results in rich self-disclosures about values and feelings. Talking about a first toy, first kiss, or first pet (all

specific topics) can be fun, but specific topics also can produce superficial levels of involvement and diminish the positive group effects.

4. Add gender-, ethnic-, or culture-specific topics when appropriate for the membership. For example, a group of older women may benefit from relating how their roles changed during their lives, such as a group of older Japanese Americans' resolving residual negative feelings about their experiences during World War II.

The Sessions

The sequence of a 10-session life review group that follows these guidelines is presented in the following pages.

Session 1: A Happy Time

The leader begins the group with a brief get-acquainted activity, reviews the group goals and procedures outlined during the screening, and reminds the members of group rules such as maintaining confidentiality and refraining from giving advice. Then the leader introduces the topic for the session by asking the members to think of a happy time and to share their memories about that time. If a response is brief, the leader can stimulate an expanded response by asking who was with the person, what made this a happy time, what were some long-term effects, or how the time changed the person's life.

As the members share their happy times, the leader

- finds connections between past and present;
- attends to the members' present feelings about the past, present, and others;
- brings isolated members into the discussion;
- fosters interaction and identification among members;
- points out the ongoing developmental aspects of living; and
- utilizes opportunities for closure.

Toward the end of the session, the members are asked to share with other members the ways in which they identify with these other members. Finally, the leader introduces the topic for the next session so the members can anticipate their next involvement.

Session 2: An Unhappy Time

Following the same procedure as used in the first session, the members share an unhappy time. The leader may want to stimulate further discussion by asking about lessons learned or positive outcomes from that experience, residual feelings, or how the experience changed the members and their lives.

The leader begins to shift responsibility gradually to the group members for making the connections, looking for central themes, and finding similarities between and among the participants. The members are encouraged to interact with one another and help each other put their stories together. As with all sessions, the leader introduces the topic for the next session.

Session 3: Holidays and Vacations

By the third session, group members' stories probably will begin to reveal core values central to their lives and self-disclosure of deep feelings. For example, when asked about the most valuable gift they ever received at Christmas, one member in a life review group described a cherished item of clothing she received from a poor, elderly, female relative. The woman who gave the gift roamed over the hills to find wool where sheep grazed and rubbed against fences, trees, and bushes. She collected the small pieces of wool, then spun the wool and wove it into items of clothing for her family members. The man who had received the gift quietly expressed a myriad of feelings as he said he could not even remember what the woman looked like but that he never would forget the beauty of that gift or its personal cost to the giver. This theme of doing rather than buying, and of finding gifts of love when economically poor, became evident in all of this member's stories. Questions to trigger memories about holidays or vacations could include queries about cultural customs or special foods associated with holidays, about modes of transportation, or about favorite vacations.

When introducing the next session's topic of cooking, tools, and toys, the leader might want to encourage members to bring old utensils, tools, or recipes to the session.

Session 4: Cooking, Tools, and Toys

The more specific topics in the fourth session typically elicit enjoyment. Members who bring old cooking utensils, tools, or toys have fun showing how they work, who used them, and how they were made. Values of ingenuity and learning to have fun despite limited resources usually emerge. For example, members often describe rattles made from blown-up pig bladders filled with peas or beans, or flutes made from cane. The value of not being wasteful emerges when members describe building furniture from cane, wood, willow branches, or discarded crates and processing clabber, butter, cream, sweet milk, or cheese from whole fresh milk.

Session 5: Historical Events

Members are asked to share two or three historical events that had significant effects on their lives, their country, or society. The members' cultural histories influence the choice of topics. For example, the Great Depression may be meaningful for older Americans but irrelevant to those who are more recent immigrants from other countries. The members are encouraged to bring photos and other mementos to the next session.

Session 6: Courting and Marriage

In this session as in the others, the group members share stories, but this time they are encouraged to show pictures or other mementos while they relate their stories. Albums and diaries consume more time than is allowed for adequate sharing, so each member is asked to show just one or two pictures or mementos that help relate meaningful aspects of their romantic relationships and marriage.

Session 7: Mischievous Escapades

Family systems, communication styles, and discipline modes often become apparent in these stories. For example, a member in one life review group told how he and some other family members visited his grandfather, who had a prized buggy in a two-story barn. The boys disassembled the buggy during the night and reassembled it on top of the large barn. The grandfather was angry, but even more, he was perplexed about how to return the buggy to the ground. The dilemma was resolved after several days of frustrating problem solving and some moderate consequences for the boys, but with no apparent residual negative feelings.

Session 8: Experiences With Failure

This session provides the opportunity to integrate negative memories into a bigger picture that balances the negative and positive aspects of members' lives. Reframing failures as stepping stones to success or opportunities for learning can help resolve old intrapersonal conflicts. The members are asked to bring heirlooms, genealogies, or other mementos that are representative of their families.

Session 9: Family Mementos

The participants share heirlooms, genograms, genealogies, or artistic representations of their families. The leader can ask many trigger questions to stimulate self-disclosure and expanded personal stories. The leader assists group members in finding connections, central themes, and similarities, and continues to encourage interaction. At the end of the session, the group members are asked to take time during the coming week to think about the stories they have shared to date and identify the importance of each in their lives.

Session 10: Closure: My Life Quilt

During this last meeting, each member is asked to put all of his or her stories together as if the stories are bits and pieces of a quilt that represents progress in the ongoing developmental aspects of living, and to show how the positives and negatives balance each other and come together to form a meaningful whole.

Finally, members are asked to relate what the group has meant to them and to evaluate the group experience. The leader may employ an appropriate evaluation measure or procedure for closure. Leaders are strongly urged to design an evaluation that can contribute to group research.

4 S DECISION MODEL FOR A BRIEF SOLUTION-FOCUSED GROUP

Many older people, because of the loss of a spouse or diminishing health, are faced with the difficult decision of leaving their home, community, and social support systems and moving closer to their adult children or other close relatives in another location. The older person's family members are often torn between balancing jobs, rearing their own children, and making frequent trips to care for the older relatives. The decision of whether an older person will remain in a familiar, comfortable environment without adequate care or move to a strange, unknown place close to family seems to be a no-win situation for both the older person and his or her family members.

The example here is of a brief solution-focused group for older people and their family caregivers who are considering changes in living arrangements for the older relative. The basic model for the group is the Schlossberg, Waters, and Goodman (1995) 4 S model, which is a system for assessing and balancing assets and liabilities in the factors associated with any transition.

Components of the Model

The 4 S's represent (a) the situation, (b) the self, (c) support, and (d) strategies.

The Situation

When applying this model to making decisions about the difficult transition of giving up one home for another, the *situation* is examined first. The counselor, the older person, and his or her family members discuss what triggered the transition, how timing affects the situation, how much of the situation can be controlled, the potential role changes caused by the transition, the permanence of the change, the amount of concomitant stress, previous experiences with similar transitions, and the attitudes of the family members and the older person about the transition.

The Self

In viewing the *self* factor, the family members and the older person assess their personal and demographic characteristics, including factors such as socioeconomic status, age, health, and stage of life. They also examine their psychological resources, such as values, ego development, and outlook.

Support

When addressing the *support* factor, the family members and the older person identify assets and deficits in the social support systems, such as intimate relationships, family units, friendships, community networks, and institutional programs.

Strategies

Finally, the family members and older person assess their *strategy*-building skills, whether they take direct action, how well they manage stress, and their facility to compromise. Once the family members and the older person identify their resources, they can balance the assets and liabilities and be better able to reach a decision. After assessing the 4 S's, they can make a decision based less on fear and more on information, strategies, possibilities, and hope.

Leadership

Cofacilitators are recommended for this group for several reasons. First, different family units display an array of family dynamics, and processing these dynamics might prove to be challenging for one leader alone. Also, the group membership will be divided into subgroups, each of which will require a facilitator.

The group leaders should be trained group counselors or therapists who have knowledge about family systems and solution-focused strategies. They should display warmth, empathy, democratic styles of leadership, support, and optimism. Finally, because this type of group is intergenerational, the leaders should have knowledge about the full range of human development and particularly issues associated with aging.

Group Goals

The goals for this group are to create options for older persons who are considering moving from their home and to help family members contribute positively to the decision by applying the 4 S coping resources model. Specifically, the goals are to help the families

1. identify resources and deficits in the community to which the older person may move,
2. compare resources and deficits in the old and new communities,
3. assess self and family to balance their strengths and liabilities,
4. learn new strategies for bridging transitions, and
5. develop a tentative transition plan with alternatives.

Membership, Screening, and Setting

Gerontological counselors working in private practice, those working in large community programs designed to help older people in transition, and those working in retirement communities often encounter families struggling with this decision. The group might consist of, say, two or three family units, each composed of an older relative and a few family members who are invested in the decision. Screening every potential family group member may be problematic, but adult children, older grandchildren, siblings, nieces, and nephews are possible candidates, provided they are supportive, nonjudgmental, and free of serious psychological or addictive problems. An important factor is an active and positive caring for their older relative.

Older people considering the move should be assessed for cognitive and physical functioning. This type of group is not appropriate for persons with severe cognitive impairment but could accommodate those with some physical deficits.

The preferred setting is the community to which the older person is considering moving. The sessions should be held in a facility that is easily reached and comfortable and can accommodate any special needs of members identified during screening.

Length, Frequency, and Duration

The recommended length of each group session is 2 hours, which may be shortened or extended somewhat depending on the size of the group. The frequency and duration of sessions will depend upon the members' abilities to attend. For example, if the older people are temporarily residing in the community to which they are considering moving, or if they are on an extended visit with their family in this new community, the group may meet weekly for a month. If the older persons visit only occasionally, the group might meet monthly. Regardless of the format, ample time must be allowed between sessions for the group members to complete the homework assignments.

Group Size and Mobility

The key to determining the size of this type of brief solution-focused group is the number of family constellations. At least two separate families of varying sizes are required, and three or four family constellations is best. The group size could vary from a total of 5 to 15 members.

The Sessions

Because this group has only four sessions, the group should be closed. Families wishing to join the group after the first session should be encouraged to be part of a new group.

Session 1

During the first session, the members introduce themselves and describe why the older group members are considering moving from their homes. They are encouraged to share their fears, how the move will change their roles, and their current support systems. Family members are asked to explain their views and the pros and cons surrounding the decision to move.

The counselors then describe the 4 S decision model and the group goals, emphasizing a future solution rather than focusing on present or past problems. In describing the goals, the group leaders caution members not to view the group as a vehicle for forcing a choice on anyone. The desired outcome is to help the group members make informed choices, with the older person empowered to make as many of the decisions as possible.

During the first session, appropriate group rules are explained. The group members are given community resource guides, lists of organizations, senior college and elder hostel brochures, descriptions of religious and community programs for older people, calendars of cultural outlets, lists of opportunities for volunteer or paid work, and any additional information available about resources in the new community.

Homework: The older family members are asked to thoroughly assess their social support system in their home communities and identify potentially similar resources in the new community. Family members may be asked to complete the same task, either alone or in cooperation with other family members and the older person. In the latter case, family members are cautioned not to push toward a single or final decision about the transition between living arrangements. Finally, the group leaders may ask the participants to complete career and leisure assessment instruments.

Session 2

The group leaders begin the second session by inviting the older people and their family members to share with the group the resources in the new community that they would like to explore more thoroughly. Whether the older persons are considering living with or near their family members, common concerns for working family members include transportation, meals, and housecleaning for the older relative. Although older people generally have some needs in common, individually they may be more interested in friendships, opportunities for social involvement, meaningful paid or volunteer work, or cultural and learning opportunities.

In this second session, assessment of personal characteristics and psychological resources that would help or hinder the transition can begin in earnest. This assessment begins with self-disclosure and any activity the leaders may create for self-assessment. Again, because the group is brief and solution focused, emphasis is placed on positive characteristics that will make the transition more successful. When deficits are noted, balancing deficits with strengths is encouraged.

Homework: The older persons are asked to further explore the resources they might wish to use if they move to the new community. They are asked to visit centers and facilities of interest to them, make appointments with coordinators of any programs in which they might want to become involved, attend meetings of organizations to meet members, or visit churches, synagogues, or religious services of their choosing. Family members may be given a similar assignment, or they may be asked to work cooperatively with the older person, again being cautioned not to push for their preferred options.

Session 3

The third session begins with the leaders' subgrouping the members into a small group for the older persons from the different families and another group for the family members. Because the first steps in exploring a transition from one home to another can be discouraging, members of both subgroups are asked to share the positive and negative experiences they had while completing their assigned explorations. Negative themes may surface, such as old familial communication blocks or differences in values and attitudes. Both subgroups may become acutely aware that the proposed transitional move may be far more difficult than they previously anticipated. If the move from one community to another is not yet an absolute necessity, both communities can be explored to balance the liabilities and assets.

At this juncture, regardless of the attractiveness of one choice over the other, strategies for remaining in the home community and for moving to the new community can be explored. For example, the subgroup of older persons may devise a plan to strengthen their support and remain in their own communities. They might transfer their major health care to medical facilities in their family members' community, thereby removing the need for the family members to travel to the older person's home community during health crises. Or they may create a plan to alternate between living in their own community and the new community.

Homework: Members of both subgroups are asked to individually focus on possibilities and plan strategies for a variety of choices.

Session 4

The subgroups are maintained for the first part of this last session so individual members can discuss their strategies for partially or wholly making the proposed transition from one home to another. At this time they might incorporate others' ideas into their own strategies. The subgroups then are brought together to share their strategies.

Closure is accomplished by members' having several possible actions from which to select one or more plans. The group members will have assessed their situations, their personal qualities, and available support. They may have devised a specific plan, but more likely they will have developed a broader picture of the possibilities. What may have seemed like a trap can be viewed now as a full range of opportunities.

Closure also is accomplished by the group leaders and members identifying needs for further counseling and follow-up. The older person or family members who will be most affected by the transition may want individual counseling. A family unit might desire family counseling. An older person may request help with grieving or with another aging issue. Follow-up is important, and the group leaders should make appropriate referrals, request permission to contact the group members in the future, and outline the follow-up procedures.

TRAINING RECOMMENDATIONS

Counseling students who intend to specialize in group work with older populations should consider training in the areas of group work and gerontological counseling in addition to training in counseling in general (Thomas & Martin, 1997). In pursuing training, students have several options. If a gerontological training program is not available, those who are interested can follow an individualized plan that combines the standards of counseling, group work, and gerontology. Numerous community and mental health counseling programs accredited by CACREP (2001) are available throughout the country. Basic counseling competencies provide the foundation for those who work with the older population. Acquiring specific gerontological skills may present a challenge because formal training may not be available in many communities (Myers, 1992).

An outline of appropriate training for a gerontological specialty within community counseling programs is included in the CACREP (2001) standards, but only two accredited programs are offered at the present time. The *Competencies for Gerontological Counseling* (Myers & Schwiebert, 1996) includes minimal gerontological competencies. Those who are unable to enroll in a CACREP gerontological program can complete their basic degree program, take additional coursework, and complete appropriate supervision to satisfy the requirements for gerontological specialty certification offered by social work or related professional associations.

The guidelines for training group specialists are specified in the Association for Specialists in Group Work's *Professional Standards for the Training of Group Workers* (ASGW, 2000). The basic knowledge and competencies for all group workers are listed, as well as the required minimum coursework and supervised practice.

Levels of training are specified for task and work groups, psychoeducation groups, counseling groups, and psychotherapy groups. Counselors conducting groups for older people should have achieved the level of training required for the type of group they plan to conduct.

Until CACREP-approved gerontological programs become more widely available, counselors who want to specialize in group work with older persons will find it necessary to pursue training, certification, and supervision from several sources. In addition to receiving basic training, counselors must intensify their training in group work, human development, and gerontology. Several noncounseling gerontological certifications are available, but these must be combined with basic counseling training. Continuing education and ongoing supervision in each of the three areas of counseling, group work, and gerontology are important in maintaining competencies. Finally, technological competencies are mandated for group counselors who adapt traditional gerontological groups to Internet formats.

LEARNING ACTIVITIES

1. Identify a 75-year-old or older man or woman in your community. Gather information about that person in an appropriate manner. You may want to conduct a personal interview, interview a family member or caregiver, or read a case history. Which type of group would be most appropriate to meet the needs of this individual? Why? What are the goals for this group? Where might this person find such a group?

2. Develop an interview outline for learning about the cultural backgrounds of potential elderly group members. What questions would you ask to better understand the older person from a multicultural perspective? What can you do to learn more about his or her cultures? Then find a person who is much older than you and conduct the interview you designed.

3. Locate a group for older people or caregivers that currently does not use an evaluation procedure that might contribute significantly to the research. Design a tentative research strategy that might help the group leader, agency, or others in the field learn more about the effectiveness of such groups, validate current practices, or produce recommendations for future groups. This exercise could form the foundation of a research paper for a subsequent class, or it could become an integral part of a practicum or internship.

4. Plan a theoretical traditional life review group similar to the example in this chapter. Assume that the potential members live too far away from each other to conduct the group in one location. Survey your community to assess the feasibility of organizing the life review group as an eGroup. What centers for older people, agencies, or educational institutions have the technology capable of being used for an eGroup? What resources are available to provide homebound older people or older people from small communities with the technological capability to participate in an eGroup? Assess the potential members for technological skills and estimate the training they will need to participate in an

eGroup. If you decide that the resources are not available for an eGroup, propose a plan to build those resources.

SUMMARY

A dramatic increase in the numbers and proportion of older adults in the United States during the 20th century generated new interest in the mental health needs of this historically underserved population. Beginning in the 1950s, a number of group counseling formats emerged to meet the various emotional, physical, and social needs associated with this lengthy developmental period.

Reality orientation groups help those with dementia more accurately interpret their experiences and take increased responsibility for their own care. Remotivation groups stimulate socialization and involvement by elderly people who are oriented but alienated. Reminiscing and life review groups foster a sense of connectedness, identity, and ego integrity for older adults in both inpatient and community settings. Psychotherapy groups focus on more intensive emotional conflicts and issues, and theme-focused groups provide support and therapy for older people as they share a variety of specific concerns.

Caregivers of the elderly, whether family members or professionals, can learn from one another and find needed support by sharing their experiences in a counseling group. A carefully planned brief solution-focused format can be successful in helping members formulate and implement plans for change at times of transition. Proposed eGroups resulting from combining emerging technology with traditional group practices undoubtedly will produce an array of groups limited only by creativity and imagination. Many of the traditional groups described previously can be adapted to technological formats. Newer intergenerational groups and career development groups for older people that are based on self-actualizing models also can be effective.

Organizing the different types of groups requires specific considerations. The initial step involves assessing the appropriateness of the group mode and choosing the type of group to be conducted. Leader skills vary for each type of group, and membership, screening, and settings are different for each type of group as well. Decisions about group length, frequency, duration, size, and mobility must be considered carefully to maximize potential group outcomes. Organizing eGroups presents additional challenges of distance screening, providing technological support, and complying with ethical standards for Internet counseling.

Wide cultural diversity is represented in the older population. Historical differences in the life experiences of older generations from diverse backgrounds add a new dimension to multicultural awareness. This added dimension challenges group counselors to expand their knowledge and sensitivity about diversity by incorporating into their knowledge base the effects of specific historically significant events on different populations.

Working with elderly people requires training in the three areas of counseling, group skills, and gerontology. Although few CACREP-approved gerontological programs are available, numerous CACREP community and mental health counseling programs and medical or social work associations offer approved gerontology programs. Those who are interested in this specialty may have to develop individualized plans for receiving training in each of these areas. Conducting eGroups requires additional technology skills for Internet counseling, specifically Internet group counseling.

As society ages and we forge ahead in the 21st century, the challenges of meeting the mental health needs of elderly people will predictably increase. Groups with older people can help join the past with the present and add continuity, wholeness, balance, and meaning to the lives of participants and group leaders. Further, these groups can build bridges from a larger community of several generations, connecting the pathways we can all travel to help transform dreams into a healthy world for future generations.

USEFUL WEB SITES

- □ AARP
  Computers and Technology: www.aarp.org/computers/
  Ageline Database: www.aarp.org/research/ageline
- □ Association for Specialists in Group Work (ASGW)
  www.asgw.org
- □ CACREP Gerontological Counseling Standards
  www.cacrep.org/2001standards.html
- □ Computers Made Easy for Senior Citizens
  www.csuchico.edu/%7ecsu/seniors/computing2.html
- □ Generations United
  www.gu.org/prog.htm
- □ Elderhostel
  www.elderhostel.org/programs/intergenerational_default.asp
- □ Legacy Project
  www.legacyproject.org/kits/index.html
- □ Links for Senior Citizens
  www.seniorjournal.com/seniorlinks.htm

REFERENCES

Administration on Aging. (n.d.). *Profile of older Americans: 2003.* U.S. Department of Health and Human Services. Retrieved October 29, 2004, from http://www.aoa.gov/prof/statistics/profile/2003/14.asp

American Counseling Association (ACA). (1999). *Ethical standards for Internet online counseling.* Retrieved October 11, 2004, from http://www.counseling.org/Content/NavigationMenu/RESOURCES/ETHICS/EthicalStandardsforInternetOnlineCounseling/Ethical_Stand_Online.htm

Association for Specialists in Group Work (ASGW). (2000). Professional standards for the training of group workers. *Group Worker, 29,* 19–28.

Bledsoe, N., & Lutz-Ponder, P. (1986). Group counseling with nursing home residents. *Journal for Specialists in Group Work, 11,* 37–41.

Burke, M. J. (1986). Peer counseling for elderly victims of crime and violence. *Journal for Specialists in Group Work, 14,* 107–113.

Burnside, I. (Ed.). (1978). *Working with the elderly: Group process and techniques.* North Scituate, MA: Duxbury Press.

Burnside, I. (Ed.). (1986). *Working with the elderly: Group process and techniques* (2nd ed.). Boston: Jones & Bartlett.

Burnside, I. (1995). Themes in reminiscence groups with older women. In J. Hendricks (Ed.), *The meaning of reminiscence and life review* (pp. 159–171). Amityville, NY: Baywood.

Butler, R. N. (1963). The life review: An interpretation of reminiscence in the aged. *Psychiatry, 26*(1), 65–76.

Butler, R. N. (1975). *Why survive? Being old in America.* New York: Harper & Row.

Butler, R. N., & Lewis, M. I. (1977). *Aging and mental health: Positive psychosocial approaches* (2nd ed.). St. Louis: C. V. Mosby.

Capuzzi, D., & Gossman, L. (1982). Sexuality and the elderly: A group counseling model. *Journal for Specialists in Group Work, 7,* 251–259.

Capuzzi, D., & Gross, D. (1980). Group work with the elderly: An overview for counselors. *Personnel and Guidance Journal, 59,* 206–211.

Capuzzi, D., & Gross, D. R. (Eds.). (1998). *Introduction to group counseling* (2nd ed.). Denver: Love Publishing.

Capuzzi, D., Gross, D., & Friel, S. E. (1990). Recent trends in group work with elders. *Generations: Journal of the American Society on Aging, 14,* 43–48.

Chandras, K. V. (Ed.). (1992). Training in gerontological counseling [Special section]. *Counselor Education and Supervision, 32*(1).

Coe, D. M., & Zimpfer, D. G. (1996). Infusing solution-oriented theory and techniques into group work. *Journal for Specialists in Group Work, 21,* 49–57.

Cohen, P. M. (1983). A group approach for working with families of the elderly. *Gerontologist, 23,* 248–250.

Corey, M. S., & Corey, G. (1997). *Groups: Process and practice* (5th ed.). Pacific Grove, CA: Brooks/Cole.

Council for Accreditation of Counseling and Related Educational Programs (CACREP). (1994). *Accreditation standards and procedures manual.* Alexandria, VA: Author.

Council for Accreditation of Counseling and Related Educational Programs (CACREP). (2001). *The 2001 standards.* Alexandria, VA: Author. Retrieved October 29, 2000, from http://counseling.org/cacrep/2001standards700.htm

Creanza, A. L., & McWhirter, J. J. (1994). Reminiscence: A strategy for getting to know you. *Journal for Specialists in Group Work, 19,* 232–237.

Dennis, H. (1986). Remotivation therapy. In I. Burnside (Ed.), *Working with the elderly: Group process and techniques* (2nd ed., pp. 187–197). Boston: Jones & Bartlett.

de Shazer, S. (1988). *Clues: Investigating solutions in brief therapy.* New York: Norton.

Dickman, I. R. (1979). Ageism—discrimination against older people (Public Affairs Pamphlet No. 575). (Available from Public Affairs Pamphlets, 381 Park Avenue, South, New York City, NY 10016)

Donahue, E. M. (1986). Reality orientation: A review of the literature. In I. Burnside (Ed.), *Working with the elderly: Group process and techniques* (2nd ed., pp. 165–176). Boston: Jones & Bartlett.

Donigian, J., & Malnati, R. (1997). *Systemic group therapy: A triadic model.* Pacific Grove, CA: Brooks/Cole.

Ebersole, P. P. (1978a). Establishing reminiscing groups. In I. Burnside (Ed.), *Working with the elderly: Group process and techniques* (pp. 236–254). North Scituate, MA: Duxbury Press.

Ebersole, P. P. (1978b). A theoretical approach to the use of reminiscence. In I. Burnside (Ed.), *Working with the elderly: Group process and techniques* (pp. 139–154). North Scituate, MA: Duxbury Press.

Ellison, K. B. (1981). Working with the elderly in a life review group. *Journal of Gerontological Nursing, 7,* 537–541.

Erikson, E. (1963). *Childhood and society* (2nd ed.). New York: Norton.

Folsom, J. (1968). Reality orientation for the elderly mental patient. *Journal of Geriatric Psychiatry, 1,* 291–307.

Gazda, G. M. (1989). *Group counseling: A developmental approach* (4th ed.). Boston: Allyn & Bacon.

Gillies, C., & James, A. (1994). *Reminiscence work with old people.* London: Chapman & Hall.

Gladding, S. T. (1991). *Group work: A counseling specialty.* New York: Merrill.

Gladding, S. T., & Thomas, M. C. (Eds.). (1991). Group work with the aging and their caregivers [Special issue]. *Journal for Specialists in Group Work, 16*(3).

Hammond, D. B., & Bonney, W. C. (1983). Counseling families of the elderly: A group experience. *Journal for Specialists in Group Work, 8,* 198–204.

Havighurst, R. G., & Glasser, R. (1972). An exploratory study of reminiscence. *Journal of Gerontology, 27,* 243–253.

Hawkins, B. L. (1983). Group counseling as a treatment modality for the elderly: A group snapshot. *Journal for Specialists in Group Work, 8,* 186–193.

Hayden, R., & Thomas, M. C. (1990, March). *Life review groups for the aging: Pathways to meaning.* Paper presented at the American Association for Counseling and Development Convention, Cincinnati, OH.

Heineman, M., & Kim, G. (2003, November). Senior citizens lead Internet growth, according to Nielsen//netratings. Neilsen//Netratings. Retrieved from http.//www.nielsen-netratings. com/pr/pr-031120.pdf

Hinkle, J. S. (1991). Support group counseling for caregivers of Alzheimer's disease patients. *Journal for Specialists in Group Work, 16,* 185–190.

Kaminsky, M. (Ed.). (1984). *The uses of reminiscence: New ways of working with older adults.* New York: Haworth Press.

Kampfe, C. M. (1995). Empowerment in residential relocation and long-term care settings. In K. V. Chandras (Ed.), *Handbook on counseling adolescents, adults and older persons* (pp. 42–53). Warner Robins, GA: Universal H. T. M. Foundation of America, Inc.

Kaplan, J. (1953). *A social program for older people.* Minneapolis: University of Minnesota Press.

Kennedy, A. (2004, July). Intergenerational activities prove beneficial to young and the young at heart. *Counseling Today,* 14.

Kiernat, J. M. (1986). The use of life review activity. In I. Burnside (Ed.), *Working with the elderly: Group process and techniques* (2nd ed., pp. 298–307). Boston: Jones & Bartlett.

Kubie, S., & Landau, G. (1953). *Group work with the aged.* New York: International Universities Press.

LaFountain, R. M., & Garner, N. E. (1996). Solution-focused counseling groups: The results are in. *Journal for Specialists in Group Work, 21,* 128–143.

LaFountain, R. M., & Garner, N. E. (1997). Solution-focused counseling groups. In S. T. Gladding (Ed.), *New developments in group counseling* (pp. 9–11). Greensboro, NC: ERIC/CASS.

Lewis, M. I., & Butler, R. N. (1974). Life review therapy: Putting memories to work in individual and group psychotherapy. *Geriatrics, 29,* 165–169, 172–173.

Lewis, M. I., & Butler, R. N. (1986). Life-review therapy: Putting memories to work. In I. Burnside (Ed.), *Working with the elderly: Group process and techniques* (2nd ed., pp. 50–59). Boston: Jones & Bartlett.

Linden, M. (1953). Group psychotherapy with institutionalized senile women: Study in gerontological human relations. *International Journal of Group Psychotherapy, 3,* 150–170.

Littrell, J. M., Malia, J. A., & Vanderwood, M. (1995). Single-session brief counseling in a high school. *Journal of Counseling and Development, 73,* 451–458.

Malde, S. (1988). Guided autobiography: A counseling tool for older adults. *Journal of Counseling and Development, 66,* 290–293.

Mardoyan, J. L., & Weis, D. M. (1981). The efficacy of group counseling with older adults. *Personnel and Guidance Journal, 60,* 161–163.

Marram, G. D. (1973). *The group approach in nursing practice.* St. Louis: C. V. Mosby.

Martin, V., Thomas, M. C., Alexander, J. J., & Loague, A. M. (2004). The role of technology in building community for older persons. *Alabama Counseling Association Journal, 30,* 52–66.

Myers, J. E. (1989). *Infusing gerontological counseling into counselor preparation: Curriculum guide.* Alexandria, VA: American Association for Counseling and Development.

Myers, J. E. (Ed.). (1990). Techniques for counseling older persons [Special issue]. *Journal of Mental Health Counseling, 12*(3).

Myers, J. E. (1992). Competencies, credentialing, and standards for gerontological counselors: Implications for counselor education. *Counselor Education and Supervision, 32,* 34–42.

Myers, J. E., Poidevant, J. M., & Dean, L. A. (1991). Groups for older persons and their caregivers: A review of the literature. *Journal for Specialists in Group Work, 16,* 197–205.

Myers, J. E., & Schwiebert, V. L. (1996). *Competencies for gerontological counseling.* Alexandria, VA: American Counseling Association.

Myers, J. E., & Sweeney, T. J. (1990). *Gerontological competencies for counselors and human development specialists.* Alexandria, VA: American Association for Counseling and Development.

National Board for Certified Counselors (NBCC). (1990). *National certified gerontological counselor application packet.* Greensboro, NC: Author.

National Board for Certified Counselors (NBCC). (2001). *National certified gerontological counselor application packet.* Greensboro, NC: Author.

O'Hanlon, W. H., & Weiner-Davis, M. (1989). *In search of solutions: A new direction in psychotherapy.* New York: Norton.

Pedersen, P. (1990). The multicultural perspective as a fourth force in counseling. *Journal of Mental Health Counseling, 12,* 93–94.

Posthuma, B. W. (1996). *Small groups in counseling and therapy.* Boston: Allyn & Bacon.

Salisbury, H. (1975). Counseling the elderly: A neglected area in counselor education and supervision. *Counselor Education and Supervision, 14,* 237–238.

Schlossberg, N. K., Waters, E. B., & Goodman, J. (1995). *Counseling adults in transition* (2nd ed.). New York: Springer.

SeniorJournal.com. (2003, February). Seniors online increase. Retrieved from http.//www.seniorjournal.com/

Shere, E. (1964). Group therapy with the very old. In R. Kastenbaum (Ed.), *New thoughts on old age.* New York: Springer.

Silver, A. (1950). Group psychotherapy with senile psychiatric patients. *Geriatrics, 5,* 147–150.

Talmon, M. (1990). *Single-session therapy: Maximizing the effect of the first (and often only) therapeutic encounter.* San Francisco: Jossey-Bass.

Thomas, M. C. (1991). Their past gives our present meaning: Their dreams are our future. *Journal for Specialists in Group Work, 16*(32).

Thomas, M. C., & Martin, V. (1992). Training counselors to facilitate the transitions of aging through group work. *Counselor Education and Supervision, 32,* 51–60.

Thomas, M. C., & Martin, V. (1997). Helping older adults age with integrity, empowerment and meaning through group counseling. In S. T. Gladding (Ed.), *New developments in group counseling* (pp. 43–45). Greensboro, NC: ERIC/CASS Publications.

Thomas, M. C., & Martin, V. (2004). *Hand me downs: Intergenerational work values.* Manuscript submitted for publication.

Thomas, M. C., Martin, V., Alexander, J. J., Cooley, F. R., & Loague, A. M. (2003). Using new attitudes and technology to change the developmental counseling focus for older populations. *Counseling and Human Development, 35(8)*, 1–8.

Walter, J. L., & Peller, J. E. (1992). *Becoming solution-focused in brief therapy.* New York: Brunner/Mazel.

Waters, E. B. (Ed.). (1990a). In-depth views of issues for aging [Special issue]. *Generations: Journal of the American Society on Aging, 14*(1).

Waters, E. B. (1990b). The life review: Strategies for working with individuals and groups. *Journal of Mental Health Counseling, 12,* 270–278.

Waters, E. B., & Goodman, J. (1990). *Empowering older adults: Practical strategies for counselors.* San Francisco: Jossey-Bass.

Yalom, I. (1985). *The theory and practice of group psychotherapy* (3rd ed.). New York: Basic Books.

Yalom, I., & Terrazas, F. (1968). Group therapy for psychotic elderly patients. *American Journal of Nursing, 68,* 190–194.

Zimpfer, D. G. (1987). Groups for the aging: Do they work? *Journal for Specialists in Group Work, 12,* 85–92.

Group Work: Gay, Lesbian, and Bisexual Clients

Bianca Puglia and Reese M. House

The counseling profession has been slow to respond to the mental health needs of gay, lesbian, and bisexual clients. Until 1973, the American Psychiatric Association labeled homosexuality as a form of mental illness. The American Psychological Association did the same until 1975. Today, the official position of the counseling profession is to train counselors to adopt an enlightened stance regarding sexual orientation. Counseling gays, lesbians, and bisexuals is like counseling other culturally different populations in that practitioners require culture-specific preparation, which in the past most counselor trainees did not receive (Buhrke, 1989; McDermott, Tyndall, & Lichtenberg, 1989). Counselors must make an effort to accurately understand the values, lifestyles, and cultural norms of gays, lesbians, and bisexuals (Gelberg & Chojnacki, 1996; Kasi, 2002).

In addition, counselors need to examine their own belief systems to ascertain whether they can offer unbiased counseling assistance to people with sexual orientations and behaviors that may be quite different from their own. Although many counselor training programs still are not providing trainees with the necessary skills, professional publications and workshops are available to improve the skills of professionals practicing in this area. In the emerging gay-affirmative atmosphere in the mental health field, it is becoming easier for counselors to develop the skills and sensitivity they need to appropriately counsel gay, lesbian, and bisexual clients.

This chapter deals with language and terminology issues related to gay, lesbian, and bisexual communities,

We would like to thank Jennie L. Miller for her contributions to this chapter in earlier editions.

including the cultures of sexual minorities in U.S. society; heterosexism; homophobia; gay, lesbian, and bisexual affirmative counseling; general group approaches with these populations; and specific groups for bisexuals, gays, and lesbians.

A WORD ABOUT WORDS

Language is important for what it communicates as well as what it implies. Throughout their lives, gays, lesbians, and bisexuals hear biased and offensive street language such as "queer," "faggot," "homo," "dyke," and "queen." This language affects the self-esteem of gays, lesbians, and bisexuals, stigmatizes them, and is just as offensive to these populations as ethnic slurs are to various ethnic populations.

Many individuals reject the term *homosexual* because it is used by dominant and often oppressing groups in our culture. Though it is commonly used in the professional literature, media, and popular fiction, the term *homosexual* reflects an inaccurately narrow, clinical focus on sexual conduct (Blumenfeld & Raymond, 1988). Thus, many regard this term as archaic, imprecise, and misleading (Krajeski, 1986). Typically, *homosexual* is used with a pejorative connotation; those who support or affirm sexual minorities seldom use the term.

The term *homoerotic*, sometimes used to describe individuals who prefer intimate emotional and physical relationships with persons of the same gender, is a similarly narrow term (Silberman & Hawkins, 1988). For these reasons, it is advisable not to use the terms *homosexual* and *homoerotic* to describe individuals. To say "He is a homosexual" or "She has a homoerotic nature" is as incomplete as saying "She is a heterosexual."

What constitutes appropriate language is subject to disagreement. One difference in opinion involves the terms *sexual preference* and *sexual orientation*. *Preference* implies that individuals choose to be gay, lesbian, or bisexual, and *orientation* suggests that sexual predisposition is innate (Blumenfeld & Raymond, 1988). Theories about the biological roots of sexual orientation have existed since the 19th century (Brookey, 2001). Some researchers support the idea that genes may influence or predispose sexual orientation but emphasize that environmental cues and social learning also play key roles (Bailey, 1995; Brookey, 2001; Byne, 1994; Johnston & Bell, 1995; LeVay & Hamer, 1994; Money, 1987).

Another topic of debate involves using *gay* as an umbrella term to describe gay men, lesbians, and bisexuals, as in "gay rights parade," "gay marriage," and "gay-affirmative counseling." Although this use of the term is meant to encompass gays, lesbians, and bisexuals, it is not always perceived as inclusive and tends to make lesbian women and bisexuals feel invisible. This usage also obscures the unique identities and issues of lesbians, gay men, and bisexuals. Nevertheless, using *gay* as an umbrella term has a practical benefit: As an adjective, *gay, lesbian, and bisexual* is more than a mouthful. We have attempted to balance the defects of using *gay* as an umbrella term with its practical advantage by using the umbrella term only as an adjective, not as a noun. We recognize that this compromise is not perfect and look forward to the emergence of an umbrella term that will be more generally inclusive and accepted.

Special consideration and care must be taken to include the term *bisexual* in our language. Only recently have bisexuals been included in theory and research about sexual orientation (Fox, 1995). As noted by Wolf (1992), "Bisexuality has been continually attacked as a nonentity, a transitional stage from heterosexuality to homosexuality or vice-versa, and as a denial of one's homosexuality" (p. 175). Bisexuals, however, see themselves as having a unique identity and prefer the word *bisexual*.

We recommend that counselors be as clear as possible in using the language. Group leaders have to be aware of their language choices and directly address the question of terminology with members. It is appropriate to ask: "How do you prefer to have your sexual orientation described?" "What terms would you like the group to use?" "How do you describe yourself?" These questions are respectful and imply to members that the leader is sensitive to the importance of language. This sensitivity indicates an openness in discussing issues of sexual orientation and sexual behavior.

CULTURAL TRENDS AND ISSUES OF SEXUAL MINORITIES

Hundreds of thousands of gay and lesbian Americans are openly integrated into our communities, families, and workplaces. Americans are not asked their sexual orientation when questioned by the U.S. Census Bureau. Therefore, exactly how many gay, lesbian, and bisexual people are living in the United States is difficult to determine. Information is compiled according to those who report living with a same-sex partner. According to the U.S. Census Bureau (2003), approximately 594,000 people were living in same-sex partnerships in the United States. Many individuals do not report same-gender activity because of the stigma attached to being nonheterosexual in U.S. society. Whatever the exact number of gays, lesbians, and bisexuals in the United States, this group is becoming more visible and active in the pursuit of equal rights.

Prior to the 1970s, gays, lesbians, and bisexuals were a largely invisible part of the American population. Remaining invisible was, to a large extent, a survival tactic. Most gays, lesbians, and bisexuals chose to avoid the stigma associated with disclosing their sexual orientation. "Hostility and discrimination at the hands of an unaccepting society created a climate of secrecy that did not permit challenges to the prevailing stereotypes" (Blumstein & Schwartz, 1983, p. 9). Over the past 25 years, gays, lesbians, and bisexuals developed a community identity to counteract the negative reactions from society. As evidence of this community, in 1969 there were 50 gay and lesbian organizations in the United States; in 1996, there were an estimated 3,000 lesbian, gay, and bisexual organizations active in North America (Brelin, 1996). That number continues to grow. An Internet search yields thousands of organizations available to the gay, lesbian, and bisexual community.

The increased public visibility has provoked a considerable anti-gay backlash throughout the United States. This most recent issue has taken the form of questioning the definition of marriage and whether it applies to gay, lesbian, or bisexual couples. According to Vaid (2001), "…engagement in cultural policy requires more than media visibility. It requires us to claim our full place in society—to engage in public debate on values, challenge sexism, defend religious pluralism, defend for others the inclusive and justice-based civil society we seek for ourselves" (p. 72).

As recently as the November 2004 election, 11 states joined several others in initiating bans on gay marriage (Roberts & Gibbons, 2004). In only 13 states do individuals perceived to be gay, lesbian, and bisexual have legal protection against discrimination in public and private employment (NOLO, 2004). Seven states prohibit discrimination based on sexual orientation but only in public employment, not private employment (NOLO, 2004). Career positions in teaching, the military, the police, and public office often are available only to those who pass as heterosexual. Gay civil union, too, is controversial in the United States. This lack of legal standing limits couples in a number of significant ways, including health insurance, hospital visitation, child custody, survivorship and estate, and other rights and benefits that are available only to married couples.

Many individuals and groups still believe that gays, lesbians, and bisexuals are committing a sin and have a difficult time accepting members of this community as a result of their religious beliefs (Lease & Shulman, 2003). Groups such as the Traditional Values Coalition post Internet articles and "fact-based reports" on the "dangers of homosexuals and homosexual behavior to children and our society."

Despite the anti-gay sentiments, the increasing openness of sexual minorities is mirrored by a slowly growing societal acceptance in the media. Television shows such as "Will & Grace," "Queer as Folk," and "Queer Eye for the Straight Guy" enjoy considerable success despite the themes of gay, lesbian, and bisexual issues. A 1996 Supreme Court decision ruled that Colorado's anti-gay Amendment 2 was unconstitutional. In September 1996, however, the U.S. Congress passed the Defense of Marriage Act, which overrides efforts by states to sanction same-sex marriage.

The Massachusetts Supreme Court decision in *Goodridge v. Department of Public Health* (2003) held that the state law barring same-sex marriage was unconstitutional under the Massachusetts constitution and ordered the legislature to remedy the discrimination within six months (NOLO, 2004). In February 2004, the court ruled that offering civil unions instead of civil marriage would not meet the requirements set forth in *Goodridge*. In May 2004, same-sex couples began to get marriage licenses and enter into civil marriages. At the time of this writing, the Massachusetts legislature is considering an amendment to its state constitution to forbid marriage between same-sex couples (NOLO, 2004).

Civil Unions, Domestic Partnerships, and Reciprocal Beneficiaries are legal classifications used in Vermont, New Jersey, California, and Hawaii to give some marriage-like rights to same-sex partners (NOLO, 2004). Even though public opinion is slowly shifting toward a more tolerant attitude toward sexual minorities, U.S. society still denigrates and discriminates against gays, lesbians, and bisexuals.

Heterosexism and Homophobia

> Unless we heal the homophobia and heterosexism deep in the
> hearts and minds of people, legislative efforts alone will not
> bring about any profound or lasting social change. (Williams,
> 1990, p. 15)

The most serious and prevalent problem that gay men, lesbians, and bisexuals face is homoprejudice based in heterosexism and homophobia (Hancock, 1995). *Heterosexism* refers to a set of political assumptions that empowers heterosexual persons, especially heterosexual white males, and excludes people who are openly gay, lesbian, or bisexual from social, religious, and political power. This system demands heterosexuality in return for first-class citizenship and forces nonheterosexuals into silence concerning this overriding facet of their lives (Mollenkott, 1985). Heterosexism also is seen when dominant groups pity sexual minorities as poor unfortunates who cannot help being the way they are (Blumenfeld & Raymond, 1988).

Because heterosexism is the societal norm in the United States, the assumption is that people will marry someone of the opposite sex. The media largely portray only heterosexual relationships as positive and satisfying. Teachers talk in class as though all students are heterosexual. These examples illustrate subtle and indirect ways by which heterosexuality is reinforced in the United States as the only viable, acceptable life option.

Homophobia, first defined by Weinberg in 1973, is an attitude of fear and loathing toward individuals perceived to be gay, lesbian, or bisexual. This belief system supports negative myths and stereotypes about these cultural minorities and maintains that discrimination based on sexual orientation is justified (Lapierre, 1990). Homophobic people downgrade, deny, stereotype, or ignore the existence of gays, lesbians, and bisexuals. Their responses range from telling or laughing at "queer" jokes to condoning, supporting, or participating in violent hate crimes committed against gays, popularly referred to as "fag bashing." These reactions create a devalued minority in the midst of a hostile society.

Internalized Homophobia

Gays, lesbians, and bisexuals often internalize the negative assumptions, attitudes, and prejudice common in the dominant culture. Internalized homophobia manifests itself in a variety of ways, including total denial of one's sexual orientation; contempt for or mistrust of openly gay, lesbian, or bisexual people; attempts to "pass" as heterosexual; increased fear; and withdrawal from friends and family. Individuals who internalize values of otherwise credible sources (such as friends, family, religious organizations, schools, and mass media) that differ from their own experience personal dissonance and low self-esteem, which becomes a major source of distress. Frequent symptoms of internalized homophobia are acute anxiety attacks, self-destructive use of alcohol and drugs, and missed work or therapy sessions. This self-hatred also can lead to depression, despair, or suicide (Kasi, 2002; Lapierre, 1990).

Counselor Homophobia

Counselors are a part of the culture that denies the existence of same-sex behaviors and/or teaches that these behaviors are morally repulsive and psychologically damaging. Furthermore, some of the counselors who are practicing today were educated at a time when homosexuality was classified as an illness. Therefore, it is not surprising that many counselors are homophobic and heterosexist and have not addressed or even recognized their own homoprejudice. Many practitioners continue to consider gays, lesbians, and bisexuals as abnormal, deviant, and in need of change.

Some counselors believe the goal of counseling with these populations is to reduce or eliminate "homosexual" behavior and substitute "heterosexual" behavior (Coleman & Remafedi, 1989; Herron, Kintner, Sollinger, & Trubowitz, 1985; Zucker, 2003). Some counselors assume that all of their clients are heterosexual. Other counselors are tolerant of nonheterosexuals but remain uninformed about issues pertaining to gays, lesbians, and bisexuals (Carl, 1992).

Although the counseling profession verbally supports a gay-affirmative position, counselors do not receive enough information about gay, lesbian, and bisexual issues in their counselor preparation programs to provide proper, adequate, and helpful services to sexual minorities (Betz & Fitzgerald, 1993; Buhrke, 1989; Kasi, 2002; Lynne, 2001; Moses & Hawkins, 1985; Newman, Dannenfelser, & Benishek, 2002). Therefore, practicing counselors have to reeducate themselves with regard to the specific issues and needs of their nonheterosexual clients.

Counselor educators must ensure that counselor preparation programs include information about and exposure to gay, lesbian, and bisexual issues. Trainees and educators alike may have to confront and overcome their own homophobic and heterosexist beliefs and behaviors. The questions in Figure 18.1 can help counselors, supervisors, and counselor educators identify their own biases about sexual orientation.

Gay-Affirmative Counseling

Gay-affirmative counseling is based on six interlocking assumptions, first articulated by Schwartz and Harstein (1986):

1. Being gay, lesbian, or bisexual is not a pathological condition.
2. The origins of sexual orientation are not clearly understood or completely known.
3. Gays, lesbians, and bisexuals lead fulfilling and satisfying lives.
4. There is a variety of gay, lesbian, and bisexual lifestyles.
5. Gays, lesbians, and bisexuals who come to counseling with no desire to change their sexual orientation should not be coerced into doing so.
6. Gay-affirmative individual and group counseling should be available.

Counselors who are sensitive to sexual orientation issues, and who have examined and challenged their own heterosexist and homophobic attitudes, are in a powerful position to help gays, lesbians, and bisexuals recognize and accept their sexual

1. Do you stop yourself from certain behavior because someone might think you are gay, lesbian, or bisexual? If yes, what kinds of behavior?
2. Do you ever intentionally do or say things so that people will think you are not gay, lesbian, or bisexual? If yes, what kinds of things?
3. If you are a parent, how would you (or do you) feel about having a lesbian daughter or a gay son?
4. How would you feel if you were to discover that one of your parents or parent figures, or a brother or sister, were gay, lesbian, or bisexual?
5. Are there any jobs, positions, or professions that you think lesbians, gays, or bisexuals should be barred from holding or entering? If yes, why so?
6. Would you go to a physician whom you knew to be or believed to be gay or lesbian if that person were of a different gender from you? If that person were of the same gender as you? If not, why not?
7. If someone you care about were to say to you, "I think I'm gay," would you suggest that the person see a therapist?
8. Would you wear a button that says "Don't assume I'm heterosexual"? If not, why not?
9. Can you think of three positive aspects of being gay, bisexual, or lesbian? Can you think of three negative aspects?
10. Have you ever laughed at a "queer" joke?

The following questions apply particularly to counseling in groups and suggest how easily values and assumptions can affect group leaders.

11. Do you assume that all members of your groups are heterosexual?
12. If a group member uses the term "partner," do you assume he or she is speaking of someone of the opposite sex?
13. If a group member uses a derogatory term for a gay or lesbian, do you let the comment pass unchallenged? What do you do when a group member uses a derogatory term for a racial minority?
14. If a group member is gay, lesbian, or bisexual, do you assume that all of his or her issues are somehow related to sexual orientation? Would you make the same assumption about heterosexual group members?
15. Do you assume that all of the past partners of members of your groups have been the same gender as the current partners?

Figure 18.1 *Personal Values Assessment: How Homophobic Are You?*

Source: From *Lesbian and Gay Issues: A Resource Manual for Social Workers*, edited by H. Hidalgo, T. Peterson, and N. J. Woodman, 1985, Washington, DC: National Association of Social Workers. Adapted by permission.

identity, improve their interpersonal and social functioning, and value themselves while living in a predominantly heterosexual society. Counselors who are unable to be open and sensitive to their client's sexual orientation are ethically obligated to refer gay, lesbian, and bisexual clients to other professionals (Chang, 2003).

Gay, Lesbian, and Bisexual Counselors

Until the late 1980s, heterosexuality was assumed to be the only suitable orientation for counselors in the United States (Rochlin, 1985). Today, the number of publicly identified gay, lesbian, and bisexual mental health professionals is growing. Many gays, lesbians, and bisexuals seek out gay, lesbian, or bisexual therapists because they are concerned that a heterosexual counselor's bias may keep the practitioner from providing appropriate care (Kus, 1990). It is becoming increasingly clear that well-prepared gay, lesbian, and bisexual counselors may better meet the needs of gay, lesbian, and bisexual clients because they provide mental health services based on the premise that gay people have legitimate mental health needs, rather than on the premise that homosexuality is wrong. Gay, lesbian, and bisexual professionals who come out can serve as role models, provide security for clients who want to see nonheterosexual counselors, and act as resource consultants in their professional and personal communities (Woodman & Lenna, 1980).

GROUPS AND ORGANIZATIONS IN THE GAY/LESBIAN/BISEXUAL COMMUNITY

> Lesbians and gay men have worked together at the local, regional, and national levels to build viable communities, to provide needed programs and services, to cope with an unprecedented health emergency, and to build a political power base for social change. (D'Augelli & Garnets, 1995, p. 306)

As gays, lesbians, and bisexuals have become more public about their sexual orientation, organized groups within the nonheterosexual community have become more common and more open. Gays and lesbians have taken the initiative and created organizations and groups to provide social support for members of their community. Although organized groups are less common in the bisexual community than in the gay or lesbian community, specific groups for bisexuals are increasing. Groups offer support to offset the isolation, oppression, and alienation of being gay, lesbian, or bisexual in U.S. society. Groups create a mini-culture in which the homoprejudice and homophobia that gays, bisexuals, and lesbians experience in the general culture are countered by social support.

Community service centers providing speakers' bureaus, hotlines, newsletters, information on community resources, referral, medical services, and other social activities such as dances and potlucks have emerged because gays, bisexuals, and lesbians often have unique and special needs that go unmet in the larger society (Blumenfeld & Raymond, 1988). Local gay newspapers list dozens of groups and organizations for bisexuals, gays, and lesbians. There are groups for women, men, racial and ethnic minorities, youth, older individuals, and persons in mixed orientation marriages (Brelin, 1996; Klein, 1990). There are groups that address coming out, relationships, career and life planning, and parenting. There are groups for parents of gays and lesbians, their children, and their spouses. In addition, there are groups addressing issues that are not necessarily related to sexual orientation, such as substance abuse and personal growth. All of these diverse groups in the gay community can be divided into three primary categories: common interest, self-help, and counseling (or therapy).

Common-Interest Groups

> The ultimate reward from developing a sense of community with other gay [or lesbian or bisexual] people is that you are no longer alone.... There are people who share your values. There are people to learn from and models to emulate.... There is the assurance of people who care and understand—people who can share familiar feelings and offer mutual support. (Clark, 1987, p. 104)

A multitude of common-interest groups is available to gays and lesbians. Examples include professional support groups for lawyers, social workers, teachers, health care providers, scientists, business owners, and artists. Organizations on many university and college campuses offer a number of group activities for gay, lesbian, and bisexual students. Also, most major religious denominations have groups that offer gays, bisexuals, and lesbians a way to participate in religious activities without homophobic overtones.

Other interest groups are organized around recreational activities, such as hiking, bowling, card games, music, and dancing. Political action committees (PACs) are another form of common interest group in which many gays, lesbians, and bisexuals are involved. PACs help empower the gay community and give members political strength and influence. All of these groups provide an opportunity for gays, bisexuals, and lesbians to be together and share common concerns and interests.

Self-Help Groups

> The self-help group functions for its members. It is organized around addressing a common concern. Individuals' separate agendas are transcended. Continual focusing on the common agenda leads to unity and a power base that is collectively sustaining and useful. (Eller & King, 1990, p. 330)

Self-help groups are effective for people who are stigmatized by the culture. These groups break down the sense of personal isolation caused by an unhealthy condition or habit and help disenfranchised individuals cope and change (Bringaze & White, 2001; Eller & King, 1990; Hall, 1985). Self-help groups are common in gay, lesbian, and bisexual communities and address a variety of issues, including alcoholism, drug addiction, incest survival, and eating disorders. Mainstream recovery groups such as Narcotics Anonymous, Cocaine Anonymous, Alcoholics Anonymous, Overeaters Anonymous, and Al-Anon often have groups specifically for gay and lesbian members. Some self-help groups address issues that are unique to the gay and lesbian experience, including coming-out groups, groups for children of gay or lesbian parents, and groups for parents of gay or lesbian children. During the past 15 years, support groups also have been developed for people living with AIDS (PLWAs) and their significant others.

Counseling Groups

> A therapy group can be a place of refuge, a place to share the most private aspects of oneself, a place to practice social skills, to get support for changing behavior. People go to groups for a variety of reasons, and that provides the diversity which makes groups so productive. (Hall, 1985, p. 68)

Gays, lesbians, and bisexuals become participants in counseling groups to address issues such as depression, anxiety disorders, panic attacks, self-esteem, sexual dysfunction, and personality disorders. Others join groups with themes of personal growth or relationship issues. Regardless of the specialty, group counseling is particularly effective with gays, lesbians, and bisexuals because groups offer a balance to the indifference and hostility of the general culture A therapeutic group environment fosters the development of a positive sexual identity (Bringaze & White, 2001). In counseling groups, gays, lesbians, and bisexuals can share their experiences and feelings and can find out how others cope with similar situations. As Lapierre (1990) noted, "Often creative forms of resolution of these kinds of negative feelings can be discovered through the group process" (p. 96).

Following the decision to participate in counseling, the first decision that gays, lesbians, and bisexuals must make is whether to attend a group organized specifically for gays, lesbians, or bisexuals or a group in which sexual orientation is not the basis for selection. When internalized homophobia is a major issue, all-gay, all-lesbian, or all-bisexual groups are more appropriate for dealing with adjustment difficulties (Conlin & Smith, 1985). Even in groups that do not specifically address sexual orientation, being gay, lesbian, or bisexual is apt to be an issue in the group. Gays, lesbians, and bisexuals who attend a group that is not organized around sexual orientation will have to decide whether and how to come out in the group. Coming out always involves risks. In counseling groups, many members will be accepting, but it is common for at least one person in the group to reject and abuse nonheterosexual members. Also, some groups have become engrossed with trying to change the sexual orientation of gay, lesbian, or bisexual members (Schwartz & Harstein, 1986; Yalom, 1995).

The distinction between counseling groups and self-help groups is sometimes confusing. One important difference is that counseling groups are almost always led by credentialed counselors who take an active role in the group. Because counselors are powerful facilitators in counseling groups, they must be sensitive to the group's attitudes and behaviors about gays, lesbians, and bisexuals. Leaders have a responsibility to recognize and confront homophobia and heterosexism among the group's members. Group leaders who fail to intervene with these issues are subtly expressing their own homophobia (Hall, 1985). Gays and lesbians frequently attend groups with a gay, lesbian, or bisexual leader or facilitator. If such groups are not available, gay-affirmative facilitators are needed to assist gays, lesbians, and bisexuals in mixed-orientation groups.

SPECIFIC GAY, LESBIAN, AND BISEXUAL COUNSELING GROUPS

> Groups are often advisable for sexual minorities who have had little or no contact with others like themselves. The group functions to "socialize" members. They typically provide a supportive atmosphere for knowledge and skill sharing about how to cope with various life problems. Groups are an important counter to the real and felt isolation which sexual minorities face in the larger social cultural milieu. (Klein, 1986, p. 28)

Groups help gay, lesbian, and bisexual members accomplish developmental tasks. They often are structured to help participants address and successfully accomplish the age-related and sexual-identity developmental tasks that all people face—sexuality, career, relationships, spirituality, parenting, aging. Although these tasks are not unique to sexual minorities, the lack of societal support systems for gay adults often exacerbates these issues. Counseling groups create a mini-culture in which the ignorance, prejudice, oppression, and homophobia that the general society directs toward gays, lesbians, and bisexuals are countered by support, acceptance, and universality. This group process allows group members to better understand and accept the issues of being gay, lesbian, or bisexual.

Human development theories identify the development of a distinct identity and a positive construct of self-worth as necessary for growth and development. Through an interactive process between the individual and his or her environment, people develop and define their identities and sense of self-worth. As gays, lesbians, and bisexuals question, "Who am I in this world?" and "How do I relate with others?" they face challenges and controversies directly related to their sexual orientation. Specific groups, such as those discussed in the following pages, can help members begin to arrive at answers to these questions.

Coming-Out Groups

> Being gay [or lesbian or bisexual] offers an uncommonly
> powerful catalyst for personal transformation. If we can stand
> the heat and give ourselves over to the full scope of the process
> of coming out, we will learn flexibility in the midst of life's chaos,
> paradox, and mystery. (Griffin, Wirth, & Wirth, 1986, p. 188)

The process of developing an identity as gay, lesbian, or bisexual is called *coming out*. As defined by D'Augelli; and Garnets (1995), "Coming out is a complex sequence of events through which individuals acknowledge, recognize, and label their sexual orientation and then disclose it to others throughout their lives" (p. 302). The first step is for the individual to come out to himself or herself by acknowledging feelings for the same gender. Then the individual has to decide whether to share his or her sexual orientation with others such as parents, friends, children, employers, and coworkers.

Coming out is difficult because gays, lesbians, and bisexuals typically are not born into gay, lesbian, or bisexual families. They suffer oppression alone, without benefit of advice or emotional support from relatives or friends. Most gays, lesbians, and bisexuals have few role models and no self-validating and visible culture on which to pattern themselves. Gays and lesbians often make statements such as, "As I became aware of my attraction for others of the same sex, I thought I was the only one with these feelings."

Each person must decide whether to identify as gay, lesbian, or bisexual. Those who choose to keep their sexual orientation secret are said to be "living in the closet." Maintaining such a secret existence supports internalized homophobia, shame, and guilt and reinforces a negative self-image by implying that certain feelings and aspects of being gay, lesbian, or bisexual are too shameful to disclose to anyone (Stone, 2003). Closeted gays, lesbians, and bisexuals lead constricted lives, constantly monitoring their thoughts, emotions, and responses. Hiding does irreparable harm to their sense of integrity and leaves them in a stressful and dissonant position that detracts from their mental health and well-being. Stress, depression, and substance abuse are all related clinically to maintaining a secret existence (Bringaze & White, 2001).

Individuals may decide to come out at any age. Some have indicated that they knew they were gay or lesbian as early as age 6 or 7. If they come out during the teenage years, development of sexual identity is congruent with adolescent development. But coming out as a teenager can be particularly difficult because adolescents are most often financially and emotionally dependent on their parents. In addition, parental and peer acceptance and approval are important to young people, and adolescents risk being disowned by parents or harassed by peers if they identify themselves as gay, lesbian, or bisexual (Silberman & Hawkins, 1988).

Many individuals do not come out until their later years and may not "enter their true adolescence until their chronological adolescence has long passed" (Coleman, 1985, p. 36). Some come out as senior citizens. Coming out is an identity crisis, and whenever it occurs, most gays, lesbians, and bisexuals will benefit from assistance with coming-out issues and developing a positive sense of self.

The stressors of addressing sexual orientation affect the function and quality of life no matter how far in or out of the closet gays, lesbians, and bisexuals are. Gays, lesbians, and bisexuals are under constant, conflicting pressure both to stay in and to come out of the closet. Every day they face decisions about whether to come out. For example, when coworkers are discussing what they did on the weekend, do gay, lesbian, and bisexual workers share with whom they spent time, or do they make up appropriate other-gender partners? At holiday times, do gays, lesbians, and bisexuals bring their partners to office parties and family dinners, or do they go alone and feign being unattached?

Gays, lesbians, and bisexuals frequently attend counseling groups to address coming-out issues in a supportive environment. These groups should focus on taking responsibility for the way one's life is developing. In groups, members can take steps to make connections with others and to move away from their isolation and secrecy.

No matter what the stage of development, coming-out groups provide an environment for members to address daily issues of being gay, lesbian, or bisexual. For example, a 45-year-old woman who has lived an active and "out" life as a lesbian may find that attending a coming-out group with people in different stages is invaluable in assessing her current issues. Group leaders must recognize the risk involved in sharing information about sexual orientation and remain sensitive to every member of the group.

Group leaders will find it useful to familiarize themselves with various coming-out models. Several provide a framework for understanding identity development for gays and lesbians (Cass, 1984; Coleman, 1985; Falco, 1987; Lewis, 1984; Sophie, 1987; Troiden, 1989). Leaders of coming-out groups, regardless of their sexual orientation, also come out in a sense when they lead these groups. They have to confront their own homophobia, face the coming-out issues in their own lives, and be comfortable discussing sexual issues, including their own sexual orientation, in the group. Otherwise they may find themselves impeding rather than helping the group process.

Youth Groups

> Models of groups for gay, lesbian and bisexual youth all suggest combining education and group interaction in a safe environment. Education is particularly important, to counter the homophobic myths and stereotypes gay and lesbian adolescents have internalized. The group also provides a place in which the adolescent can safely interact with other gay or lesbian teenagers, develop socialization skills, and combat isolation. (Hancock, 1995, p. 413)

Peer groups are important for all adolescents, and a number of organizations provide teenagers with opportunities to participate in groups. Most school, religious, and community groups, however, do not serve the special needs of youth who are struggling to identify themselves as gay, lesbian, or bisexual (Gerstel, Feraios, & Herdt, 1989). Actually, few groups are organized specifically to attract gay, lesbian, and bisexual teens (Unks, 1995). Most gay, lesbian, and bisexual teens have experienced rejection and discrimination by friends, family, church, and teachers; many also have experienced violence from their families, peers, or the community (Huebner, Rebchook, & Kegeles, 2004; Reynolds & Koski, 1995; Salzburg, 2004). The approval and inclusion that groups provide can be particularly important in helping gay, lesbian, and bisexual youth accomplish basic developmental tasks and in serving as an antidote to family difficulties, violence, hopelessness, and isolation.

Groups give gay, lesbian, and bisexual youth an opportunity to address issues of identifying themselves as gay, lesbian, and bisexual in society and to learn from and with other gay, lesbian, and bisexual teens. Sexual-minority youth typically lack positive role models and friends during their teenage years (Kus, 1990; Unks, 1995). The chance to compare experiences with other group members who are wrestling with similar identity issues enhances self-esteem and promotes emotional growth in all the participants (Gerstel et al., 1989).

Suicide

Gay, lesbian, and bisexual teens are at high risk for self-destructive behavior, including suicide (Frankowski, 2003).

> The occurrence of suicide among adolescent homosexuals is possibly the most widely publicized data about them. That this is the case is perhaps the cruelest irony in the chronicle of the woes of gay teens." (Unks, 1995, p. 7)

The National Youth Violence Prevention Organization (2002) reports that suicide is considered and attempted more seriously by gay, lesbian, and bisexual youth than by their heterosexual counterparts. This may be attributed to high incidences of depression, victimization, and substance abuse among gay teens. A youth group can act as a deterrent to suicide by providing teens with a safe place to talk about their experiences of being gay, lesbian, or bisexual in society.

Leaders of gay, lesbian, and bisexual teen groups must be prepared to address the issue of suicide in their groups. In some cases the leader may initiate the discussion to reassure members that the topic is not out-of-bounds. Group leaders also must be sensitive to the possibility that gay, lesbian, and bisexual teens exploring their sexual orientation may develop the misconception that suicide is the inevitable consequence of being nonheterosexual (Harbeck, 1995).

Coming Out

Another important issue for gay, lesbian, and bisexual adolescents is whether and how to come out to friends and family members. One fourth of gay, lesbian, and bisexual teens are homeless, and many have experienced rejection and even violence from peers and family members who were not accepting of their sexual orientation. A significant number of sexual-minority teens report that they have been physically assaulted, robbed, raped, and sexually abused (Savin-Williams, 1995). Most teen counseling groups spend considerable time discussing peer and family relationships and comparing various strategies and approaches. Members can explore their own thoughts and feelings with the group and elicit the group's feedback. As members make and implement decisions and share the reactions of those to whom they disclose, the group members gain new perspectives on their own choices.

The Los Angeles Program

Uribe (1995) described a model program developed by the Los Angeles Unified School District to address the needs of gay, lesbian, and bisexual students:

> The focus of the model is education, reduction of verbal and physical abuse, suicide prevention, and dissemination of accurate AIDS information. The method by which the model is carried out is workshops for teachers, counselors, and other support personnel, as well as support groups set up on each senior high school campus for students who are dealing with sexual orientation issues. The goal of the support groups is to improve self-esteem and provide affirmation for students who are suffering the effects of stigmatization and discrimination based on sexual orientation. (p. 204)

As this model reflects, programs focused on gay, lesbian, and bisexual teens often have to educate and involve school personnel and group facilitators as well as the teenagers. To be able to offer appropriate help to teens, adults in the teens' environment must be educated, sensitized, and helped to overcome their own homophobia and heterosexism. In the absence of such an approach, school administrators, public officials, and religious leaders may be actively hostile to the idea of gay, lesbian, and bisexual groups for young people. These adults can create an atmosphere of fear and paranoia—an atmosphere in which sexual-minority teens may hesitate to attend groups for fear of retribution and in which hostility from other teens is tolerated or even encouraged.

The Los Angeles program benefits from being located in a large, metropolitan area. Establishing and maintaining gay, lesbian, and bisexual youth groups in rural areas may be more difficult. In many small communities, these groups do not advertise their location and those who are interested are asked to phone for the time and place of meetings. Further, it may be difficult in rural areas to find group facilitators who are aware of the specific issues and needs of gay, lesbian, and bisexual youth (Ryan, 1990). Facilitators may not be familiar with or have ready access to resources. In these cases, group leaders will have to contact professional organizations, gay and lesbian task forces, and counselors who are more familiar with working with gays, lesbians, and bisexuals.

Leaders

Leaders serve a number of functions in counseling groups for gay, lesbian, and bisexual teens.

- They offer a stable hub, which is particularly important in a group in which the membership is likely to fluctuate.
- They reinforce and model the norms of confidentiality and safety within the group. These norms must be discussed explicitly whenever new people attend the group.
- They facilitate the group's process during discussions by modeling and reinforcing behaviors such as active listening and nonjudgmental acceptance of each group member.
- They can encourage linking between group members and can draw connections between what the members discuss.
- Leaders who are comfortable discussing their own sexual orientation in the group make a powerful statement and serve as positive role models for the members.

Group leaders may find that inevitably they have to advocate in the community (Frankowski, 2003; Stone, 2003). This can mean a number of things, from networking with school counselors about gay, lesbian, and bisexual students, to advocating at school board meetings for permission to advertise the group in the high school newspaper, to defending the group's existence in the "Letters to the Editor" section of local newspapers. Group leaders and the gay, lesbian, and bisexual group members alike often find themselves working as activists to promote change on a community level.

Couples Groups

Many gay and lesbian individuals live with a partner. Surveys indicate that 42.7% of lesbians and 23.5% of gay men cohabitate (Editors, 2005). With the continuation of the AIDS pandemic, more gay men are choosing to live monogamously with partners. Most often, the concerns that gay couples bring to group counseling are no different from the issues in heterosexual relationships—differences in socioeconomic and family backgrounds; differences in education, religion, or values; communication problems; previous relationships; illness; financial issues; individual emotional problems; sexual dysfunction; and jealousy. Lesbian and gay couples, however, face additional relationship problems related to their sexual orientation.

Gay and lesbian couples, as Forstein (1986) noted, "do not have the social, legal or moral sanctions that sustain opposite-sex couples. Thus, the development and maintenance of same-sex couples involves a commitment to a difficult process with many destructive internal and external forces in its path" (p. 105). For example, lesbian and gay couples frequently disagree about how open to be about their sexual orientation. One member of the couple may have come out to his or her family while the other has not. Gay and lesbian couples face a lack of visible role models for their relationship. They frequently express curiosity about how other couples deal with their everyday lives, and they bring up issues such as finances, social relationships, families, and sex.

Group counseling gives gay and lesbian couples opportunities to explore these unique relationship issues in a safe, supportive environment. Groups can help these couples look at what happens in a relationship when one member of the couple is more out of the closet than the other. Groups also can help them realize that despite a lack of modeling for gay and lesbian couples, which creates uncertainty about how to behave as a couple, the absence of strict, societal guidelines for same-sex couples allows for creativity in establishing ground rules for the relationship. The group leader and other group participants provide couples with mirrors of their relationship. The various group members offer each couple a variety of role models to consider. The group leader and group members can suggest books to read, videos to view, and lectures and other community events to attend to help couples explore alternative models of behavior.

Models for Gender-Specific Groups

Same-sex couples face the effects of societal sex- and gender-role stereotypes in their relationships. Gay couples tend to experience competition as a difficulty in relationships, while lesbian couples frequently have difficulty with fusion and separation (McCandlish, 1985; Silberman & Hawkins, 1988). Group leaders who work with male couples should know about the developmental model created by McWhirter and Mattison (1984). Their six-stage model describes and identifies the tasks that male couples encounter as they progress through predictable developmental stages in their relationship. Group facilitators working with lesbian couples may find the developmental model proposed by Clunis and Green (1993) helpful. Leaders might use these models in group counseling to assess whether the partners are moving at the same pace or are on different developmental tracks.

Domestic Violence

As a related issue, group leaders working with gay and lesbian couples may have to address the serious problem of violence and battering (Hammond, 1989; Hart, 1989; Island & Letellier, 1991; Peterman, 2003). Domestic violence is as frequent in gay and lesbian couples as it is in the society at large but has been grossly ignored and underreported (Island & Letellier, 1991; Peterman, 2003). Most victims tell no one, and authorities often fail to ask. Domestic violence is a taboo topic in U.S. society, especially in gay, lesbian, and bisexual communities (Peterman, 2003).

Battering has a profound impact on the victim. Closeness and equality in the relationship disappear, and fear, mistrust, and disillusionment take over. Counseling the victim and perpetrator of domestic violence in separate counseling groups is the ethical and effective way for group counselors to work with these couples. Although group couples counseling works effectively with most of the problems gay and lesbian couples face, domestic violence is an exception. As in all issues of violence, the victim's safety takes precedence over supporting the relationship or taking care of the batterer's current emotional needs.

Insisting on separate groups for the victim and perpetrator sends the clear message that the violence is not the victim's fault or responsibility. It also underscores the seriousness of the issue: Domestic violence is a crime, and the victim has the right, as with all crimes, to be protected from the perpetrator. Even if the couple requests to continue in the same group after disclosing an incident of domestic violence, the leader must refuse this request in order to provide safety and security for the victim.

Parenting Groups

Gays, lesbians, and bisexuals are becoming partners, having and rearing children, and challenging society's definition of what "family" means. Sometimes the children of these couples are born when one parent was in a heterosexual relationship. Increasingly, however, gay, lesbian, and bisexual couples are choosing to become parents and are bringing up their children in redefined families. Between 6 and 9 million children in the United States have one or two gay or lesbian parents (Stein, Perrin, & Potter, 2004).

Many of the difficulties of gay, lesbian, and bisexual parenting are the same stressors that heterosexual parents feel—jealousy, time spent with children, privacy, and communication. Stein et al. (2004) found that a parent's sexual orientation had little or no effect on a younger child's development and functioning. In blended families, parenting styles and responsibilities are common points of disagreement.

Other stressors are unique to gay, lesbian, and bisexual parents. Same-sex couples face difficulty if they wish to adopt children. Further, many states discriminate against gays, lesbians, and bisexuals in awarding child custody and visitation rights; in some states, these parents are considered unfit. Issues that arise for gay, lesbian, and bisexual parents who are in opposite-sex marriages include concerns about coming out to a wife or husband, to the children, and to other family members. Concerns about coming out also affect the children of gay and lesbian parents. Some children choose to hide their parent's sexuality from friends.

Gay Parents

Group counseling can help gay parents in several ways. Leaders may wish to introduce the group members to behavioral techniques to improve their child-rearing information or skills. In the group, members are surrounded by supportive people with whom they can explore specific parenting topics. The group also can problem solve and brainstorm about parenting strategies and share information on legal and other professional resources. Groups for gay fathers and lesbian mothers can be found in most urban communities and also in many rural areas.

Parents of Gay Children

Parents of gay, lesbian, and bisexual children may have difficulty accepting the sexual orientation of their children. A national organization, Parents and Friends of Lesbians and Gays (PFLAG), is a support and information network for these parents and coordinates local meetings at which parents can share the guilt, shock, and pain they may feel (Salzburg, 2004). These groups help parents overcome the cultural messages of rejection and hatred of gays and move toward acceptance and peace. The positive effects of these groups often exceed the groups' original intentions, and "the act of confronting homosexuality openly and courageously can become a source of freedom and fulfillment in the family" (Griffin et al., 1986, p. 9).

Children With Gay Parents

Children whose parents are gay, lesbian, or bisexual may have a number of issues of their own. Younger children may be confused about why their household is not like those they see in books, on television, or at their friends' homes. Older children may feel embarrassed about being different or uncertain about inviting friends home for fear of teasing or repercussions. Teenagers may try to make their parent(s) "pass" as heterosexual. Sometimes other parents restrict their children's friendships with children who live in same-sex households.

All of these issues can be dealt with effectively in children's groups. Some counselors may wish to consider running concurrent groups for children and their gay, lesbian, or bisexual parents. These groups can meet simultaneously with facilitators who help the children and parents process their own issues. The two groups can merge at the beginning or end of each or some of the sessions.

Drug and Alcohol Abuse Groups

Many mental health professionals assume that drug and alcohol abuse is higher in the gay, lesbian, and bisexual community than society as a whole. The research in this area, however, is sparse and has methodological limitations (Hughes, 2003; Paul, Stall, & Bloomfield, 1991). It is estimated that 1% of the more than 16 million people with substance abuse or dependency are gay, lesbian, or bisexual (Chang, 2003). Too often, lesbians, gay men, and bisexuals have sought and received treatment for relationship difficulties, depression, or anxiety without reporting or being asked about chemical abuse (Faltz, 1992). As a result, substance abuse problems are often unaddressed. Intake and assessment procedures with all clients should include questions about drinking and using drugs.

Internalized homophobia may explain the etiology and high incidence of alcoholism in gay men and lesbians (Browning, Reynolds, & Dworkin, 1991; Chang, 2003). Gays, lesbians, and bisexuals tend to misuse alcohol or drugs to ameliorate their feelings related to societal rejection, alienation, and stress (Deevey & Wall, 1992). Although the substance abuse may originate with internalized homophobia, counselors cannot work on a client's self-image while the client is drinking or using drugs. Accepting oneself as gay, lesbian, or bisexual does not typically happen during periods of abuse. Leaders can work with individuals in groups only after they have successfully treated the substance abuse problem—an approach consistent with that of other substance-abusing populations.

Gays, lesbians, and bisexuals who come to treatment groups that are not specifically targeted for sexual minorities may experience heightened shame and guilt as they start this new experience. Therefore, during the first group session, leaders should ask questions about the group members' sexual identity and behavior in a routine and nonjudgmental manner. By asking these questions, leaders give group members a choice about whether to reveal their sexual orientation. As noted by Finnegan and McNally (1987), "If the question [of sexual orientation] is not posed, gays or lesbians may feel heterosexuality is assumed and homosexuality is possibly unacceptable in this setting" (p. 61). Addressing sexual orientation in groups as a part of the treatment plan demonstrates sensitivity to sexual orientation issues.

Group leaders focusing on substance abuse issues should be familiar with local self-help groups and resources and be able to make appropriate referrals, because most gay, lesbian, and bisexual individuals will need to be in both counseling and self-help groups to stay clean and sober. Leaders must encourage group members to attend gay, lesbian, or gay-lesbian self-help group meetings (such as those identified earlier in this chapter) when these meetings are available.

HIV/AIDS Groups

The response of the gay, lesbian, and bisexual community to the HIV/AIDS pandemic provides a striking example of the importance of groups in the gay community. AIDS, first identified in 1981, is a usually fatal disease for which there is no known cure or immunization. Initially, gay men were the hardest-hit group in the United States. As of December 2002, there were more than 800,000 reported cases of AIDS in the United States (Centers for Disease Control and Prevention, 2004).

Groups in the gay community organized the initial, desperately needed support services for those affected by HIV/AIDS, generated the earliest self-help and safer-sex materials, and lobbied incessantly about the need for funds for care and research (McLaughlin, 1989). Gay men banded together, at first informally and then with increasing sophistication and organization, to provide and demand adequate, respectful care for their lovers and friends. The lesbian and bisexual communities responded similarly and also have been actively involved in HIV/AIDS support services.

Groups help with transportation, deliver meals, and run errands for people living with AIDS (PLWAs). Self-help and support groups were formed as well for people who were HIV positive; for PLWAs; for the friends and families, spouses and lovers, and grieving survivors of PLWAs; and for the health care providers, counselors, volunteers, and neighbors who care for people living with and dying from AIDS. Today, AIDS care continues to be provided by community groups that supplement existing services and in some instances substitute for the institutionalized medical and support services that do not exist for PLWAs.

With the advent of antiviral therapies, HIV-positive clients and PLWAs are surviving longer than before. Group leaders will have to focus on maintenance and health promotion to increase the function and quality of life for group participants (Kaplan, Tomaszewski, & Gorin, 2004).

Support Groups for PLWAs, Families, and Friends

Most mental health professionals and physicians see support groups for HIV-positive people and PLWAs as an essential element for optimum care. Eller and King

(1990) noted, "Another patient [sic] can do more toward relieving another's nagging fear than a host of health professionals" (p. 332). Support groups extend the participants' circle of support (Price, Omizo, & Hammett, 1986) and offer a powerful antidote to the isolation and alienation that PLWAs often encounter (Morin, Charles, & Malyon, 1984). In support groups, members can discuss problems related to their HIV status and share their feelings and thoughts.

Support groups provide friends and family members of PLWAs with the opportunity to vent their anger, frustrations, and sorrows regarding the illness and its effects on their lives in a safe and accepting environment (Martin, 1989). Friends and family often face issues that are similar to those confronted by PLWAs. In addition, friends and family members must deal with the exhaustion from physical caregiving, the anxiety of wondering what will happen next, and the stress of financial responsibility for a disease for which long-term costs can run into the hundreds of thousands of dollars. Support groups for significant others often are led by professionals who act as facilitators or by family members who act as peer facilitators.

Counseling Groups for PLWAs

In most counseling groups for HIV-positive people and PLWAs, members spend time discussing their individual reactions to the diagnosis and the reactions of friends and family members. The AIDS diagnosis may force PLWAs, families, and friends to face issues they previously avoided, such as sexual orientation and drug use. There are often efforts to keep the AIDS diagnosis a secret from certain family members or from people outside the family because of fears of rejection, stigma, retaliation, and isolation. Family members may try to exclude gay friends or lovers. All of these responses are brought to the group to be shared and addressed.

Other issues that group members may consider include anger, guilt, and grief over their own loss of health; the deaths of friends and loved ones and their own approaching death; recurring denial about their illness; safer sex behaviors; and the need for decision making about burial and funeral matters. The counselor has to be sensitive to the varying extent of normal distress that HIV-positive individuals experience so he or she will neither overreact to typical expressions of grief, anger, and anxiety nor minimize or ignore statements or behaviors indicating that an individual is in need of crisis intervention.

Counseling groups for PLWAs and HIV-positive individuals are closed and time limited, usually lasting 6 to 10 weeks. For people facing life-threatening illness, this group format provides stability, which reinforces their attempts to become empowered and hopeful. It also offers consistency, which is important in developing social support, trust, and comfort within the group. Group members may look at a number of different issues, including relationship issues, existential issues raised by their illness, the challenge of making lifestyle changes, or their own death and dying. The group members may vary in health status. Some may be asymptomatic, others may have had medical crises but are doing well currently, and still others may be having active illness symptoms or may develop them during the course of the group.

Whenever possible, group leaders should schedule a pre-group interview with each potential member to explain the goals and structure of the group and to assess for issues such as clinical depression, suicidal ideation, and substance abuse. Potential group members exhibiting these behaviors may not be appropriate for the group. Even though screening interviews are not always possible, preregistration is essential with a closed, time-limited group.

A GROUP MODEL FOR GAY MEN

Groups are especially helpful for people soon after they are diagnosed as HIV positive (Rabkin, Remien, & Wilson, 1994). The diagnosis almost always results in a personal crisis, and a group can help newly diagnosed individuals adjust by providing two important elements:

1. Information about HIV, treatments, and sources of support available locally
2. The chance to talk about the experience of being HIV positive in a safe, nonjudgmental atmosphere

Research has shown that with competent counseling and support, the initial anxiety and depression following an HIV-positive diagnosis dissipates in 6 to 8 weeks (Perry et al., 1993).

While urban areas may have enough HIV-positive people to offer specialized groups for newly diagnosed gay men (e.g., HIV-positive gay men with HIV-negative partners, HIV-positive but asymptomatic gay men, and dual-diagnosis HIV-positive gay men), in many parts of the country there may not even be separate groups for gay men. In smaller communities and in other areas with a low HIV population, groups for individuals newly diagnosed as HIV positive may include members of all risk groups and both sexes.

Nevertheless, when gay-specific groups are possible, they have advantages. Gay men who are HIV positive face several unique issues, including the combined stresses of the stigma of living with HIV and being gay, dilemmas about simultaneously disclosing sexual orientation and HIV status, and the deaths of friends from AIDS. These issues are more apt to be discussed in gay-only groups than in mixed groups.

The Sequence

The following is a suggested sequence for a seven-session group for gay men recently diagnosed as HIV positive.

Session 1: Telling the Diagnosis Story

The leader welcomes the group members and discusses the ground rules and structure of the group. Confidentiality and safety are emphasized at this and subsequent sessions. Each member tells the group how he came to be tested for HIV and what it was like getting the results. Some men will have chosen to be tested. Others may have been tested by medical care providers without their knowledge or consent. Telling their stories is apt to be an emotionally intense experience for all of the group participants. The leader has to pace the group to be sure that each member has time to tell his story.

Afterward, the leader facilitates a group discussion in which each member responds to the following two statements:

"The biggest change in my life since I was diagnosed is _____."
"Right now, the hardest thing about being HIV positive is _____."

Following the discussion, the leader can have the group build the agenda for the following six sessions. Alternatively, the leader could develop a schedule based on the needs identified by group members.

Session 2: Decisions About Disclosing HIV-Positive Status

Disclosure is one of the most important issues facing individuals who are HIV positive. The group leader introduces the topic of disclosure and identifies pros and cons. Disclosure generally makes support and assistance more available (Herek, 1990), whereas secrecy tends to lead to more distress and depression (Namir, 1989). Still, there are good reasons to be cautious in disclosing, because it may have negative consequences (Kain, 1996; Kaplan et al., 2004). The group leader asks members to identify people they believe it is important to tell about their HIV status—sexual partners, employers, coworkers, parents, children, other family members, neighbors, landlords.

The leader then introduces an exercise to help group members make decisions about disclosure. Each group members writes a list of 10 people and rates them along a continuum from "They already know" to "I will never tell them." They place in the middle of the continuum the names of people they may or may not tell. The group members can discuss the possible consequences of disclosing to these people and the possible consequences of not disclosing to them. The leader may ask group members to consider what might make it easier for them to disclose to these people by discussing how they would complete the sentence, "I would tell _____ if _____ were to change."

Session 3: Dealing With Emotions

In this session, group members have a chance to focus on the range of emotional responses that are typical after an HIV diagnosis. Hearing other group members express anxieties similar to their own actually may be reassuring. The discussion probably will focus on at least the following emotions: denial and disbelief, fatalism, anger, shame and guilt, and fear. The group leader can guide the group to look at how each emotion can serve a helpful function. For example, anger at the medical establishment can be helpful if it motivates a group member to become an informed consumer of medical care or to change doctors.

If positive feelings are not brought up, the group leader invites participants to discuss any positive feelings that have resulted from their diagnosis. The group members sometimes express relief at *knowing* rather than wondering if they are HIV positive and say they find it easier to plan their future. Some people who have lost friends or family members may say that being HIV positive has eliminated the survivor guilt they felt about being the only one in a circle of friends who tested negative.

Session 4: Community Resources and Financial Information

In this session, members learn about HIV-specific programs run by the health department and other local government agencies. The leader also provides information about entitlement programs, including Social Security Supplemental Income (SSI), Social Security Disability (SSD), Medicaid, Medicare, and Ryan White funds. The group leader must have current data on requirements for the various programs, as well as basic information including phone numbers, applications, and names of individuals to contact.

The group leader might want to invite to this session a resource person who can give accurate, comprehensive information about resources. It may be best to have this presentation early in the session so the group can process the information after the expert leaves.

In larger population centers, AIDS organizations may offer resource training meetings. If these meetings are available, the group leader can recommend them to the members, and this group session can be spent on psychosocial issues instead of resources.

Session 5: Self-Care

Self-care topics addressed in this session might be nutrition, safer sex practices, avoiding infections, alternative therapies, choosing a physician and evaluating medical treatment, negotiating changes in work responsibilities, changing substance-use behaviors, and stress reduction techniques. The group leader might want to provide information or bring experts to the session to assist with these issues.

In addition, participants are encouraged to look at their natural support systems in the context of who might be able to provide what type of assistance. The group leader encourages members to identify and/or develop a network of people who can provide practical assistance and emotional understanding and encouragement.

Session 6: Long-Term Planning

In this session, the leader introduces long-term planning issues that people with serious illnesses must consider, including advance health directives, power of attorney for health care, power of attorney, legal wills, long-term financial planning, and insurance options. It is particularly important for gay men to identify whom they want to involve in making decisions about their care and how they want their resources used. For example, legal wills should be completed as early after diagnosis as possible, because in some instances biological family members have challenged wills to prevent gay partners from receiving inheritances.

Some professionals consider these topics "unnecessarily upsetting" (Rabkin et al., 1994, p. 149) and defer the discussion until an individual is seriously ill. But the best time to consider these subjects and make plans is not during a serious illness

(Kain, 1996). By discussing them in a group of newly diagnosed HIV-positive people, the group leader models that long-range planning is simply one more component of good self-care.

Some group members will not be aware of all of the health care choices they have and will feel more in control of their future knowing how much say they have in their treatment throughout the course of their illness. The leader should allow enough time for group members to discuss their emotions and reactions resulting from the discussion.

At the end of this session, the leader reminds the members that the next session will be the last one and encourages them to think about what they would like to say before the group ends. The group may want to plan a celebratory element—a potluck at the beginning, or a dessert at the end of the final group session, or a ritual to acknowledge the significance of the group.

Session 7: Facing the Future

Endings have a special poignancy for people with a life-threatening illness. For some participants, the group may have been the first environment in which they could talk about their diagnosis, and for some members the group may still be the only place where they can be completely candid.

The group leader introduces a two-part exercise to help members validate the sense of loss they may be feeling. In this exercise, each member is asked to complete this sentence:

"One thing I will really miss about the group is_____."

After sharing their responses, each person completes this sentence:

"One thing I will not miss about this group is_____."

Next the leader facilitates a discussion of the most helpful elements of the past six sessions. The leader may find it useful to return to the exercise conducted in the first session and ask the men to complete the sentence:

"Right now, the hardest thing about being HIV positive is _____."

Most of the group members will list a different concern now, underscoring how quickly things can change when living with HIV.

The leader also can encourage the members to look ahead and make appropriate plans for the future. Several different exercises can be used. Group members may discuss, as a group or in pairs, their plans for the next month, 6 months from now, and a year from now. The group can do goal-setting exercises, listing what they want to accomplish or what is most important to them.

At the end of this final session, the leader ties up any loose ends. These may involve providing the phone number of the local AIDS hotline, the address of a pharmaceutical company that has a drug give-away program, and information on annuities. Participants are reminded of where they can get additional support and how to locate services they do not now need but may need at some time in the future.

GROUPS FOR OLDER GAY MEN, LESBIANS, AND BISEXUALS

The assumption that aging is synonymous with decline becomes particularly negative when generalized to older lesbians, gay men, and bisexuals who have been incorrectly portrayed as lonely and pathetically miserable. Such myths and stereotypes are not substantiated by research on the lives of older gay men and lesbians. (Reid, 1995, p. 215)

Until recently, older lesbians and gay men were generally ignored by gerontologists and social scientists. Little research was available on these populations, and services geared to their special situations rarely existed (Berger, 1996; Editors, 2005; Reid, 1995). The gay, lesbian, and bisexual community and mental health professionals alike have tended to overlook the needs of elderly gays, lesbians, and bisexuals. More recently, however, "the increased visibility and demands for civil rights by the gay, lesbian, and bisexual community have directed increasing attention to the sizable numbers of older bisexuals, lesbians, and gay men living, working, and contributing to the society in which they live" (Reid, 1995, p. 217).

As we learn more about these individuals, the stereotypes and myths of older gays and lesbians living isolated and lonely lives are giving way to greater understanding. Older gay men and lesbians are not inevitably alone and unhappy. Many have created alternative families that provide friendship and support (Shippy, Cantor, & Brennan, 2004). Most often they are integrated into their community as "out" gay men, lesbians, or bisexuals. As Friend (1991) pointed out, successful aging in gay men and lesbians is related to having a positive lesbian or gay identity. Those who reject the values of a homophobic culture and reconstruct a new meaning have been called "affirmative" older lesbians and gay men (Friend, 1991). Some older gays, lesbians, and bisexuals, however, choose not to be public about their homosexuality and to remain "in the closet." These individuals face more challenges as they confront the last years of their lives.

Older gays and lesbians face issues of aging similar to those faced by all older adults (Shippy et al., 2004), including the aging process and physical changes of aging, sensible nutrition, sex as an older adult, issues of ageism, managing finances, bereavement overload, and in some cases, isolation and loneliness. Other issues are related more specifically to aging as a sexual minority such as heterosexism/homophobia in terms of housing, job discrimination, social/human services, and institutional support. These include legal issues because same-sex relationships are not sanctioned by law. These couples need to make specific financial plans so that when one partner dies, the other will not lose the possessions and property that the two purchased together. Other arrangements, such as power of attorney for health care and hospital visitation agreements, have to be considered, discussed with family and lovers, and instituted.

Groups for older gay men, lesbians, and bisexuals have emerged to address issues of aging. These groups provide older gays, lesbians, and bisexuals with opportunities for peer sharing, socialization, and social activities. Group leaders must be aware of the variability among older gays, lesbians, and bisexuals. As Reid (1995) noted, "The recipe for a successful program is not the same for all individuals.... What is needed is an increasing variety of choices of programs and services within the community" (p. 230).

Programs or groups in urban areas may address the specific needs of older gays and lesbians. The Gay Community Services Center in Minneapolis with its Affectional Preference and Aging program, the Gay and Lesbian Outreach to Elders (GLOE) organization in San Francisco, and the Senior Action in a Gay Environment (SAGE) organization in New York City all use groups as a way to reach out to older gays and lesbians. These and similar organizations provide a variety of social activities and social support, assist with managing chronic health problems, provide transportation for homebound older adults, offer bereavement counseling, and help fight discriminatory policies in nursing homes and hospitals (D'Augelli & Garnets, 1995). In less populated areas lacking special programs and groups for older gays, lesbians, and bisexuals, group leaders will have to address these issues in a mixed-orientation group.

PERSONAL GROWTH GROUPS

Personal growth groups can be a resource and refuge for gay, lesbian, and bisexual individuals who receive limited support from friends, parents, siblings, or family members. In personal growth groups, members address their feelings of guilt and internalized homophobia. They learn to take responsibility for themselves rather than blaming society and the people in their lives for the awful state of "my world." Growth groups help members address the anger they feel toward society. Group members who learn to express their anger in positive ways are more apt to avoid the inward expressions of anger often associated with loneliness, substance abuse, and suicidal ideation.

Gays, bisexuals, and lesbians must stop asking the question "Why me?" and begin to affirm their sexual orientation. The group can encourage self-affirmative statements that allow members to embrace being gay, lesbian, or bisexual. Honest discussion in groups is liberating and lays the foundation for honest and direct interaction with other people. The ultimate reward for developing this sense of community within gay, lesbian, and bisexual personal growth groups is learning that one does not have to fight these issues alone.

LEARNING ACTIVITIES

1. You hear one of the professors in your counseling program make negative remarks about gays, lesbians, and bisexuals. These remarks are in conflict with current ethical standards and contrary to what you have heard from other professors. How would you respond to this situation?

2. In small groups, share your experiences with individuals who are gay, lesbian, or bisexual. How do these individuals support or differ from societal stereotypes? How comfortable are (were) you interacting with them?
3. On the Internet, find as many types of resources as you can for one of the various types of groups and resources for gay, lesbian, and bisexual individuals discussed in this chapter.
4. In a small group, role-play a group in which one individual is the group leader and the others in the group are gay, lesbian, and bisexual youth struggling with issues surrounding their sexual orientation. Afterward, discuss the process and outcomes of the role play.

SUMMARY

Professional groups have been slow to respond to gay, lesbian, and bisexual individuals and their unique concerns. This mirrors the attitudes of the American public, which continues to favor heterosexism. As a product of homophobia, some gays and lesbians have internalized society's negative attitudes and deny their own sexual orientation. Some counseling professionals have adopted heterosexist and homophobic attitudes as well.

What is needed is gay-affirmative counseling, in which leaders create an atmosphere of tolerance, acceptance, and advocacy. Effective group leaders are sensitive to gay, lesbian, and bisexual concerns, openly address sexual orientation issues, and create and model norms of nonjudgmental acceptance and tolerance of all group members. Some groups, particularly couples groups, might best be led by gay, lesbian, or bisexual professional counselors.

Types of groups in which sexual minorities can find support include common-interest groups, self-help groups, and counseling groups. Specific gay, lesbian, and bisexual groups include coming-out groups, youth groups, couples groups, parenting groups, drug and alcohol abuse groups, aging groups, and AIDS groups. Self-help and support groups have been developed for HIV-positive individuals; for PLWAs; for families, friends, and survivors of PLWAs; and for health care workers who care for people living and dying with AIDS.

USEFUL WEB SITES

☐ The National Gay and Lesbian Task Force
www.thetaskforce.org
☐ Parents, Families and Friends of Lesbians and Gays
www.pflag.org
☐ The National Coalition for Gay, Lesbian, Bisexual and Transgender Youth
www.outproud.org

REFERENCES

Bailey, J. M. (1995). Biological perspectives on sexual orientation. In A. R. D'Augelli & C. J. Patterson (Eds.), *Lesbian, gay, and bisexual identities over the lifespan: Psychological perspectives* (pp. 102–135). New York: Oxford University Press.

Berger, R. M. (1996). *Gay & gray: The older homosexual man* (2nd ed.). New York: Harrington Press.

Betz, N. E., & Fitzgerald, L. F. (1993). Individuality and diversity: Theory and research in counseling psychology. *Annual Review of Psychology, 44,* 343–381.

Blumenfeld, W. J., & Raymond, D. (1988). *Looking at gay and lesbian life.* Boston: Beacon Press.

Blumstein, P., & Schwartz, P. (1983). *American couples.* New York: William Morrow.

Brelin, C. (1996). *Strength in numbers: A lesbian, gay, and bisexual resource.* Detroit: Visible Ink Press.

Bringaze, T. B., & White, L. J. (2001). Living out proud: Factors contributing to healthy identity development in lesbian leaders. *Journal of Mental Health Counseling, 23*(2), 162–173.

Brookey, R. A. (2001). Bio-rhetoric, background beliefs and the biology of homosexuality. *Argumentation & Advocacy, 37*(4), 171–184.

Browning, C., Reynolds, A. L., & Dworkin, S. H. (1991). Affirmative psychotherapy for lesbian women. *Counseling Psychologist, 19,* 177–196.

Buhrke, R. A. (1989). Incorporating lesbian and gay issues into counselor training: A resource guide. *Journal of Counseling and Development, 68,* 77–80.

Byne, W. (1994, May). The biological evidence challenged. *Scientific American,* pp. 50–55.

Carl, D. (1992). *Counseling same-sex couples.* New York: Norton.

Cass, V. C. (1984). Homosexual identity formation: A concept in need of definition. *Journal of Homosexuality, 10,* 105–126.

Centers for Disease Control and Prevention. (2004). Retrieved July 19, 2005, from http://www.cdc.gov/hiv/stats.htm

Chang, Z. (2003). Issues and standards for counseling lesbians and gay men with substance abuse concerns. *Journal of Mental Health Counseling, 25*(4), 323–326.

Clark, D. (1987). *The new loving someone gay.* Berkeley, CA: Celestial Arts.

Clunis, D. M., & Green, G. D. (1993). *Lesbian couples.* Seattle: Seal Press.

Coleman, E. (1985). Developmental stages of the coming out process. In J. C. Gonsiorek (Ed.), *A guide to psychotherapy with gay and lesbian clients* (pp. 31–43). New York: Harrington Park Press.

Coleman, E., & Remafedi, G. (1989). Gay, lesbian and bisexual adolescents: A critical challenge to counselors. *Journal of Counseling and Development, 68,* 36–40.

Conlin, D., & Smith, J. (1985). Group psychotherapy for gay men. In J. C. Gonsiorek (Ed.), *A guide to psychotherapy with gay and lesbian clients* (pp. 105–112). New York: Harrington Park Press.

D'Augelli, A. R., & Garnets, L. D. (1995). Lesbian, gay, and bisexual communities. In A. R. D'Augelli & C. J. Patterson (Eds.), *Lesbian, gay, and bisexual identities over the lifespan: Psychological perspectives* (pp. 293–320). New York: Oxford University Press.

Deevey, S., & Wall, L. J. (1992). How do lesbian women develop serenity? *Health Care for Women International, 74,* 239–247.

Defense of Marriage Act, 1996. H.R. 3396 (Lectlaw, 2005).

Dworkin, S. H., & Pincu, L. (1993). Counseling in the area of AIDS. *Journal of Counseling and Development, 71,* 275–281.

Editors. (2005). Survey says. *The Gay and Lesbian Review Worldwide, 12*(1), 17–21.

Eller, M., & King, D. J. (1990). Self-help groups for gays, lesbians, and their loved ones. In R. J. Kus (Ed.), *Keys to caring* (pp. 330–339). Boston: Alyson Publications.

Falco, K. (1987). *Psychotherapy with lesbian clients: A manual for the psychotherapist.* Unpublished doctoral dissertation, Oregon Graduate School of Professional Psychology, Pacific University, Forest Grove.

Faltz, B. G. (1992). Counseling chemically dependent lesbians and gay men. In S. Dworkin & F. Gutierrez (Eds.), *Counseling gay men and lesbians: Journey to the end of the rainbow* (pp. 245–258). Alexandria, VA: American Counseling Association.

Finnegan, D. G., & McNally, E. B. (1987). *Dual identities: Counseling chemically dependent gay men and lesbians.* Center City, MN: Hazelden.

Forstein, M. (1986). Psychodynamic psychotherapy with gay male couples. In T. S. Stein & C. J. Cohen (Eds.), *Contemporary perspectives on psychotherapy with lesbians and gay men (pp. 103–137).* New York: Plenum.

Fox, R. C. (1995). Bisexual identities. In A. R. D'Augelli & C. J. Patterson (Eds.), *Lesbian, gay and bisexual identities over the lifespan: Psychological perspectives* (pp. 48–86). New York: Oxford University Press.

Frankowski, B. L. (2003). Sexual orientation and adolescents. *Pediatrics, 113*(6), 1827–1832.

Friend, R. A. (1991). Older lesbian and gay people: A theory of successful aging. In J. A. Lee (Ed.), *Gay midlife and maturity* (pp. 99–118). New York: Haworth Press.

Gelberg, S., & Chojnacki, J. T. (1996). *Career and life planning with gay, lesbian, and bisexual persons.* Alexandria, VA: American Counseling Association.

Gerstel, C. J., Feraios, A. J., & Herdt, G. (1989). Widening circles: An ethnographic profile of a youth group. In G. Herdt (Ed.), *Gay and lesbian youth* (pp. 75–92). New York: Harrington Park Press.

Goodridge v. Department of Public Health, SJC-08860. Supreme Judicial Court of Massachusetts LEXIS 814 (November 18, 2003).

Griffin, C. W., Wirth, M. J., & Wirth, A. G. (1986). *Beyond acceptance: Parents of lesbians and gays talk about their experiences.* New York: St. Martin's.

Hall, M. (1985). *The lavender couch: A consumer's guide to psychotherapy for lesbians and gay men.* Boston: Alyson Publications.

Hammond, N. (1989). Lesbian victims of relationship violence. In E. D. Rothblum & E. Cole (Eds.), *Lesbianism: Affirming nontraditional roles* (pp. 89–105). New York: Haworth Press.

Hancock, K. A. (1995). Psychotherapy with lesbians and gay men. In A. R. D'Augelli & C. J. Patterson (Eds.), *Lesbian, gay, and bisexual identities over the lifespan: Psychological perspectives* (pp. 398–432). New York: Oxford University Press.

Harbeck, K. M. (1995). Invisible no more: Addressing the needs of lesbian, gay, and bisexual youth and their advocates. In G. Unks (Ed.), *The gay teen: Educational practice and theory for lesbian, gay, and bisexual adolescents* (pp. 125–134). New York: Routledge.

Hart, B. (1989). Lesbian battering: An examination. In K. Lobel (Ed.), *Naming the violence: Speaking out about lesbian battering* (pp. 173–189). Seattle: Seal Press.

Herek, G. M. (1990). Illness, stigma, and AIDS. In P. T. Costa & G. R. Vandal Boos (Eds.), *Psychological aspects of serious illness: Chronic conditions, fatal diseases, and clinical care/master lectures* (pp. 105–150). Washington, DC: American Psychological Association.

Herron, W. G., Kintner, T., Sollinger, I., & Trubowitz, J. (1985). Psychoanalytic psychotherapy for homosexual clients: New concepts. In J. C. Gonsiorek (Ed.), *A guide to psychotherapy with gay and lesbian clients* (pp. 177–192). New York: Harrington Park Press.

Hidalgo, H., Peterson, T., & Woodman, N. J. (Eds.). (1985). *Lesbian and gay issues: A resource manual for social workers.* Washington, DC: National Association of Social Workers.

Huebner, D. M., Rebchook, G. M., & Kegeles, S. M. (2004). Experiences of harassment, discrimination, and physical violence among young gay and bisexual men. *American Journal of Public Health, 94*(7), 1200–1204.

Hughes, T. (2003). Lesbians' drinking patterns: Beyond the data. *Substance Use & Misuse, 38*, 1739–1758.

Island, D., & Letellier, P. (1991). *Men who beat the men who love them: Battered gay men and domestic violence.* New York: Haworth Press.

Johnston, M. W., & Bell, A. P. (1995). Romantic emotional attachment: Additional factors in the development of the sexual orientation of men. *Journal of Counseling and Development, 73*, 621–625.

Kain, C. D. (1996). *Positive: HIV-affirmative counseling.* Alexandria, VA: American Counseling Association.

Kaplan, L., Tomaszewski, E., & Gorin, S. (2004). Current trends and the future of HIV/AIDS services: A social work perspective. *Health & Social Work, 29*(2), 158–165.

Kasi, C. S. (2002). Special issues in counseling lesbian women for sexual addiction, compulsivity, and sexual codependency. *Sexual Addiction & Compulsivity, 9,* 191–208.

Klein, C. (1986). *Counseling our own: The lesbian/gay subculture meets the mental health system.* Renton, WA: Publication Service.

Klein, C. (1990). Gay and lesbian counseling centers: History and functions. In R. J. Kus (Ed.), *Keys to caring* (pp. 312–320). Boston: Alyson Publications.

Krajeski, J. P. (1986). Psychotherapy with gay men and lesbians: A history of controversy. In T. S. Stein & C. J. Cohen (Eds.), *Contemporary perspectives on psychotherapy with lesbians and gay men* (pp. 9–25). New York: Plenum.

Kus, R. J. (Ed.). (1990). *Keys to caring: Assisting your gay and lesbian clients.* Boston: Alyson Publications.

Lapierre, E. D. (1990). Homophobia and its consequences for gay and lesbian clients. In R. J. Kus (Ed.), *Keys to caring* (pp. 90–104). Boston: Alyson Publications.

Lease, S. H., & Shulman, J. L. (2003). A preliminary investigation of the role of religion for family members of lesbian, gay male, or bisexual male and female individuals [electronic version]. *Counseling & Values, 47,* 195–210.

LeVay, S., & Hamer, D. H. (1994, May). Evidence for a biological influence in male homosexuality. *Scientific American,* 44–49.

Lewis, L. A. (1984). The coming out process for lesbians: Integrating a stable identity. *Journal of the National Association of Social Workers, 29,* 464–469.

Lohrenz, L. J., Connely, J. C., Coyne, L., & Spare, K. E. (1978). Alcohol problems in several midwestern homosexual communities. *Journal of Studies on Alcohol, 39,* 1959–1963.

Lynne, C. (2001). Teaching outside the box: Incorporating queer theory in counselor education. *Journal of Humanistic Counseling, 40*(1), 49–58.

Martin, D. J. (1989). Human immunodeficiency virus infection and the gay community: Counseling and clinical issues. *Journal of Counseling and Development, 68,* 67–72.

McCandlish, B. M. (1985). Therapeutic issues with lesbian couples. In J. C. Gonsiorek (Ed.), *A guide to psychotherapy with gay and lesbian clients* (pp. 71–78). New York: Harrington Park Press.

McDermott, D., Tyndall, L., & Lichtenberg, J. W. (1989). Factors related to counselor preference among gays and lesbians. *Journal of Counseling and Development, 68,* 31–35.

McLaughlin, L. (1989). AIDS: An overview. In P. O'Malley (Ed.), *The AIDS epidemic: Private rights and the public interest* (pp. 15–35). Boston: Beacon Press.

McWhirter, D. P., & Mattison, A. M. (1984). *The male couple: How relationships develop.* Englewood Cliffs, NJ: Prentice-Hall.

Mollenkott, V. R. (1985). *Breaking the silence, overcoming the fear: Homophobia education.* (Available from the Program Agency, United Presbyterian Church, U.S.A., 475 Riverside Drive, Room 1101, New York, NY 10015)

Money, J. (1987). Sin, sickness, or status? Homosexual gender identity and psychoneuroendocrinology. *American Psychologist, 42,* 384–399.

Morin, S., Charles, K., & Malyon, A. (1984). The psychological impact of AIDS on gay men. *American Psychologist, 39,* 1288–1293.

Moses, A. E., & Hawkins, R. O. (1985). Two-hour in-service training session in homophobia. In H. Hidalgo, T. Peterson, & N. J. Woodman (Eds.), *Lesbian and gay issues: A resource manual for social workers* (pp. 152–157). Silver Spring, MD: National Association of Social Workers.

Namir, S. (1989). Treatment issues concerning persons with AIDS. In L. McKusick (Ed.), *What to do about AIDS: Physicians and mental health professionals discuss the issues* (pp. 87–94). Berkeley: University of California Press.

National Youth Violence Prevention Organization. (2002). *Youth suicide facts.* Retrieved June 16, 2005, from http://www.safeyouth.org/scripts/faq/suicidefacts.asp

Newman, B., Dannenfelser, P., & Benishek, L. (2002). Assessing beginning social work and counseling students acceptance of lesbians and gay men. *Journal of Social Work Education, 38*(2), 273–288.

NOLO. (n.d.) *Same-sex marriage: Developments in the law.* Retrieved November 9, 2004, from http://www.nolo.com/article.cfm/ObjectID/6DF0766E-C4A3-4952-A542F5997196 E8B5/catID/64C2C325-5DAF-4BC8-B4761409BA0187C3/118/304/190/ART/.

Paul, J. P., Stall, R., & Bloomfield, K. A. (1991). Gay and alcoholic: Epidemiologic and clinical issues. *Alcohol Health & Research World, 15*(2), 151–160.

Perry, S., Jacobsberg, L., Card, C. A., Ashman, T., Frances, A., & Fishman, B. (1993). Severity of psychiatric symptoms after HIV testing. *American Journal of Psychiatry, 150,* 775–779.

Peterman, L. (2003). Domestic violence between same sex partners: Implications for counseling. *Journal of Counseling and Development, 81*(1), 40–47.

Price, R. E., Omizo, M., & Hammett, V. L. (1986). Counseling clients with AIDS. *Journal of Counseling and Development, 65,* 96–97.

Rabkin, J., Remien, R., & Wilson, C. (1994). *Good doctors, good patients: Partners in HIV treatment.* New York: NCM Publishers.

Reid, J. D. (1995). Development in later life: Older lesbian and gay lives. In A. R. D'Augelli & C. J. Patterson (Eds.), *Lesbian, gay and bisexual identities over the lifespan: Psychological perspectives* (pp. 215–240). New York: Oxford University Press.

Reynolds, A. L., & Koski, M. J. (1995). Lesbian, gay, and bisexual teens and the school counselor: Building alliances. In G. Unks (Ed.), *The gay teen: Educational practice and theory for lesbian, gay, and bisexual adolescents* (pp. 85–94). New York: Routledge.

Roberts, T., & Gibbons, S. (2004). Same-sex marriage bans winning on state ballots. *CNN.* Retrieved November 10, 2004, from http://www.cnn.com/2004/ALLPOLITICS/11/02/ballot.samesex.marriage/index.html

Rochlin, M. (1985). Sexual orientation of the therapist and therapeutic effectiveness with gay clients. In J. C. Gonsiorek (Ed.), *A guide to psychotherapy with gay and lesbian clients* (pp. 21–29). New York: Harrington Park Press.

Ryan, C. C. (1990). Accessing gay and lesbian health resources. In R. J. Kus (Ed.), *Keys to caring* (pp. 340–345). Boston: Alyson Publications.

Salzburg, S. (2004). Learning that an adolescent child is gay or lesbian: The parent experience. *Social Work, 49*(1), 109–118.

Savin-Williams, R. C. (1995). Lesbian, gay male, and bisexual adolescents. In A. R. D'Augelli & C. J. Patterson (Eds.), *Lesbian, gay, and bisexual identities over the lifespan: Psychological perspectives* (pp. 166–189). New York: Oxford University Press.

Schwartz, R. D., & Harstein, N. B. (1986). Group psychotherapy with gay men: Theoretical and clinical considerations. In T. S. Stein & C. J. Cohen (Eds.), *Psychotherapy with lesbians and gay men* (pp. 157–177). New York: Plenum.

Shippy, R. A., Cantor, M., & Brennan, M. (2004). Social networks of aging gay men. *Journal of Men's Studies, 13*(1), 107–120.

Silberman, B. G., & Hawkins, R. O., Jr. (1988). Lesbian women and gay men: Issues for counseling. In E. Weinstein & E. Rosen (Eds.), *Sexuality counseling: Issues and implications* (pp. 101–113). Pacific Grove, CA: Brooks/Cole.

Sophie, J. (1987). Internalized homophobia and lesbian identity. *Journal of Homosexuality, 14,* 53–65.

Special report: Gays in America. (1989, June). *San Francisco Examiner*, pp. 1–78.

Stein, M., Perrin, E., & Potter, J. (2004). A difficult adjustment to school: The importance of family constellation. *Pediatrics. 114.* 1464–1467.

Stone, C. B. (2003). Counselors as advocates for gay, lesbian and bisexual youth: A call for equity and action. *Journal of Multicultural Counseling & Development, 31,* 143–155.

Troiden, R. R. (1989). The formation of homosexual identities. In G. Herdt (Ed.), *Gay and lesbian youth* (pp. 43–73). New York: Harrington Park Press.

Unks, G. (1995). Thinking about the gay teen. In G. Unks (Ed.), *The gay teen: Educational practice and theory for lesbian, gay, and bisexual adolescents* (pp. 3–12). New York: Routledge.

Uribe, V. (1995). Project Ten: A school based outreach to gay and lesbian youth. In G. Unks (Ed.), *The gay teen: Educational practice and theory for lesbian, gay, and bisexual adolescents* (pp. 203–210). New York: Routledge.

U.S. Census Bureau. (2003). Married-couple and unmarried-partner households: 2000. Census 2000 special reports. Retrieved November 10, 2004, from http://www.census.gov/prod/2003 pubs/ censr-5.pdf

Vaid, U. (2001). It's a small, homophobic world. *Advocate, 846,* 72.

Weinberg, G. (1973). *Society and the healthy homosexual.* Garden City, NJ: Anchor Books.

Williams, R. (1990). Studying sex in Sweden . . . or how I spent my summer vacation. *Christopher Street, 13*(4), 11–15.

Wolf, T. J. (1992). Bisexuality: A counseling perspective. In S. Dworkin & F. Gutierrez (Eds.), *Counseling gay men and lesbians: Journey to the end of the rainbow* (pp. 175–187). Alexandria, VA: American Counseling Association.

Woodman, N., & Lenna, H. (1980). *Counseling with gay men and women.* San Francisco: Jossey-Bass.

Yalom, I. D. (1995). *The theory and practice of group psychotherapy* (4th ed.). New York: Basic Books.

Zucker, K. J. (2003). The politics and science of reparative therapy. *Archives of Sexual Behavior, 32*(5), 399–402.

Name Index

Subject Index